ON A KNIFE'S EDGE

OSPREY
PUBLISHING

DEDICATION
For Rob

ON
A KNIFE'S
EDGE

The Ukraine,
November 1942–March 1943

Prit Buttar

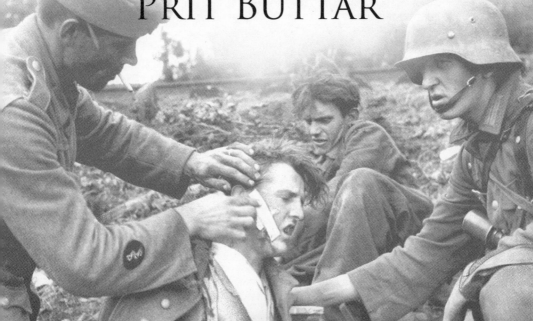

OSPREY PUBLISHING
Bloomsbury Publishing Plc
PO Box 883, Oxford, OX1 9PL, UK
1385 Broadway, 5th Floor, New York, NY 10018, USA
E-mail: info@ospreypublishing.com
www.ospreypublishing.com

OSPREY is a trademark of Osprey Publishing Ltd

First published in Great Britain in 2018

ISBN: HB 9781472828347
       PB 9781472835000
       eBook 9781472828354
       ePDF 9781472828361
       XML 9781472828378

18 19 20 21 22   10 9 8 7 6 5 4 3 2 1

Index by Zoe Ross
Originated by PDQ Digital Media Solutions, Bungay, UK
Printed and bound in Great Britain by CPI (Group) UK Ltd, Croydon CRO 4YD

Front cover: A wounded German soldier receives treatment in the Poltawa battle zone, 1943. (Getty Images)

CONTENTS

LIST OF MAPS

DRAMATIS PERSONAE

GERMANY

Oberstleutnant Wilhelm Adam – adjutant to Paulus
Major Franz Bäke – commander II Battalion, 11th Panzer Regiment
Generalmajor Hermann Balck – commander 11th Panzer Division
Field Marshal Fedor von Bock – commander Army Group South
Obergruppenführer Joseph Dietrich – commander LSSAH
Generalleutnant Karl Eibl – commander 385th Infantry Division, then XXIV Panzer Corps
Obergruppenführer Theodor Eicke – commander SS-Totenkopf
Generalleutnant Martin Fiebig – commander Fliegerkorps VIII
General Maximilian Fretter-Pico – commander of eponymous Armee Abteilung
Generaloberst Franz Halder – chief of the general staff
Leutnant Hans Hallfelz – reconnaissance platoon commander, 6th Panzer Division
Obergruppenführer Paul Hausser – commander II SS Panzer Corps
Generalmajor Otto Heidkämper – commander XXIV Panzer Corps
Generalleutnant Ferdinand Heim – commander XLVIII Panzer Corps
Generaloberst Gotthard Heinrici – commander XL Panzer Corps
General Karl-Adolf Hollidt – commander of eponymous Armee Abteilung
Generaloberst Hermann Hoth – commander Fourth Panzer Army
Oberst Walther von Hünersdorff – commander 11th Panzer Regiment
Generalleutnant Arno Jahr – commander 387th Infantry Division, then XXIV Panzer Corps
Generaloberst Hans Jeschonnek – chief of staff of the Luftwaffe
General Werner Kempf – commander of eponymous Armee Gruppe
Major Franz-Joachim Kinitz – chief of staff, 11th Panzer Division
Generalleutnant Friedrich Kirchner – commander LVII Panzer Corps

Bodo Kleine – junior NCO in 377th Infantry Division
Field Marshal Ewald von Kleist – commander Army Group A
Field Marshal Gunther von Kluge – commander Army Group Centre
General Otto von Knobelsdorff – commander XLVIII Panzer Corps
Generalleutnant Hans Kreysing – commander 3rd Mountain Division
General Hubert Lanz – commander of eponymous corps
Generalmajor (Generalleutnant January 1943) Arno von Lenski – commander 24th Panzer Division
Oberst Richard Lepper – battlegroup commander in Sixth Army
Generalmajor Hans-Georg Leyser – commander 29th Motorised Infantry Division
Major Erich Löwe – commander I Battalion, 11th Panzer Regiment
Generalmajor Walther Lucht – commander 336th Infantry Division
General Eberhard von Mackensen – commander First Panzer Army
Field Marshal Erich von Manstein – commander Army Group Don, later Army Group South
Oberst Friedrich von Mellenthin – chief of staff, XLVIII Panzer Corps
General (Generaloberst November 1942, Field Marshal January 1943) Friedrich Paulus – commander Sixth Army
Obergruppenführer Joachim Peiper – commander of Kampfgruppe Lötlampe, LSSAH
Generalmajor Wolfgang Pickert – commander 9th Flak Division
Generalleutnant Georg Postel – commander 320th Infantry Division
Obergruppenführer Hermann Priess – commander SS-Totenkopf
Generalmajor Erhard Raus – commander 6th Panzer Division
Rittmeister Heinrich Remlinger – commander I Battalion, 4th Panzergrenadier Regiment
Generaloberst Wolfram Freiherr von Richthofen – commander Luftflotte IV
Oberst Eberhard Rodt – commander 22nd Panzer Division
Oberleutnant Hans-Ulrich Rudel – commander Sturtzkampfgeschwader 2
Generaloberst Hans von Salmuth – commander Second Army
Oberleutnant Horst Scheibert – commander of 4th Panzer Company, 6th Panzer Division
Generalleutnant Arthur Schmidt – chief of staff, Sixth Army
General Walther von Seydlitz-Kurtzbach – commander LI Corps
Oberstleutnant (Oberst December 1942, Generalmajor February 1943) Rainer Stahel – commander of eponymous battlegroup
Oberstleutnant Hyazinth von Strachwitz – commander Grossdeutschland

Panzer Regiment
Brigadeführer Herbert-Ernst Vahl – commander SS-Das Reich
Brigadeführer Kurt Wahl – commander SS-Das Reich
Generalleutnant Martin Wandel – commander XXIV Panzer Corps
Field Marshal Maximilian von Weichs – commander Army Group B
Oberst Walther Wenck – chief of staff 3rd Romanian Army, then chief of staff
Armee Abteilung Hollidt
Generaloberst Kurt Zeitzler – chief of the general staff
Oberst Helmut Zollendorf – commander 114th Panzergrenadier Regiment

HUNGARY

Colonel-General Vitéz Jány – commander Second Army
Major General György Rakovsky – commander III Corps

ITALY

Lieutenant Eugenio Corti – artillery officer in Pasubio Division
General Italo Gariboldi – commander Eighth Army
General Giulio Martinat – chief of staff of Alpini Corps
Lieutenant General Gabriele Nasci – commander Alpini Corps
General Luigi Reverberi – commander Tridentina Division
Lieutenant Carlo Vicentini – infantry officer in Eighth Army

ROMANIA

General Petre Dumitrescu – commander Third Army
Lieutenant General Mihail Lascăr – commander 6th Infantry Division

SOVIET UNION

Mansoor Giztulovich Abdullin – soldier in the Red Army
Major General (Lieutenant General December 1942) Vasily Mikhailovich Badanov – commander XXIV Tank Corps

Major General Sergei Semenovich Biryusov – chief of staff Second Guards Army

Major General Vasily Gerasimovich Burkov – commander X Tank Corps

Major General Vasily Vasileyevich Butkov – commander I Tank Corps

General Nikander Yevlampievich Chibissov – commander Thirty-Eighth Army

Lieutenant General Vasily Ivanovich Chuikov – commander Sixty-Second Army

Lieutenant-Colonel Georgi Nikolayevich Filippov – commander 19th Tank Brigade

Lieutenant General (Colonel General January 1943) Filipp Ivanovich Golikov – commander Voronezh Front

Lieutenant General Mikhail Ilyich Kazakov – commander Sixty-Ninth Army

Major General Fedor Mikhailovich Kharitonov – commander Sixth Army

Major General (Lieutenant General February 1943) Nikita Sergeyevich Khrushchev – member of the military councils of Stalingrad, Southeast, Southern and Voronezh Fronts

Isaak Kobylyanskiy – soldier in the Red Army

Major General Vasily Alexeyevich Koptsov – commander XV Tank Corps

Major General Petr Kirilovich Koshevoi – commander 24th Guards Rifle Division

General Vasily Ivanovich Kuznetsov – commander First Guards Army

Lieutenant General Dimitri Danilovich Lelyushenko – commander Third Guards Army

Major General Alexander Ilyich Lizyukov – commander Fifth Tank Army, killed near Voronezh 23 July 1942

Lieutenant General Rodion Yakovlevich Malinovsky – commander Second Guards Army

Lieutenant General Ivan Ivanovich Maslennikov – commander North Caucasus Front

Lieutenant General Kiril Semenovich Moskalenko – commander Fortieth Army

Ivan Stepanovich Nosov – artilleryman in 107th Rifle Division

Major General Pavel Pavlovich Poluboyarov – commander XVII Tank Corps

Colonel Vasily Mikhailovich Polyakov – commander 25th Guards Tank Brigade

Lieutenant General Markian Mikhailovich Popov – commander Fifth Shock Army, then of eponymous mobile group

Major General Alexei Grigoreyevich Rodin – commander XXVI Tank Corps

Lieutenant General (Colonel General January 1943) Konstantin Konstantinovich Rokossovsky – commander Don Front

General Prokofy Logvinovich Romanenko – commander Fifth Tank Army

Major General (Lieutenant General December 1942) Pavel Alexeyevich Rotmistrov – commander VII Tank Corps, III Guards Tank Corps, and Fifth Guards Tank Army

Lieutenant General Pavel Semyenovich Rybalko – commander Third Tank Army

Major General Pavel Mendelevich Shafarenko – commander 25th Guards Rifle Division

Lieutenant General Sergei Matveevich Shtemenko – Deputy Head of Stavka Operations Directorate

Major Nikolai Grigorievich Shtykov – deputy regimental commander in 25th Guards Rifle Division

Major General Mikhail Stepanovich Shumilov – commander Sixty-Fourth Army

Major General Trofim Ivanovich Tanashchishin – commander XIII Mechanised Corps

Gabriel Temkin – Polish Jew, later a soldier in the Red Army

General Ivan Vladimirovich Tiulenev – commander Transcaucasian Front

General (Marshal February 1943) Alexander Mikhailovich Vasilevsky – chief of the general staff

Lieutenant General (Colonel General December 1942, General February 1943) Nikolai Fyodorovich Vatutin – commander Voronezh and Southwest Fronts

Lieutenant General Andrei Andreyevich Vlasov – commander Second Shock Army

Major General Vasily Timofeyevich Volsky – commander IV Mechanised Corps

Colonel General Andrei Ivanovich Yeremenko – commander Stalingrad and Southern Fronts

Colonel Gavril Stanislavovich Zdanovich – commander 203rd Rifle Division

Marshal Georgi Konstantinovich Zhukov – deputy commander-in-chief of the Red Army

Major General Mitrofan Ivanovich Zinkovich – commander XII Tank Corps

INTRODUCTION

A common viewpoint of the conflict on the Eastern Front in the Second World War is that the Germans fought with great tactical and operational virtuosity, but were ultimately defeated by sheer weight of numbers and the constant interference of Adolf Hitler in military affairs. Any skill on the part of the Red Army was restricted to dogged defence. Another belief, actively promoted by many German veterans, is that whilst Nazi authorities committed many atrocities in the occupied parts of the Soviet Union, the great bulk of the Wehrmacht – and many of the combat formations of the SS – took no part in such acts, and indeed were often completely ignorant of what was occurring. The truth, inevitably, is more complex.

The opening phase of what became known in Russian literature as the Great Patriotic War followed a series of dazzling triumphs in which the Wehrmacht swiftly crushed the Poles before overrunning the Low Countries and France and driving Britain from continental Europe. Even in these early campaigns, the apparent ease with which the German forces overwhelmed their opponents hid several fundamental truths. The striking power of the panzer divisions was beyond question, but their tanks were under-armed and poorly protected compared with those of Britain and France, and the great bulk of the German Army remained limited to the speed of horses and men on foot, little changed from previous centuries. The Luftwaffe had a comparatively easy time in its operations providing close support for the attacking forces, but once it stepped outside this purely tactical role, it struggled to assert itself – despite the boasts of Goering and the expectations of many within Germany, the British managed to extricate their forces from Dunkirk, and the RAF prevented the Luftwaffe from achieving air superiority over southeast England, without which any invasion of Britain was impossible.

The very speed with which Poland, Belgium, Holland and France were overrun also hid another fundamental weakness: in almost every respect, the German Army – indeed, Germany as a whole – was poorly prepared for prolonged operations. It is a longstanding axiom of military planning that sufficient reserves should be kept in hand to deal with unexpected eventualities, but partly through necessity, the Wehrmacht entered each campaign with its resources heavily committed to the initial assault. Its ability to adapt to setbacks was therefore limited, but remained untested in the early campaigns.

Logistically, there were also weaknesses. With almost no oil resources within the Reich, Germany had to depend on oil obtained from countries like Romania and from its own synthetic oil production, and this latter category repeatedly fell far short of planned levels. This was of little consequence when Germany's enemies were dispatched in a short campaign; it was possible to build up sufficient stocks of fuel to sustain the armed forces for these brief but intense efforts. Maintaining longer-term operations at even a more modest tempo would rapidly place the limited fuel supplies of Germany under far greater strain.

Nor were industrial affairs any better. At a time when western air forces were routinely supplied with more than two aero engines per mounting, the Luftwaffe had barely 1.4 engines per mounting, and there were similar shortages of other essential spare parts.[1] Partly as a consequence, the Luftwaffe started the campaign against the Soviet Union in 1941 with roughly the same number of operational aircraft as it had fielded in September 1939.[2] Tank production too remained poor, and whilst this was of little consequence in the opening campaigns, which were punctuated by pauses in fighting that allowed depleted armoured units to be brought back to full strength, it would be far more important if fighting dragged on beyond just a few short weeks. The quantity of trucks and other vehicles being produced was also poor, resulting in growing reliance on vehicles captured in France and elsewhere, for which there was a very limited supply of spare parts. Despite receiving lavish quantities of money and material resources, German industry consistently performed far less efficiently than its equivalents in other countries. Again, this was of little consequence in the era of swift victories and conquests, but if Germany's opponents were able to continue the war, their better use of resources would begin to have an effect. During 1940, for example, German industry managed to produce about 10,000 aircraft; meanwhile, with rather less consumption of resources, the British produced 15,000.[3] Production of munitions, weapons of all kinds, and motor vehicles consistently lagged far behind targets. Responsibility for German war industry rested with Hermann Goering, and its failures in the first half of the war are largely attributable to his inability to impose order upon it.

None of this mattered in the opening phases of the war, but by the end of 1942, as events on the Eastern Front took a dramatic turn against Germany, all of these limitations would become far more important. To a large extent, every German campaign to this point had been a gamble. The Polish invasion was only possible due to the inactivity of the British and French, and the strike through the Ardennes, Belgium and northern France used the great bulk of Germany's motorised forces – any setback here, or a determined attack into the Rhineland from French territory, would have been fatal. The invasion of the Soviet Union in 1941 was the greatest gamble to date, with everything staked on achieving victory before the winter, and its failure led to an even greater gamble the following year – formations along the entire Eastern Front were stripped of resources to allow the German forces in the Ukraine to launch a further advance that, if successful, might isolate the Caucasus and deprive the Soviet Union of its access to fuel. The price of this gamble was to extend the front line hugely, and with most of the Wehrmacht's striking power deployed at the points of advance, the long flanks represented a huge liability if the Red Army were able to take advantage of it.

The tactical and operational superiority of the German forces remained largely intact, but the Red Army was a quick learner. Like the Germans, the Russians had the opportunity of recent fighting, in particular the Winter War against Finland in 1939–40, to re-evaluate their peacetime plans and make alterations, but most of the lessons learned – often imperfectly – were still being implemented when Germany invaded Russia in 1941. Once war with Germany began, the learning process and implementation of change had to take place in ever more urgent circumstances. As the winter fighting in the eastern Ukraine unfolded in late 1942, the degree to which the Soviet forces had learned how to mount mobile operations, and the ability of the Germans to use their field expertise to make up for their material shortages, would be in close balance.

Inevitably, a work like this relies extensively on the memoirs of the individuals who played their parts in the great drama of the fighting of late 1942 and early 1943. The accuracy and reliability of these accounts is variable. Many of the German protagonists – Manstein, Balck, Mellenthin – have been regarded in recent years as writing misleading descriptions of the war and fostering the myth that the technically superior Wehrmacht, led with great skill by its officers, was eventually defeated by the lumbering colossus of the Red Army, which relied simply on sheer weight of numbers; these accounts also tend to give the impression that whilst parts of the SS and other German bodies may have carried out atrocities in the occupied territories, the soldiers and officers of the Wehrmacht were largely free of any blame. The accounts of the Soviet veterans are also of questionable reliability, having been written during the Soviet era and conforming to the ideological requirements of their time.[4] Yet even with these acknowledged weaknesses, these accounts remain a valuable source of information, not least in the light they shed on the personalities and attitudes of the men involved. Recent access to contemporary Soviet documentation has redressed the balance considerably, and this underlies the gradual reappraisal of the war on the Eastern Front, with growing awareness that as German power declined through a combination of inadequate industrial planning, the loss of irreplaceable personnel, and poor decisions made by Hitler, Soviet power grew as the commanders of the Red Army became increasingly skilled at the operational art. An important difference between German and Soviet development during the war is the manner in which the Soviet general staff rigorously analysed each campaign and tried to learn whatever lessons it could from its experiences; by contrast, Hitler retreated increasingly into a world in which his personal domination and the power of the 'will to win' were of greater importance than practical matters relating to battlefield experiences. During the 1960s, 1970s and 1980s, several accounts of the war written by lower ranking Russian soldiers and officers emerged, and whilst these – like many of their German counterparts – are coloured by the rhetoric of the era, with all enemies routinely described as Nazis or fascists, they give a picture of the ordinary men (and in some cases, women) who fought against the Germans. These soldiers were products of nearly a quarter century of communist rule, and this inevitably shaped the way in which they viewed their enemies; but their unquestionable patriotism and comradeship are identical to those of combatants from any nation caught up in the war.

One feature of the fighting that took place in late 1942 and early 1943 is the almost implacable lack of mercy shown by both the Germans and the Russians. This was the first occasion that the Red Army liberated areas that had been under German control for more than a short time, and whilst Russian soldiers had been made aware of the mistreatment of Russian civilians by the Germans, this was their first opportunity to witness such mistreatment first-hand. The growing anger of ordinary soldiers is almost palpable in their accounts, and the desire for revenge, coupled with the sense that the Germans had to be driven from Soviet territory as fast as possible to prevent further atrocities, contributed to the growing Russian desire to continue their offensive operations as long as possible. German accounts repeatedly highlight the manner in which Russian units killed prisoners, but the same authors are silent about similar killings by Germans.

The manner in which the Germans approached the war also changed during this critical time. Until now, the war in the east had largely been one of conquest. By destroying the Soviet Union, Germany would satisfy its long-held desire to obtain a land empire in the east, and realisation of this desire was – for many within the German hierarchy – inextricably bonded to brutal occupation policies. The resources of the conquered regions were to be exploited for maximum short-term gain without any regard for the impact upon the indigenous population, and this led to mass starvation in the Ukraine, a region that was still recovering from the excesses of Stalinist repression in earlier years; had the Germans behaved more like liberators and less like conquerors, the burgeoning partisan movement might have withered and faded away, and the outcome of the war might have been very different. Instead, forced requisitions that left the rural communities of the region without sufficient food for their own needs and the manner in which able-bodied men and women were rounded up for forced labour – many of whom were shipped off to Germany – resulted in the amount of land under cultivation falling disastrously. The mass killings of Jews, suspected communists, and other 'undesirable' elements of the population would reap a bitter harvest as the Red Army returned to the region. By the end of the winter of 1942–43, German rhetoric about the conflict was changing. The war against the Soviet Union was no longer exclusively the *Rassenkrieg* ('racial war') that Hitler had proclaimed in the summer of 1941. Instead, there was an increasing tendency – clearly expressed in the memoirs of many German soldiers and officers – that the war was being fought to save Europe from the threat of communism and the danger to western civilisation from the Asiatic hordes of Russia.

The scale of the German gamble in the 1942 campaign was so great that everything would depend upon fine margins. If the Red Army were able to take advantage of the overexposed German positions, there was a very real prospect of the war coming to a relatively swift conclusion with a crushing defeat from which the Wehrmacht would not be able to recover; conversely, if this was to be avoided, every ounce of German tactical and operational skill would have to be used to maximum effect.

CHAPTER 1

THE ROAD TO CRISIS

'When Barbarossa begins,' Hitler told his generals in early 1941, 'the entire world will hold its breath.' On 22 June 1941, 145 German divisions backed by the great bulk of the resources of the Luftwaffe, together with substantial forces from Finland and Romania – totalling perhaps three million men – crossed the border into the Soviet Union. Moscow, the prime objective at the start of the *Barbarossa* campaign, was 600 miles away; the vast spaces of Belarus and European Russia, with poor roads and railways, and huge tracts of forest and swamp, defended by 191 Red Army divisions and 37 mechanised brigades, lay between the Wehrmacht and the Soviet capital.[1]

Full of confidence after their swift victories over Poland and France, the German forces trusted that this campaign would be similar, though on a far larger canvas – a rapid advance in which the panzer divisions would cut apart the Red Army, while the Luftwaffe controlled the skies. Despite the size of the Red Army, and despite the vastness of the landscape, a victorious conclusion would come swiftly – indeed, it would have to come swiftly, because despite Goering's pronouncements and boasts as the man responsible for the production of military materiel, German industry was simply not organised to sustain a prolonged war effort. With the Soviet Union defeated, Germany would be unassailable and the future of the Thousand Year Reich would be secured.

The fighting that followed showed both the Wehrmacht and the Red Army at their best and their worst. Whilst much has been made of the all-arms striking power of panzer divisions, their successes to date were more than merely the result of concentrating armoured vehicles in a single mobile formation; the close cooperation between the ground forces and the Luftwaffe was also an important factor, as was the ability of German officers to delegate decision-making to their subordinates, allowing them to improvise in the face of unexpected developments and thus maintain a pace of operations that left their opponents bewildered and off-balance.

The customary view of the Red Army is that it relied greatly on the traditional solidity of Russian troops in defensive fighting and sheer numbers, and the Germans were further emboldened by the manner in which the Kaiser's armies had consistently outfought the Russians in the First World War. But like every other army of the era, the Red Army contained its share of visionary commanders who had written extensively about warfare in the mechanised era. Indeed, Russian military thinkers produced far more written material about the possibilities of fighting in the mechanised age than the experts of any other country apart from Germany.[2] Many of these visionaries held posts in the Soviet staff college where they passed on their ideas and more importantly their way of thinking to their students. Like their counterparts elsewhere, they articulated a multitude of ideas of variable accuracy, but the purges that ravaged the ranks of the army during the 1930s did huge damage to the manner in which new ideas were developed, tested and adopted. Mikhail Nikolayevich Tukhachevsky, perhaps the foremost thinker in the army, was arrested in 1937 and tortured until he confessed to being part of a conspiracy to overthrow Stalin, though there is little evidence to support this; he was found guilty in a trial in which he was denied legal representation and executed the same day. Five of the judges who sat in the trial were in turn arrested and executed in the ongoing purges, which also accounted for Ieronim Petrovich Uborevich, another of those who contributed to the many articles proposing new ways of waging war.

Despite the fall of Tukhachevsky and others, their ideas of conducting all-arms operations in depth remained part of Russian military doctrine and were put to good use by Georgi Zhukov in a mechanised counteroffensive against Japanese forces in border fighting at Khalkhin Gol in 1939. However, it is vital to reassess all military thinking to see how accurate it is in the light of events, and the constant interference of communist doctrine prevented the Red Army from maximising its experiences against Japan, as well as learning the lessons of the Spanish Civil War. When the Red Army was unleashed against the comparatively weak forces of Finland in 1939–40, the rigid adherence to doctrine in the face of a tough, determined enemy resulted in severe casualties for little gain. Changes were implemented, as Sergei Matveevich Shtemenko, who would serve in the operations branch of the Soviet general staff during the war and was a student at the army's staff academy in 1939 and 1940, later wrote:

The conclusions drawn by the Soviet high command from the recent war were making a noticeable impression upon the Academy … The study programme was shorn of obsolete elements. Particular stress was laid on field training and on working out complex forms of operation and combat. Training methods were being reformed to make us into commanders who could cope with any emergency.[3]

In this respect, the Russians were moving towards the German way of thinking: subordinate commanders needed the skills and knowledge to improvise in the face of unexpected events. In modern warfare, there simply wouldn't be time to wait for detailed instructions from above. However, even if training establishments could make changes in the manner in which soldiers and officers were prepared for war, it would take time for such changes to filter down through the system, and there was also a pressing need for major organisational restructuring. By 1941, Soviet formations were all too frequently the wrong size – either too big and unwieldy, or too small and weak, unable to fight alone. By contrast, the German formations, particularly the panzer divisions, appeared perfectly balanced.

In terms of equipment, the inventories of the two sides had both good and bad points. In combat against the RAF, German bombers – particularly the Stuka dive-bombers – had proved to be vulnerable, but against the Soviet air force the Luftwaffe rapidly established air superiority and its bombers were able to operate with comparative ease. On the ground, German tanks remained a source of concern – under-gunned and under-armoured – but the use of supporting anti-tank guns, excellent levels of training in close cooperation, and good communications at every level allowed them to prevail in most battles, not least because so many Soviet tanks did not have radios. Consequently, Russian troops found that changing a tactical plan once battle was joined was almost impossible, and the official means of doing so – by waving flags from turret hatches – proved to be useless. In the years leading up to the war, the Red Army acquired huge numbers of new tanks – the T-26, adopted from the British Vickers 6-ton tank and produced in larger numbers than any other tank in the world at the time; the T-28; and the T-35 – but the entire tank fleet was plagued by shortages of spare parts and skilled technicians, meaning that a large proportion of tanks was unavailable at any given time. Some, like the T-35, proved to be so unreliable that ultimately nearly all were lost due to breakdowns rather than enemy action. Others, like the T-26, were soon found to be far too lightly armoured to be of much use in combat against armoured enemies. The newest Soviet tank, the T-34, proved to be far superior to anything deployed by the Germans or indeed any other nation to date, but at the start of hostilities there were too few to have more than a local effect. The heavy KV-1 and KV-2 tanks were invulnerable to all but the best German anti-tank guns, but they too had few radios, were prone to breakdowns, and were difficult to operate. For example, changing gear often required the driver to resort to striking the gear lever with a hammer. In every other respect the performance of the army proved to be a shattering disappointment, with communications rapidly breaking down and officers struggling in vain to control unwieldy formations.

The armies of the Soviet Union floundered in the wake of their more nimble opponents, and a series of great encirclements seemed the forerunners of the rapid success on which the Germans depended. In 1939, the Soviet Union had occupied the eastern parts of Poland and had then forced the Baltic States to accept Soviet troops on their soil, prior to annexing them in 1940. This meant that the frontier was several hundred miles further west than might otherwise have been the case, but it proved to be a mixed blessing. On the one hand, there was more scope for conceding space to buy time; but on the other hand, there had been only modest progress in fortifying the new frontier. Hamstrung by Stalin's refusal to allow a full-scale mobilisation in early June, when many within the Soviet military establishment realised that a German attack was imminent, the frontier armies fought and died as they struggled to come to terms with the onset of hostilities. Their officers lacked the training to show initiative and fight their way to freedom, and their soldiers fought bravely, but then laid down their arms when the hopelessness of their situation became clear. Most would die in German captivity.

But even in the midst of disaster, the soldiers of the Red Army were learning. At a tactical level, their use of armour became increasingly skilful as the fighting progressed, to the chagrin of the Germans. Stalin ruthlessly dismissed commanders that he felt had failed to live up to expectations, though their fates varied – some were disgraced or even executed, but others, particularly those with whom Stalin had close personal ties going back to the days of the Russian Civil War, were simply reassigned to new, non-combat roles. At an operational level, the failures of the opening weeks led to rapid reappraisal of doctrine. The structure of command was repeatedly reorganised to try to improve command and control, and despite the huge setbacks there was little sense of defeatism amongst the officers and senior commanders. If the Germans could be stopped, if the Red Army could catch its breath, it would be an increasingly formidable foe.

Ultimately, the German gamble of 1941 depended upon covering a huge amount of territory before the onset of winter. The start of the campaign was delayed by poor weather and the need to secure control of Yugoslavia and Greece; despite this, the Wehrmacht seemed to be on the verge of reaching Moscow before Zhukov's counterattack threw it back. Much has been written about whether the Germans could have defeated the Soviet Union before the end of 1941, but it seems likely that, even if the final assaults had reached or even encircled the Soviet capital, the losses suffered by the army were such that there simply wasn't enough strength left to subdue the city and retain it. In particular, the infantry divisions were barely at half their establishment strength, and the panzer divisions had proved during the fighting for Warsaw in 1939 that without substantial infantry support, they were unable to fight effectively in built-up areas.[4] In any event, the Siberian divisions that Zhukov had kept in reserve were unleashed in a series of counterattacks that made the magnitude of the German gamble plain: with all its waning strength in the front line of the drive on Moscow, the Wehrmacht had almost no reserves with which to beat off the counterattacks.

With its energy spent and its forces strewn across the snows of Russia, the Wehrmacht came dangerously close to destruction in the fighting that followed. Many felt that a substantial retreat would be needed, and at first Hitler agreed to withdrawals to better defensive positions.[5] Within days though, the Führer intervened and ordered the troops to defend where they were. Many, such as Guderian and Hoepner (the commanders of the two panzer groups that had spearheaded the assault on Moscow) protested and were sacked. Through a mixture of a major effort by the Luftwaffe, local withdrawals – many unauthorised – and growing Russian exhaustion, the Germans were able to stabilise the front line.

The failure of the Wehrmacht to capture Moscow and the fighting that raged to the west of the city had major consequences for the future of the war. Hitler dismissed Walther von Brauchitsch, the commander-in-chief of the Wehrmacht, and assumed the post himself. Angered by the constant criticism and objections of officers like Guderian, he also moved to ensure that the more outspoken German generals were removed from their posts. In future, the German Army would receive its orders from an amateur, without even the support of constructive criticism from senior officers.

With the front line still so close to Moscow, Stalin remained concerned that the Germans would make a renewed attempt to take the city in 1942 and retained major reserves in the area, leading to weaknesses in the front line elsewhere. The German assault on Moscow had come in two phases, with a pause while the Germans waited for the ground to freeze and for supplies to be brought forward, and Stalin had insisted on a counterattack during this pause, despite the protests of Zhukov, who felt that the assembled forces were inadequate for the task and that there were insufficient reserves available. This was followed by a much larger counterattack after the failure of the second German attempt to reach the city, and when this eventually drove the Germans back from the outskirts of Moscow, it was the turn of the Russians to learn a fundamental truth about armoured warfare: whilst tank forces could break through front lines with varying degrees of ease, exploiting those successes and destroying the isolated German pockets was a different matter. A great deal of energy was expended effectively pushing into open space – there were no clear objectives within striking range, no geographical features against which the Germans could be squeezed or whose capture would render the German positions untenable. Writing several years later, Alexander Mikhailovich Vasilevsky, who was acting chief of staff at *Stavka* – the Soviet high command – at the time, reflected:

> A number of big shortcomings in troop control and military action came to the fore during the counteroffensive around Moscow … True, a deep carpet of snow hampered the advance, but the main factor was the lack of tanks, aircraft and ammunition where they were most needed. Formations, units and elements assumed a two-line battle order and attacked after a brief, insufficiently strong artillery bombardment; the artillery cover of the attacking infantry and tanks deep in the enemy defences was not efficient enough and sometimes was not employed at all. The tank units were usually employed as direct support for the infantry and rarely received independent missions. Gradually, however, the Soviet troops gained experience and began to act more successfully.[6]

Vasilevsky was to play a leading role in the events described in this book, and it is worth looking at his past in more detail. He was the fourth of ultimately eight siblings born to an impoverished priest in the town of Vichuga to the northeast of Moscow:

> [My father's] miserly earnings were insufficient even for the bare essentials for his large family. All of us, from the smallest to the biggest, worked most days in the fields. In winter father would do extra work as a carpenter, being commissioned to supply school desks, tables, window frames, doors and beehives.[7]

In 1909, aged 14, Vasilevsky went to the theological seminary in Kostroma, at great financial cost to his father. He was about to start his final year when war broke out and he immediately volunteered for service; in January 1915, he and several schoolmates were drafted into the town garrison and then sent to the military academy in Moscow to train as junior officers. Here he studied the writers who had developed Russian military doctrine in the preceding years, such as Suvorov, Dragomirov and Skobelev. Many of these have been heavily criticised for failing to recognise the growing power of firearms and artillery and lauding the value of close-quarter fighting with the bayonet over fire and manoeuvre, but for a young man from the provinces with no military education, the books were nonetheless greatly inspiring and he proved adept at using the texts with judicious selectivity:

> There were certain axioms in those works which I learned by heart: 'Don't describe, but demonstrate and back it up with description'; 'First convey a single idea, have it repeated and assist in its assimilation, then convey the next one'; 'Initially teach only the bare essentials'; 'Entrust rather than order'; 'Our task is to destroy the enemy – to fight to destroy without losing lives is impossible, to fight to lose lives without destroying is stupid.'[8]

By the end of the year, Vasilevsky was in the ranks of the Russian Ninth Army at the southern end of the long Eastern Front. He experienced the realities of trench warfare and would have been involved in the murderously wasteful attacks made by the Russian Army using outdated tactics in late 1915 and early 1916, but he makes no mention of them in his memoirs. Instead, he concentrates on the Brusilov Offensive of the summer of 1916, when – using innovative tactics, many of which would play a part in tactical and operational developments in the years that followed – the Russian Army broke through the lines of the Austro-Hungarian troops in the southern half of the front and briefly threatened to achieve a potentially decisive victory.[9] At the end of the year, following Romania's entry in the war on the side of the Entente Powers, Vasilevsky accompanied Ninth Army when it was deployed in support of Russia's new ally.

When the Russian Revolution broke out the following year, army units that were closest to Petrograd, the cradle of the revolution, were more likely to be seized by the revolutionary spirit than those further away. At the southern end of the front, Ninth Army was relatively untouched by the destabilising unrest that swept the Russian Army as the year progressed. For Vasilevsky, any lingering loyalty to the old order was swept away by the events of the Kornilov Affair, a series of confused events that led to the recently appointed supreme commander of the army, Lavr Georgievich Kornilov, making a failed attempt to seize power.[10]

After the October Revolution Vasilevsky spent more of his time with the revolutionary committees that were forming throughout the army, behaviour that was by no means universal amongst the officers in his regiment:

> The soldiers excitedly debated the Decrees on Peace and Land, threw away their rifles, fraternised with the Austrian soldiers, openly expressed their discontent with the commanders and welcomed the new power expressing the people's interests.
>
> The most hated officers were sometimes threatened with lynching. The split in the officers' ranks grew even wider. It was not so long ago that we had all sat round the same table, but now former comrades-in-arms looked daggers at each other. I too caught the resentful looks because I had recognised the Soviet power, was 'hobnobbing with the Bolsheviks' and visited the Soviet of Soldiers' Deputies.[11]

Like many soldiers and officers, Vasilevsky decided that he had had enough of the war and went home in November 1917, officially on leave but with no intention of returning. Within weeks, he received a letter advising him that the soldiers of his old regiment had elected him to be their commander, but given the widespread unrest across Russia and Ukraine he chose to join the local military department, where he served as an instructor for the *Vsevobuch* (the system of universal basic military training introduced by the Bolsheviks to arm the people against the residual elements of the old order). His preference was to serve with the Red Army, but as he noted, there appeared to be reluctance to allow a former officer of the Tsar's army to take up such a post. In late 1918 he accepted a job as a teacher, and the following April he finally joined the ranks of the Red Army; after the mishaps suffered by the new revolutionary army in its first engagements, there was a growing realisation that no amount of ideological purity could compensate for hard military knowledge and experience. He served in the Russian Civil War, helping to defend Moscow against the advance of General Anton Ivanovich Denikin, and in the fighting against Poland, where his division had to defend against the pursuing Polish troops after the Battle of Warsaw in 1920. Written during the Soviet era, his memoirs attempt to portray events from that era in as favourable a light for the Bolsheviks as possible, but there could be no doubt that the Red Army had suffered a major setback, as had the Russian communists' dream of exporting their revolution to the other nations of Europe.

In the years that followed, Vasilevsky held a series of commands in which he demonstrated the manner in which his experiences as an officer and a teacher combined well. He encountered several senior figures in the Soviet regime, including Kliment Yefremovich Voroshilov and Boris Mikhailovich Shapovnikov – he had a particularly close friendship with the latter, which was of great advantage to him in the years that followed. It was almost inevitable that he would be posted to the Directorate of Military Training, where he met Tukhashevsky and Zhukov, and in 1937, at a time when Stalin's purges were tearing great holes in the Red Army, he was appointed to the general staff. Vasilevsky's survival in these years was due partly to the influence of good friends like Shapovnikov, and partly to his inborn sense of diplomacy and tact. Stalin had a good personal relationship with him. When he learned that Vasilevsky had broken off contact with his father on the grounds that, as a priest, he was not a communist and was seen as an enemy of the people, he urged Vasilevsky to get in touch with his family again. There were mixed views about the diplomatic, non-confrontational style that Vasilevsky adopted – some, like Shtemenko, who in many respects followed in Vasilevsky's footsteps through the Soviet general staff, described him as a brilliant yet modest officer with a huge capacity for work, and worked alongside him for many years:

> This close and rather long period of collaboration allowed me to make a very thorough study of Vasilevsky's personal qualities. And the more I got to know him, the more deeply I came to respect this man of soldierly sincerity, unfailingly modest and cordial, a military leader in the finest sense of the term.
>
> ... What always distinguished Vasilevsky was the confidence he placed in his subordinates, his profound respect for his fellow men and concern for their human dignity. He understood perfectly how difficult it was to remain well organised and efficient in the critical early period of this war which had begun so unfavourably for us, and he tried to bring us together as a team, to create a working atmosphere in which one would not feel any pressure of authority but only the strong shoulder of a senior and more experienced comrade on which, if need be, one could lean ... Among the members of the general staff Vasilevsky enjoyed not only the highest esteem but also their universal love and affection.
>
> ... Nature had endowed Vasilevsky with the rare gift of being able to grasp essentials literally in his stride, drawing the right conclusions and foreseeing the further development of events with a special clarity. He never made any display of this, however. On the contrary, he would always listen to the ideas and opinions of others with deliberate attention. He would never interrupt, even if he did not agree with the views expressed. Instead, he would argue patiently and persuasively and, in the end, usually win over his opponent. At the same time he knew how to defend his own point of view in front of the Supreme Commander [Stalin]. He did this tactfully but with sufficient firmness.[12]

Some have speculated whether he was promoted precisely because he was so compliant to Stalin's wishes, bordering in some cases on timid.[13] Nikita Sergeyevich Khrushchev regarded him as being completely under the sway of the Soviet dictator, but as shall be seen, there were reasons for animosity between Vasilevsky and Khrushchev.[14] It is noteworthy that there is nothing remotely vainglorious in Vasilevesky's memoirs and he repeatedly goes out of his way to give credit to others. Rather than being Stalin's yes-man, it is more likely that the Soviet dictator recognised that he was a man without personal political ambition and who was therefore not likely to be a threat; consequently, he was happy to tolerate a diligent, intelligent man who knew how to disagree without causing animosity.

Immediately before the start of the Second World War, Vasilevsky became deputy commander of the general staff's Operations Directorate; he was personally involved in negotiating the ceasefire line with Finland at the end of the Winter War. He became chief of the Operations Directorate in August 1941 and deputy chief of staff, taking command when Shapovnikov was forced to step aside due to illness during the following winter. It was in this role that he became intimately involved in the fighting around Moscow – whilst the operations may have been under the control of Zhukov, Vasilevsky worked tirelessly on the logistic support needed first to stop the Germans, then throw them back. He showed himself to be a model staff officer, a man who could diligently put into practice the plans of others, modifying them as circumstances dictated without deviating from their intention.

Despite the limited successes of the winter fighting, Stalin insisted that the tide had turned and that the strength of the Wehrmacht was broken. In early January, he wrote to all higher commands:

> After the Red Army had succeeded in wearing down the German fascist troops sufficiently, it went over to the counteroffensive and pursued the German invaders to the west. So as to hold up our advance, the Germans went on the defensive and began to build defence lines with trenches, entanglements and field fortifications. The Germans intend thereby to delay our advance until the spring so that then, having assembled their forces, they can once again take the offensive against the Red Army. The Germans want, consequently, to play for time and take a breather.
>
> Our task is not to give the Germans a breathing space, to drive them westwards without a halt, force them to exhaust their reserves before springtime when we shall have fresh big reserves, while the Germans will have no more reserves; this will ensure the complete defeat of the Nazi forces in 1942. But to implement this

task we must see that our troops have learned how to breach the foe's line of defence, learned how to organise a breach in the enemy defences in all its depth and thus pave the way for our infantry, our tanks and our cavalry to move forward. The Germans have more than one line of defence; they are building and will soon have a second and a third line. If our troops do not learn quickly and thoroughly to break down and break through the enemy's line of defence, our drive forward will not be possible.[15]

There were therefore to be further counterattacks across the entire front. Again, Zhukov objected in vain that the Red Army was not yet strong enough to mount such operations, and further assaults without clear operational or strategic objectives would dissipate strength without any commensurate gains.[16] However, Stalin insisted on launching widespread attacks, believing that by doing so, he could keep the Germans off balance and prevent them from seizing the initiative and launching another major strike against Moscow, an abiding concern in his mind.[17]

The offensives that followed confirmed that Stalin's views about the Wehrmacht were far too optimistic. The counterattacks outside Moscow had left the Germans in possession of a large salient around the town of Rzhev, and further attempts in early 1942 to reduce it led only to major casualties. An attempt to destroy a large German pocket at Demyansk, south of Leningrad, was coordinated personally by Vasilevsky and proved both costly and futile, but the ability of the Luftwaffe – at the cost of hundreds of hard-to-replace transport aircraft and aircrew – to sustain the pocket for several months was something that would have consequences in the months that followed. Not far away, General Andrei Andreyevich Vlasov's Second Shock Army led a major effort to break the siege of Leningrad; when neighbouring armies failed to advance as far as Vlasov's troops, Second Shock Army found itself surrounded and was forced to surrender.

In the south, General Semyon Konstantinovich Timoshenko – another old Civil War comrade of Stalin – led a strong attack that threatened to reach Kharkov, but unknown to *Stavka* the Germans had selected the Ukraine as their prime focus for 1942, and lethal counterattacks led to a rapid reversal of fortunes and further catastrophic casualties. Zhukov and Vasilevsky both repeatedly asked Stalin to call off the offensive and withdraw the forces that had been committed, but Stalin refused until it was too late, with the result that Soviet losses climbed to 300,000, including 171,000 men taken prisoner. Critically, the Red Army lost over 1,200 precious tanks, leaving it outnumbered in armour for the coming fighting. Khrushchev, who was working as Timoshenko's political commissar, felt that Vasilevsky should have tried harder to change Stalin's mind and blamed him personally for the losses that were suffered. This criticism is surely unreasonable – the blame lay in the over-optimistic assessment and planning of Timoshenko (and therefore Khrushchev) who placed their troops in peril in the first instance, and then in Stalin's refusal to follow the advice of Zhukov and Vasilevsky, though Stalin attempted to pass blame for the mishap to Timoshenko and Krushchev:

> The [Soviet] general staff followed the development of the operation, which had been undertaken on the initiative of the command of the front, with great misgivings. *Stavka* warned the front that it could not provide any additional troops, ammunition or fuel for the operation ... But the military council of Southwest Front guaranteed success even without these.
>
> ... The position became more and more difficult until it was extremely critical. To the military council's request for help [Stalin] was compelled to reply:
>
> '... *Stavka* has no new divisions ready for action ... Our arms resources are limited and you must realise that there are other fronts besides your own ... Battles must be won not with numbers but by skill. If you do not learn to direct your troops better, all the armaments the country can produce will not be enough for you.'[18]

Given the number of occasions that Stalin had urged the front commanders to continue the winter attacks, it seems somewhat harsh that Stalin was now placing all the blame for the failures of these attacks on local commands, but regardless of who was culpable, as spring turned to summer the Germans were once more advancing, driving the Red Army before them.

The new offensive was not, as Stalin had expected, directed against Moscow. Instead, Hitler directed his forces to reach the line of the lower Volga with the intention of cutting off the Caucasus and its oilfields from the rest of the Soviet Union. Once this had been achieved, the Wehrmacht was to overrun the Caucasus as swiftly as possible, not least because Hitler believed that access to the Caucasus oilfields was vital for Germany's war effort. Stalin should have been aware of what was coming – on 19 June, a German plane carrying Major Reichel, the operations officer of 23rd Panzer Division, was shot down, and comprehensive maps showing the proposed German plan of campaign were recovered from the wreckage by Soviet troops.[19] When this intelligence windfall was presented to Stalin, he dismissed it as a German attempt at misinformation.[20] Ironically, this was at least partly due to a genuine German misinformation campaign – following the successful conclusion of the fighting around Kharkov, *OKH* (*OberKommando des Heeres* or 'Army High Command') issued instructions under the codename *Fall Kreml* ('Operation Kremlin') for a resumption of the previous winter's offensive to take Moscow. Detailed maps of Moscow were distributed down to regimental level in the German divisions facing the Soviet capital and instructions were issued for planning meetings to take place during the summer. As this fit neatly with Stalin's expectations, it is unsurprising that, given the choice of following his own belief or accepting the new intelligence recovered from the wrecked plane in the Ukraine, he chose the former.[21] The Reichel episode had another consequence: Hitler issued instructions that in order to prevent a repeat of such incidents, neighbouring units were not to have information about the orders issued to each other. The result was increasing rigidity in the German command structure, with a hugely detrimental effect on the skilful and adaptive manner in which the Wehrmacht had functioned in previous campaigns.

The losses suffered by the Red Army in the disastrous fighting near Kharkov in May left the Germans with a decided advantage. With barely any major effort, the German First and Fourth Panzer Armies erupted through the Soviet defences and headed east. The Red Army was in a period of transition; many of its pre-war troops and officers had been killed or taken prisoner in 1941, and their replacements were still learning their trade in the front line. Partly through force of circumstance and partly to avoid pointless casualties, Soviet troops fell back without risking the encirclements that had been the highlight of the previous year's campaign, as a sergeant in 3rd Panzer Division recorded:

> [It's] quite different from last year. It's more like Poland. The Russians aren't nearly so thick on the ground. They fire their guns like madmen, but they don't hurt us![22]

Attempting to stop the torrent of German armour would have been as disastrous a policy as it would have been futile, and *Stavka* issued instructions for the German breakthrough to be limited by the Red Army securing both 'shoulders' of the offensive, at Voronezh in the north and Rostov in the south. The speed of Fourth Panzer Army's advance to the Don at Voronezh threatened to derail this plan almost immediately and a new Voronezh Front was created by *Stavka* under the command of Lieutenant General Nikolai Fyodorovich Vatutin. Resistance stiffened just in time, and Field Marshal Fedor von Bock, commander of Army Group South, drew up detailed plans to throw substantial forces at the city in order to take it and secure the northern flank of the offensive.

Hitler had no intention of allowing the determined Russian resistance at Voronezh to derail his sweeping advance to the Volga and the Caucasus. Army

Group South was divided into Army Group A, tasked with driving south to the Caucasus oilfields, and Army Group B, which was to secure the line of the lower Volga. Bock was given command of Army Group B, but then dismissed when Hitler grew impatient with the delays at Voronezh. His replacement was Generaloberst Maximilian von Weichs, an aristocrat from Bavaria who Hitler judged was perhaps more compliant than the Prussian Bock.

Between Voronezh and Rostov, the Red Army continued to fall back. The lack of resistance was unnerving to some Germans, as a journalist wrote in the *Völkischer Beobachter*:

> The Russian, who up to this time has fought stubbornly over each kilometre, withdrew without firing a shot. Our advance was only delayed by destroyed bridges and by aircraft. When the Soviet rearguards were too hard-pressed they chose a position which enabled them to hold out until night … It was quite disquieting to plunge into this vast area without finding a trace of the enemy.[23]

Hitler interpreted this as a sign of terminal weakness, that the Red Army was running out of troops. In a conversation with Generaloberst Franz Halder, the chief of staff of *OKH*, he said on 20 July: 'The Russian is finished. I'm convinced of it.'[24]

At the time, Halder was inclined to agree with the Führer, but a steady stream of intelligence convinced him that the Soviet Union still possessed substantial resources that made the conquest of the Caucasus a risky venture. Indeed, such an operation only made sense if Hitler was right and the Red Army was wrecked beyond recovery – otherwise, the long flank along the Don and Volga would be hugely vulnerable to a Soviet counterattack. Unlike the previous winter, when Zhukov's counterattacks in front of Moscow ultimately ran out of steam before they could reach any meaningful objective, the Red Army would have several strategic targets within range. The most obvious option was to thrust down to the Sea of Azov and thus isolate any German forces that had penetrated into the Caucasus, but the rail crossings of the lower Dnepr were also conceivably within range, and if the Germans lost control of these, it would be impossible to supply the formations to the east of the river.

The increasingly alarming intelligence was largely correct – if anything, it underestimated the strength of the Red Army. During much of 1941, Soviet armaments production was badly disrupted as factories were hastily dismantled and shipped east, but even during this period the Soviet Union continued to produce more tanks than Germany. By early 1942, the factories had been reconstructed safe from German interference, sometimes in relatively primitive conditions; workers in the cluster of tank factories around Chelyabinsk – which earned itself the nickname of 'Tankograd' in the Soviet press – often worked in unheated buildings, many without glazing in their windows or even intact roofs. By the summer, there were sufficient tanks to create first two, then four new tank armies, but it is important to understand the difference in size and capability of Soviet formations in comparison to German ones. In 1942, a tank army consisted of two tank corps and a rifle division; each tank corps had three tank brigades and a motorised infantry brigade, with a total armoured strength of 20 heavy KV-1 tanks, 40 T-34s, and 40 light tanks. Such a corps was in fighting strength the equivalent of a weak panzer division, so a tank army could be considered as roughly the equivalent of a reinforced panzer division or an understrength panzer corps. On 6 July 1942, as the German Fourth Panzer Army fought its way into the western parts of Voronezh, the new Fifth Tank Army, commanded by Major General Alexander Ilyich Lizyukov, launched a counterattack; partly as a result of inexperience and partly due to logistic difficulties, the attack was made piecemeal with a single tank corps on the first day and the rest of the tank army being thrown in over the subsequent two days. Even this might have succeeded if Lizyukov had been opposed by infantry, but it was his and his army's misfortune that the German 24th Panzer Division, created in the winter from the personnel of the Wehrmacht's only cavalry division, lay in their path and was able to smash each attack in turn. Within a week, Fifth Tank Army had lost over 8,000 men and 73 of its tanks.[25] Lizyukov was demoted and assigned to command II Tank Corps; on 23 July, he was ordered to attack again but his brigades found themselves isolated and surrounded. Lizyukov commandeered one of the few heavyweight KV-1 tanks available and set off to try to reach his isolated units, but ran into tough German defences. Although the armour of the KV-1 proved impervious to most German anti-tank shells, the vehicle was immobilised and then overrun by infantry, and Lizyukov was killed.[26]

Despite these setbacks, the Soviet forces continued to learn. Colonel Pavel Alexeyevich Rotmistrov was at the time the chief of staff of a mechanised corps, and wrote a frank analysis of the failure of the tank corps:

> The difficulty is that while there isn't much difference in speed between the light (T-60) tank and the medium (T-34) tank on the roads, when moving across country the light tanks are quickly left behind. The heavy (KV) tank is already behind and often crushes bridges, which cuts off units behind it. Under battlefield conditions, this has meant that too often the T-34 alone arrived; the light tanks

had difficulty fighting the German tanks anyway, and the KVs were delayed in the rear. It was also difficult to command these companies because occasionally they were equipped with different types of radios or none at all.[27]

In response to this and other reports, Lieutenant General Iakov Nikolayevich Fedorenko, deputy defence minister and head of the tank and mechanised troops directorate, initiated a series of changes. Crew training was improved, particularly to promote cooperation between individual vehicles and small units. More radios were to be fitted to tanks, and handles welded to their hulls to allow infantry to ride on them as they went into battle. The KV-1s were withdrawn from tank brigades, which became made up of a mixture of T-34s and T-70s, and the overall strength of the brigade was increased to 60 tanks, so that a tank corps fielded 180 in all, making it a far better match for a German panzer division. The artillery component of the corps was also steadily enhanced, at least on paper, but it proved difficult in the short term to provide sufficient guns to satisfy the new establishment tables that were drawn up. Regardless of this, the main weakness remained in command and tactical skill. As a result, disasters like Lizyukov's disjointed counterattack continued to fritter away the hard-gained resources of the Soviet forces.

During the chaotic retreats of 1941, many Red Army units had continued to fight until they were wiped out and their few survivors were then cobbled together hastily into new formations; now, with much of the Eastern Front far quieter, there was time to pull degraded units out of the front line and bring them back up to strength with fresh drafts and to replace their lost equipment. The replenished units were then redeployed in quiet sectors to allow their new recruits time to learn their craft; instead of being thrown into the fire of battle in formations made up entirely of inexperienced men, the new troops of the Red Army learned to fight side by side with the survivors of the previous year and had the opportunity to learn from their experiences. Relationships between officers of different ranks and the men they commanded became more established and mutual trust and confidence grew as a result. If they were used judiciously, if a good operational opportunity presented itself, the units of the Red Army would be a far more formidable proposition for the Wehrmacht.

First, though, the German thrust towards Stalingrad and the Caucasus had to be brought to a halt, and trying to achieve this continued to cost the Russians major losses. Whilst Vatutin's Voronezh Front had succeeded in securing the northern 'shoulder' of the German advance, the intended bastion on the southern side – Rostov – fell to the advancing Germans on 23 July, the same day that

Lizyukov was killed. This was a major setback for the Red Army; having been caught off-guard by the German drive in the south, it was still scrambling to respond, and after capturing Rostov – and overrunning the Crimea – the Wehrmacht was in position to exploit its gains on a broad front. The local Red Army units were far too weak to cover the vast spaces that now formed the battlefield.

Nevertheless, an attempt had to be made to stop the Germans from reaching Stalingrad and the Volga. Two tank armies – First and Fourth – were available, but both were significantly below establishment strength and only First Tank Army was ready to attack. Its formations were thrown into the fighting as the Germans approached the Don crossings at Kalach; by mid-August, it had ceased to exist. Nevertheless, the German advance was slowed. Just as the Red Army was struggling to cover the terrain, so too the Germans were finding it much harder to concentrate forces, especially given the poor roads. The increasingly long northern flank of the advance along the Don had to be covered by the infantry divisions of the German Sixth Army, leaving it with reduced forces for dealing with the Russian defenders around Kalach. Gradually, the armies of Germany's allies – the Hungarians, Italians and Romanians – replaced Sixth Army's infantry formations along the Don, and these infantry divisions were sequentially added to the forces trying to reach Stalingrad; however, torn between the need to keep up attacks before the Russians could strengthen their lines and the need to pause to concentrate troops, General Friedrich Paulus, commander of Sixth Army, felt obliged to choose the former. As a result, the intermittent trickle of German divisions was more or less matched by the ability of the Red Army to send reinforcements to the area. Casualties rose steadily, and despite repeated requests from Paulus it proved impossible to secure adequate replacements. His infantry formations had started the campaign below full strength, and their steady losses through the summer left them increasingly weakened.

If the Red Army couldn't stop the Wehrmacht, Hitler could. The failure to complete the capture of Voronezh left a strongpoint from which the Soviet forces could threaten the entire flank of the German advance, but the Führer's impatience to pursue his greater goals in the south prevailed. Fourth Panzer Army was ordered south to help Kleist's First Panzer Army force the crossings over the lower Don so that it could drive on towards the Caucasus. When it was given, the order might have made sense, as Kleist was encountering substantial resistance and there was a possibility that, by concentrating sufficient mobile forces in the area, the Germans could destroy the Russian units trying to defend the river line. But by the time Hoth arrived on the Don, the Soviet forces had made good their escape. Resistance thereafter was almost non-existent, and once across the lower Don, Kleist's units rolled south as fast as fuel supplies would allow. Meanwhile, having contributed nothing to Army Group A's task – other than creating two major traffic jams, one as he passed behind Sixth Army and one on the approaches to the lower Don – Hoth was ordered to turn northeast and attack towards Stalingrad. The depleted divisions of the German Sixth Army were finding it hard to make progress as a steady flow of Russian reserve formations was deployed in their path. Had Fourth Panzer Army been available to lead the way to Stalingrad from the northwest, as had originally been intended before it was diverted first to the south and then ordered to attack Stalingrad from the southwest, it is likely that Sixth Army would have been in possession of the city and the west bank of the lower Volga before the Red Army could shore up its defences. Instead, it found itself drawn into an increasingly bitter battle of attrition in the ruins of Stalingrad. The losses suffered by its infantry divisions were now causing serious concern, and these casualties were augmented by another factor – Oberst Wilhelm Adam, Paulus' adjutant, noted with increasing concern that illness was as great a drain on the strength of German divisions as enemy action.[28] Regardless of the opinions of Hitler about the weakness of the Red Army, field commanders grew steadily more uneasy. Compared with the previous year, few prisoners were being taken. Hitler continued to interpret this as a sign that the Red Army was running out of men; the soldiers in the front line, however, increasingly feared that the Russians were preserving their strength for the coming battles.

It was a year of huge swings of the pendulum. At the beginning of 1942, the Wehrmacht was reeling from its failure to take Moscow and the subsequent Soviet counterattacks. In the weeks that followed, Stalin's over-eagerness to launch offensive operations handed back the initiative to the Germans, who first crushed the Red Army drive towards Kharkov and then opened up their own major offensive. As autumn began, the pendulum was swinging back. Sixth Army and large parts of Fourth Panzer Army were stuck in bloody street-fighting in Stalingrad, while Kleist's First Panzer Army ran out of steam – and supplies – in the Caucasus foothills. Increasingly, the Germans found that they lacked the logistic capability to support both the advance into the Caucasus and the huge demands of Sixth Army in Stalingrad. The simultaneous pursuit of both objectives had only made sense if the Red Army had been decisively defeated, and as the year drew on it was clear that this was not the case. Even when supplies were available, the attempts to mount diverging operations placed intolerable strains on combat units – the Luftwaffe could

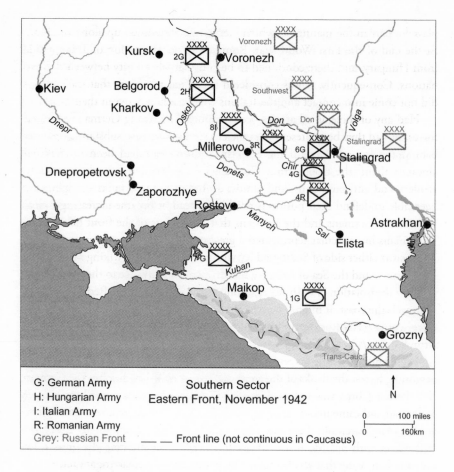

G: German Army
H: Hungarian Army
I: Italian Army
R: Romanian Army
Grey: Russian Front

Southern Sector
Eastern Front, November 1942

N

0   100 miles
0   160km

_ _ _ _ Front line (not continuous in Caucasus)

provide air support for attacks in the Caucasus or in Stalingrad, but not for both at the same time.

The long flank running from Voronezh to Stalingrad began to look increasingly vulnerable. With the bulk of Army Group B's German formations engaged in the huge battle on the shores of the Volga, security for its flanks passed to the Romanian Third Army to the northwest and the Romanian Fourth Army to the south. The Third Army consisted of ten divisions, covering a front of about 100 miles (170km); the Fourth Army was still in the process of completing its assembly in late November 1942, with seven divisions covering an even greater distance of 120 miles (200km). Beyond the Romanian sector to the north was the Italian Eighth Army of ten Italian and two German divisions, followed by the Hungarian Second Army of 12 Hungarian and two German divisions. Politics played a part in the manner in which Germany's allies lined up along the Don. At the end of the First World War, Romania seized the region of Transylvania from Hungary, and there continued to be considerable enmity between the two nations. Consequently, it was considered expedient to ensure that their troops did not come into contact and the Italians were inserted between them.

Had any of these allied armies been supported by strong German armoured forces, or had they been present in sufficient strength to have substantial reserves behind the front line, or if more German formations had been intercalated amongst them, the troops from Germany's Axis partners – weak in modern artillery and anti-tank guns, and almost devoid of modern tanks – might have been able to defend their positions reliably. Instead, it became increasingly clear to both the Germans and the Russians that the sectors of the front held by the Romanians in particular represented a great opportunity for a counteroffensive. The sectors either side of Stalingrad lay within relatively easy striking range of the Don estuary and the Sea of Azov – a successful Soviet advance to the coast might result in the isolation of both Army Groups A and B. Even if the Red Army could not reach the coast, it might encircle Sixth Army in Stalingrad, and if the Soviet forces could reach Rostov, they would be astride the long supply lines on which Army Group A in the Caucasus was dependent.

Even while the battle for Stalingrad was coming to a climax, the Red Army was beginning to test the flanks of the great salient that ended at the city. The German XIV Panzer Corps was tasked with defending the immediate northern side of Stalingrad and came under repeated heavy attack during September. Although all attacks were beaten off, there was a heavy cost, as Oberst Hans-Jürgen Dingler, a staff officer with 3rd Motorised Division, recorded, highlighting that it was not only the Red Army that was hampered by poorly trained replacement drafts:

> During these attacks our position seemed hopeless on more than one occasion. The reinforcements in men and material we received from home were insufficient. Those men who had no previous battle experience were quite useless in this hard fighting. The losses they suffered from the first day in the fighting line were staggering. We could not 'acclimatise' these people gradually to battle conditions by attaching them to quiet sectors, because there were no such sectors at that time. Nor was it possible to withdraw veterans from the front to give these raw recruits thorough training.[29]

General Gustav von Wietersheim, commander of XIV Panzer Corps, was amongst several senior commanders to express concern about the exposed flanks of the Stalingrad bulge. With Sixth Army proving incapable of suppressing the last pockets of resistance within the city and his own divisions being steadily worn down, he expressed doubt that he would be able to hold the northern flank of the salient indefinitely, particularly as the line further to the northwest was now defended by the weak Romanian Third Army. Wietersheim wrote to Paulus, his superior, suggesting that it would be safer to conduct an orderly withdrawal back to the line of the Don, where defences could be organised with greater confidence. However, this would entail abandoning the shattered ruins of Stalingrad and there was no possibility of Hitler ever agreeing to such a move, now that possession of the city had assumed such importance. Wietersheim, who had clashed with Hitler before the war and was clearly no favourite of the Führer, was dismissed and replaced by General Hans-Valentin Hube, whose 16th Panzer Division was part of XIV Panzer Corps. General Viktor von Schwedler, commander of IV Corps and heavily involved in the increasingly futile slaughter in Stalingrad, specifically highlighted the peril of concentrating strength at the point of an attack that had failed – a 'dead *Schwerpunkt*' – and advocated the movement of major forces to protect the flanks of the bulge, if necessary by pulling out of Stalingrad itself. He too was dismissed. Field Marshal List, commander of Army Group A, was removed for failing to achieve the conquests expected of him, even though he had been deprived of air support and supplies in favour of Stalingrad, and Hitler took direct command of the army group himself. Halder, the increasingly embattled chief of staff at *OKH*, whose relationship with Hitler had deteriorated badly through the second half of the year as the magnitude of the risks faced by the Wehrmacht grew ever clearer, was also sacked.

The post that Halder had occupied was hugely influential and everyone – including Hitler – was aware that it was a potent counter-weight to the Führer's military sway. Consequently, there was considerable interest in who should replace Halder. Field Marshal Wilhelm Keitel, the head of *OKW* (*Oberkommando der Wehrmacht*, 'Armed Forces High Command', the replacement for the war ministry and with overall command of German military operations outside the Eastern Front), urged Hitler to appoint Field Marshal Erich von Manstein as Halder's replacement. Like Vasilevsky, Manstein would be a key personality in the coming battles; the contrast between his origins and those of Vasilevsky could hardly be greater.

Born Fritz Erich Georg Eduard von Lewinski, Manstein was the tenth child of a Prussian general. His mother's sister, married to Georg von Manstein, was unable to have children and adopted the youngest of the Lewinski children, together with another cousin, an arrangement that was relatively commonplace at the time. Although he was aware that the Mansteins were not his natural parents, he always referred to them as 'mother' and 'father' and adopted their surname without hesitation. The family – both natural and adoptive – had extensive military links; one of his uncles was Paul von Hindenburg, who would win fame as an army commander in the First World War and would play a pivotal part in Hitler's rise to power when serving as president of Germany. As was usually the case with Prussian families, Manstein effectively joined the army as a child when he went to the junior cadet school in Holstein aged only 12; later, he became a page at the royal court and then joined the 3rd Prussian Foot Guards. In 1911, he was appointed adjutant to the regiment's fusilier battalion, and when he departed two years later to join the *Königlich Preussische Kriegsakademie* ('Royal Prussian War Academy') in Berlin to commence training as a staff officer, his battalion commander described him in glowing colours as the best adjutant he had ever known.[30]

Amongst Manstein's contemporaries in the academy were Heinz Guderian, who would lead German armoured troops with such distinction in the Second World War, and Erich Hoepner, under whose command Manstein would serve during the first months of *Barbarossa*. After completing only one of his three years in Berlin, Manstein's studies were interrupted by the outbreak of war. He joined the 1st Guards Reserve Division and took part in the successful reduction of the Belgian fortress of Namur before his division was transferred in haste to the Eastern Front. He was involved in fighting in Poland in late 1914 and was wounded, spending the next six months recovering from shoulder and knee injuries. Thereafter, he held a number of staff posts both in the east and the west. After the defeat of Germany, he demonstrated what would become one of his hallmarks: precise and detailed staffwork, produced quickly, on this occasion to organise the withdrawal of the division in which he was serving back to Germany.

Like many Prussian officers, Manstein found the abdication of the Kaiser deeply unsettling. The entire officer corps had regarded itself as bound by personal allegiance to their monarch, and now faced the difficult task of transferring their loyalty to the state. Ultimately, it was this sense of loyalty that was exploited by Hitler with the personal oath of allegiance, something that proved to be an almost insurmountable barrier for most officers when it came to trying to overthrow the Führer. But in 1918, such considerations lay far in the future. Manstein became a member of the Reichswehr, serving in a variety of roles before joining the *Truppenamt* ('Troops Office', the title under which the general staff – banned under the terms of the Treaty of Versailles – continued to function) as head of the operational planning staff. Here, he drew up plans for how the

Reichswehr – restricted to only 100,000 men – could be expanded rapidly into a much larger army should the need and opportunity arise. He was also involved in developing close cooperation with the Soviet Union, which allowed Germany to evade many of the restrictions imposed at Versailles.

Hitler's accession to power occurred when Manstein was a battalion commander in Kolberg on the Baltic coast. Like many Prussian officers, he found the Nazis generally distasteful, and when Goering visited the town, Manstein used the opportunity to make a small gesture of protest; instead of reporting to Goering with his honour guard, Manstein instructed the guard party's officer to report to the regimental commander, who then invited Goering to inspect the soldiers. It was only the smallest of snubs, but some have seen in this the roots of Goering's antipathy for the future field marshal.[31] Manstein's intervention on behalf of a part-Jewish doctor in Kolberg, a decorated veteran of the First World War who was being threatened with dismissal by local Party authorities, also did little to endear him to the Nazi hierarchy and in 1934, when he became chief of staff to *Wehrkreiskommando III* – the military district responsible for the Berlin area – he wrote to General Ludwig Beck, chief of the *Truppenamt*, to protest about regulations that forbade Jews from becoming or remaining officials either in the civil service or the military. However, these acts do not necessarily reflect a rejection of Nazi ideology regarding the Jews; the letter to Beck accepted that the legal and medical professions contained far too many Jews and that they would have to be 'cleansed', but regarded military duty as a different matter entirely. Soldiers were expected to be willing to lay down their lives for their nation, argued Manstein, and should therefore not be placed in a position where someone might question their right to be regarded as full citizens. He suggested that the Wehrmacht should be responsible for deciding the fitness or otherwise of those within its ranks to continue in service, based upon whether the individuals concerned had behaved consistently like pure-blooded Germans and possessed no foreign characteristics that might affect their behaviour. Even with these dilutions and qualifications, Manstein's letter led to some, including General Werner von Blomberg, the German War Minister, to contemplate disciplinary action. Beck – protecting his protégé in the same manner that Shaposhnikov protected Vatutin during Stalin's purges – succeeded in preventing any action being taken, and it was the last time that Manstein ventured into such political hot water.

In 1935, Manstein continued on his rising trajectory and became head of the general staff's operations branch. This was a period in which radical ideas about armoured warfare were clashing with more traditional views, and perhaps for the first time in his career Manstein found himself holding a different opinion from his conservatively minded mentor, Beck. Manstein accepted Guderian's views about independent panzer divisions forming the spearhead of the army, but also campaigned for armoured support for the infantry. This led to a paper in 1935 in which he started by reminding readers that mobile horse-drawn artillery had been added to infantry divisions in 1918 to help them overcome resistance from improvised defences, which – particularly if they possessed a few machine-guns – could bring an advance to an abrupt halt. With the advent of mechanised warfare, Manstein argued that there was a need for motorised assault artillery.[32] After some initial resistance, the concept rapidly gained ground and the first turretless *Sturmgeschütz* or assault guns began to enter service in 1937. Manstein had wished to have a battalion of three batteries – each with four or six assault guns – per infantry division, with additional assault guns assigned to panzer divisions, but providing so many weapons and crews was beyond the resources of German military industry, especially at a time when the Wehrmacht was expanding at a huge rate. The assault guns were ultimately deployed mainly in independent battalions, but consistently proved to be powerful assets both as infantry support and in anti-tank roles.

Manstein's time in the operations directorate was followed by a spell as deputy quartermaster-general, and thereafter he was appointed as commander of 18th Infantry Division, replacing Hermann Hoth, who would cross paths with Manstein in the critical weeks of late 1942 and early 1943. In 1938, Beck urged his fellow senior officers to resign en masse in protest at Germany's slide towards a war that he was convinced his nation would lose; unable to persuade them to stand by him, he resigned alone in August and commenced on a path that would lead to his involvement in, and death as a consequence of, the July Plot of 1944. Manstein regretted both his own posting to 18th Infantry Division and Beck's resignation, not least because he had aspirations of replacing Beck personally one day. Instead, the post went to Franz Halder, creating considerable ill will between the two men.[33]

As war approached, Manstein became chief of staff of Army Group South, which would be led by Generaloberst Gerd von Runstedt into Poland. He drew up the army group's operational plans, involving the concentration of its armoured assets in a powerful drive on Warsaw, and his rapid and innovative staffwork helped turn the crisis caused by a Polish counterattack into a decisive victory during the Battle of the Bzura. It was an important moment in the development both of Manstein and the German Army, as he later wrote:

[The battle] was not one which could be planned from the outset through penetration of the enemy front by powerful tank formations, but arose from counter-moves made on the German side when the enemy's own actions unexpectedly gave us our big opportunity.[34]

It was this ability to improvise during operations, and the leadership skill to execute such improvisations, that was as much a part of Germany's early successes in the war as the panzer divisions; they were powerful weapons, but it was the flexible manner in which they were wielded that led to victory. But whilst this observation by Manstein is entirely accurate, his further comments – that 'the troops had a purely military battle to fight, and for that reason it had still been possible to fight chivalrously' is naïve at best and utterly misleading at worst. Whilst later fighting in the east was on a far more brutal scale, the Polish campaign and its aftermath were marked with widespread atrocities against the Poles, and although the SS played a leading role in these, many Wehrmacht units, notably in Manstein's Army Group South, were also involved. Leni Riefenstahl, the German film director, visited the front line and witnessed either the killing of a group of Jews in Końskie or its aftermath; Manstein blamed the incident on a nervous officer who over-reacted to panic in the town. He added in his memoirs that the officer was court-martialled and sentenced to demotion and imprisonment but that such measures were undermined by Hitler, who frequently issued pardons and in 1941 removed the right of the army to prosecute cases involving civilians on the Eastern Front. Whilst it is true that Hitler did issue pardons in such cases, there is also evidence that on this occasion, prosecution only occurred at the insistence of Riefenstahl.[35] In any event, this episode surely falls far short of the 'chivalrous' conduct of war that Manstein described.

With Poland defeated, attention turned to the west and a further opportunity arose for Manstein to demonstrate his growing expertise. On 9 October, Hitler issued a directive relating to the further prosecution of the war. He started by stating that if France and Britain were not willing to discuss peace after the fall of Poland, he wished to strike as soon as possible – delay would benefit the enemies of the Reich more than the Reich itself. To that end, an offensive was to be launched on the northern flank through Luxembourg, Belgium and the Netherlands as early as possible, with the intention of defeating as large a part of the forces of the Western Powers as could be accomplished, while securing sufficient territory to protect the Ruhr and to allow further conduct of the war against Britain – i.e. the capture of the channel coast.[36] *OKH* accordingly prepared a preliminary document outlining what would effectively be a mechanised version of the Schlieffen Plan that had failed to knock out the French in 1914, the main difference being that the flanking movement would also incorporate the Netherlands. Manstein was unimpressed by this proposal and on behalf of Rundstedt's army group he submitted a series of memoranda criticising the plan. He argued that it represented what the Western Powers would expect and was likely to run out of steam somewhere in northern France, perhaps leading to the same drawn-out war of attrition that had occurred in the First World War. There were perhaps also personal issues at stake: the *OKH* plan would see Army Group B, facing Belgium and the Netherlands, as the primary attacking force, leaving Rundstedt's Army Group A, further south, to play only a supporting role, though the arguments submitted by Manstein and Rundstedt were strictly professional and logical. Furthermore, rather than aiming for what would at best be only a partial victory, Manstein argued that Germany should seek to lure British and French forces into Belgium and then annihilate them. This would leave France fatally weakened and unable to continue the war. To that end, he and Rundstedt proposed that Army Group B should make its attack appear to be the main effort, while Army Group A would concentrate its striking power for a powerful thrust through the Ardennes and Sedan to the channel coast in northern France.

Unsurprisingly, *OKH* was unimpressed by this radical proposal, arguing that there was insufficient strength available in Army Group A for such an operation. Manstein responded (on behalf of Rundstedt) that this could be achieved by transferring more forces to the south. But if *OKH* was not enthusiastic about the plan, Hitler thought otherwise. In November, he authorised the creation of a mobile armoured group for an advance on Sedan under the command of Guderian. When Manstein discussed the matter with Guderian, the latter replied that an advance through the Ardennes was perfectly possible, but should be conducted by a strike force of not just some of Germany's panzer divisions, but as many of them as possible. Discussions continued through the winter, and on 25 January there was a particularly heated encounter between Brauchitsch, the commander-in-chief of the army, and the senior officers of Army Group A; perhaps in response to this, Manstein received a new assignment just two days later, as commander of XXXVIII Corps in Stettin, far from the impending campaign.

By this stage, even Halder – who had initially been scornful about Army Group A's proposals – was coming to the conclusion that the proposed armoured force for the thrust to Sedan was too weak and would require far more force, thus effectively shifting the main effort from Army Group B to Army Group A.

The critical moment came on 17 February when Manstein and a group of fellow officers were invited to a working breakfast in Hitler's *Reichkanzlei* (Reich Chancellery). Manstein was asked to stay when the others left and had a long discussion about the plans for the west. The result was the adoption of Manstein's plan for an operation through the Ardennes to the channel coast via Sedan. Whilst Manstein had shown great skill in improvising during the Battle of the Bzura the previous year and had played a leading role in the operational plans of Army Group South prior to the invasion of Poland, this was the first time that he had devised an operation making use of most of Germany's mechanised forces, and against a far more formidable foe than the brave but outgunned Polish Army. The success of the German attack through the Ardennes, codenamed *Sichelschnitt* ('sickle cut'), demonstrated his mastery of operational thinking at every level, combining an accurate assessment of the striking power of mechanised troops, the value of surprise, the use of air power to substitute for slower moving artillery, and how to interpret his shrewd assessment of the expectations and intentions of the enemy.

Manstein's XXXVIII Corps played no role in the dramatic dash to the channel in the opening phase of the great campaign in the west. Instead, his divisions were in the second echelon and were tasked with defending the southern flank of the advance. By the end of May, he was involved in fighting off disjointed British and French attempts to strike at the Somme crossings, and in June he led his infantry corps in a swift advance across France. He had no armoured forces under his command, so he improvised as best he could; using what vehicles were available, he created motorised detachments that pushed ahead as rapidly as possible, leading personally and urging his tired men forward in the ideal manner of an outstanding officer, setting an example for others to emulate. His observations serve as a summary for anyone aspiring to leadership in any role, military or otherwise:

> The example and bearing of officers and other soldiers who are responsible for leadership has a decisive effect on the troops. The officer who in the face of the enemy displays coolness and courage carries his troops with him. He also must win their affections and earn their trust through his understanding of their feelings, their way of thinking, and through selfless care for them.[37]

The speed of advance of Manstein's infantry was astonishing. They swept forward over the Somme, Seine and Loire, some foot elements covering over 40 miles (70km) per day, and averaging about 18 miles (30km). The feat earned him the

Knight's Cross; he had demonstrated in just a few months that in addition to being an original and innovative operational planner, he was also a master of the tactical battle. After spending much of the rest of 1940 preparing his corps for an amphibious assault on the English coast, he was transferred east in early 1941 to take command of LVI Motorised Corps, later renamed LVI Panzer Corps. It was a command that he had long desired and one he embraced with enthusiasm.

LVI Motorised Corps consisted of 8th Panzer Division, 3rd Motorised Infantry Division, and 290th Infantry Division. In the coming attack on the Soviet Union, its primary task was to secure crossings over the Daugava gorge at Daugavpils, and the manner in which this was executed highlighted all the strengths of German command and training. True to the principles of *Auftragstaktik* ('task-oriented tactics'), Manstein specified what was required without dictating how it was to be achieved and gave his subordinates freedom to innovate as required. Generalmajor Erich Brandenberger, commander of 8th Panzer Division, rapidly switched the axis of his attack when the initial main thrust ran into strong resistance and proceeded to burst through the Soviet defences, spreading confusion and chaos as his troops surged forward, reaching and capturing the crossings at Daugavpils within four days – an advance of 196 miles (315km). Despite both his flanks being completely exposed, Brandenburger, with Manstein's knowledge and consent, gave his men freedom to proceed at full speed, relying on confusion and pace for security. Thereafter, progress was slower – Hoepner, Manstein's superior, demanded a pause while neighbouring units caught up, and the Red Army began to recover its balance – but the true source of the reluctance to press on was almost certainly higher. Field Marshal Wilhelm Ritter von Leeb, commander of Army Group North, was from the conservative wing of the army and unwilling to allow Hoepner's two motorised corps to thrust into the Soviet hinterland alone; in any event, logistic difficulties made the pause inevitable.

Shortly after, Manstein's troops came under attack from the Soviet Eleventh Army, commanded by Vatutin – the first encounter between the two men on the battlefield. The German 8th Panzer Division suffered heavy losses and was removed from Manstein's command, and he spent an increasingly frustrated few weeks dealing with mutually contradictory tasks – on the one hand, Hoepner's panzer group (as panzer armies were known at the time) was meant to lead an advance to Leningrad, but on the other hand the rapidly diverging axes of attack along the entire front required the panzer divisions to be used to help maintain continuity, particularly in the face of repeated Soviet counterattacks. Shortly after defeating one such counterattack and effectively destroying General Kusma

Maximovich Kachanov's Thirty-Fourth Army – which resulted in Kachanov being court-martialled and executed – Manstein was assigned to a new command: he was sent south to lead the German Eleventh Army, tasked with the conquest of the Crimea.

Manstein's new command was largely infantry, and it took him several months to achieve his objectives. At first, it seemed as if the Germans might overrun the entire Crimea before the end of 1941, but the casualties suffered by Manstein's divisions and amphibious counterattacks by the Red Army resulted in much of the initial German gains being overturned. Eventually, with substantial air support, Eleventh Army was able to subdue the eastern Crimea in May 1942 before turning to the fortress of Sevastopol, widely regarded as one of the strongest fortresses in the world. In the face of heavy resistance and considerable casualties, Manstein carefully unpicked the city's defences, completing its capture in early July, for which he was promoted to field marshal.

With this triumph in siege warfare behind them, Manstein's troops were to be deployed in the far north to repeat the feat by capturing Leningrad; it was at this point that Halder was dismissed, and Manstein's name was suggested as a replacement. Despite many feeling that Manstein was the best candidate as chief of staff at *OKH* – indeed, that he should have been given the post in preference to Halder when Beck resigned – Hitler rejected the suggestion on the grounds that Manstein was needed for the planned campaign in the north. The true reasons are probably far more complex. Manstein now had a reputation as perhaps the best strategist and operational expert in the army, and Siegfried Westphal, who as a staff captain had been his subordinate in the years before the war, sums up many of his characteristics:

> [He] was a pleasant man, a military genius. He demonstrated that in every position during the Second World War. He worked unbelievably quickly; impatiently, he couldn't stand long presentations. He was a generous superior officer, a complete gentleman, but an uncomfortable subordinate. He didn't have too many friends amongst his peers.[38]

On an earlier occasion – at the end of 1941 – when Manstein's possible transfer from the Eastern Front to high command in Berlin had been discussed, Hitler had also been ambivalent, telling Halder that whilst Manstein was a genial personality, he was too independent to fit comfortably with the manner in which the Führer worked.[39] It was therefore no surprise that Keitel's suggestion of Manstein replacing Halder was turned down. The new chief of staff at *OKH* would be General Kurt Zeitzler, a man who had held a succession of staff posts in which he had excelled and had a reputation as a logistics expert, and was a far more pliant individual than Manstein. For the moment at least, Manstein remained with Eleventh Army.

On 26 October, a day after he had attended the funeral of Leutnant Pepo Specht, a favourite aide-de-camp who was killed in an air crash while en route to take up a new post, Manstein flew to Vinnitsa where Hitler had established his headquarters to receive his marshal's baton personally from the Führer. The independent-minded field marshal took the opportunity to have a frank discussion with Hitler about the growing weakness of German infantry divisions:

> With such high losses as we were bound to have in the east while fighting an enemy as tough as the Russians, it was vitally important that the infantry regiments should always be brought back up to strength with the minimum possible delay. But when replacements never arrived on time – and none had ever done so since the Russian campaign began – the infantry had to go into action far below their proper strength, with the inevitable result that the fighting troops became more and more worn down as time went on.[40]

What particularly irritated Manstein was the fact that there were plenty of personnel available to make good the losses of the infantry. The Luftwaffe had long been regarded as lavishly over-manned by the army, and there were repeated proposals for 170,000 men to be transferred to the army after the Russian campaign began. Goering was unwilling to lose such a large body of men and persuaded Hitler to authorise the creation of 22 Luftwaffe field divisions instead, on the grounds that Luftwaffe personnel were politically more attuned to National Socialism than the army, which remained suspiciously conservative as far as the Party was concerned. Manstein had no doubt that this decision was sheer folly:

> Considering what a wide choice had been open to the Luftwaffe in making its selections for these divisions, they were doubtless composed of first-class soldiers. Had they been drafted to army divisions as replacements in autumn 1941 to maintain the latter at their full fighting strength, the German Army might well have been saved most of the emergencies of the winter of 1941–42. But to form these excellent troops into divisions within the framework of the Luftwaffe was sheer lunacy. Where were they to get the necessary close-combat training and practice in working with other formations? Where were they to get the battle

experience so vital in the east? And where was the Luftwaffe to find divisional, regimental and battalion commanders?

I covered all these aspects in detail during that talk with Hitler and a little later set them out in a memorandum I drafted for his attention. He listened to my arguments attentively enough, but insisted that he had already given the matter his fullest consideration and must stick to his decision.[41]

Goering had already specified that these divisions – lighter in manpower than regular army divisions, and far less capable militarily – would only be suitable for defensive duties on quiet areas of the front. Several were now sent to protect the flanks of Army Group B, and far from being in a quiet sector, they would find themselves caught up in a desperate battle to prevent total collapse.

Whilst the memoirs of figures like Manstein place a great deal of blame upon Hitler for the manner in which events unfolded in 1942, there is evidence that the Führer was acutely aware of the possible threat, particularly to the northern flank of Army Group B. As early as 16 August, the war diary of *OKW* recorded:

The Führer is concerned that Stalin will recall the classic Russian attack of 1920, i.e. an attack over the Don roughly at Serafimovich thrusting towards Rostov, as the Bolsheviks undertook and completed with great success against General Wrangel's White Russian Army in 1920. He fears that the Italian Eighth Army, which guards this sector of the Don, will not be able to hold back such an attack, and therefore insists anew that 22nd Panzer Division should be deployed behind the Italians as soon as possible after it has been replenished.[42]

Formed in September 1941, 22nd Panzer Division was thrown into the Eastern Front before it was ready for combat in early 1942 and consequently suffered heavy losses. It was equipped predominantly with the Pz.35(t) tank, a Czech design that was effectively obsolete by the beginning of the war with the Soviet Union. Although the division remained on the Eastern Front and saw further fighting in defeating the Red Army's disastrous drive towards Kharkov and helped in the later German advance on Rostov, it was a victim of supply priorities. At a time when so much materiel was being consumed in Stalingrad, bringing the division back to full strength was something that received scant attention. Together with the Romanian 1st Armoured Division, which had an almost identical tank in its ranks, 22nd Panzer Division was deployed in support of Army Group B's northern flank as XLVIII Panzer Corps. Due to fuel shortages, the crews of the German division's tanks dug several of their tanks into defensive positions and put straw inside them in an attempt to provide protection against frost damage; the straw attracted mice, which proceeded to damage the wiring of many of the tanks, reducing the division's strength still further. Demands for small groups of vehicles to be sent to support individual Romanian and Italian units on the front line left the division spread out and completely unable to function as a coherent force that might launch an effective counterattack against any future Russian assault.

The Red Army was indeed planning such assaults. First considerations were given as early as September and the first proposals were rapidly adopted, both codenamed after planets of the solar system. *Mars* would be a determined assault on the Rzhev salient to the west of Moscow in order to eliminate once and for all the German threat to the Soviet capital, and *Uranus* would see Soviet forces striking at both the exposed flanks of the German Sixth Army in Stalingrad in order to envelop it and destroy it. Shortly after the execution of *Uranus*, a further plan – *Saturn* – was devised, striking towards Rostov and the Sea of Azov in order to isolate and eliminate all German forces east of the Don and in the Caucasus. In his memoirs, Vasilevsky describes *Mars* as a diversionary attack, but this was far from the case; it involved more Soviet forces than were committed in the south for *Uranus*, and the fighting that raged for a month from late November was merely the preliminary step of planned operations against the German Army Group Centre. *Mars* was to be followed by *Jupiter*, which would destroy all German forces east of Smolensk. In the event, *Mars* was a costly failure and *Jupiter* was therefore never put into effect. The Red Army lost over 300,000 dead, wounded and taken prisoner; German losses were about 40,000.[43] However, it had an important consequence on the fighting further south: under such pressure, the German Army Group Centre could not spare any troops to fight elsewhere.

And it was elsewhere that the decisive turning point in the war on the Eastern Front would come: not before Moscow, where the two armies had struggled for supremacy in late 1941, and where Stalin had expected a renewal of the German effort for much of the following year. It was *Uranus* that would create the crisis that enveloped the Wehrmacht and appeared to open the way for the Soviet Union to defeat Germany entirely.

CHAPTER 2

THE HAMMER FALLS: *URANUS*

Just as Hitler and others looked at the flanks of Sixth Army – particularly to the north – with concern, senior Soviet figures were also considering their options. On 12 September, Vasilevsky, Zhukov and Stalin met to discuss once again the ultimate failure of the previous winter's counteroffensives, and how to proceed in the coming months. Zhukov started by describing – not for the first time – the way in which the attacking armies had lacked sufficient tanks and artillery to guarantee success; at the very least, he continued, these factors had to be remedied, and adequate air support would have to be available. He and Vasilevsky were sent away to discuss the issue and to return the following day with concrete plans. When they did so, they outlined what they had spent a day debating: the weakness of the German position in the south. If all German attention could be kept on the city of Stalingrad, Zhukov suggested, the Wehrmacht would be unable to release sufficient reinforcements to strengthen the positions of the Romanian troops on either flank. By committing all its reserves to assaults on these flanks, *Stavka* could ensure local superiority leading to rapid breakthroughs. The German Sixth Army could be encircled in Stalingrad where it would be destroyed, and the strategic initiative would lie with the Red Army.[1] The northern attack would start from the bridgeheads held by the Red Army at Kremenskaya and Serafimovich, about 100 miles (161km) from Stalingrad, while the southern attack would be launched from the salt lakes about 50 miles (80km) south of the city. After his two generals had outlined their plan on a map, Stalin suggested an alteration, moving the points of attack closer to Stalingrad and thus shortening the distance that the attacking forces would have to travel to meet and isolate the Germans. Zhukov refused; if the counteroffensive were closer to the city, he told Stalin, the German forces in Stalingrad would find it far easier to redeploy and block the Red Army's columns. After further discussion, Stalin agreed. The plan was adopted and under conditions of strict secrecy Vasilevsky was tasked with the detailed staffwork to turn the outline into reality, and applied himself with his customary energy and diligence.

At this stage, further exploitation of any success by advancing to Rostov and the Sea of Azov – an operation that became known as *Saturn* – was purely a speculative suggestion. The priority was to achieve two breakthroughs, for the two columns to link up and isolate the German Sixth Army, and for the surrounded German troops to be destroyed rapidly. When the three men met again on 28 September, Vasilevsky was able to describe the planned operation in far more detail. The northern pincer of the encirclement would require a larger proportion of the attacking forces than the southern pincer as its troops had the greatest distance to travel; Vasilevsky also took account of the German XLVIII Panzer Corps that was deployed in support of the Romanian Third Army, showing an awareness that even a relatively weak German armoured formation might pose a serious threat. Soviet field armies were grouped together in 'fronts' and a new such group – Southwest Front – was to be created along the Don to conduct the northern part of the planned encirclement. Its commander would be Vatutin, who had already distinguished himself in the defence of Voronezh, and he would have Sixty-Third and Twenty-First Armies and the rebuilt Fifth Tank Army at his disposal. The rest of the Soviet line was also reorganised. Between Vatutin's Southwest Front and Stalingrad would be a new group, the Don Front. Until now, this sector had been covered by Stalingrad Front, commanded by Lieutenant General Vasili Nikolayevich Gordov, a capable if somewhat unimaginative officer. In order to make his command more manageable, it had already been broken up in August, with its southern elements forming Southeast Front under General Andrei Ivanovich Yeremenko. When further elements of Gordov's command were now removed to form the new Don Front, Yeremenko's Southeast Front took over control of the Soviet forces in Stalingrad itself and was renamed Stalingrad Front; at first, Stalin appeared to want to appoint Gordov as commander of Don Front, but Vasilevsky and Zhukov advised an alternative.

They preferred Konstantin Konstantinovich Rokossovsky, a half-Polish officer who had been an ardent disciple of Tukhashevsky before the war. This had brought him into conflict with individuals like Marshal Semyon Mikhailovich Budenny, a close friend of Stalin who continued to promote the use of cavalry in future conflicts. Rokossovsky also spent considerable time in the Soviet Far East under the command of Marshal Vasily Konstantinovich Blyucker, and when the latter came under suspicion during Stalin's purges in the late 1930s, Rokossovsky was arrested and imprisoned on charges of spying. The basis of these charges was tenuous – Rokossovsky was accused of conspiring with the Japanese and deliberately failing to train his troops properly – and he was beaten and mistreated in attempts to persuade him to sign a confession, which he steadfastly refused to do. Thereafter, he was imprisoned in Leningrad until the summer of 1940, when he was released without any explanation and allowed to return to the army. He was in command of a mechanised corps when war with Germany broke out and led his troops in a counterattack in the Battle of Brody. When it became clear that the ill-coordinated Soviet forces were no match for the opposing German formations, Rokossovsky's front commander, Mikhail Petrovich Kirponos, attempted to call off the counterattack but was overruled by Zhukov; ultimately, Rokossovsky took it upon himself to extricate his own troops.[2]

In mid-July, Rokossovsky was sent to Smolensk where he was to take command of Fourth Army, but the rapidly developing German envelopment of the forces of Western Front forced a change of plan; Timoshenko, commander of Western Front, ordered Rokossovsky to form 'Group Yartsevo' out of whatever units he could scrape together in an attempt to hold back the Germans. Using a mixture of retreating formations – some of which had escaped German encirclements – and a trickle of reinforcements from the east, he fought to hold open the lines of retreat for forces further to the west. In September he took command of the Soviet Sixteenth Army, a formation brought back to something approaching full strength by the use of several penal battalions, and he and his men fought with distinction in the Battle of Moscow. Shortly after he was wounded and when he recovered he was given command of Bryansk Front, to the northwest of Voronezh. It was from this post that he was now summoned to take command of the new Don Front. He would have control of Sixty-Fifth Army (which had been formed from the remnants of, and would shortly be reconstituted as, Fourth Tank Army), and Twenty-Fourth and Sixty-Sixth Armies.

The southern pincer of the operation would be commanded by Yeremenko, and he would receive reinforcements – four tank corps and two mechanised corps – for his Fifty-Seventh and Fifty-First Armies. The son of a peasant family, Yeremenko was born near Kharkov and like Vasilevsky served in the southern sector of the Eastern Front during the First World War. He was an early recruit into the ranks of the Bolshevik forces and fought in Budenny's First Cavalry Army. In 1939, he commanded VI Cavalry Corps and led it into Poland as part of the Soviet occupation of the eastern parts of the country; despite being hamstrung by fuel shortages and having to request resupply by air merely to keep his men moving, he managed to complete his mission successfully and was given command of the First Far Eastern Army. When *Barbarossa* began he was summoned back to Moscow and given command of Western Front – the previous incumbent, Dmitri Gregoreyevich Pavlov, had been dismissed for incompetence and was soon to be arrested and executed. He had overall command of the Soviet forces that held up the German advance at Smolensk and was wounded in the fighting; thereafter, he was transferred to Bryansk Front and fought unsuccessfully to stop the thrust by German armoured forces that enveloped Kiev from the north. His weakened armies then had to deal with the renewed German attack towards Moscow and were largely surrounded and destroyed; Yeremenko was wounded again and spent the rest of the battle recovering in a Moscow hospital. In January 1942 he commanded Fourth Shock Army in the winter counteroffensive and his successes helped create the Rzhev Salient, scene of so much bloodshed in the months that followed. Despite being wounded again, he was then transferred to the south and given command of Southeast Front; in this role he oversaw much of the fighting to the west of and in Stalingrad. Even when elements of his command were broken off to create Gordov's Stalingrad Front, he continued to have authority over Gordov. His experiences had taught him the value of using armour en masse rather than in small packages and the importance of air power, a lesson learned from operating under German air superiority for much of 1941. Having launched a successful winter offensive operation the previous year, he would now have an opportunity to repeat the feat.

Zhukov and Vasilevsky visited the front line near Stalingrad, Zhukov concentrating on the northern sector and Vasilevsky the southern. In keeping with Stalin's insistence on absolute secrecy, they briefed the front commanders personally, limiting the information they gave to a strict need-to-know basis and forbidding any radio or written discussions. In mid-October, Don Front ordered the evacuation of all civilians within 15 miles of the front line, both to prevent security breaches and to free up accommodation for the soldiers who were beginning to assemble. The strain of preparation was immense in almost every area. Troops had to be moved from strategic reserve to their deployment areas, mainly at night to avoid detection by the Germans. Railway lines had to be improved and roads built, and new bridges were required across the Volga and Don – to prevent the Germans from detecting them and either interdicting them or realising that they were the prelude to a build-up of troops, most were constructed so that they were just below the surface of the water. The scale of the operation was immense: Yeremenko's forces south of the city transferred 111,000 men, 420 tanks and 556 artillery pieces across the Volga in just three weeks, together with thousands of tons of ammunition, fuel and supplies, a feat even more remarkable when one remembers that the river was full of ice floes at the time.[3] Aside from the movement of so many men, tanks, guns, ammunition, fuel and other supplies, the formations had to be prepared for the coming battle, as Vasilevsky described:

> There then began the practical work with the troops and commands on all fronts and directly on the spot so as to deal with questions associated with the impending operation. Paramount attention in the work within the troops was focused primarily on practical elaboration of measures swiftly to break down and drive through the enemy's defences in tactical depth, carefully to select methods of using each branch of the forces in actions within the operational interior of the enemy with account for the specific tasks to be carried out, and questions of coordination between the troops and their control.[4]

Despite all its care, the Red Army could not hide completely the enormous preparations that were being carried out. Increasingly, the Germans became aware of the Soviet build-up, but their interpretation of events was badly flawed. The preparations for *Mars* – intended to be the final reduction of the Rzhev Salient – were regarded by *FHO* ('*Fremde Heere Ost*' or 'Foreign Armies East', the German military intelligence section responsible for overall assessment of Soviet intentions) as representing the main Soviet effort for the coming winter. Whilst the growing concentration of forces on either side of Stalingrad was inevitably detected, the strength of the Red Army units was greatly underestimated. In any event, as Hitler reminded any doubters, the German forces on the northern flank of Stalingrad had come under repeated attack during the autumn and – despite some close calls – had repelled them all. The Red Army was simply not strong enough to mount two major offensive operations and remained tactically inferior to the Wehrmacht.[5] Additional anti-tank guns had been sent to the Romanians, and this would suffice to safeguard the flanks against whatever weak effort the Soviet forces made. Until now, the Romanian divisions had been armed with 37mm anti-tank guns, utterly inadequate by mid-1942. The additional weapons that Hitler had sent them were far more effective 75mm guns, but there were only six per division and each division was required to hold an extended sector of front line of up to 12 miles (19km). In any event, ammunition for the guns was in short supply; the ability of the Romanian formations to hold back an armoured attack with these few guns, particularly without adequate ammunition even for training, was therefore very limited.

In late October, German intelligence officers in the Stalingrad area informed their superiors of the developing threat. The growing strength of Soviet units in the Kremenskaya and Serafimovich bridgeheads and the Soviet reinforcements for Yeremenko's armies to the south were reported to Friedrich Paulus, commander of Sixth Army. He limited his response to passing the information to higher commands.[6] Whilst the passivity of the leadership of Sixth Army in later phases of the battle has been justly criticised, its failure to take any precautionary steps before the beginning of *Uranus* was just as large an omission. Hitler might well have vetoed the redeployment of the panzer divisions that were currently deployed in the city itself, but supplies could have been pre-positioned and preparations made for a swift redeployment to deal with the increasingly clear threat to Sixth Army's flanks. General Petre Dumitrescu, commander of the Romanian Third Army, had argued for a reduction of the Soviet bridgeheads at Kremenskaya and Serafimovich from the moment his troops took up defensive duties on the northern flank of the bulge, repeatedly pointing out that his relatively weak forces could not carry out their defensive tasks unless they occupied all of the right bank of the Don; even if Army Group B had been minded to support him, the huge consumption of men and resources in Stalingrad prevented any such operations.

In the second half of October, Dumitrescu repeatedly raised the alarm as Russian forces steadily built up in front of his men. As November began, these concerns became ever more pressing, with expectation of attacks within days. When those attacks turned out to be little more than raids, it was inevitable that further alarms would be more easily dismissed. The reality was that *Uranus* had to be postponed twice due to delays in moving all men and materiel into position. Luftwaffe reconnaissance also detected Russian preparations, leading to further warnings; Generaloberst Wolfram Freiherr von Richthofen, fourth cousin of the famous First World War pilot, was commander of *Luftflotte IV*, which provided air support to both Army Group A and Army Group B, and was increasingly minded to divert aircraft from what he regarded as the near-futile struggles for the last parts of Stalingrad still in Soviet hands to attack the growing Red Army concentrations facing the Romanian Third Army. His diary entry of 12 November included a clear recognition of what was imminent:

> On the Don, the Russians are resolutely continuing with their preparations for an offensive against the Romanians. *Fliegerkorps VIII*, all of *Luftflotte IV* and the Romanian Air Force are maintaining continuous attacks on them. Their reserves

have now been concentrated. I wonder when the attack will come! They have apparently been experiencing ammunition shortages. Artillery installations, however, are now starting to be equipped. I only hope that the Russians don't tear too many large holes in the line.[7]

Richthofen was wrong in one important respect. The relative lack of artillery activity on the part of the Red Army was not due to ammunition shortages. After registering their guns with a few ranging shots, the gunners were ordered to remain silent so as not to alert the Germans and Romanians to the strength of the coming attack.

Mansoor Giztulovich Abdullin was a Russian soldier from southern Siberia and saw combat for the first time in early November, when he crossed the Don with a raiding party. It was an effective way of getting new troops ready for the coming battles:

> 'On your feet!' The ominous command was given to us, the mortar men. We were loaded with weapon parts, barrels and base-plates, just a stumble and momentum would bring you down, the heavy iron striking your head.
>
> Lightly wounded mortar men wouldn't have died if it weren't for the heavy packs – our loads could finish a wounded man. We removed the equipment from a dead comrade and rushed on. I watched the company's leading *Komsomol* [a member of the *Komunisticheskiy Soyuz Molodyozhi*, the Communist Party's youth division] take all his documents, including his *Komsomol* card.
>
> We jumped over rough ground. There was a foul smell. We ran on, always forward. A purple flare hung in the sky and lit up faces of corpses – fascists and our own lying everywhere.
>
> The firing became heavier. I glanced furtively at my comrades: had they noticed? Clearly, they had. But their faces were firm and nobody hesitated – it was war, they would say, it was normal! And I was only 19 years old, knowing little …
> I jumped past the corpses, with barely any time to think; how quickly we adapt to something that we could barely imagine … I was shocked by the picture revealed by the flare's violet light – here they were, the realities of war, the real face of those announcements: 'They died a hero's death.'
>
> Like everyone else, I did what was needed. I tried not to stumble, stayed low as the bullets whistled past. I covered the last few metres almost crawling, the bullets flashing past very low – then I jumped into a trench next to another soldier: alive, unhurt. Soon we were ready to fire when ordered …
>
> My platoon commander, Pavel Georgievich Suvorov, a real eccentric, was

laughing … his good-natured laugh convinced me: from this moment, when we jumped into this trench, we were front-line soldiers. And no matter how the situation developed in the next moments, nobody would ever remember or take into account that we were just newly trained cadets from the infantry school.[8]

In mid-November, he was involved in another attack, in which his unit suffered heavy losses whilst probing the Romanian defensive positions in order to identify where the defenders' weapons were located:

I was only able to grasp the reality of that battle after it was over, when on the night of 14/15 November we were pulled back to a safe area.

In the evening, a drizzle fell and then froze under our feet, and in the dark it seemed as if we were stepping on glass. And then the full moon rose.

It was like a composition of thousands of sculptures of life-size soldiers frozen in ice – lying on their backs, hunched up, sitting, crouching, arms held aloft, frozen in mid-cry – icy faces with eyes wide and screaming mouths, bodies piled on barbed wire as they tried to press it to the ground to open a passage to the fascist trenches. Everything showed the energy of the attack. The mind resisted and did not want to accept the icy vision as reality. It seemed as if someone would turn on the film projector and the frozen frame would come to life …

I remembered clearly the September evening when all our personnel were alerted and the head of the military school read out the order of the Defence Committee about the immediate departure of the cadet brigade to join the active army. That night we oiled our weapons, in the morning we formed ranks and rushed from Tashkent towards the northwest – towards our destiny. There was laughter and singing all the way. For two days the train travelled without stopping to our destination station, where the officers of 293rd Rifle Division, which had just arrived from the front for replenishment, awaited us.

Many of my fellow cadets died in this first battle …. Did they all have a chance to learn anything from life about what they might become? Our political training too died in this battle.

Snow fell. A thick blanket hid the monstrous picture of the battle from our eyes. A huge sheet, white and heavy, like a shroud, fell in the morning. During the day, as far as the eye could see across the steppe, everything was smooth, white and quiet, as if only peace and pristine purity had ever existed.[9]

The Soviet build-up to the south of Stalingrad was also detected, and Generaloberst Hermann Hoth, commander of Fourth Panzer Army, was another who repeatedly

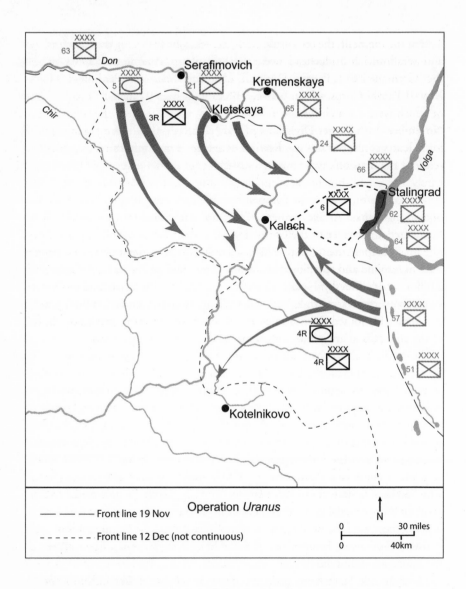

raised concerns. He had a single mobile formation available – 29th Motorised Infantry Division, which was still relatively close to full strength. On the eve of *Uranus*, this division received orders that it was to hold itself in readiness to march northwest in support of the Romanian Third Army facing the Don bridgeheads. If this were to happen, the Romanian Fourth Army in the south would be left without any armoured support at all.

For the moment, the only armoured reserves available facing the Kremenskaya and Serafimovich bridgeheads were the Romanian 1st Armoured Division and the German 22nd Panzer Division of Generalleutnant Ferdinand Heim's XLVIII Panzer Corps, which between them fielded fewer than 100 tanks, none of which were a match for the T-34s that they would face. At the beginning of November, 14th Panzer Division was ordered to withdraw from Stalingrad and join Heim's corps, but this was barely a potent force; the bitter street fighting had reduced the division's two panzergrenadier regiments to fewer than 1,000 men, barely the establishment of a single battalion, and the motorcycle battalion amounted to only a single company of infantry; the division also had few operational tanks. As November pressed on, snow and freezing fog hindered further reconnaissance by the Germans and slowed the Soviet build-up, requiring one final postponement; despite his fears that the delay might give the Germans time to respond and redeploy their troops, Stalin had no choice but to agree with Zhukov and Vasilevsky. Finally, all was ready. Zhukov was dispatched to Western Front to oversee *Mars*, while Vasilevsky took personal command of both pincers of *Uranus*. He joined the headquarters of Southwest Front in Serafimovich, full of the concerns of any senior officer on the eve of a great operation.

From dusk on 18 November, there were increasing signs of activity in the Soviet bridgeheads on the Don. The Romanians could clearly hear tank engines being warmed and reported that large troop formations had been spotted moving into forming-up areas. Early on 19 November, a Romanian cavalry patrol surprised a small Soviet scouting party and in the ensuing firefight succeeded in capturing the officer leading the group. He was promptly taken to division headquarters and interrogated, and the information he gave was alarming: the Red Army would attack in strength later that morning. Shortly after 5am, Leutnant Gerhard Stöck, who had been famous across Germany for winning the javelin gold medal and the shot put bronze medal in the Berlin Olympics and was now serving as the German liaison officer with the Romanian IV Corps, telephoned the headquarters of Sixth Army with the news. Hauptmann Winrich Behr, the duty staff officer, collated all the information, but did little more; he had already incurred the wrath of General Arthur Schmidt, Sixth Army's chief of staff, when he had woken him with similar (though lesser) reports that had proved to be false alarms. When Schmidt and Paulus did see the reports, they remained serene and indifferent. If they proved to be true, XLVIII Panzer Corps would surely be able to intercept and destroy any Soviet forces that penetrated the positions of the Romanians.[10]

As it grew light on 19 November, the waiting Soviet soldiers were dismayed to see that the entire middle Don region was shrouded in thick freezing fog.

Vatutin briefly considered a further postponement in the assault, but decided to press ahead regardless. At 7.30am local time (5.30am for the Germans, who operated on Berlin time regardless of their location in Europe – henceforth, all times are local i.e. Russian time unless otherwise stated), the massed artillery opened fire. It is one of history's ironies that the last postponement of *Uranus* had been to allow the Soviet Air Force more time to prepare, but weather conditions now rendered them impotent; in conscious emulation of the German tactics at the outset of *Barbarossa*, it had been the intention of the Soviet Air Force to spend up to three days before the battle attacking Luftwaffe airfields in order to gain air superiority. Instead, the air force officers had to console themselves with the thought that if the weather was bad enough to ground their aircraft, the same applied to the Germans.

The bombardment of the lines of the Romanian Third Army – by a total of about 3,500 guns of various calibres – continued for over an hour. Most of the batteries had 'registered' on their targets in the preceding days and weeks and struck the Romanian fortifications with great accuracy. Although concrete had been sent to the front line to build reinforced positions, rear area and headquarters units had diverted much of this to improve their own accommodation, and the infantry in the front line suffered heavy losses in their unimproved trenches and bunkers. Despite this, the attacking soldiers of the Soviet Sixty-Third and Twenty-First Armies encountered tough resistance in some sectors when they moved forward just two minutes after the end of the barrage.[11] In other areas, perhaps where the artillery preparation had been more destructive, the Romanians began to withdraw in growing disarray. Nevertheless, some units clung to their positions and threw back the first attacking wave, and a second attack with limited armoured support also made little progress. In particular, the minefields of the defenders posed a considerable obstacle for the Russians, as Viktor Kondratievich Kharchenko, a sapper, later recalled; the ground was so littered with fragments of shells and other debris that mine detectors were almost useless. Instead, the sappers had to probe the ground with metal spikes – a task made much harder by the sub-zero temperatures – and locate the mines by feel. Heavy snowfalls made the task harder still.[12]

In frustration, the Soviet forces called down a second barrage and Vatutin ordered forward the striking power of Fifth Tank Army against the lines of the Romanian II Corps, composed of 9th and 14th Infantry Divisions. Despite being hindered by the ground churned up by the artillery fire and in some cases straying into Romanian minefields, the T-34s of I and XXVI Tank Corps began to make headway, supported by VIII Cavalry Corps; the latter, compressed into a narrow front on the western edge of the assault, attacked and penetrated to the village of Blinovsky, forcing the Romanian 9th Infantry Division to pull back its eastern flank. This effectively opened the way for the neighbouring tank formations to make faster progress. Some of the Russian tanks were knocked out by defensive fire, but there weren't enough anti-tank guns or enough ammunition and the uneven struggle dragged on until midday, when the Romanian positions finally collapsed. Major General Alexei Grigoreyevich Rodin, commander of the Russian XXVI Tank Corps, motored on with his command and by the end of the day had penetrated to a depth of 12 miles (20km).[13]

Further to the east, Twenty-First Army's IV Tank Corps tore apart the Romanian 14th Infantry Division and swept forward through the resultant gap in the first hour of the attack. The Romanian V Corps – 5th and 6th Infantry Divisions, collectively under the command of the latter's Mihail Lascăr – found itself isolated between the two breakthroughs. The Romanian 9th, 13th and 14th Infantry Divisions had effectively ceased to exist as combat formations and their survivors were streaming back in disarray. A hole 48 miles (80km) wide had been torn in the front line.

When the Soviet artillery preparation started, the shellfire was audible miles away and the troops of Heim's XLVIII Panzer Corps could feel the earth trembling beneath their feet. Without waiting for orders, the men of 22nd Panzer Division prepared their few operational vehicles for action. Generalmajor Helmut von der Chevallerie, the commander of the division, had just been dispatched to take command of 13th Panzer Division and had been replaced by Oberst Eberhard Rodt. At 11.30am – as the tanks of the Russian Fifth Tank Army were smashing their way through the Romanian lines – orders arrived from Hitler's distant headquarters, ordering Heim to drive back the Soviet forces that were attacking from the Serafimovich bridgehead.

In accordance with pre-established plans, Heim had already started moving his corps towards Kremenskaya; he was aware that this was the eastern part of the sector that the Red Army was attacking, but it was also closest to Stalingrad and therefore to 14th Panzer Division, which had been assigned to his corps, and he felt that he had the best chance of concentrating his forces to maximum effect in this region first. Once the Kremenskaya penetration had been defeated, he could move further west as required. Now, Heim learned that 14th Panzer Division would join the Romanian IV Corps instead of XLVIII Panzer Corps. His mission, dictated from hundreds of miles away, was to deal with the Serafimovich penetration.

The Romanian 1st Armoured Division had already been dispatched to support the Romanian V Corps and it found itself in the path of Rodin's XXVI Tank

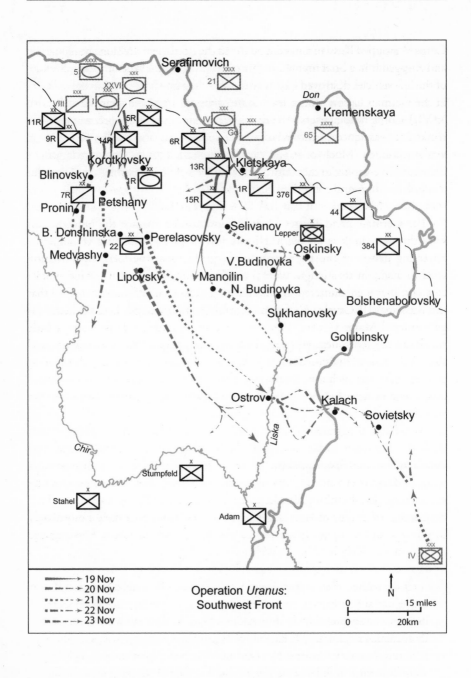

Operation *Uranus*:
Southwest Front

- 19 Nov
- 20 Nov
- 21 Nov
- 22 Nov
- 23 Nov

N

0   15 miles

0   20km

Corps. A group of Russian tanks encountered the Romanian division's headquarters and engaged it in a brief firefight before continuing on to the south; critically, one of the few vehicles destroyed in this action was the half-track carrying the radio set of the German liaison officer, leaving the division unable to communicate with XLVIII Corps headquarters. The division rapidly came under pressure on both flanks and was squeezed into a steep-walled river gully at Korotkovsky, where it was surrounded. Much of it was destroyed; short of fuel, the surviving tanks succeeded in escaping to the south where they were fortunate enough to encounter a supply column and refill their fuel tanks. Of the 84 tanks with which it had started on 19 November, it had only 30 left operational.[14]

The German 22nd Panzer Division now turned to face the Serafimovich breakthrough, in keeping with Hitler's instructions. Struggling through the retreating debris of the Romanian infantry divisions, the German formation tried to augment its strength with any of the more combat-worthy and mobile elements that it encountered. In mid-afternoon, it reached Blinovsky to find that the Russian VIII Cavalry Corps had already passed through. Late in the day, it encountered Major General Vasily Vasileyevich Butkov's I Tank Corps a little further to the south near Petshany. Fighting was confused and fragmentary, and the weak panzer division had little opportunity to demonstrate the tactical prowess that was such a hallmark of German armoured formations. Both sides lost several vehicles before the Russians broke off contact and vanished into the gathering darkness.

As the day progressed, the weather improved sufficiently for both sides to deploy a limited number of aircraft. Oberleutnant Hans-Ulrich Rudel was commanding the first squadron of *Sturtzkampfgeschwader 2*, a dive-bomber wing, and had overcome an early reputation as a poor pilot to become a leading exponent of dive-bombing, credited with hits on several Soviet warships and the destruction of dozens of land targets; he now flew from an airfield immediately to the west of Stalingrad to attack the advancing Russian forces. His language reflects views widely held in the Wehrmacht at the time:

> After the receipt of an urgent report our wing takes off in the direction of the bridgehead at Kletskaya. The weather is bad: low lying clouds, a light fall of snow, the temperature probably 20 degrees below zero; we fly low. What troops are those coming towards us? We have not gone more than half way. Masses in brown uniforms – are they Russians? No. Romanians. Some of them are even throwing away their rifles in order to be able to run the faster: a shocking sight, we are prepared for the worst. We fly the length of the column emplacements. The guns

are abandoned, not destroyed. Their ammunition lies beside them. We have passed some distance beyond them before we sight the first Soviet troops.

They find all the Romanian positions in front of them deserted. We attack with bombs and gunfire – but how much use is that when there is no resistance on the ground?

We are seized with a blind fury – horrid premonitions rise in our minds: how can this catastrophe be averted? Relentlessly I drop my bombs on the enemy and spray bursts of machine-gun fire into those shoreless yellow-green waves of oncoming troops that surge up against us out of Asia and the Mongolian Hinterland. I haven't a bullet left, not even to protect myself against the contingency of a pursuit attack. Now quickly back to remunition and refuel. With these hordes our attacks are merely a drop in the bucket, but I am reluctant to think of that now.

On the return flight we again observe the fleeing Romanians; it is a good thing for them I have run out of ammunition to stop this cowardly rout. They have abandoned everything; their easily defended positions, their heavy artillery, their ammunition dumps. Their cowardice is certain to cause a debacle along the whole front.[15]

Whilst many Romanian troops may well have fled with little provocation, it is clear that most stood and fought. Their positions were not as strong as Rudel suggests, and their artillery was chronically short of ammunition, with all supply priorities being given to Stalingrad. There is little to justify his accusation of cowardice, and the inability of the Romanians to defend their positions was more due to the failure of the Germans to honour their promises to supply them with adequate modern weapons than any moral failing on the part of the soldiers.

Comments about the hordes of Asiatic and Mongolian soldiers were increasingly common throughout 1942. From the outset, Hitler – and, indeed, the Wehrmacht, acting on his instructions – had emphasised that the war with the Soviet Union was different from the previous conflicts in the west, and represented a clash between two incompatible views of the world. As the war dragged on, it was portrayed as a crusade against everything that the Soviet Union was seen to represent from the National Socialist point of view – communism, Jewish influence, and Asian civilisation – and this would become an even stronger characteristic after the events of the winter of 1942–43. In an earlier passage in his account of the fighting in Stalingrad, Rudel wrote:

Stalingrad is Stalin's city and Stalin is the god of these young Kirgises, Uzbeks, Tartars, Turkmenians and other Mongols ... For their Stalin they are a guard of fire-breathing war-beasts, and when the beasts falter, well-aimed revolver shots from their political commissars nail them, in one way or the other, to the ground they are defending. These Asiatic pupils of integral communism, and the political commissars standing at their backs, are destined to force Germany, and the whole world with her, to abandon the comfortable belief that communism is a political creed like so many others. Instead they are to prove to us first, and finally to all nations, that they are the disciples of a new gospel. And so Stalingrad is to become the Bethlehem of our century. But a Bethlehem of war and hatred, annihilation and destruction.[16]

Precisely the same comments could have been made about the manner in which Rudel and so many other members of the Wehrmacht accepted Hitler's view of the world without question and attempted to impose it on other nations. But one of the purposes of such rhetoric, originating at the highest levels of Germany, was to demonise and dehumanise the enemy. By treating the soldiers of the Red Army as an alien horde, all manner of brutality could be justified or excused. Similarly, the Russians characterised all their opponents as fascists and Hitlerites, all equally complicit in crimes committed against the people of the Soviet Union and therefore justifying any retributive measures that might be taken.

The disinclination of Sixth Army headquarters to react in any meaningful way to the intelligence reports of the preceding days now bore its bitter fruit. Still unaware of the magnitude of the threat from Vatutin's breakthrough, Paulus ordered General Walther von Seydlitz-Kurtzbach, commander of LI Corps in northern Stalingrad, to release further troops that would be sent to the area, including all elements of 24th Panzer Division. The disparate elements of 14th Panzer Division, which had already been ordered to move to support the Romanians, struggled to reach their concentration area at Verkhne Budinovka in the face of the poor roads and fuel shortages. As a sign of what might have been achieved had more judicious preparations been made, a relatively small German battlegroup consisting of a few assault guns and supporting infantry under the command of Oberst Richard Lepper set up a strong defensive position on the eastern edge of the Kremenskaya breakthrough and obdurately beat off every attempt by the eastern elements of the Russian Twenty-First Army to push it back. The Russian III Guards Cavalry Corps had been forced to form up north of the Don due to the congestion in the Kremenskaya bridgehead and some of its units took until early afternoon to cross the river; they then encountered further problems when they attempted to advance against *Gruppe Lepper* because the Russian infantry had not marked safe lanes through the defensive minefields, and the cavalry suffered substantial casualties as a result.

Throughout the day, the German Sixth Army was – at least in theory – continuing its attacks to take the last parts of Stalingrad that were under Russian control. It was only at 10pm that Weichs sent a radio message from the headquarters of Army Group B to Paulus instructing him to break off all further attacks. In addition to 24th Panzer Division, Sixth Army was to release 16th Panzer Division and an infantry division for use in a counterattack to restore the Romanian line. Even at this stage, there was no inkling in German minds that the Russian attack was aimed at encircling Stalingrad. During the Brusilov Offensive of 1916, Russian armies along the southern part of the Eastern Front had attacked sequentially over a number of days, leading to German and Austro-Hungarian reserves rushing first in one direction, then another, without achieving anything at any location. Such tactics had become part of Soviet operational thinking, and the southern pincer of *Uranus* had deliberately been set to start one day after Vatutin's attacks along the Don. Consequently, even though the Germans had plentiful intelligence of the build-up of troops in Yeremenko's armies to the south of Stalingrad, the significance of this continued to elude them. Hoth, commander of Fourth Panzer Army, was one of the few to fear a second Russian attack in the south. To that end, he resisted all attempts to have 29th Motorised Infantry Division withdrawn from his command and sent north to help with stopping the Russian forces advancing out of the Kremenskaya and Serafimovich bridgeheads.

As the first day of *Uranus* drew to a close, Vasilevsky and Vatutin took stock. Their main attack had achieved a breakthrough, but only XXVI Tank Corps had achieved anything approaching operational freedom; I Tank Corps and VIII Cavalry Corps were still struggling to overcome stragglers and isolated pockets of Romanian resistance. The eastern flank of the breakthrough was blocked by the determined *Gruppe Lepper* and the Romanian forces on the western flank also remained undefeated. Nevertheless, there was cause for optimism. During their planning, Vasilevsky and his staff had watched carefully for signs of German reserves deploying to the area, and to date the only such reserves that had appeared – the two understrength divisions of XLVIII Panzer Corps – had been expected. In the absence of further reinforcements, it was unlikely that the resistance of the Romanians, surprisingly stubborn as it was in many cases, would continue for long. Thereafter, the armoured forces of Vatutin's front would be free to advance across the snow towards Kalach without restraint. Much, though, would depend on the southern pincer of the operation.

On the German side, there was a mixture of concern and complacency. It was clear that a major Russian attack had struck the Romanian Third Army, but its magnitude and importantly its objective remained unclear. Some, like Richthofen, expressed concerns that the Russian advance might endanger the railway line that ran through Kalach and on which Sixth Army relied for its supplies, but there was no sense of impending disaster. Nevertheless, Richthofen ordered air units still operating in the Caucasus to move north as soon as possible, so that they would be available to help deal with the Russian advance.[17] To a large extent, this complacency and passivity was because of the disjointed manner in which the German command structure was forced to work. Hitler had forbidden units from establishing communications with their neighbours, insisting on a rigid up-and-down system of command and control – even the liaison officers assigned to the Romanian formations were an unofficial arrangement. Paulus had the bulk of the local German forces under his command but they were concentrated in Stalingrad, and the Russian offensive had deliberately targeted a sector of front further away and out of reach, both tactically and in terms of command. Even had he wished to do so, Paulus was not authorised to send troops to protect his deep flanks, and Weichs – who as commander of Army Group B was at least notionally able to order such movements – had to contend with constant interference from Hitler and *OKH*.

Whilst attention was concentrated in the Don sector, Yeremenko was preparing his troops for their part in the great counteroffensive. Even from a distance of over 60 miles, the sound of Vatutin's artillery barrage was clearly audible. Yeremenko spent much of the night on the telephone to Moscow, asking for a last-minute postponement of his attack. The logistic difficulties of preparing his divisions had been immense, and many were still short of fuel, food and ammunition. Perhaps it would be better, he argued, for a delay of another day – this would allow him to bring forward more supplies and would also ensure that more German troops were diverted off to the northwest, thus facilitating his advance. Stalin overruled him and ordered him to proceed as planned.

As was the case with Southwest Front, the Germans and Romanians detected the final preparations of the Stalingrad Front, but the scale of the coming assault was successfully disguised. On the morning of 20 November, Yeremenko was dismayed to find that, as had been the case on Southwest Front the previous day, there was freezing mist, limiting visibility and effectively grounding his aviation assets. He decided to postpone the start of the attack until mid-morning and had another difficult telephone conversation with *Stavka* to explain his decision. A further telephone call followed, demanding an update; advised by his meteorological experts that the weather would soon start to clear, Yeremenko advised Moscow that the attack would begin imminently. Finally, at 10am, his artillery opened fire. After a 45-minute bombardment, the assault troops moved forward. The weather had barely changed.

The fighting against Vatutin's Southwest Front in the initial phases of its attack was marked by determined resistance by the Romanian Third Army. By contrast, the Fourth Army proved to be a less formidable foe for Yeremenko's units. Their morale was low:

> The Romanian officers and NCOs were never seen at the front, and spent their time instead in various buildings in the rear with music and alcohol ... The Romanians fought bravely, but against the waves of Soviet attack, they had no chance of resisting for long.[18]

Mikhail Petrovich Badigin was a soldier with an anti-tank gun unit in Yeremenko's forces, about to go into action for the first time:

> I clearly remember the morning of 20 November 1942. There was thick fog, drifting slowly over us. Visibility was not more than a few tens of metres. After a while, it began to snow. There was silence on the steppe. The enemy was silent. With bated breath, we waited for the first artillery preparation of our lives. And it was postponed for an hour, then for another hour. We sat in a deep trench, broke off pieces of frozen loaves. The bread crunched in our mouths, our teeth ached. Waiting the signal, many smoked, hiding cigarettes in the sleeves of their greatcoats. The tension increased steadily.
>
> Finally the Katyushas struck. With a wild roar, long tailed lightning flashed over us. On the heights, where the front edge of the enemy positions ran, pillars of fire and smoke rose. After the Katyushas, all the artillery attached to the division opened fire. It was impossible to distinguish the sound of individual batteries. The roar of heavy guns merged with the salvoes of light guns. Our guns fired at the enemy's machine-gun positions. The roar increased with every minute. Dust and smoke hung over the ridges of the high ground. The smoke was spreading to our side as well. The targets became invisible. And then dozens of signal rockets flew into the sky. Our company commander was the first to rise to the parapet of the trench with a pistol in his hand:
>
> 'For the Party, for the Motherland, forward!'
>
> Behind him came one of our cadets, then the second, the third. At that moment, we did not hear the cracks of machine-guns, or the explosions of shells, we ran and pushed the gun forward, trying not to lag behind the infantry. Fallen comrades fell alongside. Spreading his arms wide and dropping his pistol, the

company commander fell, followed by gunner Sasha Alexandrov. Thus we saw how comrades died in battle. Simply: a man falls to the ground, as if he stumbles or falls, and does not rise again.

The attack continued. Our guns moved in the fighting line of the infantry. In the first line of enemy trenches, a short but intense battle took place. It became a matter of grenades and bayonets.

The enemy couldn't stand, hesitated, edged backwards. Here it was, the cherished moment! The enemy was running! And what could be better for a soldier, more desirable than this spectacle?

'We're winning!' – joyful voices were raised.

So our baptism of fire took place.

With their hands up, the survivors of the Nazis [more likely Romanians] emerged from their shelters with grey faces. So there they were, the fascists! Many of the prisoners were in summer uniforms, their heads and legs were wrapped with whatever they had – towels, women's scarves. These were their warriors! And they considered themselves invincible. 'Now, we'll keep on beating them,' said some of soldiers.

Our regiment advanced to 13–15km [eight to nine miles] by the end of the first day of the offensive, seized a number of heights, and dug in.[19]

To the rear of the Romanians was the German 29th Motorised Infantry Division, held in position by Hoth precisely for such an eventuality, and it now went into action. Consisting of two motorised infantry regiments, a tank battalion, and assorted artillery, anti-tank, reconnaissance and engineer units, Generalmajor Hans-Georg Leyser's division was a potent force and had not been ground down in the Stalingrad battles; its tank battalion was actually slightly over its establishment strength at 55 tanks, due to previously damaged vehicles having been repaired and returned to service. As it moved forward against the northern flank of Yeremenko's forces, it encountered Major General Trofim Ivanovich Tanashchishin's XIII Mechanised Corps. Through a mixture of vehicle shortages and difficulties moving trucks across the Volga, Tanashchishin's armour was not accompanied by as many infantry as should have been the case, and the corps rapidly found itself at a disadvantage. Leyser blocked the Russian advance with one battalion of infantry and after a brief artillery bombardment to drive the few infantry who were clinging to the handholds on the T-34s running for cover, he sent his tanks streaming through the Russian columns. Hastily, Tanashchishin pulled back his exposed armour, but not before losing large numbers of tanks to accurate German fire. In an attempt to improvise a solution to the shortage of vehicles, some of Tanashchishin's infantry were advancing towards the armoured spearhead aboard a commandeered train; alerted by the sounds of battle, the infantry began to detrain, but the morning mist was now clearing and Leyser's troops had clear sight of their arrival. The train was swiftly brought under fire and left ablaze. Within moments, XIII Mechanised Corps' advance had been completely halted.

Alerted by his reconnaissance battalion, Leyser wanted to press home his counterattack to destroy Tanashchishin's corps before moving on to strike at Major General Vasily Timofeyevich Volsky's IV Mechanised Corps a little further south – as soon as he heard of the German counterattack, Volsky ordered his men to halt their advance. But even as Leyser began to draw up orders, he was forced to break off contact. The scale of the Romanian collapse was so great – only 20th Infantry Division survived the first morning's fighting as an intact formation, and the only Romanian reserves behind the front line consisted of a single cavalry regiment – that the entire southern flank of Sixth Army was exposed, and 29th Motorised Infantry Division was required to pull back to try to cover the breach. Like the action of Lepper's battlegroup in the north, the brief but powerful check delivered to XIII Mechanised Corps was an indication of how the battle might have turned out had there been less complacency in Sixth Army headquarters and at every higher level, up to and including Adolf Hitler.

Even after 29th Motorised Infantry Division broke off its intervention, Yeremenko's units continued to struggle. The columns of IV Mechanised Corps had been given unnecessarily complex orders, resulting in the few roads being choked by stationary traffic. Impatiently, Yeremenko ordered his forces to press on. Soviet records place most of the blame on Volsky, but there may be more than one reason for this. Whilst his operational orders appear muddled, they are no more so than those of other officers struggling with the inadequate roads of the region. Part of the reason why he was singled out for blame may lie in the fact that prior to the offensive, Volsky wrote to Stalin to warn him of his misgivings that the entire operation would fail. Stalin telephoned Volsky and spoke to him, as a result of which the letter was withdrawn. Nevertheless, *Stavka* may well have been minded to regard his concerns about the operation as being linked, directly or indirectly, to mismanagement in the field.[20]

While Yeremenko's troops developed their breakthrough, Vatutin's men were still mopping up the remaining pockets of resistance. Most succumbed during the day, but Lascăr's group continued to hold on to its shrinking sector of the front line. In theory, a line of retreat was still open at this stage, but isolated with only intermittent radio contact, Lascăr ordered his men to stay where they were until German and Romanian counterattacks could reach them; he fully expected the tanks of XLVIII Panzer Corps to remedy the situation. On the eastern flank of the Soviet breakthrough, the Russian 5th Guards Cavalry Division, part of III Guards Cavalry Corps, advanced in two columns. The southern column encountered Lepper's assault guns and elements of a Romanian cavalry division. Briefly, there was a scene from bygone centuries as the horsemen of both sides charged at each other, sabres drawn; the Romanians came off the worse and fell back, but the German assault guns restored the balance. Rather than get tied down in protracted fighting, the Russian cavalry began to sidestep around the southern flank of Lepper's detachment by working their way towards Selivanov, and Lepper had no choice but to pull back to avoid possible encirclement.

The gap to his south was meant to be filled by the armoured forces that Paulus had dispatched to the west, but there had been no prior preparations for their move and they had almost no reserves of fuel and ammunition immediately available. All three panzer divisions were still extensively committed to the front line in Stalingrad, where – aware at last that relief was on the way – the exhausted survivors of Lieutenant General Vasily Ivanovich Chuikov's Sixty-Second Army tried to mount local counterattacks to tie down the Germans and prevent any redeployment. The first formation to start redeploying was 14th Panzer Division, and on 20 November its assembled units probed forward to the village of Manoilin, where they encountered another regiment of III Guards Cavalry Corps. Despite being badly weakened, the Germans rapidly destroyed or scattered the Russian cavalry as well as elements of IV Tank Corps – over 19 and 20 November, 14th Panzer Division claimed the destruction of 35 Russian tanks – but with no contact on either side and growing evidence that it had been bypassed on its left flank, the panzer division pulled back to its starting position at Verkhne Budinovka. The other two armoured formations dispatched west – 16th and 24th Panzer Divisions – could do little more than send battlegroups consisting of only part of each division. Even these struggled to find enough fuel to keep moving, and as their deployment on the steppe outside Stalingrad had not been anticipated, none of their tanks had been equipped with the track extensions required to operate in deep snow. Slipping into gullies from which they had to be recovered with depressing frequency and time-consuming hard effort, their vehicles struggled west.

At the western end of the breakthrough, 22nd Panzer Division's troops in Petshany had been joined by elements of the Romanian 7th Cavalry Division. There were several uncoordinated attacks on them during the day, mainly by I Tank Corps and VIII Cavalry Corps; all were beaten off, but Rodt's division was running short of ammunition and fuel – in its move to the front line, it had been forced to beg for fuel from Romanian rear area units in its path. Towards the end of the day, Rodt pulled back to the south and the Soviet cavalry cautiously took possession of Petshany. I Tank Corps attempted to move towards Bolshaya Donshinska to the southeast to bypass the German division; the few roads in the area deteriorated rapidly under the weight of Butkov's tanks and there were regular collisions between vehicles. The detachments dispatched across country bounced across uneven ground, many of the crewmen suffering broken bones as they lurched through the snow. But if Butkov was still making slow progress, Rodin on his eastern flank was doing rather better. By the end of 20 November, his tanks had cleared Perelasovsky and Lipovsky – even if 22nd Panzer Division continued to hold up I Tank Corps, it had been outflanked and the way was open for Rodin's XXVI Tank Corps to continue its exploitation. During the night, there were further clashes between the diminishing strength of the German panzer division and Russian formations. After knocking out about two dozen Russian tanks, largely through the use of the division's anti-tank battalion – the guns of its 20 remaining Pz.38(t) tanks were almost useless against Russian T-34s – Rodt's troops continued their slow withdrawal to the south.

Once they were clear of the stubborn resistance of the remaining elements of the Romanian front-line troops, the men of Vatutin's Southwest Front found that progress was rather easier. Most of the rear area units of the Romanian Army had only the most rudimentary combat training and showed little inclination to put up resistance. Vasily Semyonovich Grossman was a war correspondent working for the Moscow newspaper *Krasnaya Zvezda* ('Red Star'); in later years, he would attract criticism for protesting about the misconduct of Red Army soldiers in Germany, but for the moment he was accompanying the advancing troops pushing out of the Don bridgeheads:

> The road is strewn with enemy corpses; abandoned guns face the wrong way. Horses roam the *balkas* in search of food, the broken traces dragging on the ground after them; grey wisps of smoke curl up from the trucks destroyed by shellfire; steel helmets, hand grenades and rifle cartridges litter the road.[21]

During the afternoon of 20 November, *OKH* began to acknowledge the developing crisis. Its first reaction was something that might have made a difference if delivered several weeks before: Germany would give the Romanian Army over 200 anti-tank guns and a similar number of howitzers, though the exact timing was not discussed. The second reaction came from Hitler. Manstein's

Eleventh Army, originally directed to prepare for an assault on Leningrad, had instead been ordered to move to Vitebsk in order to plan a winter attack to capture Velikiye Luki in the northern sector of Army Group Centre. Now, Manstein received instructions to proceed with his headquarters staff to intervene in the growing crisis in the south. He was to take command of a new Army Group Don, consisting of the Romanian Third and Fourth Armies, Sixth Army, and Fourth Panzer Army. Weichs' Army Group B would be reduced to the Italian and Hungarian armies to the immediate north, and the German Second Army beyond them at Voronezh.

This new assignment came at a difficult time for Manstein. On 29 October, his son Gero, who was serving with 18th Motorised Infantry Division near Leningrad, was killed in a Russian air raid. Manstein's personal account mirrors that of the bereaved parents of so many men in so many armies:

> We buried the dear boy on the shores of Lake Ilmen the following day [31 October]. The padre of 18th Motorised Infantry Division, Pastor Krüger, began his oration with the words:
>   'A lieutenant of the infantry.'
>   Our son would not have wished it otherwise.
>   After the funeral I flew home for a few days to be with my dear wife, for whom this boy had throughout the years been a special object of care and devotion. He had given us nothing but joy, for all the anxiety he had caused us by the ailment he had fought so bravely [he had suffered from asthma as a child]. We laid his soul in God's hands.[22]

Manstein and his staff did not leave Vitebsk until 21 November, forced by the bad weather to travel by train rather than flying to their new assignment. Due to delays caused by partisans disrupting the railways, it would take three days for them to reach their destination.

Neither at *OKH* nor within Army Group B was there any clear idea of what was happening. The loss of contact with several Romanian formations in each sector, the rapid forced move of Fourth Panzer Army headquarters as Yeremenko's troops advanced, the tendency of Vatutin's units to avoid direct battle with the few German units in their path, and poor weather hampering aerial reconnaissance all left a confused, fragmentary picture. It was only in mid-morning on 21 November that Paulus and Schmidt at Sixth Army headquarters understood the gravity of their situation. Army Group B now advised them that the two Russian attacks looked as if they would converge in the rear of Sixth Army in the region of Kalach and would thus isolate the German forces in Stalingrad. Hastily, Paulus and his staff abandoned Golubinsky, leaving a rear area party to set fire to dozens of documents, and moved to the comparative safety of Gumrak, just 8 miles (13km) from Stalingrad.

The task of Army Group Don was 'to bring the enemy attacks to a standstill and recapture the positions previously occupied by us'.[23] At first, the only additional troops assigned to the new army group were a single corps headquarters and an infantry division, and even in the absence of proper intelligence about events in the south, Manstein had little doubt that the forces at his disposal would be inadequate to the task. It is indicative of the dysfunctional manner in which the German chain of command functioned that he did not learn of the scale of the two Russian breakthroughs until he had a discussion with Field Marshal Gunther von Kluge, commander of Army Group Centre, immediately before leaving Vitebsk. He immediately sent a request by teleprinter to *OKH* requesting more substantial reinforcements; Zeitzler replied that he would try to provide a panzer division and three more infantry divisions. Even with the little information he had to hand, Manstein attempted to inject some urgency into his new command:

I also teleprinted a request to Army Group B that Sixth Army be instructed to withdraw forces quite ruthlessly from its defence fronts in order to keep its rear free at the Don crossing at Kalach. Whether this instruction was ever passed to Sixth Army I have been unable to discover.[24]

The most northern element of Sixth Army was XI Corps under the command of General Karl Strecker, who while commanding XVII Corps the previous year had repeatedly refused to authorise his men to get involved in the activities of the SS *Einsatzgruppen* behind the advancing front. With the armoured formations from Stalingrad still struggling to take up their positions, XI Corps was now exposed as the eastern flanking units of Southwest Front attempted to widen the breach that they had opened. All along Strecker's front, Rokossovsky's troops made probing attacks to try to tie down the German forces, but 376th Infantry Division, the most western formation of XI Corps, successfully withdrew to the southeast and took up a front facing west.

During the following night, the Don froze along much of its length; within a couple of days, the ice would be strong enough to support the weight of men, and when Russian infantry reached it they would find that it was no longer a physical barrier to their progress. Whilst the snow and wind reduced visibility for both sides, the Germans in particular struggled. There were further delays for their armoured forces trying to move west from Stalingrad; the leading elements of Generalmajor Arno von Lenski's 24th Panzer Division reached Kalach during the preceding night and rendezvoused with the division's workshops, which had been based in Kalach for much of the Stalingrad fighting, and took possession of a small number of repaired vehicles, but there was no time to pause and wait while the rest of the division assembled. As it grew light, Lenski was ordered to proceed across the Don bridge and take up positions to the northwest at Sukhanovsky, to defend against the Russian forces that had clashed with 14th Panzer Division the previous day. Kalach was full of stragglers and even the remnants of retreating Romanian units; only forceful action by the officers of 24th Panzer Division, some of it at gunpoint, allowed the German vehicles to cross the river and continue on their way.

The third day of *Uranus* – 21 November – brought more snow and poor visibility. At the western end of Vatutin's sector, the Russian VIII Cavalry Corps – reinforced with additional armour – drove off the Romanian cavalry division that had been holding on at Pronin and in the subsequent pursuit overran and captured the Romanian division's artillery. A little to the east, I Tank Corps clashed again with 22nd Panzer Division at Bolshaya Donshinska, but the major advance was made by the neighbouring XXVI Tank Corps, which found almost nothing in its path and was limited largely by road and weather conditions rather than German or Romanian resistance. Starting from Perelasovsky, immediately to the east of 22nd Panzer Division's positions, Rodin sent some of his tanks south to outflank the German division and the rest of his units to the southeast, and by the end of the day his leading tanks were at Ostrov on the River Liska, just 12 miles (20km) west of the vital bridges at Kalach. Had 24th Panzer Division been retained in Kalach, particularly if the entire division had been allowed to concentrate, there would have been adequate troops at hand for the Germans to counter this advance, but the lack of resistance encountered by Rodin meant that the Germans were simply unaware of the exact location of the Russian tanks.

Still largely in the dark about the locations of both friendly and enemy forces, Heim struggled to restore order even within the immediate vicinity of his XLVIII Panzer Corps. He sent 22nd Panzer Division to attack towards the northeast. It rapidly found itself surrounded and under fire from all sides; casualties mounted rapidly and the surviving elements, gathered around a single remaining company of German tanks, fought their way out to Medvashy to the southwest.

After its abortive probe to the west, 14th Panzer Division had pulled its battlegroup back to Verkhne Budinovka, and came under attack by Russian cavalry before dawn. Realising that there was no prospect of an easy advance, the Russians pulled back and sent 6th Guards Cavalry Division through Nizhne Budinovka, a little to the south. The German battlegroup attempted to counter this with an attack of its own but lacked the strength to drive off the Russians, though the appearance of a group of Stuka dive-bombers briefly scattered the cavalry force; by the end of the day, having suffered further losses, 14th Panzer Division was forced to abandon Verkhne Budinovka and retreat to Oskinsky to the east. The battlegroup from 24th Panzer Division was too far to the south to offer any assistance, and too far north to be of any help if Kalach should come under attack. Exploiting the gap between the two German panzer divisions, the Russian cavalry now concentrated on 24th Panzer Division's positions at Sukhanovsky, rapidly capturing the village and beating off a German attempt to recapture it later in the day.

Sixth Army's three panzer divisions were meant to be operating under the overall aegis of XIV Panzer Corps, commanded by Generalmajor Hans-Valentin Hube, who as commander of 16th Panzer Division had led the advance to the Volga in the summer. In his new command, he had little control over the three divisions due to the difficulties of extricating them from the Stalingrad front line and resupplying them adequately. The third German armoured formation in his corps – 16th Panzer Division – had sent a battlegroup towards the Liska, and in the confusion it missed the clashes with the horsemen of III Guards Cavalry Corps. Instead, it ran head-on into IV Tank Corps, which had followed up the success of the Russian cavalry at Nizhne Budinovka in an attempt to reach the Don to the north of Kalach. The German battlegroup was in the middle of a heated exchange of fire when it received orders to pull back to the east. After breaking off contact with the Russian tanks, the commander of the battlegroup contacted division headquarters to enquire about the reason for the withdrawal; to his consternation, he was advised that division headquarters had not issued any such order. Subsequent developments made any detailed enquiry into the circumstances of the order impossible and it remains a matter of conjecture whether it was a Soviet ruse, or the result of battlefield confusion.[25]

In the south, Yeremenko's leading units were advancing almost through open space, though isolated clashes with small pockets of German troops and armour occurred from time to time. In one such action, Mikhail Badigin's brief experience of combat came to a temporary end:

> The snowy terrain ahead of us was full of black craters from shell explosions. Four fascist tanks moved to the right along the ravine. It was the first time I saw them

in battle. I felt a shock. I tried to hide the excitement from the soldiers who could see me. The tanks were still far away, and it was pointless to fire at them yet. They moved in extended order. Sidelnikov's gun opened fire first. Shells began to explode around him, but the gun continued to fire.

When the tanks approached to within 800m, we also opened fire. I could see the tracers of our shells as they crashed into a tank, but it continued as if nothing had happened.

Finally one tank stopped, but did not catch fire. The others continued to move. At this moment our gun went out of action. The projectile didn't fire, as a part of the cartridge case had become lodged in the barrel. The loader, in his haste, probably used a dirty or rusty shell. This was the result. What to do? We couldn't take on tanks with our bare hands! And they all came on, making short stops to fire. We feverishly tried to fix the jammed gun but without success. I looked at Hashimov. He was sweating.

'Look, Hashimov, all our men have stopped firing! Probably killed!' The decision was instant. I shouted: 'Crew, follow me!'

We rushed to Sidelnikov's gun. It was only five steps away, and then something hot struck me in the side. I fell. Soon a shot rang out, then a second. The gun crew opened fire on the approaching tanks ... Then a big, unfamiliar soldier grabbed me and dragged me into cover. It was not easy for him to drag me, and I could hear his heavy breathing. The pain intensified. I clenched my teeth tightly so as not to moan. I wanted to say a word of thanks to the soldier, but suddenly everything went dark and I felt that I was flying into a dark pit.[26]

It would be five months before Badigin returned to front-line service.

Despite his earlier hesitancy and misgivings, Volsky was able to report with relief that his IV Mechanised Corps was now making rapid progress, and ended the second day of its advance about 30 miles (50km) southeast of Kalach. The logistic difficulties that Yeremenko had experienced during the build-up were now causing severe problems, with many formations running out of fuel. One division reported that it no longer had any meat or bread left.[27] In an attempt to keep his spearheads moving, Major General Mikhail Stepanovich Shumilov's Sixty-Fourth Army ordered that all vehicles, including ambulances, were to be used for moving supplies forward. Wounded men were left in the snow to fend for themselves; most died.[28] Regardless of the privations, morale was high. After so many retreats and so many setbacks, the Red Army had the Germans on the run. Some took out their anger on the Romanians, gunning down men who had surrendered.

The pincers of Vasilevsky's great encirclement were now almost within touching distance. The Germans had failed to grasp the scale and ambition of the Russian plan – the withdrawal of 29th Motorised Division to set up a defensive line in case Yeremenko's troops tried to turn north into the immediate rear of the Stalingrad positions highlights that even when it was clear that the Russians were attacking in strength on either side of the Stalingrad salient, Army Group B was still slow to draw the correct conclusions. During 21 November, Paulus sent Army Group B his personal assessment of the situation together with his recommendation:

> Sixth Army [should] break through at the southwest sector of the [threatened] encirclement by concentrating enough armour and troops to make this possible, and then open a corridor protected by armour through which all troops and essential equipment can be funnelled out to make contact with German troops in the [lower] Don-Chir area.[29]

Weichs passed the request on to *OKH* together with his personal endorsement of the proposal. Zeitzler presented the plan to Hitler with his own support, pointing out that this withdrawal would serve several purposes. It could prevent the encirclement of Sixth Army in Stalingrad; it would shorten supply lines and concentrate forces where they could protect the lines of supply of Army Group A in the Caucasus; Paulus' withdrawing divisions would be in a position to strike at the Russian armoured columns that had broken through the Romanian lines on the middle Don, potentially winning a substantial victory and blunting Russian strike power for the coming winter; and finally, it would also leave Sixth Army in a position to resume the offensive in the following year after it had spent a period of time recovering and replenishing. If the proposal was not adopted, he concluded, there was a high likelihood that Sixth Army would be cut off in Stalingrad, and – perhaps more importantly – there would be a major hole in the German lines that would be impossible to repair.[30]

This was the first German consideration of the larger consequences of the Russian attack. Regardless of the fate of Sixth Army, the retreating debris of the Romanian Third and Fourth Armies and the remnants of XLVIII Panzer Corps would not be remotely adequate to build a continuous front line. To professional soldiers like Weichs and Zeitzler, this was – perhaps slightly belatedly – very apparent. Hitler, however, took a different view. As it grew dark on the battlefields to the west of the Don, the Führer's reply reached Army Group B in the form of a radio message:

Sixth army will hold positions despite threat of temporary encirclement. Keep railroad open as long as possible. Special orders regarding supply by air will follow.[31]

Dismayed by this message, Zeitzler tried again that evening to change Hitler's mind; the Führer was currently in Berchtesgaden in Bavaria, and the two men had a long telephone conversation. Hitler was adamant: Stalingrad had to be held. If it were abandoned, he told Zeitzler, this would effectively make the year's campaign pointless. Such an attitude was almost incomprehensible to the professional senior officers of the army. The stated objective of the campaign had been to secure the lower Volga as protection for what was the ultimate aim of the entire year's operations, namely the capture of the Caucasus oilfields. Hitler's obsession with Stalin's city had then distorted the manner in which the campaign unfolded, but even if the capture of Stalingrad had been the true primary objective, clinging to it in such a manner was at best hugely risky. The previous winter, Hitler's order to the army to hold its positions in front of Moscow was probably the right one – attempting to withdraw while under heavy Russian attack might have been disastrous. Conversely, holding Stalingrad in the current circumstances was utterly wrong-minded, as circumstances were not remotely comparable. In late 1941, the Germans had no prospect of retreating to a defensible position, and the Russians had no strategic objectives within striking range – neither factor applied in late 1942. Writing many years later, Manstein felt that this fundamentally came down to Hitler's fear of taking risks at an operational level, which manifested itself in a refusal to accept temporary concession of territory in order to gain operational freedom and a reluctance to denude other sectors in favour of giving sufficient priority to the most important sector:

> There are three possible reasons why Hitler evaded these risks in the military field. First, he may secretly have felt that he lacked the military ability to cope with them. This being so, he was even less likely to credit his generals with having it. The second reason was the fear, common to all dictators, that his prestige would be shaken by any setbacks … Thirdly, there was Hitler's intense dislike, rooted in his lust for power, of giving up anything on which he had once laid hands.[32]

There was, as Manstein went on to describe, another factor. When confronted with a difficult decision, particularly where the only real option was to do something that he did not wish to do, Hitler would prevaricate and put off the decision for as long as he could, perhaps in the hope that circumstances would change and make the decision unnecessary. This was such an occasion: all of the professional opinion suggested that it was foolhardy in the extreme to leave Sixth Army in Stalingrad, but withdrawal was so contrary to Hitler's instincts that, even before he had discussed matters with Luftwaffe commanders, he was already thinking in terms of keeping the surrounded army alive by supplying it by air.

On the battlefield, the disparate German forces continued to struggle with the snow, poor visibility, chaotic conditions as Romanian soldiers retreated, and complete lack of any clarity about Russian dispositions or intentions. Finally, on 22 November, the reconnaissance battalion of 24th Panzer Division managed to extricate itself from the tangle of vehicles in Kalach and reached the rest of the division. Lenski sent its platoons out on cautious probes and discovered 14th Panzer Division's units at Oskinsky. He ordered his two tank battalions to advance north to recapture Nizhne Budinovka and Verkhne Budinovka in order to join up with his neighbouring formation, but immediately encountered armour from the Russian IV Tank Corps. Whilst this skirmish developed, two divisions of III Guards Cavalry Corps slipped through the gap between the two German panzer divisions and pushed forward to the Don at Bolshenabolovsky; here, they encountered elements of both 16th and 24th Panzer Divisions and tried with little success to infiltrate past their northern flank. Nevertheless, the bulk of Hube's XIV Panzer Corps remained tied down in confused fighting to the north of the critical Don crossings at Kalach. An attempt by the German units in Bolshenabolovsky to attack along the Don road towards the area west of Kalach – largely back along the route that 24th Panzer Division had already travelled – was abandoned in the face of crippling fuel shortages and communications difficulties.

To the west, the confused attempts by the disparate elements of the German XLVIII Panzer Corps to intervene were coming to an end. The Russian VIII Cavalry Corps had bypassed the positions of 22nd Panzer Division and began to work its way around to the rear of the division. Still out of contact with Heim's corps headquarters, the remnants of the Romanian 1st Armoured Division attempted to fight their way out to the southwest; moving roughly parallel to them but in no contact with them was a group of Romanian infantry that had broken out from the pocket under the command of Mihail Lascăr, who continued grimly to defend an original sector of the front line midway between Kletskaya and Serafimovich, now far to the rear of the advancing Russian forces. Both Romanian columns made their way to Medvashy, only to find that 22nd Panzer Division had been driven away to the southwest the day before. They fought hit-and-run battles with the few Russian troops they encountered, and left a trail of wrecked vehicles and bodies in their wake.

Early on 23 November, Rodin prepared for his most important action since the initial breakthrough. For the final advance from the Liska to Kalach, he divided his tank corps into three columns, intending to converge on Kalach from the northwest, the west and the southwest. The central column consisted of 19th Tank Brigade, under the command of Lieutenant-Colonel Georgi Nikolayevich Filippov. He had acquired two captured German tanks and an armoured car during his advance over the preceding days, and he placed these in the forefront of his forces, with the rest of his tanks – with infantry riding aboard – following a short distance behind.

The defence of such a critical location as Kalach – astride the rail link to Stalingrad, it was vital for Sixth Army's supply lines – had not been entrusted to any major combat formation. Instead, the defences consisted of a mixture of units. There was a single company from 16th Panzer Division's supply units together with much of the division's workshop teams, a small group of *Feldgendarmerie* (military police), a construction battalion, and two anti-aircraft batteries. The 'infantry' amounted to the equivalent of a weak battalion in numbers, and far less in combat value, through a shortage of officers and NCOs and in the case of the construction battalion no significant combat training. There were also hundreds of Romanian troops and German rear area stragglers who had fled to Kalach from the collapsing Don front, and the *Feldgendarmerie* troops lacked the numbers required to restore them to order; nor were there any combat officers present who might have taken it upon themselves to organise the stragglers into ad hoc combat units. A single 88mm anti-aircraft gun – a weapon that had proved itself of enormous value as a tank killer – was deployed at the bridge with perhaps a platoon of soldiers. Immediately to the east of the town was a small training unit that prepared combat engineers for street fighting and frequently used armoured vehicles, both German and captured Russian tanks. Consequently, when Filippov's column approached the bridge with its headlights blazing, the troops on the bridge assumed that it was a detachment headed for the training unit and waved it through without suspicion. A small group of T-34s then followed and they too were allowed to pass.

It was only when one of the T-34s opened fire with its machine-guns on the German soldiers around the bridge that the Germans realised that anything was wrong. Immediately, the single 88mm gun opened fire and destroyed two of the T-34s, but it had only eight anti-tank rounds available and, having fired all their ammunition, its crew abandoned it and withdrew. Meanwhile, the three captured German armoured vehicles, supported by the T-34s that had joined them, established a defensive perimeter around the eastern end of the bridge, supported by the fire of the rest of Filippov's tanks on the higher west bank. Belatedly, the scratch garrison of Kalach tried to regain control of the eastern end of the bridge so that they could trigger the demolition charges that had been prepared, but three attacks were beaten off by Filippov's men. As more Russian infantry arrived, Filippov went onto the attack and started to force his way into Kalach. One last German attack was beaten off and by mid-afternoon, Kalach had fallen. With it, Sixth Army lost its rail link to the outside world and its supply route. Whatever Hitler might have hoped from his radio message that the railroad was to be kept open as long as possible, Paulus had not made any effort to create a force capable of defending Kalach effectively. The elements of 24th Panzer Division, which passed through the town just a day before it fell, were struggling to establish a coherent line on the steppe further north; had they been in Kalach, it is highly likely that they would have had sufficient firepower to stop Filippov and Rodin, but even if Paulus had been minded to use Lenski's division in this manner, he would inevitably have had to seek permission from *OKH*, resulting in further delay, and any attempt to intercept the Russian forces further north would have been fatally weakened. Some elements of the German troops (and many of the stragglers in the town) escaped to the south and were thus able to avoid being trapped within Stalingrad, while others headed down the road to the ruined city.

After taking Kalach, Rodin paused long enough for more Russian troops to catch up; the infantry arrived the following day, by which time a Luftwaffe attack had damaged the bridge. The Russian infantry carefully crossed the frozen river, as Abdullin recalled:

> The ice was still thin and so slippery, as smooth as glass, that it was impossible to take one step after another. Carrying heavy mortar barrels, tripods and base-plates, we might break it in an instant and one slip or fall could plunge us all into the icy water.
>
> A command was given to collect sand in our helmets and our greatcoats and pour it in front of us, spreading out about five metres apart. We then carefully crossed in a chain, one behind the other. The ice creaked under our feet, as if it would break. I do not remember any [river] crossing in the entire war that was as quiet as this. For tens of metres in both directions all I heard were snorts and muffled grunts: 'Hush!' 'Don't stamp like an elephant!' 'Careful!' To the side of us was the bridge. Sappers were crawling all over it like ants. In front of the bridge was a mass of vehicles and horse-drawn carts, with more and more arriving all the time. The gunners couldn't cross the river on such thin ice and were waiting for the sappers to repair the damaged bridge.

And we, the infantry, were already on the left bank. Where were our tanks? On the entire stretch of the road from the Don to the town – in trenches, ditches, on the road – there were the corpses of fascists and abandoned enemy equipment. Our tankers had done a great job taking the fight to the Hitlerites!

We entered Kalach at dawn. In the deserted streets there were traces of a panicky retreat by the enemy. Stolen loot had been abandoned in the middle of the streets. The windows of the houses were open, the glass broken. Apparently, some Nazis had jumped out of the windows directly into the street. A dead German in a long shirt was hanging from a windowsill.[33]

Rodin now pushed on to the southeast, where Volsky was driving forward with IV Mechanised Corps as fast as his limited fuel supply would allow. Abdullin's battalion was on the northern flank of the Russian forces advancing from Kalach. Like soldiers in every army in every conflict, some of his comrades had been unable to resist the opportunity to pick up a little loot:

Loaded as always with our rifles, barrels, and base-plates, we changed our firing position at a run, close to the enemy. Our mortar teams took losses. A very good man from Bodaibo, a Siberian, was killed. Like me, he came from the mining area of Miass ... I turned him over and found a bag that seemed inexplicably heavy, and not part of the standard mortar team equipment, which had crushed the nape of his neck [when he fell]. I unfolded it – I found a hand sewing machine, carefully wrapped in tent fabric. I was shocked. This was what killed him!

The Siberian was an excellent, brave, resolute soldier. And in peacetime he was a good, caring family man. For him, the sewing machine was a symbol of prosperity. He wanted to keep the sewing machine through the war and give it to his wife. I recalled my life before the war. Only one or two people in the entire mine had sewing machines. Gramophones and bicycles were rarities. But it was this machine that killed the Siberian. I didn't find a single mark on his body, he just stumbled while running and fell. I did not tell anyone in the company about the machine, so that he wouldn't be condemned.[34]

The two pincers of the great Russian offensive met near the village of Sovietsky, completing the encirclement of Sixth Army. Soviet accounts, including a filmed reconstruction, describe how the two armoured groups guided each other to the rendezvous using signal flares and met amidst great rejoicing and the exchange of vodka and food, but the reality was somewhat different. Abdullin was with Rodin's column:

Our blood was up, and without realising that there are no more fascists between us, we collided with each other in a firefight. Like many others, I soon thought that there was something wrong: the shells flew past us without howling, the explosions were smokeless, and the automatic and machine-gun fire was different in that there were no explosive bullets.*

Heavy fire drove us to ground. We could see a lot of people fighting against us. It was strange, the figures did not look like Hitlerites. Someone then realised that the mass of troops facing us was our own! The reaction was like lightning, though belated. Suddenly the battle stopped. Everybody ceased fire. We ran towards each other, and there was only the creak of snow under our feet – such silence.

'Brothers!' we shouted in Russian![35]

Communication between the two groups was nonexistent, and both assumed that the armoured force in its path was a German battlegroup; the exchange of fire resulted in both groups taking casualties before the men realised their mistake. The commander of 45th Tank Brigade, part of Rodin's XXVI Tank Corps, submitted a report after the action that his unit had fired green flares as he had been instructed to do, but had then come under fire. After investigating the matter, Yeremenko's headquarters contradicted this, saying that no signal flares had been fired.[36]

Despite this setback, the first phase of the Russian counteroffensive was effectively complete: Stalingrad and Sixth Army – together with much of Fourth Panzer Army – had been surrounded. The elements of Sixth Army that had been sent west of the Don made their way back across the river via a series of small bridges north of Kalach and withdrew into the city. At about the same time, the final fighting around the original breakthrough area on the Don was dying down. Having held their segment of the front line since the onset of *Uranus* and with only intermittent contact with other commands, the last troops fighting under Lascăr laid down their weapons. They had received occasional airdrops of supplies, and had struggled on in the vain hope that XLVIII Panzer Corps would come to their aid. Lascăr went into captivity unaware that he had become the first non-German to be awarded the Knight's Cross by Hitler; he only learned of this when he returned to the Eastern Front at the end of the war commanding a Romanian force recruited from prisoners of war and fighting for the Soviet Union.

---

* Both sides on the Eastern Front believed that the other side used explosive machine-gun rounds, but the large wounds that led to this belief were due to the high-velocity weapons in use, at first mainly by the Germans but later by both sides.

The remnants of XLVIII Panzer Corps regrouped along the line of the River Chir, where various rear area units and groups of stragglers were coalescing into a paper-thin battle line. When he reached this area, Heim found that he had been dismissed from command for failing to defeat the Russian attack. He was also stunned to find himself under arrest for a variety of crimes: he was to blame for so few of 22nd Panzer Division's tanks being operational; he failed to provide sufficient anti-tank artillery to the Romanians; he did not keep control of his two armoured formations to allow them to cooperate effectively; and the Russian breakthrough was therefore his personal fault.[37] At no stage had he been given sufficient anti-tank weapons for his own division, let alone enough to strengthen the Romanian units, and Hitler and *OKH* had interfered in his attempts to use his corps in a coordinated attack first against the eastern part of the Russian attack, then against the western part. Nevertheless, he was singled out for blame.

Weichs knew nothing about the arrest order, and nor did Zeitzler, who was at first minded to regard it as some sort of misunderstanding. However, Keitel then confirmed that Hitler had indeed made such an order. Heim was expelled from the army, stripped of his rank and medals, imprisoned in Moabit in solitary confinement without any due process, and sentenced to death. In mid-1943, he was transferred – without explanation – to a military hospital and then released, again without explanation. Subsequently, he learned that he had been placed on the list of those who had retired from service, and his rank and medals had been restored. In August 1944, Hitler recalled him and placed him in command of 'Fortress Boulogne'. He took up the post to find that none of the extensive fortifications planned for the town had been completed and he lacked sufficient troops to man them; after a heavy bombardment, Boulogne fell to the Canadian 3rd Division after just five days. Hitler's reaction to Heim's failure to defend the city to the last man, as was the standard instruction to all 'fortress' commanders, is not recorded. Heim remained in captivity until 1948, and he died in 1971 in Ulm, not far from Reutlingen, where he was born in 1895.

CHAPTER 3

A PAPER-THIN LINE

The growth in size of armies throughout the 19th and 20th centuries, the scale of military operations, and the increasing consumption of ammunition by modern weapons made logistic considerations of ever greater importance. Even as early as the American Civil War, control of railroads was vital for the movement of supplies, and it became increasingly normal for armies to use railways as the axes of advance and retreat. The different rail gauges of the Russian Empire and the rest of Europe contributed greatly to the limitations of offensives on the Eastern Front in the First World War, and despite the increase in the numbers and reliability of motor vehicles by the Second World War, the poor quality of roads in Russia and the Ukraine, together with the sheer volumes of supplies needed, ensured that control of the railways would remain a priority, not least because the Germans lacked the quantities of trucks and fuel available to American and British forces in the west.

In the southern part of the Eastern Front, the Germans were faced with two major rail choke points for their logistic operations. The first was at the lower Dnepr, where there were only two railway crossings – one at Dnepropetrovsk and a second at Zaporozhye, the latter having been only partly restored by the time the crisis erupted on the middle Don in November. From those crossings, the rail lines continued to a second point of congestion at Rostov over the lower Don. Capture of either of these choke points by the Red Army would have devastating consequences for the Wehrmacht, and the armoured formations that had torn apart the Romanian Third Army were now far closer to both points than the bulk of German troops in the region, who were either stranded in Stalingrad or stuck in the Caucasus foothills.

The encirclement of Sixth Army made the logistic headaches of the German Army far worse. Regardless of Hitler's reluctance to abandon any territory – particularly the ruins of a city bearing the name of Stalin – it was inconceivable that Paulus and his troops could be left to fend for themselves for any length of time without supplies; having failed to anticipate the possibility of being cut off, the lack of preparations for such an eventuality began to have an immediate effect. For example, there were no facilities within the encirclement for bread to be baked on a large scale. Consequently, loaves of bread would have to be flown in rather than sacks of flour, which would have taken up far less room. From the moment they were surrounded, the physical and combat strength of Sixth Army's soldiers began to diminish, and therefore if they were to break out to the west, the order had to be given as soon as possible. In the event, Hitler accepted reassurances that Sixth Army could be sustained by air, and consequently refused permission for a breakout. This had huge consequences for the further conduct of operations on the Eastern Front and indeed for the entire war, and the events that allowed Hitler to take this position are worth closer examination – not only are they of relevance to the fate of Sixth Army and the unfolding of operations to the west of the city, they also shed valuable light on the relationships at the upper levels of the Third Reich.

Even before the two pincers of *Uranus* met on the steppe and completed the encirclement of Sixth Army, Hitler – still in Berchtesgaden – summoned Generaloberst Hans Jeschonnek, the chief of staff of the Luftwaffe, for discussions.[1] He explained to the Luftwaffe officer that the encirclement of Sixth Army was imminent, but a new army group under Manstein would restore the situation in short order. In response to the question of whether the Luftwaffe could keep Sixth Army supplied for the duration of the encirclement, Jeschonnek replied that it was perfectly possible, provided that there were adequate air bases both within the encirclement and outside it and sufficient aircraft were made available.

The basis for Jeschonnek's assurance appears to have been the previous winter's events at Demyansk. The Luftwaffe successfully sustained the pocket, but there were several critical differences. To keep the 100,000 men in Demyansk alive, 300 tons of supplies had to be delivered every day, and due to the constraints of the weather this required 500 Ju-52 transport aircraft to be made available – each aircraft could carry a little less than two tons of freight, and weather and logistic considerations meant that not all would be able to function on any given day.[2] Furthermore, the ability of the Soviet Air Force to intervene at Demyansk was minimal. By contrast, the Stalingrad pocket contained over 250,000 men, and a direct comparison with Demyansk led to the conclusion that a daily total of 750 tons would be needed. Given the far greater power of the Soviet Air Force around Stalingrad, the operations could expect a higher loss rate and even the most cursory calculations showed that the Luftwaffe simply did not have the resources for such an operation. To make matters worse, the deteriorating situation in North Africa had already resulted in much of the Luftwaffe's airlift capacity being transferred to the Mediterranean theatre to send reinforcements to Rommel's forces.

Many reasons have been suggested to explain Jeschonnek's over-hasty reassurance that an airlift to sustain Sixth Army could be carried out. Despite his personal strong loyalty to Hitler, relations between the two men had deteriorated as the war progressed due to the declining capability of the Luftwaffe, and, given the manner in which Hitler treated his subordinates, there was probably a strong desire on Jeschonnek's part to regain the favour of his master. He was also acting on the false assumption that the encirclement would be ended very quickly – therefore, even if there were a shortfall in the daily supply flights, it would be of little long-term consequence.

The commander of *Fliegerkorps VIII*, the Luftwaffe body operating in the Stalingrad sector, was Generalleutnant Martin Fiebig. On 21 November, he spoke to Sixth Army's chief of staff, Schmidt, by telephone:

I asked how they planned to keep Sixth Army supplied, especially when the supply line from the rear looked certain to be cut very soon. General Schmidt replied that supplies would have to be carried in by air. I replied that supplying an entire army by air was impossible, particularly when our transport aircraft were already heavily committed in North Africa. I warned him against exaggerated expectations. Generaloberst Paulus entered the conversation occasionally on his other telephone line. Next morning, at 0700, I telephoned General Schmidt again, telling him that he was counting too strongly on air supply. I stressed to him again that, after long deliberations, based on my experience and knowledge of the means available, supplying Sixth Army by air was simply not feasible. Further, the weather and enemy situations were completely unpredictable factors.[3]

Richthofen agreed wholeheartedly with Fiebig and spent several hours that evening and night telephoning Goering, Jeschonnek, Weichs and Zeitzler to try to persuade them that it was inconceivable that Sixth Army could be supplied by air, but although he succeeded with the latter three, it was of no consequence. Nor were he and Fiebig the only local commanders to see the folly of what was being attempted. Amongst the units that were about to be encircled in Stalingrad was Generalmajor Wolfgang Pickert's 9th Flak Division. He attended a meeting on 22 November with Paulus, Schmidt and Hoth, where the imminent encirclement was discussed. According to Pickert's account, Schmidt asked him for his suggestion on what should be done; Pickert replied without hesitation that Sixth Army should gather together all its forces and break out to the southwest. Schmidt countered that Hitler had ordered Sixth Army to continue to hold Stalingrad and that there was insufficient fuel for any breakout. An attempt to do so would involve fighting through Russian troops that had occupied higher ground to the west and several thousand wounded men would have to be left behind. Regardless of these considerations, Pickert countered, there was no realistic alternative to an immediate breakout; his division's heavy guns could offer fire support, and the smaller 20mm guns could be carried by their men. Schmidt refused to accept his advice and told him that Sixth Army would take up a position of all-round defence and would expect to be supplied by air. This was the first that Pickert had heard of this proposal, and he flatly rejected it – he told the other officers in blunt terms that based upon his knowledge of Luftwaffe capabilities, such an operation was simply impossible. Paulus, who had remained silent for much of the discussion, then made a contribution. There were two considerations that were paramount, he told the gathering. Firstly, Hitler had ordered Sixth Army to remain in Stalingrad. Secondly, he believed that a breakout would result in his army being destroyed in the open, stranded without fuel and supplies.[4] Paulus also stated unequivocally that there was insufficient fuel or ammunition for a breakout, but subsequent events showed that this assessment was at best a guess, and most likely to be incorrect.

These early exchanges were of critical importance. Every officer qualified to make a judgement – with the possible initial exception of Jeschonnek, and by this time he had changed his mind and agreed with other Luftwaffe officers – regarded the proposed airlift as impossible. The counter-argument that there was insufficient fuel for a breakout was almost irrelevant; if the army could not be sustained by air, it had to make an attempt to break through the Russian cordon, even if the consequence was that much of its equipment would have to be abandoned. After all, if an airlift was impossible, the equipment was doomed in any conceivable outcome. Caught on the hook of Hitler's insistence on clinging on to Stalingrad and with a lifetime career of obedience to orders, Paulus shut his ears to all logical consideration.

There was a clear difference of opinion developing between most front-line commanders – whether in the army or the Luftwaffe – on the one hand, and Hitler and his inner circle on the other. At Army Group B headquarters, Weichs sent a message to *OKH* on 22 November adding his weight to the argument that supply by air was out of the question and that regardless of the losses that would be suffered in an attempted breakout, it was the only conceivable course of action.[5] Within Sixth Army, the corps commanders met and came to a similar conclusion, and with the agreement of Weichs, they began preparations for an immediate regrouping with a view to breaking out on 25 November. Paulus had no knowledge of these plans and continued to hesitate between what everyone (with the exception of Schmidt, his chief of staff) was telling him and what Hitler was expecting of him. On 22 November, he requested freedom of decision if it proved impossible to reorganise his troops for all-round defence, stating that he was nevertheless prepared to hold fast if he could receive ample supplies. Given that he had recently told Pickert and others that there was insufficient fuel for any breakout, it seems odd that he should effectively have been asking for permission to conduct such an operation just a short time later – there had not been sufficient time for a thorough audit of fuel reserves, so it seems that on the earlier occasion, Paulus simply clutched at a 'fact' in order to silence Pickert. The following day, he informed Hitler that the corps commanders were unanimous in their view that an immediate breakout was necessary, and finally conceded that he had been advised that it would not be possible to supply Sixth Army by air.[6]

A day later, after returning to East Prussia, Hitler had a meeting with Zeitzler. All talk of a brief airlift while Manstein mounted a successful relief operation had gone, and instead Hitler made clear that he required a prolonged period of supply by air for the beleaguered Sixth Army. He now designated Stalingrad as a *Festung* ('fortress') and adamantly insisted to Zeitzler that it was the duty of the garrison of a fortress to withstand a period of siege. Zeitzler protested that all field commanders of the army and Luftwaffe were certain that any airlift, either short-term or long-term, was not possible. In any event, a fortress usually had the opportunity to prepare for a siege so that it could endure a period of isolation, and this was manifestly not the case with regard to Stalingrad. Hitler dismissed these arguments, telling Zeitzler not to be so pessimistic and to ignore the comments of defeatist officers.[7]

Even Jeschonnek had changed his mind. His initial assurances to Hitler had been made under pressure in his conversation with the Führer, and after discussions with his own staff – and several by telephone with Richthofen, who was a personal friend – he now contacted Hitler to advise him that his previous assessment might have been too hasty. However, Hitler was determined to hold onto Stalingrad and placed far more reliance on those who agreed with him than those who disagreed. Keitel, head of *OKW*, had a longstanding reputation for rarely, if ever, contradicting the Führer, and repeatedly proclaimed that there could be no retreat from the shores of the Volga. Generaloberst Alfred Jodl, head of the operations staff at *OKW*, was perhaps less sycophantic, but had clashed badly with Hitler over the dismissal of List in September and on this occasion chose to keep a lower profile, limiting himself to saying that there should be no withdrawal until a relief attempt had been made – which ignored the reality that the longer a withdrawal was put off, the less likely it was to succeed.

Perhaps the voice that made the greatest impression on Hitler at this time was that of Reichsmarschall Hermann Goering, head of the Luftwaffe. By this stage of the war, he was no longer held in such high esteem by Hitler; the failure of the Luftwaffe in the Battle of Britain and its gradual decline as a fighting force had disillusioned the Führer, whose opinion of Goering was further damaged by the intrigues of other senior Party figures like Martin Bormann and Heinrich Himmler, who denigrated Goering in order to advance their own interests. The multitude of posts held by Goering, with widespread responsibility for industrial production as well as the Luftwaffe, resulted in him giving less attention to any part of his sprawling empire than was needed, and by late 1942 he was anxious to recover prestige by whatever means he could. It is likely that the two men first spoke about the subject of air supply for Sixth Army shortly after Jeschonnek had assured Hitler that such an operation was possible.[8] At this stage, Hitler had already issued his order to Paulus to hold on in Stalingrad and that Sixth Army would be supplied by air. Without detailed figures immediately to hand, Goering assured Hitler that the Luftwaffe would do whatever was necessary, and then ordered his staff to divert all available aircraft for the operation. The following day, he travelled to Berchtesgaden, where Hitler asked him whether he was still in favour of supplying Sixth Army by air; Goering answered with an unequivocal affirmative.

Almost immediately, Goering received a briefing that undermined whatever remaining credibility the airlift operation had. The initial estimates on the numbers of aircraft – which cast doubt on the entire scheme – were based upon the use of 250kg and 1,000kg containers in place of bombs on bombers, but Goering now learned that this weight did not refer to their capacity, merely to the size of the bombs that they replaced. Their capacity was actually far less than this, Jeschonnek explained, and whatever diminishing hope might have existed for sustaining Sixth Army by air was thus extinguished. Despite Jeschonnek's pleas that he should inform Hitler that air supply was impossible, Goering forbade Jeschonnek from informing Hitler personally about the cargo containers. Instead, he phoned Hitler himself and assured him that the Luftwaffe could carry out the required airlift.

On a later occasion, in a conversation with Bruno Lörzer, who like Goering had been a leading fighter pilot in the First World War, Goering attempted to justify this assurance that he gave despite Jeschonnek's briefing. He told Lörzer that Hitler had started the exchange by telling him that Sixth Army was lost unless the Luftwaffe could support it by an airlift; in the circumstances, he explained, refusing to carry out the airlift would effectively have left the Luftwaffe to carry the blame for the loss of Sixth Army.[9] But such an argument assumes that the only options were either to attempt an airlift or to allow Sixth Army to be destroyed, and ignores the third option, that of an immediate breakout. However, Goering probably feared being blamed for forcing Hitler to abandon Stalingrad, the capture of which had come to mean so much.

When Zeitzler attempted to explain to Hitler that the arithmetic for an airlift simply did not add up, Hitler summoned Goering and asked him if the Luftwaffe could carry out the operation. Goering saluted and gave Hitler the required assurance, and there followed a furious argument between Zeitzler and Goering. The *OKH* chief of staff tried to persuade Goering by quoting the minimum tonnage required per day for the operation to succeed; Goering replied unequivocally that the Luftwaffe could carry the required amount, and that calculations about airlift capacity were the sole reserve of the Luftwaffe. Relieved to have heard what he wanted to hear, Hitler – who was normally obsessed with numerical data, but on this occasion discounted such data from the chief of the general staff in favour of Goering's assurances – dismissed Zeitzler with the comment that he had to believe the Reichsmarschall's assurance, and the matter was closed.[10] The exact date of this exchange is disputed, but given the movements of Goering – rather than devoting his energies to the airlift, he was in Paris from 22 to 27 November visiting art galleries – it is likely that the conversation happened after his return to East Prussia, by which time Hitler had already made his decision. In any event, the best chance for Sixth Army to escape by an immediate breakout had already passed.

Within the encirclement, Paulus finally became aware of the plans of his corps commanders to organise a breakout and immediately put a stop to them, despite their having been authorised by Weichs at Army Group B. General Walter von Seydlitz-Kurzbach, commander of LI Corps, promptly sent a heartfelt memorandum to Paulus:

> The order of Hitler to keep the encirclement and to wait for relief from outside is founded on an absolutely unreal basis. It cannot be carried through and its consequences must be a debacle. It is, however, our holy duty to preserve and save

our divisions, therefore another order must be given or another decision be taken by the army itself. Our army has only the alternative of the breakthrough toward the southwest or ruin within a few weeks. We are morally responsible for the life or death of our soldiers. Our conscience toward the Sixth Army and our country commands us to refuse the orders of Hitler and assume for ourselves freedom of action. The lives of some hundred thousand German soldiers are at stake. There is no other way.[11]

The logic of Seydlitz's appeal was impeccable, but Paulus would not be moved: Sixth Army would obey Hitler's order to hold fast. There is some irony in the thought that, when Jodl fell out with Hitler over the dismissal of List, there was talk that Jodl would be dismissed and replaced by Paulus, with Seydlitz replacing him as commander of Sixth Army – had that happened, Seydlitz would have been in a position to carry out the act of insubordination that he proposed, and that Paulus now refused to consider. Unaware that Seydlitz was actively working for a breakout and had even ordered an unauthorised withdrawal of 94th Infantry Division from the northern perimeter of the city in preparation – a move that was spotted by the Russians, who immediately put down a heavy artillery bombardment, inflicting heavy losses on the withdrawing infantry – Hitler appointed him commander of the northern sector with specific orders not to permit any withdrawals. An alternative explanation for this appointment is that by making Seydlitz personally responsible for the northern perimeter, Hitler removed any possibility of further unauthorised withdrawals. Regardless of the reason, the losses suffered by 94th Infantry Division haunted Paulus in the weeks that followed – whenever the possibility of reducing the size of the pocket in order to gather forces for a breakout was discussed, the spectre of similar events on a far larger scale dominated Paulus' fears and was used as a reason to reject any suggestions of making preparations without Hitler's prior approval.

It was in this context that Manstein and his staff had to make their own assessments and decisions. Together with Busse, his chief of staff, Manstein made his own evaluation of the situation on 24 November:

The enemy would in the first instance do everything in his power to destroy the encircled Sixth Army. At the same time we had to bear in mind the possibility that he would try to exploit the collapse of Third Romanian Army by pushing mechanised forces across the large bend of the Don towards Rostov, where he was offered the prospect of cutting off the rear communications not only of Sixth and Fourth Panzer Armies but also of Army Group A. The forces at the enemy's disposal – which he could doubtless augment by road and rail transport – would allow him to pursue the two aims simultaneously.

I further concluded that the Army Group's foremost task must in any case be the liberation of Sixth Army. On the one hand, the fate of 200,000 German soldiers was at stake. On the other, unless the army was kept in existence and ultimately set free, there could hardly be any hope of restoring the situation on the right wing of the Eastern Front. One thing was clear: even if we were able to raise the siege and re-establish contact, Sixth Army must on no account be left at Stalingrad. The city's prestige value as far as we were concerned was non-existent. On the contrary, if we should succeed in getting the army out, it would be urgently needed to give the maximum possible help in stabilising the situation on the southern wing sufficiently to bring us safely through the winter.[12]

In other words, it wasn't enough just to relieve Sixth Army; the restoration of the entire southern sector would require its troops to be redeployed to prevent a far greater catastrophe. Like many other officers, Manstein was of the opinion that the best moment for a breakout had been either before or immediately after the encirclement; now, an operation could not be launched until the end of November, by which time he expected the Red Army to have positioned sufficient troops to make success far less likely. Consequently, he concluded that – provided sufficient supplies could be brought into the encirclement by air to prevent the fighting power of Sixth Army from being degraded – it would be best to wait until he could mount a relief effort.

In his memoirs, Manstein stressed this point:

> The fact had to be faced that any delay was dangerous, since it would give the enemy time to consolidate his siege front. Such a risk could only be entertained if the Supreme Command guaranteed to supply Sixth Army by air for as long as was needed to liberate it.
>
> ... Since we considered the best chance for an independent break-out had already been missed, it was preferable from the operational point of view at the present time to wait until the projected relief groups could come to the army's aid – always assuming that an adequate airlift could be counted on. The latter factor, we emphasised [in communications to Schmidt at Sixth Army headquarters] was *absolutely decisive* [emphasis in original text].
>
> ... An absolute prerequisite for accepting the risk of not making an immediate break-out from Stalingrad was that Sixth Army should daily receive 400 tons of supplies by air.[13]

Given the widespread opinion amongst local Luftwaffe officers like Richthofen and Fiebig that an adequate airlift was impossible, it seems odd that Manstein was prepared even to consider this possibility – he must have been aware of their views about what was being proposed. To a large extent, this seems to be an attempt at rationalisation after the event, given that there was no possibility of Hitler changing his mind. But Manstein was also guided by a much larger picture. If the encircled troops were to attempt a breakout immediately, it was highly likely that they would suffer major losses in the attempt and as a consequence there would not be sufficient forces available to repair the huge breach created in the front line. This would then release the entire weight of the Russian armies surrounding Stalingrad to descend on the lower Don, thus trapping Army Group A and creating an even bigger disaster. Until such time as Sixth Army could be extracted intact and able to function as a fighting force, it was better – almost regardless of the realities of supply by air – for it to stay where it was, tying down more than half the Red Army's resources in the region. The rest of the Red Army's forces in the region were already a huge threat without this additional reinforcement.

The limited rail crossings over the lower Dnepr and the Don, compounded by constant harassment of trains by partisan groups, interfered with another vital function: the movement of reinforcements. If Stalingrad was to be reached by a relief column – indeed, if the entire southern sector of the Eastern Front was to be saved from disaster – substantial movements of troops would be necessary, either from other sectors of the Eastern Front or from the west. With the limited capacity of the rail system already stretched to the limit by supply movements, there was little capacity for still more trains, yet the effort had to be made. In the meantime, the huge hole torn in the front by *Uranus* had to be filled, or the Red Army would be free to push on to Rostov and the lower Don, sealing the fate both of the encircled Sixth Army and also of Army Group A in the Caucasus.

In the days after the completion of the encirclement of Stalingrad, the pressure exerted by the Red Army on the shattered lines of Army Group Don began to ease, not least because Vasilevsky wished to concentrate on the surrounded Sixth Army, as he later described:

> The Nazis would urgently take all measures to afford their troops maximum aid from outside and help them out of the Stalingrad encirclement; it was therefore essential for us to destroy the surrounded enemy grouping as quickly as possible and free our own forces engaged in the operation; before this fundamental task was achieved we had to isolate as best we could the encircled grouping from the

arrival of other enemy troops; to these ends we had swiftly to form a solid outer front and have enough reserves of mobile troops behind it … the troops of all the three fronts in the inner encirclement would continue their decisive actions in destroying the surrounded enemy from the morning of 24 November without any substantial regrouping or additional preparation.[14]

Had Vasilevsky known the catastrophic weakness of the German forces outside the pocket, he would have realised that preventing any relief of Stalingrad could perhaps be best achieved by a renewal of the offensive, but the Red Army was still learning the art of operations in the mechanised age, and in any event there had to be a pause to bring forward supplies and recover damaged and abandoned tanks. The retreating elements of the Romanian Third Army streamed back to the line of the Chir, where they began to coalesce around a small number of energetic officers. One such was Oberst Walther Wenck, who would later become the youngest German promoted to the rank of general. He was too young to serve in the First World War; he spent his teenage years as a cadet in a military school, and was approaching the end of his time with the academy in Berlin-Lichterfelde when the war came to an end. A fellow cadet described the mood of the cadets on the brink of manhood when they learned of the dissolution of the Hohenzollern monarchy to which their families had given service for generations:

> [We felt] the most intense pain for what was happening, [we were] effectively discarded, unable to contribute either for or against, forced to stand to one side with our wakening strength and eagerness, a reserve without a front line, held back for nothing at all, and our energy poured into a ghostly emptiness in which, even though we were still a nation, this was nothing more than a collective sentiment. This was our terror, it seemed that we were superfluous, we felt it whenever we marched as a formation through the streets, we felt it in the strange hostility in the eyes of those who stared at us.[15]

It was almost inevitable that, when demobilised soldiers volunteered to serve with the paramilitary *Freikorps* to fight against communists and other 'enemies' of what remained of the established order in 1919, many cadets like Wenck also joined their ranks. He served in the *Freikorps Reinhard* and was wounded during clashes in Berlin; for the young Wenck this was almost the equivalent of a wound received in the First World War, and he resented the intervention of his father who forcibly returned him to the cadet academy. Immediately, he escaped and joined *Freikorps von Oven*; Oberst Wilfred von Oven, who knew his father, gave him several days' leave and advised him to return home, giving him a letter for his parents. Whatever the contents of the letter were, Wenck did not find out, but he was given permission to return to the *Freikorps* from where he was sent to an infantry training school near Munich. When the peacetime *Reichswehr* was established, he joined as a junior infantry officer, and the outbreak of the Second World War found him serving as operations officer for 1st Panzer Division. After a spell as an instructor in the *Kriegsschule*, he became chief of staff of LVII Corps just as it was being redesignated as a panzer corps. As the crisis on the Don developed following the onset of *Uranus*, he was assigned both as liaison officer and chief of staff with the Romanian Third Army. He arrived in Morozovsk on 23 November and was immediately tasked with helping to bring order to the fleeing remnants of the formations that had been destroyed in the front line. He described the situation:

> The next morning I flew closer to the front in a Fieseler Storch, to the Chir bend. There was nothing left of the Romanian formations. Somewhere west of Kletskaya, the brave remnants of *Gruppe Lascar* were still fighting. The rest of the allies were in complete flight. With the limited resources at hand, we couldn't stop those retreating. I had the remnants of XLVIII Panzer Corps, the improvised Luftwaffe formations, the rear area units of the already surrounded Sixth Army, all of which were being gathered into battlegroups by energetic officers, and a constant stream of men from Sixth and Fourth Panzer Armies returning from leave ... I received my instructions and information directly from the chief of the general staff, General Zeitzler, as Army Group B had its hands full and could hardly oversee my sector properly.
>
> My main task at first was to create blocking units under the command of vigorous officers so that we could at least establish reconnaissance patrols along the front of the Don and Chir either side of the already established *Kampfgruppen Adam*, *Stahel* and *Spang*, in cooperation with the Luftwaffe units of Generalleutnant Martin Fiebig's *Fliegerkorps VIII*. I therefore literally strewed my staff along the road. The same applied to motorcycles, cars and signals equipment, in other words practically everything that one would need for staffwork. The old senior NCOs with Eastern Front experience were particularly valuable and could be given any assignment.
>
> I had no communications net of my own. By luck, I was able to make use of Sixth Army's net in its supply area and the Luftwaffe net. After countless conversations on these networks I was able to get an overall picture of the situation

in our sector where German blocking units fought on, and there were also still some Romanian formations. With just a few men I was constantly moving to get a personal impression and to be able to decide which positions should be used for elastic defence and where a definitive stand had to be made.

Our only reserve on which we could count was the returning stream of men from leave. We armed them from army group depots, workshops, or simply by 'organising' matters.

To form the leaderless groups and individual men from three armies who had been split up by the Russian breakthrough into new units often needed extraordinary, increasingly inventive and drastic measures.

I recall how in Morozovsk I sent the chief of a Wehrmacht propaganda company to set up a field cinema at a major road junction. So many soldiers and units gathered there and were reorganised and reequipped. Most then conducted themselves well.

At one point, a Feldwebel from the military police came to me and reported that near the main supply route he had discovered an almost abandoned fuel dump 'without any officers'. We actually didn't need fuel but had a pressing requirement for vehicles in order to provide transport for our newly formed troop formations. So I had signs put up along all the roads in the rear area directing people to the 'vehicle refuelling point'. Drivers desperate for fuel for their trucks, cars, and whatever else drove to our dump. The vehicles that arrived did receive fuel but were prevented from continuing on their way. In this manner the vehicles and drivers moving in the rear area or thinking about retreating were organised into new transport units so that our mobility needs were addressed. From each train transporting tanks to *Gruppe Hoth* [i.e. Fourth Panzer Army] I uncoupled a tank 'for audit purposes'. In this manner we soon had ten tanks.[16]

As the number of tanks and assault guns – acquired 'for audit purposes', or from workshops where they were being repaired – accumulated, Wenck organised them into a panzer battalion and used it to help reinforce the front line. His operations officer made the mistake of mentioning 'our panzer brigade' in a daily situation report to Manstein's headquarters, and Wenck was summoned to explain where he had obtained the tanks; despite sympathising with Wenck, Manstein ordered him to hand the tanks over to the panzer divisions that were assembling in the area. Thereafter, Wenck was more cautious, never allowing more than a company of tanks to collect at any one spot, in order to avoid attracting the attention of higher commands that might then reallocate them.

Much of the combat strength of the Luftwaffe had been operating from the airfields immediately to the west of Stalingrad in support of operations in the city, and these units redeployed in haste as *Uranus* unfolded. This had serious consequences, with much valuable equipment being left behind. In particular, de-icing equipment was in short supply and Luftwaffe ground personnel had to struggle to cope as best they could in sub-zero conditions:

> The cold caused unimaginable difficulties in starting aircraft engines, as well as engine maintenance, in spite of the well-known and already proven 'cold starting' procedures. Without any protection against the cold and the snowstorms, ground support personnel worked unceasingly to the point where their hands became frostbitten. Fog, icing and snowstorms caused increasing difficulties, which were compounded at night.[17]

The cold-starting procedures included a trick learned from the Russians the previous winter – in order to prevent engine oil from becoming too viscous in sub-zero temperatures to allow the engines to function, petroleum was added to it. Once the engine reached operating temperature, the petroleum would evaporate, allowing the engine to function normally, but the procedure increased engine wear considerably.

In an attempt to bring order to the shattered front between the Don – where the left wing of Third Romanian Army continued to hold its positions – and the Chir, where the remnants of XLVIII Panzer Corps had finally been able to stop their retreat, the German XVII Corps was moved from Army Group B's reserve to the region. It consisted of two German infantry divisions under the collective command of General Karl-Adolf Hollidt, a diffident infantry officer with a record that was superficially unspectacular, but during which he had acquired considerable skill in taking troops with low levels of training and turning them into first-rate units, an ability that was now suddenly in demand. He found his corps expanded rapidly into *Armee Abteilung Hollidt* ('Army Detachment Hollidt'), with control of the remnants of many of the Romanian divisions that had been broken during the Russian breakout from the Don bridgeheads and the new battlegroups that were being created.

In addition to Wenck's improvised units, other small groups began to form along the new front of the Chir valley. Hollidt's detachment took up positions along the upper part of the river from the Romanian I Corps on the Don to the battered XLVIII Panzer Corps with the remnants of the Romanian 1st Armoured Division and 22nd Panzer Division. Then came the first of the new ad hoc units,

Gruppe Spang, consisting of rear area units, stragglers and men who had been trying to return to their units from hospital or home leave. Its eastern neighbour was *Gruppe Stahel*, built around the staff of the Luftwaffe's *Fliegerkorps VIII* and able to make use of powerful dual-purpose flak weaponry, followed by *Gruppe Stumpfeld* and *Gruppe Abraham* – later renamed *Gruppe Adam*. With varying degrees of success, all of these units fought off Russian probing attacks in the last week of November, but despite the remarkable resilience shown by these groups, all of which contained large numbers of rear area personnel with little front-line training or experience, the new front line was paper thin. A single powerful armoured thrust would tear it apart.

Gruppe Adam was the result of a rare stroke of good fortune for the Wehrmacht. As the losses amongst junior officers mounted in Stalingrad, a decision was made to establish a school for promising NCOs from a variety of formations who could then be promoted and would serve with the infantry. The school was stationed near the mouth of the Chir at Nizhne Chirskaya, which was briefly nominated as the new headquarters for Sixth Army after the onset of *Uranus*, and Paulus' adjutant Adam was sent there before the decision was made to relocate the headquarters to the Stalingrad pocket. Adam immediately made use of the men in the school to create a series of battlegroups – the instructors became battalion commanders, the trainees, most of whom were close to the end of their training, became platoon and company commanders, and the rank and file were formed from stragglers, rear area units, and any other personnel available. The group grew rapidly to something not far short of division strength, though it lacked heavy weapons, and Adam suggested that it should be commanded by Oberst Erich Abraham, an old friend who had been serving with 76th Infantry Division in Stalingrad but had been sent to the rear due to sickness and had been working in the training school:

> To my great astonishment he turned [the post] down, as he was still ill. I have never been so surprised about a comrade as I was with Abraham at this point. We demanded the very last effort from our simple soldiers, and how did an active officer and regimental commander behave? He reported sick, although nothing noticeable in his condition had arisen during the last few weeks ... It seemed to me that the behaviour of my old comrade was due to depression.[18]

Adam continued to command the group until he was summoned back to Paulus' side within the encirclement. The group now came under command of Generalleutnant Eccard Freiherr von Gablenz; he had commanded XXVII Corps in the fighting at Moscow but was removed from his post after repeatedly ignoring Hitler's order not to pull back, and then took command of 384th Infantry Division, which was now being disbanded in the Stalingrad pocket due to catastrophic losses.

Still struggling to reach his new command along the overcrowded rail lines, Manstein arrived in Rostov on 26 November where he met General Arthur Hauffe, head of the German military mission to Romania. He informed Manstein that of the 22 Romanian divisions deployed in what had been Army Group B, nine had been completely destroyed, nine routed, and only four were still fit for battle, though given time it might be possible to return other units to the front line. By contrast, a letter from Marshal Ion Antonescu, the Romanian head of state and commander-in-chief, angrily drew attention to the repeated warnings the Romanians had given of the coming Red Army offensive and the failure of Germany to provide adequate support. As Manstein succinctly summarised: 'His letter voiced the justified disillusionment of a soldier who sees his troops lost through the mistakes of others.'[19]

Later that day, Manstein finally reached his new headquarters in Novocherkassk. It took a further day for communications lines to be established, and Army Group Don officially took control of its sector on 27 November. The previous three days had seen the first attempts by the Red Army to break into the Stalingrad pocket with the intention of dividing it into smaller segments that could then be destroyed; somewhat to the surprise of the Russian forces, Sixth Army defended its positions energetically and threw back all attacks with heavy losses. Part of the reason lay in a major underestimate of the size of the encircled German force. The Red Army had calculated on trapping perhaps 90,000 men; in reality, the German troops – together with thousands of Romanians who had retreated into the pocket – numbered nearly three times that.

Thoughts were already turning to further operations to exploit the Red Army's advantage. Vasilevsky visited the various front commanders to get their assessments of the situation, and as a result recommended to Stalin that the troops of Southwest Front should be reorganised to allow for the creation of First and Third Guards Armies. These formations, together with Fifth Tank Army, would then be unleashed against the fragile German front along the Chir and middle Don, with the intention of shattering both *Gruppe Hollidt* and the Italian Eighth Army – First Guards Army was to attack from Verkhny Mamon towards Millerovo, where it would meet Third Guards Army. Having destroyed the German defensive line, the two armies would push on to the River Donets and secure crossings, from which future operations towards Rostov would be executed. To the northwest of this force, Voronezh Front's

Sixth Army would also attack, and Fifth Tank Army would operate to the southeast along the Chir with the intention of capturing the German air bases at Morozovsk and Tatsinskaya, from where the airlift to supply Stalingrad was being mounted. Stalin approved the operation, codenamed *Saturn*. Additional reinforcements were dispatched to the area and a start date for the operation was originally set at 10 December, though delays in assembling all the required troops would force this to be put back.[20]

Meanwhile, Manstein and his staff began to look at the herculean task that confronted them. They had to restore the shattered front line and prevent a further Russian advance that would seal the fate not only of Sixth Army but of the whole southern wing of the German position and thus might cost Germany the entire war, whilst simultaneously mounting a relief operation for Paulus' beleaguered troops, with only modest forces to hand. The front along the Don and Chir might have stabilised for the moment, but Manstein was under no illusion that it represented a strong position. There was also an area of weakness immediately to the south of the Don, and if the Red Army were to advance along this route, it would pose a threat to the Rostov crossings from this direction in addition to the clear threat from the north. Whatever Hitler's orders might say about relieving Stalingrad and restoring the previous front line, Manstein intended from the outset to extract Sixth Army from the city and then pull back to a more sustainable position. Merely restoring the vulnerable line of mid-November would be to invite another Russian attack.

Having been denied permission to break out by Hitler, Paulus had reverted to his previous position that his army lacked sufficient fuel and ammunition for any major effort. Manstein wryly recorded in his memoirs: 'If these figures were correct, one could only wonder how Sixth Army had proposed to implement the breakout plan of which it had given notice four days previously.'[21]

There were two possible options for a relief march to Stalingrad. The first was to attack from the lower Chir through Kalach, which meant an advance of about 27 miles (45km). However, this meant securing a crossing over the Don and the terrain was not favourable; the area was also known to contain powerful Russian armoured forces from Fifth Tank Army. The second was to attack from near Kotelnikovo, south of the Don, along the route that Fourth Panzer Army had taken in its initial advance to Stalingrad in the summer. The distance was greater – 75 miles (125km) – and would involve crossing two rivers, the Aksay and Myshkova, but overall the terrain was better for such an operation and the opposing Russian forces were weaker. Once the Myshkova was crossed, the steppe was flat and open – the very territory where Paulus had feared his army would be destroyed as it attempted to retreat – and provided the relief column had sufficient strength to fight a battle of manoeuvre, the greater distance would not pose an insuperable problem. Manstein decided to create an armoured force under the aegis of Fourth Panzer Army to advance along this second route as the main relief effort. When it drew level with the mouth of the Chir, the German forces north of the Don would join the attack, hopefully at the same time that Sixth Army launched attacks from within the pocket.

Following the dismissal of Heim from command of XLVIII Panzer Corps, a series of individuals were briefly nominated as replacements. General Hans Cramer, chief of staff for the *Schnelle Truppen* ('fast troops', often translated as 'mobile troops') directorate of *OKH*, was the first, though he didn't get the opportunity to take up the post. Within days, Generalmajor Heinrich Eberbach was announced as the new commander; he had led the panzer regiment of 4th Panzer Division in the opening campaigns of the war with great distinction and was a popular figure amongst the armoured forces, but he was wounded within days of arriving to take up his new command. His replacement was General Otto von Knobelsdorff, who had overseen the conversion of 19th Infantry Division into 19th Panzer Division after the fall of France. His chief of staff was to be Oberst Friedrich von Mellenthin, just recovered from dysentery acquired while serving with Rommel in North Africa. He received his new assignment when visiting Hitler's headquarters in East Prussia on 27 November and immediately flew to Rostov and then on to the headquarters of XLVIII Panzer Corps. His predecessor had been dismissed at the same time as Heim and was no longer present to conduct an orderly handover; instead, Mellenthin was briefed by the remaining members of the corps staff.[22]

Knobelsdorff had held temporary command of a number of formations on the Eastern Front over the preceding months, and he now inherited the remnants of Heim's formations. The badly degraded 22nd Panzer Division consisted of no more than a few small battlegroups and was largely dispersed along the line held by *Armee Abteilung Hollidt*, and the Romanian 1st Armoured Division, reduced to only three tanks and largely composed of rear area troops who had been pressed into service as combatants, was also greatly weakened; it too was now part of Hollidt's detachment. In their place, Knobelsdorff received a new set of units: a Luftwaffe field division, Major General Walther Lucht's 336th Infantry Division (transferred from where it had been supporting the Hungarian Second Army) and 11th Panzer Division, commanded by Generalmajor Hermann Balck.

In an era where rapid changes in military technology resulted in many men having unusual careers, Balck was an individual whose path had been singular.

After serving in the First World War, he served in the Reichswehr between the wars, first as a cavalry officer and then with the infantry. During this period, he was twice offered the prestigious option of joining the general staff but declined to do so, writing in his memoirs that he preferred to stay with his front-line units. His critics would later speculate whether he turned down a role in the general staff out of fear that he would not make the grade. In 1938, he was posted to Guderian's *Schnelle Truppen* inspectorate before joining 1st Panzer Division in time for the French campaign, first commanding a motorised infantry regiment and later temporarily commanding the panzer regiment. He was a leading proponent of combining elements of panzer and motorised infantry (later renamed panzergrenadier) units into ad hoc battlegroups and led such a group from 2nd Panzer Division with distinction during the Greek campaign of 1941. Thereafter, for a man who had expressed a desire to remain with front-line units rather than take a staff post, his career took quite the opposite direction and he became inspector-general of *Schnelle Truppen*, overseeing the supply of vehicles for armoured formations during 1941 and touring the front during the winter to write a report on the state of the panzer divisions. During this time, he had frequent contact with Hitler and seems to have established a high level of trust with the Führer. In May 1942, he returned to the front line as commander of 11th Panzer Division, which had been badly worn down in the previous winter's fighting; he brought it back to full strength and took part in the drive to Voronezh before the division was withdrawn into reserve in the Bryansk region. He was now dispatched to Army Group Don with 11th Panzer Division to form the striking power of the reconstituted XLVIII Panzer Corps; despite his best efforts, some of his tanks were retained by Army Group Centre, but his division was nevertheless a powerful formation.

Balck had spent the intervening months turning the division into a first-rate unit. Showing a characteristic streak of ruthlessness, he had removed commanders whom he did not regard as being fit for serving in the manner that he required. The result was a group of subordinate commanders of the highest calibre: Oberst Theodor Graf von Schimmelman led the division's 15th Panzer Regiment, and Albert Henze and Alexander von Bosse, both with the rank of Oberst, commanded the two panzergrenadier regiments. Balck had also established an unusual system of command and control, preferring to give instructions verbally rather than committing them to writing. His experiences working alongside men like Guderian gave him valuable insights into the different themes that combined to make panzer divisions such powerful weapons – it was more than just the concentration of armoured vehicles into a single formation. The widespread adoption of *Auftragstaktik*, or 'mission-based tactics', required subordinate commanders to be fully aware of their superiors' intentions and to have the skills to innovate as required, and communication was of prime importance, as he explained many years later:

> Guderian made two very important contributions in the area of panzer warfare communications. The first contribution was to add a fifth man, a radio operator, and a radio to each tank in the panzer division. This allowed both small and large tank units to be commanded and manoeuvred with a swiftness and flexibility that no other army was able to match. As a result, our tanks were able to defeat tanks that were quite superior in firepower and armour.
>
> Guderian's second contribution was to give the panzer a signal organisation that allowed the division commander to command from any point within the division.
>
> … I always located my chief of staff in a headquarters to the rear. I commanded from the front by radio and could thus always be at the most critical point of action. I would transmit my commands to the chief of staff, and then it was up to him to make sure that they were passed on to the right units and that the right actions were taken. The result was to give us a fantastic superiority over the divisions facing us.[23]

Clearly, this arrangement required a staff team that was capable and trusted, and Balck was fortunate to have the services of Major Franz-Joachim Kinitz in the role of chief of staff. The two men had worked together for much of the year and had a clear understanding of each other's intentions and ways of working. The division's tank strength was good, with 103 vehicles, but included 28 Pz.IIs, widely regarded as too lightly armoured and armed for combat against enemy tanks by 1942, though it remained a useful reconnaissance vehicle. Only 11 of the division's tanks were Pz.IVs with the armour and firepower to engage Russian T-34s on equal terms.[24]

Balck's memoirs reveal a strongly opinionated man with a great deal of self-belief, a personality that many found abrasive; he would need all his self-belief and drive in the days ahead. He arrived in Millerovo with his division staff on 27 November and set about making all of the preparations for the arrival of his division with his customary energy.[25]

During his first days in command, Manstein had an exchange by teleprinter with *OKH* to discuss the plans for the relief effort. There had been further delays in assembling all of the forces promised to Manstein as reinforcements, and on

28 November Manstein requested permission for Fourth Panzer Army to launch its attacks without further delay. He also made it clear that he regarded it as essential for mobility to be restored:

> Above all, I told Hitler, it was strategically impossible to go on tying down our forces in an excessively small area while the enemy enjoyed a free hand along hundreds of miles of front. What we must regain at all costs was our manoeuvrability.[26]

It took five days for Hitler to reply. He disputed Manstein's figures for the strength of the Russian forces in the area, stating that all these formations were worn down by the recent fighting and short of supplies; this ignored the fact that the same was even more true of the German units in the area. Nevertheless, it was a start – there was no flat refusal to consider abandoning Stalingrad. But, characteristically, nor was there a clear recognition that this was needed. As always when faced by a decision he did not want to make, Hitler prevaricated. What is missing from Manstein's account of this period is any reassessment of the supply situation of Sixth Army. Any lingering doubts that Manstein had about the ability of the Luftwaffe to conduct the required airlift should have been dispelled by now, in which case it was surely time to reassess whether Sixth Army could wait while Hoth's relief forces were gathered. At the very least, the necessity for Sixth Army to make preparations to assist an approaching relief column by commencing attacks of its own had always been clear, and orders to this effect could have been issued at this stage.

The force that would lead the relief effort was LVII Panzer Corps under the command of Generalleutnant Friedrich Kirchner, an experienced commander of armoured forces who together with his staff had been recalled from the Caucasus for this operation, codenamed *Wintergewitter* ('Winter Storm'). Originally, Manstein had intended to concentrate three or more panzer divisions for the relief operation, but the endless delays in getting the promised reinforcements to him meant that Kirchner would have only two – 6th Panzer Division and 23rd Panzer Division. The former had been in France, where it had refitted, and was at full strength; originally dispatched east to take up a supporting position behind the Italian Eighth Army, it had been diverted to the fast developing crisis on the Don and had been assigned an assault gun battalion to increase its strength, though the assault guns would not be available immediately. The other panzer division had already been part of LVII Panzer Corps in the Caucasus and despite the casualties it had suffered was still at something approaching full strength; however, it arrived piecemeal, with many of its wheeled elements delayed by a sudden thaw that turned the few roads in the Caucasus into rivers of mud. A third formation – 17th Panzer Division – was diverted on Hitler's orders to replace 6th Panzer Division behind the Italians before being allowed to continue on its way; had it been allowed to stay with the Italians, it might have been able to intervene in the coming Russian attack, and had it been allowed to join the rest of LVII Panzer Corps on time, the relief effort would have got off to a far more forceful start, but the indecision and confusion in the German chain of command merely resulted in time being frittered away without any benefit. In addition, Kirchner would have 15th Luftwaffe Field Division, one of Goering's new formations, though nobody had any illusions about its fighting power. Two Romanian cavalry divisions would operate on the flanks of the relief attack to try to prevent Russian counterattacks.

After a period of rest and recuperation, 6th Panzer Division was in good shape. In line with other panzer divisions, it had undergone a substantial reorganisation, losing one of its three tank battalions and the staff of its rifle brigade, but its equipment was far better than that of the previous winter. The outdated Pz.38(t) tanks had been replaced with a mixture of Pz.IIIs and Pz.IVs, allowing the division to engage the Russian T-34s with greater confidence than before, but there were still concerns. Whilst the long-barrelled 50mm gun of the Pz.III was capable of penetrating the armour of a T-34, this was only possible at ranges up to 800m – by contrast, the T-34 could penetrate the armour of any of the division's tanks at maximum range. Only one panzergrenadier battalion was mounted in half-tracks, and there were concerns about mechanical breakdowns reducing the number of tanks available on any day. Nevertheless, the division made a virtue out of necessity; during training, it routinely deployed its tank regiment, the half-track battalion, a motorised and armoured battalion from its artillery regiment, and an armoured company from the tank hunter battalion in a single 'armoured battlegroup' to maximise striking power. The rest of the division would serve in a supporting role during offensive operations, forming less formidable battlegroups that would operate to protect the flanks and rear of the division's main striking force.

The men of 6th Panzer Division were in fine fettle, as Horst Scheibert, a panzer company commander, wrote:

> The losses in earlier fighting had been limited by good leadership ... [and now we had] unshakeable old corporals combined with a good core of senior NCOs and officers. After many shared operations and experiences of war, the mood was good

... Everyone regarded himself as far superior to the Russians, had confidence in his weapons and his familiar officers. All ranks, particularly in the panzer regiment, functioned as part of a team in combat, which showed itself in fruitful mutual trust. The division commander, Generalmajor [Erhard] Raus, like all regimental and battalion commanders, had risen through the division and enjoyed the confidence of all the men.[27]

On their way across Germany, the men of the division's 4th Panzergrenadier Regiment took advantage of the first snow of the winter to indulge in a mass snowball fight; their later experience of snow would be far more serious. As the dozens of trains carrying the division made their way across Belarus before turning southeast, one – carrying the headquarters battery of an artillery battalion – was ambushed by partisans. The locomotive was destroyed and the troops on the train had to take up defensive positions in a nearby wood, an early reminder, if any were needed, that even some distance from the front line, occupied parts of the Soviet Union were far from being under complete control.

As the trains made their way through Rostov, the mood of the men of 6th Panzer Division grew more sombre as they were passed by trainloads of wounded heading in the opposite direction. With progress slowed through a combination of railway difficulties and a lack of certainty about the precise location of enemy forces, the first elements of the division reached Kotelnikovo early on 27 November, having been under way from Brittany for three weeks. As Scheibert commented:

> Progress was steadily slower, the trains widely separated. Everyone looked forward to disembarkation, as the transports had already been under way from Brittany for between 18 and 20 days. Only one who has experienced living in a compartment with eight men and a constantly stinking oven, never washing properly, never able to lie down properly, and all this for up to 450 hours, understands the meaning of the expression 'transportation'.[28]

The terrain around Kotelnikovo was monotonous in its lack of significant elevation and trees. Whilst in many respects this made it ideal terrain for mechanised warfare, it was also crisscrossed with deep ravines carved by the seasonal rains; they changed almost every year, making maps of limited value, and at this time of year they were often partly or completely hidden by snow. The arrival of the first elements of 6th Panzer Division in their new area of operations was not what they might have expected, as Raus later described:

Suddenly the earth shook with a hail of shells. The ground quivered, black earth was thrown up on all sides, the windows were shattered, the brakes screamed, the wheels screeched, and with a sudden jolt, which threw men and equipment into a heap, the train came to a halt. All the troops leaped from the cars, just as they had done on the occasion of the partisan raids that they had so frequently gone through. The Russians, coming from the station building, were already storming the train with cries of 'Urrah!' At that instant our machine-guns and submachine-guns began to fire from the car roofs on the earth-brown figures advancing on the train from both sides.

In the next minute, however, the infernal din caused by detonating shells and yelling Russians was drowned out by the ear-splitting cheers from our infantrymen, who, led by Oberst Unrein (commander, 4th Panzergrenadier Regiment), rushed forward with bayonets and hand grenades to fall upon their enemies. Although it required ferocious hand-to-hand fighting, in the course of an hour our grenadiers had wrested the situation from them, then proceeded to mop up the freight cars, buildings, and other railroad installations in the area.[29]

Some of the Romanian troops in the town tried to flee to the south; a few were stopped by soldiers from 6th Panzer Division and urged back to their positions, often at gunpoint, but other Romanian troops simply took up positions alongside the new arrivals and joined the battle.[30] At one stage, Russian artillery on high ground to the north put down an accurate barrage of shells on the station, but broke off when Oberst Helmuth von Pannwitz, a cavalryman who had been tasked with raising a Cossack division to fight for the Germans, commandeered half a dozen tanks from a repair workshop at the eastern edge of the town and launched a swift attack on the artillery positions.

The presence of the Russians within firing range of the railway station – when the front line was meant to be perhaps 12 miles (20km) away – was hugely concerning, not least because it might lead to delays in the assembly of LVII Panzer Corps and therefore the start of any attempt to relieve Stalingrad. In order to ensure that Kotelnikovo was secure, there was a suggestion that the following trains be unloaded one stop down the line and the troops proceed by road, but Raus vetoed this and ordered his men to be brought directly into the town. By the end of the day sufficient elements of 6th Panzer Division had reached Kotelnikovo to be able to guarantee security. Somewhat to Raus' surprise, his division did not come under attack again and was allowed to assemble 'in essentially a peacetime fashion', though as a precaution several elements did detrain further west and proceeded by road.[31] On 1 December, the division was formally placed under the command of LVII Panzer Corps.

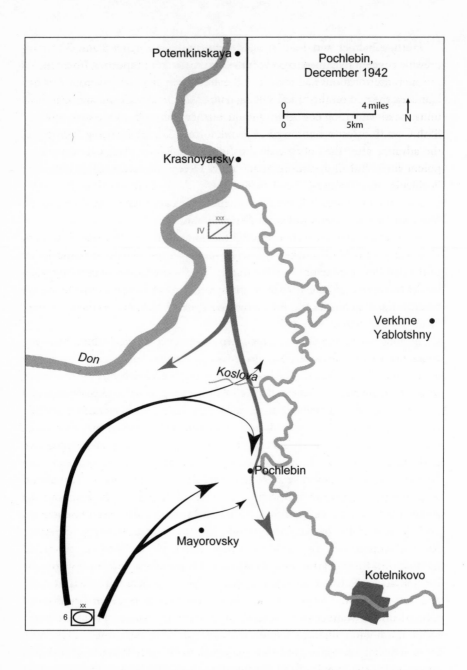

Hoth, Kirchner and Raus had a briefmeeting to discuss plans. The most pressing concern remained to prevent the Red Army from capturing Kotelnikovo; prisoner interrogations had identified the units from Yeremenko's front that had launched the raid on the town as being part of IV Cavalry Corps, and that those units remained strong enough to mount further operations. One such unit was 85th Cavalry Brigade, reinforced by a tank formation; despite being degraded in the advance after the collapse of the Romanian Fourth Army, it remained a potent force and in a surprise attack on 3 December succeeded in capturing Pochlebin, just 7 miles (12km) to the north. From there, the Russians sent a column of tanks towards Kotelnikovo, falling back only when they came under heavy artillery fire from 6th Panzer Division.

Raus wrote extensively about the fighting in December 1942, but his account is often at odds with descriptions given by other sources; in particular, the diaries of the division's regiments often contradict Raus' recollections of precisely when battles took place. Wherever such discrepancies arise, the accounts that follow are based as much as possible on the diaries and signals transcripts, as these are more likely to be accurate.

In addition to the Russian forces that had captured Pochlebin, Raus was concerned that the Russian Fifty-First Army would now join the battle from the east. He was aware that the Russian 115th Cavalry Division was moving up to support Pochlebin, so he decided to recapture the town without delay and planned an attack at first light; dense fog put paid to this, and instead the leading elements did not set off until mid-morning. Raus gives the date of this attack as 6 December, whereas the division diaries describe the fighting as taking place two days earlier.

Raus' division moved against the town with its two panzer battalions, attacking from the south and west with a total of 90 tanks – the Kurmoyarsky Aksay river (not to be confused with the Aksay) to the east prevented an encirclement from that direction, whilst also forming a barrier to prevent a Russian withdrawal. The western battalion became involved in protracted fighting with Russian armour on its northern flank and was drawn away from the main attack, which ran into determined resistance from well-positioned tanks and anti-tank guns. As the attack faltered, the panzer regiment commander, Oberstleutnant Walther von Hünersdorff, drove to the battalion that had veered to the north and redirected it towards Pochlebin. With the two battalions once more attacking on converging axes, the attack made better progress. Scheibert's company led the assault of the northern battalion, and he described the action vividly:

I now heard the order: '*Goldregen* forwards!' (this was the codename of my company) in my headset and I led with just my two leading platoons, as I did not want to collide with 7 Company which was rolling forward on my left, and the entire panorama of the Kurmoyarsky Aksay sector north of Pochlebin appeared in front of me as I crossed the last low ridge. About 1500m away I saw the road running north from Pochlebin, completely choked with Russian vehicles and supply columns. Further to the left the road ran almost along the Kurmoyarsky Aksay and then over a ridge. There too, it was full of the enemy, amongst whom I spotted tanks. Opposite me was the higher east bank of the river, and above that the endless grey sky. There wasn't much time for contemplation; we immediately took up the fight, and the enemy responded, as the lemon-yellow balls of fire from their tanks and anti-tank guns flashing from the valley showed. A glance to the right revealed Pochlebin, under artillery fire. The valley was full of clouds of dust and smoke.

We couldn't stay there as we provided a good target for the enemy defenders. On the order of the battalion commander, Major Löwe, we two leading companies leaped forward towards the road under covering fire from 4 Company. Firing from all barrels at the plentiful targets, we swiftly rolled into the midst of the Russians, scattering in all directions any who stood against us.

While Gericke (7 Company) followed the enemy retreating to the north and thus covered my rear, I turned south towards Pochlebin but also covering to the east. On either side of the Kurmoyarsky Aksay a huge crowd of Russian soldiers on foot fled from the high ground. They were under German artillery fire and were pursued by our bursts of machine-gun fire and high explosive rounds. Soon I was about a kilometre from a large trench that ran right across the road, probably from the time of the summer offensive, as it wasn't conceivable that the Russians could have dug it during the night. Later it transpired that it was part of an anti-tank obstacle south of the Koslova ravine. The Russians had established a defensive line there, and a duel rapidly developed with the anti-tank guns there. On the high ground to the south of Pochlebin we could follow the battle of II Battalion. A few tanks were burning there with clouds of black smoke above them, and through my binoculars I could see individual black figures moving amongst them. They were the crewmen from our tanks that had been shot up.

It would be hard for me to take the narrow stretch in front of me – only one road crossed the broad ditch, which was occupied by enemy anti-tank guns – without the support of heavy weapons. I requested this via the radio. Shortly after, I saw artillery shells landing in the narrow stretch. I still don't know if the

explosions were from our 4 Company in response to my request or whether the
batteries to the south came to my aid on their own initiative. In any case I decided
to attack. Either side of the road I rolled forward at high speed with my company
through the vehicles abandoned by the Russians, amongst which charged about
riderless horses and camels, swinging around to our amazement with their long
strides, and we constantly switched from fire support while halted and rushing
towards the trench, and astonishingly we were able to gain the crossing without
losses. I was the first to cross. As we drove past, I could see the destroyed anti-tank
guns and their fallen crewmen. It must be acknowledged that the enemy had
really sacrificed himself despite being outgunned. I immediately radioed back to
stop the artillery fire on this position as I had no desire to be mistaken for an
enemy tank and I asked that my location was shared [with other units]. This
transmission had barely been sent, while I was still preparing my company to
enter the village, when the artillery fire in front of us ceased as if on a training
exercise and concentrated on the village, the high ground to the east and further
to the north, where it appeared the Russians were facing Gericke's 7 Company.
That was fine work by our artillery!

The village, about a kilometre in front of me, appeared to offer only minimal
resistance. I decided to break in, partly due to the desire to be the first there with
my company. As I could see, II Battalion had made progress as a result of our
attack and was closing with the village. Fighting against little more than enemy
infantry I drove into the village. The artillery fire ceased and soon there was only
the crackling of flames from the burning huts. I was very proud to have achieved
all this with no losses.[32]

The town was rapidly overrun after a heavy artillery bombardment; there is no
mention of the fate of the town's inhabitants in any of the accounts of the battle.
Many of the Russian troops were destroyed in the area immediately outside
Pochlebin, and here the Germans encountered more camels:

A larger force thought it had found a gap between two dry riverbeds and tried to
escape westward at this point. Our covering parties had not initially spotted it due
to thick smoke, but they eventually reported the approach of something that was
neither men, horses nor tanks. Only when this mysterious unit had surged over
the crest of the range and was preparing to storm forward toward Mayorovsky was
it identified as a camel brigade. This brigade ran headlong into the fully prepared
panzers and anti-tank guns whose mission was to prevent enemy tanks from
escaping via this route … the leading elements broke down at once, and those

following behind ran back wildly. Our panzers attempted to pursue but could not do so successfully, as much of the ground was too marshy to bear their weight. The fleeing camels proved quicker and better able to move across country and, consequently, won this important race. Many of them regained their freedom since they alone were able to ford the Kurmoyarsky Aksay.[33]

By the end of the day, for the loss of 36 men killed or wounded and 12 tanks, 6th Panzer Division claimed the destruction of 56 Russian tanks and the capture of 14 guns and some 2,000 prisoners.[34] It was a satisfying success, and interrogation of the prisoners suggested that most of the Russian 81st Cavalry Division and 85th Tank Brigade had been destroyed, and 115th Cavalry Division had suffered heavy losses – in effect, IV Cavalry Corps had been reduced to perhaps the equivalent of a battlegroup. While they waited for the rest of the division and the other elements of LVII Panzer Corps to deploy, the men of the armoured battlegroup entertained themselves:

The numerous abandoned horses and camels were a pleasant diversion in the following days, particularly for the older NCOs and officers who had served in the cavalry. This 'circus' was brought to an end by a sharp order from division headquarters.[35]

But whilst the closest threat to Kotelnikovo had been eliminated, intelligence reports suggested that a larger concentration of Russian troops with perhaps as many as 300 tanks was in Verkhne Kumsky, 35 miles (56km) to the northeast. There were further Russian tank formations to the southeast. Even if all the forces of LVII Panzer Corps were able to concentrate as planned, they faced a tough task in reaching Sixth Army – they would be attacking against a numerically stronger enemy, and as a result of the fighting in Kotelnikovo and Pochlebin, there could be no doubt that the Russians knew they were coming. Even if the paper-thin front to the north could hold, LVII Panzer Corps faced a daunting task.

CHAPTER 4

DECEMBER: *WINTER STORM*

With the encirclement of Stalingrad completed, Russian plans turned to the next phase of the strategic plan: a strike against the Italian Eighth Army followed by an advance to Rostov, codenamed *Saturn*. Success in such a drive would dwarf the achievement of *Uranus*, isolating Army Group Don and Army Group A. If the operation proceeded as planned, the entire German position on the Eastern Front would be dealt an irrevocable blow, and even partial achievement would have major consequences.

Planning had begun even as the ring around the German Sixth Army was forming. On 24 November, Vasilevsky proposed that the forces of Don Front and three armies of Stalingrad Front would reduce the pocket as swiftly as possible; this was vital for several reasons. Firstly, a substantial body of Russian troops was tied up encircling Paulus' troops, and they would be needed if the Red Army was to pursue its aim of achieving a potentially war-winning victory. Secondly, there was the possibility that the Germans would succeed in re-establishing land contact with Stalingrad, allowing some or all of the trapped German troops to escape. Thirdly, the presence of Sixth Army in Stalingrad greatly complicated Russian supply movements, and the elimination of the encircled troops would improve the ability of the Red Army to transfer troops between the Caucasus and the Don region, and would also facilitate the forward movement of supplies and reinforcements.

Whilst the Stalingrad encirclement was reduced, Southwest Front – from northwest to southeast, consisting of First Guards Army, Third Guards Army, and Fifth Tank Army – was to break up the fragile German line and push south to the Donets. Once this line had been secured, Second Guards Army, reinforced with four tank corps, would be released from reserve and committed in a drive to take Rostov. At the same time, Voronezh Front's Sixth Army would cover the right flank of the operation.[1]

As a preliminary step while the necessary troops were moved into position, General Prokofy Logvinovich Romanenko's Fifth Tank Army was ordered to break up the German front line that had coalesced along the lower Chir. This would remove the Germans from their closest point to the Stalingrad pocket and – by attacking before the beginning of *Saturn* – Romanenko would draw any German reserves into the area where they could be tied down and thus would not be available to intervene when the Italians were attacked. The pressure on the fragile line of *Armee Abteilung Hollidt* hadn't ceased completely, and on 2 December *Gruppe Stahel* – one of the improvised battlegroups that had largely saved the Germans from complete collapse in the wake of *Uranus* – was finally overrun. Its mixture of army stragglers, Luftwaffe ground personnel and others had fought with great distinction and Richthofen feared that Oberstleutnant Rainer Stahel, whose 34th Flak Regiment had provided the solid core of the group, was dead or taken prisoner. To his surprise and relief, Stahel was alive and well; he gathered together the remnants of his battlegroup and fought his way back to German lines over two days. He was greeted as a hero, and – perhaps desperate to find something to celebrate amidst the widespread bad news – Hitler awarded him the Oak Leaves to the Knight's Cross.[2] In early 1943, Stahel was promoted to Oberst.

Although its tanks had played a vital role in the encirclement of Stalingrad, the Russian Fifth Tank Army had not performed as well as Romanenko might have hoped. Rodin's XXVI Tank Corps had led the way to Kalach and beyond, but Butkov's I Tank Corps had struggled from the outset; after-action reports from Vatutin's headquarters described its brigades as groping around like 'blind kittens' instead of pressing forward with determination. It was heavily involved in the running battles with the Romanian and German armoured units that tried in vain to hold back the breakthrough, and sustained substantial losses. In addition to his two tank corps, Romanenko had six infantry divisions, which were intended to have led the breakthrough and were then to be used to help seal the pocket around Stalingrad, but the initial attacks of the infantry were beaten off by the Romanians and even after the tanks had broken the defensive line, the infantry struggled to advance at a comparable rate. Instead of being able to regroup and recover broken down and damaged tanks, the two tank corps had to be employed to break up the armoured forces that Paulus had dispatched far too late to the Don. After a short period to recover, the two tank corps of Fifth Tank Army were ordered to attack over the Chir against XLVIII Panzer Corps.

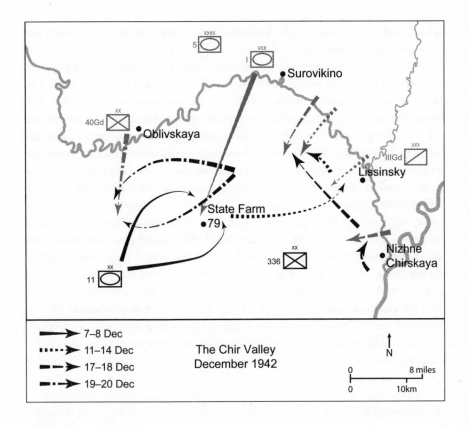

5

I

Surovikino

40Gd

Oblivskaya

IIIGd

Lissinsky

State Farm
79

336

Nizhne
Chirskaya

11

➤ 7–8 Dec

➤ 11–14 Dec

➤ 17–18 Dec

➤ 19–20 Dec

The Chir Valley
December 1942

N

0   8 miles

0   10km

By now, the German 336th Infantry Division commanded by General Walther Lucht had deployed in the area, improving considerably the strength of the defences. On 7 December, as 11th Panzer Division began to move into support positions behind the front line, Lucht reported that a Russian armoured column had penetrated the left flank of his division; this was Butkov's I Tank Corps, the first phase of the Russian attempt to break up the Chir defences. By the end of the day, the Russians had reached and captured State Farm 79, where 336th Infantry Division's supply columns had been positioned.

Mellenthin, the chief of staff at XLVIII Panzer Corps headquarters, sent an urgent message to Balck urging haste and he immediately went into action, even though much of his division was still en route. Driving through the night, the flak battalion, anti-tank battalion and combat engineer battalion of 11th Panzer Division took up blocking positions to the south of the farm. Rejecting a suggestion by Lucht that 11th Panzer Division should attack the Russians directly and drive them back – the terrain was unfavourable, Balck argued, and he intended to destroy the Russian force rather than merely push it back to its start line – the tanks of 15th Panzer Regiment, supported by 111th Panzergrenadier Regiment, circled around to the northwest and north of the farm, securing the slightly higher ground in the area. At first light on 8 December, the Russian tanks attempted to advance into the rear of 336th Infantry Division and were brought to an abrupt halt by the accurate fire of the blocking unit. Meanwhile, the force dispatched to encircle the Russians surprised a column of motorised infantry that was moving forward to support the Russian armour and destroyed it completely, following up with an assault into the rear of the Russian tanks.

Butkov's troops failed completely to spot the approach of 11th Panzer Division and were swiftly overrun. As a finale to the operation, Balck sent 110th Panzergrenadier Regiment into State Farm 79 to complete the destruction of I Tank Corps:

> As I drove through State Farm 79 a frightful picture unfolded before me. The supply units of 336th Infantry Division had been positioned there. Our brave soldiers had been brutally slaughtered en masse. The Russians had surprised and destroyed them in the early morning hours.
>
> That scene made one basic fact clear. This was all about the survival or extinction of our people ... I summarised the situation in a divisional order of the day, one of the very few that I ever published:

> 11th Panzer Division
> Staff Section Ic
>
> *Kameraden*
>
> The Bolshevist atrocities at State Farm 79, where the Russians slaughtered several hundred German soldiers, will remain in our memories forever.
>
> The interrogation of the prisoner of war Sergeant Ivan Jakovevich Kurilko ... revealed the following information: at a meeting shortly before 19 November 1942 ... at which all brigade and battalion commanders were present, two Romanians who had allegedly deserted were brought before them. Those assembled were told that these were Romanians, and that Romanians were to be taken prisoner. On the other hand, they were ordered to take no German prisoners.

They were ordered not to shoot Romanians in front of Germans, but to shoot Germans in front of Romanians. This statement corroborates with what we have seen with our own eyes at State Farm 79. It is also consistent in all details with the repeated announcements in the Anglo-American press calling for the complete eradication of the German people [this refers to the growing calls for continuing the war until Germany surrendered unconditionally, something that would become official Allied policy at the Casablanca conference in 1943].

As all of you know, this is in total contradiction to the dishonest Russian propaganda that promises German defectors and prisoners safety and return to the Fatherland after the war.

Kameraden, the tough days of fighting that are now behind us show us again that this is about the survival or extinction of our people. If in the future you falter in your courage, should you weaken during the bitter fighting, always remember the Anglo-American diatribes of hate, the slogans of the 157th Russian Tank Brigade, and the terrible sights at State Farm 79 that prove to us without a doubt the fate that awaits us if we do not win this struggle.[3]

There is no doubt that the Russians executed both German and Romanian soldiers who surrendered during the fighting in late 1942, but Balck's account is one-sided, as are those of most of the Germans and Russians who wrote about their experiences. From the early planning stages of *Barbarossa*, Hitler had made clear to his senior officers that the war would be fought without mercy – it represented a struggle between two incompatible systems, and only one could survive. Field Marshal Walter von Reichenau, commander of Sixth Army until he had a fatal stroke in early 1942, added his own instructions in October 1941 to those that had already been issued by Hitler, deliberately making a link between the two groups most hated by the Nazis, communists and Jews, and adding a third obsession, that of 'Asiatic influence':

With regard to the conduct of troops towards the Bolshevist system, there are still many imprecise ideas in circulation.

The most essential aim of the campaign against the Jewish-Bolshevist system is the complete destruction of their means of power and the elimination of Asiatic influence from the European culture.

In this regard, the troops face tasks in addition to straightforward soldiering. The soldier in the Eastern territories is not merely a fighter according to the rules of war but also a standard bearer of ruthless national ideology and the avenger of bestialities that have been inflicted upon German and racially related nations.

Therefore the soldier must have full understanding for the necessity of a severe but just revenge on Jewish subhumans. This serves another purpose, the elimination of revolts in the rear areas of the Wehrmacht, which as experience shows are always caused by Jews.

The war against the enemy behind the front line is still not being conducted earnestly enough. Treacherous, cruel partisans and degenerate women are still being made prisoners-of-war and guerillas dressed partly in uniform or plain clothes and vagabonds are still being treated as proper soldiers and sent to prisoner-of-war camps. In fact, captured Russian officers talk mockingly about Soviet agents moving openly on the roads and frequently eating at German field kitchens. Such behaviour by the troops can only be explained by complete thoughtlessness. It is therefore now high time for the commanders to clarify the meaning of the current fighting.

The feeding of locals and of prisoners-of-war who are not working for the Wehrmacht from soldiers' kitchens is an equally erroneous humanitarian act as is distributing cigarettes and bread. Soldiers should not give to the enemy things that the people at home spare at great sacrifice and things that are being brought by the command to the front with great difficulty, even if they originate from booty. It is an important part of our supplies.

The Soviets have often set buildings on fire when they retreat. The troops should be involved in extinguishing fires only if it is necessary to secure sufficient numbers of billets. Otherwise the disappearance of symbols of the former Bolshevist rule even in the form of buildings is part of the struggle of destruction. Neither historic nor artistic considerations are to play any role in the eastern territories. The command issues the necessary directives for the securing of raw material and plants essential for the war effort. The complete disarmament of the civilian population in the rear of the fighting troops is imperative in view of the long vulnerable lines of communications and where possible, captured weapons and ammunition should be stored and guarded. Should the military situation make this impossible, weapons and ammunition are to be rendered unusable. If isolated partisans are found using firearms in the rear areas, draconian measures are to be taken. These are to be extended to that part of the male population who were in a position to hinder or report the attacks. The indifference of numerous apparently anti-Soviet elements, which arises from a 'wait and see' attitude, must give way to a clear decision to work actively with us. If not, no one can complain about being judged and treated as a member of the Soviet system. Fear of German counter-measures must be stronger than threats from roving Bolshevist remnants.

Regardless of all political considerations of the future, soldiers must fulfill two tasks:

1. Complete annihilation of the false Bolshevist doctrine of the Soviet State and its armed forces.
2. The pitiless extermination of foreign treachery and cruelty and thus the protection of the lives of military personnel in Russia.

This is the only way to fulfill our historic task to liberate the German people once and for all from the Asiatic-Jewish danger.[4]

Although he later denied being aware of this order, Field Marshal Gerd von Runstedt, commander of Army Group South at the time, expressed complete agreement with Reichenau's order and advised other army commanders to issue similar instructions.[5] When Paulus replaced Reichenau, he immediately rescinded Reichenau's order – according to his adjutant – as well as Hitler's 'commissar order', which required all Red Army commissars to be executed if captured; however, when officers continued to follow Reichenau's and Hitler's previous instructions, there is no evidence that Paulus subjected them to any disciplinary action.[6]

Balck, Mellenthin, Manstein and others attempted to portray the history of the Eastern Front in a manner as favourable as possible to the Wehrmacht; most atrocities were the work of the SS, and the army generally acted honourably. Whilst this may have been the case on some occasions – and many officers did order their men not to get involved in mass killings and arbitrary acts of violence – there is no doubt that from the beginning, the Wehrmacht played a full role in the barbarous conduct of German forces in the Soviet Union. Franz Walther Stahlecker, commander of *Einsatzgruppe A*, the SS unit tasked with killing Jews and other 'undesirables' in the Baltic States, wrote in a report that cooperation with the army was 'generally good, in a few cases, for instance with the 4th Panzer Group under Generaloberst Hoepner, very close, almost cordial'.[7] During their withdrawal back into the Stalingrad encirclement, the retreating Germans found that they had too few vehicles or horses to tow their guns and used Russian prisoners of war for the task, executing those who fell by the wayside through exhaustion, and many of the Russian soldiers of I Tank Corps would have seen such cases during the fighting in November. Reports from partisans operating in the occupied parts of the Soviet Union had made the Soviet authorities aware of the behaviour of the Germans, often acting through their local allies, and these reports had been disseminated to the rank and file via the army's political commissars. Balck may have advised his troops that this was a battle for the survival of their culture; the Soviet authorities were giving precisely the same message to their men.

Gabriel Temkin was a Polish Jew who fled from his home in the city of Łódź shortly after it was occupied by the Germans in 1939, preferring to take his chances in the Russian-occupied parts of eastern Poland. From there, he first took a job in a mine in the Ural Mountains and then moved to Gomel, where he was conscripted at the onset of *Barbarossa*. Due to his Polish background, the Red Army treated him with suspicion and he was sent to a labour battalion, and he was one of the many tens of thousands of men captured by the Germans in 1942 after the failure of Timoshenko's attempt to recapture Kharkov. He later recalled how Jewish Russians were singled out after capture, with guards shouting for Jews to come forward:

> A young Soviet Jew ... responded mechanically to the German yelling and put up his hand. To this day I remember the face of that boy. I can see his grayish, scared eyes. Before he was led beyond the barbed wire fence to be shot, he sat motionless while a Russian prisoner of war, a regular army officer, was hastily removing his shoes murmuring: 'You have no need for them any more.'
>
> The Germans could not tell a Jew from a non-Jew, so they tried to enlist Russians or Ukrainians to uncover Jews. They tempted hungry prisoners with a loaf of bread for every Jew pointed out. In my presence two prisoners were denounced as 'looking Jewish' and, as it turned out, one of the suspects was indeed Jewish. As he claimed to be Belorussian, he was ordered to pull down his pants, and he failed the test. While he continued to deny being Jewish, he was mercilessly beaten and forced to dig his own grave before being shot.[8]

Temkin was able to escape detection; he had blond hair and blue eyes, and although some of the prisoners were aware of his Jewish background, none of them – even one who had previously made anti-Semitic comments about him – betrayed him.

Atrocities were committed widely by both sides from the outset of the war on the Eastern Front, as Manstein recorded at the beginning of the war with the Soviet Union:

> On this very first day the Soviet command showed its true face. Our troops came across a German patrol which had been cut off by the enemy earlier on. All its members were dead and gruesomely mutilated.[9]

Despite stating in his memoirs that he had told higher and subordinate commands that he regarded Hitler's commissar order as contrary to military conduct and that he would not be enforcing it, Manstein was later successfully prosecuted during the Nuremburg Tribunals, where it was shown that units under his command killed hundreds of commissars and were involved in mass killings of Jews; critically, the prosecution produced an order with his signature that effectively repeated the order that Reichenau had sent out the previous month.[10] It is also noteworthy that while many like Manstein claimed that they had tried to prevent the mistreatment of Soviet commissars, they are conspicuously silent on the subject of Jewish prisoners.

Balck was senior enough to have been aware of the orders Hitler gave at the outset of *Barbarossa* on how the war was to be conducted, and the additional instructions issued by the likes of Reichenau. And of course, whilst the Russians were equally guilty of atrocities on many occasions, Hitler premeditated such acts – there is no evidence that the Russians did so before the war.

To an extent, many German officers were condemned whatever they did. Ewald von Kleist, whose troops were stranded in the Caucasus while Balck was struggling to hold the Chir front, had been forcibly retired from the army before the war because of his strong royalist views and his unhidden dislike of the Nazis; he further courted disfavour by arguing with Hitler that the Hungarians, Italians and Romanians should not be used to shore up the long Don front.[11] Unlike many of his contemporaries who later questionably claimed – like Manstein – that they had opposed the brutal orders regarding commissars and others, Kleist undoubtedly treated the Russians with kindness, commenting in September 1942: 'These vast spaces depress me. And these vast hordes of people! We're lost if we don't win them over.'[12]

Ignoring the directives from Hitler, Kleist actively worked to recruit men from the Caucasus region and succeeded in raising several hundred thousand auxiliary troops, ignoring the protests of individuals like Erich Koch, the *Reichskommissar* for the Ukraine. He personally told SS and other officials that in his area of command he would not tolerate the excesses that were widespread elsewhere.[13] However, his conduct did not save him from the wrath of the victorious allies. After the war, the Soviet Union – which imprisoned and executed many Germans for their brutal misconduct on the Eastern Front – convicted Kleist of the crime of 'alienating through mildness and kindness the population of the Soviet Union'.[14] He died in captivity in 1954.

The Eastern Front brought out the worst in other nationalities too. When Hungarian troops took over control of the prison camp where Temkin was being held, there was hope amongst the prisoners that their conditions would improve, and although food supplies did briefly become more plentiful, the search for Jews continued. Temkin also found that many of the Hungarian guards amused themselves by random acts of sadism, like riding a horse over sleeping prisoners or forcing prisoners to slap each other and then punishing them for their behaviour. When a young Russian was captured after attempting to escape, he was shot in front of the rest of the camp. His last words to his fellow prisoners were '*Proshchayte, tovarishchi*' ('Farewell, comrades'). An older prisoner standing near Temkin whispered '*Proshchay, synok*' ('Farewell, son') with tears in his eyes.[15] Not long after, the remaining prisoners were moved to a new compound near Voronezh where their food was reduced to below starvation levels; the prisoners had to take wheelbarrows along nearby roads, under guard, and collect the rotting carcasses of horses killed in the recent fighting. These horses were then chopped up and boiled to make soup. In less than two months, the population of the prison camp fell from 1,500 to just 150 as a result of deaths from starvation, illness and mistreatment. When he and the survivors began a march to the west – presumably to be put aboard trains that would take them to work as slave labour in factories in Germany – Temkin managed to escape.

Regardless of the events in State Farm 79, the battle fought by 11th Panzer Division was a stunning demonstration of the use of armoured forces in defensive fighting: rather than allowing the strength of his division to be frittered away in small supporting detachments, Balck showed that it was far more effective to keep the division concentrated and to use it in a counterattacking role. His initial assessment was correct – merely stopping or pushing back the Russians was inadequate. If the front line was to be stabilised, the Russian forces had to be destroyed or they would merely regroup and attack again. There might have been an initial disagreement between Balck and Lucht – the latter had asked Balck simply to drive back the Russian penetration – but from this point onwards, the two men worked in close harmony. The troops of 336th Infantry Division did their best to hold their extended positions along the Chir while Balck and 11th Panzer Division operated in their rear, smashing every Russian attempt to break into the rear area. Balck also established a strong, mutually trusting relationship with Knobelsdorff and Mellenthin at XLVIII Panzer Corps headquarters, allowing him to function with no interference.

The next few days passed in a series of near-identical operations, with the division driving through the night to fall on the Russians early the next morning:

> It was a complete mystery to me when the soldiers actually slept during those nine days. One tank crewman added up the hours of sleep he managed during this time. Even if I had doubled his estimate it would still have been utterly implausible.

In addition, the fighting was not as easy as it may sound in this account. Quite often elements of one of my units were overrun by the Russians, encircled, and had to be rescued. Additional enemy forces always tried to exploit any successful attack. But our losses were not high because we used surprise to our advantage. 'Night marches save blood' became the slogan in the division. I often shouted at them, 'What do you want to do, bleed or march?' 'Let's march, Sir,' replied the tired and worn-out men.

    ... My General Staff Officer Ia, the brilliant Major Kinitz, sat in a position somewhat to the rear and remained in radio contact with me, the higher command, and everyone else. I remained highly mobile, moving to all the hot spots. I usually visited every regiment several times a day. While still out on the road during the evening I drew up the basic plan for the next day. After speaking by phone to Kinitz, I drove to every regiment and gave them the next day's order personally. Then I drove back to my own command post and spoke by phone with ... Mellenthin. If General Knobelsdorff agreed, the regiments received a short radio message: 'No change!' If changes were required, I drove at night once again to all the regiments so that there would be no misunderstandings. At dawn I was always back at the key location.[16]

The performance of Fifth Tank Army was a considerable disappointment for Stalin and Vasilevsky. Partly to address this, a new Fifth Shock Army was created, using the personnel of Tenth Reserve Army, under the command of Lieutenant General Markian Mikhailovich Popov. It was hoped that these fresh forces would be able to perform rather better than Romanenko's men.

    Despite being in near-continuous combat, 11th Panzer Division remained close to establishment strength. This shows the huge importance of controlling the battlefield at the end of each battle – it allowed the division's workshop teams to recover broken-down and damaged vehicles, many of which could be repaired rapidly. In a similar manner, Raus' 6th Panzer Division swiftly recovered most of its knocked-out vehicles after the fighting at Pochlebin and replaced the small number of 'total losses' with replacements from the tank repair workshop in Kotelnikovo and from new vehicles sent from Germany. As elements of 23rd Panzer Division took up positions on the right flank of LVII Panzer Corps, the moment to launch *Winter Storm* grew closer. Despite mauling the Russian IV Cavalry Corps, Raus remained concerned about a force of cavalry, infantry and a small number of tanks to his front. On 6 December, this group was reported to have advanced through the lines of the Romanian VII Corps due east of Kotelnikovo and then continued a little to the south, perhaps seeking to outflank 6th Panzer

Division at Kotelnikovo. An operational order was swiftly issued – codenamed *Otto* – to the effect that, in the event of the Russian IV and XIII Mechanised Corps advancing along this axis, the entire strength of 6th Panzer Division, together with those elements of 23rd Panzer Division that had arrived, was to be deployed in a crushing counterattack. If the two Russian corps could be destroyed, the way would be open for the Germans to advance to the Stalingrad encirclement with little hindrance. The cautiously advancing leading Russian elements entered Budarka, about 15 miles (25km) southeast of Kotelnikovo, but withdrew the following day. This is another occasion on which Raus' account differs from others – he described the Russian probe and the planned counterattack as occurring on 9 December, whereas the diary of 11th Panzer Regiment records that by this date, there was greater concern about Russian forces concentrating in the north close to the Don rather than from the east.[17]

If 11th Panzer Division was functioning efficiently, the same could not be said of other German reinforcements. One of the divisions organised from surplus Luftwaffe personnel, 7th Luftwaffe Field Division commanded by Generalmajor Wolf Freiherr von Biedermann, arrived to deploy alongside 336th Infantry Division. Biedermann had served first as an infantry officer and then as a pilot in the First World War and joined the Luftwaffe in 1934, after which he held a variety of posts in which he was responsible for training Luftwaffe personnel. He was appointed commander of his new division without any further preparation – the largest infantry formation he had commanded in the First World War was an infantry company. His men were well equipped but had undergone almost no training as infantrymen; the division's artillery was manned by men drawn from anti-aircraft formations who were experienced in defending against air attack but had no experience whatever of operating as an infantry support arm. On 10 December, two battalions were sent to occupy part of the Chir line that had been manned by elements of *Gruppe von Stumpfeld* and moved forward without taking any precautions against Russian intervention. They ran straight into an advancing Russian column and were utterly destroyed in a singularly one-sided battle. Thereafter, the rest of 7th Luftwaffe Field Division was subordinated to 336th Infantry Division and its units were deployed alongside Lucht's seasoned infantrymen.

Amidst the various weapons of war being deployed by both sides, there were some unorthodox approaches, as Mansoor Abdullin discovered:

One day I saw anti-tank dogs for the first time. Like other men from the Siberian Taiga, I love dogs very much and when I learned about the suicide dogs I was very upset. What a thing to do to a loyal animal, the joy of childhood! A dog is a devoted friend. A dog trusts a man, yet the man deceives him and sends him to his death under a tank! I felt weak when I walked over to the dogs, waiting for their moment next to their dog-soldiers. Multi-coloured, shaggy, ears hanging or erect. And this one – one ear up, the other down – it was a mongrel – while a pack of explosives of 8kg was prepared. It looked at me, tilting its head from one side to the other, hoping for a treat.

Sobakov was a middle-aged red-haired peasant from the Krasnoyarsk region – my fellow countryman. We talked about it. The dogs were trained for three months: they were fed only under a moving tank – that was the whole secret of the anti-tank dogs. An antenna emerged from the explosive pack, connected to a fuse …

Soon, German tanks appeared and we saw a black, shaggy lump running towards them. Behind him after a small interval a second, then a third.

The first dog destroyed a tank with a powerful explosion. Then came the second explosion, the third … fascist tankers began to turn their vehicles abruptly and disappeared at high speed. There was no escape from the anti-tank dogs.

A 'Urrah!' went up from our trenches. I should have been happy as the German attack had been broken, but I cried, cursing both the war and the inhuman individuals who had started it.[18]

Originally, the anti-tank dogs had been intended to release their explosives by pulling on a strap with their teeth, but it proved impossible to train them to do this reliably. The explosive charges could be detonated remotely, but such triggers were expensive and it was more usual to use timers – however, dogs often became confused and returned to their handlers, which would have been disastrous if the explosive were triggered by a timer. In an attempt to remedy this, the explosive packs were changed to have a wooden trigger sticking out of the top – the 'antenna' that Abdullin described – which would set off the explosive after the dog brushed against the underside of a tank. In battle, the dogs were generally ineffective; they became confused and distressed by the noise of combat, and most Red Army tanks, which had been used for training the dogs, were diesel-powered. German tanks, by contrast, used petroleum, and the smell was sufficiently different to confuse the dogs. Abdullin cannot have been alone in feeling relieved when they gradually stopped being used. However, the Soviet Army continued to experiment with anti-tank dogs until the mid-1960s.[19]

Manstein and Hoth struggled with conflicting pressures. On the one hand, they wanted to wait until they had three panzer divisions available to launch their relief effort, but the growing crisis in Stalingrad, where daily deliveries of supplies by the Luftwaffe averaged barely 20 per cent of what was required to keep Sixth Army functioning, meant that further delay was dangerous – indeed, Manstein's original start date for the operation had already slipped. A total of 179 Luftwaffe combat aircraft would support *Winter Storm*, and even this force was weakened by diversion of resources – fearing an attack on the Italian Eighth Army, Richthofen diverted *Kampfgeschwader 27* ('Bomber Wing 27', nicknamed 'Boelcke' after the First World War fighter pilot) and *Stukageschwader 77* ('Dive-bomber Wing 77') to the north. When the expected attack failed to appear, the order was reversed, but the planes were unavailable to Hoth's Fourth Panzer Army until 14 December, meaning that the initial assault would be made with only two thirds of the originally intended air support.[20] In addition, Richthofen had to use a large part of his fleet of He-111 bombers to fly supplies into Stalingrad, thus further reducing his ability to support ground operations. But despite the inadequacy of the supplies reaching Sixth Army, Manstein made no attempt to direct Paulus to start preparations for a breakout; given his insistence that an adequate airlift was an essential prerequisite for operations, his failure to react to the manifest inadequacies is noteworthy.

On 12 December, *Winter Storm* began: 6th Panzer Division was to break out along the axis of the railway line running from Kotelnikovo to Stalingrad, with 23rd Panzer Division on its southern flank. Thereafter, the two panzer divisions would continue their advance to the west of the railway line. The deployment of 6th Panzer Division suffered delays as columns of vehicles slowly made their way from where they had waited west of Kotelnikovo to their forming-up areas. An hour after first light – 6.30am local time, 4.30am for the Germans who operated on Berlin time – all was ready. Raus described the moment:

A sunny winter day dawned; the officers checked their watches. Everyone was fully conscious of the significance of the approaching hour.

Suddenly the sounds of explosions disrupted the silence. Every gun in the division commenced firing, and it almost seemed as if the shells were going to land within our own lines. Involuntarily, everyone flinched and stooped, but the first salvo was already screaming over the heads of the men and landing on the Gremyachi station. The earth quivered from the detonation of the heavy shells. Stones, planks, and rails were hurled into the air. The salvo had hit the centre of the Russians' chief strongpoint. This was the signal for the 'witches' Sabbath' to follow.[21]

As had been the case with the fighting around Pochlebin, 6th Panzer Division's armoured group was led by Walther von Hünersdorff, the commander of its 11th Panzer Regiment. Despite their awareness of the German forces assembling around Kotelnikovo, the Russians appear to have been taken by surprise and Hünersdorff's tanks swiftly overran the defences, capturing much of the Russian artillery intact. Two German tanks were disabled by mines and another by a Russian anti-tank gun, and many in the armoured group were surprised that the Russians did not make better use of the terrain – there was a narrow region through which all the German tanks had to pass, and a relatively modest commitment of troops to form a defensive line would have led to substantial delays. It seemed impossible that the Russians had not expected an attack, and some officers began to hope that perhaps the commitment of so many Russian troops to the Stalingrad encirclement meant that there would be relatively modest resistance in the days ahead.[22] The headquarters of the Russian 23rd Infantry Division facing 6th Panzer Division was captured shortly after the onset of the attack, followed by the corps headquarters, effectively paralysing Russian command and control. To the south, 23rd Panzer Division rapidly overcame initial strong resistance and also made good progress.

Throughout the preparatory phase, Raus had been concerned about the potential weakness of his northern flank. Releasing troops to cover the open flank would reduce the striking power of the division and thus its ability to reach Stalingrad, but it was unlikely that the Romanian cavalry division tasked with flank security would be up to the task, and the Luftwaffe field division that had been allocated to the relief attempt had not yet arrived; even when it did, it would hardly represent a potent combat force, even in a purely defensive capacity. In order to deal with the perceived threat, Raus and Hünersdorff had devised a solution that involved exploiting the initial breakthrough with a thrust to the west towards the village of Verkhne Jablochniy. A battalion of 6th Panzer Division's 4th Panzergrenadier Regiment attacked energetically from the south to simulate a major attack, and the advance of the German infantry slowed as it ran into increasingly heavy small-arms fire near the southern limits of the village. Luftwaffe reconnaissance flights reported a steady stream of Russian troops reinforcing the defences of Verkhne Jablochniy, and the panzergrenadiers launched repeated attacks to draw as much attention on themselves as possible. Meanwhile, *Gruppe Hünersdorff* was approaching from the east with the panzer regiment leading the way:

I Battalion on the right, II Battalion on the left, the anti-tank and self-propelled guns in between, II Battalion 114th Panzergrenadier Regiment following in half-tracks on a broad front. The attack progressed smoothly at first without enemy resistance, but then came to a halt due to terrain difficulties.[23]

Time was lost as the force made its way through and around a patch of swampy ground. In the meantime, the fighting at the southern edge of Verkhny Jablochniy intensified steadily. Towards the end of the short hours of daylight, Hünersdorff's panzer regiment appeared from the east and stormed into the village. In a brisk firefight, it destroyed ten of the 14 Russian tanks that had been sent to Verkhne Jablochniy; the rest were knocked out the following day by a flak detachment. Wasting no time, the panzer regiment turned back and headed off to the northeast, leaving the battalion of troops from 4th Panzergrenadier Regiment to complete the operation.[24]

In his memoirs, Raus described the fighting at Verkhne Jablochniy as a considerable success, but others were more critical; Scheibert later wrote that the vital advance towards Stalingrad was delayed, and with adequate air support the men of 4th Panzergrenadier Regiment could have secured the village without Hünersdorff's battlegroup having to divert.[25] Nevertheless, he added that it was easy to be wise with hindsight; when the attack was planned and executed, the Germans did not know the full strength of the Russian forces in Verkhne Jablochniy, and if a substantial force had been present, it would indeed have been foolhardy to leave it in place threatening the northern flank of 6th Panzer Division. The following day a group of Russian tanks was spotted to the north of the village, and the Germans called in airstrikes; the Russian tanks attempted to take shelter in a narrow gully, but when the German infantry moved forward all they found were several wrecked or abandoned tanks. Whether such an air attack could have sufficed to secure Raus' northern flank is open to question.

Raus now wanted to press on immediately to secure crossings over the Aksay, and he and Hünersdorff discussed their options at length. The attack to secure Verkhne Jablochniy had taken longer than anticipated and Raus wished to hurry forward as fast as possible. The armoured battlegroup commander was less enthusiastic about a dash across the featureless steppe in the dark, particularly after his troops had been held up by the unexpected discovery of a frozen swamp to the east of Verkhne Jablochniy. Given the few roads that were available and the relatively featureless terrain, there was a good likelihood that any night move would result in units getting lost. However, the exigencies of the situation made the taking of risks unavoidable, and after a pause for refuelling and rearming, a detachment of 11th Panzer Regiment headed for the Aksay, driving through the night. Near Tchilekov, on the direct line of advance towards Stalingrad, the road ran through a ravine, and even the tracked vehicles struggled with the heavily iced road – Scheibert's company took over five hours to negotiate it.[26] A little to the east, the division's motorised reconnaissance battalion ran into Russian tanks and requested support, but Hünersdorff decided that the priority was to continue the advance. Despite encountering two more patches of frozen swamps, the panzers finally reached the river at first light on 13 December. For the men in the armoured battlegroup who took part in this advance and those who waited for first light to follow, it was an uncomfortable few hours:

> It was bitterly cold, and the unit commanders got no sleep. The ravine [at Tchelikov], with its road no longer visible under the flattened covering of ice, constantly delayed their advance. They then had to oversee refuelling, rearming, and supply of food, they received orders for the next day, etc.
>
> Nobody was really pleased with the outcome of the day. Where were the Russians?[27]

Vasilevsky had been aware of the build-up of LVII Panzer Corps, and had hoped that the troops encircling Sixth Army would be able to crush the pocket before the Germans launched their rescue attempt. Even if complete elimination of Sixth Army was not possible, reducing the size of the pocket, particularly by eliminating the western parts, would make a relief operation a much harder undertaking and would also release troops for deployment against LVII Panzer Corps. In the first week of December, the seven encircling armies launched the opening assaults of an operation codenamed *Koltso* ('*Ring*'), and were surprised at the ferocity of resistance. Both sides suffered heavy losses – Paulus' troops lost nearly half of their remaining 140 tanks – but the perimeter held. At the southwest corner of the encirclement, the Russian Fifty-Seventh Army suffered particularly badly as it attempted to reduce the sector from where a breakout attempt might be launched, failing completely to drive the encircled Germans deeper into the pocket. *Stavka* carried out a thorough analysis of the entire campaign the following year, and its summary of the failed attempts to reduce the Sixth Army in December described clear shortcomings in the Russian Army as well as terrain difficulties:

> The command, cooperation, and the rear were not properly organised. The artillery could not give the rifle troops the necessary support in the offensive

against the enemy ...

The enemy was able to organise strong defences by withdrawing to [a] favourable line for defence.[28]

The terrain – rising from west to east, with good fields of fire and visibility, crossed by the same sudden deep ravines that were a potential hindrance to the German armoured formations involved in *Winter Storm* and providing cover where reserves and command formations could be deployed – had favoured the Russians during the German attempts to take Stalingrad, and now played into the hands of the German defenders. Conversely, had the troops of Sixth Army attempted a breakout, they might have enjoyed a terrain advantage at first, but they in turn would then have had to fight their way through a region where the landscape favoured defence. Any hope that Vasilevsky might have had about rapidly reducing the size of the encirclement rapidly vanished. Reluctantly, he and Stalin agreed that Second Guards Army, being held as reserve for the second phase of *Saturn*, should be reassigned to help reduce the Stalingrad pocket in a new attack starting on 18 December.

Vasilevsky had also hoped that Fifth Tank Army's pressure upon the Chir line would result in a breakthrough, or at the very least a diversion of the forces earmarked for the relief operation; to an extent, this hope was fulfilled inasmuch as XLVIII Panzer Corps was heavily committed to holding its positions and was thus unable to provide any assistance to Fourth Panzer Army, but the failure of Romanenko's army made the planned deep penetration to Rostov, codenamed *Saturn*, a much harder proposition. Delays in bringing forward reinforcements had already put the start date for *Saturn* back from 10 December by six days, and Vasilevsky now rushed to visit the front line, where he held urgent talks with Yeremenko. They agreed on the pressing requirement for reinforcements for Fifty-First Army to block the advancing LVII Panzer Corps, and in light of this Vasilevsky now requested the release of Second Guards Army from Rokossovsky's Don Front so that it could block the German relief effort.

Neither Rokossovsky nor Stalin were in favour of releasing Second Guards Army, which had already had its deployment altered and had thus weakened the forces available for *Saturn*. Both men wished to deploy the troops against the encircled Sixth Army, but Vasilevsky was insistent – without the support of Second Guards Army, he feared that Fifty-First Army would be insufficient to halt the advancing German troops. Stalin promised to consider the matter and, despite Rokossovsky's protests, approved Vasilevsky's proposal early on 13 December.[29] However, it would take five days for Second Guards Army to

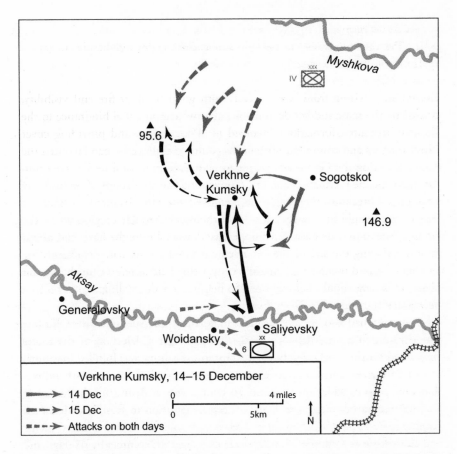

Verkhne Kumsky, 14–15 December

- 14 Dec
- 15 Dec
- Attacks on both days

0 ———— 4 miles
0 ———— 5km
N

redeploy, and until it arrived, Fifty-First Army would have to hold back LVII Panzer Corps on its own. Time was of the essence – any small hope that the Germans had of reaching the beleaguered Sixth Army would depend on 6th and 23rd Panzer Divisions achieving most of the task before Lieutenant General Rodion Yakovlevich Malinovsky's Second Guards Army could intervene. When he made the decision to divert his panzer regiment to seize Verkhne Jablochniy, Raus was of course unaware of the impending deployment of Second Guards Army, but he would have known that the Russians would move reinforcements to block the advance. It was a difficult balance – would there be greater risk in leaving the northern flank of the operation unsecured, or would the delay in advancing towards Stalingrad prove fatal? Acting on the information he had available, Raus concluded that securing his flank was more important.

Raus had been keen to lure the Russian armoured forces in the area – IV and XIII Mechanised Corps – into an ambush before the operation began in order to try to improve the chances of the operation being a success, and now ordered Hünersdorff to proceed across the Aksay in order to draw the Russians into battle. The Russian XIII Mechanised Corps – consisting of 17th and 62nd Mechanised Brigades and 41st Tank Regiment – had been ordered to stop the German advance and began to take up positions facing 23rd Panzer Division, but for the moment there was little in the path of 6th Panzer Division. But if the Russians couldn't stop Raus' division, the terrain and weather proved to be different matters. Continuation along the railway line led the armoured battlegroup into two more frozen ravines, and rather than endure further delays, Hünersdorff turned northwest. In mid-morning, he reached the advance guard on the banks of the Aksay at Saliyevsky without encountering any Russian resistance and captured its bridge intact, and his troops began to cross. The regiment's I Battalion's tanks carefully crossed the shaky bridge one by one, but when Hünersdorff tried to cross personally, his command tank slipped off the side of the bridge into the river. Every attempt to recover the tank failed and the bridge remained blocked. Originally, Hünersdorff had intended to press on to the village of Verkhne Kumsky with his entire battlegroup, supported by the armoured artillery battalion, but there would now be a considerable delay while the division's engineers constructed a new bridge; instead, Hünersdorff ordered I Battalion to continue to Verkhne Kumsky alone, and after a brief attack by Luftwaffe dive-bombers, the German tanks secured the village in the early afternoon.[30]

The village of Verkhne Kumsky would become the centre of a critical battle that largely decided the outcome of *Winter Storm*. The precise chronology of what followed is confused. Raus describes the first phase of the battle as taking place over a single day, but other accounts, notably the war diary of 6th Panzer Division, state that this phase of fighting took place on 14 and 15 December. To confuse matters still further, the Soviet account describes the fighting as occurring entirely on 15 December. For the purposes of this account, the chronology of the war diary of 11th Panzer Regiment is used, as its timings are most likely to have been recorded contemporaneously.

The German tanks in Verkhne Kumsky were joined by a motorcycle company and two dismounted platoons of panzergrenadiers. There was still no sign of the Russians, and cautiously the small group dug in and waited. A bridging column with the division advised Hünersdorff that a new bridge would be available the following morning at the earliest; until then, the advance had effectively come to a halt. Further east, 23rd Panzer Division encountered stronger resistance and some of the troops of 6th Panzer Division waiting to cross the Aksay were dispatched in a sideways thrust to help; rather than get drawn into a protracted firefight, the Russian tanks that had been holding up 23rd Panzer Division pulled back. Throughout the bitterly cold night, the German combat engineers struggled to complete their bridge at Saliyevsky and were forced to break off work several times when Russian artillery and *Katyusha* rockets bombarded the area. At 8am local time on 14 December, the bridge was finally ready and the first troops began to cross; almost immediately, Russian tanks were reported approaching from the north. A company of tanks was dispatched to the low ridge that lay between Saliyevsky and Verkhne Kumsky and destroyed a T-34 and drove off two others. At the same time, *Gruppe Remlinger* – a battalion of panzergrenadiers, an artillery battalion, and some flak detachments – attempted to widen the bridgehead by attacking the neighbouring village of Woidansky. Immediately, the attack ran into heavy resistance and was brought to a standstill, followed by increasingly strong Russian attacks.

The Russians might not have contested the ground between the Aksay and Kotelnikovo during the initial German attack, but it was increasingly clear that the next stretch – from the Aksay to the Myshkova – would be a different matter. Elements of 6th Panzer Division's tank destroyer battalion, still waiting to cross the new bridge at Saliyevsky, found themselves engaged by Russian tanks probing forward from Woidansky. Two were rapidly destroyed, and interrogation of their crews suggested that a force of up to 40 tanks would attack later that day. Even though he wanted to get as much of the armoured battlegroup as possible to Verkhne Kumsky, Hünersdorff had to leave the tank destroyers where they were to ensure that his supply lines remained open.[31]

Hünersdorff joined the troops in Verkhne Kumsky in the late morning, just as Russian infantry and tanks attacked from the north and northeast. Aware that the forces arrayed against him probably outnumbered him, Hünersdorff decided that the only way to avoid being forced to dig in and defend was to try to retain the initiative. Remlinger was ordered to make renewed attempts to capture Woidansky and thus relieve the pressure on the bridge at Saliyevsky, but once again the panzergrenadiers found they could make little progress. Remlinger requested – with the support of Raus at division headquarters – that Hünersdorff should allocate tanks to support the attack. Hünersdorff declined; he increasingly had his hands full at Verkhne Kumsky.

Leutnant Hans Hallfelz had been dispatched from Verkhne Kumsky with a platoon of Pz.II tanks, used by the division in a reconnaissance role, and a motorcycle platoon on a wide-ranging reconnaissance sweep. He first scouted to the north, where he spotted a column of at least 30 Russian tanks, and then as he slowly fell back he encountered a second group to the east of the village, and then a third approaching from the north but edging around to the west. When the reconnaissance group attempted to make its way back to Verkhne Kumsky, it came under fire; Hallfelz was forced to abandon his light tanks and ordered his motorcyclists to disperse and to attempt their escape as individuals rather than en masse. Accompanied by a few of his men, he encountered the survivors of a Russian tank crew that had been destroyed in the fighting. Shortly after, his luck appeared to have run out:

> Three more Russian tanks approached us and fired on us and we had no option – there was no cover, and our black uniforms showed up too clearly on the snow – but to play dead. On my command we threw ourselves down and lay still. We could see that these tanks had stopped about 100m from us. These minutes seemed like an eternity to us. Finally a tank drove up to us very slowly and passed within three or four metres. The second followed, and finally the third. It came so close that we feared it would roll over us. We could have touched its tracks. As soon as it was past we jumped up and took up position behind the last tank so that we could follow it in cover to the next *balka* [a small ravine or gully]. Our nerves were shredded but there were no further alarms and in the *balka* we found a few more of my platoon.
>
> From there we watched as two Russian tanks took up positions next to our abandoned tanks. Behind us and to the south we could hear sounds of fighting, but couldn't see anything of our troops. About three hours later German tanks approached and in a short firefight shot up the two Russian tanks. I asked these tanks to stay with us until we could have our tanks towed away, but they were ordered elsewhere by radio. We then returned to our tanks and found them almost undamaged. A few wires had been pulled out of the radios. Apparently, the Russians had wanted to tow away these tanks undamaged. I was soon in contact with the regiment again. If the Russians had possessed the ability and intent, it would have been simple for them to listen to all our radio traffic.
>
> Finally, after dark, German tanks from II Battalion arrived and took us on board. The remaining mobile tanks of my platoon were either towed or moved under their own power back to Verkhne Kumsky.[32]

While Hallfelz was trying to get back to the village, the rest of the regiment had an eventful day. Taking command of II Battalion, Hünersdorff turned to deal with the threat from the east. The tanks left Verkhne Kumsky heading south, and by remaining west of the road to Saliyevsky they used the intervening high ground to prevent the Russians spotting them. They then turned east and moved forward in battle formation, as Scheibert described:

After climbing a low reverse slope we were greeted by an astonishing sight: barely 1,000m from us there sat an untroubled group of about 40 tanks, painted white like us, with black numbers on their turrets, the crews sitting outside their tanks and vehicles. Surely this wasn't the enemy that the reconnaissance platoon had reported. My first thought was: they are tanks of 23rd Panzer Division. But what were they doing here in our sector? Meanwhile, we had closed to 600m, all our nerves tense, when over yonder the crews leaped into their tanks and two started to drive towards us. I had just enough time to shout 'Alert!' over the radio when the command came over the battalion net: 'Russians, free to fire!' But before a single shot was fired on our side, the two approaching enemy tanks opened fire. They fired while moving and despite the range falling to barely 300m, scored no hits. A pointless attack as already a broadside from the two companies blocking them struck the Russians with the effect that very few had time to move. The two leaders – who were in the gunsights of so many – were literally blown apart. The rest was child's play. At a range of 600m and less, every shot from our long 50mm guns was effective. With our higher rate of fire and better training we were simply better. Almost none escaped. Those fleeing were caught by the long-barrelled 75mm guns of the heavy company [equipped with Pz.IVs] at a range of over a kilometre. The last were herded into a gully and were shot up as if on a firing range. Thirty-two black clouds of smoke rose into the clear winter air.

After regrouping the battalion thrust to the north to link up with where the reconnaissance platoon [commanded by Hallfelz] was thought to be and to track down the reported enemy tanks.

The [reconnaissance] platoon crews were soon located but could not immediately be rescued as enemy tanks towards Sogotskot opened fire on us. A united attack drove them off after a short fight. Darkness prevented further pursuit.

Guided by flares fired by I Battalion, we returned to Verkhne Kumsky in total darkness.[33]

It had been a largely successful day for Hünersdorff and his regiment, with a total of 43 Russian tanks knocked out at various locations, and even if it had proved impossible to advance further towards Stalingrad, there was high expectancy that a second day of such success would break the strength of the opposing Russian forces. A further battlegroup of panzergrenadiers – *Gruppe Unrein*, made up of truck-mounted infantry – arrived at Saliyevsky, effectively securing the bridgehead against further Russian interference, and there was further welcome news from the neighbouring 23rd Panzer Division, moving up to the line of the Aksay to the southeast. Finally, the third formation earmarked for *Winter Storm* – 17th Panzer Division – was at last expected on 6th Panzer Division's northwest flank. For the Russians, it was a chastening experience. Their main armoured force sent to outflank Verkhne Kumsky had been completely destroyed, and other probing attacks from the north beaten off. Whilst Scheibert and others involved in the fighting felt that their superior rate of fire and more accurate gunsights made a critical difference, the greatest gulf between the two sides appears to have been in command and control. Hünersdorff coordinated his forces with great skill, while the Russian tank groups proved unable to deploy their overall numerical superiority to good effect.

From the German point of view, the areas of concern were twofold. Firstly, the Russians would undoubtedly make a determined effort to recover the situation the following day; and secondly, supply problems remained. Despite the best efforts of the bridging team and the combat engineers of 6th Panzer Division, supply trucks had to be towed across the icy bridge at Saliyevsky, and although ammunition, fuel and food reached Hünersdorff at Verkhne Kumsky, it was not in sufficient quantities to replenish 11th Panzer Regiment's tanks fully. For much of the day Saliyevsky was under artillery fire, and although Remlinger's group was able to prevent the Russians from making any progress in their attacks along both banks of the Aksay towards the vital bridge, the Russians were also able to prevent Remlinger from advancing towards Woidansky. At first light on 15 December, Remlinger anxiously reported that his men could hear Russian tank engines as another attack was prepared, and asked if there was any possibility of the armoured battlegroup striking the Russians at Woidansky from the direction of Verkhne Kumsky. Saliyevsky was once more under heavy bombardment, as was the road between the bridge and Verkhne Kumsky, and Hünersdorff became aware of Russian infantry and cavalry to the northeast, with a large number of tanks approaching from the northwest. Leaving Major Erich Löwe, commander of the panzer regiment's I Battalion, in command in Verkhne Kumsky with two tank companies, a panzergrenadier company, an artillery battalion and some flak units, Hünersdorff set off to engage this new Russian force in the same manner as the previous day with the intention of destroying it rapidly. At the same time, the few supply vehicles that had reached Verkhne

Kumsky would take advantage of the fighting to make their withdrawal to the Saliyevsky bridgehead.

The battle did not go as planned. Much of the success of 14 December was due to the Russians being taken by surprise, but on this occasion they were close enough to Verkhne Kumsky to see Hünersdorff's column emerging, and a duel began at long range. Once more, Scheibert was in the thick of the combat:

We soon reached open ground. Looking back, I saw the supply trucks and other wheeled vehicles disappearing south at speed, widely spread out. I felt sorry for their drivers in the unprotected cabs as they ran the gauntlet. Protected by us, almost all of them could reach Saliyevsky. Only a few fell victim to enemy tanks and anti-tank guns.

After heading north and fully deploying our four companies we soon saw a strong enemy force opposing us … The range was too great for our 50mm gunned tanks to be effective. In order to have any effect against a T-34, we had to be within 1,000m. Consequently, in this first phase of the fight only the heavy (4) company with its long 75mm guns was effective. Recognising this situation, the battlegroup commander ordered the heavy 8 Company, which was still in the village, to join us. We constantly tried to outflank the enemy to the left but here too the enemy had taken up positions. Thus an oblique front developed, slowly extending to the northwest over a width of 8km [five miles] after the arrival of 8 Company. Finally, a ravine (north of Hill 95.6) prevented further extension to the left.

At first, we were able to drive back the enemy with losses on both sides, but soon we were halted by a strong *Pakfront* [a coordinated line of anti-tank guns], which literally overwhelmed us. The Russians operated a system that they had perfected. Each tank towed an anti-tank gun, whose crew sat on the tank. Once the fighting began, they jumped off and deployed on foot. If the opposing tanks proved too strong, they re-hitched the anti-tank guns and withdrew under cover, either to regroup or to attack us from another direction. Once more they played this game with us and the anti-tank guns were particularly unpleasant as they were small targets, almost impossible to spot when camouflaged, and fired more accurately than their tanks.

Thus it continued all morning. If we used smoke to close to a more effective range, we found ourselves facing a very unpleasant *Pakfront* when the smoke cleared. Even if – largely through the efforts of the heavy companies – several Russian tanks were ablaze, our attacks only cost us casualties with little gain. The entire horizon to the north and east was full of Russian tanks and *Pakfronts*, their yellow muzzle-flashes directed at us, and everywhere – both over there and in our own line – columns of black smoke rose into the air from burning tanks. It was like a naval battle, attacks followed by withdrawals. Many anti-tank guns were silenced with high explosive shells, but the Russians seemed to have inexhaustible reserves ... Desperate orders to attack came over the radio, Oberst von Hünersdorff and Major Bäke [commander of II Battalion] repeatedly led attacks ... but our ammunition stocks were running low and finally we only had high explosive shells left.

There was wild confusion, with – including those in Verkhne Kumsky – 100 German tanks facing 300 Russians, and countless anti-tank guns. Snow flew everywhere, and the enemy anti-tank rounds left black scars on the white steppe. As a result of frequent manoeuvring and the monotony of the landscape we soon lost all sense of direction. I could only see my immediate neighbours. I could only tell where my commander was when flares were fired. Due to the confusion, there were frequent friendly fire incidents, as it was hard to recognise vehicles at long range.[34]

The Red Army developed specialised anti-tank units as early as 1929, buying its first weapons from German manufacturers before switching to indigenous production. The great majority of such guns in the late 1930s were 45mm weapons, effective against German tanks but with limited range. In order to improve survivability, the guns had been designed to allow for rapid rates of fire – they had semi-automatic loading mechanisms – and could be traversed rapidly to engage advancing enemy tanks before they were overwhelmed. In addition, divisional and regimental artillery – field guns of 76mm or larger, and anti-aircraft guns – were issued with armour-piercing ammunition, particularly after the fighting of 1939 and 1940 demonstrated the lethal power of the German 88mm anti-aircraft gun when it was used against armour. However, anti-tank guns were issued uniformly to infantry formations, but none were assigned to tank units, with the result that a division that was not facing armour would have weapons of limited use, while another division that was threatened by enemy armour might have insufficient firepower. After observing German forces in action in Poland and France, the Red Army began a programme of upgrading its anti-tank guns to 76mm calibre. Attempts to reorganise anti-tank guns into brigades were largely felt to be unsuccessful, and further redesigns both of equipment and organisation were under way in 1941 when *Barbarossa* commenced. The realities of mechanised warfare further exposed weaknesses in anti-tank weaponry, and it was rapidly concluded that guns of less than 76mm were of limited use; the complement of guns per infantry division was also too low, particularly when opposing panzer divisions attacked on a narrow front. Losses in the opening battles drastically reduced the number of weapons available – the pre-war establishment was 54 per division, but by late 1941 this had to be reduced to just 18. In order to remedy the deficiencies that had been experienced, guns were increasingly concentrated into anti-tank battalions, brigades and regiments that could be deployed en masse by corps commanders to counter German armoured threats. Equipped with a mixture of guns of different calibres (and large numbers of anti-tank rifles, which were effective only at very close range but could be used to protect the larger guns from being overrun or to stop German tank commanders from operating with open hatches), these units were increasingly effective against German armour; they would ultimately force a change in tactics for panzer divisions to prevent unacceptably high losses.[35]

Any attack against numerically superior Russian forces depended on speed for success, and the failure of 6th Panzer Division to achieve a quick victory effectively decided the issue. With ammunition almost exhausted and repeated reports that Löwe was under heavy pressure in Verkhne Kumsky, Hünersdorff had to order his tanks to break off the action. The depleted companies gathered in an area of dead ground to the west of Verkhne Kumsky and watched as columns of Russian tanks and infantry moved across their front towards the village, from where there came sounds of increasingly heavy fighting. By the middle of the day, Löwe was asking for immediate assistance to prevent the village being overrun, and after a brief discussion with Raus over the radio, a frustrated and angry Hünersdorff sent his tanks into Verkhne Kumsky:

> Major Bäke led us in, two companies up front, two following. Snow flew up from our tracks; we were in a wild mood, and we would have screamed 'Urrah!' [a frequent battle-cry of attacking Russian troops] if it had made any sense. Those who could, fired on every visible target with our machine-guns. The leading tanks, which had kept their shells until this moment, hit the Russian tanks that opposed us. Russian infantry fled on all sides; they must have thought we were crazy. But we succeeded; in a short time we were in the village, as far as I can remember without suffering any losses. To my horror several T-34s suddenly appeared from a hollow about 200m to my right. I watched as their guns turned towards us; as we had no more ammunition, I held on grimly to the sides of the turret, expecting a hit at any moment. But the most advanced one took a 75mm hit in front of the turret that made a bright flash and it immediately rolled back and disappeared into the hollow. When the next one was set ablaze, the others withdrew.[36]

Almost none of the officers from Löwe's garrison were unhurt – many were dead, others (including Löwe) wounded. Rapidly, the Germans loaded up their wounded and withdrew to Saliyevsky. Given their losses and their critical ammunition shortages, it was out of the question for the Germans to hold on to their positions in Verkhne Kumsky.

Vitaly Andreyevich Ulyanov was an anti-tank gunner in one of the many *Pakfronts* trying to stop the German attempt to reach Stalingrad, and found himself caught up in the often-frantic battles when he was ordered to pull back to a new firing position in one of the scattered villages:

We grabbed the gun and struggled with it, but we couldn't move it – our feet slipped on the ice. I then jumped out past the gunshield, on the side closer to the Germans, and pushed the gun, sliding it from the ice onto the trampled snow of the road. A machine-gun burst, rattling across the shield, broke the frame into which the sight was laid (I swore, because the gunsight was so essential), but I wasn't hit. Without waiting until the Germans opened fire again, I dived for the shield and together, pushing and pulling, we were able to move the gun ... Behind us we heard the sound of a tank – the roar of the engine and the clatter of caterpillar tracks ... We dragged the gun to a shed and turned it towards the tank, which was not slow to appear. A little before us stood a house where the wounded were collected. When we passed them, we could hear them joking and laughing – they had already won, they knew that they would soon be sent to the rear. The tank turned across the road opposite this house and began to fire with a machine-gun. I pointed the gun and fired. The projectile flew 15cm [6 inches] above the turret. Later, thinking about my blunder, I came to the conclusion that when I fired earlier at a Fritz with a machine-gun, I set up the sight for a fragmentation round, but here I shot an armour-piercing shell, whose initial speed is twice as great and the flight path is different. I hadn't thought to change the sight! After the shot, as the trails were not dug in, the gun jumped back. Second shot! Also missed! The tank turned around. It came towards us. Its machine-guns fired, bullets hit our gunshield. I fired the gun, but not accurately – we were lower than it, and the projectile flew high ...

It was only with the fifth projectile from a distance of ten metres that I hit it, and it caught fire. I jumped up, waved my hands and shouted: 'The tank is burning!' At that moment, covered by the tank, Germans in white camouflage ran up and rushed to the opposite side of us across the road, behind the house, and from there they began to fire on us with their rifles. I was wounded in the right foot, and the loader, Tolya Shumilov, in the knee. The commander of the gun,

Dydochkin, who I had not known before that day, commanded: 'Go back to the yard.' We went into the yard and ran into the barn. There was no door, and I sat at the lintel opposite the doorway. After me Shumilov ran into the barn, and Golitsyn, who was running after him, was killed by a machine-gun at the doorstep.

From the doorway, I could see a poultry house, which was about thirty metres round, woven from willow twigs. A German leaned out of it and began to shout something. I took the carbine from Tolya Shumilov as I had left mine behind. And although I knew that it was impossible to shoot without giving myself away, he shouted so brazenly that I could not stand it and I took aim and fired. The German dropped to the ground. Not understanding what had happened, a second German ran to him, presenting his back for my second shot. They started shooting from the chicken coop. I hid behind the lintel. In the exchange of fire, I hit two more. I began to reload the carbine, but the cartridge twisted and instead of pulling it out, I jammed it into the barrel, thus rendering the carbine useless. When I realized that I couldn't fire the carbine, I looked up and saw two Germans running towards me. Suddenly Dydochkin, the commander of our gun, jumped out on the right, stopped in front of the barn, took out a hand grenade, shook it like a thermometer, and threw it under the feet of the Germans. One of them bent down, probably intending to throw it back, but the grenade exploded in his hands and they both collapsed. And Dydochkin, having run past the door, disappeared. We decided to hide in the shed behind an iron barrel. Tolya somehow squeezed into the space, but I couldn't. In the courtyard the Germans were shouting something. Suddenly a German with a gun appeared in the doorway. He shouted 'Is there anyone here?' I feared that Shumilov would moan – he moaned with pain before – the German would hear, and that would be that, my luck would run out in this blasted barn, but then the German disappeared. After a while, the Germans dragged their wounded into the courtyard, from where they were soon taken away. The battle began to subside. I said 'Tolya, you must come with me.' [He replied] 'You must go, Vitya.' We lay there for a while. I said 'Let's go.' We lay still again. When I said for the third time, 'Well, let's go,' he asked me: 'Vitya, where are you wounded?' – 'In the foot.' – 'In one?' – 'In one.' – 'And I'm wounded in both legs. So you go first.'

I climbed out of the barn and as I was in my greatcoat, I decided to roll in the snow for camouflage. It was useless. The greatcoat was sound – no snow stuck to it. Realising the senselessness of this, I got up and walked to the chicken coop, I tried not to look at the dead – it was daunting. I turned left past the side of the brick building, near which there was a haystack. Next to this stack, in the light of the burning buildings of the village, I saw an old man sitting. One woman was sitting in front of him on her knees, and the second was walking back and forth nearby and moaning. I asked what had happened. It turned out that this family was in a cellar. A German raised the hatch and asked: 'Is anyone there?' They answered him from below, 'Yes. There are civilians here.' He threw a grenade into the cellar. An old woman was killed. The old man was badly wounded, and another woman wounded in her chest. Only one remained unscathed, or maybe just did not feel anything yet, being in shock. I asked them, 'The Germans are over there?' – 'Yes.' – 'And on the left?' – 'Yes.' – 'And to the rear?' – 'There too. They are everywhere.'

I asked them to change me into civilian clothes and hide me until our men came. They replied, 'What do we care about you?' I thought, we must leave, or we will be captured … I made my way down the hillside, knelt down, then took a few steps. Suddenly a shot rang out nearby. I felt the bullet fly past my head. I immediately fell on my right side and lay silently. The snow was deep and damp. I could hear the sound of footsteps: crunch, scrape. Silence. I had a Finnish knife on my belt, but lying on my right arm I could only reach it with my left hand. And what could I do with it? I decided to pretend to be dead and then strike the enemy in the face with the knife when he bent down, knowing that I would not be able to penetrate an overcoat or any other outer clothing in my position. I held my breath, so that there wouldn't be steam, but all the time it seemed to me that my heart was beating so loud that it could be heard for several metres. Again the snow creaked under his feet and – silence. I thought: 'You must come and bend over. Then I will have just one chance.' Snow squeaked again. From the sound, I realised that a man was standing and moving from right to left, trying to examine me. Suddenly the steps began to move away … And I remained lying. I was already warm, comfortable, and I realized that I was freezing. Then I climbed to my knees. I thought: 'Let him shoot!' But there was no shot, and I was afraid to look back. On all fours I climbed up the opposite slope of the hollow, along the edge of which was the road. I heard something creaking, I looked and saw a [horse] team, pulling a 45mm gun. Riders led the horses by the bridles. Two were next to the gun, and one behind. Very disciplined and strict. All ours, but the soldiers were in helmets, which we gunners did not wear: 'We're not infantry!' We had such stupid courage. And the commander made no attempt to force us. They passed me by. When I realised that they would soon be gone, I shouted: 'Comrades!'[37]

The soldiers took Ulyanov to a field hospital, where he received treatment for his wounds. There, he encountered Tolya Shumilov, who had tried to crawl after him and had encountered the same group of Russian civilians – this time, they took pity on the wounded soldier and sheltered him for two days.

Raus describes the battle in his memoirs as a considerable victory that greatly degraded the strength of the opposing Russian IV Mechanised Corps. By contrast, the Soviet staff study describes how the Russian force took Verkhne Kumsky after an 'impetuous advance'.[38] If the previous day could be regarded as a considerable tactical success for 6th Panzer Division, the abandonment of Verkhne Kumsky was unequivocally a major setback, regardless of the casualties inflicted on the Russians. In the context of the operational circumstances, anything less than a substantial German success represented an outcome that favoured the Russians – a prolonged stalemate, for example, would serve their needs perfectly well. Hünersdorff's panzer regiment lost 30 tanks, of which 20 were recovered and later repaired. They claimed the destruction of over 100 Russian tanks, but crucially – unlike the battles of 11th Panzer Division along the Chir line – they left the battlefield in the hands of the Russians, and IV Mechanised Corps occupied Verkhne Kumsky the following day and fortified the ridge immediately to the south. If it was possible for the Germans to repair two-thirds of their knocked-out tanks, it is likely that the Russians would have been able to recover a similar number. With the Russians now able to take up a strong defensive line, there was every likelihood of more time being lost, and thus there would be more time for Malinovsky's Second Guards Army to deploy. Had 17th Panzer Division been available to Hoth and Kirchner from the start of *Winter Storm*, there might have been sufficient forces to secure the Saliyevsky bridgehead and Verkhne Kumsky without the need for 6th Panzer Division to withdraw; the diversion of the division to stand guard behind the Italian Eighth Army critically reduced the strength of LVII Panzer Corps at the key moment.

Like 11th Panzer Division's actions along the Chir, the battle at Verkhne Kumsky shows German armoured units at their best, operating on internal lines to defeat converging attacks by a superior enemy. However, the battle also highlighted the numerical superiority of the Russians and their skilful use of anti-tank guns in coordination with tanks. As the Germans withdrew to the bridgehead at Saliyevsky, they knew that any further attack would require careful artillery preparation and probably air support – any chance of a swift victory in an encounter battle was gone. For the Russians, 15 December saw a degree of redemption for their failure the previous day, but their losses had been heavy.

CHAPTER 5

DECEMBER: *LITTLE SATURN*

The events on the Aksay and the failure of Romanenko's Fifth Tank Army to break through on the Chir front forced *Stavka* into a reappraisal of the situation. Having surrounded Stalingrad and having failed to overwhelm the Germans quickly, the priority was to ensure that the prize was not snatched away by the Germans, and in view of this Stalin and Vasilevsky discussed the impending start of *Saturn*, the attack on the Italian Eighth Army. On 13 December, Stalin sent a signal to Nikolai Nikolayevich Voronov, the *Stavka* artillery specialist working with the various fronts, Vatutin at Southwest Front, and Lieutenant-General Filipp Ivanovich Golikov at Voronezh Front. The original direction of exploitation for *Saturn* had been directly south, on the assumption that Fifth Tank Army and Third Guards Army would be able to advance across the Chir and through *Armee Abteilung Hollidt*, thus protecting the main force's eastern flank. There was now little prospect of this happening, and Second Guards Army was no longer available as a second echelon for *Saturn*. In view of this, Stalin wrote that the axis of the exploitation was to be shifted to the southeast, into the rear of the German forces on the Chir and those trying to reach Stalingrad. The new operation, codenamed *Little Saturn*, was to start on 16 December.[1] Vatutin was unenthusiastic about the change, maintaining that with modest reinforcements, he could still achieve the objectives of *Saturn*, but he was in a minority. After a day of wrangling, he was ordered to proceed as planned. Rostov would have to wait, though there remained the possibility that, if *Little Saturn* unfolded successfully, a rapid advance to seize the vital Don crossings at Rostov might still be possible before the end of the year.

The Russians had spent both 14 and 15 December attempting to destroy the German bridgehead at Saliyevsky. Some of their tanks reached the village and were destroyed at close quarters, and as the entry points to the village became choked with knocked-out tanks, it was progressively easier for the combat engineers, armed with magnetic shaped charge mines, to concentrate their efforts on the few remaining routes that the Russian tanks could take and to use the wrecked vehicles for cover. After sustaining further losses without any tangible gain – and little prospect of any gain – the Russians pulled back.[2]

Despite the urgent need to press on towards Stalingrad, there was nothing to be gained by an immediate attack towards Verkhne Kumsky on 16 December; the battered 11th Panzer Regiment needed to rearm, to repair its damaged tanks, and to assemble for a more concerted effort. Accordingly, the day was spent largely in improving positions around Saliyevsky; during the morning, the panzer regiment made a small advance along the Verkhne Kumsky road after artillery preparation, overrunning a further *Pakfront* and beating off an attack by a group of T-34s. The troops of 23rd Panzer Division had moved up alongside 6th Panzer Division, and there was every prospect of launching a much more powerful assault the following day. Further to the north, Malinovsky's Second Guards Army was doing its best to move into a blocking position:

> The redeployment ... had to be done by forced marching. Despite the severe frost, they managed to cover 40–50km [24–30 miles] every 24 hours ... The army commander endeavoured to ensure that when his troops reached the River Myshkova they would form a strong grouping that primarily would stop the enemy in his tracks and prevent him from getting any closer to the surrounded Paulus army; that would at once enable the army troops to go over to a decisive offensive.[3]

Whilst Stalin and Vasilevsky were able to work in close harmony – aside from the passing disagreement about the redeployment of Second Guards Army – Manstein faced a far harder task dealing with Hitler. The forces assigned to LVII Panzer Corps were far weaker than Manstein had wanted and he had no doubt that they could only reach the perimeter of the besieged Sixth Army if Paulus launched an attack to meet them. To do so, Sixth Army would have to redeploy its diminishing forces and therefore concede ground in the pocket. For Manstein, this raised two interlocking points:

> The first was that even if Sixth Army could be relieved, it must on no account be left in the Stalingrad area any longer. Hitler himself still wanted to hang on to the city – just as he had insisted on doing with the Demyansk pocket the previous winter – and to keep the army supplied there by means of a land corridor.

Army Group Don, on the other hand, was as convinced as ever that this was entirely the wrong solution and that it was essential to become operationally mobile again if disaster were to be avoided. This tug-of-war continued until the very last chance of saving Sixth Army had been thrown away.

The second issue was the reinforcement of the relief forces. Ever since the discovery that of the seven divisions originally promised us for *Armee Abteilung Hollidt's* relief bid [it was to attack across the lower Chir towards Kalach when LVII Panzer Corps drew level] we could at best expect to get XLVIII Panzer Corps with a strength of two divisions, it had been vital to strengthen Fourth Panzer Army. Anyone could see that the latter was not going to reach Stalingrad with only 6th and 23rd Panzer Divisions.[4]

Manstein had repeatedly requested that III Panzer Corps, with two armoured formations – 3rd Panzer Division and the SS *Viking** motorised division – should be transferred from Army Group A in the Caucasus to Fourth Panzer Army; but this would have required Army Group A to shorten its front line accordingly and to abandon a large salient, which went counter to Hitler's desire not to concede any ground. Another powerful unit – 16th Motorised Division – was standing guard at Elista, between the southern flank of Army Group Don and the northeast flank of Army Group A, and attempts to have it replaced by an infantry unit so that it could be assigned to Fourth Panzer Army also proved fruitless.

Hitler's refusal to countenance any concession of territory also had a direct effect on the need for Sixth Army to help with the relief attempt. Given the weakness of Fourth Panzer Army, Hoth and Manstein both believed that LVII Panzer Corps could only reach Stalingrad if Paulus launched an attack towards the approaching German force. At the very least, this would draw off Russian forces, allowing Kirchner to advance faster. However, such attacks by Sixth Army required a radical redeployment of units in the pocket, and this would only be possible if parts of the pocket were abandoned. For Manstein and his staff, this was both inevitable and necessary, and would sequentially lead to Sixth Army pulling out via the corridor that Hoth had created. In vain, Manstein repeatedly requested Hitler to approve of such an operation. Unfortunately, the Führer was able to counter with a simple argument: Paulus insisted that the fuel supplies within the pocket had fallen so low that the remaining tanks had an operating range of only 30 miles. It was therefore impossible even to consider an attack from within the pocket until

---

* Throughout this work, this division's name is spelled in the English manner; the correct German version is Wiking.

the relief column was within this distance. The argument was a spurious one: by using fewer tanks, Paulus would have been able to cover a greater distance, and in any event a powerful attack by the remaining tanks in the pocket would have made the task of LVII Panzer Corps far easier, even if the forces within the pocket were unable to advance the full distance to the relieving column. Besides, even though by this stage there had been an audit of fuel reserves, it is conceivable – indeed, highly likely, given the tendency of military units always to hoard supplies – that larger quantities remained. However, it was a convenient excuse for Hitler to use to avoid making a decision that he did not wish to make. For the moment, Manstein persisted in planning for a breakout and sequential withdrawal and simultaneously arguing with Hitler for permission to carry out such an operation; whilst he was probably increasingly aware of Hitler's intransigence on this issue, it is equally likely that he did not realise – at this stage, at any rate – the degree to which Paulus felt bound by the orders of the Führer. However, his failure to issue direct orders to Paulus to make preparations for a breakout, including redeployment within the siege perimeter, ensured that Paulus' willingness (or otherwise) to go against the wishes of Hitler was never put to the test.

In his conversations with Zeitzler at *OKH*, Hitler made clear his determination not to abandon the ruined city on the Volga:

> I have reached one conclusion ... [that] under no circumstances can we give that up. We would never win it back again. We know what that means ... If we abandon it, we sacrifice the entire meaning of this campaign.[5]

This statement shows the degree to which Hitler's priorities had changed, and the degree to which his decisions were becoming divorced from reality. At the beginning of the 1942 campaign, Stalingrad wasn't even mentioned by name – the intention was merely to reach and secure the lower Volga before pursuing the real objective, the oilfields of the Caucasus. Now, the capture and retention of Stalin's city was more important than anything else. What possible war-winning objective could be achieved by clinging to the ruins of a city that had long ceased functioning either as a communications hub or as a centre of armaments production was apparent only to Hitler, and those who blindly supported his judgement in the face of all evidence.

Despite being reduced in scale, *Little Saturn* remained a formidable undertaking. Aware of the importance of disrupting the German attempts to reach Stalingrad, Vasilevsky altered the timetable for the operation, requiring the attacking armies to make faster progress than initially planned; if the timetable were followed, XVII Tank Corps on the western side of the assault would have to cover 90 miles (150km) in just two days; XXV Tank Corps, which would lead the way to Morozovsk, would have to advance 150 miles (250km) in four days.[6] Even if Italian and German resistance was only modest, this would tax the logistic services of the Red Army to the limit. There were few good roads in the area, and although the terrain was generally flat and open, it was crisscrossed by deep gullies, which could be used as defensive positions and would force motorised units into considerable detours. Even if such an advance could be achieved, ensuring that the attacking formations remained supplied with fuel, food and ammunition both during and after the operation would be a huge task.

Although the Italians had been in their positions for some considerable time and had constructed good strongpoints, the line was brittle. There was insufficient depth to the defences, and the lack of mobile reserves meant that if the Russians could break through, there would be little to stop them exploiting their attacks. Starting from a considerable numerical advantage, particularly in tanks, the Russians further increased the odds of success by exploiting fully the prerogative of the attacker and concentrating their forces at key assault positions. Initial probing attacks to improve starting positions began as early as 11 December, and were partly the reason why a panzer division and Luftwaffe formations were diverted to the area, only to be moved away again on the eve of the true Russian attack. As the reconnaissance probes continued, the Germans began to move what few reserves they had into the area – 27th Panzer Division had replaced 17th Panzer Division, and 385th and 387th Infantry Divisions, together with an assortment of minor SS formations, were deployed to shore up the Italian lines. However, 27th Panzer Division was not remotely at full strength. It had been created in October and had yet to receive a full complement of tanks, artillery and infantry and barely amounted to a weak battlegroup; in particular, a critical shortage of trucks deprived the vital support units of the division of mobility, greatly hampering its ability to function as a mobile formation.

Many countries that found themselves embroiled in the Second World War were poorly prepared, and one of the most poorly prepared was Italy. On the eve of war, it was a predominantly agricultural economy with no preparations in its limited industrial base for war. It had no natural source of oil, and whilst much money had been spent in the 1930s on building up a substantial navy, there had been little or no regard to securing fuel for the warships in the event of a major conflict. The army was poorly mechanised, with only a few outdated tanks and completely inadequate motor transport; organisation and equipment in the army was largely unchanged from the First World War, with few automatic weapons and even fewer anti-tank guns. Within the army itself, there was a clear hierarchy of units in terms of their effectiveness. The *Alpini* formations, raised from the tough rural population of northern Italy, prided themselves on a strong *esprit de corps*, reinforced by regiments being strongly associated with localities; the infantry that formed the bulk of the army, by contrast, had a relatively poor standing, both in the eyes of the army as a whole and the infantry themselves. Given the lack of modern weaponry and sufficient industrial resources to support even the peacetime army in the field, the precipitate manner in which Mussolini committed his nation to the war represents an attitude of huge folly.

The Italian Eighth Army developed from the expeditionary force – the *Corpo di Spedizione Italiano in Russia* or 'Italian Expeditionary Corps in Russia' – that Mussolini dispatched to the Eastern Front at the beginning of *Barbarossa*. Fearing that information might leak to the Soviet Union, Hitler had not informed his Italian ally of the impending invasion of Russia and Mussolini's reaction was driven by a desire to ensure that, by contributing troops, Italy would receive a share of the spoils of victory. The Germans were not enthusiastic about Italian involvement on the Eastern Front; whilst it is possible that they did not wish for Italy to partake in any share-out after a victorious conclusion to the war, they also suggested that the Italian Army could benefit the Axis Powers rather more effectively by adding to its forces in North Africa.[7]

After it was deployed in the southern sector of the Eastern Front, the *Corpo di Spedizione* was renamed XXXV Corps, and in the summer of 1942 was joined by the *Corpo Alpini* and II and XXIX Corps, creating Eighth Army under the command of General Italo Gariboldi. With a total strength of 100,000 men, it was weak in every respect that mattered on the Eastern Front; it had only 50 tanks, few anti-tank guns (and most of those too weak to be effective against T-34s), and most of its artillery dated from the First World War.[8] When they set off for the Eastern Front, the *Alpini* assumed that they would be deployed in a mountainous region such as the Caucasus and travelled fully equipped for such warfare, with hob-nailed mountain boots, ice axes, climbing aids, and substantial mule trains. Even before they reached the front line, the soldiers became acutely aware of the gulf between them and the German forces with whom they would be serving; when their troop train travelled through the Brenner Pass, soldiers of the *Tridentina* Division found themselves alongside a German train carrying tanks. Many of the Italians felt a sense of humiliation as they stared at the equipment of their allies, who gazed back in amazement at the mules who were braying inside their railcars: 'We had one mule for every four *Alpini*, whereas the ratio was one tank for every four German soldiers … we were the ancients, they were the soldiers of modern warfare.'[9]

Once they reached Russia, the *Alpini* found that their mules were of limited value. Unlike trucks, which required fuel only when units moved, the mules needed to be fed all the time, placing additional burdens upon the badly stretched Italian logistic services. Matters were made worse by widespread corruption, with large quantities of supplies being diverted in rear areas where a thriving black market rapidly developed.

Even as they crossed occupied Poland and the western parts of the Soviet Union, many of the Italian soldiers were horrified to see the manner in which German troops treated the local population. Their disquiet grew greater as they travelled east, and many witnessed massacres of Jews and others who were deemed enemies of the Reich. After watching one such mass killing, in which 150 Jews were executed, one Italian soldier wrote in his diary: 'Until now we thought this would be an easy war; instead today our eyes were opened.'[10]

A few weeks later, after seeing action in the front line, the same soldier was shocked by the brutality shown by both the Germans and Russians:

> Our Latin soul cannot accustom itself to what we must encounter every step of the way ... I never thought I would find myself before such brutality and gestures that are highly immoral ... I used to admire the German soldier but from today he presents himself in a different light: that of a strong but profoundly barbaric warrior.[11]

Whilst the Germans were ordered to treat the civilian population with harshness, the Italians behaved completely differently. Their officers often took disciplinary action against those who committed acts of looting or worse, and almost from the start there was an instinctive affinity between the Italian soldiers, largely recruited from rural populations, and the Russian peasants of the steppe. Having escaped from German captivity, Gabriel Temkin was still in the region, working on state farms while trying to avoid detection either by the Germans or the Ukrainian police who often acted on their behalf, and he noted that whilst the Hungarians showed the same contempt for the local population as the Germans, the Italian soldiers had a far better reputation amongst the civilians of the Ukraine – if their requests for food were turned down, the Italians simply accepted the refusal rather than resorting to violence.

The conduct of the Italians towards the civilian population rapidly extended to Russian soldiery too. The Germans ordered the Italians to hand over any Russian soldiers that they captured, but as the mistreatment of Russian prisoners of war became more widely known amongst the Italian troops, there was growing reluctance to comply with this order. One day, a lieutenant of the *Tridentina* Division inspected a company of *Alpini* deployed near the Don, and was stunned to see a Russian soldier, in full uniform, standing at attention amongst his men. They explained to their lieutenant that they had captured him a few nights previously and had decided to keep him, putting him to work cutting wood, cleaning their bunker and fetching water. The officer later wrote:

> These blessed *Alpini* captured a prisoner, and instead of handing him over as required, they've kept him and turned him into their orderly. Naturally, he eats and smokes like them and they treat him with kindness and care as if he were one of them. It's incredible, I remain stunned. I thought to myself, these men are supposed to be the ferocious fascists. In a few days, they might be capable of dressing him in a uniform of the *Alpini* and even sending him out to take his turn at guard duty, as if he had been born in Vestone or the vicinity.[12]

The officer felt obliged to hand over the prisoner to the Germans, but was proud of the conduct of his men, who he felt had shown great humanity in the midst of a terrible war. Occasionally, the Italians found themselves treated kindly by the Russians; in August 1942, a *Tridentina* patrol encountered a larger group of Russians led by a political commissar. The Italians laid down their weapons, but as soon as the commissar left to visit another unit, the Russians promptly returned the guns to the Italians, handed over their own weapons, and willingly surrendered.[13]

The units deployed to support the Italian soldiers in the front line were no better equipped. The *Regia Aeronautica* – the air force of Mussolini's Italy – had deployed the *Corpo Aereo Spedizione in Russia* ('Expeditionary Air Corps in Russia') with a mixture of Macchi fighters and Caproni bombers. The Macchi MC-200 was a nimble aircraft that was initially very successful against Soviet aircraft, but by late 1942 it was widely regarded as underpowered and poorly armed. Small numbers of the more modern MC-202 had been deployed, but it too was relatively underpowered and had an alarming tendency to fall into a spin in tight turns, and its radio and oxygen supply equipment were unreliable. A shortage of equipment for operating aircraft in the wintry conditions of the Soviet Union resulted in these aircraft operating only at modest rates, and the Luftwaffe regarded air support for Germany's allies as having a lower priority than support for German units. Modest numbers of Italian transport aircraft had also deployed to the Eastern Front, but they too were of limited use in winter conditions.

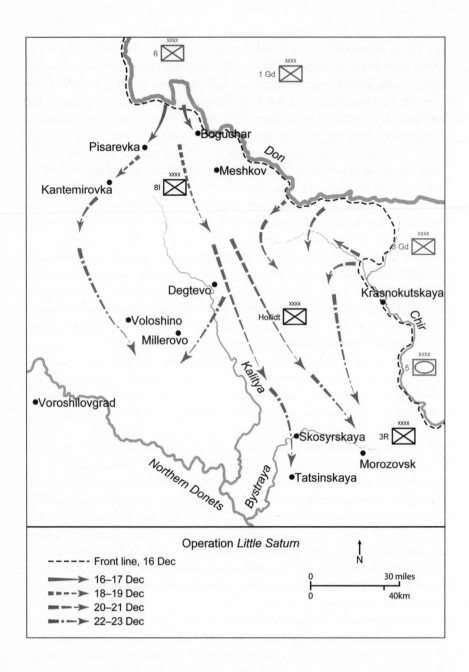

Operation *Little Saturn*

N

- - - - - Front line, 16 Dec
━━━► 16–17 Dec
■ ■ ■► 18–19 Dec
━ ━ ━► 20–21 Dec
━ ▪ ━► 22–23 Dec

0   30 miles
0   40km

As autumn turned to winter and the weather turned colder, the Italian sector of the front remained largely quiet, though there were signs of growing Russian strength and activity beyond the Don and in several small bridgeheads. By first light on 16 December, there was little doubt that an attack was coming. The artillery of the Red Army made a 90-minute preparatory bombardment, hampered by thick fog that made it impossible for observers to assess the accuracy of the fire or to redirect it; the gunners of Third Guards Army commenced their firing late in the hope that the fog would clear, and their bombardment lasted less than an hour. Similarly, the expected air support was grounded until later in the day. When the Russian infantry moved forward, in many cases crossing the thick ice of the frozen Don, they encountered varying degrees of resistance. First Guards Army in particular encountered determined defenders and repeated counterattacks, mainly – but by no means exclusively – from the German units facing the attacking divisions. Where the Russians made inroads, the thick snow hindered the forward movement of artillery to support the attacks, and during the afternoon the modest resources of the German 27th Panzer Division supported a particularly powerful counterthrust, which was only stopped when a tank destroyer battalion was hastily committed to the fighting.[14]

Vasilevsky had impressed upon Vatutin the importance of *Little Saturn* – it had to succeed in order to force the Germans to divert resources away from their relief effort further south, and it could provide a springboard for a far greater victory that might conceivably put the Soviet Union in a war-winning position. As reports accumulated of the stalled attacks, Vatutin ordered Major General Vasily Ivanovich Kuznetsov, commander of First Guards Army, to commit his tanks to the battle – originally, the plan had been to hold them back until the infantry had achieved a breakthrough, in view of the considerable distance that the armoured forces would have to cover in just a few days. Kuznetsov had XVII, XVIII, and XXV Tank Corps at his disposal and the first units went into action just before midday. It was an inauspicious start, with the first brigade advancing without adequate reconnaissance and blundering into a minefield; within an hour, 27 of its tanks had been disabled or lost.[15] Kuznetsov had no choice but to halt his armour and combat engineers were ordered to clear paths through the mines so that the tanks could advance the following day.

The weakness of the artillery preparation in Third Guards Army's sector ensured that Lieutenant General Dimitri Danilovich Lelyushenko's troops fared even worse. They crossed the frozen Chir but found that the strongpoints that the Germans had constructed on the west bank were still intact, and bitter fighting ensued; powerful counterattacks by a mixed force of Romanian troops and the remnants of 22nd Panzer Division, now formed into a single battlegroup, south of Krasnokutskaya, caused a panic amongst some of the Russian troops, who broke and ran. To add insult to injury, the Russian troops had to endure air attacks from Luftwaffe formations when their own air force remained grounded by the fog. The ambitious timetable for *Little Saturn* looked increasingly unachievable as darkness fell.

The Russian forces had a busy night preparing for the following day. The artillery formations were resupplied and tanks deployed alongside First Guards Army's infantry. There was another artillery bombardment early on 17 December, after which the Russian infantry advanced again accompanied by tanks. In the sector where Major General Fedor Mikhailovich Kharitonov's Sixth Army attacked, its 267th Rifle Division encountered tough resistance from mixed German and Italian troops in Dubovikovka, but succeeded in penetrating the defences further east. Immediately, Major General Pavel Pavlovich Poluboyarov's XVII Tank Corps was committed and pushed forward against diminishing resistance towards Pisarevka on the River Boguchar. A little to the east, XXV Tank Corps overcame the mainly German defences in its path and reached and crossed the river, while the German 298th Infantry Division and the Italian 3rd Infantry *Ravenna* Division were driven back into Boguchar itself. The front line had been broken, and the way was open for a major exploitation into the rear areas of Army Group Don.

By contrast, Lelyushenko's Third Guards Army continued to struggle. Its infantry found that the morning's 30-minute bombardment had been relatively ineffective and were unable to overcome the defensive lines, and even the commitment of I Guards Mechanised Corps failed to achieve a breakthrough. It mattered little; the units of Vatutin's other two armies continued to press forward through the night, securing crossings over the Boguchar. The breakthrough might have taken two days rather than the single day that had originally been planned, but it had been achieved.

On the same day as Vatutin's breakthrough, LVII Panzer Corps advanced again towards Verkhne Kumsky. Now that 23rd Panzer Division had reached the Aksay, Kirchner ordered the combined tanks of his two divisions, under the overall command of the energetic Hünersdorff, to roll up the Russian line that had developed along the hills immediately to the north of the river. At the same time, *Gruppe Unrein* was to try again to drive the Russians out of Woidansky and thus safeguard the western flank of *Winter Storm*. Finally, 17th Panzer Division would strike at Generalovsky, further to the west; its arrival released the third battlegroup of 6th Panzer Division, *Gruppe Zollenkopf*, a welcome boost to the German forces in the Saliyevsky bridgehead.

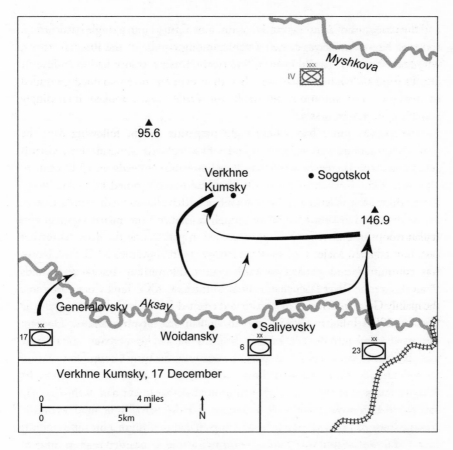

Verkhne Kumsky, 17 December

0   4 miles
0   5km   N

The panzer regiment of 23rd Panzer Division, reinforced by other elements of the division, formed a distinct battlegroup under the command of the panzer regiment commander, Oberstleutnant Georg-Hennig von Heydebreck. It deployed in the division's own bridgehead across the Aksay at Shestakov, about 4 miles (7km) east of Saliyevsky, but was delayed in forming up, and the initial attack by which it and *Gruppe Hünersdorff* would move to link up with each other was largely carried out by the latter. Two hours later than planned, the two groups met up; aware that precious time was slipping away, Hünersdorff turned north and attempted to force the Russian defences at Hill 146.9, part of the low ridge that ran between Saliyevsky and Verkhne Kumsky. Here, the Germans ran into a defensive position but swiftly overran it. Nevertheless, attempts to drive on to Sogotskot and thus outflank Verkhne Kumsky failed in the face of another line of defences:

This position before us was excellently laid out – fairly small but deep trenches, occupied by a very tough defender. None gave up even though our entire battalion stood in the midst of the positions. The Russians had to be shot out one by one. We avoided driving to and fro in order to prevent tracks coming adrift on the broken terrain. Each tank was assigned to a number of foxholes and waited until a Russian showed himself. It was a singular scene when I glanced around through the viewing periscopes. The tanks stood like elephants with their trunks extended and appeared to be sniffing at the earth. Finally the riflemen arrived in their half-tracks and under our protection cleared the entire position relatively quickly. It was about time, as tanks and *Pakfronts* further north, firing with increasing accuracy, were making their presence felt unpleasantly. During this time, our stationary tanks formed unmissable targets for even the poorest anti-tank gunner.[16]

The panzergrenadiers of 6th Panzer Division, supported by a battalion of assault guns, attempted to force their way directly north from Saliyevsky but made little headway, while the armoured battlegroup moved around to the west to try to attack from that direction – due to the lack of progress by the panzergrenadiers, the assault had to be made without infantry or artillery support. Despite an airstrike by Stukas, the defences proved too strong for the Germans to penetrate into Verkhne Kumsky. The short hours of daylight soon drew to an end and with Russian tanks trying to work their way around the western flank of the German force with a view to cutting its lines of retreat, Hünersdorff called off the attack. Briefly, Raus considered a night attack, but fuel and ammunition were running low and Hünersdorff was rightly reluctant to allow his depleted armour to venture into the village in darkness. Near midnight, the Germans pulled back to their starting line to regroup – a further day lost for the relief column, a day gained for Vasilevsky to move Second Guards Army into position.[17] As they returned to the bridgehead, the German officers glumly reflected on another demonstration of the ability of the Russians to dig in and construct effective defences in just a day, despite the frozen ground.[18] The troops of 11th Panzer Regiment were beginning to show the strain of constant action, as the regiment's diary recorded:

Due to continuous operations in the past days, which allowed no time for technical maintenance of the vehicles, the operational capacity of the regiment is greatly reduced. In addition, the crews – who have had no roof over their heads and almost no time for sleep, are exhausted. In these circumstances, a further operation in the next day offers little prospect of success and in the view of the [regiment] commander will result in losses that are utterly disproportionate to any gains, as the last days have demonstrated.[19]

18 December would, in Manstein's words, prove to be 'a day of crisis of the first order'.[20] After struggling to penetrate the Don defences for two days, Vatutin's front started to advance faster. The western shoulder of the assault continued to experience strong resistance; here, 14th SS Police Regiment and the Italian 3rd Alpine *Julia* Division – the only Italian division that had been held in reserve rather than being committed to the front line – had joined the German 385th Infantry Division and 27th Panzer Division, but after breaking through further east, Poluboyarov's armour threatened to envelop them from the south and the line was gradually levered back. Similarly, the Soviet armour pouring through the widening breach in the front line endangered the defences of the German 298th Infantry Division at Boguchar. There was growing confusion amongst the Germans and Italians; with the Italian 9th Semi-Motorised *Pasubio* Division – a hybrid formation with a mixture of motor transport and mounted troops, though in reality it possessed too few trucks even to reach the same level of motorisation as a German infantry division – beginning to give ground to the east, 298th Infantry Division began to withdraw without informing the neighbouring Italian *Ravenna* Division, which then gave way under the weight of Russian pressure. It was a pattern that would be repeated in the next few weeks: German units withdrew repeatedly without informing neighbouring units from other nations. The 5th *Cosseria* Infantry Division, caught in the direct path of the advance, effectively disintegrated, losing its artillery and what few heavy weapons it possessed, and by the end of the day the leading Russian tanks had penetrated to Degtevo, an overall advance of nearly 50 miles (80km). In Hollidt's sector the Romanian I Corps pulled back in disarray, unhinging the defences along the upper Chir; German formations also began to buckle under the strain, and there was the growing danger that *Armee Abteilung Hollidt* would be rolled up from the north. However, determined resistance a little to the south allowed Hollidt to pull back his northern flank in a more-or-less orderly manner, and complete collapse was avoided. Despite being composed predominantly of units cobbled together from broken formations or rear area troops, Hollidt's command was proving remarkably resilient.

Meanwhile, Kirchner's LVII Panzer Corps tried again to advance towards Paulus' beleaguered troops. The modest resources of 17th Panzer Division had finally arrived and were deployed on the western flank of the advance, with orders to advance and capture Collective Farm Marta before aiding the attack on Verkhne Kumsky; with 23rd Panzer Division covering to the east, 6th Panzer Division was to thrust forward to the River Myshkova, where Hoth hoped it would soon be able to link up with Sixth Army.[21] Most of the panzer regiment was held in reserve to allow the crews a break from combat and a chance to carry out maintenance while the panzergrenadiers of *Gruppe Zollenkopf* led the attack – if it proved to be successful, 11th Panzer Regiment would be committed to exploit any breakthrough. The division's operations officer recorded in his diary:

> It is becoming ever clearer that the battle for Verkhne Kumsky is of great – if not decisive – importance in the fight to break through to the Stalingrad encirclement … once more a bitter struggle develops. Already after just a short time *Panzeraufklärungsabteilung 6* [the reconnaissance battalion of the division] reports substantial casualties, particularly amongst its NCOs. Veteran East Fronters who played a part in earlier years in combat that certainly wasn't easy, later state that this attack was the toughest that they endured. Even when individual Russians are hemmed in from all sides, they don't give up but keep firing at the shortest range imaginable. The steppe grass gives the defenders good cover. Consequently, our own attack makes progress only slowly. The hoped-for aid from an armoured attack by 17th Panzer Division from the west does not occur because 17th Panzer Division's panzer regiment is pinned down by enemy tanks that attack Collective Farm Marta from the north. Furthermore, the enemy's heavy weaponry plays a part. Just in the sector of *Panzeraufklärungsabteilung 6* … the haul of booty is 30 light machine-guns, ten heavy machine-guns, 14 anti-tank rifles, six anti-tank guns, and 10 field guns and mortars. To the right, in I Battalion, 114th Panzergrenadier Regiment's sector, the advance is somewhat more straightforward and by dusk a platoon even manages to penetrate into Verkhne Kumsky via a ditch. But this surprise success can't be exploited and the platoon has to withdraw back to I/114's positions.[22]

To make matters worse, Luftwaffe flights spotted the arrival of fresh motorised forces further north: Second Guards Army was taking up positions along the Myshkova. In recognition of their achievements, Stalin redesignated the undefeated survivors of IV Mechanised Corps in and around Verkhne Kumsky as III Guards Mechanised Corps. In view of the way that they had frustrated every attempt by 6th Panzer Division to retake Verkhne Kumsky and renew its advance towards the Stalingrad perimeter, the accolade was completely justified.

Hoth and Kirchner discussed the situation that evening. They concluded that if it proved impossible to capture Verkhne Kumsky the following morning, it would be necessary to redeploy the entire panzer corps somewhat further east in an attempt to bypass the Russian defences – they were aware of the growing crisis to the north and knew that time was rapidly running out for them to break through to Sixth Army. Despite a day in which only two tank companies were committed to the battle, the fighting had reduced 6th Panzer Division's tank strength to just 57 tanks.[23] Manstein had to assess this against the widening emergency across his entire army group and spent much of the day in terse exchanges with *OKH*. The collapse of the Italian Eighth Army required urgent attention, and the only mobile forces available were the divisions still struggling to reach Verkhne Kumsky. It seemed inconceivable that the rapidly dwindling strength of LVII Panzer Corps would be able to march all the way to the Stalingrad encirclement, particularly now that reconnaissance flights had spotted the fresh forces of Second Guards Army deploying in its path – the best that could be hoped for was that Kirchner would be able to get to and perhaps across the Myshkova, as Manstein made clear in a signal to *OKH*:

> As LVII Panzer Corps by itself obviously cannot make contact with Sixth Army on the ground, let alone keep a corridor open, I now consider a break-out to the southwest to be the last possible means of preserving at least the bulk of the troops and the still mobile elements of Sixth Army.
>
> The breakthrough, the first aim of which must be to make contact with LVII Panzer Corps on the Myshkova, can only take place by forcing a gradual shift of Sixth Army towards the southwest and giving up ground sector by sector in the north of the fortress area as this movement progresses.[24]

It was a further iteration of the issue that had been raised repeatedly in the past few days. At *OKH*, Zeitzler added his weight to Manstein's views, but Hitler remained unmoved; furthermore, the trickle of reinforcements to Fourth Panzer Army was now stopped completely so that troops could be sent to try to restore the situation further north where Vatutin's armies were threatening to unhinge the entire German line. Worried that a personal trip into the encirclement might result in him being cut off from his headquarters as the crisis around his army group continued to develop, Manstein sent his intelligence officer, Major Eismann, to brief Paulus and Schmidt. Eismann advised those at Sixth Army headquarters that the developing crisis on the upper Chir and middle Don could not be ignored, and it would not be possible for Fourth Panzer Army to continue its relief efforts for long; a breakout was therefore essential for the survival of Sixth Army. With characteristic understatement, Manstein later wrote that the outcome of Eismann's mission was 'not encouraging'. Whilst Paulus and other senior officers appeared to accept the inevitability of such a breakout, Schmidt apparently insisted that Stalingrad could still be held, allegedly telling Eismann that 'All you people have to do is to supply it better.'[25] Ultimately, Paulus fell back on Hitler's insistence that Stalingrad was to be held. Unless the Führer rescinded that order, a breakout and abandonment of Stalingrad was out of the question.

It is debatable whether Manstein might have had more chance of persuading Paulus and Schmidt to face reality if he had travelled to the pocket himself, or perhaps more likely if he had summoned the senior officers of Sixth Army to fly out to meet him in Novocherkassk – at the very least, he could have used their respective positions in the chain of command to issue a direct order for a breakout, though it must be remembered that he studiously avoided doing so throughout the crisis. Schmidt might have been able to cling to the belief that simply increasing the size of the airlift would be sufficient in his discussions with a relatively junior visiting officer, but it would have been a different matter if he had been confronted with the facts in the headquarters of Army Group Don. In any event, no such meeting occurred, and Schmidt – and to a slightly lesser extent Paulus – were able to persist in their repeated position that they would remain bound by Hitler's orders and that the Führer's will would prevail in the issue of the airlift. Ultimately, this appears to have been the crux of the problem, and in the absence of Hitler's agreement, Manstein seems to have been unable to issue a clear order on his own behalf, either because he did not wish to defy Hitler or because he believed that Paulus and Schmidt would refuse to follow an order that was directly contrary to Hitler's instructions.

The original plan for *Winter Storm* had called for XLVIII Panzer Corps to advance across the Chir towards Kalach at this point of the operation, with 336th Infantry Division attacking across the Don to link up with LVII Panzer Corps while 11th Panzer Division drove forward to the Don bend and the Kalach area, but the bridgehead across the Chir from which the operation was originally intended to begin had been lost to Russian attacks. Balck had moved 11th Panzer Division to the lower Chir on 15 and 16 December facing Nizhne Chirskaya to launch an attempt to recapture the town and thus start the thrust towards Kalach when he received news of another Russian penetration to the west at Lissinsky and Nizhne Kalinovsky, separated by about 13 miles (22km). Balck moved against Lissinsky first, attacking early the following morning and destroying the Russian forces that had broken through. He would have liked to have another day to complete the destruction of the Russians, but Mellenthin contacted him from XLVIII Panzer Corps headquarters to overrule him – a rare event, occasioned by the threat of the Russian penetration at Nizhne Kalinovsky. If this thrust was left unattended, the Russians would be able to threaten the Luftwaffe airfield at Oblivskaya, and the tired drivers of 11th Panzer Division turned their vehicles northwest and drove to Nizhne Kalinovsky through the night, losing tanks – albeit temporarily – when they slipped on the icy road and found themselves stranded in the roadside ditch. When the armoured battlegroup reached Nizhne Kalinovsky, it had only 29 tanks ready for action.[26]

When he arrived at the new sector, Balck conducted a rapid reconnaissance and acted with characteristic vigour. A panzergrenadier regiment turned towards the north to block further Russian columns, while the second panzergrenadier regiment deployed in the path of the Russian penetration. The strike force, as ever, was 15th Panzer Regiment, which moved against the rear of the Russian force:

> At 0500 the Russians arrived. Their tanks and other formations were rolling past us toward the south. Then Schimmelmann released Karl Lestmann's formation [one of the two panzer battalions]. Just like on the training area, our tanks pivoted around and followed the Russians. The Russians had no idea that the tanks following their columns were German. In just a few minutes Lestmann's 25 tanks destroyed 42 Russian tanks without loss. Then they disengaged and in the bottom of a valley prepared for the Russian second wave. As the Soviet tanks advanced over the crest of the ridge our guns fired from below. Again, the fighting was over in a few minutes. Twenty-five German tanks had shot up 65 Russian tanks without loss. The accompanying Russian infantry escaped at first but then a Russian relief column was stopped with heavy losses [by the blocking panzergrenadier regiment].[27]

South of the Don, aware that time was against them, the weary troops of LVII Panzer Corps set out again on 19 December for Verkhne Kumsky, driving through the bright early morning towards the village. The tanks of the three divisions – reinforced by vehicles that had been repaired overnight – attacked together. Scheibert described the events:

> Finally, 17th Panzer Division appeared on the high ground to the left, taking over protection of that flank and releasing forces for a further attack. Everything was to be concentrated on Verkhne Kumsky. It was a systematic attack, and as every enemy position was now known, the attacking Stukas were accurately directed onto their targets. Shortly after, the grenadiers managed to break into the village,

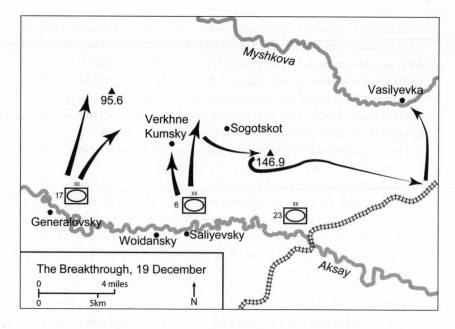

The Breakthrough, 19 December

0   4 miles

0   5km

N

supported by the assault guns. We tanks immediately moved up, having observed the entire spectacle from 3km further back, rolled through our own troops in a broad front and ran into fleeing enemy troops between Verkhne Kumsky and Sogotskot. As there was no further resistance and the enemy was surrendering everywhere in groups, I ordered no further firing. We just rounded them up with our tanks, disarmed them if required, and sent them back where the grenadiers following us gathered them together. Sogotskot was taken almost without a fight.

At this moment we received a radio message and we were assigned a new mission: pursuit as long as we still had fuel! The first objective was Hill 146.9, well known to all of us. I was at the spearhead of II Battalion. The day was drawing to a close as I came under fire just before reaching 146.9 after passing south of Sogotskot. The entire skyline to the east was lit up with muzzle flashes, and tanks could be made out in the fading light. Behind us was the western sky, still light. The commander immediately ordered a mass attack by the battalion; targets could only be identified when they fired and against the western sky we must have stood out in silhouette for the Russians. As our losses mounted, the [battalion] commander (Major Bäke) broke off the action and led us via the shelter of a fold in the terrain in a new attack. In complete darkness we launched a right flanking assault on the enemy. On Major Bäke's orders this attack was conducted at high speed without regard for losses and before I could believe it we were in the midst of the enemy.

There followed a murderous action. The enemy's muzzle flashes blinded us, tanks drove towards us like shadows. I and all the other tanks that had broken in fired as fast as we could. Enemy tanks passed us barely ten metres away; one had to take care not to ram them. Soon several tanks were ablaze and lighting up the battlefield. Then we were through and once more had darkness and stillness around us; behind us flames flickered on the steppe and the firing died down. Other companies battled to widen the breach, intending finally to hand it over to the grenadiers. Sadly, my company had dead and wounded, and tanks that had lost their tracks when overrunning enemy anti-tank guns and were no longer operational.

We assembled and, with Oberst von Hünersdorff and Major Bäke leading, we drove on towards the east, as I could determine from the clear starry sky. All I knew was that, regardless of what it cost, we were to secure a vital crossing over the Myshkova. We were told that at this crossing, comrades breaking out of the Stalingrad encirclement would link up with us. These thoughts had been with us all day.[28]

Pushing on through the darkness, the German tank column missed the first turning to the north and the bridge at Vasilyevka. Hünersdorff ordered his men to avoid firing if at all possible and Scheibert and his comrades rolled forward in an epic advance through the darkness:

The march towards the east seemed almost endless to me, somewhat unreal in the complete stillness around us. The moon rose slowly and allowed us to see the surroundings better. It was crystal clear and the snow seemed to glow from within. Our only concern was not to lose sight of the man in front. Sometimes we drove fast, then we stopped while the spearhead sought the right route. As several tracks crossed our route and the roads marked on the map could barely be made out in daylight through the continuous snow sheet, the leading elements frequently chose the wrong turning. They often ran into ravines that were difficult to traverse. In order to lose no time, the companies still on the right road were assigned to lead the way while those in the rear followed. The shortest route ... was missed; we made a detour and then came across a good road running to our objective from the south. Here it was almost impossible to lose our way as a telegraph line ran alongside the road.

Eventually I found myself in the middle of the battlegroup. More ravines, their icy overhangs shimmering with greenish moonlight ... I have to admit that I had no idea where we were on the map, but trusted the spearhead and the commander completely. Either side of the road I saw positions that seemed to be fully manned. My astonishment knew no limits and it seemed ever more unreal, not least because of the complete stillness all around.

Then we had a prolonged halt. My watch showed 2200, which meant midnight local time. We sat one tank behind another, closed up on the road. To the right the telegraph line, further in front a dark area and beyond it rising ground, apparently with a village on it. Right across the road, near this rise, a well-constructed anti-tank ditch and positions could be made out. It was very cold, and suddenly – I don't know exactly how – armed Russian soldiers were standing amongst our tanks! More and more emerged from the darkness to right and left. We stared – my crew at least, peering out of their hatches – at these guys, not sure if we could believe our eyes. My gunner made me aware that the Russians were still armed. I hissed 'Be still, they think we're Russians!' in his ear and waited, expecting a shot at any moment.

But nothing happened – on the contrary, they leaned on our tracks and tried to chat to us. There were no shots. Couldn't they tell that we were just babbling instead of speaking Russian, couldn't they actually see the black crosses on the sides of our wagons? I fingered my pistol and put a hand grenade behind my seat. My God, what were we to do? This couldn't go on forever. I glanced at the vehicles in front of and behind me and saw the same scenes there.

It isn't clear to me how we got into that situation. There was only one explanation: that as we had rolled into their positions during the night without any sounds of combat, the Russians assumed we were their tanks, especially as we had appeared in peacetime marching formation and Vasilyevka was about 20km [12 miles] behind the front line. While the Russians on Hill 146.9 were fighting with *Gruppe Küper* at that time and still had to deal with *Gruppe Zollendorf*, between 30 and 40 tanks had broken through and were somewhere in their rear area. The Russians here had not been made aware of an armoured group breaking through.

It couldn't go on, we could simply have gunned them down, but leaving aside that we had been forbidden to open fire, we were reluctant to shoot at the curious Ivans. In this manner, we passed an amicable quarter of an hour.

Suddenly, the peace was broken from up front. From the high ground that could just be made out came a shot, followed by further shots and machine-gun fire. We swiftly disappeared into our turrets, the Russians into the darkness either side of the road, and then we advanced slowly but surely against the village that we could soon see clearly.

I later discovered that our leading tank was hit by a T-34 at a range of 10 metres at the northern exit from the village. The Russian tank suffered the same fate, but our outstanding spearhead leader, Oberleutnant Michaelis, died a hero's death. In the next days we saw the two tanks still standing side by side.

Just before the bridge we heard loud cries from further ahead. As I looked out of the turret, a reconnaissance vehicle came back past our column. In its turret was a face wearing a leather jacket and helmet. His face passed three metres from me. A Russian! By the time the moment of shock had passed, the vehicle had disappeared. It was shot at as it passed the end of the column, without success. Now the Russians were certainly aware what had happened.

We broke into the village, the few grenadiers with us dismounted, and by dawn had largely secured the widespread village of Vasilyevka, and most importantly were in control of the undamaged bridge.[29]

Shortly before 2am local time, Raus received a signal from Hünersdorff:

We have only two weak half-track companies with us. I am in combat with enemy tanks and infantry in the attack objective. The bridge is secured. A rapid advance by Zollenkopf is urgently needed; we have no more fuel.[30]

Zollenkopf's panzergrenadiers struggled forward through the night, in almost constant contact with Russian defenders. A small contingent succeeded in delivering much-needed fuel and ammunition to Hünersdorff's toe-hold on the far bank of the Myshkova. The Stalingrad perimeter was just 29 miles (48km) away. Hünersdorff's regiment had been reduced to 20 tanks, and its communications with the rest of Fourth Panzer Army were precarious to say the least.

Whilst there was a glimmer of light for the Germans south of the Don, the situation in the north continued to move in favour of the Russians. After overcoming the initial resistance of the Italian Eighth Army, Vatutin's forces in the north continued inexorably to exploit their gains. The Russian Sixth Army was transferred from Voronezh Front to Southwest Front, and Vatutin ordered his armoured formations to push on to cause maximum disruption – XXV Tank Corps and I Guards Mechanised Corps were to reach Morozovsk by 22 December, XXIV Tank Corps was to capture Tatsinskaya a day later, and XVII and XVIII Tank Corps were to reach Millerovo on 24 December.[31] These objectives would leave the Russians not far short of the original aims for *Saturn*, though the timetable remained ambitious. Nevertheless, the two tank corps were in excellent condition, with an establishment of 159 tanks, of which 96 were T-34s. Their personnel had been rested and trained extensively, and were anxious to get into combat.[32] However, they were not without their problems, as Colonel Burdeyny, chief of staff of XXIV Tank Corps, had discussed with Vatutin on 12 December. There was a shortage of anti-aircraft firepower and field artillery in the corps, and there was particular concern about diesel fuel shortages, which meant that it might not be possible to refuel all the tanks once operations began. Whilst Vatutin was able to order the transfer of additional field and anti-aircraft artillery, there was little he could do about the fuel shortage.[33]

In the northern part of the Russian breakthrough was the town of Kantemirovka, astride the railway line that provided lateral communications for Army Group B. The first units of XVII Tank Corps moved towards the town early on 19 December, and a full-scale battle developed as the garrison – a mixture of retreating stragglers, army rear area units, and police and SS formations – struggled to retain control. By the end of the day, the town was in Russian hands. The remnants of 27th Panzer Division, with only ten tanks still running, took up covering positions to the west of Kantemirovka. Now that they were clear of the German defences around the town, the brigades of XXIV and XXV Tank Corps made swifter progress through open ground, but were limited by a number of factors. As they advanced, they outstripped the range of their air support and were repeatedly struck by Luftwaffe attacks, and their lengthening supply lines were constantly disrupted by the retreating fragments of German and Italian units still falling back from the shattered front along the Don. Fuel shortages, enemy action and breakdowns reduced both corps to barely half their starting strength in just a matter of days. The troops of Third Guards Army encircled the Romanian 7th Infantry Division on 19 December, destroying it the following day, and linked up with elements of First Guards Army to the south to complete a tenuous encirclement of the northern part of *Armee Abteilung Hollidt*; retreating elements of the German 62nd Infantry Division succeeded in fighting their way through, as did parts of the Romanian Army, though losses were heavy.

If *Uranus* created a sense of crisis in the Wehrmacht, this was doubly so as *Little Saturn* unfolded. The Russian tanks were motoring across open ground towards the vital airfields of Morozovsk and Tatsinskaya with no organised defences in their path, and the utterly inadequate air supply of Sixth Army would come to an end if the airfields were lost. Using the last of its strength, LVII Panzer Corps had reached the Myshkova, but a further advance was out of the question – in any case, in the absence of substantial reinforcements from elsewhere, Manstein would have to call on its panzer divisions to try to intercept the Russian armour pouring into the rear area of Army Group Don. The moment of decision for Hitler was at hand, and further prevarication would be fatal: if any of Sixth Army was to be saved, a breakout was now essential.

CHAPTER 6

NOW OR NEVER

There has been much criticism of Manstein for not issuing a clear order to Paulus to initiate a breakout, and for not personally meeting the man who was, technically at least, his subordinate, either by summoning him to Army Group Don headquarters or by flying into the Stalingrad pocket.[1] This is part of the insoluble debate about whether Sixth Army could have been saved had the local commanders behaved differently. Manstein appears to have been aware of this potential criticism of his conduct of operations and wrote at some length to justify his behaviour.[2] In preparation for this moment, Manstein had drawn up a brief outline of a second operation to follow *Winter Storm*. Codenamed *Donnerschlag* ('Thunderclap'), it would see Sixth Army carrying out a phased withdrawal from Stalingrad towards the southwest. In order to help alleviate the supply problems of Paulus' troops, Army Group Don had assembled a column of vehicles carrying 3,000 tons of supplies and numerous tractors so that as much of Sixth Army as possible could be made mobile, and as soon as LVII Panzer Corps established contact with the encircled troops, this column was to rush through. But as will be seen, Manstein did not trigger *Thunderclap*.

The remnants of the Russian forces that had held Verkhne Kumsky with such determination – 1378th Infantry Regiment and 55th Independent Tank Brigade – withdrew across the Myshkova, and were absorbed into the ranks of Second Guards Army. The commanders of the two formations, Lieutenant Colonels Diasamidche and Aslanov – were awarded the title 'Hero of the Soviet Union'. It was an apt medal; the determined stand made by their men and a supporting anti-tank regiment had played a critical part in delaying LVII Panzer Corps' advance.[3] On 20 December, fighting continued around Hünersdorff's fragile bridgehead, and one account of the fighting records ominously that the lack of troops in the German contingent made it impossible to take prisoners, and the Russian forces holding on in parts of Vasilyevka outnumbered the Germans.[4] It took until late afternoon for significant reinforcements to reach Hünersdorff, and the disparate elements of the division were left to reflect upon the consequences of the previous day's advance – the thrust by the division's tanks to Vasilyevka with little infantry support left them in desperate need of infantry reinforcements, while at the same time the division's panzergrenadiers struggled to reach the bridgehead without the support of the division's tanks. Zollenkopf couldn't set off immediately in pursuit of the tanks after the capture of Verkhne Kumsky as he had to extract his troops from the village and wait for supplies of fuel, food and ammunition to be brought forward, not least so that he could take some of these supplies with him to Hünersdorff; by the time he was ready to move with I Battalion, 114th Panzergrenadier Regiment, the tanks were long gone and Russian forces had once more blocked the road to Vasilyevka:

The march in the dark night was particularly difficult. The vehicles slithered through the frozen ravines, and everyone frequently had to dismount and push them up slopes. In other places, the tracks left by the tanks hindered the progress of the wheeled vehicles; the column frequently broke up, resulting in prolonged pauses. East of Hill 146.9 the battalion encountered elements of II Battalion 114th Panzergrenadier Regiment (in half-tracks), which had lost contact with Hünersdorff and had no idea where it was. As Russians constantly attacked out of the darkness, they had formed a hedgehog position in order to defend against attacks from all directions. As they saw the approaching lights of I Battalion the Russians thought that they were probably about to be attacked by tanks again and disappeared into the darkness.

The staff of 114th Regiment lost its radio apparatus in the darkness when it took command of I Battalion. It was later discovered that the radio set had developed technical faults and thus contact with the division and *Gruppe Hünersdorff* was lost. At midnight [2am local time] the rifle companies reached the railway line. This was clearly too far to the east. After brief reconnaissance they saw that the tanks had turned north. The entire column followed.

After a few kilometres' drive the leading company came under rifle and machine-gun fire. As dawn broke, Russian positions could be made out. While the companies deployed for an attack and the [artillery] battery took up positions, the battalion was attacked by Russian aircraft with bombs and fixed weapons. There were few losses. The attack by I Battalion was successful; at 10am [midday local time] resistance was overcome and the battalion was able to assemble and mount up.

The advance continued over a wide open plain; the terrain gradually fell away to the Myshkova valley. Soon, a few houses in Vasilyevka could be seen. Sounds of fighting came from this direction. *Gruppe Hünersdorff* was fighting a defensive battle there. Radio contact wasn't possible. I Battalion deployed with the intention of entering Vasilyevka dismounted on a broad front. The commander assumed that the enemy would not be particularly strong and that the tanks would eventually be able to overcome any anti-tank guns that had been deployed. There was therefore great surprise as artillery and anti-tank fire struck the battalion from the nearby high ground. The battalion had to incline to the right where a ravine ran towards the village and offered protection. Here it dismounted in order to fight through to the isolated bridgehead of *Gruppe Hünersdorff*. Shortly before darkness the leading company reached the southern part of the village and came under fire from a few houses near the bridge.[5]

The air attack that is mentioned in this report also features in the memoirs of a Russian pilot. The Russians had identified the need for a dedicated ground attack aircraft in the early 1930s but at the time the available aero-engines lacked the power needed for a relatively heavy aircraft to perform effectively. In 1938, Sergei Ilyushin designed a two-seater aircraft with substantial armoured protection built into its structure, but when the plane flew the following year it failed to demonstrate the required performance and was redesigned as a single-seat low-altitude aircraft. In this form, it entered service in 1941 as the Ilyushin Il-2. Originally, it was armed with two 23mm guns that were fed ammunition in clips, but after extensive trials a single belt-firing 23mm weapon was adopted; Yakov Grigoreyevich Taubin, the inventor of the original clip-firing guns, experienced a fate that was widespread in the paranoid days of the purges of the 1930s. He was arrested on the charge of deliberately producing a substandard weapon and executed shortly before the German invasion of the Soviet Union.[6] Only 249 planes were available at the beginning of *Barbarossa*, crewed by men who had almost no training in their use and most of whom had never fired their weapons even in practice, but after the initial disruption caused by the relocation of Soviet industry to the east, production of the Shturmovik, as the plane had become known, increased steadily. After the loss of many aircraft as a result of German fighter interceptions, the Shturmovik was modified back into a two-man design with a rear gunner in the cockpit when more powerful engines became available. The aircraft grew to be popular with its crews, largely because its substantial armour made it almost invulnerable to hits by any weapon of less than 20mm calibre; however, this armour did not extend to the rear of the cockpit, leaving the rear gunner exposed to the fire of attacking enemy fighters. In addition, this armour added considerably to its weight and thus reduced the quantity of weapons it could carry. Alexander Alexeyevich Karpov was a pilot in a squadron equipped with Shturmoviks and took part in attacks to try to disrupt the operations of LVII Panzer Corps. His account of one such raid shows the difficulty of operating in marginal weather conditions:

Our task was to destroy an enemy tank column. A few minutes passed and we flew into clouds. We reduced altitude to 100m. The leader's aircraft was a dim grey shape ahead. A blizzard was coming. Finding a column on the march in this weather was not simple ...

Suddenly, a snowflake appeared on the windscreen. All around it became white – we plunged into a snowstorm. I lost sight of the squadron. My right hand grasped the rubber tip of the control knob as I tried to maintain course so as not to crash into the next plane. Suddenly it grew brighter. My plane was very close to Hitali [the squadron commander] ...

If it were not for the increasing snowfall obscuring the horizon, Hitali would have found the enemy column without much difficulty. We had flown in bad weather before, and every time he had found the target, attacking accurately. Now a white veil suddenly obscured the earth rendering it invisible, making it difficult to orientate. I wondered whether we would turn back.

To arrive exactly on target and conduct a surprise attack – this could be done only with good visibility, and with the slightest deviation from the route we lost our direction. We listened attentively to the voice of the squadron commander. During a flight in difficult weather conditions, every word caught on the air was vital ...

For more than a quarter of an hour we circled over white fields. Many of us would perhaps have been happy to return to our airfield, but our leader remained steadfast. For Hitali, apparently, everything was clear. It was necessary at all costs to find the enemy tanks to prevent them from advancing and breaking through the ring of encirclement ...

Still everything was white around us. Under our wings was an unspoiled silent steppe, covered with a flat, white, even layer of snow. But then I heard our callsign on the air. This was the highest reward for long patience, for our belief in success! I heard Hitali's voice, telling us the location of the enemy column. Now the weather didn't feel so terrible!

Making a u-turn, we approached a barely discernable road. Now I noticed a dark long strip crossing a white flat field. The column slowed suddenly, small dots separated from it: soldiers jumping to the ground from their vehicles. Before my eyes I could see gun barrels being elevated. Having spotted us, the fascists deployed their anti-aircraft batteries in a hurry.

'Attack!' The long-awaited command was eagerly welcomed, and one by one bombs fell on the Nazis' heads. Snow flecked with earth rose over the field, trucks and tanks drove away from the road, many getting stuck sideways on the verge. Our gunfire flashed across the white field. Bombs fell from an extremely low altitude. They are exactly on target … Trucks, tractors, wagons lay stranded on the road. Some were burning, some were damaged, though many trucks and tanks tried to escape from our attack aircraft.

The yellow glare from burning vehicles created circles of light on the road, illuminating the fascists who had fallen to the ground. In the middle of the column, several new fires erupted. Now we attacked from the windward side, masking ourselves with smoke, thus preventing the enemy anti-aircraft gunners from engaging in targeted fire.

The dead steppe came to life. Enemy tanks, the bright flames of burning trucks, exploding ammunition. It was hard to judge the altitude of the plane. You needed some special intuition to pull the plane out of the dive in time.

I heard a command: another attack. The plane turned tightly again. I felt the pressure as I was compressed into my seat. It was almost impossible to move a foot or a hand. There was little time to think, I had to grip the control column tightly …

There were black spots before my eyes. I felt there wasn't enough air and I wanted to stick my head out of the half-open window of the cabin … I was close to the sword-blade shape of Hitali's wing. We came out of our steep turn in horizontal flight and again brought our guns to bear on the enemy.

After our attack we turned away, leaving behind the blazing steel boxes of fascist tanks, enemy infantry cut down by machine-gun fire, killed by the last bursts from our cannon. It was an uncompromising brutal battle with the enemy and bad weather, and we won it.[7]

Just like the descriptions of German pilots like Rudel, this account almost certainly overstates the effect of the attack. The efficacy of the Shturmovik remains disputed; whilst Russian accounts describe the destruction of dozens of German tanks and other vehicles, these accounts are not consistent with the known strength of the formations that came under attack, or their returns to higher commands about casualties suffered. This example is a case in point: the Russian account describes the German column as taking substantial losses, whereas the German account mentions the air attack only in passing, and specifically states that its impact was minimal. Nevertheless, the appearance of the armoured aircraft overhead had a considerable psychological impact upon German soldiers, who were aware that they could do little to drive them off unless they were accompanied by flak units.

From the beleaguered bridgehead over the Myshkova, Major Bäke managed to reach the approaching column of German troops in an armoured car, and the panzergrenadiers successfully attacked the small cluster of Russian-held buildings. A limited amount of fuel and ammunition reached the stranded tanks of 11th Panzer Regiment, but barely enough to allow them to continue to hold the bridgehead. The regiment's war diary entry for that evening paints a bleak picture:

> The commander of the leading company of I Battalion 114th Panzergrenadier Regiment arrived at 4.45pm [6.45pm local time] but accompanied by only a few men. By 7pm [9pm local time] the first two platoons of I Battalion were in the bridgehead. It was still not possible to dispatch armoured cars through the southern perimeter, but this was planned for the night. As a result, a penetration in the northwest of the bridgehead could not yet be cleared. The commander planned to mount an attack towards the west from the bridgehead at dawn after the arrival of Hauenschild [i.e. the rest of I Battalion] against the high ground northwest of Vasilyevka so that it is possible to push further from there.
>
> The lack of water for the bridgehead garrison greatly reduces its strength, and in particular the wounded suffer as a consequence. Since yesterday midday, a total of 25 tanks have been lost, some due to breakdowns but most due to being shot up. I Battalion has only seven operational tanks.[8]

The troops opposing 6th Panzer Division were the first elements of Second Guards Army. This powerful force was originally composed of I and XIII Guards Rifle Corps and II Guards Mechanised Corps, but on 18 December was additionally given control over VII Tank Corps, III Guards Mechanised Corps (the former IV Mechanised Corps, which had frustrated 6th Panzer Division for so long at Verkhne Kumsky), IV Cavalry Corps and the independent 300th Rifle Division.[9] Even if some of these formations – III Guards Mechanised Corps in particular – were heavily degraded, the odds piling up against Kirchner's LVII Panzer Corps were insuperable. The various elements of 6th Panzer Division were strung out right across the battlefield – Hünersdorff's battlegroup was in the Vasilyevka bridgehead, still desperately short of ammunition, food and fuel; panzergrenadiers from 114th Regiment were in the southern part of the village;

and the other battalions were still struggling forward, hindered as much by the poor roads and freezing conditions as by constant harassment from the Russians. The neighbouring panzer divisions were still trying to advance on either flank in order to reach the Myshkova.

One of the units of Second Guards Army was Major General Petr Kirilovich Koshevoi's 24th Guards Rifle Division. It was ordered to take up positions to the west of the Vasilyevka bridgehead along the Myshkova, opposite the farm of Nizhne Kumsky. When he reached the Myshkova, Koshevoi studied Nizhne Kumsky through his binoculars and, concluding that the German forces there were modest, he decided to launch an attack on the night of 19–20 December to secure the village:

> Our artillery put down a particularly heavy bombardment that night.
>
> We had to work without fire correction, but we shot well. The shells struck the centre of the farm where we believed the enemy command post was located. The village was in turmoil. There was a roar of engines from the fascist tanks. The enemy tried to get them out of the shelling. The commotion on the streets grew into a panic.
>
> At this time, one of my battalions, the Kazakhs, broke into the enemy's position and engaged the Hitlerites amongst the houses. Fierce fighting ensued around the outskirts. The company of Lieutenant Krechetov, which advanced to where the fascist tanks were parked, had a particularly heated battle and was supported by Lieutenant Orumbekov's mortars. They did not give the German tankmen time to start their cold engines. Krechetov's men fought bravely and energetically, killed the crews of two dozen tanks, and damaged the vehicles themselves.
>
> In the centre of the farm meanwhile, the shells of our artillery continued to explode. Unable to restore order, the Hitlerite officers rushed to their vehicles and tried to leave the danger zone. At that moment the machine-gunners of Captain Cazac, who had occupied the windmill, opened fire. One by one they shot the occupants of three vehicles. This added to the enemy's confusion. The resistance of the Hitlerites became increasingly disorganised. They retreated to the southern part of the farm, away from our fighters ...
>
> We had no contact at all between the Kazakh battalion and our observation post. We waited for a report, but fighting was raging in the village, there was a fierce exchange of fire, and probably there was no time for it. Standing on the start line, the Tymoshenko battalion waited in vain for the signal, as did other troops. I tried to contact the [Kazakh] battalion commander myself, but we were told that the captain was in the front line. I requested his chief of staff. The answer was

the same. Both commanders, apparently, were carried away by the battle, forgetting about everything else.

It was only before dawn, when the enemy was driven out of the central part of the village, that Yasyrev finally reported: 'I'm sitting by the mill, and the battalion is heavily engaged, and I'm wounded.'

'Do you need help?' I asked Yasyrov.

'No,' he answered, 'we'll manage.'

And the battle in the farm became increasingly fierce. We undoubtedly achieved what we hoped for: the enemy was not able to drive us back, but that did not mean at all that he was giving up. On the contrary, the Nazis came to their senses in different parts of Nizhne Kumsky and put up organised resistance. It was necessary to break it, stretching the enemy's forces and inflicting new blows. It was time to attack with Kukharev's and Tymoshenko's battalions.

I called Kukharev to the phone. His battalion was waiting for orders in the vegetable gardens on the northern outskirts of the farm. 'Attack!' I ordered.

Tymoshenko received the same command.

A few minutes later, fresh units broke into the streets of Nizhne Kumsky. There were more flashes of light in the darkness. I knew that now it would be easier to break the enemy in the centre of the farm, where the struggle continued with the same intensity.

While we watched Nizhne Kumsky, responding to reports and giving orders, we constantly looked to the east. There on the horizon appeared a faintly visible white stripe – a sign of the imminent dawn. It was time to get a full account of the results of the battle in the farm, but I still had little information. I became increasingly anxious. Every 20 minutes I picked up the phone to the 3rd [Kazakh] battalion and spoke with Yasyrev. He reported tersely that the enemy had taken heavy losses, but could not confirm that he had been defeated: it was not possible to determine this in the dark. But it was clear that in some parts of the farm the resistance of the enemy had weakened noticeably, and in some places he was trying to break off the battle and retreat to the southern and western parts of Nizhne Kumsky. The battalion commanders were all fighting with their men and weren't in their battalion command posts.

The time was five o'clock. I decided it was time for me to move to Nizhne Kumsky. There, at dawn, I would be able to look around and intervene. The main forces of the division had not yet been drawn into the battle and we had reserves to parry any enemy counterattack that might occur. I took Saprykin with me, got into the car and along the road on which the German tanks had approached the river the day before, and rushed to the farm.

176

On the outskirts of Nizhne Kumsky, there were hundreds of corpses of enemy soldiers, broken German weapons, smoking tanks. Heat and the stench of burning radiated from the steel wrecks.[10]

It seems from this account that Koshevoi attacked Nizhne Kumsky initially with just one battalion out of nine that he had available. The account is also inconsistent in that it describes increasing German disorganisation and panic, yet at the same time stresses that the fighting was fierce with little progress being made. When Yasyrev's troops proved unable to secure victory unaided, he committed a further two battalions – still only part of the forces available to him. It is possible that some elements of his division were still marching up to the Myshkova, but Koshevoi appears to have made no attempt to bypass the defences or to encircle the Germans, options that were surely available to him given the troops at his disposal. On this occasion at least, the Russians showed that their tactical approach was unsubtle: an artillery bombardment followed by a frontal attack.

There are other problems with this account. The German forces around Nizhne Kumsky were the leading elements of 17th Panzer Division, which had a total tank strength far lower than the 65 tanks that Koshevoi claimed his men destroyed. According to the division's war diary, the farm and surrounding village had been occupied by the leading elements of the German division, and although Koshevoi's troops managed to capture the position they suffered heavy casualties.[11] The vehicles that he described being destroyed were probably a mixture of armoured cars and light tanks from the reconnaissance platoon, but even if a number of trucks is included, a total of 65 seems improbably high and there is no mention of such a major setback in the records of the German division. The rest of 17th Panzer Division assembled over the next day, and Koshevoi watched cautiously for signs of an attempt by the Germans to force a crossing of the Myshkova.

As the columns of the German division moved up to the Myshkova and Nizhne Kumsky, they continued to be harassed by scattered Russian units. Vasily Semenovich Krysov was the commander of a T-34 platoon and, together with another tank commanded by his friend Mikhail Marder, covered the withdrawal of the rest of his unit as the surviving tanks pulled back towards the Myshkova:

We waited for darkness and then moved to the river crossing. Marder and I covered the retreat with our two tanks. We found the pontoons at last and thought we were out of danger when we came under heavy gunfire from behind. I managed to tell Misha by radio: 'We are burning!'

And he answered: 'We're alight too!'

It was a tank battalion of 17th Panzer Division sent forward by Hoth! And we had stumbled upon it! They saw us and opened fire with sub-calibre projectiles from a short distance. The Germans had sub-calibre shells as early as 1941 but we only received them in 1943, before the Battle of Kursk.

The Germans managed to set both our tanks on fire with hits in the rear. A projectile hit our transmission and the engine caught fire. The crossing and the shore were suddenly illuminated by flares. Heavy fire! We couldn't jump out through the turret. We opened the emergency manhole-hatch in the middle of the combat compartment, taking the most essential things – machine-guns, grenades, a first aid kit – and lay under the tank. All in my crew were still alive and weren't injured. But what about Mikhail? By the light of the flares I saw Marder's crew getting out of the tank, also through the emergency escape hatch, which meant that some at least were still alive. Hiding, we waited: when would they get tired of firing flares? Soon a group of enemy scouts appeared. We pressed ourselves against the ground. But the Germans, without stopping, passed by. At last everything calmed down. I crawled over to Marder's crew. Misha said that he heard the scouts say: 'Ten Ivans were burned alive here.'

It was necessary to get to our own side. By the light of a pocket torch we studied the map, outlined an escape route and set off. Before dawn, we came to a ravine where we decided to stop. We set up a shelter to protect us from the wind, and, burying ourselves in snow and numb from the cold, sat in cover for the whole day.

When it was dark, we set out again. The northeast wind blew, carrying fine snow. Misha Marder was ahead as he could speak German if necessary, and we walked on, stretching our frozen legs. After a day of exposure we were very cold, although we had all the winter accoutrements – felt boots, cotton trousers, quilted jackets under greatcoats, and fur tankers' helmets on our heads. Ahead of us a column of smoke rose into the air. When we approached, we made out a whole series of dugouts with a sentry walking the perimeter. The German at first was frightened, but Marder threw up his hand in a fascist salute. The guard had only started to raise his hand in response when Misha Tvorogov from my crew charged and hit him hard on the head, and the German fell. He had no time to raise the alarm.

We went on and suddenly came across another guard. We had no time to hesitate and threw a grenade at him before hurrying away. The Germans realised what was happening and opened fire with a machine-gun, and then a mortar. Many of us were injured, but we had already reached our trenches. Misha Marder was seriously wounded in the back and we immediately sent him to the medical battalion. I had a piece of shrapnel in my right forearm, but I refused to go to the medical battalion.

We had walked more than a day to reach our lines and we could say we were lucky, all were alive, although many were injured.

I do not know the fate of Misha Marder. His full name was Moses Borkovich. His fellow soldiers searched for him for a long time, but without success, and we do not even know whether he survived after being wounded. At school, Mikhail was a good student, intelligent, gifted, very bright; kind, but clever; happy to talk about any topic; he was also an artist and made posters for the school. In battle he always acted decisively, he didn't hold back. In short, he was a good fellow, a really fine person, a steady comrade and a brave soldier.[12]

Bitter fighting continued around Vasilyevka on 21 December; Hünersdorff tried to enlarge the bridgehead, in particular to secure the high ground to the north, without success, and as a result the entire bridgehead remained under Russian fire. The pressure was so intense that it was impossible to pull the remaining tanks out of the fighting in order to regroup them into a strike force, and the panzergrenadiers' half-tracks were generally too damaged or disabled to be usable in an attack. Nevertheless, the panzergrenadiers were able to reach the neighbouring village of Kapkinsky, where they encountered further resistance, as a non-commissioned officer later recalled:

The Russians ... had dug a huge anti-tank ditch in a corner and defended themselves from within it. We were only able to advance very slowly. I crept along a trench almost parallel to the Russian position. Our I Platoon was behind me. We succeeded in breaking into the anti-tank ditch with comparatively few losses. Only Jupp Hohenbrink was hit in our platoon as we lay without cover in the open. As we moved up to the anti-tank ditch we captured a lot of booty – we counted about 40 prisoners and even more dead. But what I experienced I would not forget for the rest of my life. Without waiting for orders I stormed along an anti-tank ditch that ran at right angles to the one we had already cleared with only a few men from my group. My plan was to use the enemy's confusion in order to clear as much of the anti-tank ditch as possible so that the Russians could no longer occupy strong positions in front of ours. We chased after the fleeing Russians. The men in a bunker wanted to surrender. A white rag was waved on the end of a bayonet. One of my riflemen dragged a belt of machine-gun ammunition into the bunker. Then a shot rang out and right next to me Rifleman Collin fell, mortally wounded. We had to pull back as fast as possible. On the evening of 23 December we carried Collin back and laid him to rest in the military cemetery at Kotelnikovo.[13]

During the day, 17th Panzer Division had succeeded in reaching the Myshkova further west but was unable to secure a crossing; it launched a powerful attack on Nizhne Kumsky that led to further losses on both sides, but the village remained in the hands of Koshevoi's division. Rather than waste further time on trying to secure a second bridgehead, Kirchner ordered 17th Panzer Division to move its forces to Vasilyevka, where they were to release 6th Panzer Division's forces for a further advance and simultaneously were to try to work their way west along the north bank of the river. Hünersdorff was ordered to push forward to State Farm Krep and thence to Verkhne Tsarinsky, a further advance of 21 miles (35km). It was an ambitious objective and unachievable given the forces arrayed against the Vasilyevka bridgehead, but there was still no sign of any activity from Sixth Army. Scheibert and the other men in *Gruppe Hünersdorff* had experienced hard days of fighting with little rest at Verkhne Kumsky, but their ordeal was now far worse:

> Almost every hour, during the day or the night, the Russians – either individually or in groups – directed their weapons against us. We were driven into a smaller area and couldn't leave our vehicles. The few panzergrenadiers with us were under our tanks or dug themselves in nearby, emerging only for occasional counterattacks under cover of our fire. Without fuel, we couldn't move. Each tank was assigned a sector, overall control was no longer possible – one could see only one's own stretch, one's own grenadiers and crewmen. It was hugely disagreeable and most casualties were caused by the almost constant artillery and rocket bombardment, whose sudden intensification always presaged new attacks. In this manner, one tank after another was knocked out, and amongst others I lost my best platoon commander, Feldwebel Reusch. The wounded were our greatest concern. We no longer knew where we could put them, the last houses were ablaze or reduced to ruins. There was no water and it was bitterly cold outside.
>
> For the first two days we were completely cut off from supplies, without our own artillery which might have subdued the enemy, and only Stukas, in greater strength each day, provided us with palpable support. From low altitude they dropped their bombs just a few metres from us amongst the attacking Russians. Just as we suffered heavy losses, the Russians carpeted the outer parts of the village with their dead.
>
> I too was hit when travelling to the regiment commander whose command post was in a trench under his tank. Shrapnel across my ribs. It was a wonder that

my winter uniform, my tobacco pouch and my cigarette case absorbed much of it. The blow knocked me down. Comrades pulled me under a tank and the doctor was able to pull the fragments out right there.[14]

In a period that seemed to be a constant series of crises, the last week of December was perhaps worse than ever. Manstein had to contend with the increasingly clear fact that Paulus was a longstanding stickler for complying to Hitler's orders; late on 19 November, even as the Red Army was erupting out of the Serafimovich and Kletskaya bridgeheads, Paulus had told Adam, his adjutant:

> There is still the order whereby no commander of an army group or an army has the right to relinquish a village, even a trench, without Hitler's consent. Of course the decision of every army commander has been paralysed. But how will we get through the war if orders are no longer complied with? What effect would this have on the troops? However large the command of the general is, the men must be given an example of his soldier's obedience to orders.[15]

It should be noted that Adam's account is consistently far more favourable towards Paulus than other accounts, but all are agreed on his rigid adherence to orders and near-abhorrence of taking independent action contrary to those orders. In such circumstances, even if Manstein had ordered Paulus to commence *Thunderclap*, it is highly likely that Paulus would have insisted on confirmation of the order from Hitler, in particular that the previous orders to hold Stalingrad had been rescinded, and there was no possibility whatever of such confirmation being forthcoming. But time was running out: whatever Kirchner's intentions might be to advance closer to Stalingrad, the reality was that LVII Panzer Corps was at the end of its strength. Sixth Army should have been redeploying its forces in anticipation of this moment, in particular concentrating its remaining tanks in the southwest, but no such measures had been taken – Paulus was fearful that without the support of the tanks, his exhausted and half-starved infantry would be unable to hold out elsewhere in the perimeter, and in any event the pressures on the pocket were so great that even a modest redeployment would have required the front line to be pulled back, something that Hitler had expressly forbidden.

The situation in the Stalingrad encirclement raises another curious fact. Over 200,000 men had been trapped by *Uranus*, yet the 20 German divisions in Sixth Army had been unable to scrape together more than modest battlegroups for the final assaults in the city prior to the encirclement. Energetic officers along the Chir had managed to organise rear area personnel into effective battlegroups after *Uranus*, and without the presence of significant armoured forces – despite Wenck's improvised panzer brigade – these battlegroups repeatedly repelled Russian attacks. By contrast, Sixth Army made little attempt to prepare for its rescue – the armour that had been dispatched across the Don in a futile bid to stop the northern pincer of *Uranus* was dispersed, and the only steps taken within the encirclement to help LVII Panzer Corps consisted of simulating signals traffic in an attempt to persuade the encircling Russians that a breakout was imminent.[16] One armoured formation – 3rd Motorised Division – had been positioned at the southwest tip of the pocket, but it received no additional supplies in order to retain its mobility and was not given any warning orders to prepare for active operations. Whilst ammunition shortages, a lack of winter clothing, the effect of inadequate food supplies, the loss of so many junior officers in the fighting in the city, and the constant Russian pressure undoubtedly placed great strains upon the surrounded troops, a degree of passivity and resignation appears to have been present from an early stage of the siege, with Schmidt merely repeating his assertion that responsibility lay with those outside the pocket to ensure that the airlift promised by Hitler was adequate. With much of the siege perimeter running through the ruins of Stalingrad and thus favouring the defence, it should surely have been possible to improvise battlegroups in order to release troops to prepare for a possible breakout. At the moment that Army Group Don's crisis had reached its peak, Sixth Army was in no position to start an attack towards LVII Panzer Corps – even if Paulus were inclined to order such a move, it would take days to organise, and time was absolutely of the essence.

Having received no response to his signal of 19 December, in which he had advised Paulus that Sixth Army would have to start moving towards the Myshkova if a link-up with Hoth's Fourth Panzer Army was to be achieved, Manstein finally gave Paulus explicit instructions to commence operations:

> Sixth Army will begin *Winter Storm* attack [i.e. its move towards the Myshkova bridgehead] earliest possible. Aim will be to link up with LVII Panzer Corps ...
>
> Development of situation may make it necessary to extend [the breakout] ... up to Myshkova. Code-word *Thunderclap*. In this case the aim must likewise be to establish contact with LVII Panzer Corps in order to get convoy through [i.e. the supply column that stood ready behind Kirchner's divisions], and then, by covering flanks on the lower Karpovka, to bring army forward towards the Myshkova simultaneously with sector-by-sector evacuation of fortress area.
>
> It is essential that *Thunderclap* should immediately follow *Winter Storm* attack ...
>
> All weapons and artillery which can be moved, primarily guns needed for the

fighting and also any weapons and equipment which are difficult to replace, will be taken along. To this end they will be moved in good time to the southwest of the pocket.

All necessary preparations to be made ... Only to be implemented on express issue of *Thunderclap*.

Report day and time on which you can attack.[17]

This order has been the subject of much controversy and criticism. It did not directly order the immediate evacuation of Stalingrad, but made such an evacuation inevitable – Sixth Army was to commence its attack towards the southwest as soon as possible, and *Thunderclap* was to follow 'immediately'. In his memoirs, Manstein argued that he did not immediately authorise *Thunderclap* because of two factors: firstly, it was important that the evacuation of Stalingrad would have to coincide with the plans of Fourth Panzer Army; and secondly, he still wanted to try to secure Hitler's agreement to abandon Stalingrad – it should be remembered that at this stage of the war, the utter irrationality of Hitler's orders was not widely understood and few officers were minded to ignore the directives of the Führer. Manstein added that whilst responsibility for not complying with Hitler's order to hold the city at all costs would lie with him as army group commander, 'the commander of Sixth Army would still feel his hands were tied as long as it remained in force.'[18] *OKH* had its own liaison officer in Sixth Army headquarters, and even if Paulus had been minded to ignore Hitler's order, there was no possibility of Hitler not becoming aware of it.

The response was, to say the least, disheartening. Paulus replied that it was impossible to release any forces for a breakout without giving up parts of Stalingrad, and he could not do so unless and until Hitler's order to hold the city was rescinded. Even worse, he informed Manstein that it would take six days for him to organise a breakout, even if Hitler were to give permission. In addition, the commander of Sixth Army added that the physical state of his men was now so poor that success was very unlikely; finally, the fuel situation remained unchanged and it was impossible for him to consider a breakout of more than 20 miles. At least 4,000 tons of fuel and other supplies were needed for Sixth Army to achieve the desired degree of mobility. Aware of the fuel shortage, Hitler refused to accede to Manstein's plans – if Paulus was unable to cover the required distance, he would have to stay where he was. However, Hitler added, he would order the Luftwaffe to increase the amount of fuel it was flying into the pocket to improve Sixth Army's mobility.

According to Adam, Paulus complained repeatedly that he was kept in the dark about developments outside the pocket. It could therefore be argued that Manstein should have issued explicit instructions to Paulus to prepare for an attack towards LVII Panzer Corps at an earlier date, and in this context his dispatch of a lower ranking staff officer into the pocket is relevant. If he had met Paulus and Schmidt personally, either by flying into the pocket or summoning Sixth Army's senior officers to meet him outside the pocket, such instructions would surely have been issued and there would have been no possibility of Schmidt dismissively declaring that all that was required was a greater effort to sustain Sixth Army by air. It should have been clear to Sixth Army headquarters that as Fourth Panzer Army approached, the moment would come for the troops in the encirclement to exert pressure – indeed, this had been explicit in Manstein's original operational order for *Winter Storm* – and Schmidt and Paulus must be criticised for making so few preparations, even though further instructions about a breakout from Army Group Don were not sent to Sixth Army until this late stage.

When Fiebig learned of Hitler's latest pronouncement about the airlift, he wrote in his diary that the instructions were simply impossible. The previous four days had seen an average of only 145 tons of supplies of all kinds reaching the pocket each day, and at that rate it would take nearly six weeks to deliver the required fuel, even if all airlift capacity was used purely to transport fuel.[19] In other words, there was not the remotest possibility of restoring Sixth Army's mobility by flying in sufficient fuel.

Manstein's assessment of Paulus' situation was even-handed, and he placed due importance on the problems faced by Sixth Army. Even allowing for Army Group Don taking responsibility for ignoring Hitler's order to hold Stalingrad, there remained the very daunting task that Paulus faced. His army would have to fight its way through the encircling Russian forces and then cover at least part of the distance to the Myshkova while being assailed on all sides. If it were to fail in its breakout, or become stalled once the breakout began, or if its flanks or rear were to be forced by the pursuing Russians, the army would perish on the open steppe.

Writing many years later, Paulus' chief of staff Schmidt insisted that a breakout had never been possible, and that the weakened troops of Sixth Army would have been crushed had they attempted an escape.[20] An obvious riposte is that Schmidt was one of the main proponents of holding onto Stalingrad at all costs, and that as chief of staff he had to share responsibility for the complete lack of any preparation for a breakout – the six days that Paulus insisted that he needed were utterly unrealistic given the pressure on the Myshkova bridgehead and the collapse of the Italian Eighth Army. It is of course possible to speculate what might have happened had *Thunderclap* been attempted, but no such attempt was ever made. Manstein wanted breakout preparations to begin before he would order *Thunderclap*, not least so that Hitler would be unable to stop it; Paulus said that he could only begin a breakout by abandoning parts of Stalingrad, and he would only do so if Hitler sanctioned it; and Hitler hid behind Paulus' fuel shortage and refused to give permission on the grounds that a breakout was pointless unless LVII Panzer Corps managed to move closer. While the arguments continued, Army Group Don's situation worsened steadily and precious time slipped away.

The initial resistance of Italian and German units along the middle Don had been replaced by chaotic conditions as the Russian tank formations pushed on as fast as they could while the surviving defenders simply tried to get to safety. The Russian XVII Tank Corps tried to make up for the time that had been lost achieving the breakthrough, dispatching a tank brigade to race forward to Voloshino and disrupt the German defences before they could coalesce; such exploitation groups rapidly became a feature of Red Army tactics. On 23 December, other elements of Poluboyarov's tank corps helped First Guards Army encircle Millerovo, where much of the German 3rd Mountain Division – one of the formations initially promised to Manstein and endlessly delayed due to its regiments being tied down in fighting elsewhere – had been concentrating. Elsewhere, Badanov's XXIV Tank Corps motored on towards the vital airfields from which the Stalingrad airlift was being conducted, leaving the supporting Russian infantry far behind. At first the advance of the tanks had been delayed by pockets of resistance, particularly near the village of Raskova where a reconnaissance group of three T-70s ran into one of the few German units in the area with adequate anti-tank guns. In moments, two of the tanks had been knocked out. A further probe, this time by T-34s, was also repulsed, forcing XXIV Tank Corps' leading formation, 4th Guards Tank Brigade, to make a time-consuming detour. Even after he found a way past the German strongpoint, Colonel Kopylev, the commander of 4th Guards Tank Brigade, continued to move with too much caution for the likes of XXIV Tank Corps headquarters, and when the neighbouring 130th Tank Brigade reported faster progress, Badanov switched the main axis of advance away from 4th Guards Tank Brigade and this allowed the position at Raskova to be outflanked, opening the way for Kopylev to press forward. Perhaps spurred on by criticism from Badanov, Kopylev now showed greater energy. Early before dawn on 19 December, his tanks overran a German column and swiftly crushed it. The following day, another column of German trucks was overwhelmed.[21]

Through a mixture of breakdowns and enemy action – predominantly in the form of air attacks – the tank corps' strength declined steadily from its initial 160 tanks to fewer than 100, but this was still far more than the entire armoured strength of the Wehrmacht in the area. Despite their losses, Badanov's men had reached Skosyrskaya by 21 December and were within range of Tatsinskaya.[22] Russian bombers attacked the Morozovsk airfield and Fiebig, currently stationed in Tatsinskaya, discussed the situation by telephone with Richthofen. The latter turned down Fiebig's request for an immediate evacuation of Tatsinskaya but advised him to organise whatever ad hoc defences he could. In the meantime, he contacted higher commands for permission to withdraw; when the reply came back from Goering two days later, it was not what he had hoped: Tatsinskaya was to be held at all costs.

The Russian XXV Tank Corps had a somewhat harder time than XXIV Tank Corps and was embroiled in almost continuous combat with a variety of German formations; it succeeded in reaching Uryupin on 23 December, but lacked the strength to advance any further. The infantry support for these armoured elements was frequently held up in running battles with groups of Italian and German soldiers trying to escape. Such actions continued until 26 December, and although large numbers of prisoners were taken and most of the few determined strongpoints that tried to hold out were overrun – Millerovo proved to be a notable exception – other stragglers succeeded in making their way to comparative safety. The capture of Meshkov on 19 December threatened to cut the escape route for many Italian troops withdrawing from the Don, and groups of varying sizes of Italian and German soldiers tried to recapture the town in the following days – although they failed to do so, they tied down the Russian XVIII Tank Corps for two days until Russian infantry arrived to take over the defence of the town. The northern wing of *Armee Abteilung Hollidt* narrowly escaped destruction, with many units breaking and trying to flee while others – all badly worn down in earlier fighting – continued to struggle against the Red Army. On the lower Chir, Fifth Tank Army made further attacks against XLVIII Panzer Corps with as little success as before, but even if the assorted battlegroups and 336th Infantry Division, supported by Balck's 11th Panzer Division, continued to hold the line, they were rapidly being outflanked by the collapse further to the northwest.

Millerovo had been captured by the German 23rd Panzer Division and 71st Infantry Division during the summer advances in 1942 and was an important logistic centre. This applied both for supplies being brought forward and items being sent to the rear, and an area of low-lying ground near the town became the location of a notorious transit camp for Russian prisoners of war. The leading units of 3rd Mountain Division took up defensive positions in Millerovo on

18 December and fought off the first major attempt by Russian tanks to penetrate the northern defences five days later.[23] Together with fragments of other units that retreated into Millerovo, Generalleutnant Hans Kreysing's troops – originally an alpine division of the Austrian Army – fought off repeated attacks by both tanks and infantry, making good use of the stores in the town. The attacking Russians soon reached the abandoned transit camp; although any remaining prisoners had been evacuated, the Russians had no difficulty in finding some of the mass graves of those who had died in German captivity.

The Italian *Pasubio* Semi-Motorised Division had fought well until 19 December when it received orders to pull back to Meshkov. Unaware that the Russian XVIII Tank Corps was already in the town, the Italians found that their diesel vehicles were unusable as they had no winter additive to keep the fuel sufficiently liquid; after the few gasoline-fuelled vehicles had left, the rest of the men set off on foot. Eugenio Corti, an artillery lieutenant, described the scene:

In what was now complete darkness, on the road of beaten snow leading to Meshkov ... the most formidable column of men I had ever encountered was gathering.

There were thousands and thousands of us, dark figures moving across the white road that twisted and turned across the endless wastes of untouched snow.

... we came across one of our 2nd Battery guns that had skidded downhill and off the road. A man had been crushed under the wheels of the gun carriage: he lay on the ground, an oblong heap of dark rags against the white. Together we pulled the gun back up onto the road, and it set off again swinging this way and that behind its tractor.

We resumed our march in the flood of men and vehicles heading south.[24]

The men of the *Pasubio* division struggled on in bitterly cold conditions, encountering Germans from 298th Infantry Division as well as fellow Italians from the *Torino*, *Ravenna*, and *Celere* divisions and men from two of Mussolini's 'Blackshirt Legions', broadly equivalent to the German SA paramilitaries before the war. The column of men gradually become increasingly disordered, with the Germans showing little inclination to help their Italian allies, partly because they blamed the entire catastrophe on the poor combat performance of the allied armies. But, as Corti recorded, the men of his division had few anti-tank weapons or heavy machine-guns, and their light machine-guns were notoriously unreliable in cold weather. The refusal of the Germans to share weapons, rations and fuel with allies they regarded as having failed them created widespread antipathy amongst the Italians. In truth, relations between the Germans and Italians had been relatively poor from the outset, for a variety of reasons. As already described, the Italians were horrified by the behaviour of the Germans towards civilians and prisoners, and it should be remembered that just a generation before, the fathers of these Italian and German soldiers had been on opposing sides during the First World War. One of the battleships of the Italian Navy, *Vittorio Veneto*, bore the name of the battle at which the Italian Army finally achieved victory over the forces of Germany's ally, Austria-Hungary. Nor had the Germans honoured their assurances that they would provide Italian troops on the Eastern Front with modern equipment, particularly anti-tank guns. For their part, the Germans regarded the Italians as poor soldiers with no commitment to the war and little inclination to fight. However, it should be pointed out that on many occasions, Italian troops fought just as hard as their German counterparts, within the limits of what they could achieve with their antiquated weapons. To a large extent, the Germans only had themselves to blame for the poor performance of their allies.

As they laboured closer to Meshkov and realised that the town was already in Russian hands, the soldiers in the column veered away to the west in an attempt to find an alternative escape route. Their line of march was littered with the debris of defeat – broken-down vehicles, dead and dying horses and men, abandoned equipment of every description. In a valley around the village of Arbuzov, they congregated in and around the few buildings available, most of which were commandeered by German troops; the Italians were forced to rest outside in the bitter cold. Officers tried with limited success to reorganise the men into coherent military units and to take up defensive positions against the Russians who appeared to be everywhere, but the exhausted, frozen, starving soldiers continued to slip away from the positions where they were deployed. Nevertheless, the Germans and Italians were able to expand their perimeter on 23–24 December and a confused battle broke out, resulting in losses on both sides. As the fighting died down, Corti returned to Arbuzov:

> The whole valley … seemed to be strewn with the dead. There were also a vast number of wounded. With anguish we felt that we wouldn't be able to take care of them: all of them, or nearly all, were doomed to die within a matter of hours.
>
> Some 'dressing stations' had been created: I particularly remember the one in Arbuzov by the infirmary hut.
>
> The two rooms forming the hut and the stable were now so crammed with men that it was utterly impossible to walk around in them.
>
> The wounded were even lying on top of one another. Even from outside, their

groaning and screaming could be heard – it sounded so small in the terrible cold.

When one of the few soldiers who had devoted himself to looking after them came in with a little water to ease their plight, the groaning was joined by the shouts and oaths of those he inadvertently trod over.

But the most wretched spectacle of all wasn't what we found inside the house, but outside on the ground around it.

Here the snow had been levelled a bit by straw, and on this straw several hundred wounded men were lying.

They had been left in every kind of position by those who had hurriedly brought them there – but they weren't touching each other, so that one could walk among them.

Most of these men kept silent. It must have been between -15 and -20 degrees [Celsius]. Most of them were huddled under wretched blankets that were encrusted with snow and, as usual, as stiff as sheet metal; some had no blankets, and all they had to protect them were their overcoats. Dead men already intermingled with the wounded: their wounds, some of which were monstrous, had been just barely bandaged, and they had been unable to resist the terrible struggle against a conspiracy of loss of blood, hunger and cold.

It was hard to distinguish them from the wounded; both were equally motionless.

One, just one, doctor went the rounds of this vale of tears, exhausted, trying as best he could to treat the men.

Somewhere or other I heard – I can't recall whether it was that day or in the days that followed – that he had been wounded no less than twice by enemy shell splinters while performing amputations with a cutthroat razor.[25]

Having been driven back from the village and surrounding buildings, the Russians started to shell the concentration of stragglers, at first in a desultory manner but then with periodic intensifications. Casualties continued to mount inexorably, particularly when shellfire struck the helpless wounded lying in the open. Occasionally, German aircraft appeared overhead and dropped supplies to the encircled men, but if they managed to reach the supply canisters first, the German soldiers refused to share them with the Italians. Rumours – which proved to have no substance to them – circulated that a German armoured column was on its way to rescue them, but other rumours that the Germans had killed all the Russian prisoners captured during the expansion of the pocket proved to be correct. Equally, Corti encountered an Italian straggler who told him that he had been part of a column of 5,000 Italians captured by the Russians, but that the guards had suddenly fired upon the prisoners and killed most of them.

An Italian officer later related what happened when a column of vehicles from an Italian field hospital ran into Russian troops:

> The most seriously wounded, about 150, were then separated from the rest, herded against an old hut and machine-gunned. The tracks of the powerful T-34s then completed this misdeed by grinding that poor flesh into the ground ... Some 30 officers and soldiers, incapable of standing on their feet, and still lying in an *isba* [Russian hut], were barbarously butchered, and the *isba* itself set fire to. The Russian machine-guns can't have killed them all, though, because as soon as the flames rose we heard cries of desperation which changed into spasmodic screams of agony ...
>
> When they had completed this massacre, the Russians put the survivors into columns ... We walked across the steppe for 14 days, only once receiving a small piece of bread ... During this long march the men escorting us missed no opportunity to display their cruelty. Dozens and dozens of prisoners who were no longer able to follow the column were machine-gunned and their corpses left at the edge of the track to mark the column's sad progress.[26]

It seems that neither side was inclined to show any mercy, though as will be described later, there were many occasions when the Russians treated Italian prisoners far better than German prisoners.

Reinforcements for Army Group B arrived in a trickle. After a summer of heavy combat with Army Group South, 19th Panzer Division had been pulled out of the front line in October and sent to the Orel sector where it was to take up winter quarters, but was then moved to Bryansk where it was once more embroiled in hard combat. With barely a pause for rest or recuperation, it was then extracted from the front line and sent to the Ukraine, forming up on the southern flank of 27th Panzer Division. In order to take command of the remnants of the Italian Eighth Army and the various improvised units that had been created to try to salvage something from the general collapse, Weichs created a new 'army detachment' under the command of General Maximilian Fretter-Pico, who had been commanding XXX Corps in Army Group Centre – together with his headquarters staff, he now tried to bring order to the front, much as Hollidt had the previous month.

The battles that followed are noteworthy examples of how both sides used formations that had been worn down after combat. None of the German units were remotely close to their establishment strength – Balck recorded that his 11th Panzer Division was reduced to just 20 tanks – and the Russian armoured columns were operating at the end of extended supply lines, often with chaotic fighting continuing in their rear. The leading brigade of the Russian XXIV Tank Corps reached Skosyrskaya on 22 December and its first attack into the town was beaten off, not least because so many tanks had broken down or been lost in combat that the brigade lacked the punch to deal with properly organised defences. After regrouping overnight and gathering strength as another tank brigade arrived, another attack was launched the following day. Fierce fighting continued until the evening, when the German 306th Infantry Division finally pulled back. Many of the inhabitants greeted the Russian tank crews with stories of arbitrary civilian executions by the retreating Germans.[27]

Badanov, the commander of XXIV Tank Corps, considered pausing to regroup – his formations were strung out over 60 miles (100km) of snowbound roads. Fuel was taken from disabled tanks and captured German vehicles, but it was of limited use as German tanks had petroleum engines, whereas the pressing need was for diesel fuel. Sufficient supplies reached the leading units to keep them barely mobile and after a brief conference with the commanders of the brigades that were present, Badanov decided to press on rather than wait for all units to catch up, which would have improved tank strength as the following units were meant to be recovering salvageable tanks. Fearing that delay would give the Germans time to recover their balance, he gave his crews just a few hours' rest and then ordered them to push on to Tatsinskaya in the expectation that the leading elements of Third Guards Army would reach the same area within the next few days. The following morning dawned with thick fog as the Russian tanks approached the vital town, shielding them from view, and after a brief but violent bombardment with *Katyusha* rockets, Badanov's force surged forward. Two of his tank brigades attacked the airfield to the south of Tatsinskaya, while the third seized positions to the west. The startled defenders had little chance against the Russian tanks, which raced onto the airfield, firing at ground installations and parked aircraft. In conditions of extremely poor visibility, some pilots tried to get their planes airborne – Fiebig and his staff scrambled aboard one of the last Ju52 transports to leave, and the plane limped with only one functioning engine to Rostov. Within hours the airfield – one of the two main bases for the Stalingrad airlift – was in Russian hands. Of 170 airworthy aircraft on the airfield, 46 were captured or destroyed, and trainloads of supplies were captured both at the airfield and the railway station in Tatsinskaya.[28] There was a darker side to the Russian success – as had been the case in several incidents on both sides, the Russians showed little inclination to take prisoners. Many Luftwaffe ground personnel, wounded men in the airfield hospital, and other German soldiers were executed summarily. Some were deliberately mutilated.

The commander of the infantry battalion of 4th Guards Tank Brigade was Major Nikolai Pavlovich Yudin:

> When we burst into the western part of Tatsinskaya from the Talovsky farm, the Germans jumped out of the houses and fired with automatic weapons and rifles. Amidst the turmoil, I saw a truck towing an anti-tank gun heading west at high speed. The commander of the T-34 tank advancing with us also saw the departing vehicle and fired at it with the main gun, smashing the anti-tank gun and the entire rear of the truck. The surviving fascists threw themselves out of the vehicle. Submachine-gunners ran after them, and I chased one who was wearing a long coat and was separate from the main group of fascists. On the run he shot at me with a pistol and ran past the house. I threw a grenade towards the house, and it exploded as he climbed through the wattle fence. At the same time, the Komsomol of our battalion, Sergeant Nicolai Poloskin, struck the same fascist with a burst of gunfire. Upon reaching the dead man, we saw that he was dressed in a senior officer's uniform with medals. I cut off the officer's epaulettes, took a case full of documents and, after the battle, presented it to the corps commander, Badanov. To my surprise, instead of gratitude I received a big scolding.
>
> 'Why did you kill him?' he said, 'We could have taken a senior officer prisoner!'
>
> I was a bit surprised and taken aback and answered: 'Comrade General, I did not know that he was a senior officer, he was hardly going to show me his documents, he shot at me with a pistol and almost killed me.' After that, Vasily Mikhailovich [Badanov] calmed down.[29]

The appearance of Russian tanks at Tatsinskaya, far to the rear of the forces of *Armee Abteilung Hollidt*, meant that time had finally run out for Hoth's attempt to reach Stalingrad. Whilst Second Guards Army was assembling between the Myshkova and the siege perimeter, Vasilevsky stayed with Malinovsky in the latter's headquarters in Verkhne Tsarinsky, the intended objective of the next push by the German LVII Panzer Corps. To date, stopping the Germans had been the primary objective in this sector, but now it was not enough; as soon as sufficient troops had gathered and in any case no later than 24 December, Vasilevsky wanted Malinovsky to go onto the attack and drive the Germans back towards and through Kotelnikovo. In addition to attacking 6th Panzer Division in its bridgehead at Vasilyevka with I Guards Corps and VII Tank Corps, Second Guards Army was to deploy II Guards Corps and VI Mechanised Corps in an assault against the eastern flank of the German force. It was hoped that this latter attack would fall on Romanian forces and it would be possible for the Russian attackers to move into the rear of LVII Panzer Corps, after which the German armour would be destroyed before it could withdraw.[30]

Whilst preparing for a further advance on 22 December, 6th Panzer Division had to beat off repeated Russian attacks on the bridgehead at Vasilyevka on both sides of the river throughout the preceding night, and by dawn all of the division's panzergrenadiers had been committed to defensive positions. Kirchner visited the division that morning and urged Hünersdorff to advance as planned to Verkhne Tsarinsky. The division's operations officer recorded in his diary:

> The enemy pressure on the bridgehead lasted all day … the forward positions have nevertheless reached the conclusion that, given the situation in the rear and the forces available, a further thrust towards the encirclement is beyond question. Under these circumstances, the desired 'corridor' [down which Sixth Army was meant to withdraw] would merely be the creation of a road along which one could drive into the encirclement but would not be able to return.[31]

Columns of Russian infantry were detected approaching the bridgehead from the north as the Russian Second Guards Army began to step up its pressure, but the timely intervention of Luftwaffe bombers broke up the attack before it could develop. Elements of 23rd Panzer Division reached Birzovoi to the east but, whilst they prevented further pressure on the bridgehead from that direction, they were not strong enough to capture the town or to force another crossing over the Myshkova. It was now increasingly clear to everyone that a further advance towards Stalingrad was impossible, especially when aerial reconnaissance detected the approach of yet more Russian armour as VII Tank Corps moved into position. The arrival of the last elements of *Sturmgeschützabteilung 228* with 40 assault guns provided a welcome increase to the strength of the German forces on the Myshkova, but it was clear that the firepower of the assault guns would be needed to beat off the coming Russian attacks rather than helping in a further advance. Kirchner and Hoth reluctantly abandoned any plans of trying to push on to Stalingrad, ordering 17th Panzer Division to secure Verkhne Kumsky and thus hold open the lines of communication of the troops on the Myshkova. Any last chance for Sixth Army to be rescued was about to disappear.

CHAPTER 7

A DESPERATE CHRISTMAS

Manstein could have no doubt about how bad the overall situation was becoming. As early as 20 December, he had informed *OKH* that the Russians would seek to exploit their breakthrough in the Italian Eighth Army's sector to press on first to the Donets and then to Rostov, thus guaranteeing the isolation and ultimate destruction of both Army Group Don and Army Group A. He received no response – according to his memoirs, Hitler was busy with *OKW* leaders in discussions with the Italians and was unavailable to give permission for any changes. It was surely the last possible chance for Sixth Army. If it was to escape, an order for an immediate breakout was needed before LVII Panzer Corps was driven back – there was little prospect of it staying on the Myshkova if its eastern flank came under sustained pressure, and even if the bridgehead could be held, the Russian advances towards the Donets rendered all else irrelevant. At *OKH*, Zeitzler made one last attempt:

> [I tried] to explain how desperate everyone was, how hungry, how they were losing trust in the high command, how the wounded were succumbing and freezing. But none of it made any impression on Hitler.[1]

As an act of solidarity, Zeitzler had put himself on the same rations as the encircled men in Stalingrad. He lost weight drastically, and when Hitler finally noticed he irritably ordered Zeitzler to desist.

By the evening of 23 December, Manstein concluded that he could no longer wait for Hitler either to allow Paulus to abandon Stalingrad or to send reinforcements to stop the Russian forces threatening to bypass Hollidt and thereafter isolate the entire southern wing of the German position on the Eastern Front. For weeks, he had been asking that 16th Motorised Division, the sole unit covering the vast gap between the southern flank of Army Group Don and Army Group A in the Caucasus, should be relieved by an infantry division from the latter army group – this would have provided vital additional firepower for LVII Panzer Corps. On 20 December, *OKH* had finally ordered SS Panzergrenadier Division *Viking* to the area in order to release 16th Motorised Division, but this move would take at least ten days, far too long to make any difference. With a heavy heart, Manstein was forced to reshuffle the forces available to him. Balck's 11th Panzer Division had been holding the line of the lower Chir for all of December and it was now ordered north to deal with the Russian forces approaching Tatsinskaya. This would leave XLVIII Panzer Corps exposed, so Manstein had no choice but to ask Hoth to release a panzer division from LVII Panzer Corps in order to replace Balck's troops. Aware of the scale of the crisis to the north and the impossibility of holding on any longer for Sixth Army to break out, Hoth ordered his best formation – 6th Panzer Division – to pull out and move to XLVIII Panzer Corps' area. Manstein informed Paulus of the development in a brief signal late in the afternoon of 23 December, concluding with the words: 'You can draw your own conclusions about the consequences of this on further cooperation with you.'[2]

In his account of events, Adam – Paulus' adjutant – repeatedly states that Army Group Don did not make the overall situation clear to Paulus and kept him in the dark about developments elsewhere – the implication is that had Paulus known what was happening, he might have acted differently. Whilst Manstein might not have given detailed information to Paulus about the collapse of the Italians and other troop movements, it should be remembered that Sixth Army had its own *OKH* liaison officer who was in radio contact with Zeitzler's staff, so it is hard to imagine that Paulus and Schmidt were completely in the dark. In any event, it rather begs the question: what difference would any such knowledge have made? Paulus repeatedly told Adam that he felt bound by Hitler's orders and could not contemplate direct disobedience. This applied equally to the order to hold onto Stalingrad and to any later thoughts of surrender. Even if he had been completely aware of the developments elsewhere, Paulus' record suggests that his conduct would have been exactly the same.

Regardless of how much information about the overall situation was passed to Paulus, either by Army Group Don or *OKH*, any lingering doubts about the success or failure of *Winter Storm* were now gone. The daily exchanges between Manstein and Hitler took on an increasingly surreal tone: Hitler promised to send 7th Panzer Division as reinforcements, but Manstein pointed out that it would arrive far too late to save Sixth Army; Hitler countered by speculating whether the new *Schwere Panzer Abteilungen* – heavy tank battalions equipped with the new Tiger tank – would swing the balance back in Germany's favour, and Manstein was left wondering what possible difference one or two battalions of a new combat vehicle, still going through its teething process, might make. On the battlefield, Hollidt rushed whatever units he could scrape together to the aid of 306th Infantry Division at the northern end of his battered line, and several of his staff officers took on the task of bringing order to the retreating stragglers and sending them back into action. The first elements of 6th Panzer Division had been dispatched from the Myshkova late on 23 December and the rest of the division withdrew south of the river the following day, destroying the bridge and thus ending the brief life of the precarious bridgehead – given the threats to either flank of Fourth Panzer Army and the apparent inability of Sixth Army to make a breakout attempt in a realistic timescale, there was nothing to be gained by continuing to expose the few mobile elements of Army Group Don to possible encirclement and destruction. It was little consolation to the disheartened men of 6th Panzer Division that it was announced that Hünersdorff had been awarded the Knight's Cross in recognition of his conduct in the recent fighting.

Even if 6th Panzer Division had not been forced to leave the Myshkova bridgehead in order to deal with the critical situation further north, it is likely that it would have been driven back. With all its forces now assembled, the Russian Second Guards Army was ready to attack, and Koshevoi's 24th Guards Rifle Division was ordered to advance and recapture Verkhne Kumsky as part of the western flank of the Russian advance. On 22 December, 24th Guards Rifle Division and the neighbouring 300th Rifle Division beat off attempts by 17th Panzer Division to destroy the enclave that Koshevoi had established at Nizhne Kumsky, and the following day the Russians launched their own attack, swiftly advancing to Verkhne Kumsky and showing rather more tactical acumen than they had in their first attack across the Myshkova:

> We attacked the enemy in Verkhne Kumsky around noon, while simultaneously bypassing the farmstead to the east and west. The battle lasted four hours and was stubborn and bloody. The enemy fought for every house. Many of his tanks, because of a lack of fuel or damage to the running gear, were buried in the ground and used as armoured fire points. They were relatively simple to counter: we engaged them with direct fire and anti-tank grenades. The enemy was unable to repel the attack of the guardsmen and withdrew from Verkhne Kumsky to the south with losses.[3]

North of the Don, the ordeal of the retreating Italian troops continued. Some retreating elements had reached the comparative safety of the fragile new front line, where attempts were being made to dispatch help. Lieutenant Carlo Vicentini was told to return to Krinichnoye, a small village further east, with two ambulances to evacuate the wounded soldiers who had gathered there. With a young driver, the officer set off on the night of Christmas Day, finally reaching an improvised aid station near Krinichnoye:

> The dirt floor was covered with wounded men; bandaged heads, legs, hands; dead men covered with greatcoats; pale faces, feverish eyes; Italians and also many Germans. In a shed at some distance, two doctors covered with blood were working around a table.[4]

The two ambulances were fitted out to take two stretchers each, but Vicentini managed to squeeze eight men into the back of each vehicle and another two into each cab. When they attempted to leave, the ambulances were surrounded by other desperate wounded men, and Vicentini was only able to drive off after promising to return as many times as necessary to evacuate everyone. When he unloaded the wounded in Rossosh, he was told that the ambulances were needed in another sector, but managed to get permission to return to Krinichnoye with one vehicle.

> I will never be able to forget what we saw as we drove around the bend in the road. The shed didn't exist any more. Fragments of wood and sheet metal were scattered all over the place, along with body parts, and burned rags containing shapeless objects. There was an enormous black mark on the ground ... A group of *Alpini* sought in vain for any signs of life in that apocalyptic scene.[5]

Vicentini found some of the wounded who had been in the hut where the doctors were working were still alive and loaded them all into his ambulance. As they returned to Rossosh, both Vicentini and his young driver wept uncontrollably. In addition to the wounded, Vicentini wrote, the ambulance 'carried two men, each with a terrible wound that would never heal. And every Christmas that same wound reopened.'[6]

North of Tatsinskaya, 11th Panzer Division moved into action with its customary energy and speed. Although he had only 20 tanks and a weak panzergrenadier battalion with him, Balck had been able to bring the bulk of the division's artillery to the new sector, and rather than wait for the rest of the division

– which in any case would not amount to a major increase in combat strength – he attacked early on 24 December. The German column swiftly recaptured Skosyrskaya after a sharp battle with the Russians, thus isolating the rest of Badanov's tank corps. Balck directed the rest of his division still en route to march on Tatsinskaya and his signals battalion picked up a radio message from Badanov ordering all of XXIV Tank Corps' remaining tanks to converge on a nearby hill.

Some elements of Raus' division managed to snatch a brief rest in the town of Potemkinskaya on Christmas Eve, where a bridge across the Don had been assembled, and drank a small ration of mulled wine while they listened to Christmas carols played by the division's band:

> How fortunate for these soldiers who were able to experience the evening of Christmas Eve in the midst of the battles of 1942. From here to an area north of Vienna in May 1945 [where the division finally surrendered] there were still a few years of defence and attack, of counterthrust and retreat, of victory and setback to endure, if any had the good fortune to remain with the division for such a long time. And it was also good that none who listened to carols in the regimental chapel on the Don knew that with the withdrawal from the Myshkova the long march towards home had definitively started.
>
> And Stalingrad? It was clear to all members of the division that evening that it had been finally lost.[7]

Throughout Christmas Day, Balck pressed the Russians into a tighter pocket as the first elements of 6th Panzer Division began to arrive – the reconnaissance battalion, the assault guns of *Sturmgeschützabteilung 228*, a company of the anti-tank battalion, and an anti-aircraft battery. The rest of the division deployed in and around Morozovsk, some elements not arriving until the following day. In the meantime, the leading elements were subordinated to Balck's 11th Panzer Division for an assault on the encircled Russians at Tatsinskaya. Struggling through the snow, the Russian infantry was still labouring to reach Tatsinskaya in time to support Badanov, as Colonel Gavril Stanislavovich Zdanovich, commander of 203rd Rifle Division, later recalled:

> It was a tough march – suffice it to say that the normal daily march of the division in good conditions weather was 30km [18 miles]. Now we had to cover 45–50km each day on foot!
>
> There was a severe frost. A piercing wind was blowing. In numerous dells and ravines, the roads disappeared into continuous snowdrifts and the soldiers

sometimes had to carry tools and equipment literally on their shoulders. In addition there were defeated enemy units moving in parallel to our columns to the south. Their paths often crossed the division's route and they set up ambushes in populated areas, firing on our columns. This, of course, delayed the advance. And German aircraft were active overhead.

When we approached the village of Skosyrskaya we found that it was defended by a large force ...

After giving the division a short rest and determining the enemy's positions, I ordered an assault without artillery preparation or waiting for more ammunition to be delivered. I knew that I was acting contrary to current rules, but the situation required it.

Two regiments – the 592nd and 619th – attacked the southern outskirts of the Grinev farm. As soon as the Nazis noticed them, 15 tanks with infantry mounted on them rushed there from Skosyrskaya at high speed. Our companies lay in the snow and opened fire. Approaching to within 500m, the enemy infantry dismounted and advanced supported by shellfire from the tanks. But the aim of our anti-tank guns was perfect: in just a few minutes, four tanks were burning on the field. The rest couldn't continue and began to withdraw into cover.

Having repulsed the counterattack, my regiments again went onto the offensive. And again up to 20 tanks with mounted infantry came from the village to attack us. The battle dragged on until dark. At dusk it could clearly be seen that several more enemy vehicles were ablaze.

... It was clear that the Nazis would not easily yield their positions. They would not give up because this was the most direct route to Rostov.

At night, both sides stopped their attacks and on the morning of 29 December my regiments again went on the offensive. And again without artillery preparation: there had not yet been time to deliver ammunition. It remained on the Don, and there was no fuel to move it.

Instead of taking up the defensive, the fascists rushed into the oncoming battle. At high speed, tanks reappeared: five, ten, 15, 20. Only 11 shells remained in the battery of Lieutenant Makarenko from the 592nd [Anti-Tank] Regiment. 'Don't rush, guys!' He shouted. 'Just one shot for each armoured target!' The first shot missed. 'The first gun's crew is to leave the gun and repulse the enemy infantry attack with small arms fire,' the lieutenant calmly commanded: he gave all the shells to a better crew. 'Fire!' The enemy tank shuddered and stopped. Gradually, acrid black smoke began to rise above it. 'Fire!' And the second tank was set on fire! 'It's all on target!' cried the excited lieutenant. Meanwhile, the artillerymen of the third crew fired well-aimed shots with their anti-tank rifles.

Not far from Makarenko's battery, Sergeant Tyrashchenko worked dispassionately. The Ukrainian behaved as if he knew no fear. Aiming at an enemy vehicle about 200m away, he fired an accurate shot from his anti-tank rifle and the tank was hit ... he killed a second tank. Then an armoured car. Gunners Norzulaev and Kinzhanov disabled another three tanks ... Thus, the division's soldiers successfully repulsed all attacks outside Skosyrskaya and inflicted heavy losses on the fascists. But in our ranks shells and cartridges were almost completely used up.[8]

Like so many accounts written by the soldiers of both sides, this description records an improbable number of enemy tanks destroyed in the action, and it is likely that some – particularly those knocked out by anti-tank guns – were half-tracks, as it was not common practice for German infantry to attack riding on the backs of tanks, and anti-tank rifles would be almost ineffective against the frontal armour of any tanks belonging to 11th Panzer Division that remained operational. But regardless of any exaggeration, the reality was that the Russian infantry could get no closer to Tatsinskaya than the village of Skosyrskaya, whether this was due to the strength of German resistance or ammunition shortages in the Russian ranks. Badanov would have to fight on alone.

Originally, Balck had intended to carry out an attack to recapture Tatsinskaya on 26 December but *Sturmgeschützabteilung 228* was slow to assemble due to fuel shortages, and without its firepower he lacked the strength to deal with Badanov's forces. On 27 December, he finally began the assault, making only modest progress. To the northeast, Hünersdorff beat off a Russian infantry force that was attempting to advance towards Tatsinskaya by slipping past the flank of the blocking force at Skorsyrskaya. In Tatsinskaya, Badanov carefully assessed the strength of his remaining forces. He had 57 T-34s and 32 T-70s, with another ten tanks undergoing repairs. In addition, he had a mortar regiment, the artillery and an infantry battalion of 24th Motorised Rifle Brigade, approximately a battalion of infantry who had ridden into combat on the backs of the tanks, and a company of combat engineers. It might be a substantial force, particularly in terms of tanks, but ammunition was desperately short – between them, the tanks had only about 250 rounds for their main armament.[9]

The remnants of the Italian Eighth Army were still struggling to escape. Late on 24 December, concluding that there was no armoured column on its way to them, the mixed Italian and German troops gathered in and around Arbuzov set off on foot. Corti and perhaps 1,500 others were left behind, sleeping in whatever shelter they could find and unaware that the escape attempt had begun. As the Russians moved in, Corti and other officers tried to get the remaining men moving towards the southwest, in the direction that the rest of the column had travelled. Even as the Russians overwhelmed the small pocket, Corti managed to catch up with the main column and the slow retreat continued with the German soldiers leading, the Italians following. On Christmas Day, Corti came across further evidence of the pitiless nature of the fighting near a wrecked German truck:

> Some partisans had fired at the truck, setting fire to its precious cargo of gasoline. They had been surrounded in a house, and taken alive – six or seven of them in all. The Germans had doused them in the flaming liquid, then left them like that.
>
> Eyewitnesses told me that the poor wretches had started running and leaping about, screaming helplessly. They had then ripped off their flaming clothes and thrust themselves completely naked into some pools that appeared through the ice on the stream's surface and had gone on screaming until they were dead.
>
> … As for the Russians … when all is said, they were certainly no less murderous than the Germans.[10]

Like many regular army officers, Corti had regarded the Blackshirt battalions with contempt, but their conduct during the retreat forced him into a reappraisal. Their officers remained with them on foot, leading by example, and they showed a willingness to fight their way to freedom – by contrast, many of the officers of the regular army had vanished, leaving their men to fend for themselves. By the end of Christmas Day, the tattered column had reached a village about 24 miles (40km) from Millerovo. Here, Corti fell asleep through exhaustion and awoke to find that, as had been the case in Arbuzov, the main column had left; rounding up the remaining troops in the village, he set off in pursuit, catching up before dawn. Daylight on 26 December brought them to a village that was in Russian hands, and the Germans in the column led an assault to wipe out the Russian infantry. Occasionally under fire, the group continued across the countryside, hoping that Millerovo remained in German hands; unaware that the column had veered to the north, away from Millerovo, they reached Chertkovo early on 27 December. Corti estimated that about 30,000 Italian troops had commenced the retreat, but only 8,000 entered Chertkovo. The rest had either died of exhaustion, cold and wounds, or had been taken prisoner. Here, finally, there was a semblance of order; the town contained a supply depot and the exhausted men were able to get new clothing and the first proper meal since their ordeal had started. In theory at least, Corti and those with him had escaped encirclement in that Chertkovo had communications still open to the west, but over the next three days, as the exhausted men rested and tried to recover their strength, the front line moved again and they were once more isolated.

The utter unreality of Paulus' requirement for six days' preparation time prior to a breakout was underlined by the events on the Myshkova. With the forces of Malinovsky's Second Guards Army now fully deployed, the Russians increased the force of their attacks, with VII Tank Corps attacking in strength on 24 December and forcing a withdrawal from the Myshkova. By the end of Christmas Day, Saliyevsky was under heavy Russian fire. Regardless of his orders to-hold his forward positions as long as possible, Hoth had no choice but to allow his hard-pressed troops to withdraw towards Kotelnikovo. In Verkhne Kumsky, the Russian rifle divisions of I Guards Rifle Corps paused for just one day to recover their breath and bring forward supplies before resuming their advance, and 17th Panzer Division, supported by what remained of a Romanian infantry division, could do little to stop them – even if they managed to hold any given point, the Germans and Romanians lacked the numbers to maintain a continuous defensive line and it was always possible for the Russians to outflank them. When describing the fighting, Koshevoi acknowledged the casualties that his men suffered, but felt that compared with the desperate battles of earlier months, the fact that they were almost always advancing greatly helped the morale of his men:

> Although many were bleeding and comrades were dying, we moved towards the goal unceasingly and unshakably. We advanced day and night, fighting battles, smashing the infantry, artillery and tanks of the Hitlerites and their allies. We decisively attacked the evil enemy.
>
> We had become sufficiently experienced and mature warriors and held in our hands the new weapons that the heroic workers of our country had given us. Now the Soviet bullet sped towards the enemy everywhere. In the air, we no longer conceded to the fascists either in speed or in the maneuverability of the aircraft. Our pilots shot down German aviators, and smoky plumes from enemy vehicles regularly arose in the frosty sky. The soldiers followed them with their eyes, remembering the beginning of the war. Those bitter times were a thing of the past. This was a great turning point.[11]

Despite their clear successes, the infantry of I Guards Rifle Corps felt that they were inadequately supported by their armoured formations. In a chance meeting with Vasilevsky at the corps headquarters, Koshevoi raised this issue and was advised by his corps commander to contact the tank units directly in order to improve coordination. The Russian VII Tank Corps reached the eastern outskirts of Kotelnikovo on 27 December but it in turn complained of a lack of infantry support – II Guards Mechanised Corps should have been operating close behind but was still held up on the line of the Aksay, west of Saliyevsky. Aware of the weakness of Hoth's army, Malinovsky directed VI Mechanised Corps to bypass the town, while III Guards Mechanised Corps and XIII Mechanised Corps were ordered to strike even deeper in the rear of the German positions and to attack Zavetnoe, over 50 miles (80km) further to the southeast. VII Tank Corps and I Guards Rifle Corps were to take Kotelnikovo together.

Still trying to improve cooperation with the neighbouring tank units, Koshevoi finally managed to make personal contact with Rotmistrov, commander of VII Tank Corps, near an airfield to the west of Kotelnikovo. Rotmistrov's tanks had failed in their first attempt to take Kotelnikovo by storm, as he later wrote:

> From my command post, I watched the progress of our tanks and saw that the leading KV-1 stopped, then two T-34s started to burn, followed by a T-70. My frustration can be imagined. I ordered the crews to withdraw from the zone of enemy anti-tank fire immediately. But one of the battalions of 3rd Guards Tank Brigade broke through to Hill 84.0 and crushed the firing positions of the enemy anti-tank batteries there. There was thus a gap in the enemy defences, into which rushed a tank and motorised rifle battalion of the same brigade. However, the Hitlerites again brought down on them powerful artillery and mortar fire directly from the outskirts of Kotelnikovo. Even German aviation appeared, making a series of bombing runs against our combat formations.[12]

Rotmistrov told Koshevoi that his tanks were unable to penetrate into the town due to German anti-tank defences, and Koshevoi promised to support the attack with his men. The Luftwaffe units that had supported the German defenders had also reported on the strength of the gathering Russian forces around the town and, rather than get tied down in a defensive battle that he could not win, Kirchner decided to abandon Kotelnikovo. The defenders withdrew to the west on 29 December, leaving the town in the hands of the Russians – in only five days, all the hard-won gains of the German relief effort were gone and even their starting positions had been lost. Even if, by some miracle, LVII Panzer Corps had been able to link up with Sixth Army, it is questionable how many of Paulus' hungry troops could have escaped such an onslaught.[13]

The long flanks of Fourth Panzer Army had been obvious targets for the Russian armoured columns, and the Romanian divisions tasked with defending them proved once again that their ability to resist tank attacks was very limited. Manstein was critical of the commanders of the Romanian VI and VII Corps for failing to sustain their men's morale, but without better armaments it is difficult to see what they could have achieved. The morale of the Romanian troops had been dealt an irreparable blow during *Uranus* and they fell back in disarray at the first appearance of Russian tanks. Manstein ordered their withdrawal from the front line.[14]

Vasilevsky visited Kotelnikovo shortly after VII Tank Corps captured the town, and it is worth remembering that, whilst the Germans were dealing with the consequences of their failure to reach Stalingrad, the same events were a great cause for joy in the Red Army:

> It was a magnificent starry night. Pure moonlight streamed down on the frost-bound steppe. Here and there in the darkened houses of Kotelnikovo gleamed a cigarette end or a cigarette lighter. Occasionally I could catch the short rat-tat-tat of a machine-gun in the distance. I breathed in lungfuls of the good wintry air of my homeland. Victory filled my heart with joy, and the breeze from the not so distant Caspian burned my cheeks and seemed somehow to herald fresh big successes for us in the near future.[15]

In view of its successes in the operations of Second Guards Army, Rotmistrov's VII Tank Corps was renamed III Guards Tank Corps shortly after the capture of Kotelnikovo. For Rotmistrov, it was a bittersweet moment; he was justly proud of the efforts of his men, but his nephew Petr Leonidovich Rotmistrov was amongst the dead in the fighting for Kotelnikovo.

Despite the setbacks between Kotelnikovo and the Myshkova, Manstein had not completely dismissed the possibility of still being able to reach Stalingrad. On 26 December, he had a meal with Richthofen and the two men shared their frustrations. Richthofen noted in his diary:

> We both complained together. Manstein suggested that the Reichsmarschall himself [Goering] should assume command of both the army group and *Luftflotte IV*, since he always claims that the situation here or at Stalingrad is not as bad as we report. Our motto: 'Assign the confident commander to the post he is confident of fulfilling!' The Führer now refuses to speak to Manstein by telephone, to summon him to his headquarters, or to come out here himself.[16]

On the same day, Manstein sent a signal to *OKH* with several key requests. Firstly, the situation on his army group's northern wing had to be stabilised by the transfer of further reinforcements, including 7th Panzer Division, promised for Fourth

Panzer Army by Hitler but unable to arrive in time to make a difference. Secondly, the German Seventeenth Army in the Caucasus needed to send an infantry division to Rostov in order to safeguard the lines of communication of Fourth Panzer Army and all of Army Group A. Thirdly, Manstein still believed that if sufficient strength could be concentrated in Fourth Panzer Army, the Russian Second Guards Army and Fifty-First Army could be defeated and driven back and a second relief attempt made. To that end, he wanted III Panzer Corps and an additional infantry division transferred from Army Group A, together with 16th Motorised Division from its long vigil at Elista, between Army Group Don and Army Group A. If these forces could be gathered within the next week, there was sufficient time to fly adequate food and fuel to Sixth Army to overcome Paulus' objections to mounting any attacks from within the encirclement, though clearly this would fall far short of the 4,000 tons previously described.[17]

Such redeployments would have major consequences. The transfer of so much strength from Army Group A would mean that it was highly unlikely that the Germans would be able to remain in the Caucasus. For Manstein, a withdrawal from the Caucasus had long been inevitable – the presence of German troops there was predicated upon a strong presence on the Volga, and if a column were able to reach Stalingrad, there was not the remotest possibility of Sixth Army staying where it was. Indeed, Manstein's new proposal accepted that it was highly likely that much of Sixth Army would be destroyed during a breakout and retreat, but at least something might be saved. Given Hitler's refusal to countenance the abandonment of any territory, it can hardly have come as a surprise when *OKH* advised Manstein that Army Group A could not afford to release the required troops. However, Zeitzler was of exactly the same opinion as Manstein, Hoth, Weichs and Richthofen with regard to the situation on the Eastern Front, despite being surrounded by the likes of Jodl and Keitel, who clearly believed Hitler's assertions that Stalingrad could be held through the winter and Sixth Army could somehow be kept alive. Late on 27 December, Zeitzler faced Hitler again and made a further appeal for the withdrawal of Army Group A, concluding his presentation with a stark warning: 'Unless you order a withdrawal from the Caucasus now, we shall soon have a second Stalingrad on our hands.'[18]

The situation had deteriorated to a level where even Hitler could no longer procrastinate, and after a brief pause, he gave his approval. As soon as he returned to his office, Zeitzler issued the orders by telephone, instructing his staff that they were to be passed to Army Group A immediately; it was a wise precaution. Within moments, he received a message to telephone Hitler, who told him to take no action until the morning. Zeitzler advised the Führer that it was too late, and Hitler had no choice but to leave the matter as it was. By his swift action, Zeitzler almost certainly avoided a further round of prevarication and delay.

Manstein was informed on 31 December that the armoured formations of the SS were to be concentrated as the SS Panzer Corps – later renamed II SS Panzer Corps – near Kharkov; from there, Hitler advised that they would mount a new relief effort. However, the limitations of the railways meant that it would take until early February before this force could possibly be ready. Manstein's opinion of this was typically blunt and uncompromising:

How Sixth Army was to be kept alive in the meantime was not stated ... There was no basis whatever for assuming that the forces of the SS Panzer Corps would ever suffice to carry an offensive as far as Stalingrad. What might well have been achieved over the relatively short distance of 80 miles [133km] from Kotelnikovo to Stalingrad in December, when the reinforcement of Fourth Panzer Army had been entirely feasible, could only be regarded as sheer fantasy in February, when it was a matter of covering 350 miles [580km] from Kharkov ...

When Hitler rejected all of Army Group Don's requests for the speedy reinforcement of Fourth Panzer Army at the end of December, the fate of Sixth Army was finally sealed.[19]

In reality, the fate of Sixth Army had been sealed long before.

At Tatsinskaya, the Russian 24th Motorised Rifle Brigade succeeded in fighting its way past 11th Panzer Division and linked up with Badanov's encircled troops. Balck was acutely aware that the Russians in the town outnumbered his force; however, he would also have known from monitoring their radio nets that the Russians were desperately short of fuel and ammunition – 24th Motorised Brigade had only its own modest ammunition stocks, and little to spare for the forces already in Tatsinskaya. On 26 December, elements of 6th Panzer Division began to deploy west of the town, as an NCO in 6th Panzer Division's 4th Panzergrenadier Regiment later recorded:

Thus, after two days on the road and covering a good 300km [180 miles] from the Myshkova, we reached the area of Tatsinskaya on the day after Christmas. The temperature the preceding day remained below freezing, and during the night fell to 20°C below. A strong, icy wind blew from the east. Many vehicles of our company were already showing signs of wear after their journey across the Don; some were being towed and others were greatly delayed. Nevertheless, although some were still absent despite their best efforts, we went straight into an attack towards Tatsinskaya.

The trucks – we were only a panzergrenadier regiment in name [i.e. they were not mounted in half-tracks] and had Renaults as vehicles – were left behind in a hollow and we trudged forward accompanied by assault guns on a very broad front. Other companies were alongside us, also spread far and wide. The snow was 30cm (1ft) deeper than south of the Don.

There wasn't much of the enemy to be seen. The first fighting came after 5km [3 miles] between the assault guns and enemy anti-tank guns and tanks. We could only advance laboriously, often lying in the snow rather than moving, and as darkness fell we came to a halt behind a hill. We apparently had no contact to right or left and we feared that once again we would have to spend a night on the steppe, hungry and shivering.

Finally, we found a village in a small valley to one side, free of the Russians and occupied by another of our companies.

Just as we were about to set off to deploy again the following morning there was the shout 'Tanks!' As a sentry had apparently fallen asleep, they were already in the village and at first there was chaos. Lacking any other targets, the tanks fired with their main guns at individual men and everyone hustled to find some cover. Here too we saw that those who were the first to be killed were those who lost their heads, took their eyes off the enemy, and sought safety purely in fleeing. But we also had to defend ourselves against enemy infantry that had dismounted amongst the tanks.

Finally our anti-tank guns intervened and the first tank went up in flames. Then Oberleutnant Herwig from our 7 Company damaged one with a magnetic mine. His attempt at a second failed and sadly he was killed in the attempt. Slowly we gained the upper hand and were able to drive the enemy from the village.[20]

On the same day, the Russians in Tatsinskaya received a morale-boosting message: in recognition of its achievements, XXIV Tank Corps was renamed II Guards Tank Corps, and Badanov was awarded the Order of Suvorov 2nd Class. At the end of the day, they received rather more practical help – a small airdrop of ammunition, though barely enough to replace what had been used during the day's fighting.

During 27 December, the panzergrenadiers probed into the outskirts of Tatsinskaya and were briefed in the evening that they were to attack the town during the night, supported once more by the assault guns:

For most of us it was our first major night action, and that too in a town. Personally, I have to say that I much preferred fighting in a built-up area to an attack across an open field. At least here we would find more cover and one could work forwards from house to house, throwing hand grenades through windows and waiting for their detonations.

We set off at 2000 (2200 local time). To our left was 7th Company. The attack began at 2300. We formed a long firing line. Shots soon rang out barely 150m ahead of us – machine-guns. The first men fell. A scouting group moved forward and disappeared into the darkness. We followed slowly and after a while reached a deep trench behind which we could make out the first houses on the edge of Tatsinskaya. To our horror, we found many dead German soldiers in the trench, apparently from when the Russians arrived three days previously.

To our left, some assault guns were fighting Russian tanks. We took up positions on this side of the trench. We heard shots in front of us; it was probably our scouting group. Then they appeared; they had brought some Russian trucks to a standstill with their fire as they withdrew. Some of our men had been wounded. We could now hear enemy tanks in front of us and could see a few, perhaps only 50m away. We stood ready for another attack, tried to link up with our neighbours, summoned the assault guns and agreed how to proceed.

But before we could, we heard a clatter in front of us. The enemy tanks were pulling back. We could soon see that there were only weak enemy forces before us. The Russians were giving up the town and pulling out. To where?[21]

Badanov had drawn up plans for a possible breakout in the event of further Russian reinforcements failing to reach him. The first option was a withdrawal broadly along the route that his men had followed to reach Tatsinskaya, but it was clear that this was now blocked by German armour at Skosyrskaya. The second option required his remaining men to head towards the northwest; whilst the distance they would have to travel to reach friendly forces was further, this route had a better likelihood of success as it did not lead directly through strongly held German positions. Early on 28 December, Badanov ordered his remaining mobile elements to commence the operation. The leading formation was 4th Guards Tank Brigade, and it soon ran into German anti-tank guns; two tanks were set ablaze almost immediately as fighting erupted. Badanov promptly dispatched his chief of staff to take command of the engagement, while 26th Guards Tank Brigade was ordered to find a way past the flank of the German defences. As 4th Guards Tank Brigade attempted to force its way through, another two tanks were lost, but in confused fighting the Russians found gaps in the German line and, breaking off the battle as rapidly as they could, managed to escape in the darkness.[22]

Balck calculated that perhaps a dozen tanks and 30 trucks succeeded in escaping; according to Burdeyny, Badanov's chief of staff, the three tank brigades of the corps had between them 42 tanks when they reached Russian lines, though this would have included previously disabled vehicles that were now recovered on the line of march.[23] The rest of II Guards Tank Corps was destroyed as 11th Panzer Division's regiments recaptured the town and then proceeded rapidly to Skosyrskaya where they overwhelmed the leading elements of the Russian 203rd Rifle Division, which was still trying to break through and march to Badanov's aid. Although the Germans could claim a tactical victory by recovering Tatsinskaya, Badanov's men had fulfilled their mission despite their losses. The already inadequate airlift to Stalingrad had been badly disrupted and a vital airfield knocked out; in future, Luftwaffe flights would have to be made from further away, reducing the number of operations possible each day.

The front line began to stabilise a little. German reinforcements helped shore up the fragments of units that had escaped the destruction of the Italian Eighth Army, and the aggressive intervention of 6th and 11th Panzer Divisions brought the southward exploitation of the breakthrough to an abrupt halt. On 27 December, 6th Panzer Division had made radio contact with the headquarters of the German XXIX Corps, which – with three Italian divisions under its command – had been part of the Italian Eighth Army and had been retreating for days with a mixed group of about 5,500 men, most of them Italians. The following day, the panzer division's reconnaissance battalion was able to reach the 'roaming pocket' and bring the survivors to safety.[24] Whilst Tatsinskaya had been recaptured, the Russian forces in the area still threatened to advance upon the nearby airfield at Morozovsk, and reducing this force now became a priority. Attempts by the division to push back the Russians to the northeast of Morozovsk met with mixed success, as a panzer company commander later wrote:

> It was still dark when we took up positions ready for a counterthrust south of the road to Skosyrskaya, west of the village of Novo Nikolayev. The final discussions took place there between my commander, Major Bäke, Oberst Unrein who was commander of 4th Panzergrenadier Regiment, and the commander of 11th Panzer Division's panzer regiment. While elements of 11th Panzer Division were to encircle from the west the enemy who had broken through, we together with the panzergrenadiers of Remlinger's battalion were to advance northwards and reoccupy the lost ground. I had arrived the previous day in Novo Marievka from

Kotelnikovo via Tsimlianskaya with replacement tanks from our workshops and had taken over several more tanks of my battalion there, and using the rear area elements of my company had assembled a bunch with representatives of almost every company of the battalion.

Thus, I led 15 tanks against the enemy. The terrain, particularly to the west of me, was quite flat to the skyline, with the village of Nikolayev about 3km away, and beyond it running to right and left there was a substantial ridge and the northern bank of the Bystraya river running from east to west. We set off somewhat echeloned with the encircling attack by 11th Panzer Division. The enemy before us was swiftly driven back. He seemed weaker than expected. Actually, it was just his picket line. Soon though we came under increasing anti-tank fire from the high ground; we also spotted tanks there. We could only hit them with our not exactly numerous Pz.IVs with their long 75mm guns.

At the same time the plain around us began to be splattered with heavy mortar fire. It was like the beginning of a heavy rainstorm on a smooth surface. It seemed particularly strong to me as the ground was so improbably flat and white and one could see a long way without hindrance. I had the feeling that I was on an ice sheet on the sea in my tank.

This was the point at which the unprotected panzergrenadiers, who until now had been able to follow at the speed of the tanks, were forced to halt. I had a decision to make: should I slow down to the pace of the panzergrenadiers, or should I attack further on my own? If the former, we would be left scattered on the plain and over time would be shot up one after the other, but if the latter, I might be able to overrun and destroy the mortar positions, or at least penetrate to a section of their second line of defence and thus reach the protection of the village that lay before me. From there, with better cover, I could engage the enemy on the nearby high ground from effective range.

After a brief conversation with Hauptmann Remlinger, the commander of the infantry forces, and after reporting my conclusions to my commander, I gave the order to attack. At that moment I took an anti-tank hit in my engine which forced me to switch to another tank. On this occasion I chose a Pz.IV, on the one hand for its radio equipment, which was better suited for command, and also in order to fire personally on the tanks on the high ground. It isn't always right, as the leader of a panzer company should primarily lead and fight as a secondary consideration. But which other company commander would criticise this? The love of the hunt often ran through us and, so long as it was only to a limited extent, it was acceptable.

We rapidly reached the village, since everyone was clear that we had to rush forwards. Here we smashed up all manner of things, destroyed a few anti-tank guns and also took prisoners. We were also able to shoot up the tanks on the heights, as the rising columns of black smoke showed. It was a still, sunny and cold day.

But the panzergrenadiers didn't follow us; I couldn't blame them, as there was still heavy fire on the plain, which now looked like a tablecloth splattered with black marks. I wished we had our artillery with us.

After a while the Russians seemed to have rallied and infiltrated across the unobserved riverbank into the village and caused us problems with all their weapons at close range. Without the grenadiers I couldn't hold on without heavy losses in ground that was now becoming unsuitable for us. Finally I had to give up the village, but as you might expect with casualties, though none dead. There were harsh but, as is often the case on these occasions, unfair words with the panzergrenadiers. The grenadiers had actually suffered many casualties on the flat plain.

After what seemed an endless wait it was possible to bring up artillery.

With its support, which included putting down smoke on the high ground, the second attack succeeded. We were able to take the village and the heights swiftly and almost without casualties.

A short while later, Grinev and Malo-Katchalin fell into the hands of the panzergrenadiers almost uncontested. This day cost me nine tanks shot up and for the panzergrenadiers and us it was a Pyrrhic victory.[25]

The Luftwaffe's bombers – particularly those under the command of Oberst Ernst Kühl – played an important part in bringing the Russian advance to an end, conducting repeated missions against the Russian armour. But this meant that those aircraft were unavailable for airlift operations into the Stalingrad encirclement; thus, even though the Russian armour did not succeed in reaching Morozovsk, its presence was sufficient to divert Luftwaffe strength in their direction, thus having a further detrimental effect on the trapped Sixth Army.

The Russians were at the end of their supply lines and it was proving difficult to sustain both Vatutin's operations and the assault by Second Guards Army on Kirchner's LVII Panzer Corps. However, the outcomes of both *Little Saturn* and *Winter Storm* could justifiably be viewed with satisfaction by the Red Army. Some of the objectives of the assault along the Don, such as the permanent capture of the airfields at Morozovsk and Tatsinskaya, had not been achieved, and although it had suffered heavy losses, *Armee Abteilung Hollidt* succeeded in pulling back its line more or less intact. The entire Russian operation had struggled in the face of a demanding and probably over-ambitious timetable, but there were nonetheless significant gains. In particular, Manstein had been forced to divert forces from Fourth Panzer Army, thus ending whatever dwindling prospects remained of reaching Stalingrad. Whether the Red Army would have been able to carry out the far more ambitious objectives of *Saturn* is highly questionable, and it is at least possible, if not likely, that such an operation would have stalled due to logistic difficulties. Whilst, as has been suggested by some, the use of Second Guards Army to maintain the initial advances made in *Little Saturn* might have allowed the Red Army to reach Rostov and render any relief operation conducted by Fourth Panzer Army irrelevant, there are simply too many imponderable factors in such a scenario.[26] With so many German forces cut off by such an advance, and in particular with them under the command of Manstein rather than Paulus, it is highly likely that the static battles around Stalingrad would not have been repeated on a larger scale – instead, the Germans would have attempted to keep the fighting as fluid as was possible within the constraints of fuel supplies, and at a tactical level they were still a force to be feared.

The total losses suffered by the Italians exceeded 84,000 killed, captured or missing, with over 29,000 wounded or sick. Only the *Alpini* Corps at the northern end of Eighth Army's sector was left intact, and most of the German formations involved in the fighting also suffered heavy losses. Russian casualties were not light – over 80 per cent of the tanks committed were either knocked out or suffered mechanical breakdowns, though many of these would be recovered in the following days. Infantry losses in the Red Army were also heavy, particularly during the initial breakthrough; 203rd Rifle Division, for example, lost about 70 per cent of its troops.[27]

The Red Army began its evaluation of the battle almost immediately. Many of the tank losses after the initial breakthrough were caused by Luftwaffe attacks, and there was an urgent call for the improvement of anti-aircraft firepower. All too often, tank units found themselves isolated without infantry support, and there was a recommendation for closer cooperation between mechanised brigades and tank formations to overcome this deficiency.[28] The structure of tank armies was reviewed and changes were made, though it would take several months for these to be put into action. All Russian armoured units reported incidents of their lines of supply being disrupted by the movements of German and Italian stragglers in their rear areas, and in order to address this recommendations were made that infantry forces should always be within two or three days' march of the leading armour. In order to help achieve this, some tank corps gained rifle divisions, and enterprising commanders attempted to motorise these forces so that they could keep up with the armoured spearheads.[29] Future operations would also see more determined efforts to mop up the debris of broken enemy units following a breakthrough, to reduce to a minimum their ability to disrupt further Russian advances and the movement of supply columns.

The question of whether Fourth Panzer Army could have reached the encircled Sixth Army has been the subject of great debate. If so much time had not been lost after the first crossing of the Aksay, if 17th Panzer Division had been available from the outset, if Hitler had agreed to the timely transfer of 16th Motorised Division, if III Panzer Corps had been moved from the Caucasus – any combination of these might have permitted LVII Panzer Corps to reach Sixth Army. However, most such discussions concentrate on what the Germans might have done differently and pay little regard to how the Russians might have acted in response. Even if it had proved possible to advance from the Myshkova to Stalingrad, there was not the remotest possibility of Hitler agreeing to the evacuation of the ruined city with sufficient alacrity – he might eventually have been forced to concede the point, but only if he had absolutely no alternative, and even then he would probably have prevaricated until the withdrawal resulted in disaster, and would then have used this disaster as justification for refusing any withdrawals in future. Nor is there anything to suggest that Paulus would have agreed to disobey instructions from the Führer and thus take the necessary steps to save his army. Had LVII Panzer Corps reached the siege perimeter, the supply column that had been prepared would have been able to relieve at least some of the shortages in Sixth Army, but given the imbalance of military strength in Fourth Panzer Army's sector, it is hard to see how the corridor could have been kept open for long, particularly as the events on the middle Don would still have required the diversion of forces to the north at some point. Ultimately, the outcome for Sixth Army would probably have been much the same, though its final act may have been prolonged by the provision of supplies. Instead, Paulus' army was left to its fate in Stalingrad, where hunger, illness, the cold weather and Russian action continued to eat away at its strength. Paulus and Schmidt might demand better air supply, but the Luftwaffe lacked the means to provide it and had now lost the air bases nearest to the city. Every day brought the end of Sixth Army closer.

CHAPTER 8

THE OSTROGOZHSK-ROSSOSH OPERATION

The situation that presented itself to Manstein at the end of December was one that offered few if any grounds for optimism. By contrast, viewed from the Russian side, the same situation offered almost too many enticing opportunities. To a degree, that profusion of choice had already played a significant part in the conduct of the fighting.

The initial intention of *Uranus* was to encircle the main grouping of German forces in Stalingrad, and the operation worked perfectly. Immediately, it created new opportunities, largely because of the size of the hole that it tore in the German line. Just as he had done the previous winter, Stalin became enthusiastic for pursuing multiple targets – whilst Vasilevsky wanted to concentrate on destroying Sixth Army in Stalingrad, Stalin was keen to launch *Saturn* in order to destabilise the entire German position in the Ukraine, but given the number of Russian troops required to encircle and contain Sixth Army in Stalingrad, such ambitious operations were only realistic if the pocket could be reduced rapidly. It was only when the number of German troops encircled became clear and it was necessary to divert more forces to deal with them that Stalin agreed to scale down the operation to *Little Saturn*. While fighting continued at a slower tempo after the end of *Little Saturn*, the Germans were able to rebuild their line much as they had after *Uranus*, creating a new group under Fretter-Pico from the debris of the retreating forces, but both this group and its predecessor – *Armee Abteilung Hollidt* – were hardly strong enough to beat off a sustained assault. Was it still possible to achieve a victory that would dwarf the success of *Uranus* and potentially win the war?

Manstein received some news on 29 December that eased his concerns a little: bowing to reality, Hitler finally confirmed the instructions that he had given to Zeitzler two days before, allowing Army Group A to withdraw from its positions in the Caucasus. The advance towards the oilfields of Maikop and Grozny had been predicated upon two factors: firstly, that the Red Army was effectively a defeated force; and secondly, the Wehrmacht would maintain a strong position in the Don-Volga region to protect the rear of the southward advance. Both of these factors had been rendered invalid by the events of late November and December, and the troops of Army Group A were badly needed to salvage the deteriorating situation further north. But whilst Hitler had agreed to the withdrawal of Kleist's army group, progress was painfully slow. It had been deprived of adequate fuel for weeks, and it would take – from Manstein's point of view – an eternity to pull back its eastern flank even as far as Pyatigorsk and Praskoveya, still 250 miles (420km) southeast of Rostov.

Whether the delays were due to Hitler's prevarication, Kleist's reluctance to withdraw, or genuine fuel shortages – and all three probably contributed – Manstein had to buy sufficient time for fuel and trains to be moved into position. Consequently, even though there was no longer any realistic prospect of rescuing Sixth Army, it was essential that Paulus' troops continued fighting. They continued to tie down substantial Russian forces, and if these were allowed to move elsewhere, there was no prospect whatever of Army Group A being able to withdraw; if it found itself trapped in the Caucasus, its destruction would make the German position on the Eastern Front completely untenable.

It is one thing to ask soldiers to fight a tough battle in appalling conditions if this plays a part in their own salvation; it is quite another to ask them to continue that battle when there is no hope of rescue. Manstein's insistence on Sixth Army continuing to fight the surrounding Russian forces, even after 9 January when the Don Front called on Paulus to surrender to avoid pointless suffering, has been criticised by some.[1] Aware of his responsibility in prolonging the agony of the encircled soldiers of Sixth Army, Manstein wrote at length about what he clearly saw as a difficult decision:

Every extra day Sixth Army could continue to tie down the enemy forces surrounding it was vital as far as the fate of the entire Eastern Front was concerned. It is idle to point out today that we still lost the war in the end and that its early termination would have spared us infinite misery. That is merely being wise after the event. In those days it was by no means certain that Germany was bound to lose the war in the military sense. A military stalemate, which might in turn have

215

led to a similar state of affairs in the political field, would have been entirely within the bounds of possibility if the situation on the southern wing of the German armies could in some way have been restored. This, however, depended first and foremost on Sixth Army's continuing the struggle and holding down the enemy siege forces for as long as it possessed the slightest capacity to resist. It was the cruel necessity of war which compelled the Supreme Command [i.e. Hitler] to demand that one last sacrifice of the brave troops at Stalingrad. The fact that the self-same Supreme Command was responsible for the army's plight is beside the point in this context.[2]

This passage from Manstein's memoirs is correct from a strategic point of view, but badly flawed in another, more political respect. It was by this stage common knowledge that the Allied Powers would accept nothing less than unconditional surrender by Germany as the price of peace. Whilst a military stalemate might have been technically possible, it is almost impossible to conceive of the political circumstances in which this might have led to some form of negotiated peace. The Soviet Union was determined to ensure that Germany would never pose a significant threat to it again, particularly as the magnitude of the atrocities committed during German occupation was becoming increasingly clear, and Manstein's hopes of some form of 'honourable draw' in the political arena reflect the naivety of German officers when it came to politics. In some respects, the distaste for political matters shown by the sons of Prussian Junkers families owed a great deal to the glittering ostentation of the Wilhelmine era immediately before the First World War; the capital of the young nation of Germany, flushed by its victory over France in the Franco-Prussian War of 1870–71 and enriched both by industrialisation and French reparations, came to embody much that was completely the opposite of traditional Prussian values of austerity, a strong sense of duty, and obedience to the head of state. Further serious damage was done to the relationship between politicians and the army by the events of late 1918 that led to the Armistice and eventual defeat for Germany. The bitter recriminations after the end of the First World War, in particular the widespread promotion of the *Dolchstoss* ('stab in the back') myth that the undefeated German Army was betrayed by cowardly politicians, made soldiers even less inclined to pay heed to politics. Instead, they retreated into a purely military world, divorced from the political consequences of their actions. It is therefore unsurprising that they lacked the acumen for accurate analysis of what might be politically possible.

Before Hitler combined the offices of Chancellor and President in 1934, German officers and civil servants had given an oath of allegiance, or *Reichswehreid*, to the state and the country's constitution, but this was now changed to an oath of loyalty directly to Hitler. Although this worked hugely to Hitler's advantage, the change was actually on the initiative of Generals Werner von Blomberg, the War Minister, and Reichenau, who was serving as chief of the Ministerial Office at the time; their motive for this was apparently that such an oath would bind Hitler more closely to the army and would thus force him to distance himself from the SS and the Nazi Party. The consequence was completely the opposite, with army officers, conditioned by a lifetime of obedience and duty, regarding themselves as permanently bound to the Führer. Although thousands of army officers claimed to be sick on the day that the oath was to be taken in order to avoid taking it, they were all forced to take it when they returned to work. Only a small number of officials, mainly civilians in the civil service, refused to take the oath. A few were forcibly retired, but the majority were executed, either immediately or not long after. For the army's officers, the consequence of the oath, in which they swore unconditional obedience to Adolf Hitler, the leader of the German Reich and people, was that they were ill-equipped to deal with a reality in which the head of state to which they had sworn obedience then exploited that obedience and devotion to pursue policies that ensured Germany's foes would seek nothing less than unconditional surrender.

Some of those closest to Paulus wrote later that it was unacceptable for Manstein and Hitler to force him to continue fighting when all hope of rescue was gone, and that humanitarian concerns should have outweighed operational considerations.[3] Whilst this is an arguable point of view, it is surely wrong to place all the blame for the suffering of the soldiers of Sixth Army on higher commands. Ultimately, Paulus was the man in charge in the front line and could have acted according to his conscience. His inflexible adherence to orders contributed greatly to the fate of Sixth Army, from its encirclement and the arguments around the various moments when a breakout might have been possible, to the terrible suffering of his men throughout January. Indeed, his role in the events in and around Stalingrad is a stark reminder of the limitations of always adhering to orders from above. If he felt bound by Hitler's orders, it is surely somewhat hypocritical for him to have expected Manstein to have acted in direct contravention of those same orders.

On the first day of the new year, Vasilevsky received fresh instructions from Stalin: he was to order Yeremenko's front – renamed Southern Front instead of Stalingrad Front, to reflect the fact that it had now moved away from the fighting around the city – to drive on to Tsimlyanskaya, Konstantinovskaya, Shakhty, Novocherkassk (all on the Don and progressively closer to Rostov), and Salsk in the first week of January, while the forces in the Caucasus were to reach Tikhoretskaya in the second week. If such gains were achieved, they would place the Russian tanks barely 40 miles (68km) from the Sea of Azov and astride the railway line running south from Rostov to the German Army Group A, still slowly withdrawing from its high-tide mark. However, Vasilevsky was not to oversee the operation personally:

> Stalin told me that *Stavka* ... was instructing me to leave at once for the Voronezh Front where, as the *Stavka* representative, I was to take part in preparing and implementing the offensive operations planned on the upper Don; I was also responsible for the organisation of joint action between the Voronezh Front and the Bryansk and Southwest Fronts.[4]

The intention of this offensive further north was to achieve breakthroughs either side of the German Second Army and to try to envelop it, or at the very least force it into a major retreat. Whilst the overall aim of *Saturn* had been to reach Rostov and thus isolate Army Group A in the Caucasus, the same result could be achieved by Yeremenko's front advancing south of the Don, while successes further north would ensure that the German troops operating immediately north of the Don were also endangered by the prospect of Russian forces pressing down to the Sea of Azov or seizing the Dnepr crossings. Whether the Red Army had the logistic capability of conducting both operations simultaneously while at the same time trying to put pressure upon Army Group A to stop its withdrawal and completing the reduction of the Stalingrad pocket was questionable, particularly given the logistic breakdowns during *Little Saturn*. But – as had been the case in the fighting near Moscow the previous winter – Stalin was buoyed up and confident after the successes that had already been achieved. In the summer, Hitler had fatally misjudged the Red Army, believing that it had effectively been defeated and his armies were therefore free to advance almost at will; Stalin now risked making a similar mistake.

As well as urging on the formations of Yeremenko's armies – which had suffered substantial losses in their attacks to drive back Fourth Panzer Army – and sending Vasilevsky to oversee the new offensive by Voronezh Front, Stalin also issued orders to the Russian forces in the Caucasus. Here, a combination of stubborn defence and the diversion of German logistic and air support to the fighting in Stalingrad had left the Germans short of their objectives – although Maikop was captured, its oil wells had been severely damaged by the retreating Russians and it proved impossible to push on to Grozny or Baku. Nor was it possible to eliminate the Russian forces defending a narrow strip of territory along the east coast of the Black Sea, from where they could threaten the western flank of Army Group A. On 4 January, Stalin sent a signal to General Ivan Vladimirovich Tiulenev, commander of Transcaucasian Front, advising him that his northern group was to be separated to create a new Northern Caucasus Front under the command of Lieutenant General Ivan Ivanovich Maslennikov. The signal emphasised an important point:

> It is not in our interest to expel the enemy from the northern Caucasus. It would be more useful to hold him up so as to encircle him by an attack from the Black Sea group [the semi-autonomous part of Transcaucasian Front operating on the Black Sea coast against the western flank of Army Group A] …
>
> … Your … main task is to select a powerful column of troops from the Black Sea group, take Bataisk [immediately south of Rostov] and Azov, break into Rostov from the east and thereby bottle up the enemy's North Caucasus Group so that you can either capture or wipe it out. You will be assisted by the left flank of the Southern Front whose task it is to arrive to the north of Rostov.[5]

In order to ensure that his subordinates carried out their orders, Tiulenev was to join the Black Sea group and supervise its attack towards Rostov. Whilst there was clear operational sense in Stalin's instructions, they added still further to the demands faced by the Red Army's logistics service, which would have to supply armies up to 300 miles (500km) apart, attempting to advance over ground that had already seen heavy fighting and would suffer further degradation as the Germans destroyed infrastructure during their retreat – all in the middle of winter. Tiulenev had doubts about the feasibility of the plans:

> Having received these orders, Ivan Efimovich [Petrov, Tiulenev's chief of staff] and I became very thoughtful. In fact, *Stavka* has set us an incredibly difficult, if not impossible task. The goal stated in the directive was tempting: with the capture of Bataisk we would put the enemy in a desperate situation. However, considering this plan as a whole and carefully analysing the current situation, we ran into insurmountable obstacles.
>
> The main one was the area of the upcoming military operations – the spurs of the main Caucasian range. We had to overcome them at the most unfavourable time of year, when the temperature on the coast was above freezing, and in the mountains it dropped to -15 to -25°C. During this period, the rugged spurs of the ridge were covered with a deep blanket of snow.

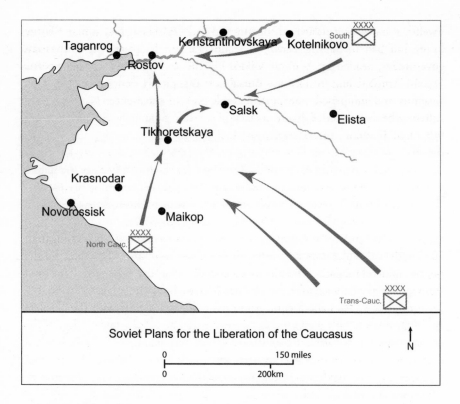

Soviet Plans for the Liberation of the Caucasus

And what of the lack of roads for delivering ammunition and food? Their construction required a large number of road and engineering battalions. On our front, there were very few such battalions.

The second difficulty was the transfer of troops from Ordzhonikidze [now Vladikavkaz]. It could only be carried out in two steps: to the port of Poti by rail, and then by sea [to the new North Caucasus Front]. It would take considerable time.

Even Petrov, who had seen and overcome many difficulties in the heroic defense of Odessa and Sevastopol, sighed regretfully: 'I had a hard time in the Crimea, but what we face now is much more difficult.'[6]

The target for Voronezh Front's assault was the sector of the front held by the Hungarian Second Army. In early 1942, Hitler requested that the Hungarians send a larger contingent to the Eastern Front; to date, the Hungarian Army's *Gyorshadtest* ('Rapid Corps') had been the only significant formation fighting the Russians, operating first to protect the southern flank of the German Seventeenth Army and then helping to close the Uman pocket where the Russian Sixth and

Twelfth Armies were destroyed, but by the end of 1941 it had suffered heavy losses and had to be withdrawn to recuperate.[7] In its place, the Hungarian government, headed by Admiral Miklós Horthy de Nagybánya, dispatched its Second Army, strong in numbers but almost completely deficient in anti-tank weapons and motorised transport. It took part in the fighting at Voronezh, suffering heavy casualties due to its lack of modern weaponry – the Hungarian 9th Light Division, for example, lost half its strength in forcing the Russian defences after German artillery and armoured support failed to appear – and was then assigned to defend the line of the Don from the northern flank of the Italian Eighth Army to the positions of the German Second Army. Like many parts of the Eastern Front, it received a very low supply priority throughout the second half of 1942 as resources were poured into Stalingrad – as had been the case with the Romanians and Italians, the Germans had promised to supply their Hungarian allies with anti-tank weapons but largely failed to do so, and when they did the poorly trained Hungarian recruits were generally unable to use them. Even food supplies became haphazard as the year progressed. The Hungarian 1st Armoured Division, like its Romanian equivalent, was equipped mainly with the obsolete Pz.38(t), and had only a handful of German Pz.III and Pz.IV tanks. Most of the Hungarian infantry formations on the Don were termed 'light' divisions and had only two infantry regiments, compared with three in the Russian divisions that faced them. In short, their fighting power was minimal, especially in the context of the brutal Eastern Front.

On the southern flank of the Hungarian forces was what remained of the Italian Eighth Army, largely the *Alpini* Corps of three divisions. Its southern neighbour was the German XXIV Panzer Corps; despite its imposing title, it was not a powerful formation, with the weak 385th and 387th Infantry Divisions, the survivors of the Italian *Julia* Division, and 27th Panzer Division, which at this stage of the war had only 13 tanks. In addition, it included a cavalry brigade under the command of SS Oberführer Hermann Fegelein, described by Albert Speer as 'one of the most disgusting people in Hitler's circle'.[8] Before the war, Fegelein was a keen equestrian who used his personal friendship with Heinrich Himmler to his advantage, being given the task of organising a riding school for the SS in Munich. Despite having no formal military training, he commanded the *SS-Totenkopf Reiterstandarte* (*Totenkopf* 'mounted regiment') in Poland, which was then rapidly expanded after the successful campaign and played a leading role in the eradication of Polish intellectuals and clergy, including the massacre of nearly 2,000 people in the Kampinos Forest in December 1939.[9] During his time in Poland, Fegelein was charged with complicity in looting, but his court martial was blocked by his friend Himmler; he was also charged with unlawful sex with a Polish woman, which resulted in her becoming pregnant, and then forcing her to have an abortion. Himmler blocked this investigation too, as well as other attempts by his rival Reinhard Heydrich, the head of the *Reichssicherheitshauptamt* (*RSHA*, the 'Reich Security Head Office') to investigate other allegations.[10] After the beginning of *Barbarossa*, Fegelein's cavalry proved unable to keep up with the pace of the German advance and were instead used in wide sweeps through the Pripet Marshes region of Belarus. After Himmler complained that Fegelein's men were killing too few partisans, actions became more indiscriminate in order to increase the body count. By 18 September, Fegelein reported that his men had killed over 14,000 Jews and nearly 2,000 soldiers and 'partisans'; other accounts put the number of Jews killed by the SS cavalry at closer to 24,000, though it is arguable that many of these victims were just civilian Russians who were rounded up by Fegelein's men.[11] After a spell away from the front line for much of 1942, he returned in the winter to take command of a brigade of SS cavalry; he was wounded by Russian snipers shortly after, and was therefore absent from his command when the storm broke against Army Group B in early 1943. His troops, more accustomed to massacring civilians than fighting the Red Army, would find themselves in the thick of the fighting; the absence of their commander was unlikely to play any part in their performance, particularly given his complete lack of military training and dubious experience of real combat.

Golikov's Voronezh Front had spent the late summer in a futile attempt to recapture the German-held parts of Voronezh. Although little progress was made in the city, a valuable bridgehead was secured about 29 miles (47km) to the south. After another failed assault on western Voronezh in September 1942, the front went over to the defensive and allowed its armies to recover their strength. Following the success of *Little Saturn*, attention returned to this sector; if the Hungarians proved as fragile as the Italians and Romanians, there was the potential for gains on both flanks. To the north, the German defences immediately south of Voronezh would be outflanked, and to the south, the defensive line hastily constructed by the Germans would be destabilised before it could firm up, thus facilitating further advances towards Rostov. To help Golikov achieve a breakthrough, the Russian Third Tank Army was dispatched from *Stavka* reserve to give his forces added strike power. Even without this, he probably had enough strength to force the Hungarians back, but with the armour of Third Tank Army, a breakthrough was effectively guaranteed. Vasilevsky might have been concerned that numerically, the German and Hungarian forces had similar or even more

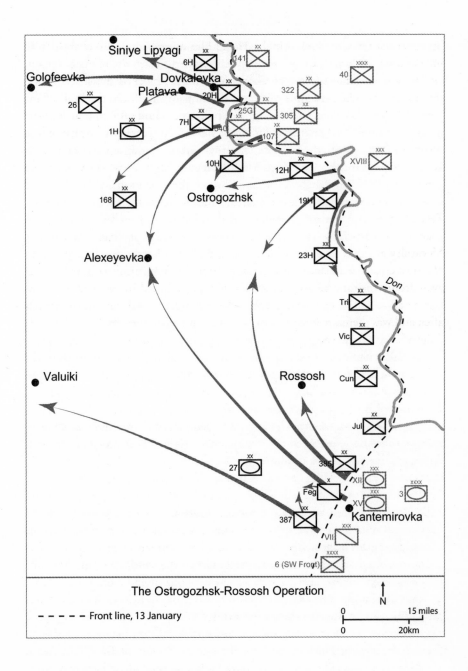

The Ostrogozhsk-Rossosh Operation

– – – – – Front line, 13 January

0   15 miles

0   20km

N

infantry, but the reality was that the Hungarian contribution was unlikely to be able to resist for long.

Zhukov joined Vasilevsky in Golikov's headquarters to plan the new attack. They created a northern group around Fortieth Army, reinforced by IV Tank Corps, in the bridgehead that had been secured south of Voronezh, and a southern group consisting of Third Tank Army and VII Cavalry Corps, which would attack from Kantemirovka. The two groups would aim to link up at Alekseyevka with other pincers meeting further to the east, while the southern group's cavalry shielded the southern flank of the operation. If the operation succeeded, it was expected to encircle and destroy 15 enemy divisions.[12] Unfortunately for the newly promoted Lieutenant General Kiril Semenovich Moskalenko's Fortieth Army, IV Tank Corps was late in deploying and would not be available at the beginning of the operation, but given the modest strength of the Hungarian forces, Moskalenko was confident that his army would be able to prevail with the tanks that it already possessed. The lessons learned from *Uranus* and *Little Saturn* were already being put into effect; the attack would include several smaller thrusts intended to prevent the defeated enemy from forming large pockets capable of prolonged resistance.

It was increasingly routine practice for the Russians to try to take prisoners before an attack in order to interrogate them about the opposing forces – such prisoners were known amongst the troops as 'tongues'. Nikolai Petrovich Pustyntsev was a soldier in a reconnaissance unit that specialised in such tasks, and he and his comrades were ordered into action. After a preliminary scouting mission, a raid was prepared for the following night but as was often the case with such operations, things didn't go to plan:

> The next day the soldiers returned empty-handed. They had suffered casualties. Two wounded men were dragged back on wooden sleds. On one I saw Boris Erastov, on the other Mikhail Peklov. Both had been wounded by grenades. Boris was particularly badly wounded: the guy was, as they say, riddled from his feet to his waist. He turned to me, tried to smile, but the smile was weak, barely discernible. 'I'm lying here like stuffed poultry,' he said. The boys were sent to the hospital that same morning.
>
> 'The three of us, the snatch squad, crawled to the German trenches,' Nikolai Vakhrushev, who took part in the raid, later told us. 'We saw the silhouette of a sentry's helmet: it stood out very clearly in the snow. Mikhail whispered to us: "We'll take him," and rushed forward. We were behind the sentry. We jumped into the trench. Mikhail swung his arm and struck the fascist on the head with a rock in

General Nikolai Vatutin in January 1944. (Getty)

Soviet reinforcements run to take position in the Factory District of Stalingrad, Autumn 1942. (Courtesy of the Central Museum of the Armed Forces, Moscow via Stavka)

Soviet cavalry ride past an abandoned German 37mm anti-tank gun during the advance westwards from Stalingrad. (Courtesy of the Central Museum of the Armed Forces, Moscow via Stavka)

Soviet infantry advance past a downed German aircraft.
(From the fonds of the RGAKFD in Krasnogorsk via Stavka)

The Red Army made extensive use of cavalry throughout the war for both pursuit and reconnaissance
missions. (Courtesy of the Central Museum of the Armed Forces, Moscow via Stavka)

Soviet trophies: two German armoured cars lay abandoned, awaiting removal and evaluation.
(From the fonds of the RGAKFD in Krasnogorsk via Stavka)

Romanian POWs, many of whom would go on to serve in the Soviet-sponsored
'Tudor Vladimirescu' Rifle Division, await the order to march off. (Courtesy of the Central
Museum of the Armed Forces, Moscow via Stavka)

Axis POWs cross the frozen waters of the Volga River, February 1943.
(Courtesy of the Central Museum of the Armed Forces, Moscow via Stavka)

German POWs trudge eastwards into captivity. (Courtesy of the Central Museum of the
Armed Forces, Moscow via Stavka)

A column of Soviet T-70 tanks waits to advance, February 1943. (Nik Cornish at www.Stavka.org.uk)

Razvedchiki (scouts) pose for the camera on the outskirts of Kharkov.
(From the fonds of the RGAKFD in Krasnogorsk via Stavka)

Soviet forces move into suburban Kharkov.
(Courtesy of the Central Museum of the Armed Forces, Moscow via Stavka)

16 February 1943: Soviet armour drives past the Palace of Industry on Dzezhinsky Square in Kharkov on the day it was liberated. (From the fonds of the RGAKFD in Krasnogorsk via Stavka)

T-34 tanks in an ambush position during the German offensive February–March 1943.
(Courtesy of the Central Museum of the Armed Forces, Moscow via Stavka)

Soviet soldiers celebrating the liberation of an unidentified town with the daily 100gram issue of vodka.
(From the fonds of the RGAKFD in Krasnogorsk via Stavka)

Soviet heavy artillery: a 280mm Br-5 M1939 mortar prepares to fire.
(From the fonds of the RGAKFD in Krasnogorsk via Stavka)

A 152mm ML-20, M1937 howitzer is moved into position by a Stalinets S-65
tractor with spare fuel and munitions on a sledge. (Nik Cornish at www.Stavka.org.uk)

Soviet 76mm anti-aircraft guns watch for the approach of Luftwaffe aircraft.
(Nik Cornish at www.Stavka.org.uk)

A tracked 203mm B-4, M1931 howitzer takes aim. (Nik Cornish at www.Stavka.org.uk)

Soviet refugees wend their miserable way to safety.
(Courtesy of the Central Museum of the Armed Forces, Moscow via Stavka)

Carrying its quota of *tank desant* men, a T-34 goes into the attack.
(Courtesy of the Central Museum of the Armed Forces, Moscow via Stavka)

Gathered around the latest issue of *Pravda*, Red Army men, several of whom are armed with SVT-40 automatic rifles, listen to the news. (Courtesy of the Central Museum of the Armed Forces, Moscow via Stavka)

Razvedchiki (scouts) set out on their next mission.
(Courtesy of the Central Museum of the Armed Forces, Moscow via Stavka)

Soviet sub-machine gunners man the front line as the Germans advance, March 1943.
(Courtesy of the Central Museum of the Armed Forces, Moscow via Stavka)

Happier days for the Axis: central Stalingrad, September 1942. The soon-to-be iconic *Barmaley* Fountain
can be seen to the right of the gun. (Nik Cornish at www.Stavka.org.uk)

The price of defeat: dead Axis soldiers heaped outside Stalingrad awaiting burial in mass graves. (Courtesy of the Central Museum of the Armed Forces, Moscow via Stavka)

A column of Panzer IIIs waits while a supply unit clears the road. (Nik Cornish at www. Stavka.org.uk)

A German machine-gun position somewhere on the eastern Ukrainian steppe. (Nik Cornish at www.Stavka.org.uk)

Opposite • Field Marshal Friedrich von Paulus surrenders, 1 February 1943. (Getty)

As the Soviets advance, so the Germans retreat. Here a 150mm sFH howitzer waits for the order to leave. (Nik Cornish at www.Stavka.org.uk)

Well-camouflaged German infantry in the front line. (Nik Cornish at www.Stavka.org.uk)

On the sleeves of these Germans' jackets can be seen the red stripes that identified them to friendly forces. (Nik Cornish at www.Stavka.org.uk)

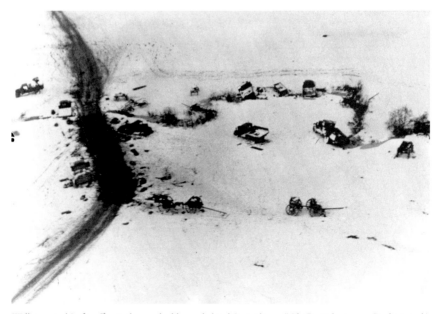

Well-executed Luftwaffe attacks wreaked havoc behind Soviet lines. (Nik Cornish at www.Stavka.org.uk)

The emptiness of the steppe behind German lines. (Nik Cornish at www.Stavka.org.uk)

German troops retreat during February 1943.
(Nik Cornish at www.Stavka.org.uk)

A Waffen SS mortar team takes a break during
the battle for Kharkov. During close-range
fighting mortars were an effective way of giving
close support to an attack.
(Nik Cornish at www.Stavka.org.uk)

Light 20mm German anti-aircraft guns west of Kharkov, February 1943.
(Nik Cornish at www.Stavka.org.uk)

The end of a T-34 tank, March 1943. Third Tank Army suffered heavy losses during this period. (Nik Cornish at www.Stavka.org.uk)

Field Marshal Erich von Manstein on whose 'Backhand Blow' all German hopes hung after the fall of Stalingrad. (Getty)

SS Panzer Grenadiers enjoy their lunch during the fighting for Kharkov.
(Nik Cornish at www.Stavka.org.uk)

A Panzer IV of II SS Panzer Corps moves into Kharkov. (Nik Cornish at www.Stavka.org.uk)

A German patrol poses following its debrief. (Nik Cornish at www.Stavka.org.uk)

As the weather became milder, mud became a major concern for the Germans.
(Nik Cornish at www.Stavka.org.uk)

German heavy artillery: a 210mm M18 mortar prepares to fire. (Nik Cornish at www.Stavka.org.uk)

German troops clean and check their weapons after battle. (Nik Cornish at www.Stavka.org.uk)

German armoured cars pause to refuel during Manstein's counterattack.
(Nik Cornish at www.Stavka.org.uk)

As they pulled back the Germans scorched the earth to deny their enemy any shelter from the elements.
(Nik Cornish at www.Stavka.org.uk)

his fist. But he overdid it: the Hitlerite fell dead. And then another emerged from the dugout. We seized him, but he was quick and nimble. He knocked me down with a blow to my head and rushed off down the trench. Without stopping to think, Boris rushed after him. He overtook him at the bottom of the ravine. Boris only needed to grab the German and disarm him – and we would have our "tongue". But Boris fumbled in his haste and grabbed the head of a grenade on the German's belt. There was an explosion. The fascist went to the next world, and Boris was riddled with shrapnel.' Thus ended the first raid by our scouts in 1943.[13]

A day later, Pustyntsev led a second raid:

We put on fur coats and white camouflage trousers and headed for our forward positions, grabbing our submachine-guns and grenades. Freshly fallen snow lay all around, squeaking under our felt boots.

We left our forward positions behind us. We lay in the snow and gently crawled along the dark bushes at the edge of the field. There was a heavy frost, but we felt hot. Our bodies were covered with perspiration. Oh, those snow-covered metres of 'no-man's land' were tough!

Ahead, about 15m from us, we saw the enemy trenches. The edge of the parapets looked almost blue. We crouched with bated breath, often stopping. Finally, we could see the shape of the dugout. At the entrance was the dark silhouette of a sentry. The door of the dugout creaked. A German appeared on the threshold. He said something to the sentry and again ducked inside.

Silence. We lay still. Against the dugout the figure of the sentry looked awkward and too bulky. The head was wrapped up in some black scarf, thick ersatz-boots on the legs. Not a hardened soldier. Now we were aware of the frost. Despite our warm clothing, we began to freeze. Our bodies gradually cooled, and cold started to bite to the bone.

It became a competition in endurance. Who was better tempered, who was better suited to the cold? The German cracked first. He stamped his ersatz-felt boots, walked to the other side of the trench, and turned his back to us. That was what we were waiting for. Shmelkov whispered: 'Forward!'

Lykov and I quickly grabbed the German and pushed a rag into his mouth. We hurried to rejoin Shmelkov, Ziganshin and Danikirov. The five of us dragged our prey. There was silence for a while. But suddenly the lights of flares exploded into the sky. Machine-guns began to chatter when the Hitlerites realised the sentry was missing. We hurriedly tumbled into a ditch. We watched as the bullets scattered the snow. We made it back safely.[14]

Despite the customary measures taken by the Russians to disguise their preparations, the Hungarians knew that an attack was coming, but the underestimation of it by several senior commanders would prove to be catastrophic. In a signal at the end of 1942, Major General György Rakovsky – commander of III Corps – wrote: 'Only local Soviet attacks are expected … My impression is that we can take care of these attacks ourselves.'[15]

Whatever the views of Rakovsky, the commander of the Hungarian Second Army – Colonel-General Vitéz Jány – and the men in the front line had no such illusions. Without anti-tank guns, they were helpless. Ironically, the Germans had huge numbers of captured Russian 76mm guns that would have turned the Romanian, Italian and Hungarian Armies into far more formidable defensive formations, and it was surely not beyond the abilities of industrialists either in Germany or the allied nations to set up facilities for the production of appropriate calibre shells. But Hitler had a deep-seated reluctance to using military equipment captured in Russia, even to passing it to his allies, and in any event the armies of the allied nations were deployed along the Don at a time when Hitler – and, it should be remembered, Halder for a considerable period – believed that the power of the Red Army had been broken. In such circumstances, it is possible that many in Germany were unenthusiastic about devoting resources to improve the defensive firepower of nations that might prove to be enemies one day.

Morale amongst the Hungarians was low and the disaster at Stalingrad had reduced their confidence still further. The Russians were of course aware of this. Nikolai Grigorievich Shtykov was a deputy regimental officer in 25th Guards Rifle Division, and in preparation for the coming attacks his men also brought in prisoners:

> From the documents that came into our hands and from the testimony of the captured Hungarians, we knew that many of them had begun to realise that they were participating in another nation's criminal war. All they wanted was to return home. Entries in the diary of the soldier Istvan Bolachek from the 1st Motorcycle Brigade, killed in a skirmish with our division, made this eloquently clear. Here is an excerpt:
>
> 'Yesterday I was in battle and I survived by a miracle. The lieutenant-colonel and several captains were killed. Morale is low. It's cold and freezing. Help us, Holy Mother of God, to return home.'
>
> A soldier from the Hungarian 20th Infantry Division, taken prisoner by our scouts, stated during interrogation that he could have resisted capture but did not do so, since he did not want to fight for the interests of the Horthy government, which he didn't share.[16]

Reinforcements in the form of fresh, inexperienced recruits arrived in the Hungarian lines just a few days before the Russian attack. The men had received only basic training before being sent east, and in other circumstances they would have been rotated through the front line to allow them to get used to conditions while undergoing further training. Instead, they found themselves in the thick of the fighting. On 12 January, the Russians carried out energetic reconnaissance probes preceded by heavy bombardments. Major General Pavel Mendelevich Shafarenko's 25th Guards Rifle Division, in which Shtykov was serving, would be in the first wave of the attack, with the first objective being the village of Orekhovaya:

> With the consent of the army commander, we decided to leave a two-minute gap between the end of the artillery preparation and the Katyusha volley. The idea was simple. As soon as the artillery switched its fire into the depth of the enemy's defences, our infantry, without leaving their trenches, would open fire with small arms and shout 'Urrah', as was usually done at the beginning of an attack. The Nazis would come out of cover to repel us. At that moment, they would be struck by the Katyushas. Only then would the Guards make their real attack.
>
> At 0900, my artillery commander [Colonel Nikolai Ivanovich] Novitsky, who had replaced Soloviev, came to the command post of 81st Guards Regiment.
>
> The fog did not dissipate. Everything had been prepared and checked the previous evening. Aircraft had carried out reconnaissance of targets and artillerymen had aligned their guns. Sappers had made passages at night through the minefields, carefully camouflaging them. Passages in enemy wire entanglements would be made during the attack, using tanks with bulldozer blades. Two battalions of 81st Guards Regiment were in position, waiting for the command.
>
> Only at 1000 did the fog clear a little, and we heard the roar of aircraft coming from the east. The attack planes of Colonel Vitruk's 291st Assault Aviation Division appeared overhead. One after the other, the planes flew over Orekhovaya, dropping bombs and striking the enemy with shells from their quick-fire cannon. Fighters patrolled high in the sky. Enemy aviation was not visible.
>
> As soon as the last attack planes left, our artillery rumbled and the army, divisional, regimental and battalion guns and mortars opened fire. Heavy artillery shells rushed over our heads, rising from the east bank of the Don. Using direct fire, the guns of 53rd Guards Artillery Regiment demolished the enemy's front line bunkers. Orekhovaya was enveloped in smoke. Dugouts and shelters collapsed, wire and anti-tank obstacles and trees were smashed.
>
> An hour later, the thunder of artillery fire began to ease.
>
> Then there was a loud 'Urrah!' from our front line and the crackle of small

arms fire. Still reeling from the bombardment, enemy soldiers jumped out of their shelters to repel the attack. There were muzzle flashes from the positions in Orekhovaya.

And then the sky over our heads was lit by red flashes – the salvoes of two Katyusha battalions. A signal flare climbed from Kazakevich's observation post. Tanks and infantry set off to storm Orekhovaya.[17]

Several hundred Hungarian troops – largely the new recruits – surrendered; others put up a spirited fight, but overall the opposition encountered by the Russians was modest at best. In some areas, the progress made by the reconnaissance thrusts was sufficient to trigger an early deployment of the main forces, though bringing forward the timetable of the assault by a day taxed the resources of the headquarters personnel of the Red Army formations, who had to issue revised orders to all the troops involved to ensure tight cooperation and had to move supplies forward a day earlier than anticipated. Nevertheless, the leading elements of Moskalenko's army secured several penetrations into the depth of the Hungarian defences.

The main attacks of the northern group of Russian forces began the following day. For the first 24 hours, the Hungarian IV Corps held its lines with dogged determination, even though the Russian infantry managed to make deep penetrations in some sectors, but the corps was too weak to sustain its defence; it had been forced to commit all its formations to the front line, and as these began to run out of ammunition there was only one possible outcome. The lack of local reserves was particularly critical with regard to the Russian penetrations, which could not be sealed off, let alone driven back. In vain, the Hungarians repeatedly requested support from the German *Korps Cramer* with two infantry divisions, the Hungarian 1st Armoured Division and an assault gun battalion, but this formation – designated as the sector reserve – could only be deployed on the express orders of Hitler. It was only as the day drew to a close that 168th Infantry Division was permitted to move from its reserve location towards Ostrogozhsk. If the division had been at full strength, its intervention might have made a difference, but its regiments had less than half their establishment strength and its tardy deployment had little effect.

Shafarenko's 25th Guards Rifle Division encountered gritty resistance and despite its successes the previous day made only limited progress. Demonstrating the growing skill of the Red Army in adapting to rapidly changing battlefield situations, Moskalenko contacted Shafarenko and advised him that the neighbouring 340th Rifle Division was advancing with greater ease; Shafarenko immediately dispatched two of his regiments and 116th Tank Brigade to his left flank to take advantage of this and was able to unhinge the stubborn defences to his front. By the end of the day the Hungarian front line had disintegrated and the main Russian armoured forces were unleashed.[18] The leading Russian forces rapidly penetrated at least 10 miles (17km), tearing open a breach of 30 miles (50km). Shafarenko's advancing regiments and supporting tanks ran into the 429th Infantry Regiment of the German 168th Infantry Division near Dovkalevka, and opted to launch a night attack to deny the Germans sufficient time to dig in:

> Before dark, the units prepared for the attack, restoring order to their formations and replenishing ammunition. The Guardsmen had a few moments' rest and consumed the dry rations issued for the day. It grew dark and colder. The Nazis fired occasionally with small arms and mortars, illuminating the terrain in front of their position with flares. Time passed slowly until the appointed moment. Then in the frosty silence came the crash of Katyushas. Bright trails of fire cut through the cold night sky from different directions towards Dovkalevka and Vesely Khutor. Fires broke out and ammunition stores in Dovkalevka began to explode. The Guardsmen attacked.
>
> The tanks of Captain Lagutin's company with assault submachine-gunners from 81st Guards Regiment were the first to break into Dovkalevka, cutting down the fascists who ran out of the houses. A battle broke out in the nearby farm. The blow was so unexpected for the enemy that he fled, abandoning weapons and serviceable vehicles. On the streets of Dovkalevka alone the enemy lost up to 350 soldiers and officers, dead and wounded.
>
> Our losses are two killed and one wounded.
>
> ... Bilyutin, the commander of the 78th Regiment, showed sensible initiative after capturing Vesely Khutor – he immediately organised the pursuit of the enemy and at 0800 on 14 January, together with a battalion of 253rd Infantry Brigade, he led his men into Mastyugino. The thrust by the regiment was extremely important. It took us into the enemy's second line of defence, which had not yet been occupied by defenders. It was necessary to take the most effective measures to preempt the Hitlerites. In our orders, overcoming the second defence zone was one of the main tasks of the division.
>
> We decided to create an advanced detachment of 81st Guards Regiment and a tank battalion of 116th Tank Brigade and deployed part of the second echelon – 73rd Guards Regiment – to advance on Platava, an important enemy strongpoint in the second line.[19]

Shafarenko's estimate of friendly and enemy casualties is probably as inaccurate as those in other accounts written by combatants on both sides, but the outcome was clear: the German 429th Infantry Regiment was driven back with substantial losses, and pursued energetically.

On 14 January, the attack widened in the north. Many Hungarian units put up stubborn resistance but the outcome was rarely in doubt. By the end of the day, some tank units had advanced 14 miles (23km) and the Hungarians were in disarray – the 12th Light Division had been almost completely destroyed. It took the intervention of parts of the German 26th Infantry Division – from *Korps Cramer* – to slow the Russian advance.

On the same day, the southern group of Russian forces attacked XXIV Panzer Corps. It took the commitment of the Russian XII and XV Tank Corps during the afternoon to break the initial resistance of the German lines. Both tank corps had problems in the preparation phase of the operation; the commander of XII Tank Corps was killed in an air attack while his units were detraining, and several sections of XV Tank Corps were delayed by bad road conditions. By the end of the day parts of the SS cavalry force and 387th Infantry Division were encircled. Somewhat predictably, Fegelein's SS horsemen proved to have even less combat value than the Hungarians and were rapidly defeated. The most dramatic episode of the assault to date occurred when Russian units from XV Tank Corps overran the headquarters of the panzer corps. Most of the personnel were killed, either during the fighting or were executed immediately afterwards, including the corps commander, Generalleutnant Martin Wandel; command passed to Generalleutnant Arno Jahr, the commander of 387th Infantry Division.

Gabriel Temkin, the Polish Jew who had escaped German captivity, was in a village in the Hungarian sector when the storm broke. Along with other able-bodied men, he was rounded up and ordered to join a column marching west. During the march, he encountered a labour battalion composed of Hungarian Jews, struggling under heavy loads and the curses and blows of Hungarian guards; when the column reached a small village, the men in Temkin's column were herded into a barn but the Jews were left outside, where many froze to death during the night. Whilst most of the persecution and mass murder of Hungary's Jewish population occurred in mid-1944 and Hitler repeatedly expressed frustration that the Horthy government was obstructing his racial policies, there was widespread mistreatment of Hungarian Jews in the preceding years. Although their plight was better than that of Jews in Poland or the occupied parts of the Soviet Union, it was by no means comfortable. Horthy was personally opposed to pogroms against the Jews, having protested about such acts in the chaotic days following the collapse of the Austro-Hungarian Empire, but even in those days his criticism was tempered by his need of forces to oppose communists in the newly independent Hungary, and he repeatedly refused to condemn the actions of some of the groups responsible for what became known as the 'White Terror'. In October 1940 he wrote a letter to his prime minister, supporting the widespread anti-Semitic views of many in Hungary but at the same time attempting to rationalise his distaste for measures against the Jews:

> As regards the Jewish problem, I have been an anti-Semite throughout my life. I have never had contact with Jews. I have considered it intolerable that here in Hungary everything, every factory, bank, large fortune, business, theatre, press, commerce, etc. should be in Jewish hands, and that the Jew should be the image reflected of Hungary, especially abroad. Since, however, one of the most important tasks of the government is to raise the standard of living, i.e., we have to acquire wealth, it is impossible, in a year or two, to replace the Jews, who have everything in their hands, and to replace them with incompetent, unworthy, mostly big-mouthed elements, for we should become bankrupt. This requires a generation at least.[20]

The Jewish population of Hungary was increasingly persecuted as the war continued, and in August 1941 about 20,000 Jews deemed not to have Hungarian citizenship – mainly those who had fled to Hungary from Poland and Czechoslovakia after the arrival of the Germans, but including many who had lived in Hungary all their lives but had no documentation to prove their citizenship – were shipped to the Ukraine and massacred at Kamianets-Podilskyi. The men who carried out the killings were a mixture of Germans, Ukrainians and Hungarians, operating under the overall control of Friedrich Jeckeln, who was *Höhere SS- und Polizei-Führer* ('Senior SS and Police Commander') of Russia. Known for his ruthlessness and infamous for conducting mass executions in which victims were stripped and forced to lie face down in pre-dug pits, often on top of previous victims, before being shot in the back of the head – a practice known as *Sardinenpackung* ('sardine packing') – Jeckeln oversaw several such massacres in the second half of 1941, for which he was awarded the War Merit Cross with Swords. Some 40,000 Jewish men were later sent from Hungary into the Ukraine as labour battalions, usually under the command of violently anti-Semitic Hungarian officers; only 5,000 returned to Hungary after the withdrawal of Hungarian troops in mid-1943.[21] Taking an opportunity to slip away from the combined column of Hungarian Jews and Ukrainian civilians, Temkin hid in a village until Red Army units caught up with him.[22]

Throughout 15 January, the Russian units in the north struggled to finish off the battered Hungarian divisions, rapidly accumulating prisoners and loot; Shafarenko wrote that his division alone took over 600 prisoners and captured 112 guns and mortars and numerous other items. However, it is worth noting that he included 54 anti-tank rifles amongst the booty, but such weapons were not in use in the Wehrmacht; this is therefore either a mistake or an exaggeration, and makes the accuracy of his other figures questionable.[23] The following day there was a major breakthrough as the various elements of Cramer's corps were scattered. An attempted counterattack by the German 26th Infantry Division and the Hungarian 1st Armoured Division was first brought to a halt and then reversed by a major counterattack and as the German infantry units pulled back in increasing disarray, the neighbouring Italian *Alpini* Corps' flank was exposed. Lieutenant General Gabriele Nasci, the corps commander, struggled in vain to get accurate information about the Russian attacks – the only information trickling down from above was that there had been some enemy penetrations, but the scale of these was completely underestimated in the reports sent to the *Alpini* Corps. Nasci's troops were the last major Italian formation left on the Eastern Front, and he had every intention of avoiding the fate of the units that had been caught up in *Little Saturn*. Any decision that he made would depend upon timely, accurate information if it was to be successful. Instead, he found himself having to rely upon reports that were at odds with reality.

The Russian XVIII Corps, an independent formation to the south of Fortieth Army and tasked with making one of the subsidiary thrusts to prevent the isolated enemy forces from forming a large, durable pocket, drove forward through the broken Hungarian units and threatened Ostrogozhsk from the east while troops from Fortieth Army approached from the north. If the two Russian columns converging on Ostrogozhsk met, a significant number of Hungarians would be encircled with little opportunity to set up any sort of perimeter. Other formations of the Russian XVIII Corps pursued the Hungarians and Germans towards the west while the southern Russian group also made rapid progress. Rossosh came under attack by XII Tank Corps early on 15 January, and a mixed group of troops – a few German assault guns, headquarters staff and a battalion of *Alpini* – supported by a timely Stuka attack managed to beat off the first attempt by the Russians to capture the town. The following day, the Russians attacked in greater strength and captured the town, and the arrival of infantry freed the armoured formations to exploit further to the northwest; XII Tank Corps turned north, while XV Tank Corps raced towards Alekseyevka, the prime target for both Russian attack groups. However, as had consistently been the case throughout the winter, the Russian tanks began to struggle with the limitations of their supply lines. In an attempt to improve matters, most tanks had been fitted with a barrel of fuel and carried boxes of additional ammunition, both strapped to the rear deck, but many tanks were running low on diesel and supply levels were too low to guarantee that they would be able to reach Alekseyevka. In order to ensure mobility, fuel was transferred to the tanks of 88th Tank Brigade and the vehicles that were left without fuel took up all-round defence to await the arrival of further supplies and reinforcements from the rear.[24]

The effective destruction of the headquarters of XXIV Panzer Corps began to have serious consequences. Believing that the Italians were already withdrawing, Jahr issued orders for what remained of his corps to start pulling back to the west; at first, this was countermanded by Army Group B, but permission was finally granted late on 15 January and the Germans began to pull out – given that they thought that the Italians had already started to move west, they made no attempt to inform the *Alpini* of their own withdrawal. The Italians, who had not yet started to withdraw, widely interpreted this as a cynical attempt by the Germans to leave the Italians behind effectively to cover their own retreat.[25] General Italo Gariboldi, commander of the Italian Eighth Army, had indeed requested permission from Weichs at Army Group B for a withdrawal, but at the headquarters of the *Alpini* Corps, Nasci – acting on the basis of the information that he had received about the modest scale of the Russian attacks – ordered his men to launch local counterattacks. These made little progress, but the result was that his formations lost connection with the German units of XXIV Panzer Corps. Late on 15 January, Nasci realised that his men were being left behind and issued orders for the withdrawal of the *Alpini* to begin.

After the fall of Rossosh, Gariboldi was able to make contact with XXIV Panzer Corps. He was informed that the Germans were almost out of ammunition. Orders from higher commands were often contradictory; at dawn on 17 January, Nasci received a message from Weichs: 'To leave the Don line without orders from Army [Group B] is absolutely forbidden. I will hold you personally responsible for executing this.'[26]

Shortly after, fresh instructions arrived from Gariboldi stating that XXIV Panzer Corps and the *Alpini* Corps were to break out to the west. An attempt to recapture Rossosh on 17 January failed, and it became clear to the Italians that any escape would have to be through the terrain to the north of the town, across roads that were less suitable for large-scale movements. In addition to the withdrawal of XXIV Panzer Corps on the southern flank of the Italians, news arrived that the Hungarians to the north were also pulling back – this was in fact not entirely correct, and whilst many Hungarian formations had been overrun or driven back, others were still clinging to their positions. Nevertheless, Russian forces were able to press south against the exposed flank of the Italians and a withdrawal became vital if the *Alpini* were to escape destruction.

The leading elements of the Russian 107th Rifle Division, on the southern flank of Fortieth Army, reached Ostrogozhsk on 17 December. Ivan Stepanovich Nosov was an artilleryman who took part in the assault on the German defences:

And then the artillery preparation began. Shells and mortar bombs began to explode on the enemy positions. Smoke swirled over our gun barrels and, rising slowly into the sky, dispersed in the frosty blue.

Soon the line of riflemen moved forward. We too followed with our gun. But then some sort of enemy strongpoint came to life. Several of our infantry fell. The gun crew prepared to fire. 'Straight ahead, a bush. The bunker is to the right,' the gun commander directed me. I quickly spotted the target. There it was, a snowy hillock. In its centre – the firing aperture of the bunker. From there, a machine-gun blazed away incessantly. I also saw that several figures had moved away from the line of riflemen. Brave individuals were crawling towards the bunker, leaving behind deep furrows in the snow.

'Fire!' shouted the team. I pulled the trigger. Smoke and snow obscured the target, but the fascist-machine gun continued to fire. The sergeant made an adjustment. Again, we aimed carefully. This time the projectile hit the top of the hillock, raising a cloud of snow.

'What are you doing?!' [Sergeant] Artamonov [the gun commander] was upset. I was overcome by irritation and anger. I tried to pull myself together, calm down. And as soon as the smoke cleared, I fired a third shell at the bunker. A flame flashed right in the embrasure. The machine-gun fire stopped. 'We should have done that quicker,' the gun commander said, calming down.

As soon as we destroyed this bunker, the Nazis began to withdraw, still firing. The line of our riflemen rose and moved forward. Plunging waist-deep through the snow, the crew rolled the gun after them. Sweat poured down our faces, my throat was dry and I was desperate for a drink. I felt my strength was running out. And the sergeant hurried us onward: 'Faster, faster, guys! We are behind the infantry.'

With great difficulty we covered the snow-covered field, and then a hollow with a few bushes. When climbing the far slope, we reached the end of our strength. Fuelled by anger alone we managed to push the gun to the next firing position.

We caught up with the infantry during the evening … We stopped. The usual tension of battle was replaced by deadly fatigue. We could not move any further.[27]

As the Germans pulled back, the men of 107th Rifle Division secured Ostrogozhsk and linked up with troops approaching from the east; the northern flank of the Hungarian Second Army was either broken and fleeing to the west or encircled. A day later, XV Tank Corps reached Alekseyevka. Alexander Alexeyevich Vetrov, the deputy technical officer of the corps, was with the leading elements:

It was already getting dark when elements of 88th Tank Brigade, with whom General Koptsov [the corps commander] was advancing, approached the southwestern outskirts of Alekseyevka. From a small hill, they were surprised to see everyday activity at the large railway station: the locomotives were smoking on the tracks, trains were being assembled, and people were busily fussing around the railcars. The Nazis clearly did not expect us.

'We must attack before we are spotted,' said the corps commander, without taking the binoculars from his eyes.

The commander of the 88th Tank Brigade, Lieutenant-Colonel Sergeev … shrugged his shoulders. He objected uncertainly: 'But I have only 20 tanks and two companies of motorised rifles, Comrade General. According to intelligence reports, there is a large police unit in Alekseyevka, as well as several regiments of Hungarians and Italians. Would it not be better to wait for the approach of the remaining tanks and rifle units?'

'No, not better. An immediate attack by our small squad will suffice – surprise, take the enemy by surprise. And this will give us a great advantage,' Koptsov answered, and immediately switched to detailed orders for the combat mission.

In the darkness, one company of 34 men burst into the southwest outskirts of the city. Its attack was so quick and impetuous that the enemy, many times superior to us in strength, wavered from the very first minute. And then our submachine-gunners, supported by the tanks, struck the city from the opposite side. In a short time a railway station was captured, together with many prisoners, steam locomotives under steam, and wagons loaded with valuable material.

In the city, things were different. Our tank company, which at first quite easily mastered the central Factory Street and the plant itself, was then stopped by strong artillery and mortar fire from near the monastery. There, as it turned out, a fairly large Hungarian garrison was stationed. And in general, after recovering from the first confusion and realising that they were dealing with only a small body of our troops, the enemy soon increased resistance everywhere. Moreover, bringing up reserves, they even launched a counterattack. Having repulsed it, the tank company passed to active defence. But at the end of the next day, unable to hold out until the arrival of 52nd Mechanised Brigade, we were forced to abandon the city centre and pull back to the southern outskirts of the city.

At dawn on 19 January, the main corps forces with artillery and motorised rifle battalions joined us. The 2nd and 3rd Battalions of Lieutenant-Colonel Golovachev's 52nd Mechanised Brigade joined the company of tanks that had been driven back to the southern outskirts of Alekseyevka. After a short artillery preparation they made a fresh attack. Fierce street battles began. The enemy resisted desperately, repeatedly making counterattacks. Some locations changed hands several times. The men of 2nd Motorised Rifle Battalion under the command of Senior Lieutenant Lapsin particularly distinguished themselves.

By noon, after breaking the stubborn resistance of the enemy, our units once more seized the railway station, where 37 locomotives and 476 wagons with military equipment had accumulated. And an hour or two later the tank brigades completely encircled Alekseyevka from the south, west and east. Finally, realising the pointlessness of further resistance, the garrison of the city began to surrender. The first to put up white flags were the Italians. Hungarian soldiers and officers weren't far behind them. Finally the Germans waved white rags and went to captivity. Another Soviet city was thus liberated from the enemy.[28]

The following day, a local teacher led Koptsov and his fellow officers to the charred ruins of a barn on the northern edge of Alekseyevka. He explained that just a day before, a group of SS soldiers had arrived with a large number of Russian prisoners, many of them wounded soldiers, and including many women and children. The prisoners were pushed into the barn, the doors were bolted, and the building was set alight. Other witnesses described how the side wall of the barn collapsed in the flames and a woman attempted to crawl from the inferno, clutching a dead child; a German soldier shot her. The Russians also learned of a nearby camp where the Germans had held forced labourers:

Taking with us a military doctor and two townspeople and a few vehicles, we set off. Soon our vehicles reached a dense barbed wire fence around an open camp, exposed to the wind on all sides.

Here, too, we saw a terrible scene. In the barracks were thousands, exhausted by their intolerable labours, hunger and cold, and the unimaginable abuse of their captors. Many were so exhausted that they could not even rise from their wooden bunks.

Among the prisoners were Russian speakers. From them we learned that the camp, guarded by SS police, was under the responsibility of the Todt organisation's road construction team. Jews from many countries of Europe had been brought here. Among them were prominent scientists, lawyers, writers, doctors, and musicians.

We were told that in the camp each prisoner was given a certain period of hard labour, after which he was subject to mandatory execution.

'I still had a long time to serve, five months and nine days,' our volunteer guide interpreter from amongst the prisoners told us, grunting with the pain of a back injury, 'but my friend, an Austrian artist, had only eight days left.'

We approached a tall, thin old man with feverish, glittering eyes and long grey strands of hair, wearing a broad yellow strip with a black six-pointed star on the left sleeve of his striped jacket. We asked who he was.

'I'm a lawyer from Budapest,' the prisoner answered. 'I am 41 years old. I worked as a digger for over a year. If it had not been for the Red Army, I would have been killed in 12 days.'[29]

The Todt Organisation was created in 1933 when Fritz Todt, in his post as *Generalinspektor für das deutsche Strassenwesen* ('General Inspector of German Roadways'), used the *Reichsarbeitsdienst* ('Reich Labour Service' or *RAD*) and its conscripted workforce to increase the rate at which Germany's Autobahn network – originally built with workers recruited on the open labour market – was being constructed. This labour force was given its eponymous title in 1938, and from 1939 the Todt Organisation was increasingly involved in military construction rather than the civil engineering projects of earlier years. As the demands on the organisation steadily increased, labourers were acquired from prisoners and civilians in occupied territories, not least because Germans were now being conscripted into the armed forces. Within months of the invasion of the Soviet Union, Todt became convinced that the war on the Eastern Front could not be won and used his high standing within the German government to make his opinions known to Hitler. He was killed in an air crash shortly after in February 1942, leading to speculation that he had been assassinated because of his views; Albert Speer, who replaced him, wrote in his memoirs that the enquiry held by the Reich Air Ministry concluded that the possibility of sabotage was ruled out, and consequently further measures were not required – in other words, there was no attempt to determine the true cause of the accident, something that Speer regarded as 'curious'.[30] On the Eastern Front, Todt labour battalions were used widely for the construction of field fortifications, airfields, and almost any other requirement of the occupying forces, and as the war progressed larger numbers of concentration camp prisoners and local civilians were used.

Vsevolod Pavlovich Shemanskiy was a junior signals officer with the Russian 116th Tank Brigade, operating as part of the northern group of Red Army forces. On 20 January, the brigade received orders to accelerate the advance with a penetration to the town of Golofeevka, on the main railway line running from Voronezh to the Donbas region:

I must say, the task was not easy. Golofeevka was comparatively deep behind enemy lines. To get to it, we would need swiftly to pass through a number of settlements in which there were German garrisons of variable strength. But by seizing this rail station, we would disrupt enemy communications and deprive the enemy of the opportunity to transfer reserves to the area of our offensive. Also, once we secured the station, we would cover the left flank of our troops from possible strikes of German units surrounded in the Ostrogozhsk area if they tried to escape from the encirclement. The tankmen could achieve this objective with a quick thrust, suddenly appearing at the location where the enemy did not expect them.

... The tanks moved towards Golofeevka in a column. Ahead was a combat reconnaissance patrol – the light tank platoon of Lieutenant Vasily Stepanovich Tkachev. Sergey Zhelnov was on the back of one, with one of our radio sets. Behind the reconnaissance platoon, at the requisite distance, was the leading element of the KV tank company. It was led by Bobrovitsky. Behind it was the rest of the detachment. The night was dark, a violent blizzard was raging, and the flanking patrols maintained radio silence.

... We moved cautiously. We tried to bypass settlements and avoid combat with minor units. The main thing was to approach Golofeevka quietly and suddenly attack the enemy.

The drivers drove the tanks at low speed, guided by the track marks of the reconnaissance vehicles and by the barely discernible marker sticks that stood along the side of the road [protruding above the snow]. In order not to wander off the road, the tank commanders opened their hatches and leaned forward in their turrets, straining their eyes, peering into the snowy haze, ready for any surprise. The infantry were sitting silently behind the turrets. Some were dozing, warmed by the heat from the engines, others were lost in the endless thoughts of soldiers. Nobody smoked. The howl of the blizzard and the gusty wind covered the noise of the engines.

Judging by the map, we were near a large village where there should be enemy units. The reconnaissance tanks turned into a field to bypass it. The rest followed. A long time passed before we again reached the road. Before that, we came upon a familiar scene. About 2km from the village a column of enemy vehicles was found stranded in the snow: about a dozen trucks. German drivers were dozing in the cabins, waiting for dawn. But here came our tanks. Our soldiers quickly rounded up the Germans, who were taken by surprise. We decided not to waste time with the trucks. Bobrovitsky left a tank and a detachment of submachine-gunners to protect them and hastened on to Golofeevka itself. When the main forces of our detachment approached the stuck column, they tied the trucks to their tanks. Our soldiers took the wheel of some, and disarmed German drivers drove the rest.

Before dawn Tkachev's tanks approached Golofeevka. The enemy did not show himself. A squad of submachine-gunners was sent to the railway station. In white coats, they seemed like ghosts, quickly dissolving in the mist and falling snow.

Minutes of waiting. Only those who wait for the return of scouts know how slowly time passes. Just as they had disappeared, the pale silhouettes of men in long white coats suddenly came into view. The scouts reported that there were three trains with locomotives under steam in the station. Apparently, the enemy hadn't enough manpower for them. Near the crossing of the railway line, there was a bunker. The station and the freight trains were guarded.

Tkachev's decision was immediate – to attack without delay, using all the advantages of surprise ...

The tanks spread out and moved towards the station. The outlines of the buildings appeared, the trains on the tracks. One of the trains started to move. Yamigin's tank was closest to it. Two shells fired by Yamigin hit the target precisely: the locomotive froze in place. Pashcha's tank hit the bunker at the crossing and eliminated its garrison. Tkachev's tank broke through to the station, firing on the railway commandant's office.

Enemy soldiers ran from the station building in haste, but directly into the fire of our submachine-gunners ... When Selivanov came up with his tanks, Golofeevka was already taken ... It was morning of the 22nd of January. Stupin and Selivanov organized the defense of Golofeevka and sent scouts to nearby settlements. They examined the captured trucks and found food in them.

The village residents emerged. They gathered in groups around the tankmen and began to ask impatiently for news from the fronts. The soldiers answered them and persuaded everyone to go home. Time was passing and we feared air attack by the fascists.

The blizzard stopped. The sun came out. Returning scouts reported that there was no enemy in nearby villages, and the policemen, having learned that Soviet troops were in Golofeevka, had fled.[31]

In their haste to advance, some Russian units found themselves facing unexpected difficulties. One of Shafarenko's regiments approached the village of Siniye Lipyagi under the belief that it was not occupied by the Germans, and Bilyutin, the regiment commander, hastily summoned help. When the regiment led by Shtykov arrived, Bilyutin swiftly informed him of events:

The pace of march had greatly accelerated. All wanted to reach the village as quickly as possible and rest there at least for half an hour after exhausting off-road movement.

Suddenly, when the regiment was about 5km from Siniye Lipyagi, the commander of the forward detachment [who had reported the village free of Germans] sent a new, alarming message: 'I am engaged by large enemy forces. [I am] Surrounded. I need help.' It turned out that a large column of Nazis with tanks and artillery had just arrived in the village. The advance detachment was trapped. They engaged in combat, taking up positions for circular defence in the centre of Siniye Lipyagi.

'We can still hear shooting,' Bilyutin said, nodding toward the village. 'So the advance detachment is still holding on. But how long will they last? After all, they don't have any heavy weapons. And against the tanks and the artillery, what can they do with rifles?' He winced and continued: 'I pity them. They are waiting for us in hope. And we've just made our sixth attack, we've already put in a big effort.'

I understood his plight. Of course, every minute was precious now. After all, there, in Siniye Lipyagi, people were dying. Our brave people! And we had to help at all costs!

Quickly we organised artillery to strike the enemy's firing points, identified in previous attacks. While the artillery was moving up, the battalions of my regiment bypassed Siniye Lypyagi on both flanks. We agreed that Bilyutin's regiment would continue to attack from the front.

Our artillery fired its shells. Fire and smoke marked the outskirts of the village. For some reason the Nazis were silent. Perhaps they were stunned by such a powerful bombardment and they realised that new reinforcements were approaching and were now preparing for a particularly strong onslaught.

A red flare flew into the grey sky. It was the signal. Bilyutin's regiment rose for its seventh attack. My battalions led by Golovin, Nikifortsev and Obukhov hit the flanks and the rear of Siniye Lipyagi. The well-coordinated attack of the two regiments was successful: we burst into the village. But for several hours a fierce melee continued on its streets, sometimes resulting in hand-to-hand fighting.[32]

Eventually, the Germans were driven off. The Russians claimed to have killed or captured 1,500 Germans and to have destroyed many tanks; however, there were few German armoured units operating in the area, and this claim is therefore questionable.

On 21 January, after fending off German counterattacks, XV Tank Corps was able to continue its advance, linking up with elements of Fortieth Army approaching from the north and creating a second encirclement. For the moment, the ring around each encirclement remained incomplete and there was still an opportunity for the Hungarians, Italians and Germans to escape, but this would require urgent action. With his army disintegrating around him, Jány sent an urgent signal to Army Group B. Unless he received clear instructions to pull back by the end of 18 January, he intended to take matters into his own hands. Gariboldi meanwhile had lost patience and ordered his men to pull back, despite further orders from Weichs to continue to hold the front line for as long as possible. In freezing weather, the now familiar columns of disorganised troops and rear area units began to struggle through the snow. Elements of the *Alpini* and XXIV Panzer Corps became entangled, leading to clashes and even exchanges of fire. Late on 17 January, Gariboldi received further orders from Army Group B instructing him to continue to hold the front line in order to cover the withdrawal of XXIV Panzer Corps; even if such instructions had been realistic, they arrived too late.

The Italians and Germans pulled back across the valley of the River Rossosh, north of the town of the same name. The southern columns included men from Jahr's 387th Infantry Division as well as parts of the Italian *Julia* and *Cuneense* Divisions, and as they struggled along the frozen roads, the retreating troops were forced to abandon many of their vehicles. As a consequence, most communications equipment was lost, further disrupting command and control. The troops on the southern flank of the retreat suffered the most from Russian pressure, suffering heavy losses from constant Russian attacks, both by Red Army units and partisan formations.

Having moved north of Rossosh, a force consisting largely of a regiment from the *Julia* Division reached the village of Novaya Postoyalovka on 19 January, where it ran into Russian infantry. At this stage of the retreat, the Italians still had some of their artillery with them, and nine howitzers supported an attempt to storm the village; although the *Alpini* succeeded in securing a lodgement in the eastern edge, they were unable to make further progress and the appearance of seven Russian tanks forced them back. Fighting continued all day, and during the following night the Italians attempted to regroup. Before dawn on 20 January,

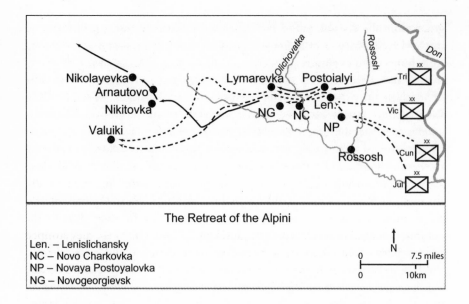

The Retreat of the Alpini

Len. – Lenislichansky
NC – Novo Charkovka
NP – Novaya Postoyalovka
NG – Novogeorgievsk

they tried once more to take Novaya Postoyalovka, but the Russians had been reinforced by units moving north from Rossosh and drove the *Alpini* off with heavy losses. As further Italian units arrived, they joined the increasingly desperate attacks and during the afternoon there was a final assault on a ridge that blocked the Italians from continuing their retreat, little more than a human wave led by a few determined officers:

> A desperate throng hurled itself towards the enemy ... pushed by the frenzy of wanting either to outrun death or embrace it. Behind the first ones, they rose from the snow and thrust themselves forward in an incredible jumble of machine-gunners without weapons, quartermasters, telephonists, non-commissioned officers, medical corpsmen, drivers, doctors, mule drivers, artillerymen, and *Alpini* who had fired their last bullets.[33]

Despite this attack, the Russians remained in the western edge of the village, blocking the line of retreat. By this stage, the *Alpini* had abandoned all materiel that was not essential to combat, and there was therefore little that could be done for the wounded from the fighting.

The surviving German troops from 387th Infantry Division succeeded in crossing the crest that had cost the Italians so much blood, but, together with parts of 27th Panzer Division and much of Fegelein's SS Cavalry Brigade, a large group from the division found itself encircled by Russian forces in and around the Soviet collective farm at Lenislichansky. Out of ammunition and suffering from hunger and exposure, the Germans had no choice but to surrender; rather than become a prisoner, Jahr shot himself. Generalleutnant Karl Eibl, commander of 385th Infantry Division, had already been ordered to take command of XXIV Panzer Corps, largely because Jahr was unable to reach the corps headquarters and was out of communication with higher commands.

An attempt to outflank the Russians in Novaya Postoyalovka by moving to the north ended in failure, but after a long, difficult march through deep snow the following night, a column of men from *Julia* managed to slip through the Russian cordon and reached the Voronezh-Rossosh road. By this stage, most of the men had been without any food for four days.[34] The column managed to reach Novogeorgievsk on 22 January, where they stopped to rest. Before long, Russian tanks and infantry appeared and it was clear to the Italian officers that their men were incapable of further exertions. The commander of the 8th *Alpini* Regiment of the *Julia* Division opted to negotiate a surrender to spare his men further casualties. A few small parties managed to slip away through the Russian lines and joined up with other retreating columns. However, the struggles of the men of *Julia* had not been in vain; by engaging the Russians in and around Novaya Postoyalovka, they prevented them from moving further north to attack the retreating column of the *Tridentina* Division.

Conditions for the retreating soldiers were as terrible as those experienced by others in the bitter retreats from the Don. In Lymarevka, the schoolhouse was used to shelter the wounded, but other soldiers tried desperately to escape the cold outside, as an Italian chaplain later described:

> [The soldiers] literally intoxicated by the cold, broke through the fragile line of the sentinels and men spilled into the schoolrooms, stepping on the wounded and dying men on the floor. It was a tangle of bodies, screams, curses, and pleas in the shadows of that hopeless hovel.[35]

Many of the villages through which the retreating soldiers passed were defended by groups of partisans, while others had been abandoned entirely. Some were still inhabited, and despite the widespread merciless brutality experienced by so many in the campaign, there were moments of rare compassion and kindness. One Italian soldier, Vittorio Trentini, had lost his gloves and his hands were developing frostbite. A Russian woman in an *isba* where he sought shelter from the cold looked at his discoloured hands silently, and then took up a sheepskin from the floor and left the room. She returned having made mittens for him:

> Lovingly she urged me to try them on, smiling once she was certain they fitted well. I have kept those mitts; they saved my hands ... I shall always remember that dear mother whom I hugged with intense emotion ... I shall always remember her with infinite gratitude.[36]

Others too experienced similar events when the peasants – who had so little themselves – took pity on the frostbitten Italians with their inadequate worn-out boots wrapped in rags. The kindness and good behaviour of Italian soldiers in the second half of 1942 was clearly widely known amongst the local population. A lieutenant later wrote:

> It was during the withdrawal that we discovered the genuine humanity of Russian peasants, ready to share their humble *isbas* and what little food they had. Then, as well as much later, they accommodated us not as aggressors, but as victims of a common catastrophe.[37]

North of Lenislichansky, where the predominantly German group under Jahr had surrendered, the retreating *Alpini* of the *Tridentina* Division managed to evade the Russians who had blocked the attempts to escape further south and approached Postoialyi. Suspecting the village was occupied by Russian troops, General Luigi Reverberi, the commander of *Tridentina*, ordered a battalion to secure the buildings; the *Alpini* picked their way into the village and suddenly found themselves caught in an ambush. As they desperately defended themselves, other *Alpini* rushed to their aid, driving the Russians off; as was consistently the case, the poorly armed *Alpini* paid a heavy price in blood for their success.

From Postoialyi, the *Tridentina* column continued west to the River Olichovatka. Here they found a Russian force blocking their retreat at Novo Charkovka, but an attack by *Tridentina* managed to capture the village and reopened the route; during this period, the Russians were struggling to bring forward fuel to their leading armoured formations, and were thus unable to block their retreating enemies as effectively as they would have wished. Eibl was with the last of the troops to reach Novo Charkovka and as his truck approached the village, there was an explosion. Whether this was the result of the truck passing over a landmine or a hand grenade thrown by Italian troops who mistook the Germans for Russians, Eibl suffered a severe wound to his leg.[38] Two Italian

Army doctors treated him and concluded that the only way of saving his life was a field amputation, which they carried out in the most primitive of conditions without any morphine or other drugs. Despite their efforts, Eibl died from loss of blood the following day.[39] In Generalmajor Otto Heidkämper, XXIV Panzer Corps acquired its fourth commander in less than a week.

Not far away, Nikolai Pustyntsev and his reconnaissance team were out ahead of their division. They encountered a small group of partisans outside a farm during a night march and asked about the location of any Germans; the partisans told them that a rear area unit was in a nearby village. They moved to the village, which was actually free of Germans, where they were offered shelter by the locals, but awoke to noise and confusion: a German unit, one of the many attempting to retreat to the west, was also seeking shelter in the village. They fled into nearby woodland where the partisans they had met earlier took them to an encampment. Here, the partisan commander – who had served briefly with the cavalry before the war – advised them that a group of about 200 Germans and Hungarians had gathered in the village of Vakulovka. He suggested that the small reconnaissance group should attack them in conjunction with the partisan band, and the combined force deployed rapidly:

In the darkness, a shadow approached. A boy crept up to us. I heard his muffled voice: 'It's me, Vasek. They asked me to tell you that the second group is ready.' The partisan commander nodded in approval and, lifting a flare gun, shot upwards. The night sky was lit up with a pink flame. The wooden huts were clearly visible with caps of snow on the roofs, hedges, vegetable gardens and snowdrifts, all looking pink in the flare's light.

Someone began to fire a machine-gun. From the opposite outskirts of the village came rifle volleys. The partisan group broke into the centre of the village. The Nazis ran out of the huts in panic and fell to the ground, struck by partisan bullets.

The partisan commander ordered our group to search an isolated house. We approached cautiously and threw open the door. Before us was a curious sight: on a table in the corner, an oil lamp flickered dimly. Soldiers threw themselves to the floor. '*Hände hoch!*' we shouted. We aimed the muzzles of our three submachine guns at the men on the floor. They quickly jumped up and raised their hands. I turned on my flashlight. They were thin, their faces covered with bristles. They had a hungry gleam in their eyes. 'German? *Soldaten?*'

'*Nix German. Wir Ungar,*' they muttered in fear, looking at us hopefully. Who could tell: were they Hungarians or just calling themselves that to ease their fate, having been captured by the partisans? They knew how great was the hatred of the

Soviet people for the Hitlerite invaders, whose hands were stained with the blood of millions of innocent children, women, and the elderly. The hour of retribution had come.

We took the prisoners' weapons, and led them to the collecting point – the rural schoolhouse. It was crammed full. More than a hundred enemy soldiers and officers were captured.[40]

The retreating troops had been acting on the assumption that they were trying to reach the small town of Valuiki, but late on 21 January a radio message reached the radio set used by XXIV Panzer Corps – one of the few amongst the retreating troops that was still functioning – that they should try to reach Nikitovka instead. Retreating on an axis a little further north than the main body, the *Tridentina* Division continued towards Nikitovka and captured it after a brief fight on 25 January. The rest of the retreating troops reached Valuiki, fighting off constant attacks by Russian units, both from the Red Army and the local partisans, unaware that they were meant to be following the *Tridentina* Division further north. The Russian VII Cavalry Corps – redesignated VI Guards Cavalry Corps in recognition of its successes in this operation – blocked the way further west. The exhausted Italians, together with the remnants of the German formations that had been swept away by the Russian advance, tried in vain to break through the Russian defences. Many were killed, and most laid down their arms after a brief battle.

After passing through Nikitovka, the *Tridentina* Division led a column of perhaps 40,000 Italians, Hungarians and Germans to the next village, Arnautovo. Here too the way was barred, and the *Alpini* made three attacks that were bloodily repulsed. After five hours of fighting, the *Alpini* pulled back a short distance to try to gather their strength. The *Tirano* battalion of *Tridentina* then launched a further attack and succeeded in driving off the Russians; after the fighting, the battalion was reduced to just 150 men.[41] Other elements of *Tridentina* bypassed Arnautovo and approached the village of Nikolayevka. Here, the vanguard encountered an Italian soldier fleeing towards them; he told them that he had been a prisoner of the Russians but had escaped, and warned the column against trying to force the defences in the dark.

On the morning of 26 January the vanguard (two weak battalions and one fairly strong battalion) ventured forward, supported by three German assault guns. The eastern approach to Nikolayevka was across an open snow-covered slope and the Russian defenders inflicted heavy losses on the advancing men; at the bottom of the slope they engaged in close-quarter fighting amongst the houses and buildings around the railway station. Losses mounted steadily on both sides for little gain. Reverberi, commander of the *Tridentina* Division, and Heidkämper met to discuss their options, and were surprised when a German Fieseler Storch landed nearby. Heidkämper boarded the plane and conducted a quick reconnaissance of the area before returning; the pilot of the plane offered to fly him and Reverberi to safety, but they chose to stay with their men. As darkness fell, Reverberi climbed onto one of the German assault guns and shouted encouragement to his men, bellowing '*Avanti Tridentina!*' a cry that was taken up by thousands, both armed and unarmed, and a human wave swept towards the Russians. Despite their clear superiority in firepower, the Russians withdrew; General Giulio Martinat, chief of staff of the *Alpini* Corps, was killed leading the assault, but the village was overrun and the exhausted Italians and Germans sheltered in Nikolayevka overnight. When the spring thaw came, the Russians counted about 11,000 dead of all nationalities in and around Nikolayevka.[42]

Even in the midst of the fighting, there continued to be moments of surprising compassion. A sergeant of the *Alpini* entered an *isba* in the hope of finding some food, and was shocked to stumble into a room where heavily armed Russian soldiers were sitting around a table, sharing a meal. As he stood rigid with fear, a woman in the *isba* offered him some milk and food. Silently, he slung his rifle over his shoulder and took the food. When he had finished, he returned the bowl to the woman, thanked her, and left, watched in silence by the Russian soldiers.[43] Immediately after the battle, an Italian lieutenant found five Russian soldiers in another *isba*, sitting at a table and waiting for a woman who was cooking them a meal. They smiled at him and pointed at a vacant seat. The woman served him as well as the Russians, who then lay down next to the stove to sleep, encouraging him to join them. The following morning, they woke him and pointed him to the west, sending him on his way with smiles and waves.[44]

Led by the last surviving German assault gun, the column set off again on 27 January, brushing aside a Russian defensive position immediately to the west. Harassed from the air, the men marched on through the snow, many falling by the roadside through exhaustion, cold and hunger. As the few mules with the column faltered and died, wounded men were abandoned, crying out in vain not to be abandoned or for someone to put them out of their misery. Finally, on 29 January, the survivors reached German lines.

From the Russian perspective, the Ostrogozhsk-Rossosh Operation, as it was known to them, was a complete success. In his memoirs, Moskalenko, the commander of Fortieth Army, claimed that over 71,000 prisoners were taken and 52,000 Hungarian, Italian and German soldiers were killed; in addition, huge stocks of military equipment, ammunition, food and other supplies were captured. He therefore calculated that the enemy had lost over 123,000 men killed or taken prisoner, compared with his army's losses of 4,527.[45] Even if casualties for the other Russian armies involved in the operation were proportionately heavier, the outcome was still a huge victory for the Soviet Union. Unsurprisingly, morale was high, contributing to the growing sense of confidence:

> A curious detail: there were so many prisoners that we were not able to transport them under guard. Therefore, so-called meeting points were created. Our soldiers confined themselves to explaining to the prisoners where to go. They then walked in the specified direction, asking people they met for further directions.
>
> Columns of prisoners were marching east, and Soviet troops, among them the Fortieth Army, were hurrying westward. The enthusiasm was great, our chests bursting with joy: the long-awaited hour had come! We beat the fascists, liberated our native land and our fathers, mothers, sisters, brothers and children who were languishing in captivity. In that glorious, unforgettable January of 1943, we all seemed to have grown wings to drive the enemy west ever more quickly.[46]

The Hungarians later estimated that in less than three weeks, they lost 35,000 dead and a similar number wounded, with perhaps 26,000 taken prisoner.[47] The total Italian losses on the Don were greater. Only 25,000 men of the *Alpini* Corps escaped, leaving behind tens of thousands of dead, and a total of at least 75,000 taken prisoner as a result of *Little Saturn* and the battles of the Ostrogozhsk-Rossosh Operation. Most of those who fell into Russian hands died, usually as a result of illness or exposure, but many were also executed out of hand. However, those who survived later recalled the manner in which the Russians dealt with different nationalities. One *Alpino* watched two soldiers searching a group of prisoners:

> They make two people advance, they search in their coats and jackets, grabbing watches, rings and all personal possessions, then they look at the nationality. If the soldier is German he is stabbed with a bayonet, or shot point-blank; if he is Italian or Hungarian, his life is saved.[48]

Some died as a result of the 'accidents' of war. One group of Italian prisoners was loaded into railway freightcars in Valuiki and locked in; before the train could leave, it was attacked by German aircraft. Hundreds of those aboard were killed, and those who survived were forced to march for days – often unsupervised, as

Moskalenko described, and without food – until they reached rudimentary prison camps.[49]

Even when they reached the new front line, the retreating Italians who escaped capture often had further ordeals ahead of them. The pressure upon logistic services and the almost complete loss of the Italian Eighth Army's own rear area units meant that there was little by way of transport to take the survivors away from the front line, and the frostbitten, starving men had no option other than to continue their march. Eventually, they were put aboard trains and transported back to Italy; most of them were in need of medical care, but there weren't enough hospital beds available and care often had to be improvised. In an attempt to hide the magnitude of the disaster, Mussolini ordered that families should not be allowed to greet the returning trains, leading to wretched scenes at railway stations where military police had the unhappy task of holding back civilians desperate for news of their husbands, brothers, fathers and sons. When they were allowed to visit the temporary hospitals where the men were taken, many civilians were horrified by the stench of gangrene from frostbitten limbs. With no access to antibiotics, the medical staff carried out thousands of amputations, adding to the despair of the soldiers who faced a return to their rural homes without legs or arms, knowing that there was no possibility of them being able to work on the farms they had left when they were sent east. The men of Eighth Army paid a huge price for Mussolini's arrogant folly and lack of preparedness for the realities of war.

German losses in this battle amounted to just 6,500, but the total German combat strength in the fighting was barely 10,000 men. The personnel of 385th and 387th Infantry Divisions were reorganised as a new 387th Infantry Division, with 385th Infantry Division being disbanded. Weichs' Army Group B was left commanding nothing more than a few battered remnants and the formations arriving from the west, and as will be described later it was disbanded a few days after the conclusion of the Ostrogozhsk-Rossosh Operation, its remaining troops being assigned to the neighbouring Army Group Centre in the north and Manstein's Army Group Don in the south. Remarkably, Weichs escaped criticism from Hitler and was promoted to Field Marshal; after a spell in the 'Führer Reserve' he was given command of German forces in the Balkans, from where he conducted a highly skilful withdrawal under heavy pressure from all directions towards the end of the war. He went into captivity after the war with the Western Allies but was released while awaiting trial for war crimes due to his ill health. He died in 1954. Gariboldi returned to Italy with the remnants of his army, and was awarded the Knight's Cross by Hitler in recognition for his services on the

Eastern Front. Thereafter, he was caught up in the collapse of the fascist government. The Germans imprisoned him and sentenced him first to ten years' imprisonment and then to death the following year on charges of treason, but he was liberated by the advancing Western Allies. He died in 1970; his son followed in his footsteps and served as a senior officer in Italy's post-war army. Jány was heavily criticised by the Germans for the failings of the Hungarian Second Army, even though he had given repeated warnings that his forces would not be able to hold back a major Russian attack. After the war, he was briefly held by the Americans but then returned voluntarily to Hungary in 1946, where he was prosecuted the following year on charges of war crimes. The Communist Party in Hungary portrayed him as the 'Don Executioner', responsible for the deaths of so many Hungarian soldiers, and he was found guilty and executed by firing squad. After the fall of the Iron Curtain, he was posthumously acquitted of the charges against him.

CHAPTER 9

THE STRUGGLE FOR BALANCE

The Red Army had every reason to be pleased with the outcome of the Ostrogozhsk-Rossosh Operation, but it is arguable that it represented a diversion of resources from more decisive areas. Gains along the middle Don were undoubtedly welcome, particularly as they unhinged the German line further north and potentially opened the way towards the Dnepr crossings, but there were no objectives within range of the advancing troops that could be regarded as essential for a decisive victory. Had the troops used in the operation been deployed against Hollidt or Fretter-Pico in the south, it is possible that the Russians could have reached Rostov and the coast of the Sea of Azov from the north, completing the isolation of the German forces in the Caucasus. But just as Hitler had succumbed to strategic greed in the summer, believing that the Red Army was irrevocably broken, so the Russians were overcome by the multitude of choices that presented themselves. From their point of view, every assault since the onset of *Uranus* had succeeded. The German Sixth Army was entering its last days in Stalingrad, and the relief attempt had been beaten back. Even if German forces around the lower Don and in the Caucasus remained intact and able to withdraw, it seemed only a matter of time before they were isolated.

The Ostrogozhsk-Rossosh Operation had resulted in the destruction of Axis forces along the Don to the south of Voronezh and had also exposed the southern flank of the German Second Army, which now found itself in an exposed salient. The northern part of this salient had been relatively stationary for several months and was heavily fortified, but the rapid Russian advance in the south now offered an inviting opportunity – yet this, too, was a diversion of attention to the north at a time when potentially decisive opportunities continued to beckon to the south. Vasilevsky devised a plan to try to envelop Second Army with converging attacks against its salient and submitted his proposals as early as 19 January. Stalin gave his approval the same day and detailed planning began immediately. On 24 January, forces of the Russian Fortieth Army, which had led the advance in the northern sector of the operation against the Hungarians, turned north in strength, reinforced by the fresh IV Tank Corps and three rifle divisions, as Moskalenko later described:

> A snowstorm began on the morning of 24 January 1943. The roads were frozen. The temperature fell to -20°C. Most importantly, visibility was extremely limited. The beginning of our assault had to be postponed to 1200. But by noon the snowstorm hadn't stopped. Nevertheless, once again postponing the attack would mean that it would be abandoned on that day altogether. Therefore, we went ahead at 1200. Despite the poor visibility, the artillery was to carry out a 30-minute bombardment. Although this was carried out according to plan, its result was insignificant. The artillerymen could not see their targets and therefore couldn't suppress most of them. Air operations had to be abandoned because of the strong blizzard.
>
> All this complicated the actions of our infantry and tanks. The infantry, approaching to within 300–350m of the front line of the enemy's defences during the artillery preparation, attacked the enemy positions immediately when the bombardment ended, supported by tanks. They were met with artillery and machine-gun fire. A fierce firefight broke out all over the front. However, an hour later we managed to break the resistance in some areas and started to move forward. Fending off enemy counterattacks, my infantry divisions entered the enemy's defences in the areas of Bocharov and Staro-Nikolaevskaya by the end of the day.
>
> IV Tank Corps was more successful. It broke the resistance of the units of the German 68th Infantry Division, and in two hours advanced 8km [five miles] and captured the Lebyazhye area. Next, it was to attack towards Arkhangelsk. Large snowdrifts forced General Kravchenko to choose the shortest route, through the settlements of Staromelovo and Novomelovo.
>
> Conditions were extremely difficult here for an assault. Attempts to move off the roads in order to bypass populated areas, fortified by the enemy for all-round defence, were futile. Tanks became stuck in deep snow, skidding and consuming large amounts of fuel. The roads were also covered in many places with snow.[1]

The Germans were driven from Voronezh the following day by Sixtieth Army, and the forces on the northern flank of the German salient began to advance on 26 January. Generaloberst Hans von Salmuth, commander of Second Army,

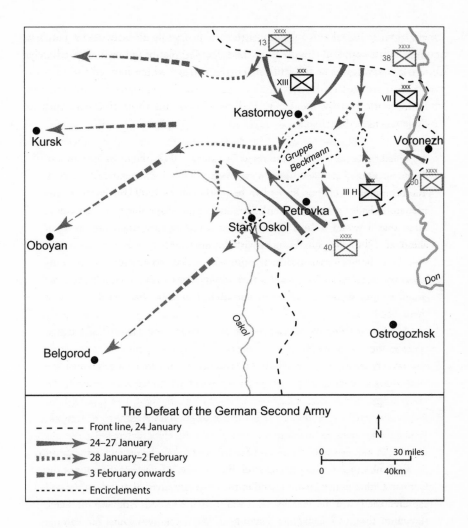

The Defeat of the German Second Army

- - - - - Front line, 24 January

➤ 24–27 January

➤ 28 January–2 February

➤ 3 February onwards

---------- Encirclements

N

0   30 miles

0   40km

found himself hamstrung by Hitler's insistence on holding untenable positions and reluctant permission for a withdrawal came too late; eight German and two Hungarian divisions were encircled. As the advancing Russians attempted to make the most of their opportunities, the task of containing and reducing the encirclement was given to the Russian Thirty-Eighth Army under General Nikander Yevlampievich Chibissov.

Bodo Kleine was a junior NCO in 377th Infantry Division, one of the formations encircled by the Russians. There had been little fighting in his sector with the main Russian thrusts passing to either side, and he and his comrades were suddenly ordered to abandon their trenches and withdraw to the west. His account illustrates the chaotic conditions of the retreat, as well as continuing tensions between troops from Germany and other Axis nations:

At dusk we left our positions and assembled in an abandoned village (Krimskaya), from where the battalion began its retreat. We marched all night. After midnight we rested in a Russian village. We couldn't go into the houses because they were occupied by Russian civilians. In the village a house was burning brightly. We lay down to rest in the snow next to this house, so that we could at least warm ourselves a little. After an hour's rest we continued. It slowly became light. Now we saw an endless column of vehicles, heavy weapons and marching men on the main road. Amongst them were simple sleds drawn by one or two horses on which all manner of equipment had been loaded.

We were the rearguard, which meant that we had to protect the rear of the column from Russian attacks. Next to the main road lay masses of abandoned materiel, from typewriters to radios, and all manner of everyday goods – blankets, tents, rucksacks and wash kits. Roughly every 50m lay a dead horse at the roadside. These were horses that couldn't be taken with us due to a shortage of fodder. They had been shot.

We marched thus along the main road through the harsh cold and icy wind, with snow showers constantly sweeping over us. Vehicles, horses and men had to labour through the deep drifts. The cold created powdery snow that was very loose and particularly difficult for marching, constantly causing the smooth leather soles of our boots to slip.

… We had procured an *akja* – a Finnish sled in the shape of a boat – for our equipment and machine-gun, and we were also able to get a cover in a village with which we covered our *akja*. We thus saved our strength and were also able to take turns to sit on the sled. The terrain was gently hilly and rose for several kilometres before then falling away again. When the main road ran through valleys, we often came under mortar fire from partisans who were hiding along the road and fired on us.

As we had almost no heavy weapons, we couldn't engage them. Consequently we crossed the valleys at a run as fast as we could to escape the mortar fire. Usually though there were a few soldiers in the valleys who had been hit who we couldn't take with us, even though we were the last to pass. But we were lucky and managed to come through relatively unscathed.

When we came to villages in the evening and wanted to spend the night in the Russian houses, we found that these were full of Hungarian soldiers who had thrown away their weapons. We then turned the Hungarians out and moved in. The Hungarians usually spent the nights in stables, where they had some cover.

… The retreat went on and on. We now marched by day and night and were utterly exhausted. The Russians were trying to encircle the retreating troops. We were often attacked during the day by Russian aircraft. They flew low over the retreating column. Most were Il-2 ground attack aircraft or fighters. We opened fire with all our weapons but we couldn't damage the Il-2s with our infantry weapons as they were well armoured. But the Russians crisscrossed our column to avoid taking serious damage. If they had flown along the column, they would have had more success.

We were apparently within an encirclement that was moving towards the west, and individual Russian tanks constantly passed us about 500m away, firing wildly at the column. There would then be shouts of 'Anti-tank guns, forward!' – but anti-tank guns were nowhere to be seen. After firing, the tanks drew away and disappeared in the next fold of the land. As the Russians were still dealing with the Stalingrad encirclement, they apparently didn't have enough troops to attack us more forcefully.

… When we were spending the night in the last house in a village, we were suddenly wakened from a deep sleep at dawn by gunfire. We pulled on our camouflage jackets and boots and ran out of the house.

As I had struggled to pull on my boots, I was still alone inside. A shell exploded in the front room of the house. I ran out and saw parts of a horse plastered to the wall, and two horses that we had brought with us lay dead in the snow. Our sled had also been hit. Then I saw three Russian light tanks escorted by about 25 men driving towards us.

A field gun detachment was in the last house on the other road. The gunners aimed their weapons and fired almost simultaneously at the tanks, which were now about 500m away. I couldn't believe my eyes, all three tanks were hit and knocked out. Only the infantry continued to advance.

Meanwhile I had taken cover behind a dungheap next to the house and calmly opened fire on the brown-uniformed Russian soldiers. After they saw that the tanks were out of action, they withdrew. I then ran into the house to seek out my comrades. But the house was empty. There was a wounded man in the front room who was unable to move. I asked him where the others were. He said: 'They all left. Take me with you, don't leave me here.' I told him I would look for a sled onto which we could load him. I ran from the house. But there were no Germans to be seen near or far.

The first Russian civilians had already come out of their houses. I asked if they had seen any German soldiers. They indicated the other end of the village, where the land rose again. There I saw the last of our group, at least 500m away, running up the hill through the snow. I ran after them as fast as my feet could carry me and finally caught up with the last soldier, who was carrying the baseplate of a mortar on his back. With his heavy load, he couldn't keep up with the others in the deep snow … I couldn't help our comrade in the house, as I couldn't carry him with me in this situation. Sadly, I didn't know his name. What became of him?[2]

Given the widespread presence of partisans and the shortage of medical services for Russian troops let alone for prisoners, it is likely that the wounded man did not survive.

Kleine's 377th Infantry Division, together with the German 75th and 340th Infantry Divisions and the Hungarian 6th and 9th Infantry Divisions, was part of *Gruppe Beckmann*, one of three groups of men trying to escape to the west. Harassed by partisans, attacked from the air and occasionally encountering Red Army detachments, the rearguard laboured on through the cold. In one village, they came across a small column of vehicles at dusk and realised that they were Russian – their line of retreat was blocked. Quickly, Kleine and the others deployed for an attack, but when Kleine attempted to fire his machine-gun, he found that the breech was frozen solid, a recurring problem with the MG-34s that were in widespread use. He watched as his comrades attempted to storm the village in the face of heavy Russian fire, including from a 20mm anti-aircraft gun mounted on one of the vehicles; it was only when this was silenced that the German infantry was able to press home its attack and clear the village. Afterwards, Kleine was left behind by his company to pass instructions to another element of 377th Infantry Division; he now discovered that, just as Hungarian and Italian soldiers were shunned by the Germans, so he was now shunned as a straggler:

Like other stragglers, I now had to flee back with the crowd and received nothing to eat, not even a cup of coffee or tea from other units.

If I came across a field kitchen that was handing out hot drinks or even soup to its soldiers, I was asked my unit and, as I was not from the relevant formation, I was refused a cup of coffee or tea, or bread or other food.

This is what they called camaraderie. Thus I was forced to get food by whatever means I could. I used snow to quench my thirst, chomping it slowly in my mouth and letting it melt. But this just seemed to make my thirst even worse.[3]

Despite feeling abandoned, Kleine was actually fortunate; several days later, he passed a column of wrecked vehicles strewn with dead Germans, including the rest of his infantry company. It was well into February before he reached the safety of German lines at Sumi, to the northwest of Kharkov – a march of about 140 miles (230km) in bitter cold and with uncertain food supplies. Most of his division, together with the rest of *Gruppe Beckmann*, had been destroyed.

Salmuth had only recently been promoted and this perhaps protected him to some extent from being saddled with the blame for the near-destruction of his army. Nevertheless, given the scale of the casualties suffered by his forces – Russian estimates came to 80,000 Axis troops killed, wounded or taken prisoner – it was inconceivable that he would emerge unscathed. He was replaced as commander of Second Army by General Walter Weiss and placed in reserve, before returning to the Eastern Front during the summer.

On occasions, the speed of the Russian advance created problems for the Red Army as different units attempted to keep up with events. Shafarenko's division suffered the consequences of one such episode:

> My 78th Regiment, along with the division's training battalion, advanced rapidly after liberating Berezovo and Petrovka and reached the settlement of Nizhne Gniloe. There, it was counterattacked by the Hitlerites. Heavy fighting lasted a whole day. Developing the fighting, the regiment captured Bogoroditsky and by the evening of 28 January was already moving towards Gorshechnoye when it was hit by our aircraft. As a result, there were 20 casualties, including the deputy commander of the training battalion, Captain Solomin.
>
> At that time we were engaged in heavy fighting. A number of sectors didn't have a continuous front line and the situation changed rapidly. The error of our aviation was not entirely an accident. As it turned out, neither the infantry nor the pilots used identification signals. When Bilyutin [the commander of the regiment] gave me a report about what had happened when he arrived in Gorshechnoye, I had a very harsh conversation with him, which was hard for both of us; for me, because I saw how he completely understood the mistake. The division headquarters immediately instructed all units to ensure close monitoring of identification signals.[4]

Shtykov was heavily involved in the battle for Nizhne Gniloe:

> [The German counterattack] first fell on the training battalion of the division, with which our regiment did not have good communications. It was defending on one flank, facing the 'Kauchuk' state farm. It was from there that no less than a regiment of enemy infantry attacked. The training battalion immediately found itself in a difficult situation.

We tried to help the cadets. In particular, our regimental artillery so accurately covered the fascist lines that they immediately took cover and then seemed to pull back. Success? By no means. Soon the Nazis resorted to an artful trick which, unfortunately, neither we nor the commander of the battalion of cadets, Major Generalov, grasped at first.

And what happened is this. When the attack was repeated, when the enemy line approached most closely to the cadet trenches, the Nazis suddenly stopped firing their rifles and, rising to their full height and throwing up their hands, ran to our men, shouting: '*Russki*, do not shoot, prisoner!'

The cadets stopped firing because the Germans were surrendering. Belatedly, one of our men shouted, 'Drop your weapons!' And then the fatal trick was played. The fascists who had 'surrendered' suddenly lowered their hands and almost at point-blank range opened a hurricane fire at the cadets. A minute's confusion was enough to allow the enemy to reach our trenches. The training battalion was literally cut into two parts. One group, consisting of about 120 men, withdrew to the positions of our regiment, and the other retreated to the village of Klyuchi, where the division headquarters was located at the time. In this battle, the cadets suffered heavy losses. It was the price for a brief loss of vigilance.

Almost simultaneously with the attack of the positions of the training battalion, the enemy struck a blow against our regiment. He managed to put Captain Golovin's battalion under pressure, but he did not achieve much more. The Guardsmen fought furiously, although to resist the greatly superior forces of the enemy (more than a thousand Nazis attacked the positions of the regiment, which was badly bled out from previous actions) was very difficult.

… Night came, but the Hitlerites still didn't weaken the onslaught. Now the battle was fought by firelight. Gorshechnoye was ablaze. The houses collapsed, strewing the streets with debris … By the morning of 31 January, the situation of our regiment was particularly complex. By this time, we held only the school building, the dairy and the station buildings. And during the afternoon the enemy struck two more powerful blows against our positions. To repel them, we mobilised all the forces we could. Even the wounded rejoined the fighting line. Armed with submachine-guns, staff officers also fought alongside the rank and file.

We suffered heavy losses in two days of fighting in Gorshechnoye … But we were all particularly grieved by the news of the death of our illustrious battalion commander, Captain Alexei Petrovich Golovin. I, too, had a hard time dealing with this loss. After all, I have often shared difficult moments on our journey from the Don with Alexei Petrovich, I was able to see personally his unmatched courage, and his outstanding leadership. And now this man was gone. Damn you, war![5]

After taking heavy losses, Shtykov's regiment was driven out of Gorshechnoye. Even at a time of general Russian successes, this setback attracted heavy criticism and Belov, the regiment commander, was dismissed. Shtykov took over the diminished regiment and was ordered to retake Gorshechnoye; after receiving a small draft of reinforcements, he led a successful attack on 4–5 February. When the modest haul of prisoners was drawn up into columns, Shtykov was surprised to learn that the Germans refused to march in the same column as the Hungarians.[6]

Having escaped from the Hungarians and hidden until the Red Army arrived, Gabriel Temkin reported to the newly established Russian military authorities in Stary Oskol. He found that large numbers of other soldiers and escaped prisoners were doing the same thing:

> The atmosphere was unfriendly and tense. Some were saying nervously in low voices that former prisoners suspected of desertion or collaboration with the Germans were sometimes shot on the spot without any court ... I entered the commandant's office smiling, but he did not reciprocate, and our conversation was very brief. He told me, like he did all the others, to go to ... Kalach, to an NKVD camp *na provyerku* (for a 'checkup').[7]

Temkin and other former prisoners travelled to Kalach by hitching rides on army trucks and reported to the NKVD camp, located in a former poultry farm. Here, he was interrogated about his name – both his real Polish name and the non-Jewish pseudonym he had adopted whilst in captivity – and whether there was anyone who could corroborate that he had not assisted the Germans. In many respects, Temkin was the sort of person who, in other circumstances, the NKVD would have regarded as 'guilty until proven innocent', but such was the pressing need in the Red Army for replacements that, after he recovered from a severe fever that hospitalised him, he was permitted to join the army.

Meanwhile, events continued to unfold further to the southeast. During 1942, Kleist had advanced swiftly over the open plains of the northern Caucasus before slowing to a crawl as he approached the mountains to the south; attempting to advance in the opposite direction in winter, the Russians found that they faced huge difficulties. The road network, barely adequate in the summer, was completely unsuited to major operations in the winter, and Kleist's troops conducted an efficient and orderly withdrawal, giving the pursuing Russian troops little or no opportunity to disrupt matters. Both the Black Sea group and the forces advancing out of the Caucasus mountains proceeded slowly and cautiously, and Tiulenev and Maslennikov were later criticised for their lack of energy, apparently fearing that Kleist would suddenly launch a counterattack and strike towards the Caucasus oilfields. Shtemenko, who had been sent to the region to oversee operations, later wrote:

> The main forces of First Panzer Army succeeded in breaking away from our Northern Group, whose pursuit of the enemy was belated and badly organised. Our signals communications were not prepared for control of offensive operations, and the result was that the units got mixed up on the very first day of the pursuit. The staffs were unable to find out the exact position or the state of their forces. Fifty-Eighth Army lagged behind its neighbours until it was almost part of the second echelon. V Guards Cavalry Corps and the tanks were unable to get ahead of the infantry. The command of the front tried to put matters right but with little success.[8]

There were also problems with the depleted strength of the units that were being asked to pursue and cut off the Germans. Shtemenko noted that 10th Guards Cavalry Division had fewer than 2,000 men, only six field guns, and four heavy machine-guns. Its sister formation, 9th Guards Cavalry Division, was barely any better, with about 2,300 men, seven guns and eight machine-guns. The horses of both divisions were exhausted and incapable of prolonged marches. In the First World War, all armies had clung to their cavalry units in the hope that when it became possible to conduct mobile operations, mounted troops would finally come into their own, but the Germans discovered during the fighting in Romania in late 1916 that when pursuing a defeated enemy, infantry could be urged to make greater efforts whereas horses simply collapsed if the same was attempted with cavalry units, and the logistic requirements in terms of fodder further limited their value – at one stage during the First World War, the Russian Army was using more railway capacity to move fodder for horses than food for soldiers. Now, in the Caucasus, the Russians were learning the same lesson. On 8 January, Stalin impatiently urged Maslennikov and Tiulenev to show greater energy:

> You have ... lost touch with [your troops]. It cannot be ruled out that with such a lack of order and communications in the Northern Group your mobile units will be surrounded ...
>
> This situation is intolerable.
>
> I command you to restore communications with the mobile units of the

Northern Group and regularly, twice a day, to inform the general staff of the state of affairs on your Front.

This is your personal responsibility.[9]

Helped by Shtemenko and his team from the general staff's operations department, Maslennikov and Tiulenev drew up plans for two operations to try to achieve Stalin's objectives. *Gory* ('Mountain') would see Fifty-Sixth Army advancing to Krasnodar by 18 January, and then on to Tikhoretskaya; Shtemenko and the others were aware that Stalin wanted the advance to continue to Bataisk, but they were doubtful that the weakened units of Fifty-Sixth Army would even be able to reach Tikhoretskaya. The second operation, *Morye* ('Sea'), was a joint operation between the Black Sea Fleet and Forty-Seventh Army. Its objective was to recapture Novorossisk by the third week of January and then to advance into the Taman Peninsula in order to prevent any German withdrawal towards the Crimea. Stalin approved this second plan but – as predicted by Shtemenko – objected to *Mountain*, repeating his insistence that the ultimate objective should be an advance to Bataisk. Accordingly, the plan was altered to include a third phase that would envisage the advance requested by Stalin, though the senior officers in the Caucasus remained doubtful that there would be sufficient strength to achieve it.

Despite the best efforts of Maslennikov, Tiulenev and Shtemenko, deteriorating weather with alternate snow and rain made movement of heavy equipment, particularly artillery, almost impossible. Stalin allowed the two operations an additional day or two of preparation. When the advance began, the forces on the eastern flank of the Black Sea Group achieved surprising progress and by 16 January were close to Krasnodar. By contrast, neither Fifty-Sixth Army nor Forty-Seventh Army succeeded in gaining much ground.

Regardless of whether the German withdrawal from the Caucasus mountains was successfully conducted due to German skill or Russian tentativeness, the consequence was that Kleist was able to pull back Army Group A to the planned line slightly ahead of schedule; however, the northern flank of his army was still in Petrovskoye, with a gap of nearly 140 miles (233km) to Fourth Panzer Army – only two formations, *SS-Viking* and 16th Motorised Division, stood in this expanse. Whilst much of the muddy valley of the Manych was almost impassable for the Russians, there were still plenty of opportunities for a strike against the inner flanks of either panzer army.

The herculean task that faced Manstein was taking a huge toll. The relief operation mounted by Fourth Panzer Army had been predicated upon Hitler's promise of a steady stream of reinforcements, but these had failed to appear, not least because of the crises that broke out along the Don. In addition to failing to produce the promised reinforcements, Hitler continued to issue orders demanding that the depleted units of Army Group Don did not retreat and held arbitrary lines, something that Manstein dismissed as a policy that would be 'about as effective as a cobweb'. In growing frustration, Manstein wrote to Zeitzler on 5 January asking that he be relieved of his command:

> Should these proposals not be approved and this headquarters continue to be tied down to the same extent as hitherto, I cannot see that any useful purpose will be served by my continuing as commander of Army Group Don. In the circumstances it would appear more appropriate to replace me by a 'sub-directorate' of the kind maintained by the Quartermaster-General.[10]

The request was inevitably declined, and Manstein continued to wrestle with the tasks he faced. The tribulations of Hoth's Fourth Panzer Army were just part of the overall crisis, but to a large extent they typified the difficulties confronting Manstein. Pressured by the Russian Second Guards and Fifty-First Armies driving his forces back from Kotelnikovo, Hoth had to try to keep his army intact whilst also blocking any Russian drive towards Rostov. At the same time, he had to try to prevent major incursions into the rear of First Panzer Army to the south. An attempt by the Russians to bypass Hoth's army with Twenty-Eighth Army and strike between First and Fourth Panzer Armies was intercepted by 16th Motorised Division, but the consequence of this was that this division, which had been intended to join LVII Panzer Corps, was now tied up in defensive duties.

Hitler had finally released 7th Panzer Division from reserve and the desperately needed armour was immediately thrust into action north of the Don, assembling in Belaya Kalitva (known to the Germans as Forschtadt). Outside the town were the remnants of a work camp that had been set up the previous summer; Russian civilians from as far away as Stalingrad had been brought there and the stronger and fitter individuals selected for work details across occupied parts of the Soviet Union and even Germany. Those who were not selected were simply turned out onto the steppe to fend for themselves, and unknown numbers perished as the weather turned cold in late 1942.[11] As soon as it arrived, Hollidt ordered the division – commanded by Generalleutnant Hans Freiherr von Funck – to move east to intercept advancing Russian forces. On 6 January, it encountered Russian armour about 18 miles (30km) northeast of Belaya Kalitva. An account by an officer in the division's 7th Panzergrenadier Regiment described both the nature of the fighting and the extent to which the disaster at Stalingrad was still being concealed from ordinary troops:

> The situation didn't look particularly rosy, but we were unaware of the extent of the Russian breakthrough after Stalingrad and the encirclement of Sixth Army. We were certainly troubled by the large crowds of Romanians and Italians fleeing to the rear, but we were convinced that the situation could soon be brought under control. Whilst we explored operational options to the east of Shakhty, we were suddenly ordered into action on the Donets near Forschtadt. A front line was being established there in great haste against powerful enemy forces that had broken through at Millerovo and were pressing forward. While the bulk of the division then deployed east of the [River] Kalitva for an attack, *Kampfgruppe Steinkeller* followed a little later to the west of the river. We first encountered the enemy during the afternoon of 7 January. After an initially rapid advance, Grünert's battalion (I Battalion, 7th Panzergrenadier Regiment) suddenly came up against a strong, well-constructed enemy position, which made good use of the terrain. Despite the use of all available forces it was not possible to break through the enemy's position. While the regiment staff was pulled out during the night in order to take command of another battlegroup made up of parts of the division and other units for deployment at Novocherkassky, the rest of the division was thrown into another threatened sector of the front. During this period, Grünert's battalion endured particularly difficult days. Without any artillery support, the battalion had to beat off one powerful attack after another, repeatedly fight its way clear of threatened encirclements, and engage in bloody house-to-house fighting with the enemy.
>
> On 11 January the battalion took over a position between the Kalitva and the Donets with orders to prevent the enemy from advancing against the vital bridgehead at Forschtadt. The 18km [11-mile] sector consisted of a series of strongpoints, which in the event of strong enemy pressure had to fight alone under the command of their experienced officers. Meanwhile, the battlegroup led by the commander of 7th Panzergrenadier Regiment, consisting of a battalion of the panzer regiment and Walsberg's battalion (II Battalion, 7th Panzergrenadier Regiment), found itself in heavy fighting against attacking enemy forces that grew stronger by the hour. Over 30 T-34s were shot up … During the night of 17–18 January the enemy broke through a sector of the front that was not manned due to inadequate forces in strength and attacked the regimental headquarters. Only at dawn, when our numerical inferiority became obvious, did we pull back to a position that had been prepared during the night. But by then the enemy had cut

off and completely encircled Walsberg and van Gember's panzer battalion. In an almost insane manner, Oberstleutnant von Steinkeller, the regiment commander, drove through the enemy lines in his half-track, pursued by a T-34, but succeeded in reaching the surrounded troops. From here he attacked the enemy tanks in Novocherkassky, destroyed them, and broke through to our lines with most of the encircled troops.[12]

Meanwhile, any doubt about the threat to Rostov was dispelled on 7 January when Russian troops succeeded in bypassing Hoth's northern flank and pushed forward to a point only 12 miles (20km) from Novocherkassk (not to be confused with the similarly named village where Steinkeller's group was fighting), where Manstein's headquarters was based; Rostov was a mere 20 miles (33km) further to the southwest. Hastily, an ad hoc battlegroup built around armoured vehicles from repair workshops drove the Russians off, but whilst the threat to Novocherkassk and thereafter Rostov was eased for the moment, the Russian armoured force began to apply pressure to the southeast along the valley of the Manych, thus threatening the northern flank of Fourth Panzer Army.

Many of the Russian forces advancing towards Rostov contained large numbers of relatively inexperienced men; some, particularly those recruited from urban populations, had little knowledge of spending long periods in the open steppe during winter and there were many cases of frostbite. The urban background of others was exposed in other ways; Isaak Kobylyanskiy was a sergeant in an artillery unit within Second Guards Army, but despite his rank he had only been in action since the autumn. He had grown up in Kiev and suddenly found himself with responsibility for the horses allocated to pull his unit's artillery, and had to learn quickly about how to care for them. Others found that occasionally, they had more to fear from their own side than from the enemy, as Kobylyanskiy later recalled, describing what happened to Sergey Zvonarev, a man in his unit, when they were deployed close to the Don when he decided to try his hand fishing through a hole in the ice at night:

> He came upon three men bent over ... holes in the ice. They were wearing snow-white camouflage coveralls and seemed to be engrossed in fishing. At a distance of about ten metres from the three, Zvonarev called out: 'Hey, Slavs! Are the fish biting?' Unexpectedly all three drew themselves up to full height and instead of a response, Sergey heard: '*Hände hoch!*'
>
> ... He reappeared in our march column during a stop ... The ill-starred fisherman told us that before dawn the Germans, who had captured him, left

their position and in the ensuing week had retreated southward, taking the captive Sergey with them. They treated him kindly and fed him well … Nobody was appointed to look after him round the clock, and at a convenient moment Sergey hid in a villager's house. Then he found his way back to the regiment.

Not more than a half hour had passed since the prodigal son's return, when a NKVD officer of the regimental Special Department (*Osoby Otdel*) appeared and ordered Zvonarev to follow him. We never heard another word about that reckless guy.[13]

Whilst the unfortunate Zvonarev had been lucky to fall into the hands of Germans who treated him well, he would have been treated with great suspicion by the Soviet authorities on his return out of fear that he had been sent back as a spy, particularly in view of his apparently good treatment. Even in the opening weeks of the war, it was made clear to soldiers that their chances of survival were low if they surrendered to the Germans, but whilst surrender if incapacitated by wounds was acceptable, men who were capable of fighting but still laid down their weapons would be regarded as deserters. Their families would be denied any benefits or aid, and the only manner in which these men could redeem themselves was to escape, or die in the attempt. In the case of Zvonarev, even this appears to have been inadequate. It is likely that, after extensive interrogation, he would have been assigned to a penal battalion, in which his prospects of survival would have been very poor. Like soldiers in every army in every era, the men of the Red Army dealt with events like this with grim humour: if you fell into the hands of the military police or the NKVD, they told each other, you had to be prepared to prove beyond doubt that you weren't a camel.[14]

After its initial withdrawal, Army Group A was now expected to hold its new line while rear area units were withdrawn and Hitler decided on just how far he was prepared to pull back. Despite the disasters to the north, he remained obsessed with holding onto some of the gains that had been made in 1942, even if only so that he could try again in 1943. The incursion into the Caucasus had been based upon a strong German presence along the Don and Volga, and the Red Army being sufficiently weakened by defeats to prevent it from interfering; neither of these two factors could be expected in the foreseeable future, and purely on operational grounds this should have been sufficient to dictate a complete withdrawal from the Caucasus. This was precisely what Manstein wanted – all of Germany's successes were based upon mobile operations, and in the current circumstances mobility could only be achieved by abandoning territory that in any event could no longer be held. Yet Hitler continued to prevaricate and delayed coming to any conclusion.

North of the Don, Hollidt's collection of exhausted divisions and ad hoc battlegroups, backed by the tireless panzer divisions, continued to struggle to hold back the Russians. The gradual withdrawal towards the west from the line of the River Zymlia resulted in a shortening of the front line, allowing at least local reserves to be created, but at the same time the Russians too benefited from this and were able to concentrate their forces more effectively. After its catastrophic losses in November, 22nd Panzer Division was to be disbanded and orders to this effect were issued on 9 February, but were not fully implemented until the following month; in the meantime, the remnants of the division fought alongside Raus' 6th Panzer Division. Just like Hoth, Hollidt was threatened on both flanks; in the north, Fretter-Pico's group was still trying to restore the front after the disasters of *Little Saturn* and was steadily being driven back, while in the south, Russian units continued to move along the Don and then threaten either Hollidt or Hoth. If the Russians were to break through on the northern flank, they might threaten Voroshilovgrad (now Luhansk) and the crossings on the Donets – were these to fall into Russian hands, it would be almost as catastrophic as losing the Don crossings at Rostov.

In almost constant combat, 6th Panzer Division fell back to the line of the Donets, forced repeatedly to assign small groups of tanks to infantry formations in order to provide them with moral support as well as much-needed anti-armour firepower. A rabbit farm to the west of the valley of the small River Bystraya became the scene of confused fighting after a Russian column managed to reach the cluster of buildings in early January, and as a consequence of having to loan vehicles to support other formations, 6th Panzer Division struggled to concentrate sufficient strike power to eliminate the penetration. On 7 January, *Gruppe Hünersdorff* was deployed to the east of the Bystraya in order to outflank the Russian penetration and render it untenable. The icy conditions and slippery roads delayed the assembly of 6th Panzer Division's units and only limited progress was possible; the following day, too, the attackers struggled to make any impression. Ultimately, events elsewhere along the front intervened – if such counterattacks were to be carried out, they had to succeed quickly so that the Germans could then redeploy their tanks elsewhere. Even though much of the line of the Bystraya was in German hands, it had to be abandoned so that the panzer divisions could concentrate their units.

Constantly mounting limited operations, 6th Panzer Division crossed the Donets on 17 January; it had been reduced to 39 tanks, but within just two days the repair workshops and fresh supplies from Germany increased this to 71 tanks. Although the division's Pz.III tanks had provided valuable service, there was little doubt that they were of limited value in the prevailing conditions and were fast becoming obsolete, as Hünersdorff wrote in a report:

> The Pz.III is in no way suited to the requirements of fighting in the east. Its armour is too thin, and the calibre of its gun is inadequate. By contrast, the assault guns have provided outstanding service in the fighting on the steppe, even though they do not have a rotating turret and must face the enemy to aim. The reason for [their good performance] is their substantially stronger armour and their large guns.[15]

Production of the Pz.III was coming to an end; it was planned to re-equip all panzer divisions with one battalion of the slightly larger Pz.IV equipped with long-barrelled 75mm guns, and one battalion with the new Pz.V or Panther tank. Although Hitler gave approval for production of the Panther in May 1942, a variety of delays meant that it did not start until December. Ultimately, it would prove to be an effective tank, but the first vehicles were plagued by teething problems and it did not enter combat until the summer of 1943 and throughout the war it was beset with reliability issues. The heavyweight Pz.VI or Tiger, armed with a deadly 88mm gun, had been in production since July 1942 but was available only in small numbers, in special heavy tank battalions; the panzer divisions would have to continue to rely on their Pz.IIIs for the time being, regardless of their inferior armour and firepower.

Not far away, 7th Panzer Division was also pulled back across the Donets, occupying a defensive line in and to the west of Kamensk. There was heavy fighting while the division drove back Russian forces that had established small bridgeheads across the river, but even after it had secured the line, the division had no rest; Russian forces had crossed the frozen Donets about 24 miles (40km) to the northwest, and Steinkeller's battlegroup had to be dispatched to deal with this. Morale remained high as a result of repeated successes, but casualties continued to rise, particularly amongst irreplaceable junior officers.[16]

The various enclaves that had been created during and after the Russians launched *Little Saturn* were abandoned. After a prolonged defence, the German 3rd Mountain Division pulled out of Millerovo towards the southwest. The nearby German and Italian forces that had gathered in Chertkovo endured intermittent encirclement, with much of their supply being brought in by air (and thus diverting aircraft away from the Stalingrad airlift). It rapidly became too dangerous for aircraft to land, and thereafter supplies were dropped from low-flying planes, often without parachutes. Many of the Italian troops were reorganised into new formations, and together with the Germans these fought off two major attempts by the Russians to storm the town in the first part of January. It was even possible to launch a counterattack on 7 January to recover a section of the perimeter that had been overrun. Fighting died down the following week and on 15 January the garrison received orders to break out to the west. Accompanied by a few armoured vehicles, the soldiers assembled into columns in the bitter cold and set off towards dusk, leaving several thousand wounded behind. Hundreds of men towards the tail of the retreat were cut off by the Russians and overwhelmed, and a major Russian tank attack against the rest was beaten off with the timely aid of a Stuka attack. With order breaking down even amongst the units that had managed to hold together the longest – largely German front-line troops and the Italian Blackshirts – the men staggered on. Eventually, after two days and nights, their path made its way up onto a plateau:

> We passed a number of field artillery pits, with German guns pointing our way. Behind them, the uneven mounds of earth covering the gunners' shelters were sticking out of the snow.
>
> Did I have any idea what those gun pits meant?
>
> I don't rightly remember.
>
> What I do remember is that in front of those cannon in the snow lay a great number of dead Russians. One, a Mongol, was lying practically across the track; he was wearing a fine, thick balaclava, which covered his whole face apart from his eyes.
>
> I took it off him; I had some difficulty, because the dead man's ears were like ice. I noticed that the balaclava was stained with blood; the dead man's broad face was likewise sullied with frozen blood.
>
> I slipped his balaclava over mine: soon it unfroze a little, and started giving off a mild, strange odour. 'The smell of a Siberian,' I thought with a smile; but now, though still lacking my service cap, I no longer needed to hold the blanket over my head to keep the wind off me.[17]

Corti and a handful of his comrades had succeeded in making their way to safety. They later estimated that their XXXV Corps had originally numbered about 30,000 Italians, and of these about 8,000 managed to reach Chertkovo. Some 5,000 left the town on 15 January, and only 4,000 – most of them wounded or suffering from frostbite – managed to reach German lines. Even now, their ordeal was not over and they faced a further long march along frozen roads to the areas that had been designated for the survivors of the Italian Eighth Army.

The tanks of the SS Panzergrenadier Division *Viking* had finally arrived from the Caucasus, completing a journey of 360 miles (600km) by rail. Endlessly delayed, the SS tank crews later estimated that their average speed during the journey had been no more than 6 miles (10km) per hour. They were deployed to cover the yawning gap between the southern flank of Army Group Don and the northern flank of Army Group A, releasing 16th Motorised Division for deployment with LVII Panzer Corps – originally, Manstein had hoped that this would be possible in time for a resumption of *Winter Storm*, but instead the division joined the desperate defensive struggle to hold back the Russian advance on Rostov. As they moved forward to the front line, the men of *SS-Viking* saw dispiriting scenes:

> Along the road leading to the front, we were met again and again by innumerable columns coming our way. You almost feel abandoned when you head toward the enemy all by yourself. After the traffic on the road had died down, you could see what sorts of things had been abandoned along the side of the road. Valuable vehicles and special-purpose vehicles were simply left behind due to the smallest of problems that could have easily been fixed. They often had important and valuable cargoes.[18]

SS-Viking was formed as a division around the regiment *SS-Germania* in 1940; the division's name was originally to be *Germania*, but this was changed by Hitler almost immediately to recognise the presence of large numbers of Dutch, Danish, Flemish and Norwegian volunteers in its ranks. After the war, it was widely believed that *SS-Viking* had a relatively 'clean' record, but like the other SS units deployed in the front line alongside the Wehrmacht in Russia, it was later implicated in a number of war crimes, including the massacre of hundreds of Jews in Zloczow (now Zolochiv in Ukraine), in which its troops were enthusiastically aided by Ukrainian militiamen. The killings continued until a detachment from 295th Infantry Division under the command of Oberstleutnant Helmuth Groscurth arrived and took over control of the town.[19] However, whilst Groscurth made frequent protests about the misconduct of SS personnel in the area where his troops were operating, Wehrmacht cooperation and collaboration in war crimes was – as already mentioned – widespread.

The weakness of German infantry formations in the face of armoured attacks had been laid bare by the events of recent weeks, and there were constant demands for armoured support:

> As a result, the [*SS-Viking* panzer] battalion was employed carved up in companies. A company wherever it threatened to become hot.

The battalion commander no longer had any direct influence on his company commanders, since they often had to make decisions on their own that were born of the momentary circumstance.

And frequently the infantry commander was constantly in the ears of an oft-plagued commander: he should do this or that. As a result, it was easy to get in the dangerous position of serving two masters, his battalion commander or the infantry commander.

That nothing good came of that was clear. You frequently had to employ the entire force of your personality to ensure that your tanks remained firmly under your control. Otherwise, it could happen that the infantryman tried to take on the job of being a tanker as a secondary profession. And that was the worst possible thing: bungling in warfare is paid for in blood.[20]

In such a vast area, neither side had sufficient troops for continuous lines and there were frequent incidents where units of the two armies became intermingled. This led to wild encounters, as a junior officer in *SS-Viking* later recalled:

Towards midnight, we went through the outpost line of the *Nordland* Regiment, talked to the platoon leader for a little while and saw his men squatting in their holes, sleepy-eyed and exhausted … we were able to get two Russian huts at the edge of the village to sleep in. It was comfortably warm, and the persons who dwelled there were friendly.

… Early in the morning, at 0500, I was shaken awake by a messenger from the battalion headquarters. There was no mistaking it: alert! He had barely given me his message when a burst from a submachine-gun went through the window, and the messenger collapsed on me, dead. In less than a second, the light was swept from the table and we were flat on the floor. Soon there were several Russians in the room: *Ruki Werch!* – Hands up! Initially, we were frozen in place. Young Rötzer's entire body started shaking and – God knows! – the entire situation was damned precarious.

In the meantime – all of this happened in a matter of minutes – Russian and German commands were being shouted outside. A burst from a MG-42 smashed against the walls of the house, and ricochets rocketed through the shot-out window. A quick decision: my Belgian FN pistol out of the holster on my rear, unload a full magazine in the direction of the flustered Russians and then Rötzer and I zigzag through the enemy – cut and run!

Rötzer was grazed, but we managed to get out. Teeth chattering and bathed in sweat, we reached an empty hut and took two Russian steppe jackets and felt boots.

In the meantime, the village had become a witch's cauldron. The *Nordland* outposts received us in our Russian garb with rifle fire.[21]

In constant action, *SS-Viking* pulled back to the line of the River Manych, abandoning the east bank on 19 January. Although losses through enemy action were not heavy, many tanks were damaged in combat and there were constant breakdowns as tanks struggled to cope with the frozen roads; the repeated redeployments put a considerable strain upon the division's workshops, which had to move all the disabled vehicles as well as their own equipment.

The strain of conducting so many operations simultaneously was beyond the capacity of the Red Army's logistic services, despite their best efforts to improvise, as Rotmistrov – recently promoted to Lieutenant General – wrote:

On my instructions, the chief of staff of the corps, Colonel [Vladimir Nikolayevich] Baskakov, repeatedly reported to the headquarters of Second Guards Army about our supply problems, but without any result.

Finally, the front commander, Colonel-General Yeremenko, member of the Military Council of the Front [Nikita] Khrushchev and Commander of Second Guards Army Lieutenant General Malinovsky arrived at my command post. I reported to them that the resistance of the enemy was increasing, and the corps was starved of all types of supplies.

Extremely frustrated, Yeremenko – leaning on a cane (he had an old wound) – walked about the room excitedly and said irritably: 'I don't have anything I can give you, but the mission must be carried out! It is necessary to take Rostov – the Germans are pulling back there.'

'Well, how can we?'

'Listen,' interrupted Yeremenko, 'You will lead a mechanized group. I am transferring II and V Guards Mechanized Corps to your command. Combine your tanks, drain the fuel from the damaged and broken vehicles. Do whatever you want, but capture Bataisk and Rostov. More than that, I'll give you aero-sled battalions. They will terrify the Germans.'

It was the first time I had heard about the aero-sled battalions and asked in bewilderment: 'And what are they?'

'Plywood structures with a propeller on skis,' replied Malinovsky with an ironic smile.

When I happened to see this curiosity, I could not help but be amazed at the absurdity of the idea of its creators. A machine-gun was mounted on each aero-sled and several submachine-gunners were seated on it. It was assumed that

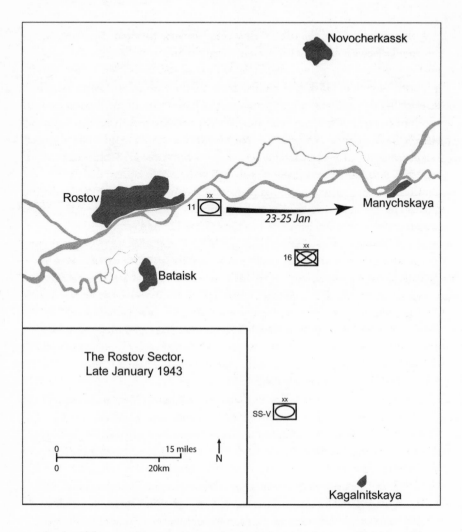

the use of these machines during combat operations in winter conditions would have a great effect, especially in a moral sense.

But in actual fact it turned out that aero-sleds were not suitable not only as combat vehicles, but even as a means of transportation, especially on the Don, where frost in winter often alternates with slush and even rain. They often crashed, and most importantly were easy prey for enemy aviation.[22]

The *Aerosani* or aero-sleds had been in use by Russian forces since immediately before the First World War in a variety of manifestations. They proved to be versatile as transports and reconnaissance vehicles in northern Russia, seeing service in the war against Finland, but as Rotmistrov described they were far less effective further south. Some were even fitted with light armour to try to improve their survivability, but the additional weight simply made them slower and easier to destroy.

Balck's 11th Panzer Division continued to engage Russian spearheads energetically:

> The engagements mostly followed a common pattern. The panzergrenadier regiments moved into an extended position, and the panzer regiment attacked to the front of them and destroyed everything that moved toward us. Then we would have some peace while the Russians turned toward an adjacent unit, which I then supported with the panzer regiment.[23]

To a large extent, Balck's successes with his division – now significantly under strength – were due to the weakness of the opposing Russian units. Had they been reinforced by the formations thrown at the Hungarians and Germans further north, the outcome would surely have been very different, and at the very least 11th Panzer Division might have found itself tied down in prolonged combat, but the Russians couldn't pursue all of the opportunities that presented themselves. Nevertheless, the threat posed by the Red Army along the Don, with forces now gathering on the Manych, required attention, and Manstein ordered Balck's division south. Even this move required considerable wrangling with Hitler, but orders were issued on 22 January. Rear area units from the Caucasus were withdrawing towards the north while supplies continued to flow towards Kleist's army group in the opposite direction, and the vehicles of 11th Panzer Division now struggled along the same routes as they attempted to cross to the south bank of the Don. To make matters worse, the fuel shortages that constantly plagued German movements left many of his formations barely able to move and despite the pressing urgency of dealing with the approaching Russians – the 'mechanised group' created by Rotmistrov's III Guards Tank Corps – Balck had to pause for a day in Rostov while he awaited further supplies. On 23 January, 11th Panzer Division attacked the leading Russian units and he wrote that he rapidly threw them back; by contrast, Rotmistrov wrote that his mechanised group made good progress at first, but were then forced back by superior German numbers – despite following the advice of Yeremenko and Malinovsky, Rotmistrov had not been able to keep more than a modest number of tanks running, and even moderate losses resulted in the mechanised group's tank strength dropping rapidly.

The Russians were driven back to the town of Manychskaya, on the banks of the river itself. On 24 January, 11th Panzer Division made an initial attack that made little headway, but was more successful the following day. Having observed the positions of the defenders, Balck ordered a heavy bombardment on the northeast perimeter of the Russian defences followed by an advance by his division's reconnaissance battalion and a large number of half-tracks and trucks, shielded by a smokescreen. The Russian tanks in Manychskaya moved to face the threat, and immediately Balck's artillery switched its fire to the southern perimeter, followed by an attack by the panzer regiment. The Russians were taken completely by surprise and – according to German sources – about 20 Russian tanks were knocked out, with 11th Panzer Division suffering only minimal casualties (one dead and 14 wounded). The bridge over the Manych was captured intact.[24] It should be noted, however, that almost every German account of this battle is based upon Balck's memoirs. Whilst he claimed that III Guards Tank Corps was destroyed as a result of his capture of Manychskaya and the subsequent pursuit of the retreating Russians, Russian accounts show that it was reassigned to a new assault group the very day that Balck was recapturing Manychskaya.[25] It is therefore likely that the formations he overran were, at best, what remained of the mechanised group that Rotmistrov had assembled in his attempt to reach Rostov.

Despite the success of Balck and other energetic commanders, the situation south of the Don was growing ever more precarious for the Germans. *SS-Viking* abandoned the line of the Manych around Proletarskaya late on 19 January and fell back towards Rostov, having to fight its way through Russian forces that had already bypassed it:

> Salsk, a few kilometres away, had already been burning for hours. Our companies formed convoys so that the immobilised tanks could be towed along. We were the last to fight our way through a burning Salsk and headed in the direction of Rostov, our next objective, by way of Gigant.[26]

Constantly outflanked and occasionally almost surrounded, *SS-Viking* fell back in stages. By the end of January, reduced to the strength of barely a single tank company, the division's panzer battalion fell back to Kagalnitskaya, 30 miles (48km) southeast of Rostov. It stayed in this area for several days, its strength slowly edging up as repaired tanks were returned to the front line.

On 23 January, Stalin sent a signal to Yeremenko's Southern Front urging him to push on as fast as possible. In particular, he demanded that Yeremenko drive on to Bataisk, while the Black Sea Group cut off the German lines of retreat towards the Taman Peninsula. The Northern Group of the Transcaucasus Front was now transformed into the North Caucasian Front, but despite energetic efforts by all concerned, a combination of poor roads, supply problems, and determined German resistance prevented a second Stalingrad south of Rostov.

Throughout this period, the ordeal of Sixth Army continued. Convinced that the failure of Hitler to recognise the direness of the situation was because he was inadequately informed, Paulus dispatched General Hans-Valentin Hube, commander of XIV Panzer Corps, to meet the Führer just before the end of 1942. He returned on 7 January with the news that another relief attempt would be made in February and Sixth Army would have to hold out until then; however, Hitler had promised an improvement in the airlift. Such promises were utterly empty; the Luftwaffe lacked the capacity to provide adequate supplies at the beginning of the encirclement, and now – after the loss of so many aircraft, and the necessity to fly from further to the west on account of Russian advances – there was no question of keeping Sixth Army alive and combat-worthy until it could be rescued. In any event, the second relief attempt was the proposed advance by the SS Panzer Corps from Kharkov, an operation that Manstein had already dismissed as impossible.

Hube's return to Stalingrad coincided with a call from the encircling Russians for the surrender of the trapped troops. In accordance with his orders, Paulus refused. Hube left the pocket for the last time a few days later, leaving behind a few who still believed that Hitler would rescue them; most, however, had accepted reality. On 10 January, the Russians responded to Paulus' rejection with a major assault preceded by heavy artillery fire. Two days later, Pitomnik – the main airfield within the pocket – was overrun by a raiding group of Russian tanks. Although they were driven off, the airfield was lost permanently four days later. Gumrak was the only remaining airfield in the pocket and had a considerably lower capacity than Pitomnik; it was also under artillery fire, and the end was clearly in sight.

By this stage, many of the Russian troops that had originally been deployed to encircle Stalingrad had already begun to move away as the fighting power of the German Sixth Army, and the perimeter it held, was steadily reduced. The role of the trapped army to tie down Russian forces was therefore increasingly ineffective; nevertheless, as late as 19 January Manstein was still telling senior Luftwaffe officers that the service provided by Sixth Army was still of huge benefit and it had to receive adequate supplies to continue its resistance.[27] Just three days later, Manstein's opinion had changed. He had what he later described as a 'long and violent dispute' with Hitler to the effect that it was now time for Sixth Army to surrender. Unsurprisingly, Hitler refused, insisting that resistance should continue even if the pocket were broken into smaller parts. Surrender was futile in any case, he pointed out to Manstein, as the Russians would not honour any agreements regarding welfare of prisoners:

> When Hitler turned down my request for Sixth Army's capitulation, I was naturally faced with the personal problem of deciding whether to register my disagreement by resigning command of the army group.
>
> ... It is, I think, understandable that one should have wished to be released from responsibilities rendered almost unbearable by the interminable, nerve-racking battles that had to be fought with one's own supreme command before it would accept the need for any urgent action. The extent to which this wish preoccupied me at that time is apparent from a remark made by my Ia, the then Colonel Busse ... [whose] words were: 'If I had not kept begging him (Manstein) to stay for the troops' sake, he'd have chucked the job back at Hitler long ago.' ...
>
> ... [But] a senior commander is no more able to pack up and go home than any other soldier. Hitler was not compelled to accept a resignation, and would hardly have been likely to do so in this case ...
>
> ... At the time in question I had not only Sixth Army to consider. The fate of my entire army group was at stake, as well as that of Army Group A. To throw up my task at this moment ... struck me as a betrayal of those brave troops who were also involved in a life-and-death struggle outside the Stalingrad pocket.[28]

On 24 January, Paulus sent a despairing signal directly to *OKH*:

> Fortress can be held for only a few days longer. Troops exhausted and weapons immobilised as a result of non-arrival of supplies. Imminent loss of last airfield will reduce supplies to a minimum. No basis left on which to carry out mission to hold Stalingrad ... [I] shall give orders just before final break-up [of the pocket] for all elements to fight through to southwest in organised groups. Some of these will get through and sow confusion behind Russian lines. Failure to move will mean end of everyone, as prisoners will also die of cold and hunger. Suggest flying out a few men, officers and other ranks, as specialists for use in future operations ... Please detail officers by name, obviously excluding myself.[29]

Zeitzler replied that he had made an almost identical request four days before. Hitler's response was the same on both occasions: he reserved any decision regarding a breakout, though characteristically he did not flatly reject the requests. It was another example of his procrastination when confronted with a decision that he did not wish to make.

On 26 January, the pocket was split in two. Several of Paulus' generals pleaded in vain on 27 January for permission to surrender; the following day, the northern pocket was further split in two. On 29 January, the Russians sent envoys to call on the surviving Germans to lay down their weapons. A day later, the tenth anniversary of Hitler becoming Chancellor of Germany, Paulus sent a further signal to Germany:

> On the anniversary of your seizure of power, Sixth Army congratulates its Führer. The swastika still flies over Stalingrad. Our battle has given the living and coming generations an example, also in the hopelessness of never surrendering, that Germany will win.
> Heil mein Führer.[30]

It seems extraordinary that he sent this signal at a time when Adam claims he was increasingly bitter and disillusioned with the German high command. This discrepancy suggests that perhaps Paulus did not feel as let down by Hitler as Adam – writing about two decades later – claimed; alternatively, this signal may have been drafted by Schmidt, whose personal devotion to Hitler remained unshaken right to the end.

On the last day of January, Hitler promoted Paulus to Field Marshal in the expectation that a German field marshal would rather commit suicide than surrender his forces to the enemy. Instead, Paulus – a devout Catholic who was strongly opposed to suicide – met Russian envoys and surrendered personally; at the same time, the southern pocket laid down its arms. Paulus was thus able to claim at a later date that his act of surrender had applied only to himself and not to Sixth Army. The central pocket surrendered later the same day, followed by the northern enclave on 2 February. Of approximately a quarter of a million men who were surrounded by *Uranus*, nearly 91,000 remained alive and were taken prisoner; the rest had either died during the siege or had been evacuated after being wounded. Typhus ravaged the camps to which the exhausted, emaciated prisoners were taken, leading to tens of thousands of deaths. Only 5,000 survived to return to Germany after the war. This was not – as claimed by many, including Manstein – evidence that Hitler had been correct in his statement that the Russians would not look after prisoners; the number of captives was simply overwhelming, and they were in such a debilitated condition that even had plentiful supplies of food and medicine been available, many would still have died. The Russians struggled to feed their own army and civilian population during the war, and had no capacity to cope with having to take responsibility for such a large number of sick, emaciated prisoners.

Mansoor Abdullin was present when the fighting stopped with what seemed unnatural suddenness:

> I awoke to someone's amazed exclamations. It was dawn. Several lads, close together, were looking at the opposite side of the street. What was there? I scrambled through them to look and nobody protested, even though it must have been uncomfortable – they were so carried away by the spectacle. I looked at the empty eye sockets of the windows of the house opposite and at first couldn't understand what it meant. From the windowsills white cloths were hanging askew. Small white rags were neatly arranged on piles of broken bricks. And quiet.
>
> Not a single sound.
>
> Surrender.
>
> I don't remember which of the guys spoke the word, carefully, as if afraid to frighten it away.
>
> Should we reveal ourselves? What if it was a trap? The Germans had fought bitterly the previous evening. Curiosity prevailed: is it really capitulation? What should we do now, at this moment? I suddenly saw that the lads were embarrassed, they exchanged glances with hesitant but joyful smiles; they said, 'We're as dirty as devils, covered in dust and soot. Accepting surrender isn't the same as battle. Perhaps we need a representative.'
>
> Yes, where can we find someone who looks respectable? I thought. We must accept their surrender as soon as possible or the Germans may decide we are afraid and change their minds about giving up!
>
> I jumped out over the guys and went to the middle of the street. With feet like clay, I walked slowly. There were white rags and cloths in many houses where we didn't even think there were any fascists.
>
> All around I saw people like me, 'representatives', hesitantly walking into the middle of the street. We looked at each other with embarrassed glances; we were happy, but exposed like fools, and if shooting came now, it would be more than awkward.
>
> I slung my gun over my shoulder as a gesture [to the Germans]; it was so dirty I didn't think it would work anyway.
>
> And suddenly they emerged from the ruins, from their burrows, all at the same time. They too walked slowly, threw their guns onto the snow and raised their

hands. They were indifferent to my grubby appearance. Someone dropped a gun at my feet. It was the only reason I could tell that the scarecrow wrapped in a blanket was an officer. A pistol, thrown at me in such a way to make sure I realised …

I suddenly realised with relief that there would be no tricks: the Germans were disciplined people. And this was a real surrender.

The boys, seeing the Nazis behaving like this, poured into the street, dancing. Next to us, the Hitlerites looked like scarecrows. What rags they wore! They threw their weapons onto piles and silently formed up in columns of eight to ten men in breadth.[31]

Inevitably, much of the analysis of the Battle of Stalingrad has concentrated on where blame lay, with only a few – such as Adam – seeking to exonerate Paulus. Balck had known Paulus for some considerable time before the war, and his analysis is perhaps a reasonable one:

> Paulus spent almost his entire life serving in staff posts. He had never personally made decisions. He just received them and then passed on orders. He was a typical background figure, indispensible and of the greatest value if led by a strong personality, for example Reichenau … Being a weak man, he remained true to what he had always done – he presented his case, asked for a decision, and then turned it into orders for others. Nor had Paulus been prepared properly for command. He moved from chief of staff of an army immediately to command of an army. He did not pass through the positions of regiment, division and corps commander.
>
> Paulus cannot be burdened with the entire blame for Stalingrad. Stronger soldiers would have failed in such chaos.[32]

Towards the end of the siege, Paulus singled out the Luftwaffe for blame, making no distinction between distant figures like Goering and Jeschonnek, who had given Hitler utterly unjustified assurances about the transport capability that would be available, and the aircrews who had risked – and frequently lost – their lives trying to fly supplies into the encirclement. On 19 January, the Luftwaffe's Major Erich Thiel, whose He111 bombers had been involved in the airlift, met Paulus in his headquarters and was stunned by the verbal attack that the commander of Sixth Army made on him:

> When [aircraft] don't land, it means the army's death. It is too late now, anyway … Every machine that lands saves the lives of 1,000 men … Airdrops are of no

use to us. Many canisters are not found because we have no fuel with which to retrieve them ... Today is the fourth day in which my troops have had nothing to eat ... The last horses have been eaten. Can you imagine it: soldiers diving on an old horse cadaver, breaking open its head and devouring its brain raw? ... Why did the Luftwaffe say that it could carry out the supply mission? Who is the man responsible for mentioning the possibility? If someone had told me that it was not possible, I would not have reproached the Luftwaffe, I would have broken out.[33]

This was an extraordinary statement: several Luftwaffe officers – and almost everyone other than Hitler – had informed Paulus that the airlift proposals were utterly unrealistic, but he had adhered rigidly to the orders he received from Hitler. At no stage did he or his chief of staff visit any of the airfields in the pocket to ascertain the situation for themselves.

He wasn't the only senior figure to cling to deluded beliefs about the events in Stalingrad. Two weeks after Paulus' surrender, Goering spoke to a meeting of senior Luftwaffe officers: 'Paulus was too weak. He failed to turn Stalingrad into a proper fortress ... [His] army just relied on the Luftwaffe and expected it to perform miracles.'[34]

At no stage, either at the time or later, did Goering accept any responsibility for his role in the events that led to the destruction of Sixth Army. When he met Richthofen in early February, he tried to justify himself on the grounds that he had been forced to comply with Hitler's wish to hold onto Stalingrad at all costs, and the true blame lay with the Italians – if their lines had not disintegrated as a consequence of *Little Saturn*, Tatsinskaya and Morozovsk could have been held and LVII Panzer Corps would have broken through to the encirclement. Richthofen's response was scathing: the airlift was already failing before the Italian Eighth Army was defeated, and Goering would have known far more about the realities on the ground had he troubled to visit the front personally. There can be no doubt that Hitler understood the widespread criticisms of Goering, and the relationship between the Führer and the head of the Luftwaffe, already in decline, cooled still further in the weeks after Paulus' surrender as Hitler attempted to spread the blame for the disaster.[35]

Over the following months, the senior officers who were captured in Stalingrad were interrogated and received repeated visits from German communists who had fled to the Soviet Union to escape the Nazis. At first, Paulus refused to cooperate with the Russians but after the failed assassination attempt against Hitler in July 1944 he became a vocal critic of the Nazis, joining the *Nationalkomitee Freies Deutschland* ('National Committee for a Free Germany') and broadcasting to German troops, calling on them to stop fighting for the Nazi regime. He had sent his wedding ring back to his wife on one of the last planes to leave Stalingrad, and never saw her again; she died in 1949, when he was still being held captive. In 1953 he was allowed to move to East Germany. He died in 1957, part-way through writing his personal account of the battle with which his name will always be linked.

Hitler ordered that the German people should be told that all of Sixth Army had perished. This was in keeping with previous policy – many letters sent back to Germany via the Swedish Red Cross by German prisoners of war in the Soviet Union were destroyed in order to perpetuate the myth that the Russians took no prisoners. As this account has shown, the fighting on the Eastern Front was brutal and there was widespread disregard on both sides for what passed as normal conduct elsewhere, but in the front line it was generally known that the Russians often took prisoners – there were plenty of cases of men escaping back to their own side and reporting on their experiences. However, in the particular case of Stalingrad, senior Nazi figures rapidly tried to portray the hopeless fight to the bitter end as being analogous to episodes of history that would have been familiar to Germans of the era. One was the battle between King Leonidas' Spartans and the Persian invasion army at Thermopylae in 480 BC – the Spartan king deliberately chose to stay and fight to the last man in order to buy time for other Greek forces to pull back in safety. Speaking in a radio broadcast on 30 January, Goering argued that the war against the Soviet Union was one taken on by the German people to protect all of Europe from Bolshevism, a further manifestation of the change of emphasis with regard to the reasons for the German attack on its eastern neighbour. Stalingrad, he told his audience, was proof that Germany would win this critical struggle. Future generations would come to regard it as the most heroic battle in German history, because people who could fight like that would triumph in the end. It mattered little to a soldier whether he died in Stalingrad or North Africa or elsewhere: the law that they obeyed was one that called for them to die for their country, and the defenders of Stalingrad had done that.[36] He specifically quoted the epigram of Simonides engraved upon a memorial at Thermopylae, rewording it to reflect what had happened at Stalingrad: 'If you come to Germany, go tell them that you saw us fight at Stalingrad, obedient to the law laid down for the security of the German people.'[37]

This speech was broadcast before the final surrender and was heard by soldiers in the city; the effect of such a bombastic funeral oration from a man who had directly contributed to the disaster – though few of his listeners would have known this at the time – can only be imagined.

Newspapers took up the theme. In the *Volks-Zeitung* on 4 February, Georg Dertinger, like Goering, used the Spartans at Thermopylae and the defiant last stand by the Burgundians in the *Nibelungenlied* for inspiration:

Only a few hours have passed since we heard the song of 'Good Comrades' over the radio that announced to us the end of the battle of Stalingrad...

...This is not a matter of victory or defeat. This is not a matter of the ebb and flow of the war ... This is a matter only of heroism, of courage, of military testing ...

Remember, German mother, when as a child you heard for the first the heroic song of Kriemhild or of the heroes of Etzelburg? ... Remember, German father, when with glowing cheeks you heard for the first time about the heroism of Leonidas and his 300 Spartans who died at the narrow pass of Thermopylae so that their people could live? ...

...There have always been individual heroes. Never before have all in a battle been heroes. There is no historic example of this scale. That is the gift of our age ...

... The soldier fought next to the general. All barriers and distinctions fell away, leaving only the community of warriors. They had but one thought: People and Fatherland. That is what they fought for, that is what they bled for. They died so that Germany could live.[38]

But if the Nazi regime was to salvage anything from the disaster and claim some sort of lofty moral victory, it had to persuade the German people that all those in Sixth Army had perished in the fighting. There was also the expectation that this would stiffen the resolve of German troops to fight harder against a foe who would show no mercy if they tried to surrender. As the months after the battle passed and many of those who surrendered made radio broadcasts on behalf of their Russian captors, and when news of those broadcasts filtered back to Germany, families who had believed that their menfolk had died began to hope that some might have survived. Even decades after the end of the war, a few still hoped that loved ones might one day be released by the Soviet Union.

Both sides attempted to create a mythical version of the war. The soldiers in their armies were universally heroic and self-sacrificing, determined to fight to the last man; the enemy was portrayed as monstrous and merciless. The latter was largely true for both sides, as the mistreatment of many prisoners of war showed, but an abiding tragedy of the war is that the mythology created by the Soviet system persisted for decades after the war, and indeed still exists today amongst the dwindling band of surviving veterans. Even memories of the suffering of the Russian people, soldiers and civilians alike, were suppressed if they were felt to detract from the glory of the Red Army; for example, mass graves of hundreds of soldiers bore the names of perhaps a dozen or so, and citizens of Leningrad were forbidden from mentioning the near-starvation of those in the city during radio broadcasts.[39] The Soviet legend was that Russia had undoubtedly suffered greatly, but the reality of the true magnitude of the suffering was too vast to be faced. For many years, Red Army veterans were discouraged from writing memoirs about their experiences, and those that did emerge had to comply with the orthodox view of the war. German writers, too, were bound by an orthodoxy, albeit less official, producing accounts in which the Russians were rarely if ever credited with any tactical skill, were usually portrayed as attacking in overwhelming strength against Germans who fought with great expertise, and atrocities against Russians were rarely mentioned.

As the final act of the Stalingrad tragedy was being played out, even Hitler had to accept that there were limits to prevarication and that he could no longer put off a decision about Army Group A. On 27 January, he issued definitive orders. First Panzer Army was to withdraw behind Fourth Panzer Army and across the Don at Rostov, as Manstein had been demanding for several weeks. However, it was reduced in strength – several of its formations were to be transferred to Seventeenth Army, which would withdraw with Kleist's army group headquarters into the Taman Peninsula, where it would be supplied via the Crimea. Stalin had hoped to prevent this by pushing forward with the Black Sea group of forces, but the pursuit of the withdrawing Germans was too cautious and the rearguard action too skilful. Analysing the lessons of the winter's fighting, a Soviet report the following summer drew the following self-evident conclusion:

> The offensive and energetic pursuit should be completed by the destruction of the withdrawing enemy. Tank, mechanised and cavalry formations should try to reach the routes of withdrawal of the enemy.[40]

Given the poor roads and the lack of supplies, such an energetic pursuit was beyond the capabilities of the Black Sea group, regardless of how audacious its commander might have been.

At last, Manstein was to be allowed to pull back the long, exposed southern flank of the German line on the Eastern Front. Whether there was still time to do this, and whether the forces thus released would be able to remedy the series of disasters further north, remained to be seen.

CHAPTER 10

FEBRUARY: RETREAT FROM THE DON

In a little over two months, the Red Army had changed the situation of the Eastern Front in a manner that probably exceeded all its most optimistic expectations and certainly to a greater extent than the most pessimistic German might have anticipated. The first operations to exploit the successes of *Uranus* and *Little Saturn* tore apart what was left of the Italian Eighth Army, wrecked the Hungarian Second Army beyond repair, and came close to destroying the German Second Army. Moskalenko's summary was perhaps a little wide of the mark in not finding the situation surprising, but in other respects was a view widely shared by other Russians at every level:

> The sudden change in the situation that occurred as a result of the resolute actions of the Soviet troops in the middle and the end of January 1943 was not unexpected either for the commanders of the Fortieth Army or for its soldiers. Undoubtedly, the situation that was taking shape then seemed very novel to us. Just a few days after the beginning of an operation, the enemy was everywhere in complete flight and fighting was increasingly reduced to cutting his escape routes, fragmenting the surrounding troops and then capturing or destroying them. But did not each of us expect this moment, did we not know from the first day of the war and in the worst weeks and months of retreat that the hour of retribution would inevitably come one day?
>
> I will never forget this feeling, nor the joyful wave that swept through us after the November-December events in the Stalingrad region and then again in the days of our January offensive. The long-awaited hour has come! This was evidenced

by everything: the fact that the Soviet troops were now advancing on a broad front, and the fact that they were striking with increasing force, and especially that these were skillful blows – not driving the enemy back, but surrounding him and destroying him.

In the unfolding events, it was not difficult to see a clear sequence. It became obvious that they were engendered by a single conception, grandiose in scale and purpose, and that the management of its implementation was carried out from a single centre, according to a well thought out plan and with unprecedented breadth and art. First – the encirclement of the enemy in the Stalingrad area. Then – the defeat of the enemy in the Middle Don. Now – the liquidation of the enemy's Ostrogozhsk-Rossosh group. And it was clear: more attacks on the enemy were being prepared.

… The position of the German Second Army reminded me of another bulge formed in September 1941 in the vicinity of Kiev. It was not extended to the east, like now, but to the west, and it was not enemy troops that defended it, but ours. And it was the German Second Army, together with Guderian's panzer group, who then inflicted a blow from the north on the right wing of the troops of the Southwest Front.

How noisily jubilant the enemy was at that time. He announced to the whole world – not for the first time! – the destruction of the Red Army and the imminent end of the 'eastern campaign.' More than a year had passed since then, but victory in this war was even further away for the enemy. Perhaps now the German-fascist command could with good reason speak of the approach of the end of the 'Eastern campaign.' But it would be an infamous, shameful end. It would bring with it the defeat of Hitler's Germany, the destruction of fascism.

Yes, the situation had changed. For us it was time to get even with the enemy.[1]

Whilst it may have seemed to men like Moskalenko that the series of blows that had wrecked the German position was part of some huge master plan, the reality was that each operation created new opportunities, and the Red Army had built up sufficient reserves to exploit these in a more or less opportunistic fashion. But despite all these successes, a decisive conclusion to the campaign remained to be achieved and reserves – and time – were beginning to run out.

Substantial reinforcements were now beginning to assemble for Manstein's hard-pressed armies. For many years, Heinrich Himmler, head of the SS, had planned to develop substantial military units as rivals to the Wehrmacht and the first such *Waffen-SS* formations were created before the war. The first engagements against Polish troops in 1939 were not encouraging; the first combat unit, at this stage barely a regiment in size – *Leibstandarte SS Adolf Hitler* or *LSSAH* – formed part of XIII Corps and allowed itself to get embroiled in close-quarter fighting rather than exploiting the exposed flanks of the Polish defences, and Weichs, who was at the time the corps commander, was especially critical of the poor leadership of the division.[2] Even a year later, there were concerns that despite getting high quality recruits, the SS units were built largely around men whose loyalty to the SS was seen as more important than their military skills; Fedor von Bock, who held the rank of Generaloberst at the time and would command Army Group Centre during the opening phases of *Barbarossa*, wrote in April 1940:

> The combat-readiness of the SS NCOs and formations is insufficient. We will pay for that with unnecessary bloodshed. It is a pity to waste such excellent human materiel.[3]

The *Waffen-SS* formations were steadily enlarged and had reached the size of divisions by the summer of 1941. Despite substantial improvements in their training, there remained considerable problems and there were protests about the manner in which troops from *SS-Totenkopf* became involved in looting and attacks on civilians during the drive into Latvia, leaving their neighbouring units exposed and costing unnecessary casualties; Generalmajor Otto Lancelle, commander of 121st Infantry Division, was killed by a Russian sniper just a day after he filed a report that was deeply critical of *SS-Totenkopf*.[4]

In addition to purely German formations, the growing *Waffen-SS* also raised formations from other nations. The first of these was *SS-Viking*, and like the other early SS units, it steadily grew in strength and quality. In 1942 many of the divisions were pulled out of line to be reorganised and re-equipped as motorised or panzergrenadier formations. *SS-Viking* was part of Army Group A in the Caucasus and late in 1942 it was transferred north to cover the gap between Kleist's group and Manstein's Army Group Don, releasing 16th Motorised Division for operations, but several other SS divisions – *LSSAH*, *Totenkopf* and *Das Reich* – had been grouped together to form the SS Panzer Corps in France, and these formations now began to assemble in the Ukraine. Himmler ensured that his divisions were lavishly equipped; in addition to panzergrenadier and panzer regiments, the SS units had a heavy tank company which, during the coming fighting, would be equipped with new Tiger tanks, and a battalion of assault guns. In combat power, these panzergrenadier divisions were actually at least as powerful as Wehrmacht panzer divisions. Many of the defects in the training of the rank and file had been remedied, but several of the officers of the divisions had followed careers in the SS and lacked the combat experience of their Wehrmacht equivalents; others were veterans like Obergruppenführer Paul Hausser, the commander of the corps – who had lost his right eye after being wounded by shrapnel in October 1941 – and had served in the First World War and in the Reichswehr between the wars, and was rightly seen as a skilled and forceful leader.

However, the assembly of this powerful force would take time. Until then, Manstein continued to struggle with the resources available to him. Fourth Panzer Army was to continue to protect the vital crossings at Rostov, while First Panzer Army was brought north through the city in order to be available for operations further north. This was Manstein's overall plan – in order to deal with the Soviet forces steadily outflanking his army group and moving west, he would leapfrog his formations west, with First Panzer Army withdrawing behind Fourth Panzer Army and *Armee Abteilung Hollidt* before being thrown at the Russians; thereafter, Fourth Panzer Army would in turn pull back covered by Hollidt's troops and be available to launch a counterattack on the west flank of First Panzer Army.

The diversion of forces from First Panzer Army to Seventeenth Army – particularly 13th Panzer Division – was an ongoing source of frustration, but at least there was the prospect of being able to achieve a degree of mobility at long last. But releasing troops from the Caucasus and bringing fresh units from France was only part of the solution; in addition, Manstein needed to be able to trade space for time, and to draw the Russian forces into a position where an effective counterblow could be delivered. Here, he came up against Hitler's reluctance to consider withdrawals. The arguments now centred on the eastern parts of Ukraine around the Donets, a centre of coal mining. Hitler repeatedly argued that possession of these mines – or at least their denial to the Russians – was essential. Without coal from the Donets basin, or Donbas, he told Manstein and others, the Soviet Union would not be able to keep its coking plants operating and ultimately this would cripple tank and munitions production. Manstein had his doubts, later writing that despite not having access to these coal mines for 1942 and much of 1943, the Soviet Union managed to manufacture thousands of tanks and millions of shells without any apparent coke shortages. Nor was the coal absolutely vital for the German war effort – whilst it was suitable for coking, it was too poor to be used for locomotives, and as a result every train that was used to move Ukrainian coal back to Germany had to be provided with coal for propulsion brought from Germany, placing further demands on the already badly stretched railway network.[5]

For professional officers like Manstein and Zeitzler, all considerations of economic desirability or necessity were secondary to military capability – unless sufficient forces could be deployed in the region, it would be impossible to retain control of the Donbas region regardless of how much Hitler might wish it. Whilst Hitler frequently used economic arguments to overrule the military practicalities of his generals, his record in such matters was already questionable by the end of 1942. The entire focus of the 1942 campaign – the capture of the Caucasus oilfields – had been based upon Hitler's view that control of these oilfields was vital both for Germany and the Soviet Union, but despite being unable to extract oil from much of the region for large parts of 1942, the Red Army showed no sign of being short of fuel. By contrast, the Wehrmacht was repeatedly crippled by fuel shortages, and even when Maikop was captured, it proved almost impossible to get the damaged oil wells into production – the total amount of Caucasus oil extracted by the Germans during their period of occupation has been calculated to amount to just seven tons.[6] If the Caucasus region was so vital to Germany's interests, the folly of Hitler's obsession with the sterile battle to capture the ruins of Stalingrad seems even greater.

Manstein summed up the situation with characteristic precision:

> Should we be unable to do this [deploy new forces in strength] … we should simply have to accept the consequences. The southern wing of the German armies could not close the gap with its own forces if it remained on the lower Don. Nor could it go on fighting there in isolation if the expected reinforcements took a long time to arrive and deployed far to the rear … The battle being fought by the southern wing and the deployment of the new forces must be so attuned to one another in a special sense as to become operationally coherent. Either the new forces must be made to deploy swiftly and relatively far to the east, in which case it would be possible for the army group to remain on the lower Don and Donets, or else they could not, and the army group would have to be pulled back to join them. If one of these two courses were not taken, the enemy would have an opportunity to cut off the whole southern wing before any reinforcements could make their presence felt.[7]

That opportunity had been beckoning since the successful completion of *Uranus* and continued to do so. Hitler repeatedly told Zeitzler that such fears were misplaced as the Russian formations had to be badly worn down after the losses they had suffered. Aware of the Russian forces moving north and west from the Caucasus and Stalingrad, Manstein had little doubt that the Red Army would still be able to concentrate sufficient strength to overwhelm his troops, whose worn down state was repeatedly ignored by Hitler. The disparity between the opposing forces was amply demonstrated when a powerful Russian force crossed the Donets on 2 February to the east of Voroshilovgrad while another Russian force began to push southwest from Starobelsk. These two formations threatened to combine and drive down to the Sea of Azov or directly towards Rostov. In order to deal with this, Manstein intended to use First Panzer Army in a counterattack, but at the same time he needed to pull back Fourth Panzer Army so that it too could be used in a counterattacking role further to the west. He outlined his proposal in a long teleprinter message to *OKH*, emphatically stating – not for the first time – that continued occupation of the Donets basin was simply impossible. Even if the line could be held in the short term, Army Group Don would be left in a vulnerable salient that could be threatened at any time in the future. Instead, Manstein proposed drawing the Russian armies towards the lower Dnepr while he concentrated his own strength to their north, from where he would then attack towards the Black Sea, aiming to break up the Russian armies and to isolate and destroy them.

Such an operation called for the abandonment – even if only temporary – of far more than just the Donbas region, and given Hitler's unwillingness to make even modest withdrawals, it was surely no surprise to anyone when he steadfastly opposed Manstein's suggestion. Instead, Manstein had to opt for his second-best option, namely an operation in which the two panzer armies would attack northwards once they had withdrawn from the Don, while the SS Panzer Corps attacked towards them from the northwest. Impatient for a turn of the tide, Hitler now ordered the first SS division that had deployed in SS Panzer Corps' new location in the Kharkov area – *SS-Das Reich* – to attack on its own towards the south to restore the front line. This ignored the fact that *SS-Das Reich* was already heavily involved in defensive fighting near Volchansk to the northeast of Kharkov, and even if it had been available for such an attack, it would have required substantial support to protect its rear areas as it advanced towards the south – and no such support was available.

On the battlefield, events continued to move in the Red Army's favour. The few Romanian troops still in the front line showed little inclination to fight, as Major General Sergei Semenovich Biryusov, chief of staff with the Russian Second Guards Army, personally discovered as he drove through morning fog, trying to locate the Russian III Mechanised Corps:

> Gradually the fog began to dissipate a little. In front of us, we noticed marching
> columns travelling in the same direction as us. Our car appeared to be between

two such columns moving along converging roads. 'That's good, we've made good time,' Subbotin [a staff officer with Biryusov] said. 'This is undoubtedly part of III Mechanised Corps!'

'Something looks wrong,' I replied doubtfully, 'there aren't enough motor vehicles, and the men on foot don't look like Guards.' In the meantime, we approached to within 200m of one of the columns. The soldiers were now clearly visible. It became obvious: these were enemy troops before us. In the column, too, they noticed us: they looked back at us, pointing. The thought flashed through my head: 'They are deploying that gun right now,' but then I saw that there were several men just tinkering with the gun. And what should we do? 'Drive to the head of the column!' I ordered the driver. At full throttle we raced along the road to the front of the large column. It was not hard to guess by the uniforms that we were dealing with Romanians.

I got out of the car and raised a hand. The column stopped. Many people shrugged their shoulders, not understanding what was happening. I asked for a senior officer. The Romanian colonel came up and formally introduced himself. 'Where are you leading the column?' I asked severely. 'You are about to run into our artillery and machine-guns.'

The colonel blinked his eyes guiltily and in broken Russian began to explain: 'The Romanians do not want to fight anymore. We want to surrender. But we don't know where to go.'

I took his map and pointed at it, indicating where they should go. Then I wrote a note to my rear area commander, so that the Romanians who surrendered were fed and ensured their further evacuation. I also had to leave one of our submachine-gunners with the Romanian colonel as a guide. It was absolutely necessary, not so much to ensure the Romanians didn't wander down the wrong road, but rather to notify our troops moving along the roads that this column had already surrendered.[8]

An attack by 6th Panzer Division against a large Russian bridgehead over the Donets failed to make headway after it ran into well-positioned anti-tank guns that put down an accurate fire on the attacking German armour, but despite scoring hits on ten tanks the Russians didn't succeed in knocking out any of them. Given the penetrative power of most Russian anti-tank guns at the time, this seems a remarkable outcome at first glance, but despite the prodigious output of Russian factories it was not possible to equip all anti-tank formations with 76mm guns, and many still used large numbers of anti-tank rifles instead. Even these weapons would prove lethal at closer range, and rather than risk losses,

Hünersdorff called off the attack. Shortly after, the division was pulled out of line and temporarily assigned as army group reserve, giving its men a much-needed break to allow for repairs and fresh drafts to be incorporated into its depleted ranks, particularly the panzergrenadier and reconnaissance battalions.[9] Further west, Russian troops pushed forward through almost empty space towards Izyum, and Manstein could do nothing to intervene – 6th Panzer Division was the only formation not already committed and he needed it to recover its strength if it was to be of use in the critical counterattacks that lay ahead. For several days, Army Group Don had wanted to pull back *Armee Abteilung Hollidt* to the line of the River Mius, but Hitler had refused to permit such a withdrawal, and even if Hollidt were able to reach the Mius line now, the Russians would already have outflanked it. Given the Russian attack towards Izyum, Manstein now demanded that he be allowed to pull back to the Mius without further delay, and that additional rail capacity was urgently needed. In addition, substantial forces currently in the Taman Peninsula – particularly 13th Panzer Division – should be moved to the lower Dnepr, and preparations made for a possible airlift in the event of the Russians being able to reach the coast of the Sea of Azov.

The Russian plans to turn the flank of the German forces pulling back to the Taman Peninsula by way of a joint operation between Forty-Seventh Army and the Black Sea Fleet – codenamed *Sea* – failed to achieve its objectives. After failing to reach Novorossisk in late January, Forty-Seventh Army tried again on 1 February without gaining any ground. Four days later, the amphibious part of the operation was ordered to proceed, even though it was doomed to failure in the absence of any advance by Forty-Seventh Army. The bombardment of German defences was ineffective and the main landing at Yuzhnaya Ozereika, to the west of Novorossisk, ended in ignominious defeat – only 1,400 men even managed to get ashore, and suffered heavy losses before the survivors were withdrawn. A second landing at Stanichka survived rather longer, but was also a failure.[10]

Amongst the formations pursuing the retreating Germans from the Caucasus was 588th Night Bomber Regiment, which was renamed 46th Guards Regiment in early February 1943. It was an unusual formation in that its aircrew and ground personnel were all women, known to the Germans as the *Nachthexen* ('night witches'). Their Polikarpov Po-2 bombers were fragile biplanes with plywood and canvas structures and could carry only a limited number of small bombs. Despite their fragile appearance, the aircraft were remarkably difficult to shoot down as they were able to fly slower than the stalling speed of German fighters and often made their bombing runs at night in a gliding attack with the engine switched off. Operating from airfields – any clear area of ground would suffice – close to the front line, the planes were able to carry out several annoyance raids every night. Whilst their bomb-loads might have been modest, their value for harassment was considerable, and the planes – variously nicknamed the *Nähmaschine* ('sewing machine') or *UvD* (*Unteroffizier von Dienst* or 'duty NCO', who would make rounds of the trenches at night to ensure men were awake and keeping guard properly) were a constant irritation to the Germans, who eventually emulated such formations with *Störkampfstaffel* ('harassment combat squadrons') of their own, using a variety of obsolete open-cockpit biplanes. As 588th Night Bomber Regiment advanced in the wake of IV Guards Cavalry Corps, Natalia Fedorovna Kravtsova, one of the pilots, had the disconcerting experience of seeing corpses from the recent fighting, an experience that – like so many air force personnel on all sides – she found deeply unsettling:

> Rasshevatka was all ablaze. Low smoke spread over the railway station. In the warehouses, grain was alight, and the smell of burning hung in the air. Everything was smoky, dirty. There were signs of horses everywhere, hoof-prints in the snow. The cavalry corps of General Kirichenko had passed through here, pursuing the enemy. There was fighting here. Corpses had not yet been removed. Dead horses lay here and there.
>
> On the roadside leading to the airfield, Ira Sebrova and I stumbled upon the corpse of a dead German. He was lying behind a hillock, and I nearly tripped over him. We stopped and stood silently, gazing at him.
>
> The German was young, without uniform, in blue underwear. His body was pale and waxy. The head was thrown back and turned to one side, and his straight fair hair hung down to the snow. It seemed that he had just turned and looked down the road in horror, expecting something. Maybe death.
>
> It was the first time that we saw a dead German so close. Each of us already had three hundred sorties to our accounts. Our bombs had sown death. But how this actually looked, this death, we had only imagined rather vaguely. We just didn't think about it, and most likely did not want to think about it.
>
> 'Suppress the firing point,' 'Bomb the crossing,' 'Destroy the enemy personnel' – all this sounded so familiar and mundane that it did not cause any ambiguity. We knew: the more damage we inflicted on the enemy, the more Nazis we killed, the sooner the hour of victory would come. To kill the fascists? It seemed that it was as simple as that. For this, we went to war. So why, now, looking at the dead enemy, on his white, bloodless face, on which the fresh snow rested and did not melt, on the hand with his fingers twisted to one side, did I experience a mixed

feeling of depression, disgust and, oddly enough, pity? Tomorrow I would fly again on bombing missions, and the day after tomorrow, and on and on until the war was over or until they killed me. Against Germans just like this one. Why then did I feel this pity?[11]

Po-2 aircraft continued to be used in harassment attacks throughout the war and even in later conflicts; the North Koreans used them during the Korean War, achieving some notable successes when they attacked airfields. Much like Luftwaffe pilots, the aircrews of night fighters operating with the United Nations forces against North Korea found them almost impossible to engage – their wood-and-canvas structure gave poor radar echoes, and on one occasion a US F-94 Starfire jet fighter was lost when it stalled while trying to fly slowly enough to engage a Po-2.

The units of *SS-Viking*, which had played such an essential part in holding the Russians at arm's length while First Panzer Army completed its withdrawal through Rostov, received orders to fall back to the city on 4 February. It took two days to complete the journey, with the tanks struggling to cope with icy slopes already made smooth as glass by the passage of previous vehicles. In conditions of -30°C with an icy wind blowing, the troops arrived in Rostov to find the city choked with traffic as a multitude of units struggled to escape to relative safety further north. While they took a day's rest to repair their vehicles and find some warm shelter, the men of *SS-Viking* had time to reflect on all that had happened since they had crossed the Don at Rostov on their way south nearly seven months previously. Two of the panzer battalion's three company commanders and most of its platoon commanders were dead or wounded, as were thousands of other men in the division. Then they were on the road again, ordered to move to Sambek, between Rostov and Taganrog. It took 15 hours to travel the 33 miles (53km) to their destination along badly degraded roads where all manner of military traffic jostled for priority. From there, *SS-Viking* moved on to Taganrog, where it was subordinated to XL Panzer Corps.

On 6 February, Hitler summoned Manstein to a conference and the hard-pressed field marshal boarded a plane for Germany with mixed feelings. On the one hand, the battles raging across the front held by Army Group Don continued to demand his constant attention; but on the other hand, he needed to force Hitler to make key decisions so that he could deal more effectively with those battles. Slightly to Manstein's surprise, Hitler showed an adroit touch by starting the conference with the declaration that he accepted full responsibility for the disaster at Stalingrad. Discussions then moved on to the vexed issue of the

Donets basin. Manstein repeated his view – shared by Zeitzler – that the region could not be held, and the only question was whether its loss was to be accompanied by the destruction of significant parts of Army Group Don. Only the immediate withdrawal of Hollidt's forces to the Mius and permission for Fourth Panzer Army to pull back through Rostov on the heels of First Panzer Army would remedy the situation. Hitler countered with his usual argument about the economic importance of the Donets, a discussion that dragged on for several hours. Nor was the Führer minded to listen to the benefits of shortening the front line to release resources – if this was done, he argued, the Russians too would be able to concentrate their formations more effectively. In any case, after such a prolonged spell of offensive operations, the Red Army had to be approaching the end of its resources. Finally, the abandonment of the Donbas region would, according to Hitler, have adverse diplomatic consequences, particularly in terms of relations with Turkey.

Aware of Hitler's probable line of argument, Manstein had prepared carefully for the conference and countered patiently that he had recently met the president of the German Coal Union, who had assured him that the Donets basin was in no way indispensible for Germany. Hitler then suggested that the approaching thaw would render the roads unusable and would bring all operations to a halt; Manstein dismissed this, pointing out that this would require the thaw season to start unprecedentedly early. Even if an early thaw did happen, the German forces would then face renewed Russian attacks in the spring, still in their exposed positions. He then attempted to move discussions on to another matter: the command of the Eastern Front. Since the first winter of the war with the Soviet Union, Hitler had assumed the position of commander-in-chief, but Manstein now suggested that, combined with the Führer's other responsibilities, this was not a sustainable arrangement. Many had proposed in the past that Manstein should be appointed commander-in-chief on the Eastern Front, which would allow him to move formations from one sector to another without constant delays, but Hitler wasn't interested in such discussions. Previous army officers who had held such a post had disappointed him deeply, he told Manstein, and he felt it would be impossible to appoint someone to a post that would – in Hitler's opinion – be above Goering.

After four hours of exhausting talks, a conclusion of sorts was reached with regard to the Donets basin. Hitler grudgingly gave permission for Manstein to carry out his planned withdrawals, though at the last moment he succeeded in imposing a delay of an additional day. Such a delay was utterly pointless, as an additional day of occupation of the region was of no material benefit for the Germans, and instead left Hollidt's forces exposed for longer than was absolutely necessary. Nevertheless, it was finally possible for orders to be issued to Hollidt to withdraw to the Mius and for Fourth Panzer Army to begin its redeployment. It would take at least two weeks for Hoth's formations to reach their new area of operations further west, and it remained to be seen how much damage could be inflicted on the German line by the Russians in the meantime.

Having pursued the retreating German Fourth Panzer Army down the Don valley to Rostov, the Russian Second Guards Army was now pressing *Armee Abteilung Hollidt*, but the Russians were constantly frustrated by tenacious defence and determined counterattacks. Kobylyanskiy's regiment was deployed in an attack into the village of Novaya Nadezhda, north of Taganrog, and after the infantry had secured a foothold in the village, Kobylyanskiy moved his two field guns forward to provide close support. They suddenly found themselves caught up in a surprise German counterattack at night:

A sudden rattle of machine-guns and the hiss and explosion of mortar shells shattered the silence. Tracer rounds flashed across the nighttime darkness in brilliant arcs. Flares rose one after another in the depths of the village. A few mortar shells exploded just where our limbers were standing. One haystack burst into flames, then the others began to burn.

Our gun crews quickly prepared to fire down the street, but all we could see were gun flashes and we were afraid of firing on our own troops. Suddenly the loud rattle of several German submachine-guns firing simultaneously rang out, and just a moment later, a few of our infantrymen ran past us toward the river in a half crouch, followed by a few more. Then another group ran past our guns, with two or three machine gunners dragging their guns behind them. A real *drap-marsh* [colloquial army term for a rout] had started. From the first moment that it started, nobody could stop this panicked flight.

I realised what was going on and ordered: 'Bring up the limbers double quick! Prepare guns to march!' One limber appeared, but the second limber no longer had any horses. We hooked up Senchenko's gun, and I directed it to the river to join the retreating infantry. Simunin ran to help the second horseman drag away his limber. Ismaylov's crew with my assistance struggled to manhandle their horseless gun through the snow, but the river was still so far! Occasionally, several tardy infantry soldiers scurried past us for the river.

Finally, a group of mortar men with their dismantled 'samovars' [army slang term for mortars] on their shoulders ran by and left us behind. We remained the lone group, struggling slowly across the snow-covered plain. We were exhausted, but we continued rolling the gun.

By this time the Germans were beginning to emerge onto the outskirts of the village and began directing aimed fire at us … When we were at a distance of some 70m from the river, an explosive bullet struck the gun shield. We dropped into the snow … Then we abandoned the gun and crawled to the river.

… Fortunately the Germans remained in Novaya Nadezhda. Otherwise, they could have arranged a real slaughter on the river ice.[12]

The following night, Kobylyanskiy led a group of six men back into Novaya Nadezhda and recovered the abandoned gun.

Manstein returned to his headquarters in Stalino – now Donetsk – on 7 February. Hitler's grudging permission had not come a moment too soon; the staff at Army Group Don headquarters informed their commander that Russian forces had penetrated into the southern suburbs of Rostov. Petr Alexeyevich Belyakov was a sniper in the Russian Twenty-Eighth Army and was with the first Russian troops to enter the city. He found himself in a tough battle with German units, and his account – whilst full of the anti-Nazi rhetoric often found in Soviet-era descriptions – gives an insight into the manner in which snipers fought:

We were surrounded by Rostov citizens. They had joyous expressions, tears in their eyes. We heard cries of 'Our liberators! Our people! At last!'

'A truck! A German truck!' It was a truck with tarpaulin on the back. Spesivtsev aimed at the driver and killed him. The officer sitting next to him managed to jump out of the cab but fell immediately, caught in a burst of machine-gun fire. German soldiers jumped out of the rear and they met the same fate.

Inspired by our first success, we moved on. But then there were alarming shouts: 'Tanks! Tanks!'

'The bastards have spotted us!' cursed our commander, Tuz. He gave orders to Spesivtsev to go up to the top floor of the house and find out how many tanks the enemy had. Just a minute later we heard Spesivtsev's voice:

'Four! There's a truck behind the tanks!' Soon one of the tanks stopped near the house from the window of which the sniper Spesivtsev was watching, and we lost contact with him.

One of the tanks, its tracks clattering, crept along the middle of the street, where a German vehicle lay smashed by us. There were men with submachine-guns behind the tank. We retreated to Dolomanovsky Road. And again an alarming warning: 'Tanks!'

'Cover!' Ordered Lieutenant Tuz. We occupied a corner house. There were already several fighters in it. Among them was a small, broad-shouldered commander with stern features. He was wearing a white sheepskin coat. On his belt were a pistol and two grenades. This was our new battalion commander, Tuz said – Senior Lieutenant Oreshkin.

From the street we heard firing. Our house was surrounded by fascists. We thought we'd have a fight to the death. We weren't alone. A group of soldiers led by Lieutenant Manotskov joined us, cut off from the station where the main units of the brigade were concentrated. We numbered about fifty. We organised a circular defence. Everyone had their task. My place was near the corner window. I hid behind the first thing I found – a Viennese chair, which I put on the windowsill. We watched. Through the optical sight, the nearest streets, a railway track, and a house on a hill could be seen clearly. An excellent position for a sniper! A group of Hitlerites ran out from behind the vehicles. Ahead of them, apparently, was an officer. He wore a high cap, with binoculars on his chest. I pressed the trigger – a good shot. The fascist dropped the pistol and fell to the ground. I knew from experience that the soldiers would try to carry away the corpse of their officer. So it happened: a Hitlerite crawled towards the dead man. And again a shot rang out. On the right, someone appeared running, wrapped in a check shawl. Was it a woman? I peered through the telescopic sights and saw the muzzle of a machine-gun. 'Marauder,' I decided, and I fired.

'Well done!' I heard the voice of the battalion commander, 'Just look for more targets.'

... Now the enemy soldiers were more cautious, lying on the ground. It wasn't easy for officers to get them to attack. The head and shoulders of a Hitlerite emerged from behind a concrete wall. In a sheepskin coat: so, an officer. 'We're giving up!' he shouted in Russian.

'If they're giving up, why do they keep their guns ready?' – the thought flashed through my mind. 'They don't know where we are,' said the battalion commander, 'they want to spot us. Shoot, shoot!' I aimed the crosshairs of the sight at the target. I pulled the trigger smoothly. And the Hitlerite officer waved his hands helplessly.

Firing began to die down. We were running out of ammunition. My rifle magazine was empty. I reported this to the lieutenant with alarm. He thought for a moment. 'Comrade fighter,' he said, turning to the machine-gunner Zavalishin – 'you have a dozen cartridges left in your magazine. Give them to the sniper.'

'What?' exclaimed the machine-gunner, turning pale. 'I can't give them up! How will I fire?' The machine-gunner glared, a defiant stare. I understood how precious the rounds were. 'I won't give them up,' Zavalishin repeated, 'take anything, comrade commander, greatcoat, felt boots – but cartridges?'

'The sniper needs them,' the lieutenant said in a tone that was not to be contradicted. The gunner emptied the magazine, handed over a cartridge, then another. He passed them one at a time, like a hungry man giving up his last piece of bread. There were 11 cartridges. What a pity that there were so few!

A short distance away, hiding behind a drainpipe, was a fascist. I could see his feet, shod in boots. He stamped his feet – evidently he was trying to keep warm. And my trigger finger itched to shoot him in the heel! … But I forced myself to move the optical sight to the left: in a large crater – a group of Hitlerites. They looked around. I checked each one, alas, and there wasn't a single officer there. None of the targets were important. I would have to wait. However, if any of the soldiers decided to move, I would have to use up one of my cartridges.

There was an explosion. It was from the rear of our house, where a fascist tank was firing. Through a cloud of dust, I saw a soldier lying on the floor. Part of his abdomen was torn apart. Senior Lieutenant Oreshkin carefully covered him with a sheepskin coat …

From the top of the destroyed wall, Lieutenant Tuz shot at the machine with short bursts. The attic of the house was burning. The lieutenant ran over, looking for me: 'Finish the scoundrel, over there.' Apparently one of the Hitlerites had moved down the street, pushing a woman ahead of him. The lieutenant wounded him. Despite this, he crawled to the cellar of the neighbouring house, hoping to hide there. My shot killed him.

The encirclement around us became tighter. The enemy realised that we were running out of ammunition and began to show more boldness. The tank came around the turning from Engels Street. It stopped in front of our house. The Germans rushed to the tank, breaking cover. They knocked on the armour with rifle butts, shouting something, pointing in our direction. We watched with alarm. After all, two or three shots from the tank would be enough – and we would be buried under rubble. And indeed, the tank slowly began to turn its turret. A shot seemed imminent. But what was this? The hatch opened and the tankman's head emerged from it. He asked the soldiers something.

'Sniper!' whispered the battalion commander who had come up behind me. 'Kill him.' I pressed the butt into my shoulder, I fired. The Nazi slumped on the edge of the hatch. The battalion commander put a hand on my shoulder: 'Keep it up!'

Meanwhile, the tank made a sharp turn. For what purpose? To take a more advantageous position for firing? But it turned right around and left the street. We wondered: had the tank run out of ammunition? Or after taking losses, was its crew demoralised? Anyway, the tank disappeared. And without its support the

Hitlerite soldiers did not dare to storm our house. They also withdrew in the direction of the station from where the thunder of battle came.

It was evening, and then night. The commanders gathered in the courtyard of the house. They discussed how to get out of the area. Of course it made sense to make our way to the station where the main forces of the brigade were fighting. But according to intelligence, the enemy had strong combat units in that direction. And we lacked the most essential things – ammunition.[13]

The Russian soldiers left Rostov under cover of darkness and made their way to Bataisk, where they were reunited with the rest of their unit.

Fourth Panzer Army was ordered to withdraw north of the Don and the first elements of First Panzer Army were thrown into the struggle to hold the line of the Donets. Further to the north, the attack by *SS-Das Reich*, which Hitler had promised would go far towards stabilising the front line, failed to make any headway in the face of strong Russian forces. Indeed, it was the Red Army rather than German forces that was advancing. The rout of the German Second Army after the collapse of the Hungarian Second Army had left a huge hole in the front line; the only forces in the gap were grouped together as *Armee Abteilung Lanz*, another ad hoc agglomeration of battered front-line units, assembling reinforcements, and rear area formations. Until the SS Panzer Corps finished concentrating, the main forces available to General Hubert Lanz were *SS-Das Reich*, 320th Infantry Division, the weak 298th Infantry Division, 168th Infantry Division, and parts of the Panzergrenadier Division *Grossdeutschland*. Whilst this might sound like a substantial force, it had to cover a huge area of open space to the east of Kharkov against greatly superior Russian forces. The first elements of *Grossdeutschland* to deploy in the region consisted of the modest *Kampfgruppe Pohlmann* with just a rifle company, a heavy weapons company, and a single company of tanks; this first battlegroup fought alongside 298th Infantry Division on the River Milova at Chertkovo in January before the rest of *Grossdeutschland* began to assemble around Kupyansk. From here, it was dispatched north along the line of the River Oskol to try to stop the Russian forces driving west. From here, the division gradually pulled back towards Belgorod under constant pressure.[14] Originally, the intention had been for *Grossdeutschland* to restore contact with Second Army to the north, but even in the absence of heavy Russian pressure, the gap was simply too large.

Amongst the units pursuing *Grossdeutschland* was Nosov's artillery battery, still supporting the infantrymen of the Russian Fortieth Army. Like many soldiers, Nosov and his comrades were in the middle of their first campaign.

They had been told a great deal about the atrocities committed by the Germans on Soviet soil, but now came across the evidence themselves as they advanced:

The battery had been in battle for a month and a half. We were already accustomed to the inconveniences of front life, forcing ourselves to do without many things. We learned to doze sitting or standing, building a fire in the snow, preparing food. Every day we gained experience, expanding our understanding of war ...

Destroyed towns and corpses of civilians demanded revenge. We no longer just heard about the barbarity of the fascists on our land. Every newly discovered crime brought us more heartache.

One day the battery was moving forward slowly through snowdrifts. In the evening the column stopped. Lieutenant Cherednichenko, having taken out the map, began to consult with our platoon commander about something. While they were talking, the men jumped out of the truck and gathered around the heat of the engine. We could see a chimney ahead of us in the twilight. The rest of the village was invisible.

... Yuri Kozlov, who was now in our crew, was given permission by the sergeant to run forward. Not for the sake of curiosity, of course: he was to find suitable lodging for the night, or maybe get hold of some food. The delivery of food, ammunition, and fuel had been much reduced for the past few days.

Kozlov came back quickly. At first he couldn't speak. He breathed heavily for some time. Finally he shouted: 'The monsters! Beasts! Even children! And a baby! The animals!' He swore profusely. No one reprimanded him. Even the commander of the platoon's first gun, Sergeant Fyodor Simakov, who did not tolerate any foul language, was silent. 'Comrade Sergeant!' Kozlov finally asked in an imploring tone, 'see what's here!' He pulled Artamonov's sleeve.

Lighting a flashlight, we went down into a cellar, which apparently served as someone's dwelling. The greenish light swept along the walls and the earth floor. Kozlov stopped in a corner. A woman lay there, her head thrown back and arms outstretched. There were three children, one just in underwear. One next to the other. One was a baby. They were aged between two and six years. They lay face down. There were clots of blood on the pale napes of their neck. They had been shot at point-blank range.

One of the men groaned loudly and ran out of the dungeon. The rest were silent, with faces darkened by pain and anger. We returned to our vehicles. We were silent. The frost was sharp, but we were hot with anger. 'The reptiles should be strung up!' said Kashutin through gritted teeth, clenching his fists in fury. 'Hang them!'[15]

On the occasions that German accounts mention such incidents, they often blame them on the activities of partisans, either executing suspected collaborators or trying to besmirch the reputation of the retreating Germans. Whilst partisans probably carried out such acts on some occasions, there is also no question that the Germans or their locally recruited allies committed the majority. Regardless of who had actually executed this family, the effect upon the Russian soldiers can easily be imagined, particularly as many had family members living in the areas occupied by the Germans.

Petr Afanasievich Traynin was a political officer serving with the Red Army. He noted the change in the demeanour of German prisoners compared with earlier in the war, and a change in the manner in which they were treated:

After the defeat of the enemy at Kantemirov and Ostrogozhsk-Rossosh, our troops seized a large number of prisoners. There were so many of them that sometimes there weren't enough soldiers to accompany the columns. On those occasions, the captive Nazis were sometimes escorted by armed women collective farmers. I personally saw one of these columns. The Nazis trudged past, unshaven, ragged, many frost-bitten. Their harassed faces had long since lost the brazen self-confidence that I had occasion to notice from the prisoners of the Hitlerite soldiers near Moscow in the difficult autumn of 1941.

I gazed at them now and thought: 'Look at these creatures that look just like me.' Like me, all of them were probably doing something useful before the war, quite mundane, making something, ploughing the land, baking bread, loving and cherishing children, taking care of their wives. What made them change their own lives so abruptly, to exchange all this for the dirty work of robbery, murder, violence? The orders of the Führer, submission to an evil will? Surely not! But then what?

By nature, I was never a cruel or vindictive person. But now I looked at the captured prisoners without regret, even with some sense of joyful vengeance – they got what they deserved, the bastards!

Yes, my heart was hardened. This war made me so. And the deeds of these men, now trudging obediently to our rear zone.

I remembered the first battles near Moscow and the first encounters with the captured Nazis. Then we still did not know the true face of fascism. That was why we offered bread and food to prisoners, gave them tobacco, because an unarmed soldier was no longer our enemy. But then – then I saw a village near Moscow, Ozherelye, in which only eight out of 200 houses survived. The rest were burned not by war, but by fascist incendiarists – soldiers of special units intended for torching villages, towns and cities, from which the Nazi troops retreated. Yes, these soldiers razed homes in cold blood, leaving old people, women and children in the snow and frost without homes.

In the same place, near Moscow, in Krasnoye Selo, we managed to liberate some people who had been locked in a barn. They had been detained there by force of arms, and they remained there without water and food for eight frozen December days! Three infants froze to death in their arms.

And one day the soldiers showed me a photograph taken from a captive Nazi tankman. It depicted the moment when the fascist monsters buried alive a Soviet lieutenant. In the picture, a bleeding five-pointed star was clearly visible, carved by a knife on the forehead of the officer. And who knows, maybe those who buried this lieutenant were now in the ranks of the Hitlerite warriors trudging past. And certainly there were some who did evil deeds near Voronezh, those who wiped the village of Korotoyak from the face of the earth and left another village, Strozhevskoye, ablaze.

Once in one of the villages we came upon the ashes of a burnt house. Only the stove survived. And on it, on this stove, a naked and mutilated man and woman were crucified. A little to the side lay the corpse of a young mother. On her chest was the stiffened body of a child. The woman had her hands chopped off. Could such a thing have been done by soldiers just obeying orders? No! Only those who fully believed in the hateful idea of the superiority of the Aryan race could burn, crucify, shoot 'inferior' people, 'subhumans', calmly and with pleasure.

That was why now I had not a drop of compassion for the listless prisoners![16]

This passage is a little disingenuous – during the retreat of the Red Army in 1941, it was official policy to destroy infrastructure in order to hinder the German advance, and it is quite conceivable that the destruction of Ozherelye was carried out by Russian units during their withdrawal. However, there is no question that hundreds of thousands of Russian civilians were killed during the period of German occupation; many starved to death because of forcible confiscation of grain and other foodstuffs, while others were executed because they were Jewish or suspected of helping partisans, or as reprisals for the activity of partisans.

The continuing successes of the Red Army seemed to create endless opportunities for further gains. With such huge holes torn in the German front line, Stalin was keen to press home his advantage and perhaps seek an early end to the war – given the rate at which his armies were advancing, it seemed as if only logistic difficulties stood in the way of a successful drive to the Dnepr and

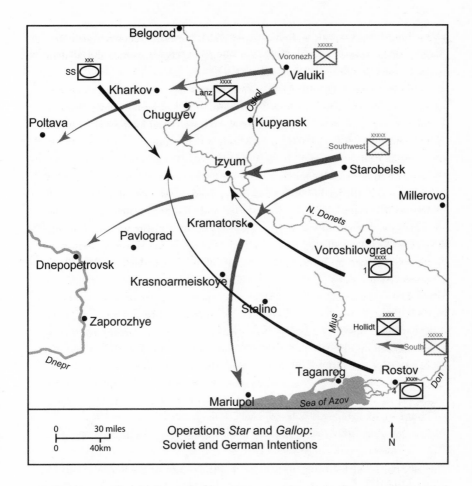

Operations *Star* and *Gallop*:
Soviet and German Intentions

0   30 miles
0   40km

N

beyond. Even if the Wehrmacht survived until the spring thaw brought all operations to a standstill, it would surely be so weak that the summer would see a resumption of Russian advances. The key was to maximise the gains that could be achieved.

To that end, Russian commanders considered their options. Vatutin was keen to exploit the continuing weakness of the northern flank of Army Group Don, created by the disintegration of Army Group B. In order to exploit this, he submitted proposals to *Stavka* on 19 January for a powerful thrust to the west from Starobelsk, and then from there to the south into the rear of Manstein's hard-pressed forces. Either the Germans would be surrounded and destroyed, or they would be forced to retreat precipitately to the west, abandoning irreplaceable quantities of equipment as they did so. Either outcome would result in the German defences in the Ukraine becoming untenable. Convinced that the Germans had already suffered irreparable damage, Stalin approved the proposals the following day, assigning them the codename *Stachok* (usually translated as *Gallop*).[17] Vatutin's Southwest Front would mount the main attack and deep penetration, with Southern Front driving back the German forces withdrawing through Rostov; Vatutin would attack first, with Southern Front launching its assaults on 29 January. At the same time, the huge hole created by the rout of the Hungarians and the near-destruction of the German Second Army was also to be exploited. Here, the main target was to be the recapture of Kharkov, followed by a westward pursuit of the retreating Germans by the victorious Voronezh Front. On 23 January, *Stavka* issued orders for this operation, codenamed *Zvezda* (*Star*), to commence on 1 February.

In the midst of victory, there were further discussions about the optimum structure of combat formations, and Rotmistrov was summoned to a meeting in Moscow:

Poskrebyshev [head of the Special Section of the Central Committee of the Communist Party] invited me to the office of the Supreme Commander-in-Chief. At a long table sat members of the Politburo, *Stavka* and government. First my gaze turned to [Foreign Minister] Molotov, adjusting his pince-nez. Stalin, standing in the depths of the office, moved slowly towards me. I stopped and reported in a formal way, placing myself at his command. 'I did not order you here, I invited you, Comrade Rotmistrov,' Stalin shook my hand. 'Tell me how you thrashed Manstein.'

I was somewhat embarrassed: after all, the Supreme Commander certainly knew in detail about the battles with the enemy that had torn apart Paulus' forces, surrounded in Stalingrad. But as he asked, I began to tell him, analysing these battles, the tactics used by III Guards Tank Corps in the offensive towards Rychkovsky and Kotelnikovo.

Stalin walked silently around the table, occasionally asking me short questions. He and all the others present listened attentively to me. I wondered whether the Supreme Commander invited me to describe the battles with Manstein for their benefit. Gradually, Stalin moved the conversation to tank armies. 'Our tank armies,' he said, 'have learned to successfully smash the enemy, and inflict shattering and deep penetrations on him. However, why do you think it is not advisable to have infantry formations in the tank army?' The Supreme Commander stopped and gazed at me with narrowed eyes. I realised that someone had told him my opinion.

'During offensive operations, rifle divisions lag behind the tank corps. As a consequence, the interaction between the tank and rifle units is disrupted, and it is difficult to keep control at the same time of the tanks that have moved forward and the lagging infantry.'

'Still,' Stalin objected, 'as the bold and resolute actions of General Badanov's tank corps in the Tatsinskaya area showed, tankmen without infantrymen face difficulties retaining positions captured in operational depth.'

'Yes,' I agreed. 'Infantry is needed, but it must be motorised. That is why I believe that, in addition to tank corps, motorised rifle units rather than ordinary rifle units should be part of the tank army.'

'You propose to replace the infantry with mechanised units, but the commander of the tank army, Romanenko [who had commanded Third, Fifth and Second Tank Armies since the beginning of the war], is pleased with the infantry divisions and asks for another one or two such divisions to be added to his command. So which of you is right?' asked Molotov, who had been silent before.

'I gave my opinion,' I replied. 'I believe that the tank army should be a tank army, not by name, but by composition. Its best organisational structure would be two tank and one mechanized corps, as well as several regiments of anti-tank artillery. In addition, we should ensure mobility of headquarters units and reliable radio communication between them and all subordinate units.'

Stalin listened to me attentively, nodding approvingly and, smiling, looked at Molotov, who again interrupted me with a question: 'It seems that you do not like anti-tank rifles and, in essence, you want to replace them with anti-tank artillery. But they are successfully used against tanks and firing points. Is that not so?'

'The fact is, Comrade Molotov, that anti-tank rifles were and are an effective means of fighting enemy tanks in defensive operations when used in trenches from a distance of not more than 300m. But in mobile operations they cannot combat the cannon fire of enemy tanks, which have a range of 500m or more. Therefore, it is desirable to have at least one anti-tank brigade [with 76mm guns] in tank and mechanised corps.'

The discussion lasted about two hours. Stalin was also interested in my views on the use of tank armies in offensive operations. They boiled down to the fact that the tank armies should be used by a front commander or even *Stavka* to deal massive strikes, first and foremost, on the tank groupings of the enemy on primary axes, but without stipulating to the armies the route for their offensive, which would only hamper ability of the tanks to manoeuvre effectively. I felt that Stalin was well aware of the importance of the massive use of tank forces.

'The time will come,' he said, as though reflecting aloud, 'when our industry will be able to give the Red Army a significant amount of armoured, aviation and other military equipment. We will soon attack the enemy with powerful tank and air strikes, we will mercilessly drive and smash the German fascist invaders.' Stalin glanced at the notebook on the table and again moved around the office, continuing to reason: 'Already now we have the opportunity to form new tank armies. Could you lead one of them, Comrade Rotmistrov?'

'As you wish,' I quickly got up from my chair.

'This is a soldier's answer,' the Supreme Commander said, and again looking at me intently, he added: 'I think you will. You have sufficient experience and knowledge.'[18]

The following day, Rotmistrov was given command of Fifth Guards Tank Army, which now included his old III Guards Tank Corps.

There was little doubt that the Wehrmacht was still reeling from the blows that had been inflicted upon it, but the Red Army had also suffered substantial losses. Nearly all of the reserves that had been built up over the late summer of 1942 had been expended, and stocks of fuel and ammunition were beginning to run low. In order to mount their attacks, both Golikov's Voronezh Front and Vatutin's Southwest Front would have to commit almost all of their forces to the initial assault, with few major formations left as second echelons. Nor would there be any operational or strategic reserves available to deal with any unexpected exigencies. Nevertheless, *Stavka* was understandably in an optimistic mood, and issued a confident directive on 26 January:

> As a result of the successful attacks by our forces of the Voronezh, Southwest, Don and North Caucasus Fronts, enemy opposition has been overcome. The enemy defences have been broken on a broad front. Lacking strategic reserves, the enemy is forced to deploy arriving formations in isolation directly from the route of march. Many gaps have formed, and other sectors are covered by disparate small groups. The right wing of Southwest Front threatens the Donbas region. There are favorouble opportunities for the encirclement, isolation and destruction of the enemy forces in the Donbas region, the Caucasus and along the Black Sea.[19]

Of all the Russian operations since the beginning of *Uranus*, these two carried the greatest risk. The attacks to encircle Stalingrad and the operations against the Italians and Hungarians on the Don might conceivably have encountered unexpected German resistance, but had they not unfolded as planned, neither

Little Saturn nor the Ostrogozhsk-Rossosh operation would have left the Russian forces exposed to devastating counterattacks. These latest proposals were heavily reliant upon the assessment by *Stavka* that the Germans were weak and in disarray, and if this assessment proved to be inaccurate there was a real danger that the attacking formations would be vulnerable to a counter-strike. Whilst the Russians would have been aware of the trickle of formations arriving from France, and the abortive attack by *SS-Das Reich* had already revealed the presence of the first elements of the SS Panzer Corps, they believed that these would be swept away in what would turn into a growing rout. The impact of German reinforcements during the preceding weeks – particularly 6th, 7th and 11th Panzer Divisions – might have suggested that *Gallop* and *Star* would be risky undertakings, but confidence was high. Supply heads remained largely where they had been in early December – even in the prevailing chaotic conditions, the retreating Germans had done sufficient damage to railway lines and bridges to ensure that Russian supplies were detrained some distance to the rear of the current front line and thereafter had to be brought forward by motor transport. This would also be the first major operation since the beginning of *Uranus* to be conducted entirely by Russian units that were below full strength; instead of their establishment strength of about 10,000 men, rifle divisions had only 6,000 to 8,000, many of them relatively new recruits who – unlike the troops deployed to such lethal effect in November and December – had not been given the opportunity to learn their craft on 'quiet' sectors of the front. Armoured formations were also below strength, with many tank corps fielding only 30 to 50 tanks each.[20] Given that each tank corps was meant to be as powerful as a reinforced panzer division, these were worryingly low strengths at the beginning of an offensive operation. Admittedly, LVII Panzer Corps – with the exception of 6th Panzer Division – had mounted its relief operation towards Stalingrad with similarly degraded formations, but its eventual failure showed the degree of risk that was being taken.

Nevertheless, the collective strength of Vatutin's Southwest Front remained substantial. Between them, the First and Third Guards Armies, Sixth Army, Fifth Tank Army, and 'Mobile Group Popov' – the equivalent of a further army – fielded 325,000 men with over 500 tanks, and on its northern flank Voronezh Front could add a further 190,000 men and 315 tanks. Against this, Manstein had only modest forces. *Armee Abteilung Lanz*, standing before Kharkov, consisted for the moment of two infantry divisions and *SS-Das Reich*, with a further two SS divisions still assembling. To its south was Mackensen's First Panzer Army, withdrawn through Rostov and deployed along the Donets, with a paper strength of two infantry divisions and three panzer divisions, but only 40,000 men and 40 tanks; it included in its strength the new XXX Corps, which was the new designation for Fretter-Pico's group of stragglers, rear area units and broken combat formations. *Armee Abteilung Hollidt* had survived the various blows directed against it and still had seven infantry divisions and two panzer divisions, together with battlegroup remnants of two other infantry divisions, totalling perhaps 100,000 men and 60 tanks. In total, the Germans were outnumbered eight to one in armour – not counting about 250 tanks of the SS formations – and over two to one in manpower. How long the Russian formations would be able to supply their armour, and how long those tanks would continue running in the face of mechanical and other difficulties, would go a long way towards deciding the campaign.

CHAPTER 11

FEBRUARY: A WAR OF MOVEMENT

The terrain on which *Gallop* would be fought was not entirely favourable for mobile operations. Although the low hills offered little encouragement for defenders, there were – as had been the case further east – numerous ravines and gullies, and the lack of paved roads meant that any thaw would render movement very difficult, particularly as the roads were in poor condition at the outset of the campaign. In conjunction with Third Tank Army from Voronezh Front to the north, the Russian Sixth Army, commanded by Lieutenant General Fedor Mikhailovich Kharitonov, was to advance rapidly on the northern flank of Southwest Front, passing to the south of Kharkov and penetrating 66 miles (110km) in just a week. Starting a day later, Lieutenant General Vasily Ivanovich Kuznetzov's First Guards Army was to attack a little to the south, rapidly wheeling south into the rear of the German defences after its initial breakthrough. Mobile Group Popov would be inserted between Sixth Army and First Guards Army and had the important task of penetrating deep into the rear of the German positions before reaching the Sea of Azov at Mariupol. The lessons of the Russian penetration to Tatsinskaya during *Little Saturn* were already being put into effect; in an attempt to prevent the armoured spearheads from being left stranded without infantry support, tank corps were assigned rifle divisions either with sufficient vehicles to allow them to keep up with the tanks, or with the infantry assigned to ride aboard the tanks as they advanced. Rotmistrov's proposals for mechanised infantry formations to be embedded within tank armies would take longer to implement. However, despite attempts to improve the infantry support of tank formations, Popov's group was far from its paper strength, and its logistic support in particular was weak. It would start the operation with sufficient supplies for the tanks to be refuelled and resupplied with ammunition just once

– thereafter, it would be dependent upon the long lines of communication stretching back to the railheads beyond the Don. Supply levels for his infantry units were even lower.[1]

Starting almost at the same time was *Star*, the operation to retake Kharkov and drive back the Germans in the northern parts of the Ukraine. First details of the plan were decided on 23 January, with the aim of continuing the pursuit of the defeated German forces. There would be no time for lengthy redeployments or other preparations and Golikov was to commence operations on 1 February. However, three days later, Golikov was granted an additional day's grace, but the tasks assigned to his Voronezh Front were extended to include the recapture of Kursk; Vasilevsky later wrote that this was because of a desire to maximise gains before the arrival of the SS Panzer Corps, but there may also have been a degree of operational greed involved.[2] The two northern armies of the front – Thirty-Eighth and Sixtieth – would push west towards Kursk, while the three southern armies – Fortieth, Sixty-Ninth and Third Tank Armies – would move against the German forces defending Kharkov. Although Moskalenko's Fortieth Army was numerically strong, with 90,000 men and 100 tanks grouped into eight rifle divisions, a tank corps and three tank brigades, many of its units were still busy mopping up areas of resistance left behind in the recent advance, and maintenance requirements left many of his tanks unavailable for the start of the operation. However, losses during the Ostrogozhsk-Rossosh Operation had been very modest, and morale remained very high. Third Tank Army, under Lieutenant General Pavel Semyenovich Rybalko, had two tank corps and a Guards cavalry corps, and in total had 165 tanks; it was to form the main striking force for the assault, and Golikov could expect that the forces he sent against Kharkov would amount to a total of about 200,000 men and 300 tanks. Opposing them would be the northern part of *Armee Abteilung Lanz* – even after the arrival of SS reinforcements, it would have only 70,000 men and perhaps 200 tanks available to defend Kharkov, a city that Hitler had given express orders to the SS Panzer Corps to hold at all costs.[3]

Unlike the earlier Red Army operations of the winter, *Gallop* and *Star* started while previous advances were still occurring, and at first there was little sense amongst the Germans that a new phase had started. Starobelsk fell to Russian forces late on 29 January, and other columns pushed closer to Kupyansk, driving the German 298th Infantry Division back across the River Krasnaya on either side of the town. Here, the advance temporarily came to a halt as the German infantry put up spirited resistance, with both 298th Infantry Division and *SS-Das Reich* to its north proving difficult opponents. By the end of 1 February, Rybalko's

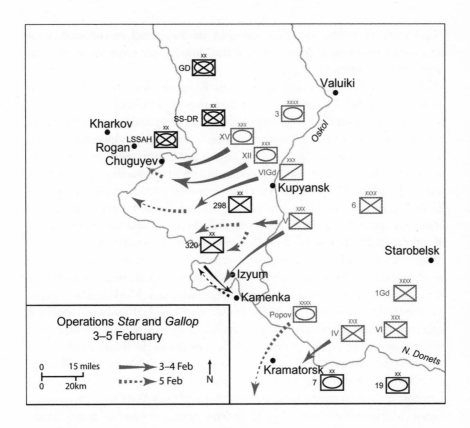

Operations *Star* and *Gallop*
3–5 February

0 ___ 15 miles ___ 3–4 Feb
0 ___ 20km ___ 5 Feb   N

Third Tank Army had succeeded in making several deep penetrations, turning the flanks of 298th Infantry Division. Worried that further German reinforcements were reportedly en route, Rybalko ordered XII and XV Tank Corps and VI Guards Cavalry Corps to join the battle the following day, changing the emphasis of his army's attack to the south in order to make the most of the successes of 1 February. Despite this, progress remained disappointing. Although some elements reached the northern Donets, many continued to be held up, particularly by the relatively powerful units of *SS-Das Reich*; however, VI Guards Cavalry Corps was able to report that it had successfully cut the main line of retreat of the German 298th Infantry Division towards Chuguyev.[4] To the north, the Russian Sixty-Ninth Army collided with *Grossdeutschland* and also made disappointing progress; the town of Veliko-Mikhailovka proved to be a particularly stubborn strongpoint, and heavy fighting continued until late on 4 February, when the defences were outflanked and the Germans withdrew. It was only further north

311

that Moskalenko's Fortieth Army managed to advance against relatively weak opposition, threatening to cut the German lines of communication between Kursk and Belgorod; the speed of its advance towards the latter city was such that even if the German lines further south continued to hold, there was a serious danger of them being outflanked and rolled up from the north.

With both flanks vulnerable and bypassed and threatened with encirclement, Generalmajor Herbert Michaelis ordered his 298th Infantry Division to break out to the west, only to run directly into the Russian VI Guards Cavalry Corps, which had worked its way into the rear area of the German division. Forced to abandon much of its artillery and other equipment, 298th Infantry Division began a fighting retreat towards the first units of *LSSAH* that were beginning to deploy further to the rear, but even though Michaelis was retreating, the running battles fought by his men continued to interfere with the Russian advance, which was now falling behind schedule.[5]

By the end of 3 February, the Germans had determined the broad intentions of the Russian forces committed to *Gallop* and *Star*, through a mixture of prisoner interrogations and aerial reconnaissance. Popov's group had been recognised and Lanz was finally able to reckon with sufficient SS forces to be present for a planned attack on 5 February in an attempt to restore the front line from the north; *SS-Das Reich* was in position to the east of Kharkov, while the first elements of *LSSAH* were to the southeast.[6] However, it was important for the Russians not to be allowed to advance too quickly and 320th Infantry Division was ordered to launch a counterattack to stop a Russian attack to the south of Izyum. Generalleutnant Georg Postel reported that it would be difficult for his division to assemble sufficient forces for the attack on account of deep snow on the roads, but Lanz overruled him and ordered him to proceed as planned. Early on 4 February, a regiment of 320th Infantry Division succeeded in capturing the northern part of Kamenka, to the south of Izyum, but other elements of the division in Izyum itself reported increased activity from partisans and the leading elements of Kharitonov's Sixth Army. By midday, Russian tanks were probing into the northeast parts of the town and cavalry had cut the roads running west.

To make matters worse, the regiment that Postel had been ordered to commit to the attack south of Izyum was also cut off through a mixture of advancing Red Army units, partisans, and roads blocked by snow. Postel made repeated requests to be allowed to pull back to the west and was finally given permission late on 4 February. During the night that followed, he began his attempt to escape, breaking through the Russian troops that had bypassed Izyum to the north. Early the following morning, Kharitonov's men took possession of Izyum itself.

The timetable for the Russian Voronezh Front was ambitious if it was to secure protection for the northern flank of *Gallop* and Golikov urged his troops forward, seeking to break up the retreating German 320th Infantry Division as rapidly as possible. The first attempts to secure crossings over the northern Donets on 4 February by the leading units of Rybalko's Third Tank Army were repulsed by *LSSAH* and the following day was spent bringing up reinforcements. Early on 6 February, a second attempt was made by XV Tank Corps with infantry support and it too failed; casualties mounted steadily, and by the end of the first week of February XV Tank Corps had only 10–15 tanks in each tank brigade and most of its mechanised infantry battalions had barely the strength of a single rifle company. Although the tank strength would fluctuate according to how many repaired tanks could be returned to service, the striking power of Rybalko's various armoured formations was considerably below establishment and likely to remain so for the rest of the campaign.[7] At the seam between Third Tank Army and Sixth Army, VI Guards Cavalry Corps' success in bypassing the German 298th Infantry Division seemed to offer a more promising line of advance and Rybalko ordered it to push on to the west, hoping that by outflanking the stubborn defences of *LSSAH* he would soon be able to resume the advance elsewhere. This was a risky undertaking – VI Guards Cavalry Corps was a mobile force but in no measure a substitute for the armoured forces that had ground to a halt on the northern Donets, and its thrust to the west would expose its northern flank to counterattack. But under pressure to make up for lost time and to a large extent swept along by the prevailing belief in the Red Army that the Germans had already been defeated, Rybalko was prepared to take the risk; after all, every such operation in the preceding weeks had succeeded spectacularly. On this occasion though, the opponents were entirely Wehrmacht and SS formations, not the weak units of Germany's allies.

At first, the gamble seemed to be justified; by 9 February, 201st Tank Brigade, the leading unit (and main firepower) of VI Guards Cavalry Corps, had penetrated to Taranovka. In the meantime, Rybalko ordered the units that had failed to force the northern Donets line a little to the north to regroup and prepare for a deliberate assault. Three days passed, much to the irritation of Golikov and other higher commanders, who believed that Rybalko was being overcautious, but many of his units were still engaged with the retreating German 298th Infantry Division. At the northern end of Rybalko's sector, his troops were surprised by powerful counterattacks by *SS-Das Reich* on 5 February, which inflicted heavy losses. Repeated frontal attacks on *SS-Das Reich* failed to make progress, but 184th Rifle Division succeeded in bypassing its southern flank.

Other Russian units followed and on 9 February the SS division was pulled back to a line closer to Kharkov.

On 10 February, Rybalko's main forces made another attempt to force the line of the northern Donets. This time they were successful, largely due to the fact that the Germans had already decided to pull back and *SS-Das Reich* had abandoned plans for further counterattacks. With XII Tank Corps to the south and XV Tank Corps to the north, the Russian attack progressed well at first, reaching and securing Chuguyev. Just 7 miles (12km) further west, however, the Germans had set up their next defensive line at Rogan and the advance came to a sudden stop. That evening, Rybalko took stock and made further changes. With the support of additional infantry and a tank brigade, XV Tank Corps would continue to attack directly towards Kharkov from the east, while XII Tank Corps attacked from the southeast. In addition, VI Guards Cavalry Corps was to push back the German forces from the south.[8]

As one of the largest cities of the Soviet Union, Kharkov was regarded by both Hitler and Stalin as a highly prestigious location, and the Führer expected his loyal SS to defend the city with determination. For Manstein, such an obstinate defence of a fixed position – particularly if it involved the only concentration of fresh armoured units available to him – was pointless and foolhardy; it would surely lead to the isolation and destruction of the SS Panzer Corps, whilst depriving the Germans of the only hope that they had of restoring the situation through a battle of mobility. In addition, the infantry-weak SS panzergrenadier divisions were unsuited for urban warfare. As would increasingly be the case as the Wehrmacht withdrew towards Germany, Hitler declared Kharkov a fortress and appointed a commandant to hold the city at all costs. Despite mobilising tens of thousands of people – mainly civilian forced labour – to dig fortifications, the city garrison had only a single security division and a few ad hoc rear area units available to defend it. Regardless of Hitler's orders, Lanz had already drawn his own conclusions by the evening of 5 February, as the war diary of his *Armee Abteilung* recorded:

> A prolonged defence of Kharkov is not possible. The troops at hand are to be concentrated in the individual suburbs under their separate commands. Their task is to hold open the route for the retreating front line troops.
>
> *LSSAH* and *SS Das Reich* will bypass Kharkov. Between them, the units [of the fortress commandant] are tasked with delaying the enemy's advance and preserving their combat strength. All necessary demolitions are to be prepared.[9]

For the moment though, Hitler's order that Kharkov was to be held at all costs remained in force, even though Manstein had other preferences. The bulk of the Russian Third Tank Army was now to the southeast of the SS Panzer Corps and it was tempting to use the corps' forces in a counterattack, particularly towards the south against the exposed Russian VI Guards Cavalry Corps. From there, Hausser's forces could conceivably push on to try to restore contact with German forces further south – at the same time, as the first part of his westward shift of the forces that had come perilously close to being cut off south of the Don, the units of First Panzer Army were to attack from the south. Once Fourth Panzer Army in turn had redeployed after pulling back behind *Armee Abteilung Hollidt* and First Panzer Army, it would join this attack, and ultimately the two panzer armies would seek to link up with the advancing SS and thus destroy the Russian forces that were thrusting towards the Dnepr.

Once the Russian offensive started, Vatutin's orders were to insert the forces of 'Mobile Group Popov' between his Sixth Army and First Guards Army in order to carry out the deep penetration and envelopment that would destroy the German forces in southeast Ukraine; the objective of Popov's units was ultimately Mariupol on the coast of the Sea of Azov, with Krasnoarmeiskoye (now Pokrovsk) as an intermediary objective. Given the pressure upon the Russian logistic services, Popov's units started with shortages of both fuel and ammunition, but nevertheless were able to provide support for the adjacent flanks of Sixth and First Guards Armies in the initial phases of the attack. On paper, the mobile group was a formidable force with III, X, and XVIII Tank Corps, IV Guards Tank Corps, two further tank brigades, three rifle divisions, 3rd Guards Motorised Rifle Brigade, and – by the second half of February – three ski brigades. However, all of these units were significantly below establishment strength, with the tank formations collectively fielding only 180 tanks – still substantially more than the opposing German forces had available to them.[10] IV Guards Tank Corps succeeded in reaching and capturing Kramatorsk but ran headlong into determined German resistance and called for reinforcements, finding once again that without infantry support, armoured units found it difficult to overcome stubborn defences.

The fighting that erupted around Kramatorsk marked the first attempts by Manstein to strike to the north with the forces that he had pulled back through Rostov, but the situation remained precarious. Mackensen's First Panzer Army was threatened on both flanks – Third Guards Army had crossed the Donets at Voroshilovgrad and was trying to sever the connection between First Panzer Army's southeast flank and *Armee Abteilung Hollidt*, while Popov's group attempted to push past the northwest flank via the valley of the Krivoi Torets. Manstein ordered Mackensen to deal with both Russian penetrations, concentrating on the forces in the Krivoi Torets first in order to restore contact with German units nearer Kharkov, but was informed that much of First Panzer Army's strength was already committed to the fighting at Voroshilovgrad and there was therefore little available for the proposed counterthrust towards the northwest. The only force that could be sent north was XL Panzer Corps, with the depleted *SS-Viking* and elements of 3rd and 13th Panzer Divisions, and Generaloberst Gotthard Heinrici, the corps commander, informed Manstein that it was impossible to manoeuvre around the western flank of the Russian forces in the Krivoi Torets valley due to terrain difficulties. Instead, the modest assets of XL Panzer Corps were thrown into a frontal battle with the advancing Russians, in which there was little prospect of the sort of rapid success that was required. Slightly to the north, where the Russian Sixth Army was pressing on towards the west, Balck's 11th Panzer Division was committed to combat before it had fully concentrated, something that Balck had always tried to avoid. Not surprisingly, the initial attempts by the division to recapture Kramatorsk failed but the Russians suffered heavy losses, with IV Guards Tank Corps reduced to just 37 tanks on 4 February. The following day, the Russian III Tank Corps arrived in Kramatorsk, but it could only contribute an additional 23 tanks, and the force remained weak in infantry – precisely the problem that had bedevilled the Russian attack on Tatsinskaya earlier in the winter.[11] Further reinforcements were dispatched, but it would take time for them to make their way along damaged and congested roads.

The problems with moving forward supplies and reinforcements from the railheads showed no signs of improving, despite the attempts to learn from earlier operations and to make what changes were possible. Lieutenant General Nikolai Semenovich Skripko, a bombing specialist, was deputy commander of the Soviet Eighteenth Air Army at the time, and later wrote about the difficult demands that were placed upon his aircrews by a profusion of targets, the weather, and the need to help with supply movements:

Rain in early February interfered with combat work, but on the night of 5 February the weather improved somewhat, and we immediately fielded 253 aircraft. Our air units bombarded railway junctions in Bryansk, Kursk, Orel, Lvov, Gomel, Kharkov, Zaporozhye, and Rostov …

On the following night, 218 of our aircraft bombarded the same targets … Forty-eight crews struck at a German airfield in the Stalino area.

... We used every opportunity to get into combat. On the night of 8 February, difficult meteorological conditions ruled out flights to the west. The weather in the south was slightly better and 116 crews attacked railway junctions. The most important of them was Kharkov, which at that time was on the enemy's main traffic route. In a night raid, 54 aircraft struck this large railway junction. ... Photo reconnaissance showed that the raid was very effective. Five German rear area concentrations were ablaze, and the fires were accompanied by violent explosions.

The second most important railway junction in the south was Rostov. Our troops seized Bataisk and came very close to this large industrial centre, which was rightfully considered the gateway to the Caucasus. Due to unfavourable weather, only 23 crews managed to attack Rostov. They made accurate attacks on German rear area echelons and station facilities, disrupting the functioning of the railway junction.

About 50 long-range bombers struck a powerful blow at a large enemy airfield in the area of Stalino. From there, enemy aircraft made frequent raids on Soviet troops that had attacked towards Starobelsk, Lisichansk, and Voroshilovgrad and had begun the liberation of the Donbas region. Using heavy bombs, our crews severely damaged the German airfield and disrupted air force activity. They bombarded the aircraft with small incendiary and fragmentation bombs, caused numerous fires and explosions and damaged many enemy vehicles.

And on the morning of 8 February, our long-range aviation began to carry out emergency transport tasks. The troops of the Southwestern Front ... that had seized Kramatorsk, Barvenkovo and other settlements the day before had advanced far ahead and were out of contact with their supply bases, 300km [180 miles] or more behind them. The retreating Nazis destroyed railways everywhere and it took a long time to restore them, and continuous snowfalls and snowstorms made it difficult to transport goods with the few worn out vehicles that were available. *Stavka* ordered us to help the troops of General Vatutin, who were experiencing serious interruptions in supply. We were forced to remove 47 aircraft from combat missions and send them to deliver ammunition, food and specialists to Southwest Front. The return flights evacuated the seriously wounded.[12]

Like air force personnel throughout the 20th century, Skripko overstates the effectiveness of his forces. There is no doubt that the air attacks on railways and airfields caused disruption, but the impact was modest as best; even the far heavier raids on railway junctions by the Western Allies failed to stop rail movements. The Soviet bomber formations used a variety of aircraft, many produced by domestic industry, like the Ilyushin Il-4, the Petlyakov Pe-2, the Tupolev Tu-2, and the heavier Pe-8, and western aircraft like the Douglas A-20 and North American B-25. Some proved to be very vulnerable to defensive fire and fighters, and others were difficult to fly; the controls of the Pe-2, for example, were so heavy that when it was flown by female crews, it often took two people – the pilot and navigator – to exert sufficient backwards pressure on the control column to get the plane off the ground. As was the case with the Luftwaffe, aircraft types that rapidly became obsolescent in the more crowded skies of Western Europe – where there was a higher likelihood of being intercepted by modern fighters – continued to provide effective service throughout the war.

The fighting around Voroshilovgrad included engagements between the Red Army and units that caused a mixture of surprise, consternation and anger, as Gavril Zdanovich, commander of 203rd Rifle Division, later wrote:

On 13 February there were sudden cheers from the German trenches, and several hundred Russian soldiers ran towards us.

At first, we thought that some Soviet unit had broken through from the enemy's rear, and therefore did not open fire. But this assumption quickly proved false: the attack was made by traitors, the Vlasovites.

With fierce hatred our fighters fought with the traitors of the Motherland! The battalion in which political instructor Khorunzhiy was the deputy commander had only a hundred men at the time. Our soldiers met the Vlasovites with heavy machine-gun fire, and then fixed bayonets and drove them across the field. Fifty marauders were forever left to lie on the very land that they had betrayed.[13]

General Andrei Anreyovich Vlasov had fought with distinction in the ranks of the Red Army in 1941, and in early 1942 he led his Second Shock Army in an attack to try to lift the siege of Leningrad. Although his troops made good progress, other units failed to advance on either flank and Vlasov and his men were surrounded, with the pocket finally being destroyed in June. Vlasov had been offered evacuation by air but chose to stay with his men; he hid in the countryside but in July was betrayed by a Russian farmer. In German captivity, he became an increasingly outspoken critic of Stalin and repeatedly offered to create an anti-communist army from the ranks of Red Army soldiers captured by the Germans, and ultimately he was permitted to create the Russian Liberation Army – often known as the Vlasov Army – in 1944. His motivation for this has been the subject of fierce debate, with many Russians claiming that he was merely acting in an opportunistic manner, but he – and many other Russian officers who served in his 'army' – had personally experienced atrocities committed by the NKVD or had suffered during Stalin's purges of the Red Army, and Vlasov was understandably bitter about the manner in which the failings of other formations left his Second Shock Army isolated. Given that Vlasov's proposals for an anti-Soviet army of Russians did not bear fruit until later in the war, it is highly unlikely that Zdanovich and his men fought against elements under the command of Vlasov, but there were many formations of Cossacks, Ukrainians and others operating under German control in 1942 and 1943. Most of these were used in rear area duties, often willingly aiding the Germans in the massacres of Jews, 'partisans' and other undesirables, and it is likely that one of these police-like paramilitary formations had been thrown into the front line near Voroshilovgrad.[14] The bitterness and desire for revenge amongst the soldiers of Zdanovich's division was hardened by what they found in the town of Krasnodon (now Sorokyne), 28 miles (45km) southeast of Voroshilovgrad:

When the division headquarters arrived in Krasnodon, the central square was full of people. When liberating towns, we had become accustomed to the fact that the residents were happy to greet our soldiers. But these people's faces were grim and gloomy. I immediately understood: something had happened. And I was not mistaken.

'We've suffered a terrible tragedy in the city,' an old woman told me. 'In recent days, the Nazis discovered an underground youth organization. Dozens of people were arrested for their involvement. Many were killed. And many were thrust alive into the shaft of a mine and the exit was blocked.'

... Here I met Major [Ignaty Fedorovich] Bespalko. He approached and said that the shaft of the mine was piled with corpses. And the people gathered here were relatives of those who died or disappeared into fascist captivity. 'The Krasnodon citizens believe that there might still be some alive in the mine,' said Ignaty Fedorovich, breathing hard. 'The residents themselves tried to clear the entrance, but it turned out to be mined.'

'Take the sappers, render all necessary help, see to it personally,' I told the head of the political department.

A soldier in wartime saw everything: burned villages, where the victims were sitting amidst the ashes, as if petrified by grief; roads on which hungry, homeless children wandered after losing their parents ... We lost comrades-in-arms: one moment they were talking, arguing, joking, and then they were gone; we saw collapsed bridges, and the water in the river running red with blood. But what we witnessed in Krasnodon shocked even experienced warriors.

After we had cleared the entrance to the mine, the corpses could be removed. Ten, 20, 30, 50. They were neatly packed in layers of snow that now melted, like in spring. And the Red Guards, who had been standing by the mine for several hours, cautiously approached these frozen rows, anxiously peered at the disfigured, blue-faced bodies and walked slowly on if they did not find their relatives.

But suddenly someone froze in the midst of these lifeless rows, cried out in a despairing voice, knelt down and, wrapping his arms around the wet snow, shook a body, as if trying to wake the deceased.

'Comrade fighters,' Major Bespalko said at a rally organised afterwards, 'today we bow our heads before the fallen heroes of Krasnodon. We mourn their loss, but we know what those who are no longer with us also knew: others will take the place of the fallen. The partisan movement in the fascist rear is growing and growing. The earth burns under the feet of the invaders: they are beaten at the front, they are beaten far behind the front line. Our entire nation is at war with Hitler's evil spirits. And our duty as soldiers is to fight even better, to exterminate the fascist invaders even more thoroughly. We will avenge ourselves for you, the heroes of Krasnodon, and we will always remember your sacrifice. We will reach the den of the fascist beast, and there will be no mercy for him.'[15]

Much to Manstein's irritation, the Russians soon demonstrated that the terrain difficulties described by Heinrici did not apply to their T-34s with their broad tracks and superior cross-country ability, and IV Guards Tank Corps – extracted from the fighting in Kramatorsk – threatened to break out to the southwest. Although other sectors of the Eastern Front had been reluctant to part with troops as they faced crises of their own, 19th Panzer Division had grudgingly been released by Army Group Centre for redeployment in the south after being extensively involved in mobile operations against Russian penetrations in a similar manner to 11th Panzer Division's operations on the Chir. At first, the division was intended to support the Italian Eighth Army, but this had effectively ceased to exist long before Generalleutnant Gustav Schmidt's men could arrive and instead 19th Panzer Division found itself assigned to Fretter-Pico's group, now known as XXX Corps. After heavy fighting, the division was forced to concede the town of Kremmenaya, appearing to open the way for a Russian advance south across the Donets on a broad front, but for once the weather interceded to the advantage of the Germans: a sudden rise in temperature melted much of the snow and rendered most roads impassable for a day. By the time that movement was possible again, 7th Panzer Division had moved into a blocking position around Slavyansk. Fighting for the town began on 3 February and both sides rapidly reinforced their troops. It became a key battle – if the Russians could take Slavyansk, they could bear down on Army Group Don from the

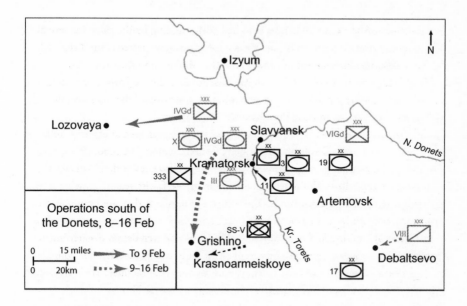

Operations south of
the Donets, 8–16 Feb

0 — 15 miles — → To 9 Feb
0 — 20km — ▪▪▪▶ 9–16 Feb

north, but 7th Panzer Division continued to put up determined resistance. With the exception of IV Guards Tank Corps, the forces of Mobile Group Popov had ground to a halt and were far behind their ambitious timetable.

Still believing that the Germans intended to pull back to the Dnepr, *Stavka* issued orders to Vatutin on 10 February to do everything possible to pin Army Group South against the coast of the Sea of Azov. Vatutin ordered Kuznetsov to advance on Zaporozhye with his First Guards Army whilst at the same time capturing both Slavyansk and Artemovsk. Given its limited resources, this was a considerable undertaking for First Guards Army, which attempted to push on to Sinelnikovo and Zaporozhye with one of its rifle corps while the other was thrown at Slavyansk. On 11 February, after receiving some much-needed supplies, 14th Guards Tank Brigade – part of Popov's force – took Grishino in an early morning attack, following this up with an advance into Krasnoarmeiskoye later that day and thus cutting one of the important lateral railway lines upon which Manstein's army group was dependent. Such a development needed urgent action, and a planned attack to recapture Kramatorsk was cancelled in favour of retaking Krasnoarmeiskoye. At first, the only formations available for this were *SS-Viking* and part of 333rd Infantry Division, and in an attempt to make his limited resources stretch to maximum effect, Mackensen proposed instead that while *SS-Viking* and 333rd Infantry Division attacked Krasnoarmeiskoye, the combined forces of 7th and 11th Panzer Divisions would attack the Russians from Slavyansk, pushing west into the rear of the Russian force that had reached Krasnoarmeiskoye. In this manner, Kramatorsk too could be recaptured.[16]

SS-Viking was feeling the strain of constant combat and, like most formations on both sides, was far from its establishment strength. When it attacked on 12 February, striking from the east and northeast, it fought its way into the edge of Krasnoarmeiskoye but then found itself involved in a bitter fight with IV Guards Tank Corps. A German regiment had been dispatched to retake Grishino but found the roads were almost impassable and instead was forced to take a detour to the west in the hope of bypassing the defences. Like the force sent into Krasnoarmeiskoye, it was soon bogged down in difficult combat amongst the buildings of Grishino and the nearby villages. Casualties increased steadily for little gain.[17]

Most of the German 333rd Infantry Division had been tasked with holding the front to the north of Slavyansk and ultimately re-establishing contact with German forces near Izyum, but its lines had been penetrated on 3 February and much of the division driven back by the northern elements of First Guards Army; this thrust also captured the town of Lozovaya, an important railway junction. Critically, the regiment that had been intended to help *SS-Viking* in its attacks was also driven west, leaving the SS unit to struggle on without any support. The rest of 333rd Infantry Division was pushed back to the southwest of Slavyansk, exposing 7th Panzer Division and leaving it in danger of encirclement. But just as it seemed as if First Guards Army was finally about to break open the German lines, 3rd and 11th Panzer Divisions at last began to make some impression in their attacks and succeeded in taking the eastern parts of Kramatorsk; at the same time, 7th Panzer Division was able to push southwards from Slavyansk, ensuring that it was not completely encircled in the town. However, the planned attack deep into the rear of Popov's forces at Krasnoarmeiskoye had to be abandoned.

Conditions were extremely taxing for the soldiers on both sides. The medical officer of one of 7th Panzer Division's panzergrenadier regiments submitted a report to the division medical officer on 4 February:

Since 29 January, Walsberg's battalion has been in constant action without any opportunity for shelter ... The manpower of the battalion consists of just two officers, 21 NCOs and 94 men, which includes the crews of an anti-tank gun and an infantry support gun, meaning that there are only 78 men available for use as infantry ... As a result of the current manner of deployment, the daily incidence of frostbite is particularly high. The men are lying on an open plain in icy wind and can only be fed at night. Food is brought forward in canisters and when it reaches the last combat outposts, is barely lukewarm. Due to the reduced strength of the battlegroup to which Walsberg's battalion is subordinated [*Kampfgruppe Steinkeller*], its replacement has not been possible. Every single man has now endured seven days in the open in icy conditions with inadequate food and practically no sleep. The men are at the end of their physical strength and losses through frostbite and illness rise daily. Many are ridden with lice, and it is not possible to take countermeasures in this situation …

In the conditions described above, it is not possible to give any medical guarantee about the continuing operational status of the remnants of the battalion and its replacement seems essential.[18]

Despite the difficulties it faced – particularly by *Kampfgruppe Steinkeller*, which repeatedly found itself isolated – 7th Panzer Division managed to retain control of Slavyansk until, on 16 February, it was ordered to pull out to the south so that it could be redeployed for a further attack on Krasnoarmeiskoye. At the end of the battle in Slavyansk, General Funck, the division commander, wrote:

The division can look back with pride on the tough but successful days of battle of *Gruppe Steinkeller* from 2 to 17 February, when through the unshakable bearing of its leader it succeeded in holding this vital cornerstone of the Donets front against superior enemy forces and this made possible a decisive change in the outcome of the winter fighting. *Kampfgruppe Steinkeller* repeatedly repulsed Russian assaults with determined defence and stubborn counterattacks in particularly difficult combat during days and nights filled with the highest stresses. From the strong-willed commander down to the last outstanding individual soldier, the regiment has truly upheld the honour of German soldiers and once more maintained the proud tradition of Viazma [where the regiment had fought with distinction earlier in the war] … the Slavyansk battlegroup has my particular thanks and recognition for this outstanding and significant achievement.[19]

Whilst the combat performance of 7th Panzer Division was undoubtedly worthy of praise, especially in such terrible conditions, its conduct in battle was little more 'honourable' than that of almost any other unit on either side during the winter's fighting. Few prisoners were taken by either the Germans or the Russians in the pitiless struggle for the ruins of Slavyansk.

Like the Wehrmacht's advance to and beyond the Don the previous summer, the entire *Gallop* operation had been predicated upon the belief that the enemy was already defeated and in full retreat. The bitter fighting at Krasnoarmeiskoye and Slavyansk exposed how badly stretched the Russian units were; by this stage, the divisions of Kuznetsov's First Guards Army each barely had the strength of a full infantry regiment. Despite the clear presence of substantial German forces in and around Slavyansk, Kuznetsov continued to shift the weight of his army further west in accordance with Vatutin's orders. Popov was also trying to regroup his forces, ordering X Tank Corps to move to support IV Guards Tank Corps at Krasnoarmeiskoye. Using roads that had already been damaged by the passage of IV Guards Tank Corps and were then suddenly hidden by a fresh and heavy fall of snow, Major General Vasily Gerasimovich Burkov's tanks laboured south, averaging less than a mile every hour, and as they passed to the west of Slavyansk they were further delayed by an encounter with 11th Panzer Division, still trying to attack west from the Slavyansk area. They finally reached Krasnoarmeiskoye on 15 February, having travelled 36 miles (60km) in five days.[20]

Whatever the views of Hausser and Lanz might be with regard to operations around Kharkov, higher authorities had a different opinion. Aware that the weight of Russian forces bearing down on his corps from the east required the commitment of too many units to leave enough troops for the planned attack towards the south and southwest against VI Guards Cavalry Corps, Hausser requested permission for the attack order to be cancelled so that he could fulfil the 'Führer Order' to defend Kharkov. Manstein had already recommended that if necessary, Kharkov should be abandoned, albeit temporarily, in order to ensure sufficient units were thrown into the attack – if it succeeded, there would be ample opportunity to recapture Kharkov, and if it failed, any prolonged defence of the city would be pointless as the Russians would succeed in reaching the Dnepr crossings and would thus seal the fate of Army Group B. To the north of Kharkov, *Korps Cramer* reported the rapid advance of Russian forces towards Belgorod, making any success by Hausser's divisions of limited value – indeed, the push by Moskalenko's Fortieth Army towards Belgorod and the resultant outflanking of the German defences to the east of Kharkov was the main threat to the city. For the moment, the wishes of higher commands prevailed and the counterattack – ordered by Army Group B – remained in place. This left the rest of Lanz's command under constant pressure, and he waited anxiously for news from the two infantry divisions pulling back also under intense pressure. Since it began its retreat, 298th Infantry Division had been completely out of communication, and contact with 320th Infantry Division was intermittent; the fate of the regiment that had been deployed by the latter in an attack towards the south of Izyum was completely unknown. Early on 7 February, *SS-Das Reich* began the attack against VI Guards Cavalry Corps but almost immediately ran into strong resistance and had to call a halt – the Russians had been deploying for an attack of their own, and both sides suffered heavy losses. However, over the next day, the greater firepower of *SS-Das Reich* made itself felt and VI Guards Cavalry Corps was driven back.

The ability of *Korps Cramer* to protect the northern side of the counterattack – and the northeast approaches to Kharkov – was thrown into question when the reconnaissance battalion of *Grossdeutschland* reported that it was encircled and had to fight its way to safety, and other Russian formations threatened Belgorod. The only fragments of good news for the Germans were that 320th Infantry Division reported small groups from its lost regiment had succeeded in fighting their way through Russian lines – the division continued to struggle towards Balakleya to the west, receiving intermittent supplies by air and carrying 500 wounded men – and that the remnants of 298th Infantry Division had reached the lines of *LSSAH*, reduced to no more than a battlegroup. However, both of the infantry divisions had delayed the Russian forces, buying invaluable time for the rest of the SS Panzer Corps to arrive.

Despite the pressure upon *Armee Abteilung Lanz* and a substantial gap between its northern flank and what remained of the German Second Army, Hitler's obsession with never conceding ground continued to prevail and *OKH* insisted that Belgorod had to be held, even at the risk of encirclement.[21] Throughout this period, the refusal of higher commands to accept reality continued to hamper the German forces. Hausser had repeatedly warned that the attack by his divisions towards the south was unlikely to succeed on account of snowbound roads, fuel shortages and the strength of the enemy, but Weichs continued to insist on the attack proceeding – late on 7 February, Weichs informed Hausser that the attack was the subject of a 'Führer Order' and no further objections would be tolerated. Lanz too had changed his mind and was now insisting on Hitler's instructions being followed to the letter. Much as Manstein had found during his recent journey to Germany, Hitler remained convinced about the invincibility of his SS and regarded Hausser's corps as perfectly capable of holding Kharkov whilst simultaneously attacking towards the south.[22] Tiring of what he saw as obstinacy on the part of Weichs, Hausser contacted Zeitzler at *OKH* directly, thus bypassing the chain of command via Lanz and Weichs. This was at the very least a serious breach of protocol, but further signals followed during the night and a degree of reality prevailed. The attack would still proceed, but on a far lesser scale; the threat of *Korps Cramer* being driven from Belgorod was too great, and there were signs that the Russian Sixth Army was beginning to pick up the pace after its prolonged battle with the retreating German infantry divisions. There was therefore a high likelihood of Kharkov being outflanked both to the north at Belgorod and to the south at Balakleya, and in order to avoid the possibility of encirclement the arriving elements of *SS-Totenkopf* were ordered to form up in Poltava, 80 miles (125km) to the southwest of Kharkov. Nevertheless, although *SS-Das Reich* and *LSSAH* were permitted to make local withdrawals, Hausser was ordered to form a new mobile group to the south of Kharkov from where it could attack further to the south into the rear of the Russian forces that were now beginning to move against the exposed northern flank of Army Group Don, seeking both to disrupt these forces and to establish contact with Manstein's northern flank.

By now, the various battlegroups of *Grossdeutschland* defending Belgorod had been driven back to the city itself. At first, they were delighted to find supply dumps that had been hastily abandoned by withdrawing rear area units and, like the retreating elements of 168th Infantry Division, helped themselves to items like food, wine and even toothbrushes, but then found themselves involved in increasingly hard fighting covering the retreat of 168th Infantry Division to the west and northwest while falling back themselves towards the southwest along the road to Kharkov. One survivor of a battlegroup that had been hastily assembled from the *Grossdeutschland Führer Begleit* battalion responsible for escorting Hitler and had then been dispatched to the front line later described the battle as he and his comrades fell back through Belgorod late on 8 February:

At about 1900 the enemy suddenly attacked, firing everything they had. In barely an hour the city behind us was blazing fiercely. Most of our men now experienced heavy street fighting for the first time. The front as such had ceased to exist; for the front had now become the corner of a house. None of us knew whether the roaring of engines was caused by our own or by Russian tanks. There was firing in front, but then also from the right and then again on the left. At ten metres no one recognised friend or foe. The crews of the *Grossdeutschland* company's anti-tank guns gave their all in the close-quarter struggle with the enemy tanks. I can still see the crew of one gun, on a narrow street which led to the cemetery to the right of the road, which literally held out to the last man, until he too lost his life to a direct hit.

The clear winter night was brightly lit. Our winter clothing no longer gave any protection against the snow. Every movement could be seen from a distance. Our company's platoon leaders tried desperately to hold together and assemble their people.[23]

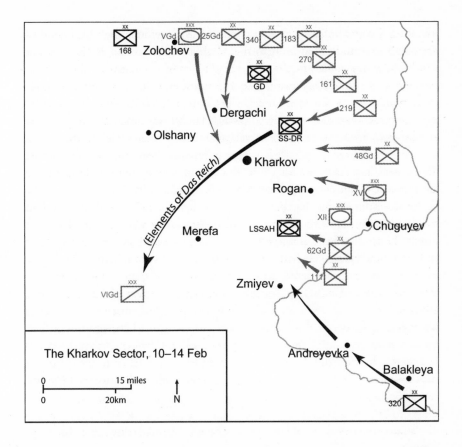

The Kharkov Sector, 10–14 Feb

Carrying their dead and wounded with them, the battered units of *Grossdeutschland* abandoned Belgorod and fell back towards Kharkov. There could be no question of obeying Hitler's edicts and continuing to defend Belgorod without almost certainly allowing the complete destruction of *Grossdeutschland*.

Postel's 320th Infantry Division was still trying to reach safety. Early on 9 February, it attacked Balakleya from the southeast; the most advanced elements of *LSSAH* were in Zmiyev, 27 miles (44km) to the northwest. Between the two units, Russian troops continued to push west and southwest across the Donets. In an attempt both to hinder this Russian advance and to bring 320th Infantry Division to safety, Postel was ordered to continue to push northwest. The following day, still carrying their growing number of wounded – attempts to evacuate them by air failed repeatedly – and receiving only minimal supplies of fuel and ammunition from the Luftwaffe, Postel's troops reached Andreyevka, but there was still no end to their ordeal; the SS units hadn't been able to move any closer to them, and 320th Infantry Division would have to continue further. On 11 February, while the exhausted soldiers pressed on, the SS started their attack from south of Kharkov. At first, the attack made good progress, but soon encountered strong resistance and failed to reach its objectives for the day; as intended, the advancing Russian forces had established a firm shield to protect the northern flank of the Russian attack against Army Group Don. However, the determined resistance of 320th Infantry Division and the presence of the SS Panzer Corps' formations along the Donets – together with the limited counterattack of 11 February – meant that the Russian Sixth Army was somewhat further south than originally planned.

By the end of the day, *Armee Abteilung Lanz* was effectively out of touch with both of its neighbours. Contact with Second Army to the north had still not been re-established and the gap had actually worsened with the loss of Belgorod, and there remained a substantial gap to First Panzer Army in the south. On 12 February the Russians began a direct attack towards Kharkov from the northeast and east. In the early afternoon, the survivors of 320th Infantry Division finally managed to make contact with SS units immediately to the east of Zmiyev. The division had lost most of its heavy equipment and over half its personnel, but had survived as a coherent formation and had contributed substantially to slowing the advance of Kharitonov's Sixth Army. Even now, it was not possible to grant its remaining troops a chance to rest and recover; they were subordinated to the SS Panzer Corps to help in its ongoing efforts to attack towards the south.

Whilst the attack by the SS Panzer Corps – mainly by elements of *SS-Das Reich* – towards the south made some progress, a definitive breakthrough continued to elude Hausser, with Russian cavalry formations proving more mobile through the snow-covered landscape than the German tracked vehicles. Hausser wanted to redirect the attack towards the southwest in an attempt to find a way through weaker resistance, but he was overruled by Army Group B and ordered to continue the attack towards the south. However, by the end of the day there had been a further rearrangement of command. Army Group B was to be dissolved and its headquarters personnel ordered back to Germany; *Armee Abteilung Lanz* would now come under the command of Manstein's Army Group Don. In the difficult circumstances facing the Germans, Army Group B's personnel remained in the front line until the summer. In addition to the disbandment of Army Group B, *Korps Cramer* also received a new commander: Erhard Raus, who had led 6th Panzer Division during *Winter Storm* and the fighting between the Don and Donets. Walther von Hünersdorff, the energetic and charismatic commander of 6th Panzer Division's panzer regiment, now took command of the division.

Manstein later wrote that he was not in favour of the dissolution of Army Group B on the grounds that his headquarters now had to take control of forces to its north in the midst of an intense battle for survival, without having the necessary communications networks in place. The problems in communications between different German formations were indeed a cause for concern at several levels, with many division commanders complaining that they were often out of contact with higher bodies and corps commanders – particularly Hausser – often communicating with *OKH* directly rather than via their army and army group headquarters. But Manstein was also frequently critical about the lack of coordination between different commands on the front line, and at least the new arrangement gave him personal control over all the formations involved in trying to hold back the Russian attacks in the Ukraine.

Rybalko's Third Tank Army continued to batter its way towards Kharkov. In three days, XV Tank Corps ground forward about 6 miles (10km) until reaching the outskirts of the city. Meanwhile, Hausser's counterattack continued to come up against strong resistance. But even though the German defences to the east of Kharkov remained strong and took a heavy toll on Rybalko's troops, the Russian Sixty-Ninth Army steadily drove back *Grossdeutschland* along the road from Belgorod, suffering heavy losses as it did so. Its northern neighbour, Fortieth Army, completely outflanked the defences of Kharkov to the west by exploiting the discovery that *Grossdeutschland* and 168th Infantry Divisions were retreating on diverging axes. Moskalenko dispatched V Guards Tank Corps – the new name of IV Tank Corps, which had served as Fortieth Army's main strike force in earlier operations – into the gap and broke through to Zolochev. From here, elements of Fortieth Army continued towards the northwest suburbs of Kharkov itself, guided by civilian volunteers who knew the locations of the German defences.[24]

Brigadeführer Herbert-Ernst Vahl, who had taken command of *SS-Das Reich* only three days earlier, was increasingly aware that his room for manoeuvre was constrained and getting worse. If he fell back further in the face of the Russian attacks from the east, he would face the prospect of costly urban warfare, and in any case the thrust by the Russian Fortieth Army towards the northwest parts of Kharkov completely outflanked both his division and *Grossdeutschland*. He made his corps commander aware of his concerns; his warning was passed up via Hausser and Lanz to Manstein, who forwarded it to *OKH*, but early the following morning he had to pass back Hitler's decision, which was probably as unsurprising as it was disappointing:

> The commander [of the army group] … advises the subordinate corps that in keeping with the Führer Order the positions at Kharkov are to be held. Attempts will be made to release units through the [southward] attack of the SS Panzer Corps to deal with the enemy penetration towards Kharkov.[25]

Lanz reinforced the instructions with a personal visit to Hausser's headquarters in mid-morning on 14 February. Although he had made clear his own view that Kharkov could not be held, he was – not unlike Paulus – a man who would rigidly obey Hitler regardless of his view of reality on the ground. All he could suggest to Hausser was that the mobile group being formed by *LSSAH* to the south of Kharkov could be used to beat back the advancing Russians. By this time, Russian forces had bypassed Kharkov to the north and were reported to be advancing westwards either side of Bogodukhov, 34 miles (55km) to the northwest of Kharkov. Most of the elements of *Grossdeutschland* fighting near Kharkov had been in almost constant action for the past two weeks and living in their vehicles or out in the open. Casualties from frostbite began to add to the losses in combat, and many companies had to be merged to try to maintain sufficient fighting strength. The Russian forces that had pushed west after taking Belgorod were also turning their attention south, forcing *Grossdeutschland* to extend its lines ever further to prevent an encirclement. The village of Dergachi was captured by the Russian 25th Guards Rifle Division, and from there, Shafarenko's division threatened to cut the lines of retreat to the west; a *Grossdeutschland* battlegroup succeeded in recapturing Dergachi on 12 February, but the Russians merely moved further west before edging south again. When 25th Guards Rifle Division launched a second attack on Dergachi, the *Grossdeutschland* battlegroup fell back rather than fight a futile battle.

In his memoirs, Balck described several occasions during the war when Wehrmacht officers found it difficult to maintain tight control of SS formations, which often chose to submit reports via their own lines of communications or, as had been the case with Hausser, simply bypassed their superior headquarters and took up matters directly with *OKH*. In an attempt to restore normal chains of command, Manstein issued an order that such parallel reports were to stop with immediate effect. In any event, the growing confusion of the battlefield, coupled by German demolitions and destruction of key installations, made it increasingly difficult for the different headquarters to communicate. As darkness fell, Hausser spoke to Army Group Don headquarters by radio and reported that on the eastern side of Kharkov, the position of *SS-Das Reich* was now so unfavourable that an immediate withdrawal was required to prevent the division from suffering major casualties as well as the loss of Kharkov itself. Unless he received orders to withdraw, Hausser warned, he would issue such orders himself. Lanz learned of this exchange and contacted Hausser directly, repeating Hitler's order that the SS Panzer Corps was to defend the city if necessary 'to the last man'. This led to a further radio discussion between Hausser and Lanz, as recorded in the diary of *Armee Abteilung Lanz*:

> OB ['*Oberbefehlshaber*' or 'Senior Commander', in this case Lanz]: Asks about the situation.
>
> SS-OGrF ['*SS-Obergruppenführer*', i.e. Hausser]: Major preparations and a penetration to the southern airfield, which is now in enemy hands.
>
> OB: Can positions still be held today?
>
> SS-OGrF: For the moment, yes, [but] an order for withdrawal was issued half an hour ago.
>
> OB: This order is contrary to the Führer Order, and must be countermanded.
>
> SS-OGrF: I doubt that a counter-order can be executed.
>
> OB: The Führer Order is to be obeyed. 320th Infantry Division is to be used in a counterthrust.
>
> SS-OGrF: The division is still in Zmiyev and is not available.
>
> OB: It is to be brought forward immediately.
>
> SS-OGrF: It lacks the strength for combat, its horses are too weak for any movement.[26]

Hausser had done something that nobody else had been prepared to do during all of the crises of the winter: he had issued his own orders in direct contravention to Hitler's instructions, despite those instructions being repeatedly reinforced. There could be no question about who was right – in addition to penetrating the southeast perimeter of the Kharkov defences and capturing the airfield, the Red Army had made any prolonged defence of the city impossible. The leading elements of Shafarenko's 25th Guards Rifle Division had advanced past the north of the city and reached Olshany, some 16 miles (26km) to the northwest of the city. The road between Kharkov and Poltava was under fire too – if the city wasn't completely encircled, such a development was imminent. All of the professional soldiers – Hausser, Lanz, Manstein and Zeitzler – were in agreement, but the habit of adherence to orders remained strong and Manstein immediately raised the matter with Zeitzler and Hitler, asking that the order to defend Kharkov to the last man be rescinded. In the meantime, the southward attack was to cease, and all attention turned to holding the city. Despite this, Lanz reported late in the morning that his forces lacked the strength to drive the Russians out of Kharkov and that complete encirclement of the remaining troops in the city was imminent.

The situation worsened by the hour. *Korps Raus* reported that its front line to the north of Kharkov had been penetrated at several points and powerful Russian formations were advancing on Kharkov from the northwest and north. In the early afternoon, a signal arrived from Hitler's headquarters: the city was to be held. As the day drew to an end, the escape route to the west narrowed still further and Hausser concluded that there was no possibility of the mobile group from Dietrich's *LSSAH* arriving in time to restore the situation – in any event, a single battlegroup would make no difference to the outcome of the battle. Regardless of the Führer Order, he told his units to pull back as he had previously directed. Paulus might have been a 'weak man' in the opinion of Balck and others; Hausser was a completely different personality, and had no intention of allowing his divisions to be encircled and destroyed. Under heavy fire and constantly threatened by superior Russian forces, the elements of *SS-Das Reich* still fighting in the east of Kharkov pulled back to the southwest, suffering substantial losses from Russian infantry and partisans in combat at close quarters. Almost by chance, the headquarters of *Grossdeutschland* became aware of the withdrawal of the SS and issued its own orders to pull out; by the time *Korps Raus* learned that the SS Panzer Corps had decided to abandon Kharkov, *Grossdeutschland* was already withdrawing:

> Assault guns and tanks barred the main and secondary roads into the city from the north and northwest, while the vehicle columns poured quickly, but in an orderly fashion, into the city and out of it to the southwest. In the city itself there was shooting everywhere, although the populace took no serious part in it. Fires still smouldered here and there. Pioneers had prepared important fixtures such as bridges, dumps and hangars for demolition. They waited beside houses in small groups for the order to detonate. It was nearing midnight; the bulk of the units were through, only lone vehicles and dispatch riders still drove through the streets toward the exits from the city. On the street corners the vehicles of the *Grossdeutschland* assault gun battalion stood out as dark shadows against the night sky. They were to be the last to follow, transporting the pioneer demolition squads. It was just before midnight when a tremendous explosion shattered the night stillness. The big road bridge flew into the air, not without causing considerable damage to the nearby houses.
>
> ... When we rolled across the rail bridge we saw the station. It had been blown up, and the wreckage covered the tracks. We left the jumble of houses and drove

into the open of the workers' settlement at the western edge of the city. The road climbed somewhat near a brickworks and the column stopped. The squad in front of us had a bottle of schnapps and we were a little jealous, for in that cold a little drink wouldn't have hurt. While we were shouting to them that they should leave us a little, someone noticed soldiers with white snow smocks and guns on a road about 300m to our left on the far side of a hollow. They also stopped and looked over at us, and as we watched they began moving an anti-tank gun into position to fire on us. 'Man, those are Russians!' Our column began moving, engines roared. Away from the road and into cover! The truck pulled away, drove slowly up the hill and stopped behind a house. We got down. The driver was supposed to follow the other vehicles but most of them had got stuck. Suddenly we came under small-arms fire and a Russian heavy machine-gun rattled from the brickworks. Behind us a 20mm flak gun on a self-propelled chassis opened fire; it was hit. Boom! Crash! A scream, and there was nothing more to be seen of the anti-aircraft gun. Direct hit; a wounded man was dragged away by his comrades …

… There was sporadic shooting. Cautiously we ran from house to house. We had almost all made it when a single shot rang out and one of us fell, shot through the head. We peeked cautiously around the corner of a house. There was a ping and the bullet hissed past our heads, missing by a hair …

After half an hour we heard the sound of tanks in the distance behind us. We listened expectantly, but would they find us? The roar of engines drew ever nearer and then stopped about 200m behind us. A messenger came to us: 'Leave here quietly at once and assemble at the tank.'

… The column rolled out of the city in a southwesterly direction. Flames leapt from the burning buildings. Entire houses collapsed with loud crashes and showers of sparks as we broke out of the encirclement to the southwest. Behind us the sky over burning Kharkov was red.[27]

Immediately, a message arrived from *OKH* demanding an explanation for the abandonment of Kharkov. Functioning increasingly as little more than a relay between signals to and from front-line units and higher commands, Lanz replied that there simply hadn't been sufficient troops to hold Kharkov at the same time as mounting an attack towards the south, and that the forces defending the city had been opposed by an estimated 20 rifle divisions, four rifle brigades, ten tank brigades, two tank regiments, two motorised brigades and two cavalry divisions. Whilst this was undoubtedly an overestimate, the facts were undeniable: holding Kharkov would have led to the encirclement of *SS-Das Reich*, one of the few precious mobile formations upon which so much depended. In any event, the infantry-light armoured formations of the SS Panzer Corps were utterly unsuited to defending a built-up area.

There were, inevitably, repercussions. Manstein's pressing concern was whether the unilateral action on the part of Hausser had endangered *Korps Raus* to the north, particularly the *Grossdeutschland* division, which extracted its units from around Kharkov with difficulty and suffered substantial losses. He also recorded his unhappiness at the sparse nature of communications between the SS Panzer Corps and his headquarters, and succeeded in having *SS-Totenkopf* subordinated directly to Army Group Don rather than Hausser's corps; in addition, army staff officers were to be assigned to each SS division to ensure an improvement in communications. Questions were raised about whether the SS Panzer Corps' units should all be subordinated directly to higher commands and Hausser's headquarters should be withdrawn; for the moment, it remained in place. There were also questions about Hausser himself – in his memoirs, Manstein suggested that had he been a Wehrmacht officer, he would undoubtedly have been brought before a court-martial for such a brazen act of disobedience to the Führer. Ferdinand Heim had been dismissed from command of XLVIII Panzer Corps in the aftermath of *Uranus* for far less, and at the time of Hausser's withdrawal from Kharkov was under arrest and sentenced to death. However, Hausser had been awarded the *Goldene Parteiabzeichen der NSDAP* ('Gold Party Badge of the National Socialist Party'), the third highest award for Party members, just three weeks previously. Perhaps fearing the loss of prestige if such a prominent Party member were subjected to disciplinary action, Hitler turned a blind eye to Hausser's disobedience.[28]

Writing many years later, Moskalenko – whose Fortieth Army played a leading part in the recapture of Kharkov – offered his own views on the failure of the SS to obey Hitler's orders to hold the city to the last man:

> Soviet troops attacked Kharkov a week after the end of the period of mourning announced in Germany on the occasion of the death of Sixth Army, which was destroyed in the Stalingrad area. The fascists then continued to ring the funeral bell – for those armies that were defeated on the middle Don, in Ostrogozhsk and Rossosh, Voronezh and Kastorny. This series of powerful attacks by the Red Army so thoroughly frightened the Hitlerite warriors that they were now horrified at the thought of any encirclement that threatened them. The SS and their generals, apparently, were no exception, which is why the escape of the SS Panzer Corps from the half-encircled Kharkov is not surprising.

But it was regrettable that the SS Panzer Corps succeeded [in escaping encirclement] because, if it had followed the orders of the Führer, I have no doubt that all three of its divisions – *LSSAH*, *SS-Das Reich* and *Totenkopf* – would have ceased to exist. Who knows, perhaps, this was the reason why Hitler decided not to punish the commander of the SS unit.

And Hitler could hardly have acted differently, given that – undoubtedly on his instructions – the press of fascist Germany concealed from the German people the very fact of the liberation of Kharkov by the Red Army! At that time, as the news of this event flew all over the world, the German Information Bureau on 18 February asserted that fighting was continuing in Kharkov. The Nazis were afraid to tell the truth to the German people, since the loss of Kharkov was a very sensitive blow to them, especially since it occurred literally immediately after the catastrophe at Stalingrad and the defeat of the fascist troops on the Don.[29]

Hausser, too, wrote some thoughts about the events many years after the war, highlighting the limitations of complete obedience:

There will always be different opinions when assessing a situation. In such cases, orders are decisive. Without obedience there can be no armed forces.

If a subordinate thinks an order is wrong, he must report his opinion, justifying it and requesting an alteration. If the higher authority adheres to its decision, the subordinate must obey. If he believes that he cannot do so, he takes personal responsibility and must be prepared to answer for it. Whilst disobedience may be reported as an act of wilfulness, this overlooks the duty of a commander of men: 'responsibility for subordinate troops'!

The threatened destruction of the troops must awaken the conscience of the commander! Thus it was at Kharkov!

A decision to disobey is not taken lightly by a responsible man, particularly against a thrice-reiterated order of the highest command. It helped that all intermediate superiors agreed inwardly. Besides, there was the menacing example of Stalingrad, which had concluded catastrophically two weeks earlier.

But the intermediate superiors cannot be assessed by the same measure; the decision to disobey was *not* required of them. Only the immediate commander, who experienced the combat of the troops every day and also heard from them, was in that situation.

Correct assessment requires training, personal experience, and also probably a degree of courage.[30]

335

These words must have been chosen deliberately to contrast Hausser's decisions with those of Paulus in Stalingrad. The latter had certainly benefited from the excellent training of the German general staff, but lacked the experience and the courage to take personal responsibility and disobey orders that were manifestly wrong.

Whilst much of the local population had greeted the Germans with enthusiasm in 1941, the mood was very different by early 1943, after 18 months of brutal occupation. Generally, Ukrainian civilians welcomed the returning Red Army, though many in the Ukraine still remembered the mass deaths from starvation in the 1930s due to Stalin's policies. Some took the opportunity to take revenge on those who had collaborated with the Germans, such as the men who had volunteered to serve as police officers, though this was not without risk, as one Russian artillery lieutenant later recalled:

In February 1943, the battery was stranded in a village ... due to mechanical problems with our vehicles. Until then, I had not slept for two days. I lay down on the floor of the nearest hut to sleep, when suddenly I was awakened by Malyshev who said, 'We caught a policeman. What do you want us to do with him? Beat him up or send him to headquarters? The locals want to execute him.' All I could say was, 'Go to hell, do what you like, just leave me to sleep.' A few minutes later, there was a gunshot in the courtyard. I left the house – in the snow lay a dead policeman surrounded by a crowd of villagers interspersed with my men. The peasants shouted 'A dog's death for a dog!' and they told us how badly the German collaborator had behaved. A week later, a representative of the special department of the regiment [i.e. the NKVD detachment] summoned me for interrogation about the events in the village. I told him what had happened and he smiled amiably, shook my hand and wished me success in battle. The following week I was called to division headquarters ... in the building of a rural school. The legal department officer approached me and ordered me to follow him. I entered a classroom – it was a division tribunal!

Without listening to my explanations, three rear area types accused me of murdering a civilian ... [After a brief recess] the chairman read their verdict: 'Eight years' imprisonment!' I was furious. 'For what?' He continued in a monotonous voice, 'The verdict can, on the recommendation of higher commands, be commuted if you show courage and heroism in the battles for the socialist homeland.' There was nothing about a penal battalion or postponement of the sentence until the end of the war. They turned and left the room. I sat there for two hours waiting for the guards to arrive and to tear off my buttons, and to take my belt and pistol. Nobody came. I did not know what to do. I left and rode my horse quietly back to the battery without hindrance. I was sick at heart, thinking, 'Chekist* swine! They should be on the front line, the bastards!'

I met the battalion commander and told him what had happened. He replied, 'Just carry on fighting and don't worry about this nonsense, we'll sort it out.' Others in my place might have deserted or gone over to the Germans, but I am a Jew, a Communist, and a patriot, and the word 'homeland' isn't an empty phrase for me ... After another fortnight I was ordered by telephone to relinquish command of the battery and report to division headquarters. I was certain that this was the beginning of the road to the camps in Siberia. The battery sergeant put some food in a bag for me. I bid farewell to my comrades, gave all my 'trophies' to my friends and went on foot to headquarters. I found four other artillery commanders there and we were offered posts in a new anti-tank unit. None of us refused. And I have no idea what happened about my 'criminal case'. There were no tribunal documents in my personnel file when I was demobilised.[31]

---

* The Cheka was the first state security police force organised by the Bolsheviks after the Russian Revolution.

CHAPTER 12

FEBRUARY: THE SWING OF THE PENDULUM

After the end of the SS Panzer Corps' attack against the Russian VI Cavalry Corps and the abandonment of Kharkov, 17 and 18 February were quieter days as both sides took stock. The latter day was the anniversary of the founding of the Red Army a quarter of a century earlier, when the fledgling Bolshevik Russia was desperately trying to fend off the rapacious German Army prior to the humiliating peace terms that were imposed at Brest-Litovsk, and Stalin issued a proclamation to mark the day:

> The Red Army is an army of defence of peace and friendship among the peoples of all countries. It was created not for the conquest of foreign countries, but for the defence of the frontiers of the Soviet country …
>
> … the Red Army has become an army of life-and-death struggle against the Hitlerite troops, an army of avengers of the outrages and humiliation inflicted by the German-fascist blackguards on our brothers and sisters in the occupied districts of our country.
>
> … For twenty months the Red Army has been waging an heroic struggle, without parallel in history, against the invasion of the German-fascist hordes. In view of the absence of a second front in Europe, the Red Army alone bears the whole burden of the war. Nevertheless, the Red Army has not only held its own against the onslaught of the German-fascist hordes, but has become in the course of the war the terror of the fascist armies.
>
> … Three months ago the troops of the Red Army began their offensive at the approaches to Stalingrad. Since then the initiative in military operations has

remained in our hands and the pace and striking power of the offensive operations of the Red Army have not weakened. Today, in hard winter conditions, the Red Army is advancing over a front of 1,500 km [950 miles] and is achieving successes practically everywhere. In the north, near Leningrad, on the central front, at the approaches to Kharkov, in the Donets Basin, at Rostov, on the shores of the Sea of Azov and the Black Sea, the Red Army is striking blow after blow at the Hitlerite troops.

... It does not follow ... that the Hitlerite army is done for and that it now only remains for the Red Army to pursue it to the western frontiers of our country. To think so would be to indulge in unwise and harmful self-delusion. To think so would be to over-estimate our own strength, to under-estimate the strength of the enemy and to adopt an adventurist course. The enemy has suffered defeat, but he is not yet vanquished.[1]

The caution of the closing words was not necessarily reflected in the mood of confidence in army commands, but the Russians took the two days as a much-needed break to reorder the formations that had become badly entangled in the assault on Kharkov, and to bring up fuel, ammunition and reinforcements; at the same time, the Germans tried to reorganise the units that had pulled back under heavy pressure.

Losses were beginning to accumulate amongst the Russian formations that had achieved so much success. Prior to commencing the attack that recaptured Belgorod and Kharkov, Shafarenko had been forced to reorganise the men of his 25th Guards Rifle Division into two regiments instead of three, and the fighting to the west of the city, as he and others tried to cut the German lines of retreat, depleted the ranks still further; in addition to losing an experienced regimental commander, the division was dangerously weakened. It had started this latest operation below full strength, and now had less than 50 per cent of its establishment. In an attempt to remedy matters, Shafarenko – like other Red Army commanders – accepted volunteers from the civilian population of Kharkov into his ranks. By doing so, he increased his nominal strength by perhaps 1,500 men, but operating so far from their supply depots and still involved in ongoing operations, the Russian units were short of everything needed to turn these volunteers into useful soldiers: uniforms, guns, ammunition, and time for training.[2]

It was probably little consolation to Hitler that the capture of Kharkov was something of a disappointment to the Russians. Whilst they had liberated the fourth largest city in the Soviet Union from German occupation, they had failed to encircle any German formations and their attacking armies had been badly mauled. Nevertheless, revised orders were being sent out by Golikov's Voronezh Front even before the capture of Kharkov was complete, and despite Stalin's words of caution the mood in higher commands remained hugely optimistic, as Shtemenko later described. His observations about the personality of one of the front commanders are interesting, as they show how one man's enthusiasm and opinion could influence the decisions of higher commands:

> By the middle of February ... Golikov reported every day to *Stavka* that large forces of the enemy were withdrawing westwards. Similar news was arriving from Southwest Front ... Vatutin also assessed the enemy's behaviour as a flight across the Dnepr.
>
> In reality, however, the German command had no intention of withdrawing its troops to the other side of the Dnepr. During this fighting withdrawal the enemy was preparing a counterattack ...
>
> ... The movement of enemy convoys during remarshalling [i.e. deploying for the counterattack] continued to be regarded as headlong retreat and an attempt to avoid battle in the Donbas and to reach the western bank of the Dnepr as soon as possible. The command of Southwest Front firmly maintained this mistaken point of view, although facts that should have put them on their guard were already in evidence.
>
> General Vatutin's personal opinion was highly regarded on the general staff and had, of course, strongly influenced the planning of the Soviet operation in the Donbas. We all knew Vatutin well and not without reason considered him a gifted and original strategist with a strong dash of romanticism in his make-up. He was always full of energy and prepared to work desperately hard.
>
> ... Vatutin believed that all enemy resistance would soon be crushed. Golikov laboured under the same fatal delusion, which spread from the front commanders to the general staff, and from the general staff to *Stavka*. In Moscow, it was also assumed that these offensive operations were going more or less to plan.[3]

These accounts, and those written by other senior Soviet officials of the era, place most of the blame for over-optimism mainly upon Vatutin and to a lesser extent on Golikov, but regardless of their personal views, there appears to be considerable hindsight in these accounts. And if the 'facts that should have put them on their guard' were indeed already in evidence, *Stavka* and the general staff were as guilty of ignoring them as Vatutin and Golikov. To an extent, Vatutin was a convenient scapegoat after the war; he was mortally wounded in an ambush by Ukrainian nationalists in February 1944 and thus did not survive to write his memoirs.

Although the advancing Russian tank units had engineer teams assigned to them in order to allow for rapid repair of damaged vehicles, the capacity and capability of these teams were limited and the tank formations tried to find ways of improvising. In his role as deputy technical officer for XV Tank Corps, one of the formations of Third Tank Army, Vetkov used every resource available:

> Wanting to speed up the repair of armoured vehicles and to use local industrial resources, I decided to visit the Kharkov tractor factory with personnel from the tank brigades ...
>
> What we saw in the factory area was a scene of terrible, barbaric destruction. One of the largest mechanical manufacturing plants in our country lay in ruins. And nor was it the only one! As we personally discovered, the German fascist invaders had done the same to the electro-technical and other factories in Kharkov, and to the generator turbines.
>
> Late in the evening, when we had lost all hope of finding any suitable workshops, some elderly workers who had previously worked in a tank factory came to us and in a few brief words offered their services in the repair of our tanks. They said that they had already found a suitable workshop, the necessary equipment, tools, and even some repair materials. What a stroke of luck!
>
> In short, the very next day we began to repair military equipment. We worked literally around the clock. I directed our tank repair teams, technicians and drivers and our corps' 96th Mobile Tank Workshop to join the [civilian] workers.
>
> To the credit of the young and energetic chief of Captain Ivanov's vehicle repair workshop, the team subordinated to him with the assigned task coped brilliantly. After several days of selfless labour, the vehicle repair mechanics returned a half dozen T-70 tanks to service, rendering a considerable service to our tank brigades.
>
> The Kharkov workers did not lag behind them. Thanks to their skilled hands, 24 T-34s were repaired. The thinned-out ranks of tank brigades thus received new forces.[4]

Golikov's new instructions outlined operations that were to follow the capture of Kharkov. As soon as the city was secure, his Fortieth and Sixty-Ninth Armies were to drive forward towards Poltava as rapidly as possible; Moskalenko was to exploit towards the west and northwest, reaching Krasnopolye and Slavrograd before pushing on to Lebedin, reaching the latter no later than 21 February, while Sixty-Ninth Army advanced west to Bogodukhov. Third Tank Army would work in cooperation with the neighbouring Sixth Army to advance towards

Poltava and Krasnograd, and the orders explicitly stated the intention to proceed beyond these objectives to Kiev and the Dnepr.[5] This would require a further advance of 78 miles (126km) to reach Poltava, and from there another 64 miles (103km) to Kremenchug on the Dnepr. Reaching Kiev from Kharkov would require a total advance of 252 miles (406km). Even if the Wehrmacht had been defeated, the physical demands of covering so much ground before the spring thaw turned most roads to mud were daunting, especially given the very high likelihood that the retreating Germans would continue to destroy bridges and other vital installations. Simply moving sufficient fuel to the advancing units for such a push was surely beyond the capabilities of the Red Army's logistic services, and regardless of how strongly *Stavka* was influenced by Vatutin's optimism, the lack of any sense of reality amongst higher commands is extraordinary.

Golikov's orders were badly behind schedule before they were issued – initial instructions had been sent out on 12 February in the expectation that Kharkov would fall the following day, and even after the Germans were driven from the city, it took another three days to reorganise the forces that had become so badly intermingled. Casualties had reduced the average strength of Fortieth Army's rifle divisions to fewer than 4,000 men; some of Sixty-Ninth Army's divisions were in an even worse state.[6] Moskalenko wrote that since the beginning of the year, his Fortieth Army had mounted three major operations with barely a pause between them: the Ostrogozhsk-Rossosh Operation, the attack on the German Second Army, and the advance to Belgorod and Kharkov. Whilst the first two had resulted in modest casualties, the fighting in and around Kharkov had been much harder, and as a result his formations were badly in need of reinforcements and rest. Vasilevsky – who was promoted to Marshal of the Soviet Union on 16 February – visited Kharkov the day after the city was liberated and concluded that in order to bring Voronezh Front back to a semblance of its proper strength, it required 300 more tanks and 19,000 men; since the beginning of *Star*, it had received only 1,600 replacements.[7] Regardless of this, the instructions to continue the advance remained in place.

Some German units took advantage of the reduced tempo of the fighting to recuperate and rest, while others chose to settle old scores. Obergruppenführer Joachim Peiper, commander of a battlegroup of *LSSAH*, had led the column that fought its way through to the retreating 320th Infantry Division and allowed the latter to escape. When Peiper's battlegroup withdrew, it found that Russian forces – either part of the Red Army or partisans – had attacked a rear area medical unit of the SS division. Some accounts describe the deaths of 25 Germans, while others record that just two Germans were wounded.[8] The SS

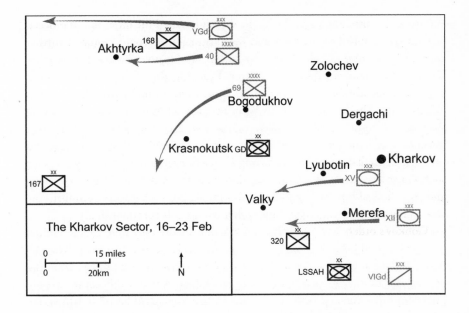

The Kharkov Sector, 16–23 Feb

0   15 miles
0   20km   N

battlegroup responded with an act of violence that had become all too commonplace on the Eastern Front; Peiper ordered his men to retaliate by burning down two villages and slaughtering the inhabitants, resulting in the deaths of 872 civilians of all ages.[9] Peiper's battlegroup became known as 'Lötlampe' ('Blowtorch'), and whilst this may reflect the motif of a blowtorch stencilled on its vehicles, both the motif and the nickname may in turn have originated with Peiper's personal enthusiasm for ordering the torching of villages. Peiper continued to be involved in actions that were at least questionable for the rest of the war. In September 1943, after *LSSAH* was transferred to Italy, he ordered his men to set fire to the village of Boves after two German soldiers were captured by partisans, and 22 Italian civilians were killed either in the flames or shot trying to escape. In early December, he was back on the Eastern Front, once more implicated in the razing of a village and the massacre of its population, and in December 1944 his eponymous battlegroup infamously machine-gunned over 80 US soldiers who had surrendered to the Germans during the Ardennes offensive. This was only one such episode involving the battlegroup during the Battle of the Bulge; over the course of the fighting, Peiper's men killed 362 prisoners and 111 Belgian civilians.

The Russian Sixty-Ninth Army resumed its advance on 19 February towards Bogodukhov with Fortieth Army to the north applying additional pressure.

The German 168th Infantry Division was, like all such formations involved in the battles of February, badly below establishment strength and was unable to defend the entirety of its sector with any guarantee of success, resulting in a rapidly developing risk of it being outflanked and rolled up. Lanz immediately flew to 168th Infantry Division's headquarters to get a personal view of the situation and learned that radio intercepts suggested that the Russians intended to bypass the division. By mid-afternoon, there were reports of Russian troops in Bogodukhov, and even more alarmingly the road west of Akhtyrka had been cut by the leading reconnaissance elements of the Russian forces. When he returned to his own headquarters, Lanz contacted Manstein's chief of staff and requested that *SS-Totenkopf* be deployed to shore up the line to prevent the Russians overwhelming 168th Infantry Division; his request was turned down, though a small SS battlegroup was sent north. Manstein needed the bulk of the division for his counterstroke, and if necessary the army group would have to concede further territory on its northern flank – once the situation had been restored to the south, it would be possible to direct armoured forces to the north to drive back the Russians, and if it proved impossible to restore the front line to the south, blocking the Russian advance towards Akhtyrka would be irrelevant.[10]

Grossdeutschland also came under pressure, with Russian forces attempting to penetrate between it and the neighbouring 320th Infantry Division. Having detected the Russian units preparing to attack, *Grossdeutschland* tried to cover the attack by moving three infantry companies into a blocking position, but these were unable to hold back the Russians and were driven back. Whilst the soldiers of 168th Infantry Division continued to put up dogged resistance, they were almost entirely without anti-tank weapons, leaving them completely exposed in the open ground around Bogodukhov; in an attempt to restore the situation, an anti-tank company was moved from *Grossdeutschland*, which had just received its first Tiger tanks. By mid-afternoon of 20 February, there were gaps between *Grossdeutschland* and 320th Infantry Division to the south and 168th Infantry Division to the north, and one of its regiments was threatened with being encircled in Lyubotin, where it found itself engaged in fighting with the Russian XV Tank Corps from Third Tank Army; casualties were heavy on both sides. During the night that followed, elements of 320th Infantry Division were able to restore contact from the south, but the situation remained precarious. On 21 February, attacks by Stukas helped relieve some of the pressure on 168th Infantry Division, but Bogodukhov was abandoned. The northern flank of the division was bypassed by the leading elements of the Russian Fortieth Army, which pushed on to the west and crossed the River Vorskla at Akhtyrka. To the south of Lyubotin, the Russian XII Tank Corps found it difficult to advance when it ran into the remaining elements of 320th Infantry Division and elements of *Grossdeutschland*. Lyubotin was finally occupied on 22 February when Russian forces succeeded in pushing past the southern flank of the defences, but the toll on the attackers was heavy and XV Tank Corps – already below establishment strength at the beginning of the battle – was reduced to just a small handful of tanks. Giving up Lyubotin was actually advantageous to *Grossdeutschland*, as the division was able to concentrate its forces in a somewhat smaller sector. After the fighting retreat through Belgorod and Kharkov, the slackening Russian pressure along its front was greatly welcomed, particularly as *Grossdeutschland* would soon be required to launch an attack as part of Manstein's counterthrust. To the south, the line began to stabilise with the arrival of further reinforcements – 167th Infantry Division had been brought east from garrison duties in the Netherlands, though it would be early March before all its elements arrived. Whilst 168th Infantry Division remained under great pressure, with no local reserves left, the transfer of 4th Panzer Division by Army Group Centre to the southern flank of Second Army posed a considerable threat to the northern flank of Fortieth Army, thus forcing the Russians to divert units to block any German thrust.

In so many respects, the Red Army was now experiencing a phase of the war that was an eerie replica of the conditions that the Wehrmacht had faced the previous summer. Its higher command firmly believed that the enemy was defeated, and it was being ordered to pursue a presumably broken opponent with little regard for caution. At the same time, front-line commanders were acutely aware of how run-down their units were, and were operating with supply lines of increasing length and fragility. Unlike the panzer divisions, the Red Army's armoured formations at this stage of the war still had very limited capacity for recovering and repairing damaged tanks, and the Germans were thus able to 'recycle' such vehicles far faster, allowing for quicker recovery from intense periods of combat. In some cases, for example on the southern flank of the Russian advance around Slavyansk and Krasnoarmeiskoye, the field commanders had little doubt that the Germans were far from defeated, but higher commands continued to think otherwise. Vatutin believed that there was no cause for concern:

> His reports to *Stavka* were still infused with optimism, which was fuelled by the breakthrough of the tanks to Krasnoarmeiskoye. Vatutin believed that all of the enemy's resistance would soon be broken.[11]

Just as had been the case during Paulus' advance to and battle for Stalingrad, the Russian advance across the Ukraine carried huge risks. Any resurgence of German strength could leave the Russian armies dangerously exposed, and with all their forces committed – as had been the case for the Germans during the Stalingrad battles – a reversal of fortunes could prove catastrophic. Another parallel is the manner in which the commanders of Russian armies had to deal with changes in orders imposed from above, but lacked sufficient knowledge of what was happening elsewhere to judge the context, as Moskalenko wrote:

> By that time, the offensive of [the Russian] Third Tank Army, as well as Sixty-Ninth Army, had indeed been stopped by the enemy. The German-fascist command, which had already recovered considerably after a number of major defeats, concentrated considerable forces on the southern flank of the Soviet-German front. Having created superiority on key axes, with the help of strong tank attacks it stopped the advancing Soviet troops and soon began to push them to the east and northeast.
>
> I did not know all this at that time, since I did not have full information about the situation in the units of the Southwest and the left wing of the Voronezh Fronts. Therefore, at first I was disturbed only by the fact that Voronezh Front unreasonably complicated the tasks of Fortieth Army. But, I thought, they probably still reflect some very real plan. And there was a hope that Sixty-Ninth and Third Tank Armies would help the Southwest Front to defeat the enemy and then return to their previous sectors, after which our Fortieth Army would also breathe more freely.
>
> However, the content of the directives of the front became more and more alarming. One spoke of a certain delay in the advance of Thirty-Eighth Army, the next about the slowing down of the advance of Sixty-Ninth Army. All this happened to the right and left of us, and therefore could not be disregarded when determining the nature of further military operations by Fortieth Army, because its flanks were not secured. As a result of these reasons, gaps appeared on the right and left, reaching about 50 km [30 miles] by 25 February.[12]

But in order to create the reversal of fortunes that he was trying to engineer, Manstein needed more troops. Despite the timely arrival of 167th Infantry Division, Manstein continued to fret about the rate at which reinforcements were reaching him. Earlier in February, he had raised the matter with Zeitzler at *OKH* and was assured that the number of troop trains dispatched to his army group would be increased to 37, but on 14 February he received only six. Whilst the deployment of 4th Panzer Division with Second Army was a welcome move, Field Marshal von Kluge, the commander of Army Group Centre, advised Manstein that the best he could do was try to stop the retreat of Second Army

– an intervention into the Ukraine from the north could not be expected. It was at this moment that Hitler announced that he would be visiting Army Group South personally. Whilst Manstein welcomed the opportunity for face-to-face talks with his supreme commander, he expressed concerns about his ability to ensure the Führer's safety; his headquarters was now situated in Zaporozhye, and Russian forces were moving closer every day. Despite Manstein's misgivings, Hitler left for Zaporozhye on 17 February, while the repercussions of the abandonment of Kharkov were still playing out. However, the threat to Hitler was apparently not purely from the Russians. The personnel of Army Group B were still in place, and according to one source there had been an expectation that Hitler would visit Weichs instead of Manstein; if this occurred, an attempt would be made to remove him from power.

The panzer regiment of *Grossdeutschland* was under the command of Oberstleutnant Hyazinth von Strachwitz, an energetic tank commander who had been seriously wounded on more than one occasion, the latest being when serving with 16th Panzer Division in Stalingrad. Whilst recovering from his wounds, he met Oberst Wessel Freiherr von Freytag-Loringhoven, who was the signals staff officer in Army Group South's headquarters. He had clashed with Obergruppenführer Hans-Adolf Prützmann, who in his role as commander of German police forces in the occupied Ukraine had overseen widespread executions of Jews and others, and Freytag-Loringhoven now made Strachwitz aware of the atrocities being committed by the SS and others, and the dishonour that these acts brought upon Germany as a whole and the military in particular.

In early 1943, Strachwitz took command of the new *Grossdeutschland* panzer regiment and met Oberst Hans Speidel, who had served as a staff officer with the Italian Eighth Army and was now on the staff of *Armee Abteilung Lanz*. Whilst Speidel – like many conservative army officers – had considerable sympathy with many of the territorial aspects of Hitler's ambitions, in particular regarding the recovery of territory removed from Germany after the end of the First World War, he was strongly opposed to the racial policies that were being carried out with such brutality throughout German-occupied Europe. He had a brief conversation with Strachwitz on 8 February, during which both men agreed that, given the disaster at Stalingrad and the manner in which Hitler had led to the disaster, the time had come to remove Hitler from power; prior to Stalingrad, conspirators had feared that loyalty to Hitler within the army was simply too strong.

Later that day, the two officers met Lanz. At this stage, it should be remembered that Lanz had been saddled with orders to hold Kharkov at all costs – orders that he knew were futile and would only result in another Stalingrad if he obeyed them – but despite his personal misgivings, continued to pass on the orders and tried to enforce them. The three men allegedly agreed that when Hitler next visited Army Group B's headquarters, Strachwitz would use his panzer regiment, which he regarded as being completely loyal to him personally, to encircle Hitler and his bodyguard. Hitler would then be informed that he was under arrest, and if he resisted, Strachwitz would use force.[13]

In the event, the plan came to nothing, as Hitler visited Zaporozhye instead. Just how much truth there is in this account is open to question; Strachwitz's cousin, who was an active anti-Hitler conspirator, later said that Strachwitz had told him that if Hitler was killed by conspirators, this would constitute an act of murder, and that Strachwitz was too tightly bound by his Prussian code of honour to get involved in such matters.[14] However, it is undeniable that many officers on the Eastern Front were prepared to take extreme measures against Hitler. Just a few weeks later, the Führer visited Army Group Centre's headquarters in Smolensk. A large group of conspirators intended either to kill or arrest Hitler, but the personal security arrangements of the Führer – several teams of bodyguards and unexpected alterations to routes of travel within Smolensk – prevented any action being taken. However, when Hitler and his entourage departed, one of the conspirators – Oberst Henning von Tresckow – asked Oberstleutnant Heinz Brandt, a staff officer with *OKH*, to take a parcel back to Berlin for a friend. The parcel, wrapped to resemble two bottles of alcohol, contained explosives and a timer that was set to trigger the bomb whilst the plane was still over Russian territory – the death of Hitler could then be blamed upon an accident, or even interception by Soviet fighters. The plotters waited anxiously to hear of the loss of the plane, but were appalled to learn that Hitler's group flew back to Germany without incident. Desperately trying to salvage the situation and at least prevent discovery, the conspirators managed to recover the parcel; when they dismantled it, they found that the timer had worked as intended and its vial of acid had eaten through its casing and had triggered the detonator, which had burned normally – but the explosives, consisting of two British magnetic clam mines, had failed to explode, possibly because the package had been stored in an unheated cargo compartment aboard the plane and was therefore too cold.[15] It is intriguing to speculate what might have happened if Brandt had kept the parcel with him within the cabin of the aircraft. In the context of plots such as this, it is certainly possible that similar conspiracies existed in other parts of the Eastern Front.

It is highly likely that Manstein was approached by military conspirators in the first weeks of 1943. On 26 January, while his headquarters was still in Taganrog, he received a group of visitors that included Major Claus Schenk Graf von Stauffenberg, the man who would place a briefcase bomb in Hitler's bunker in July 1944. Alexander Stahlberg, who was serving on Manstein's staff as an adjutant, later claimed to have heard exchanges between the two men through a half-open door, a heated conversation about the practicality of changing Germany's political leadership.[16] Inevitably, Manstein did not make any record of the conversation in his diaries, and the death of most of the anti-Hitler conspirators in the aftermath of Stauffenberg's failed attempt of July 1944 and the mythology that has grown up in the years after the war have made it almost impossible to judge with any certainty what passed through the minds of individuals at the time, when any hint of dissent was likely to lead to arrest, imprisonment and worse. However, in a letter to his wife, Manstein commented on those who visited his headquarters in January:

> I had a long discussion with Schmundt [Hitler's adjutant] ... The others came with their worries as if I could provide them with remedies. The trust is always very touching, but how should I change things that are not within my power and possibility?[17]

Balck wrote in his memoirs that as the Stalingrad fighting drew to a close, many in higher commands seemed increasingly vocal in their complaints about Hitler. Like many Prussian officers who prided themselves on their refusal to consider political issues, Balck appreciated the lack of trust between Hitler and senior military figures, but felt that soldiers should concentrate on soldiering and not become involved in such issues.[18] Others had different views. Many of the civilian conspirators against Hitler were shocked that so many senior officers had refused to consider taking action because of their oath of loyalty to the Führer, yet had surrendered to the Russians at Stalingrad. The conspirators had always believed that it would be impossible to move against Hitler until there was a substantial military setback, yet it now seemed that far from triggering widespread revolt, the disaster at Stalingrad seemed to bring senior officers closer to Hitler.

When Hitler arrived in Zaporozhye on 17 February, the first day of discussions revealed the gulf between him and Manstein. After a winter of frustrations and disasters, Manstein finally had the two things that he had wanted, and regarded as essential to restore the situation: mobility and reinforcements, particularly with armoured forces. He was also aware that the Russians were dangerously over-extended, and – with the right timing – Army Group South could use its mobile assets in First and Fourth Panzer Armies and the SS Panzer Corps to inflict a damaging reverse on the Red Army. It was only by doing this that the integrity of the front line could be restored and the persisting threat to the entire southern sector removed. On top of his previous problems, he was now running out of time; at best, he could expect a further month before the spring thaw brought all operations to a halt for several weeks. Both sides would use the thaw to rebuild their strength, but unless the danger to the Dnepr crossings was eliminated, the Russians would simply resume their threatening attacks in the summer. Manstein therefore informed Hitler that he wished to use his forces to destroy the Russian forces in the southern Ukraine at the earliest opportunity; this would be achieved by First and Fourth Panzer Armies striking north while the SS Panzer Corps attacked towards the south, on converging axes. Thereafter, he would turn his attention to recapturing Kharkov.

By contrast, Hitler's priorities were the exact reverse. Still smarting from Hausser's decision to abandon Kharkov, he wished to recapture the city as soon as possible and demanded that this take priority over the planned operations against the Russian forces further south. He rejected Manstein's objections – that a counterattack at Kharkov would either fail or be forced to abandon any gains made if the Russian threat further south remained in place, and given that the spring thaw could be expected to set in along the Black Sea coast before it occurred further north around Kharkov, the priority should be on operations in the south. Once the thaw started in this region, there would still be time to recapture Kharkov provided the Russian forces in the south had been defeated. Nor was Hitler convinced by the arguments about the size of the Russian forces that were advancing in the gap between the southern wing of *Armee Abteilung Lanz* and the northern wing of First Panzer Army, or those that were attacking *Armee Abteilung Hollidt* on the Mius. At best, Hitler insisted, these represented a few burned-out formations, and it was wrong to prioritise their destruction over the recapture of an important city like Kharkov. Finally, he fell back on one of his favourite themes when having difficult discussions with military experts: if the Russians were left in possession of Kharkov and the Donets basin, the economic and industrial benefits they would accrue would be huge.

The preceding weeks had taught Manstein that it would take considerable patience to overcome Hitler's objections. On the first day of the conference, the best he could achieve was agreement that as it would take until 19 February for the SS Panzer Corps to complete its concentration in the area between Krasnograd and Kharkov, a final decision on whether it was to be sent north or south could be deferred until then. On the second day of Hitler's visit – 18 February – Manstein was able to report that the Russian forces that Hitler had repeatedly dismissed as being near the end of their strength had achieved several penetrations along the Mius. In addition, a substantial force was operating behind Hollidt's lines at Debaltsevo; although it had been restricted in its activities by a variety of units, it had not been possible to eliminate it. More importantly, Russian units from Kharitonov's Sixth Army had been identified south of Krasnograd, and Kuznetsov's First Guards Army had captured Pavlograd. Finally, Manstein informed Hitler that an immediate attack to retake Kharkov was impossible because a sudden thaw around Poltava had left wheeled elements of *SS-Totenkopf* stranded axle-deep in mud. This last argument was somewhat more tricky, as the previous day had seen Manstein insisting that the thaw would affect operations further south before reaching the Kharkov area, but nevertheless any immediate deployment of the SS Panzer Corps to retake Kharkov was impossible for the moment. Consequently, the available forces would be better used in a strike towards the south, as Manstein had proposed. Grudgingly, Hitler had to agree.

Manstein then moved on to discussions about the longer term. Even if his planned operations were successful, he doubted that the threat posed by the Red Army would be completely eliminated – come the summer, it was almost inevitable that the Russians would once more try to pin his forces against the Black Sea. The only way to avoid this was to start considering operational plans for the entire year, involving further mobile operations – in other words, the ceding of ground where necessary in order to draw the Russians into positions where they could be attacked and destroyed. The two men rapidly found themselves arguing at cross-purposes. The Russian units were badly degraded, Hitler insisted. But the German units were no better, retorted Manstein. The Führer replied that this would be remedied in the summer, and when Manstein pointed out the same applied to the Russians, Hitler diverted the argument into an insistence that Russian armaments production would be even greater if the resources of the Donets basin were to be held by the Red Army, and the new weapons that would soon be available to the German Army would remedy matters. Manstein's closing comments about the second day were succinct: 'We lived, it seemed, in two entirely different worlds.'[19]

The last day of Hitler's visit was 19 February, and Kleist was summoned from Army Group A to join the discussions. To Manstein's relief, Hitler ordered that the forces in the Kuban Peninsula should serve as a reservoir from which they could be dispatched to Army Group South when needed. Unfortunately, this would prove to be an almost empty gesture, and few troops would be withdrawn via the Crimea to help out in the Ukraine. Any doubts that might have persisted about the threat from the advancing Russian units were surely dispelled when it was reported that Russian tanks from Kuznetsov's First Guards Army had captured Sinsinokovo and cut the main railway line upon which the southern half of Manstein's army group depended; this also placed the Russian spearheads less than 40 miles (70km) from Hitler's current location. As the Führer's entourage boarded their planes and headed back to Germany, elements of the German 15th Infantry Division, which was part-way through being transferred from France to Fourth Panzer Army, were able to deploy against the Russian forces in Sinsinokovo and further north. With Russian tanks so close to Zaporozhye, it was also important to organise defences around the key city, and local Luftwaffe anti-aircraft units were formed into an ad hoc battlegroup, much as had been the case throughout the winter. The new group was placed under the command of none other than Rainer Stahel, who was enjoying a meteoric rise and had just been promoted to Generalmajor.

Countermeasures were already being taken to deal with the threatening Russian forces, though Manstein was forced to take considerable risks – in order to have any chance of success, his counterattacks would require all of the mechanised troops available, which meant that he had no choice but to strip the rest of the front line of armoured support. In particular, the Mius line held by *Armee Abteilung Hollidt* was left with just a few assault guns, but Manstein's calculation was simple: the counterstroke had to succeed, and he had to take whatever risk was necessary to achieve this. If it failed, the situation would tilt irrevocably in favour of the Russians anyway. The Russian forces that had penetrated the German defences along the line of the Mius and reached Debaltsevo belonged to VIII Cavalry Corps. Like all such units caught up in the fighting, the corps was badly below establishment strength and soon found itself stranded without fuel and little ammunition. It was isolated by 17th Panzer Division, but the consequence was that the German unit was tied up for critical days and unavailable for deployment elsewhere; in recognition of their breakthrough and prolonged resistance, the surviving elements of VIII Cavalry Corps were renamed VII Guards Cavalry Corps. Finally, late on 23 February, the remnants of the Russian cavalry broke out to the east. Both sides regarded the episode as a victory; the Germans felt that they had effectively knocked the corps out of the line of battle, whereas the Russians believed that the penetration had destroyed several German units and had tied down valuable German armoured forces.[20]

The Russian IV Guards Mechanised Corps also found itself isolated after forcing a path through the German defences along the Mius. The headquarters of Second Guards Army – to which the mechanised corps belonged – struggled to make contact with the isolated unit, and when radio communications were

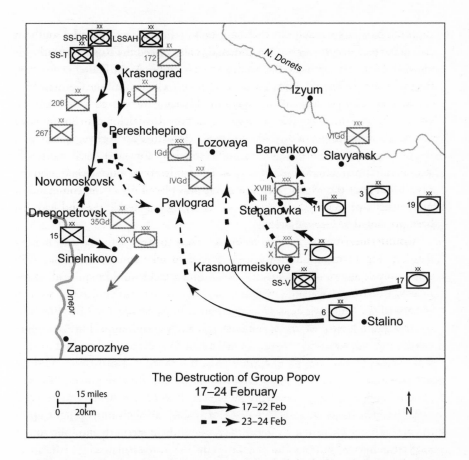

The Destruction of Group Popov
17–24 February

0   15 miles
0   20km

——▶ 17–22 Feb
- - ▶ 23–24 Feb

N

briefly restored, the orders from Biryuzov, chief of staff of Second Guards Army, for a withdrawal back to the Mius were dismissed as a German ruse. Finally, radio contact was established for long enough to allow for properly coded instructions to be sent:

> Fumbling for weak points in the enemy's defences, IV Guards Mechanised Corps first moved south, then was forced to turn back, and then began a fighting retreat carried out at night towards the east. It was unable to return to where it had broken through and thus didn't reach Second Guards Army, but further to our left it ran into Fifty-First Army. This caused new complications: in the dark it was taken for the enemy and came under fire.
>
> Soon, however, the misunderstanding was clarified, the artillery ceased firing, and IV Guards Mechanised Corps (or rather, the combat core of this once-formidable

formation) was again among its own. It was withdrawn for rest and replenishment. For skilful leadership in combat, the corps commander Lieutenant General [Trofim Ivanovich] Tanaschishin and chief of staff Colonel Zhdanov were awarded the Order of the Red Banner. For courage and bravery, orders and medals were also awarded to a large group of officers, sergeants and soldiers.[21]

The first of Manstein's counter-blows against the Russian forces was to be delivered by XL Panzer Corps. After pulling 7th Panzer Division out of Slavyansk, Heinrici was able to concentrate his forces for an attack on Krasnoarmeiskoye. Balck's 11th Panzer Division attacked immediately south of Kramatorsk on 18 February with an improvised team of snowploughs clearing the approach roads; each plough was followed by a squad of motorcycle-mounted infantry from the division's reconnaissance battalion, with tanks and half-tracks close behind. Within a few hours, 11th Panzer Division was firmly established astride Popov's supply lines. At the same time, *SS-Viking* and 7th Panzer Division moved against Krasnoarmeiskoye and Grishino.

The Russian IV Guards Tank Corps and 3rd Guards Motorised Rifle Brigade were almost annihilated by the German attack; by 18 February, the entire tank strength of IV Guards Tank Corps was just 17 tanks.[22] Although X Tank Corps had succeeded in reaching Krasnoarmeiskoye, it was only in marginally better shape and both corps were desperately short of fuel. Major General Pavel Pavlovich Poluboyarov, commander of IV Guards Tank Corps, did what he could to organise his defences and as 7th Panzer Division pushed into the centre of Krasnoarmeiskoye his troops launched determined counterattacks. In one such attack, the commander of the Russian 14th Guards Tank Brigade was killed, but he succeeded in bringing the German advance to a standstill. The attack by *SS-Viking* from the south also ran into strong resistance despite substantial air support by German dive-bombers.

Popov tried to respond to the calls for help from his subordinates. The armoured elements of Group Popov that were holding the line at Slavyansk and Kramatorsk were ordered to hand over their sectors to the group's infantry divisions, which were now arriving after struggling forward on the snowbound roads; once they had pulled out of their current positions, these units together with two ski brigades were to proceed with all possible speed to Krasnoarmeiskoye. But it would take at least two days for these forces to reach Poluboyarov, and his attempts to recapture key parts of the town with his own forces late on 18 February failed with heavy losses. The following day, 7th Panzer Division bypassed the northern defences of Krasnoarmeiskoye while *SS-Viking* and parts of 333rd

Infantry Division pushed into the town itself. To the north, the first attempts by III Tank Corps to march to Poluboyarov's aid were blocked by 11th Panzer Division. The last fighting in Krasnoarmeiskoye died down on 20 February, and the attacking Germans liberated a large group of prisoners – soldiers from Germany, Italy and Romania, railwaymen, and construction teams from the *Organisation Todt* – who had been held in the town since the arrival of the Russian armour. Abandoning their positions, the survivors of IV Guards Tank Corps infiltrated through the German cordon and ultimately managed to reach Barvenkovo, where they were later re-equipped with new tanks.

Despite this substantial setback and other signs that the Germans were about to launch a counteroffensive – aerial reconnaissance detected the concentration of German vehicles near Krasnograd and fresh forces moving east from the Dnepr crossings, rather than retreating as might have been expected – the Russians remained confident. Even during the desperate fighting in Krasnoarmeiskoye, Poluboyarov received an order demanding that he encircle the German units in the area and prevent their withdrawal. During the afternoon of 20 February, Lieutenant General Semen Pavlovich Ivanov, chief of staff of Southwest Front, still believed that the assembly of German forces near Krasnograd – two divisions of the SS Panzer Corps – was a precursor to a withdrawal from the Mius line towards the lower Dnepr, and accordingly urged all the mobile units in Southwest Front to press forward and reach their objectives 'at any cost'.[23] The German armour, according to Ivanov, would be used in an attempt to defeat the leading elements of any Russian units that stood in the way of the planned retreat, and the battle for Krasnoarmeiskoye was interpreted in this light, as evidence that the Germans were still planning a major withdrawal and the counterattack was merely an attempt to buy space and time for this to happen. The problem was not so much one of failing to detect German movements, but rather of misinterpreting them, and many senior Russian officers were in the dangerous position of interpreting whatever they saw to fit what they already believed.

Whilst Ivanov's assessment may seem hugely over-optimistic, it is worth considering what the overall picture must have looked like from the perspective of *Stavka* and commanders down to army level. The opening offensive of the winter – *Uranus* – had effectively knocked the Romanian Third and Fourth Armies out of contention, and had led to the encirclement and ultimate destruction of Paulus' Sixth Army, easily the densest concentration of German forces on the Eastern Front. The attempt to break the Stalingrad encirclement had been defeated with substantial losses on both sides, and at the same time

Little Saturn tore apart the Italian Eighth Army and further damaged the few German forces available along the middle Don. The Germans had been forced to abandon substantial territory in the Caucasus and despite their best efforts had left behind large quantities of equipment, and the Ostrogozhsk-Rossosh Operation had eliminated the Hungarian Second Army. In total, one German army had been annihilated at Stalingrad, another – Fourth Panzer Army – had been badly damaged during the fighting for the city and the failed relief attempt, and four armies of Germany's allies had been destroyed. Following on from this, the German Second Army had also been smashed and driven back in complete disarray.

Although the opening phases of both *Gallop* and *Star* had fallen behind schedule, they had still succeeded in making substantial gains, despite starting the offensives with units that were far from being at full strength and were operating at the end of badly stretched lines of supply and communication. The forces of Southwest Front had struggled to sweep aside the German defences at Slavyansk and Popov's group had not been able to sustain its drive towards the Sea of Azov, but success appeared to be tantalisingly close. The German abandonment of Kharkov also contributed to Russian optimism; *Stavka* would have been aware of Hitler's order to hold the city at all costs, yet the supposedly loyal SS had chosen to pull back – this had to be a sign that the Germans were close to the end of their strength.

When the empires of Europe rushed headlong into the First World War, there was a prevailing doctrine – despite evidence from recent conflicts such as the Anglo-Boer War and the Russo-Japanese War – that offensive operations were the only way to win a conflict, and a similar belief about offensive operations seems to have existed in *Stavka* in the Second World War. To an extent, this derived from the extensive writing on armoured and mechanised warfare by Red Army theoreticians between the wars and was further reinforced by the clear successes of German armoured forces in the opening campaigns of the war. However, there was as yet little awareness of the equal value of armoured forces in counterattacks against over-extended attacking formations – instead, the Red Army chosen to counter German armoured units by the extensive use of anti-tank guns employed in large numbers as a *Pakfront*. Balck had demonstrated perhaps better than anyone the manner in which a concentrated, well-led armoured force could defeat disjointed but numerically superior enemy forces in a series of attacks carried out with energy and precision, but it was perhaps too soon for those lessons to have been recognised and learned. For the moment the pre-war predilection of the Red Army for offensive operations had been reinforced by the apparent inability of German forces to stop attacks, and this, combined with over-optimistic interpretations of the current situation, led the Russians into a dangerously exposed situation.[24]

Manstein now had his forces broadly in position for his planned counterstroke, and equally importantly the Russians had inadvertently positioned their armies in vulnerable positions. Hoth's Fourth Army headquarters had successfully pulled back from the lower Don, covered by *Armee Abteilung Hollidt*, to Dnepropetrovsk, and was now given control of Hausser's SS Panzer Corps in addition to XLVIII Panzer Corps, which consisted of 6th and 17th Panzer Divisions. These two corps would be used to attack either side of the Russian forces penetrating between Krasnograd and Krasnoarmeiskoye. *LSSAH* was detached from the SS Panzer Corps and would remain under the control of Lanz and would protect the northern flank of this counterattack, and once the two panzer corps' attacks had met in or near Lozovaya, their divisions were to continue towards the Donets and thus outflank from the south the Russian forces that had taken control of Kharkov. First Panzer Army's XL Panzer Corps, with 7th and 11th Panzer Divisions and *SS-Viking*, was to attack north from Krasnoarmeiskoye towards Barvenkovo, thus eliminating the units of Group Popov. Only after the Russians had been driven back to the line of the Donets would the German forces move to recapture Kharkov.

After a winter of miscalculation and misfortune, it was inevitable that sooner or later, the Germans would experience some good luck, and Manstein benefited from this in two ways. Firstly, as already described, his leapfrogging of First and Fourth Panzer Armies to the west was perceived by the Russians as evidence of headlong retreat, encouraging them to strive harder to reach the Dnepr before the Germans could escape. Secondly, Hitler's near-endless prevarication probably delayed the beginning of Manstein's counterstroke considerably, giving the Red Army more time to plunge headlong towards the west and thus expose its forces to the coming German attack. Even with this good fortune, the planned operation would be a risky endeavour, with many of the formations used to launch it – particularly the divisions of First and Fourth Panzer Armies – badly depleted after months of near-continuous combat.

It is hard to overstate the magnitude of Manstein's achievement in getting his forces into position for the counterstroke. Getting permission to withdraw German forces from the Caucasus was of course an essential element, as was the arrival of fresh troops from the west to replace those lost in Stalingrad and the collapse of the armies of Germany's allies. The former had taken endless arguments with Hitler, and delivering sufficient fuel and train capacity to achieve the withdrawal had stretched the logistic capabilities of the Wehrmacht to the limit. It is worth remembering that this was achieved against the context of constant partisan harassment of supply lines that stretched for hundreds of miles across occupied territory. Both the logistic effort and the transfer of troops to the Ukraine were further hindered by developments elsewhere. The disaster at Stalingrad coincided with Montgomery's comprehensive victory at El Alamein, followed by *Torch*, the American landings in North Africa; characteristically, Hitler refused to cut his losses and instead of salvaging what he could from the forces that had been sent to North Africa, he insisted on dispatching further reinforcements to what was effectively a lost cause. Fighting continued until May when the last remaining German forces surrendered in Tunisia, but the unwillingness of Vichy French forces to fight the Americans ensured that ultimately, even if Rommel's *Afrika Korps* could recover from its defeat at El Alamein, it would be comprehensively outflanked by the predominantly American forces advancing from the west. The diversion of troops and more importantly logistic capacity towards North Africa added to the considerable strains of supplying and reinforcing the German forces in the Ukraine, but from the Russian point of view, this was far less than what they expected from the Western Allies.

Stalin had been pressing the British and Americans to open a front against Germany in the west, and at first the Americans at least had been inclined to comply. In March 1942, Roosevelt wrote to Churchill:

> I am becoming more and more interested in the establishment of a new front this summer on the European continent, certainly for air [operations] and raids … And even though losses will doubtless be great, such losses will be compensated by at least equal German losses and by compelling the Germans to divert large forces of all kinds from the Russian front.[25]

A few weeks later, General George Marshall, the US chief of staff, visited London with two proposals. One, codenamed *Roundup*, was for major landings in France by 48 Allied divisions in the spring of 1943, but the other, codenamed *Sledgehammer*, was a more modest attempt to capture either Brest or Cherbourg – or potentially both – in the autumn of 1942. This latter operation would be carried out initially by mainly British Empire forces, as the US Army was not yet ready to contribute substantial numbers of troops. The intention was to secure control of either Brittany or the Cotentin Peninsula and then build up substantial forces there during the winter of 1942–43 as American divisions became available before attempting a breakout. The British were not at all enthusiastic for a variety of reasons. Firstly, they believed that there was insufficient amphibious capacity for *Roundup* or even the more modest *Sledgehammer*. Secondly, British forces were already heavily committed elsewhere, for example in North Africa and the Far East. Thirdly, even if a port could be captured on the French coast, it was highly likely that the Germans would be able to deploy mines and U-boats in sufficient numbers to make it almost impossible to reinforce the landings as planned. Finally, the British suggested that it might be better to commit the inexperienced US Army to battle first in a less critical sector, such as North Africa, before taking on the might of the Wehrmacht in continental Europe. Despite American enthusiasm, *Sledgehammer* was in reality an utterly impossible undertaking. At best, six divisions could have been landed, and would have been opposed by at least 30 German divisions, several of them panzer divisions that had been resting and re-equipping in France. It was wildly unlikely that any ground seized in the initial operation could be held through the winter – the forces in the captured port, with their supplies dependent upon the ability of the Allied navies to clear German minefields and U-boats, would potentially have had to face substantial German counterattacks and even if they had survived, a breakout would have had to force defences that would have had ample time to be reinforced. The result would almost certainly have been losses on the scale of the First World War. Any lingering doubts were ended by the failure of Operation *Rutter* at Dieppe on 19 August 1942, when about 6,000 men, mainly Canadians, were deployed to test the feasibility of capturing a port for a short period. Over 60 per cent of those who were put ashore were lost, leaving the German propaganda service triumphantly proclaiming that they had defeated a full invasion attempt, though the Wehrmacht forces were left puzzled by the entire operation – one interrogator asked Canadian prisoners: 'Too big for a raid, too small for an invasion. What were you trying to do?'[26] *Rutter* demonstrated conclusively the gap between current capabilities and those required for a successful invasion of continental Europe, with the result that *Roundup* was postponed from mid-1943 to mid-1944, and eventually metamorphosed into *Overlord*. In the meantime, the British and Americans decided to proceed with the invasion of North Africa as an opportunity to develop further their amphibious capability and to build up the experience and fighting power of the US Army.

But whilst the invasion of North Africa resulted in the diversion of considerable German logistic resources, it fell far short of Moscow's demands for a second front, and there was a widespread belief that the failure of the Western Allies to establish such a front was largely responsible for the German recovery on the Eastern Front – if German troops had been tied down in France or elsewhere in Western Europe, it would have been impossible for Manstein to receive the stream of reinforcements that allowed him to restore the front line. In the years after the war, many Soviet writers interpreted the delay in creating this second front as a deliberate policy by the capitalist west to allow Germany a free hand against the Soviet Union, and that far from drawing off German forces to the west in order to ease the pressure upon the Russians, the Red Army drew ever more German forces against it to the benefit of the Western Allies. In his memoirs, Vasilevsky wrote:

> Stalin told me [on 16 February 1943] that ... a message had been sent on behalf of the Soviet Government to ... Roosevelt and ... Churchill. This had said that instead of the promised help to the USSR by diverting the German troops from the Soviet-German front the opposite had happened: because of the feeble British-American operations in Tunisia, Hitler had been able to move additional forces to the Eastern Front ... Therefore, the Soviet government insisted that the second front be opened in Europe, in particular in France, before the latter part of 1943.[27]

Whilst they were clearly delighted that, after all their losses and setbacks, they were finally getting to grips with the German invaders, Russian soldiers in the front line also speculated on when the Soviet Union's allies might be able to divert German resources away from the Eastern Front. Zdanovich, whose infantry division had struggled in vain to reach Badanov's tanks at Tatsinskaya, asked Lieutenant General Alexei Sergeyevich Zheltov, a visiting staff officer from Southwest Front, about the prospects of a 'Second Front' in the west:

> Zheltov thought about it. Approaching the table on which my map was spread, he looked at it, then at me. A merry spark flashed in his eyes.
> 'In the old days there was a good proverb: rely on God, and do your best. God, as we now know, doesn't exist. Similarly, the Second Front of the allies still doesn't exist. We will wait for it – for now. But as for ourselves, we have to rely on our own strength.'
> And [he] began to tell in detail how the economic and military potential of our country was growing day by day. The selflessness of the workers of the rear and the rapid introduction of new techniques made it possible to give the army

an ever-increasing number of tanks, guns, and aircraft. The task of the front-line soldiers was to pursue the Nazis as quickly as possible, in spite of any difficulties.

'In general, rely on yourself and do not give the enemy any respite,' summarised Zheltov.[28]

Regardless of these arguments, the redeployment of German forces from the Caucasus and Western Europe to help restore the Eastern Front was a huge logistic undertaking for the Wehrmacht, particularly as Army Group Don succeeded in moving considerable quantities of supplies in to the Kuban region at the same time to replenish Seventeenth Army. Moreover, this merely provided the military forces for Manstein to attempt to restore the front. In addition, his planned operation could only succeed if the Russians were where he expected them to be – in other words, he had to anticipate Russian intentions and modify his own plans accordingly. Finally, the timing of the counteroffensive called for careful coordination across a vast battlefield – Kharkov lies about 206 miles (332km) from Mariupol on the coast of the Sea of Azov. Some units – such as XL Panzer Corps at Krasnoarmeiskoye – had to start their attacks earlier than others for local tactical reasons, yet it was vital that this did not alert the Russians to what was coming. The timing of the entire operation was of course critical – too soon, and the Russians would be able to react and take countermeasures, but too late, and the Red Army would have cut the German supply lines and the spring thaw would bring all mobile operations to an abrupt end. It speaks volumes about his intellectual capabilities that, whilst conducting repeated and exhausting negotiations with Hitler, Manstein was able to keep abreast of the constant flow of intelligence and reconnaissance material arriving in his headquarters, correlate this with the current locations of his own forces, and modify his plans as required. The ability to juggle the variables of force, space and time is a rare attribute, and to do so under immense stress, with so much depending on the outcome, is rarer still.

But even with all of these factors considered and exploited to the full, there remained the matter of executing the plan. Although the Russian forces were badly depleted by months of fighting and were operating at the end of long supply lines, they remained numerically stronger than the German forces facing them. Manstein's subordinates had the prerogative of all attackers in that they could – within certain constraints – concentrate their forces where they chose, but success in the coming fighting would depend hugely on the manner in which Manstein's plans were carried out down to the lowest level. Throughout the war, German troops – particularly those in the panzer divisions – had demonstrated a flair and skill for mobile warfare that generally left other armies floundering in their wake, but the Red Army had improved hugely from its clumsy efforts in the first weeks of *Barbarossa*. With considerable justification, officers in the Wehrmacht continued to believe that at a tactical level, they and their men were more than a match for any forces deployed against them, but on the Eastern Front the gap had narrowed considerably. The philosophy of *Auftragstaktik* – the doctrine of delegating a task to a trusted, highly trained subordinate, but making the subordinate aware of the overall mission and thus giving him as much autonomy and room for improvisation as possible – had contributed hugely to the German victories of the opening years of the war. That doctrine and the excellence that underpinned it would be vital in the coming days.

After a brief pause to regroup and take on supplies, the SS divisions were ready to resume operations. On 19 February, even as Russian forces attempted to advance west from the Kharkov area, *SS-Das Reich* attacked suddenly from its forming up area south of Krasnograd in three columns and made good initial progress. However, the German attack started with signs of friction between the Wehrmacht and SS. When the chief of staff of the SS Panzer Corps, Standartenführer Werner Ostendorff, contacted Manstein's headquarters in mid-morning to give an update on progress, he added that he regarded the intention of Army Group South to send a liaison officer to the SS Panzer Corps as a 'vote of mistrust' in the staff officers of the corps. In response, Manstein's chief of staff agreed to refer the matter to *OKH* for resolution. During the afternoon, the reply came back from *OKH*: Zeitzler had sided with Manstein. However much the SS resented the arrangement, they would have to live with it.[29] Resistance to *SS-Das Reich* grew through the battle, but late the following night its troops managed to secure the town of Pereshchepino, an advance of 18 miles (30km). Importantly, the road and rail crossings over the river that ran through the town were captured intact, allowing for continuation of the attack towards the south. Without a pause, the advance continued and by mid-morning on 20 February the town of Maryanovka, a further 21 miles (34km) to the south, was in German hands. During the afternoon, the leading elements reached Novomoskovsk and linked up with elements of the German 15th Infantry Division, which had advanced from the west.

The fallout that resulted from the Soviet recapture of Kharkov claimed one more victim on 20 February. Hubert Lanz, in whose eponymous *Armee Abteilung* the SS Panzer Corps had been operating when Hausser deliberately disobeyed Hitler's orders to hold Kharkov at all costs, was removed from his post and replaced by General Werner Kempf. The official reason was that Lanz's previous command experience was with mountain troops and infantry, whereas Kempf had commanded 6th Panzer Division during the French campaign and then led XLVIII Panzer Corps from the beginning of *Barbarossa* until September 1942, when he was briefly placed in reserve. Now, Hitler nominated him as Lanz's replacement, justifying the decision on the grounds that an experienced commander of armoured forces was required. This was more than a little harsh on Lanz, who had shown no weakness in handling armour, and had assiduously attempted to enforce Hitler's order that the SS Panzer Corps should not retreat from Kharkov. Unable or unwilling to punish Hausser for his act of disobedience, Hitler chose instead to dismiss Lanz.

After a short spell in reserve, Lanz was dispatched to the Balkans where he took command of XLIX Mountain Corps and then XXII Mountain Corps. Here, he was heavily involved in the actions to disarm Italian troops on the Greek islands after Mussolini was overthrown and the new Italian government negotiated an armistice with the British and Americans. The German troops under Lanz's control were responsible for carrying out orders that the Italians were not to be taken prisoner on the grounds that their nation had betrayed Germany, and over 5,100 Italian soldiers were killed on Cefalonia alone. When his troops occupied Corfu, Lanz ordered the execution of nearly 30 Italian officers and the disposal of their bodies at sea. These incidents weren't the first occasion that Lanz had been involved in war crimes; in 1941, he was commander of the German 1st Mountain Division when it captured Lvov, and the troops found that the retreating Soviet authorities had carried out mass executions in the city prison. The Germans blamed this on Jews working for the NKVD and a bloody pogrom against the Jewish civilian population of Lvov followed. Initially at least, the perpetrators of the pogrom were Ukrainians who had formed an ad hoc militia, and their actions were praised in a report by the RSHA:

> During the first hours after the departure of the Bolsheviks, the Ukrainian population took praiseworthy action against the Jews ... About 7,000 Jews were seized and shot by the police [i.e. the self-appointed militia] in retribution for inhuman acts of cruelty.[30]

Even if many of the killings were carried out by the Ukrainian population of the city, the SS *Einsatzgruppe C*, operating in Army Group South's area, rapidly took control and thereafter the Ukrainian militia operated under German supervision. In any event, Lanz's troops made no attempt to stop the slaughter, which accounted for over 4,000 Jews in just a few days – Lanz even published a proclamation blaming the Jews for their 'provocation' of the Ukrainian population of the city.[31] Nor were the events on the Greek islands the last atrocities with which he was associated. In late 1943, after a German officer was murdered by partisans, Lanz ordered the indiscriminate artillery bombardment of a Greek village, resulting in the deaths of 82 civilians. After the war he was convicted of war crimes and sentenced to 12 years' imprisonment in the Nuremberg Trials, but released in 1951. His alleged involvement in plots to arrest or even kill Hitler should be seen in this context – he was not the only senior German figure charged with war crimes who tried to claim that they had been part of one or other of the anti-Nazi groups. However, it is worth bearing in mind that those who opposed Hitler did so for many reasons. A few, such as Freytag-Loringhoven, Groscurth and Kleist, were genuinely appalled by the racial policies of the Third Reich and the brutal mistreatment of civilians in Poland and the Soviet Union, but others, particularly those from the traditional Prussian *Junker* families that had always provided Prussia and Germany with its officers, were motivated more by fear that Hitler was leading Germany to military defeat, and such motivation was not incompatible with collaborating with and participating in the behaviour of the SS and other organisations against Jews, communists and other 'undesirables'.

The advance by *SS-Das Reich* had serious consequences for the Russian attempts to advance towards the west. The division established a series of strongpoints along its line of march and these fended off several Russian attacks both from the east, as Russian reinforcements and supply formations moved up, and the west, where 267th Rifle Division and 106th Rifle Brigade suddenly found their lines of communication had been cut. *SS-Totenkopf* was ordered to assemble at Krasnograd so that it could support its sister division and the attack could be continued beyond Novomoskovsk towards Pavlograd, and in the meantime *SS-Das Reich* and 15th Infantry Division did what they could to fend off Russian counterattacks through the morning of 21 February. As elements of *SS-Totenkopf* took over many of the strongpoints along the line, *SS-Das Reich* was able to concentrate its forces in and around Novomoskovsk. However, despite the clear evidence of a strong German counterattack and the isolation of perhaps half the combat strength of Kharitonov's Sixth Army, the Russians remained confident that they still held the initiative. In an attempt to give his front's advance renewed impetus, Vatutin ordered I Guards Tank Corps and XXV Tank Corps – effectively his entire armoured reserve – to move rapidly to the area around Pavlograd, not to block the German attack but to advance further to the west. This new mobile group was ordered to push on to the Dnepr and secure crossings by the end of 22 February.

Whilst the SS Panzer Corps consolidated its position around Novomoskovsk, Vatutin's new mobile group began its thrust towards the Dnepr, bypassing

German positions in Sinelnikovo and advancing to within 15 miles (25km) of Zaporozhye. The only concession to the German threat from the north was the deployment of two of I Guards Tank Corps' brigades to cover the northwest approaches to Poltava – the entire corps would have been hard-pressed to deal with a powerful 'panzergrenadier' division like *SS-Das Reich*, and two weak brigades represented a completely inadequate force.[32] In addition, Vatutin asked Voronezh Front to divert its forces towards the south in order to put pressure upon the German forces moving towards Pavlograd, but at this stage he saw this merely as dealing with an irritating local problem rather than the decisive switch in momentum that was actually occurring.

Having regrouped in and around Novomoskovsk, *SS-Totenkopf* and *SS-Das Reich* set off on 22 February towards Sinelnikovo and Pavlograd; however, icy roads delayed the arrival of much of *SS-Totenkopf*. One of the formations of *SS-Das Reich*, Panzergrenadier Regiment *Deutschland*, reached the outskirts of Pavlograd in mid-morning, and shortly after other elements of the division linked up with 15th Infantry Division's units that had been holding Sinelnikovo. The Russian units in the path of the advancing SS formations – mainly from First Guards Army's IV Guards Rifle Corps – were put to flight, and fresh columns of Russian troops crushed as they arrived.

Even now, Vatutin continued to urge his units on. The mobile force's orders remained to push up to the Dnepr and to seize crossings, while Sixth Army – much of which had been left isolated by the advance of *SS-Das Reich* – was ordered to secure Krasnograd with its northern flank as soon as possible. The reality on the ground was very different; almost out of ammunition and other supplies, the soldiers of 267th Rifle Division and 106th Rifle Brigade abandoned their heavy equipment and filtered back to the east through the thin line of strongpoints that the SS had established in their rear. Having advanced as far as it could, the mobile force committed to reach and cross the Dnepr was – like almost every Red Army formation at this stage of the campaign – desperately short of fuel, ammunition and food, and almost stationary. *Stavka* issed orders late on 22 February to Voronezh Front confirming that, as requested by Vatutin the previous day, it was to send Third Tank Army and Sixty-Ninth Army towards the south. This in turn required Fortieth Army further north to expand its sector, depleting its forces for any further local advances. The success of the SS counterattack towards the south thus helped the hard-pressed northern wing of *Armee Abteilung Kempf*, as the Russian forces that had been applying pressure to 168th Infantry Division were now forced to cover a larger segment of front line and could no longer concentrate their forces for further attacks. Despite this, the

Russians succeeded in enveloping the northern flank of the German division at Akhtyrka and driving it back with heavy casualties and the loss of almost all its heavy equipment and artillery. Regardless of the successes further south, there was now a danger that Russian forces would succeed in breaking apart the northern flank of Kempf's group and then push deep into its rear areas. The bulk of *Grossdeutschland* was being extracted from the front line in order to create a motorised strike force and further reinforcements from the west were expected in the first week of March, but until then it was necessary to make do with what was available. As if to underline the absurdity of Hitler's assertion that a few battalions of Tiger tanks would be sufficient to turn the tide, Strachwitz reported that the efficacy of his new tanks was limited both by supply shortages and teething problems. Within days, most of them had been temporarily withdrawn from service in the panzer regiment of *Grossdeutschland*, though they continued to see action with the SS divisions.[33]

At this point, Hoth – under whose Fourth Panzer Army the SS Panzer Corps was currently operating – unleashed the southern component of his counterattack. XLVIII Panzer Corps now consisted of 6th and 17th Panzer Divisions, and these struck north on 23 February. Despite their losses through the long winter's fighting, they remained formidable units, especially when their various components were able to cooperate and the divisions were able to work together. At first, this was hindered by snow-clogged roads that prevented all of 6th Panzer Division's units being available on 23 February, but the attack rapidly gained momentum. Even if supplies had been available for the Russian I Guards Tank Corps and XXV Tank Corps, their lines of communication were cut when 6th Panzer Division linked up with *SS-Das Reich*. To make matters worse, the isolated Russian tanks now came under sustained air attack. Over the next few days, the surviving personnel abandoned their vehicles and, like the infantry that had been cut off by *SS-Das Reich* in its opening attack, set off on foot towards the east.

SS-Totenkopf was also beginning to make its presence felt. On 23 February, it attacked towards the southeast either side of Popasnoye (a little to the north of Pavlograd), making good progress against a weak Russian tank brigade and 35th Guards Rifle Division; as the advance continued to Vyasovok, it encountered increasing resistance as Russian forces began to concentrate to try to prevent encirclement of units further west and south. At the same time, *LSSAH* launched a sudden attack on the Russian infantry facing it, overrunning the headquarters of 172nd Rifle Division, but in view of the danger to the northern flank of *Armee Abteilung Kempf*, all of the formations west of Kharkov were ordered to shorten their front line to allow for mobile forces to be released, particularly the formations of *Grossdeutschland*. However, the orders from *Stavka* for Russian forces to switch their efforts to the south greatly reduced the ability of Fortieth Army to exploit its successes against 168th Infantry Division at Akhtyrka. Although further ground was gained in the coming days, progress was slow and the crisis for the German defences had actually passed.

24 February saw little sign that the Russians were aware of the impending catastrophe, other than trying to speed up the redeployment of forces towards the south – in particular, they made no attempt to stop further attacks in the north. As a result, energy continued to be dissipated on attempts to advance, and troops continued to move in directions that effectively placed them in ever greater danger. Shafarenko's 25th Guards Rifle Division had been transferred from Fortieth Army to Third Tank Army on 19 February, and now found itself under the command of Sixty-Ninth Army; for the tired men, short of ammunition and other supplies, it made little difference as they laboured forward through thick snow. Shtykov and his fellow regimental commanders were summoned to a conference:

> There was an acute shortage of ammunition.
>
> As it turned out, our regiment wasn't the only one in this situation. The other regimental commanders at the meeting said the same thing: there was no ammunition, nothing with which to fight. Listening to all these complaints, the acting head of the rear echelons of the division, Captain Pisarev, finally replied: 'Where can I get more? The division has been transferred to Rybalko's army. And its stores are literally empty. If only there were more transport. We have one hope – Fortieth Army, our former command. Maybe they'll help out for old times' sake? They have ammunition in Kazachia Lopani, it's not far. I'll try to negotiate. But the regimental commanders must help me. You need to find horses, carts, and trucks. Otherwise I can do nothing.'
>
> 'And I think the commanders shouldn't have to worry about such matters,' said Pavlov, the head of the political department of the division, who was present at the meeting. 'Better that they concentrate on leading the military operations of their regiments. The situation is complicated, comrades. But as for the provision of transport – we, the political section of the division, will do this. And immediately! Time does not wait. In the south, our troops are already withdrawing to the Donets. This blue arrow on the operations section's map marks the position of the Nazis – we must move in this direction, and then hold on!'
>
> 'We will keep going, we are Guards,' said Colonel Guselnikov, the artillery commander of the division, thoughtfully. 'But for how long? After all, the infantry

[of Third Tank Army] is already engaged. Its units have almost no anti-tank resources. And the army started to run out of T-34s long ago. It's only a tank army in name.'

Briefly, the division commander assured us then that he would take all measures to provide units with ammunition. And in conclusion he said, 'Tomorrow, on the day of the 25th anniversary of the Red Army and the Navy, we will fight with all our resources. I will transfer to the regiments all the transport assets of the division. And the commanders of the units themselves should share with each other everything they can. We must again drive the enemy back. This will be our battle gift to the glorious anniversary.'[34]

This shows the continuing level of complacency – there was still no awareness that the Germans were mounting a powerful counteroffensive, and all concerns were centred on trying to find sufficient supplies to continue the Red Army's advance. Despite the best efforts of all concerned, ammunition remained critically short, particularly for the artillery, thus greatly reducing its ability to support the division's infantry.

Meanwhile, after bringing forward supplies overnight, SS-Totenkopf continued its advance; repeated attempts by the Russians to attack SS-Das Reich from the northwest were beaten off on the outskirts of Pavlograd, and during the afternoon both SS divisions converged on Verbky, immediately to the northeast of the town, and linked up. Thereafter, the Germans were able to secure the rest of Pavlograd as well as strengthen their grip on the ground over which the two SS divisions had advanced. The remnants of the Russian 35th Guards Rifle Division, still supported by the surviving nine tanks of 16th Guards Tank Brigade, struggled in the face of heavy pressure both on the ground and from the air before falling back to the east; together with other Red Army units caught in the advance of the Germans, it was forced to abandon much of its heavy equipment. From the south, XLVIII Panzer Corps also continued to advance, with 6th Panzer Division clashing with the Russian 41st Guards Rifle Division. The Russian division was badly below strength, reporting on 21 February that it had barely 3,000 men and was almost out of ammunition, and could do little to stop the Germans. Major General Nikolai Petrovich Ivanov, the division commander, was killed in the fighting along with his second-in-command, the division commissar, and a regimental commander, and the broken remnants of the division escaped to the east, skirting around the outskirts of Pavlograd and leaving all their artillery behind on the battlefield.[35] To the east, 17th Panzer Division – reduced to just eight tanks and 11 assault guns – continued to advance against the Russian

III Tank Corps, but the weakness of the German forces was beginning to make itself felt; in its diary, 6th Panzer Division recorded that the advance was too fast to allow for thorough destruction of bypassed enemy formations, and in any case the advancing spearheads lacked the strength to maintain tight contact with each other and thus maximise their haul of prisoners.[36] Instead, they pressed on as best they could while the Russians slipped away between the German battlegroups, albeit at the cost of abandoning their heavy weapons.

Having started both *Gallop* and *Star* with formations that were significantly below full strength, the front and army commanders of the Red Army had already committed their modest reserves and had all of their available units in the front line. The only way to respond to the German attacks was to try to shift units from one sector to another, just as the Germans had been forced to improvise during and after *Uranus*. For the Russians, there were additional difficulties. The rear area behind the German, Romanian, Hungarian and Italian armies had been largely under the control of Axis forces for several months, whereas the Red Army was operating over newly re-conquered territory, with damaged roads, bridges and railways. Even if forces could be found to move laterally, their redeployment was a time-consuming business, adding to traffic problems as the redeploying units repeatedly encountered supply units struggling to move from east to west.

To make matters worse, the enforced withdrawal of Luftwaffe units to air bases further west proved to have a substantial silver lining: these new bases were far closer to supply depots and the German homeland, and it was therefore far less difficult to provide spare parts in a timely manner. At times during the late summer and autumn of 1942, Luftwaffe units had struggled to get more than 30 per cent of their aircraft into usable condition, but availability now increased steadily. By contrast, Russian fighters and bombers were still operating from their original airfields to the east – even if new airfields could be captured or improvised as the Russian armies moved west, providing them with adequate fuel and ammunition placed unachievable demands on the hard-pressed logistic services. The combination of reduced Russian air cover and a slowly recovering Luftwaffe meant that the constant traffic jams in the rear areas of the front line came under repeated air attacks, adding further to delays both in redeployment of fighting units and the movement of vital supply columns.

The *Voyenno-Vozdushnye Sily* ('military air forces') or VVS had, like the Soviet Union's ground forces, started the war with huge disadvantages. Its ranks had been badly affected by Stalin's purges; 15 out of 16 air army commanders were removed, and more than 75 per cent of all senior VVS officers were executed, imprisoned, demoted or dismissed.[37] Much like the Soviet Union's armoured forces, the air force was equipped with a large inventory of equipment of varying usefulness. Even if the planes had been modern and effective, the fleet was crippled by shortages of spares of all kinds, and the opening phases of *Barbarossa* saw huge losses as the experienced Luftwaffe fighter pilots rapidly established control of the air and Luftwaffe bombers hammered Russian airfields – for the loss of only 35 aircraft (and only 20 in combat), German forces destroyed over 2,000 Russian planes in the first few days of the invasion.[38] By concentrating production largely on the highly effective Ilyushin Il-2 ground attack aircraft and the Yakovlev Yak-1 fighter, the *VVS* gradually recovered, but as the Luftwaffe had found in late 1942, even the best-equipped and best-trained air force struggled when confronted with long supply lines and difficult weather conditions.

While Vatutin might still have believed that victory was imminent, Popov had no such illusions. His X Tank Corps was reduced to only 17 tanks by 21 February and III Tank Corps was in even worse shape, with only 12 tanks. Together with XVIII Tank Corps – with only eight functioning tanks – these formations found themselves opposed by the increasingly aggressive forces of XL Panzer Corps, consisting of *SS-Viking* and 7th and 11th Panzer Divisions. Popov first requested permission to withdraw from his exposed positions before dawn on 21 February, but Vatutin brusquely refused, telling his subordinate that such a move would allow the Germans to withdraw safely to Dnepropetrovsk, and was contrary to the mission assigned to Popov's mobile group.[39] Far from withdrawing to the west, the Germans were intent upon destroying Popov's stranded tanks and 7th Panzer Division struck hard against X Tank Corps; whilst one battlegroup attempted to pin the Russians in their defensive positions, a second group moved northeast and tore into the rear area formations, reaching and capturing Stepanovka. To the west, *SS-Viking* advanced against III Tank Corps while 11th Panzer Division clashed repeatedly with XVIII Tank Corps, driving its survivors north. Together with the remnants of IV Guards Tank Corps and the infantry formations of Mobile Group Popov, the retreating Russian armour attempted to regroup as they withdrew, creating several short-lived ad hoc formations that managed to put up variable levels of resistance, but by the end of 24 February Popov's remaining troops, with almost no operational tanks, had been driven back to a line about 9 miles (15km) south of Barvenkovo. The forces of XL Panzer Corps were now moving north with XLVIII Panzer Corps on their left flank, driving all before them.

At this stage, even Vatutin had to face reality. The report sent by his headquarters to *Stavka* late on 24 February described the desperately weak state of his armoured spearheads; in an attempt to keep his tank formations moving, he (and other Russian commanders) had tried to emulate the Germans by ordering repair teams to accompany the advancing tank corps, but these units had now either been destroyed or overrun by the Germans and forced to abandon their equipment. He had no reserves left with which to combat the advancing Germans, and he ordered a halt to all offensive operations; he also made a further urgent request to *Stavka* for support from his northern neighbour. Regardless of the steps that the Russians took, the initiative had passed firmly to Manstein's formations. On 25 February, the SS units of XLVIII Panzer Corps, which had driven south to meet up with 6th and 17th Panzer Divisions, now swung their axis of advance towards the northeast, and together with XL Panzer Corps to the east, the German armoured formations launched a remorseless drive. From its starting positions immediately to the northeast of Pavlograd, *SS-Das Reich* was ordered to advance 28 miles (45km) to Lozovaya with *SS-Totenkopf* on its left flank. The advance began at first light and the leading elements reached Lozovaya in the middle of the day, where the Russians had set up a strong defensive line supported by artillery and anti-tank guns – the first properly constituted defensive line that the Red Army had set up to deal with the German counteroffensive. Throughout the day, the main forces of the SS divisions fought their way forward, struggling to make progress both due to Russian resistance and the badly degraded state of the roads, many of them choked by abandoned Russian vehicles and the wreckage created by Luftwaffe attacks, and as darkness fell Hoth urged both divisions on, but to no avail. Resistance, while still relatively disorganised in some sectors, was sufficient to prevent a rapid advance, and both SS divisions were having to contend with large bodies of Russian stragglers to the rear of their spearheads; many were simply trying to escape, while others were prepared to stand and fight.

A little to the east, XLVIII Panzer Corps was moving forward in the same direction. The immediate eastern neighbour of *SS-Das Reich* was 6th Panzer Division, and in a battle waged by units that were badly below strength on both sides, the Germans made steady if unspectacular progress against the Russian 41st Guards Rifle Division and 244th Rifle Division, which dug in around the village of Bogdanovka and mounted a determined stand. To the east of 6th Panzer Division, the leading elements of 17th Panzer Division enjoyed greater success, penetrating the thin defences of the Russian 195th Rifle Division, as the division commander later described:

> Our advance led us deep into the mass of the retreating Red forces. I saw long Russian columns battered by unopposed Stuka dive-bombers. Then my few tanks

would overrun the scattered remnants. Fierce fighting developed … The road was blocked by abandoned armoured scout cars, horse-drawn vehicles, wounded men and horses, and many dead. It was difficult to get through.[40]

Despite the difficulties of advancing through the debris of the Russian retreat, 17th Panzer Division finished the day significantly ahead of its neighbours; 6th Panzer Division was some distance behind to the west, while the divisions of XL Panzer Corps to the east ran into determined Russian defences south of Barvenkovo. Kuznetsov had thrown everything he could gather into the path of the German advance in order to prevent his First Guards Army from being torn apart, and mixed elements of three rifle divisions and four tank corps – which collectively fielded perhaps 50 tanks – succeeded in holding up the German panzer formations.

Whilst Vatutin might have woken up to the threat that his forces faced, a few commanders were still urging their subordinates forward. On the same day that Vatutin and Kuznetsov struggled desperately to hold back the determined advance of Fourth Panzer Army, Moskalenko's Fortieth Army received orders from Voronezh Front to aid the advance of Sixty-Ninth Army on its southern flank towards Poltava, while still trying to advance towards Sumy in the north. The sum total of troops available to Moskalenko consisted of six rifle divisions and one tank corps, all badly under strength, and these were now required to operate across a front of 100 miles (146km). Largely because German strength was concentrated in the south, Fortieth Army was able to edge forwards, but as its leading elements approached Sumy, they encountered increasing resistance; the German 332nd Infantry Division, newly arrived from France, had just taken up positions in the town. Trying to capture Sumy before defences could be organised, Moskalenko fed units into the battle as they arrived rather than pausing to regroup, much as Paulus had done on a far larger scale in the advance to Stalingrad – weak infantry regiments, tank brigades with almost no tanks, and anti-tank regiments, all short of ammunition and other supplies. Fighting continued for several days with escalating losses, but the Germans remained in control of Sumy; it was one thing to probe forward through the thinly held German lines, but quite another to try to force defended positions with the exceedingly limited forces available. Increasingly worried about the exposed flanks of his army, where he had lost contact with the armies to either side, Moskalenko urged Voronezh Front to allow him to cease offensive operations. On 1 March, he finally received permission to do so and to take up defensive positions.[41]

Kuznetsov might have been able to gather 50 tanks to reinforce the defenders of Barvenkovo against First Panzer Army's XL Panzer Corps, but fuel shortages remained severe and almost all of the tanks were used in a stationary role, greatly reducing their efficacy. In heavy fighting, *SS-Viking* succeeded in advancing past the western edge of the defences while 7th Panzer Division bypassed them to the east. Leaving 11th Panzer Division to attack the Russians from the south, the two flanking divisions pressed on towards the Donets and Izyum. Amongst the Russian defenders of Barvenkovo were the men of 38th Guards Rifle Division; they had played a part in the bitter streetfighting in Stalingrad in the autumn and after a brief pause for replenishment had been involved in *Little Saturn*, and their thinned ranks now had to withstand the attacks of the resurgent Wehrmacht alongside what remained of 52nd Rifle Division, as Ivan Frolovich Klochkov, a junior officer at the time, later recalled:

> Surrounding the city, the Nazis brought down on its defenders heavy fire with mortars, artillery and massive air strikes. Wave after wave of enemy bombers, up to 60 at a time, flew to our positions, their tanks attacked, but the Guardsmen courageously repulsed the onslaught of the enemy, holding back his considerable forces. In these battles, we suffered heavy losses. The commander of 38th Guards Rifle Division, Major-General AA Onufriev, chief of staff of the division, Colonel Sachuk, many other officers, NCOs, and soldiers died bravely. Together with our commander, we had marched with IV Airborne Corps in the forests of Byelorussia, participated in bitter battles near Moscow, the Don, Stalingrad, Voronezh, Rostov and the Ukrainian lands. We loved and respected him for his courage and strove to follow his example. The commander of the division, the chief of staff and other heroes were buried in the city of Novy Liman with all military honors and we vowed over the graves to take revenge on the enemy for their death.
>
> After three days of hard fighting for Barvenkovo our division was ordered by the command of Southwest Front to leave the city and retreat to Izyum. The breakthrough was organised in several places. The commander of our 115th Regiment, Colonel Drobyshevsky, led the breakthrough of the enemy's positions on the northern outskirts of Barvenkovo ...
>
> For three days, the guardsmen conducted defensive rearguard battles with the enemy right up to the Northern Donets River. On the night of 1 March, near the village of Kamenka, the regiment broke through to the Northern Donets and occupied defensive positions along its left bank, near the town of Izyum ... Defensive battles began with the enemy units on the right (western) bank. In comparison with the hard winter battles, these seemed to us relatively low-key.[42]

Although 38th Guards Rifle Division and the neighbouring Russian units succeeded in pulling back to the line of the Donets, they were forced to abandon most of their heavy equipment.

The drive by the SS towards Lozovaya also resulted in bitter fighting as the Russian 58th Guards Rifle Division, supported by what remained of I Guards Tank Corps and I Guards Cavalry Corps, tried to hold back the German advance. *SS-Das Reich* gradually fought its way into the town while *SS-Totenkopf* advanced from the west, both towards Lozovaya and threatening to outflank the Russians to the north. During the afternoon of 26 February, the Russian defenders pulled back to the industrial sector in the northwest part of the town where they dug in once more. Whilst the German progress wasn't spectacular, it was remorseless and the defenders were running out of men and ammunition, but if the remnants of the Russian formations attempting to retreat were to escape, it was essential to hold back the Germans for as long as possible. While 58th Guards Rifle Division battled with *SS-Das Reich*, the weakened divisions of XV Rifle Corps fended off *SS-Totenkopf* and bought valuable time for 35th Guards Rifle Division and 267th Rifle Division to fight their way towards the northeast. A curious pattern began to develop, with the units of both sides moving broadly in the same direction; the German armoured formations lacked the infantry strength to create a continuous front and thus prevent the Russians from retreating, while the Russians were unable to outpace the German spearheads. Clashing regularly, both sides struggled towards the northeast along badly damaged roads that were choked with the wreckage of fighting and snow, often compounded by sudden thaws. Spring was drawing closer, and time was rapidly running out for a successful conclusion to Manstein's counteroffensive.

The day saw a notable casualty for the Germans. Obergruppenführer Theodor Eicke, commander of *SS-Totenkopf*, had lost contact with his division's panzer regiment and decided to fly to the unit in a light aircraft. The Fieseler Storch that was used for such tasks was a nimble machine, capable of operating from almost any open strip of ground, but it was vulnerable to ground fire. In the early afternoon, as it flew over a group of Russian troops attempting to escape from the advancing SS divisions, the plane was hit by ground fire and crashed. Eicke, a fellow SS officer, and the pilot were killed; the command of the division passed to Obergruppenführer Hermann Priess, the division's artillery regiment commander. Like many senior SS figures, Eicke was, to say the least, a man with an unsavoury past. He volunteered for service in the Bavarian Army at the outbreak of the First World War and spent the conflict as a regimental paymaster, and after the war, he became a policeman but was dismissed because of his involvement in violent demonstrations against the government. By this stage, he had become a member of the Nazi Party and was convicted of planning to bomb the meetings of political opponents; he fled to Italy, returning after Hitler came to power in 1933. Almost immediately, he clashed with *Gauleiter* Josef Bürckel, who had him detained in a mental asylum. However, Himmler had already taken an interest in Eicke and soon had him released. Shortly after, he was appointed commandant of the Dachau concentration camp, where he established a regime of strict discipline both for the guards and prisoners, a policy that was rapidly adopted as standard for all concentration camps. He played a leading role in Hitler's purge of the SA in 1934, personally executing Ernst Röhm, the leader of the SA, and became chief of the *Inspektion der Konzentrationslager* ('Concentration Camp Inspectorate'). He sided with Himmler in the struggle between the head of the SS and Reinhard Heydrich for control of the concentration camp network and was given command of the new *SS-Totenkopf* division when it was created in late 1939 using personnel from concentration camp guard units. Eicke had already seen action, leading a mixed force of SS cavalry and infantry into Poland, where his unit was heavily involved in attacks on the Polish Jews, notably in Włocławek and Bydgoszcz. Almost inevitably, *SS-Totenkopf* continued in a similar manner, with its personnel massacring 95 British prisoners of war in Le Paradis in Belgium in May 1940. During the opening months of *Barbarossa*, *SS-Totenkopf* saw service with Army Group North and was involved in the massacre of Russian soldiers and Baltic Jews; as has already been described, the tendency of the division to allocate time and resources to such activities resulted in less support for neighbouring Wehrmacht units engaged in battle against the Red Army, leading to repeated (and futile) protests. Given his loyal service to the Nazi Party and his brutal enforcement of discipline in the concentration camp system, Eicke was regarded with great favour by Hitler and he was treated as a hero after his death. One of the regiments of *SS-Totenkopf* was renamed in his honour.[43]

A little to the east of *SS-Totenkopf,* the fighting for Lozovaya continued to rage. *SS-Das Reich* attacked into the northern parts of the town after a powerful Stuka attack on 27 February and finally secured control of all but the industrial area, which was the centre of Russian resistance. Elements of the SS division had already started to exploit to the north beyond Lozovaya, leaving the last Russian defenders in their wake. To the west of *SS-Totenkopf,* there remained a small gap to the southern flank of *Armee Abteilung Kempf,* where *LSSAH* had fended off repeated Russian attacks for several days whilst also noting the southern movement of large Russian formations as units of Third Tank Army responded to orders to move their axis of advance towards the southwest. None of the Russian attacks succeeded in making any significant headway and the SS division rapidly recovered from the losses it had suffered in and around Kharkov through a mixture of reinforcements and the efforts of its repair teams. Perhaps the only consequence of the Russian attacks was that *LSSAH* was unable to withdraw units from its front line to form strike forces for a resumption of offensive operations. The southern flank of the division came under heavy pressure at Yeremeyevka, and Obergruppenführer Joseph 'Sepp' Dietrich, the commander of *LSSAH*, made repeated requests to be allowed to pull back the endangered units, but after a lengthy exchange of signals with Raus' headquarters it was agreed that the line would be held for the moment – *LSSAH* would use its modest mobile reserves to launch a series of counterattacks to break up the Russian forces threatening Yeremeyevka.[44]

As darkness fell on 27 February, Manstein spoke to Kempf by telephone. The concentration of the limited forces of the Russian Third Tank Army between the front line held by *LSSAH* and the advancing units of *SS-Totenkopf* had been observed by German reconnaissance units and it was time to deal with this threat; Manstein wanted *LSSAH* to advance towards the east, into the flank of Third Tank Army. Kempf replied that he had doubts whether *LSSAH* could free up sufficient resources for such an attack, as it was fully committed to holding its current sector of the front line. Luftwaffe reconnaissance suggested that the Russians were pulling back in front of the northern flank of *LSSAH*, but Kempf responded that this did not reflect the situation on the ground, where pressure remained strong. Further discussions followed between Kempf and Dietrich, and the latter reported that, slightly contrary to Kempf's doubts, he was confident that he could attack with at least one battlegroup with a good chance of success.[45] Given Dietrich's earlier requests to Raus for permission to withdraw his southern flank, it seems at the very least that the SS division was sending mixed messages to higher commands.

On 28 February, *Stavka* transferred command of Third Tank Army to Southwest Front with orders for it to attack towards Lozovaya so that it could come to the aid of Sixth Army's retreating units. Although Sixty-Ninth Army was to extend its front to allow Third Tank Army to concentrate on its new task, the former formation was still required to pursue its previous orders to advance towards the Dnepr – despite later suggestions that Vatutin was largely to blame for the excessive optimism that gripped higher commands, *Stavka* appears still to have been pursuing the drive to the Dnepr at the end of February, by which time Vatutin had no doubts about the magnitude of his mistake. Kazakov's troops were badly overstretched and he signalled Voronezh Front Headquarters that he doubted that he would be able to achieve his objectives. Golikov's response was appropriately acerbic: 'There remains a distance of 400–450km [240–270 miles] to the Dnepr, and 30–35 days until the spring thaw. Draw your conclusions and calculations from this.'[46]

The Russian plan to restore the situation called for an attack by Third Tank Army against *SS-Totenkopf*, and Rybalko's men struggled to get to their designated start line. XV Tank Corps and three rifle divisions marched through the last night of February and took up positions around Kegichevka, where they waited for XII Tank Corps. VI Guards Cavalry Corps, on the eastern flank of the planned attack, immediately came under pressure from elements of *SS-Totenkopf* as the German attack towards the north from Lozovaya continued. The headquarters of the SS Panzer Corps had a nasty surprise early on 28 February when it came under attack by Russian troops, presumably one of the many fragments of units that were trying to escape towards the northeast, and the soldiers of the corps signals battalion suffered substantial losses before a nearby anti-aircraft battery drove off the Russians; shortly after, the flak gunners called in a Luftwaffe airstrike, which rapidly dispersed the Russian attackers. A little to the north, the resistance of the Russian troops who had struggled to hold Lozovaya began to fall away and the bulk of *SS-Das Reich* made steady progress, advancing about 12 miles (20km) during the day. Further west, 6th Panzer Division moved up alongside, with 17th Panzer Division reaching the banks of the northern Donets; only the remnants of I Guards Cavalry Corps stood between the rest of the advancing German armour and the river. *SS-Viking* and 7th Panzer Division also reached the northern Donets, the latter penetrating into the southern parts of Izyum.

Even at this stage, the German counteroffensive had achieved a great deal. Realistically, any Russian hope of penetrating to the Dnepr and isolating the southern wing of the German forces to the east of the river was gone, and the material losses of the Russian forces were substantial – even if the haul of prisoners was relatively modest, the loss of tanks, artillery and other heavy equipment would take some considerable time to be remedied. The final magnitude of Manstein's success, though, would be determined by how the operation now unfolded. For the Russians, their last hope of ending the winter campaigning season still in a position to threaten the Dnepr crossings would depend on Third Tank Army's ability to engage with and destroy the German armoured forces; for the Germans, the next phase of the battle had to be won if Manstein's recovery was to be sustained.

CHAPTER 13

KHARKOV

At every level, the Russians had been slow to recognise the scale and threat of Manstein's counterstroke. At first, field commanders interpreted the German attacks as local counterthrusts intended to try to restore the front line; when it became clear that the attacks were larger and more significant, Vatutin and others believed that they were purely attempts to fight off the Russians while the Germans continued their withdrawal to the Dnepr. The scale of the German setbacks through the winter created a deep-seated belief that the tide had turned irrevocably. Any German recovery would only be on a local scale, and could be overcome – either the local Russian forces would suffice to defeat the Germans, or further Russian successes elsewhere would render any German advance irrelevant. Even in the last days of February, when local commanders and *Stavka* finally woke up to the scale of the counteroffensive that was rapidly unfolding, there continued to be such miscalculations. There was a curious similarity between the views of Hitler and those of senior Russian commanders – the losses suffered during the winter fighting must have left the enemy too weak to launch successful attacks. This was largely what lay behind the failure to pull Popov's group out of danger, though fuel shortages would have made implementation of any order to retreat very difficult; it also explains the inadequate attempts to stop the advance of Fourth Panzer Army by throwing local units against the Germans. To a large extent, such a policy was inevitable, given that the Russians had already committed all their reserves, both at a local and regional level – the only alternative would have been to order a rapid withdrawal, and given the prevailing belief about the overall strategic situation, this was unthinkable. However, by the end of February, it should have been clear that local redeployments would be insufficient to halt Manstein's forces. Nevertheless, *Stavka* continued to behave as if the situation could be restored if the worn-down, poorly supplied units already in the Ukraine were used in counterattacks against the equally depleted German units – hence the decision to send Third Tank Army towards the south against Hoth's Fourth Panzer Army. This particular move was based upon the expectation that the German forces of *Armee Abteilung Kempf* had been sufficiently beaten to ensure that it would remain passively on the defensive; but as has already been described, *Grossdeutschland* was already making preparations to join Manstein's counteroffensive, and the SS divisions were far from defeated.

As First and Fourth Panzer Armies reached the banks of the Donets, Manstein considered his options. His assessment of the damage inflicted on the Russian Southwest Front was similar to the assumptions that the Russians had made about *Armee Abteilung Kempf*, but was rather more accurate – Vatutin's armies had been neutralised and sufficient damage had been inflicted upon them to make further Russian attacks impossible. The next objective was to deal with Voronezh Front, though Hitler continued to call for an early attack to recapture Kharkov, as Zeitzler repeatedly reminded Manstein in several signals. Manstein regarded the city as irrelevant as an objective – if the Russian forces in the area were defeated, the city would inevitably fall into German hands, but if they remained in the field, any attempt to recapture it risked a second Stalingrad with German troops tied down in bloody streetfighting.[1] Already, the spring thaw was beginning along the banks of the Black Sea and time was therefore fast running out – further armoured warfare was almost impossible along the Mius, much to the relief of the exhausted troops of *Armee Abteilung Hollidt*. The choices open to Army Group Don were to pursue the defeated Russians across the Donets before turning north into the deep rear of the forces around Kharkov, or striking north. This latter option raised two further possibilities. The Germans could either tackle the Russian forces head-on and storm into Kharkov from the south and southwest, or they could bypass the city to the west, circle around the northern outskirts, and then move southeast to isolate the garrison before making an attempt to capture Kharkov itself. Unlike Hitler and Stalin, the professional soldier did not succumb to strategic greed. A pursuit of the Russians over the Donets carried two substantial risks. Firstly, the imminent thaw could leave the German forces stranded east of the river. At the moment, the river ice along the Donets and elsewhere was strong enough to allow infantry to cross practically anywhere, but once this ice broke up, the floes on the Donets would make even pontoon bridges impossible to use and any forces committed across the river risked being isolated. Secondly, to advance northeast while the Russian forces around Kharkov remained undefeated invited a Russian counterattack into the flanks of First and Fourth Panzer Armies. In any event, the divisions that had successfully pursued the Russians back to the Donets were themselves exhausted and would be unable to operate at anything approaching optimum performance without a pause while supplies were laboriously brought forward. Consequently, the decision was made to stop at the Donets and turn north. Even this decision required further careful management by Manstein – aware that they had attracted Hitler's ire for abandoning Kharkov, the SS formations were desperate to redeem themselves, and Manstein used his new system of liaison officers to ensure that the SS obeyed his instructions. The planned manoeuvre – to bypass Kharkov to the west and then encircle it to the north and northeast – required the German armoured forces to travel further and potentially exposed their northern and northwest flanks to Russian counterattacks, but it was surely preferable to getting embroiled in urban combat.

Luftwaffe attacks to prepare the way for an advance by *LSSAH* began at first light on 28 February and were reported to be highly successful, though as has already been described, the accuracy of such observations, made when flying through anti-aircraft fire at high speed, was questionable; the bomber crews kept up their efforts all day, striking at Russian defences and rear area units alike with little intervention by Russian aircraft. Dietrich had assembled his division's assault group in Kegitchevka, and reconnaissance soon spotted a strong Russian column of perhaps 800 men, two tanks and 50 other vehicles heading for the same area.[2] Air attacks rapidly followed and the Russian forces were hit repeatedly and brought to a halt. For the moment, *LSSAH* continued its preparations to attack towards *SS-Totenkopf*, limiting itself to local counterattacks, but nevertheless by the end of the day Dietrich reported that his men had accounted for 18 Russian tanks, including one Pz.IV that the Russians must have captured in earlier fighting and put to use with their own forces. Such losses represented considerable damage to the Russian VI Guards Cavalry Corps, which had been tasked with protecting the rear area of the elements of Third Tank Army that were concentrating against Fourth Panzer Army, though as ever these claims of enemy tanks destroyed should always be treated with caution. Despite the losses suffered by the cavalry corps, the additional time taken by Dietrich's division to prepare for its major assault confirmed the view of *Stavka* that the German counteroffensive was limited to the drive by First and Fourth Panzer Armies and there would be little or no threat from the west; the Russian Third Tank Army continued to move the bulk of its resources south. However, despite the pressing urgency of dealing with the German advance, Rybalko informed higher commands that he would not be ready to attack on 2 March as originally intended, and that he would have only 30 tanks.[3] When his corps commanders briefed their men about the coming operation, they were met by reactions of disbelief, as Vetrov later wrote:

Lieutenant-Colonel Fedotov [in charge of rear area units of XV Tank Corps], who was sitting next to me, looked at me in bewilderment and, lowering his voice, asked: 'But how can one advance when each tank has only ten shells left, and all vehicles have half-empty fuel tanks?'

I only shrugged my shoulders in agreement. Yes, what to say? I was also well aware of the extremely difficult situation with the provision of ammunition, diesel and gasoline for the tank brigades. I also knew that because of the lack of fuel the artillery units, mobile tank repair teams and other combat support units that were attached to the corps were stuck in Merefa. But this was not due to negligence on the part of our logisticians. Firstly, we were getting further from our supply bases day by day, and traffic routes and areas of deployment had changed frequently. The situation at the front was complex. And: the weather. Snowfalls and storms had raged throughout January and a part of February, but now an early spring thaw had struck. It was difficult for tanks to move, and even more so for the wheeled vehicles, including fuel tankers.

At that moment, as if guessing what the chief of the corps rear area units had whispered to me, [Major General Vasily Alexeyevich Koptsov, commander of XV Tank Corps] said: 'Comrades! I know that we have completely exhausted both corps and army supplies of fuel and ammunition. Yes, and our personnel have been considerably thinned out. The remaining tanks are barely enough for even one combined brigade. However, I ask you to understand: an extremely complicated combat situation requires the most energetic and decisive actions from us. The Hitlerites, as you know, have pushed back the troops of Southwest Front. So how can we not help them, how can we not take some of the heavy burden on ourselves?' Koptsov rubbed his broad forehead with his hand and finished: 'We'll deliver ammunition and fuel.' This would be in the very near future, even if it had to be by air, the commander assured us.

And indeed, soon we were delivered a certain amount of ammunition and fuel.[4]

Whether the supplies that were received would be sufficient remained doubtful. With all formations so far below establishment strength, every last available vehicle was scraped together and dispatched to the front line. When Vetrov visited XV Tank Corps' workshops and managed to find five T-34s and two T-70s

– the mechanics had even managed to locate sufficient fuel and ammunition for them, and volunteered to crew them in action – Koptsov greeted him with relief and gratitude; this modest force, he told Vetrov, amounted to more than the strength of one of his tank brigades.[5]

For several days, *Grossdeutschland* had been recovering from the losses it had suffered in Belgorod and Kharkov and was assembling in a rear area, hindered as much by fuel shortages as enemy activity. By late afternoon on 27 February, the division reported that it had sufficient fuel for operations up to a radius of only 48 miles (80km). Nevertheless, a stream of replacement drafts and new equipment arriving from Germany had brought the division back to full strength and further fuel was delivered the following day, improving the situation considerably. The division had recovered sufficient strength that Manstein now began to consider how to add it to his developing counteroffensive by attacking towards the northeast to threaten Belgorod. The response from *Armee Abteilung Kempf* was not encouraging: the division could not be expected to be ready for operational deployment until 4 March, and an attack as proposed would be over roads already badly degraded in recent fighting.

On 1 March, the state of the roads in the sector held by *Armee Abteilung Kempf* was discussed at headquarters. The chief of the groups' pioneer units reported that most roads were in poor shape, and there were signs of a spring thaw in some areas; time was rapidly running out for Manstein's counteroffensive. Increasingly, units were being forced to divert supply columns via secondary routes, where there was a greater threat of them encountering partisans or retreating stragglers of Red Army units. Generalmajor Friedrich Fangohr, chief of staff of Fourth Panzer Army, added his concerns; whilst the attack from the south had made excellent progress and German armoured columns had reached or were approaching the Donets at many locations, the roads were deteriorating rapidly. He was assured that *LSSAH* would attack towards *SS-Totenkopf* as planned, but Dietrich also contacted Kempf's headquarters to warn about delays due to difficulties moving through the thawing mud. Despite this, orders were issued for *LSSAH* to attack as planned on 2 March – if the attack were delayed further, it was probable that the Russian forces currently between *SS-Totenkopf* and *LSSAH* would withdraw before they could be brought to battle.

Late on 1 March, Dietrich contacted Kempf again. He reported that the Russian units facing his division in Kegitchevka looked like they were preparing to withdraw, and proposed an immediate pursuit. A series of conversations between different headquarters followed, and shortly before midnight Manstein issued definitive orders. Whilst *LSSAH* could make strong reconnaissance probes,

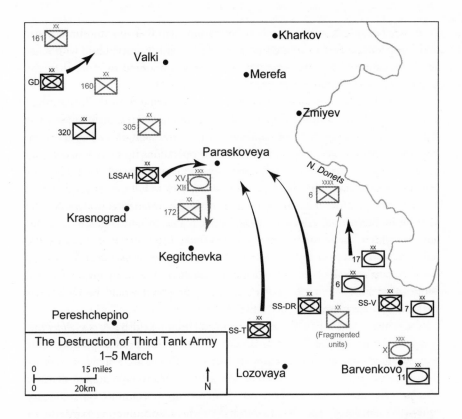

The Destruction of Third Tank Army
1–5 March

its main effort would take place the following day, at the same time as a further northerly thrust by *SS-Totenkopf*. Throughout the day, both *SS-Totenkopf* and *SS-Das Reich* had continued their advance, occasionally being brought to a halt by determined Russian rearguards but always either breaking resistance or bypassing it. The neighbouring Wehrmacht divisions to the east also continued to push forward to the line of the Donets where the Russians had dug in and stood ready for a determined defence, but it was now clear to the Germans that the Red Army did not intend to try to halt the German spearheads south of the river. Most of the fighting in the sectors of XLVIII Panzer Corps and – to its east – First Panzer Army's XL Panzer Corps took place behind the German front line, as groups of retreating Russians clashed with German columns. For the moment, the German units that had carried out the advance to the Donets could take a couple of days' rest – a badly needed opportunity to bring forward supplies and reinforcements, and, for troops who had been in almost continuous action for several weeks, to get some long-overdue sleep.

LSSAH began its advance at first light on 2 March. By mid-morning, the division reported that it was gaining ground against Russian forces that put up little resistance in most areas, though – contrary to the reports of the previous night – Kegitchevka remained in Russian hands and there was fierce fighting as the SS division attempted to force the defences. To the east, both *SS-Totenkopf* and *SS-Das Reich* continued their advance, though some elements of the Russian Third Tank Army launched limited local attacks of their own in an attempt to secure better start lines for the planned attack of 3 March. In confused fighting, a group of Russian soldiers supported by tanks – most probably stragglers from one of the units already bypassed by the SS divisions – encountered a German artillery position and swiftly overwhelmed it, but such setbacks for the Germans were isolated and had little impact on the general tempo and momentum of operations. On 3 March, *LSSAH* was returned to the control of Hausser's SS Panzer Corps in order to ensure better coordination with the other SS divisions in their convergent attack, and during the morning its leading elements thrust forward about 6 miles (10km) to Paraskoveya, directly in the rear of Rybalko's units.

Early on 2 March, Rybalko finally launched his attacks against the SS Panzer Corps. With his XV Tank Corps reduced to just a handful of tanks and aware that the Germans were threatening to encircle his forces, Koptsov asked for permission to withdraw to the north, but Rybalko felt that he had to make at least an effort to attack. He sent XV Tank Corps with a rifle division south against *SS-Totenkopf*, only for it to run head-on into the Germans who were launching a further attack of their own. Almost immediately, XV Tank Corps and its accompanying infantry were forced onto the defensive, while elements of *SS-Totenkopf* and *LSSAH* met to the north, encircling the Russian force. The war diary of the SS Panzer Corps described the day's combat:

> All of the day's operations were marked by wild, mainly uncoordinated attempts
> by the encircled enemy to break out and by the most difficult road conditions that
> greatly hindered the advance and the achievement of assigned objectives.[6]

The rest of Rybalko's armour – XII Tank Corps – was to attack towards the east against *SS-Das Reich*. It too ran directly into German forces advancing in the opposite direction. The temperature had risen above zero, and the deep mud on roads that had already borne the weight of heavy traffic during the Russian advance proved more of a hindrance to the Germans than Russian resistance. As the advancing elements of *LSSAH* approached from the west, the Russian XXII Tank

Corps found that, like the neighbouring XV Tank Corps, it too was encircled. Any thought of Third Tank Army restoring the situation by attacking the SS divisions was now out of the question, and as darkness fell, Rybalko called off further attacks towards the south. The combined forces of XII and XV Tank Corps, together with three rifle divisions – in reality, they collectively had the strength of a single rifle regiment – were put under the overall command of Major General Mitrofan Ivanovich Zinkovich, the commander of XII Tank Corps, who was to extract them from their encirclement. Zinkovich ordered XV Tank Corps to attack to the east supported by a rifle division, with XII Tank Corps following with a second rifle division; the third rifle division would form the rearguard.

Koptsov ordered his troops to form up in two columns for their breakout attempt. They set out at dawn on 3 March; almost all of their heavy weapons were out of ammunition and there was barely enough fuel for a single day of operations. The northern column reached a small village but was driven off by machine-gun fire from German troops that had taken up a blocking position, and as the Russians attempted to detour around the village they came under heavy shellfire. The solitary tank in the northern column was knocked out, and Vetrov, who was leading the group, decided to turn back and try to follow the southern column, which was led by Koptsov:

> About 11am, somewhere on our left we heard shots, and to our front shells began to explode on the road. 'German tanks!' – Shouts of alarm were heard. People poured from our vehicles and hid in a roadside ditch, exposed to rifle and machine-gun fire from our flank.
>
> We soon realised that we couldn't avoid a major battle. General Koptsov immediately organized a circular defence. When he gave orders, his voice was firm, and the orders themselves were brief, precise and accurate.
>
> Through my binoculars, I saw a column of 15–20 enemy tanks about a kilometre from us. It would not be easy to hold out against such an enemy force. In the meantime the enemy fired on us with a few tanks and anti-tank guns. An artillery duel ensued. But of course, we couldn't sustain it for long: as already mentioned, we had very little ammunition.
>
> The earth trembled with the frequent explosions and the snow melted. Shrapnel rained down. Suddenly, General Koptsov groaned and fell to the ground. I rushed to him. But at that very moment I felt a piercing pain in my left shin. The submachine-gunners from the commandant's platoon and the commandant's lieutenant Nikolai Yudin ran up. Laying the general on a fur coat, they carried him to the shelter of a vehicle.

'Vetrov! Stay here for me and hold on!' These were the last words of Koptsov. He lost consciousness. Without even having bandaged my wounds, I tried to keep the corps moving. Relying on a stick, I moved from gun to gun, from tank to tank. My boot squelched unpleasantly as it filled with blood, but I ignored it. It was necessary to adjust the fire [of our guns].

The enemy tanks tried to attack us several times, but the organised and brave actions of our artillerymen, who fired albeit rarely but with great precision, stopped the enemy from approaching. Admittedly, our losses in people and especially in motor vehicles grew, but there were also three smoky pillars of fire rising on the German side, after which the enemy became less brash.

During the evening, I was wounded again. The ambulance orderlies took me to the staff bus where the captain of the medical service, Darya Grigorievna Shinkarenko, washed the wound with alcohol. When her expression became concerned, I realised that things were not good. And the doctor confirmed this. 'You have a twenty-centimetre laceration on the right side of the rib cage with a fracture of three ribs, as well as a wound to the left leg,' she said. 'And I do not have anti-tetanus serum or even anything for the pain. Everything went up in flames in the ambulance.'

I assured her that nothing would happen to me if I didn't get a tetanus shot, and then inquired about the health of General Koptsov. 'Vasily Alekseyevich lies in the next vehicle, he has a wound to the right leg and has lost a great loss of blood,' answered Darya Grigorievna.

After the doctor left, the adjutant of the corps commander, Senior Lieutenant Vladimir Revushkin, entered the vehicle. He reported: 'We are still surrounded. But as soon as it gets dark, we'll get off the highway and make our way north.' It was the right thing to do. We just had to hold out until the evening.

And we held out. As soon as it got dark, two T-34s with men armed with submachine-guns riding them went ahead. They were followed by a car carrying General Koptsov. The school bus, in which I lay, slowly followed the car. Other motor vehicles followed behind, and the last of the remaining T-34s brought up the rear of the column.

With me in the bus were Military Technician Mikhail Chernyak and my driver Fedor Demeshko. They did everything they could to keep me from being jostled, but in vain. And soon the worst happened: the bus ran out of petrol. We had to attach it with a cable to the tank at the rear of the column, and now such sharp jolts were added to the continuous shaking that my head grew numb and I vomited.

For a long time our bus followed our tank. But then on the next sharp turn it suddenly strongly heeled and skidded to the side. The steel cable broke and we were left alone. The crew of the tank didn't notice what had happened in the darkness.[7]

Koptsov died shortly after Vetrov lost touch with the rest of the column, and only a handful of men from XV Tank Corps managed to escape on foot; Vetrov was amongst them, and remained in hospital for two months recovering from his wounds.

With much of his army destroyed, Rybalko struggled to set up a defensive line that might have a chance of stopping further German advances. He received reinforcements in the shape of a rifle brigade, two tank brigades, 25th Guards Rifle Division and a Czech battalion, but most of these units were simply being transferred from other sectors of the front line and were far below their establishment strength. To his northwest, Kazakov's Sixty-Ninth Army also attempted to organise a defensive line, abandoning any remaining intentions of trying to press on to the Dnepr. Moskalenko's Fortieth Army was also ordered to stop its advance, though it was to hold its current positions; in addition, it was to release three rifle divisions for use further to the southeast where they would be committed to counterattacks to restore continuity of the front line. This would leave Fortieth Army with three rifle divisions and one badly weakened tank corps covering 72 miles (120km) of front line.

Shafarenko's 25th Guards Rifle Division – reorganised into just two regiments because it had lost so many men – faced a tough march to reach its new area of operations:

> We were marching to a battle that would be no easier than our previous engagements. We were required to cover about 80km [48 miles] in a day – and this was at the beginning of the *rasputitsa* [muddy season], along roads in our immediate rear which, undoubtedly, were kept under surveillance by enemy aircraft. It was clear to everyone that these unusually tight deadlines were forced upon the commanders due to the prevailing situation. We were gambling too much, but it was absolutely necessary.
>
> Advanced detachments of the regiments set off with cars and sleds. They led the way for our weakened main formations to their new lines. The political workers and communists explained the situation to the Guardsmen, and people did everything to keep within the specified schedule.
>
> As soon as the march began, I rode along with the unit commanders, artillerymen, engineers and scouts. It was necessary to understand the situation, to conduct reconnaissance and ensure cooperation. Only thus would the commanders be able to link up with neighbouring units and, without losing time, occupy their defensive positions.
>
> From our knowledge of the terrain, we expected the main attack of the enemy from the south and southwest – good roads led from there to Kharkov. The few

roads from our sector of the front towards the southeast [i.e. the direction of travel for the division] turned out to be difficult to reach, especially in the vicinity of Zmiyev, at the confluence of the Mzha River and Northern Donets. These would also be useful for the enemy.

To the right and left of us there we had no contact with neighbouring units. Our reconnaissance detachment, sent along the northern bank of the Mzha River, finally encountered a battalion of NKVD troops at the southern outskirts of Merefa.[8]

There were increasing signs of a lasting thaw. Roads rapidly turned to mud and although *Grossdeutschland* was more or less ready to launch attacks, it was difficult to determine the best route of advance given the deteriorating state of the ground. Although the component units of *Grossdeutschland* began to move to their designated forming up areas on 5 March, it remained doubtful that they would be able to attack the following day as planned. Meanwhile, the divisions of the SS Panzer Corps set to work reducing the surrounded elements of the Russian Third Tank Army and other formations; rear area units of the SS divisions were organised into *Jagdkommandos* ('hunting groups') and *Säuberungskommandos* ('cleaning up groups') in order to avoid using the main combat elements if at all possible. At midday on 4 March, a military police detachment of the SS Panzer Corps found the corpse of General Koptsov, and while *SS-Totenkopf* helped with the elimination of the remaining encircled Russian formations, *LSSAH* and *SS-Das Reich* resumed their advances, making limited gains. Throughout 5 March, scattered units clashed behind the front line as the last elements of the encircled Russian formations were dispersed or destroyed; by the end of the day, *SS-Totenkopf* reported that it had captured 36 tanks, 11 armoured cars, 159 guns, and over 500 trucks. There was no report regarding the number of prisoners that were taken.[9] Whilst many of the Russian troops simply abandoned their equipment and managed to slip away towards the east, it is possible, perhaps even likely that – given the past conduct of *SS-Totenkopf* – many of those who did surrender were executed.

With order largely restored to the rear areas of the SS Panzer Corps, major offensive operations could resume on 6 March. Assessments of aerial reconnaissance photographs and prisoner interrogations confirmed Manstein's view that the forces of Vatutin's Southwest Front had been comprehensively defeated and he could now turn his attention to Golikov's Voronezh Front without any great concern, and he intended to push towards Kharkov with Fourth Panzer Army – the SS Panzer Corps, with XLVIII Panzer Corps on its

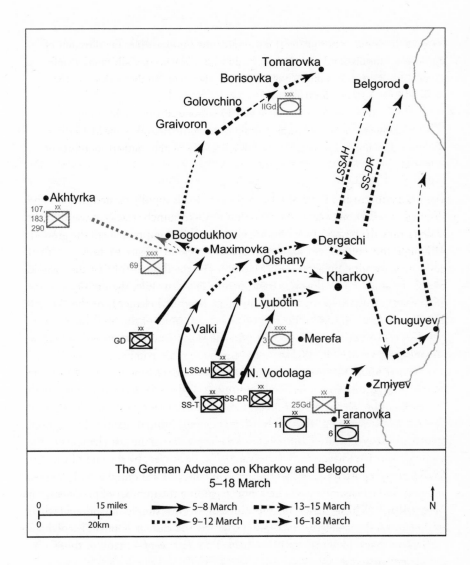

The German Advance on Kharkov and Belgorod
5–18 March

0 — 15 miles
0 — 20km

➤ 5–8 March   ➤ 13–15 March
➤ 9–12 March   ➤ 16–18 March

N

eastern flank, would lead the assault. At the same time, the infantry divisions of *Armee Abteilung Kempf* and the *Grossdeutschland* motorised infantry division were to launch powerful attacks further west; the latter was to advance on Bogodukhov and create a breach between the Russian Sixty-Ninth Army and Third Tank Army. Manstein was careful to ensure that the instructions issued were clear: the intention was to defeat the Russian forces defending Kharkov and then to bypass the city to the west. Aware of the strong desire of the SS to recapture the city as soon as possible to appease Hitler, Hoth carefully reiterated these instructions.

The SS divisions – *LSSAH* on the left, *SS-Totenkopf* in the centre (though due to its involvement in clearing up the encircled elements of the Russian Third Tank Army, it would not be available immediately for the attack), and *SS-Das Reich* on the right – were opposed by the reinforcements that Rybalko had received. The two flanking SS divisions attacked the hastily deployed Russian defensive line in strength with powerful support from Stuka squadrons, and the eastern part of the attack rapidly outflanked the Russian defences at Novaya Vodolaga. After a brief but determined fight, the Russian units facing *LSSAH* pulled back, allowing Dietrich's division to move forward. To the east of the SS Panzer Corps, 6th Panzer Division fought its way into Taranovka, held by 25th Guards Rifle Division, and a protracted battle for the town began. Having been assigned to Rybalko's Third Tank Army only two days previously, 25th Guards Rifle Division was now placed under the command of the Russian Sixth Army to Rybalko's southeast. This was more than a purely administrative adjustment – unlike Third Tank Army, Sixth Army still had ammunition and fuel available and was able to send both supplies and reinforcements to Taranovka, immediately to the southwest of Zmiyev.

Shafarenko's badly weakened division was determined to hold Taranovka for as long as possible. The initial probing attack by 6th Panzer Division's reconnaissance battalion was beaten off just outside the town by a single Russian platoon, supported by a solitary 45mm anti-tank gun, with what seemed remarkable ease, but Shafarenko wondered why the Germans had pulled back:

> Soon we had a clue – more than three dozen 'Junkers' [Stuka dive-bombers] appeared in the sky and attacked in two waves. The first wave flew towards Taranovka, the second, having circled overhead while gathering, began bombing the positions of the platoon, striking at the entire area. The air was filled with the howl of sirens, the roar of engines, and the whistle of falling bombs, and thick smoke mixed with fine blowing snow.
>
> Fortunately, the Nazis dropped most of their deadly cargo on dummy positions that had been dug the day before. One of the bombs exploded near Lieutenant Shironin. He was thrown to the bottom of the trench by the blast, and when he staggered to his feet he saw smoke rising from the ravaged landscape all around. Taranovka was ablaze.
>
> In this raid, the crew of the 45mm gun were knocked out.[10]

When the Germans attacked a second time, Shafarenko's troops fought with great determination, but with their anti-tank gun out of action, they came under increasing pressure. However, the main German effort was elsewhere and other elements of 6th Panzer Division bypassed the isolated platoon and entered Taranovka itself, where bitter fighting erupted.

The following day, Rybalko's Third Tank Army continued to retreat in the face of the advancing SS divisions. Novaya Vodolaga, outflanked the previous day, was abandoned. *SS-Totenkopf* was redeployed, pulling out of its position between its sister divisions, and deployed on the western flank of the SS Panzer Corps with explicit instructions to lead the drive to encircle the city by passing its western and northern outskirts. Immediately to the west of *SS-Totenkopf*, *Grossdeutschland* was finally able to commence its attack. As was the case with the panzer divisions earlier in the winter, *Grossdeutschland* concentrated much of its strength in an armoured battlegroup, commanded by Strachwitz, and its advance began smoothly. By early afternoon, Strachwitz had advanced a considerable distance, though progress was slowed by the need to make a sideways thrust with his tanks to the west in order to facilitate the advance of an infantry battlegroup of *Grossdeutschland*. Losses were reported to be minimal, with the Russians generally pulling back rather than making a determined stand. Further to the northwest there was considerable confusion in Russian commands about the status of the three rifle divisions that Moskalenko had been ordered to release from his Fortieth Army in order to help Sixty-Ninth Army; Moskalenko believed that they were now under the command of Kazakov's Sixty-Ninth Army, while Kazakov maintained that they remained part of Fortieth Army, which would be responsible for using them in a counterattack to restore the front between the two Russian armies. In any event, the three divisions – all badly depleted by the losses they had suffered in earlier fighting and short of artillery ammunition – struggled to move to their new area of operations, retracing the route they had taken with such confidence only two weeks earlier. For the moment, the southern flank of Moskalenko's Fortieth Army remained out of contact with its neighbour.[11]

While the Russians struggled to respond to the rapidly changing situation on the battlefield, the German advance continued. In Taranovka, 6th Panzer Division was joined on 8 March by elements of 11th Panzer Division and drove the Russian 25th Guards Rifle Division out of the town; thereafter, the Germans pushed forward to Sokolovo, between Zmiyev and Novaya Vodolaga, where they encountered the Czech battalion that had been sent to Rybalko as part of his reinforcements. The Czech troops – deployed in a setting that favoured the defence – fought with great determination despite being outnumbered and outgunned, and temporarily brought the Germans to a halt, as a member of 6th Panzer Division later wrote:

> After the exertions of the previous weeks with almost constant operations the troops were beginning to show signs of exhaustion. Through the example set by their officers – the division commander, and the commander of 4th Panzergrenadier Regiment who advanced at the head of his grenadiers with a rifle in his hands – the troops moved forward once more and at 1400 the first companies of I Battalion and the reconnaissance battalion penetrated into Sokolovo. The village was strongly held by Czech troops supported by numerous anti-tank guns. It had to be cleared in tough streetfighting.[12]

Both sides' accounts describe the battle for Taranovka as being as fierce as any that had been fought on the Eastern Front. The survivors of a battalion of the Russian 78th Guards Rifle Regiment held out in the old church in the centre of the town, sheltering behind its thick walls. When their ammunition was exhausted, they prepared to try to escape under cover of darkness, but even as they were preparing to withdraw a Russian tank managed to reach them, bringing much-needed supplies. Eventually, the remnants of 25th Guards Rifle Division and the Czech battalion were driven back.

If XLVIII Panzer Corps was held up, the same was not true of the SS Panzer Corps. *SS-Totenkopf* was able to join the other two divisions and advanced through Valki towards the north; together, the SS formations drove all before them and isolated Lyubotin. The weather had turned cold once more and a little to the west, Strachwitz's battlegroup advanced through blowing snow to Stary Merchik, immediately to the west of Lyubotin, hindered more by the difficulties encountered by the division's wheeled elements than by Russian action. It was expected that the truck-borne infantry would be able to rejoin the leading elements of *Grossdeutschland* overnight, after which the division would resume its advance towards Bogodukhov. The SS divisions were rapidly approaching the southern outskirts of Kharkov, and if *Grossdeutschland* continued its advance, the western flank of Hausser's corps would be protected from any Russian counterattack. This would have serious consequences not only for the defence of the city, but also for the Russian troops of Sixty-Ninth and Fortieth Armies that were to the west.

There were further snowfalls overnight, and *Grossdeutschland* – advancing in three columns – struggled forward along roads choked with snow. Many of the division's infantry still hadn't caught up with the leading armoured elements, and by midday the most eastern column had effectively come to a halt – although the temperature had fallen once more below freezing, this just transformed recently melted snow into a sheet of ice on which fresh snow had now fallen. Helplessly, the leading elements of the stranded column reported that Russian forces could be seen to their front escaping towards the northeast, largely on foot.[13] However, Strachwitz remained mobile and his battlegroup – with the Tiger tank company now once more in action – pushed forward and cut the main road from Bogodukhov to Kharkov at Maximovka. Immediately, the tanks and the few half-track infantry that had managed to accompany them found themselves involved in heavy fighting with Russian troops trying to escape to the east; these were the leading elements of the three infantry divisions that Moskalenko had been ordered to dispatch towards Sixty-Ninth Army. None of the Russian attempts to re-open the vital road succeeded, and Strachwitz requested sufficient fuel supplies to allow him to continue advancing towards the northeast. However, Manstein's chief of staff advised Generalmajor Walter Hörnlein, the division commander, in a radio conversation that the previous instructions – for the division to guard the western flank of the continuing German counteroffensive – remain in force. It was to capture Bogodukhov and only then would it be able to drive on to the north and northeast. Already, there was considerable traffic congestion in rear areas as the supply columns of different units struggled forward along the few usable roads, and Manstein's headquarters was anxious to avoid exacerbating this by compressing the breadth of the German advance.

Lyubotin was captured by *SS-Das Reich* early on 9 March. A little to the west, *SS-Totenkopf* established contact with *Grossdeutschland* and its leading elements advanced to Olshany – even if the Russian attacks on Strachwitz were to succeed in re-opening the road from Bogodukhov, it was now blocked at a second point. The only Russian forces in the area were the remnants of VI Guards Cavalry Corps, trying to maintain contact between Third Tank Army and Sixty-Ninth Army, and these fell back without putting up prolonged resistance. During the afternoon, encouraged by the speed of the advance, Hoth contacted Hausser to discuss how to proceed. In particular, was it possible to take advantage of the disarray of the Russian forces to secure Kharkov quickly, before the Russians could organise a proper defence? Hausser's reply was equivocal. His divisions would not be able to make such an attempt until the following day at the earliest, and even this would require fuel and ammunition to be delivered to the leading formations. However, by the evening, he issued clear orders for *SS-Das Reich* and *LSSAH* to attack Kharkov directly, without confirming the operation with Hoth. The commander of Fourth Panzer Army had been prepared to consider a rapid thrust against Kharkov if it would lead to its swift capture, but Hausser seized the opportunity to try to recapture the city regardless of the level of resistance.

For the Russians, the situation had worsened beyond their darkest fears in what seemed like an astonishingly short time. Moskalenko's Fortieth Army still had no contact with units on either flank, and now Sixty-Ninth Army had also lost touch with its neighbours. A little to the south, several Russian units launched determined counterattacks against XLVIII Panzer Corps and managed to fight their way back into Taranovka, but were unable to hold onto their gains and were forced back once more. Izyum lies in a loop of the Donets, and Russian forces infiltrated across the still-frozen river to the south of the town, exploiting the fact that 7th Panzer Division lacked the strength to secure the full line of the river. Immediately to the south of the Donets, at the base of the north-projecting loop that runs towards Izyum, the Russians captured a low ridge at Donetske and held it in the face of a determined counterattack by the panzer division; further Russian attacks succeeded in overrunning parts of the division's defensive line and threatened to break into the rear areas. Major Richard Grünert, commander of one of the division's panzergrenadier battalions, rallied his men and led them in a counterattack, but with other elements of 7th Panzer Division being driven back he too was forced to withdraw. Once the division had gathered its strength, a determined series of counterattacks was launched:

> Suffering extraordinarily heavy losses, the enemy was smashed and driven back. It was only in Donetske, which had no particular value for us, that the enemy was left in control of the battlefield. Our losses were also heavy.[14]

German casualties were severe enough to force the panzer division temporarily to disband one of its panzergrenadier battalions. Grünert continued to lead his men from the front. Late on 13 March, he personally led a counterattack by a motorcycle company against another Russian penetration before moving to a neighbouring sector where another of his companies was under pressure. Here, he was caught in the blast of a Russian artillery shell and killed. He was posthumously awarded the Knight's Cross with Oak Leaves.

The series of attacks at Izyum and Taranovka were designed to help counter the German counteroffensive, but the gains were negligible. At best, the Russians could console themselves that they had tied down some elements of Fourth Panzer Army to stop them joining the continuing drive towards Kharkov. With the fighting now perilously close to Kharkov, Stalin issued instructions for Moskalenko to travel to the city to assess its defences, even though Kharkov lay outside the zone of operations of Fortieth Army:

I went to Kharkov with a small operational group. At that time, Lieutenant General Dmitri Timofeyevich Kozlov, deputy commander of the Voronezh Front, had been appointed to oversee the defence of the city and tried to organise the defence with the help of a small garrison. Having pressed back the weakened Sixty-Ninth and Third Tank Armies with superior forces, the enemy was already fighting on the southwest and southern outskirts of Kharkov. Enemy tanks and infantry were fighting their way towards the centre of the city.

It was too late! An attempt to hold the city by strengthening its defences with some of the forces of Fortieth Army should have been made much earlier. Now it was impossible to think about the transfer of troops and the organisation of defence in those few hours that remained at our disposal. I reported this to the front commander. He agreed that it was no longer possible to reinforce the city, and ordered me to return to my army to take action against the enemy's attempts to bypass the city's right flank.[15]

In fairness, the pace at which the situation had deteriorated for the Red Army was such that any earlier consideration for organising the defence of Kharkov would have seemed overly pessimistic – just two weeks before, there had been high expectations of reaching the Dnepr and of pinning the Germans against the shores of the Black Sea. Now, the only forces available to defend the city were 19th Rifle Division, newly arrived from *Stavka* reserve, 86th Tank Brigade, the remnants of 48th Guards Rifle Division, and 17th NKVD Rifle Brigade, together with whatever front-line formations might be driven back into Kharkov. Even if Moskalenko had been ordered to transfer troops from his army to reinforce the garrison, he had none to spare. His remaining forces were stretched out over a huge front, with each division holding over 21 miles (35km) of front line.

There was no let-up for the Russians on 10 March. Both Moskalenko and Kazakov were worried about the forces of Fortieth and Sixty-Ninth Armies that were in danger of finding themselves isolated as the SS Panzer Corps and *Grossdeutschland* advanced northwards, and everything would depend on the attack by the three divisions released by Fortieth Army, which were to restore contact with Sixty-Ninth Army. Once this had been achieved, forces would be transferred further east to repeat the attack with a view to restoring contact between Sixty-Ninth Army and Russian forces further east. After only modest artillery preparation, the Russian infantry moved forward only to run into the armour of *Grossdeutschland*, which was itself deployed for an attack. The uneven contest was soon over with the Russians falling back in disarray towards Bogodukhov, unable to press home an attack without armoured support.

Whilst Strachwitz might have been unimpressed by the reliability of the division's Tiger tanks, they were now proving their worth as the Russians found to their alarm – much as the Germans had discovered in 1941 – that their anti-tank weapons were almost useless against the enemy's best tanks. Moskalenko later wrote about a report from the commander of III Tank Corps, which was now thrown into the fighting in an attempt to hold back *Grossdeutschland*:

> I remember General [Ivan Antonovich] Vovchenko met me near Borisov and reported that his tanks could not penetrate the frontal armour of the German tanks. I was surprised, since there had been no reports like that until then. Lieutenant-General Fedor Fedotovich Kuznetsov, a member of the Military Council of Voronezh Front, and a member of the Military Council of Fortieth Army, Colonel Ivan Samoilovich Grushetsky, were also present at the meeting. Together we went to General Vovchenko's observation post to check if he was right. Through our binoculars, we saw how the shells of our tank guns created a burst of sparks when they hit the frontal armour of the German tanks and ricocheted to the side.
>
> This 'problem', however, was soon solved by our artillerymen. They took into account that the frontal armour of the new German tanks was very strong and they decided that if this was the case, they should not be engaged head-on but against their side or rear armour. This, of course, was a new idea, and it required not only a different arrangement of weapons in anti-tank support positions, but also the greatest strength of mind. After all, it was now necessary to let the German tanks pass them first, and only then to engage them. But as is known, both the strength of spirit and courage of Soviet soldiers were up to the task. Consequently, the Tigers proved to be no worse than all the other fascist tanks.[16]

The Tiger had frontal armour that was 100mm thick, compared with side armour of 60mm; this compared with 50mm frontal armour and 30mm side armour for the Pz.IIIs and Pz.IVs in service at the time. By comparison, the T-34 had frontal armour of 45mm and side armour of 40mm, though the sloping of the armour effectively increased its thickness and also increased the chance of a ricochet. In order to improve the odds of surviving enemy fire, Tiger crews were trained to engage targets by turning the tank slightly to one side rather than directly facing the target, so that any incoming ordnance would strike the frontal or side armour obliquely. Whilst Moskalenko's account is correct in saying that Russian anti-tank units altered their tactics to try to avoid engaging Tiger tanks against their tough frontal armour, these changes would take time to implement, and the side and rear armour of the Tiger was still sufficiently thick to prevent penetration by most Russian guns. In the short term, particularly during the fighting around Kharkov, the Russians continued to fear the Tigers and German battle losses were minimal. The SS divisions deployed just nine Tiger tanks each in their heavy panzer companies; *LSSAH*, *SS-Totenkopf* and *SS-Das Reich* lost only two tanks in each division, and not all of these were a consequence of enemy action.[17] The casualties suffered by *Grossdeutschland* were much the same, and it would be some considerable time before the Russians succeeded in coming to terms with their powerful opponent. Nevertheless, the Tiger units did not have an easy time. The 50-ton tanks were close to the limit of technological capabilities, and their engines and transmissions were prone to breakdown; in order to avoid excessive strain on their engines, tank crews were discouraged from running the engine at maximum power. The weight of the tanks limited their deployment, despite using wide tracks to try to reduce ground pressure, with bridges being a particular problem, especially in the Ukraine where all crossings had endured heavy traffic for several weeks. Fuel consumption in rough ground was also far greater than anticipated – at a time when the Wehrmacht was constantly plagued by fuel shortages, this was a major limiting factor in the usefulness of the new tanks. But whatever their limitations in terms of mobility may have been, their 88mm gun provided their crews with a weapon that could easily destroy any tank in the world at ranges of over a mile.

Whilst *Grossdeutschland* moved closer to Bogodukhov, Hitler made another visit to Manstein's headquarters in Zaporozhye, and a morning conference was attended by all the army commanders in the region. Numerous matters were discussed, with Hitler concentrating particularly on plans for the summer; equipped with the newest tanks, the panzer divisions would field a mixture of Pz.IVs with long-barrelled 75mm guns and the new Panther tank, and would launch a crushing blow against the Russians. During discussions, the salient around Kursk that projected towards the west between Army Group Centre and Army Group South was suggested as a possible objective for a summer offensive. As was often the case, Hitler was more interested than his generals in the new equipment that would be available; for the army officers, the new tanks were merely the tools with which they would be working, and the use to which those tools were put was of far greater importance. If the wrong objective was selected, the operation would fail, regardless of the excellence of the equipment that was available.[18]

After a working lunch, the officers who had attended the conference returned to their commands, which had been continuing to push towards Kharkov. The intention of the SS Panzer Corps for the day was to push north rapidly to the west of Kharkov and then turn towards the city and to capture it from the northwest before defences could be organised. Russian resistance in the path of *LSSAH* was stiffening and there was heavy fighting in and around Dergachi to the northwest of the city. As a result of the efforts of the stubborn Russian rearguards and the huge difficulties faced by all vehicles, tracked or wheeled, in moving through the slowly melting snow and over roads that had almost completely disintegrated, the SS divisions were late in concentrating for their new tasks and it became clear that it would not be possible to capture Kharkov in a rapid thrust as Hoth had intended. Despite this, orders remained in place for an assault on the city. Meanwhile, after successfully defeating the Russian infantry counterattack, *Grossdeutschland* paused to bring forward supplies before attempting to push on towards Bogodukhov.

Whilst *SS-Totenkopf* had encountered frustrating Russian resistance throughout the day, it had still succeeded in driving back the various Russian units deployed against it – VI Guards Cavalry Corps, 160th Rifle Division, and 48th Guards Rifle Division – and had inflicted further damage on them. On its right flank, *LSSAH* turned towards Kharkov and penetrated into the outskirts from the northwest and north. Kozlov, the deputy commander of Voronezh Front, had appointed Major General Evtikhi Emilianovich Belov, who had been deputy commander of Third Guards Tank Army, as the 'battle commander' for Kharkov, and in order to deal with the SS units threatening the city from the north, Belov was forced to move troops from the western and southwest defences. This reduced the strength of the resistance in the path of *SS-Das Reich*, allowing it to close up to the city, but the Germans were repeatedly frustrated by the rapidly disintegrating roads and were unable to gather sufficient strength to force their way past the Russian rearguards. Reluctantly, Hausser issued orders for his divisions to regroup overnight with a view to launching a decisive attack the following day.

Golikov, the commander of Voronezh Front, had placed his last hope of restoring the situation in the counterattack by the three rifle divisions released by Moskalenko's Fortieth Army, and with their defeat he had to move quickly to prevent Sixty-Ninth and Fortieth Armies from being isolated and destroyed. Kazakov was ordered to pull back with his Sixty-Ninth Army to protect the road from Kharkov to Belgorod and to set up a defensive line north of Kharkov; he was also ordered to hold Bogodukhov, but this was beyond his resources and a hasty transfer of units between his army and Moskalenko's Fortieth Army was organised to provide the latter with sufficient resources to hold the town. Meanwhile, Moskalenko's headquarters in Graivoron came under heavy German air attack and he was forced to move northeast to Kryukovo.[19] At a higher level, *Stavka* ordered the Russian First Tank Army and Twenty-First Army to deploy north of Belgorod from where they would be available to intervene in the battle for Kharkov, and Sixty-Fourth Army, which had been rebuilding in the Stalingrad area, was also summoned back to the front line.[20]

As had repeatedly been the case for both sides, translating orders into reality on the ground proved to be a considerable challenge, and none of the three armies dispatched to the region were likely to be able to contribute anything to the battle for Kharkov before the end of March. In the meantime, the Russian forces around the city had to do the best they could. Early on 11 March, *Grossdeutschland* resumed its attack on Bogodukhov, and the infantry divisions of *Armee Abteilung Kempf* exerted pressure on the wide bulge held by the Russian Fortieth and Sixty-Ninth Armies. From the north, the revitalised German Second Army made limited attacks against the northern parts of Moskalenko's forces and recaptured Lebedin. *Grossdeutschland* soon encountered tough resistance and asked for help from the Luftwaffe to help break up the Russian defences; then, while the division's armour closed in from the north, its infantry battlegroups attacked from the south. By early afternoon, Bogodukhov was in German hands. From there, *Grossdeutschland* moved towards Graivoron, overrunning and destroying several columns of retreating Russians as it did so.

The SS divisions that had drawn the anger of Hitler when they disobeyed the Führer's orders and retreated through Kharkov were now fighting in the outskirts of the city and were eager to restore their reputation. In constant battle with the Russians, Hausser's troops fought their way into the western parts of the city. Realising that despite Manstein's express orders, the SS had used his suggestion of a rapid strike to capture Kharkov as a pretext for launching a full-scale assault on the city, Hoth now ordered *SS-Das Reich* to withdraw from the fighting so that it could be deployed north of the city – this would then allow *SS-Totenkopf* to move east and southeast with its rear area secure from Russian interference. Hausser responded that it would be difficult to extract the division which, contrary to all instructions from higher commands, was now increasingly tied down in streetfighting. Towards the end of the day, he sent a summary to Manstein and Hoth, highlighting both the gains his corps had made and the problems that it faced:

> Throughout the evening there have been increasing indications that, shielded by strong rearguards equipped with anti-tank guns and tanks, the enemy is evacuating Kharkov. An enemy [counter]attack from Zolochiv [to the northwest of Kharkov]

is expected. Most of *SS-Das Reich* and *LSSAH* are firmly established along the eastern, northern and western edges of the city. We have penetrated into the northeast part. The junction of the roads to Volchansk and Chuguyev [i.e. the main roads to the southeast and northeast] is temporarily in our hands. We are shifting the main point of effort of *LSSAH* to its eastern flank.

SS-Totenkopf is defending a front of 45km [27 miles] with just two regiments. One of the division's panzer battalions is with *SS-Das Reich*.

Road conditions to the north of Kharkov are such that moving *SS-Das Reich* there will take 36 hours. Bridges have been partially destroyed. The ice is no longer strong enough to bear weight. There is no guarantee of supplies reaching *LSSAH*.

Therefore, I conclude: a continuation of the attack in current deployment with a further shift of the point of main effort to the eastern flank. After taking Kharkov, the bulk of the corps will concentrate east of the city for a thrust towards the south.[21]

In fairness, it should be pointed out that although the SS divisions had been involved in heavy fighting and in one sector had been temporarily driven out of the city by a Russian armoured counterattack, they had done considerable damage to the defending forces deployed by Belov.[22] Despite Hoth reiterating his order for *SS-Das Reich* to be withdrawn, the division launched a successful night attack to overcome a stubborn line of Russian defences that had been the scene of costly fighting through much of the afternoon, but Hoth had no intention of tolerating what he saw as a deliberate attempt to ignore his instructions. He now sent written orders to the SS Panzer Corps: *SS-Das Reich* was to deploy to the north to facilitate the continuing envelopment of Kharkov by *SS-Totenkopf*. Hausser replied that he remained responsible for the divisions and expressed doubts about whether they would be able to carry out Hoth's orders. In an attempt to make Hoth change his mind, he submitted a further situation report in which he said once more that Russian resistance in the city had been broken, and that the state of the roads made redeployment of *SS-Das Reich* almost impossible, but Hoth would not be swayed. Shortly before midday on 12 March, Fourth Panzer Army issued unequivocal instructions for the division to be deployed as previously ordered. There were further delays as Brigadeführer Wahl, the commander of *SS-Das Reich*, found reasons to prevaricate and claimed that he could not disengage, but by late afternoon he too received written orders from Hoth. No further obstruction would be tolerated.[23]

On the same day, *Grossdeutchland* continued its pursuit of the defeated elements of Moskalenko's Fortieth Army. After a further air attack, the Germans captured Graivoron towards the end of the day, forcing the Russians to pull back to Golovchino. This effectively eliminated any remaining threat to the SS Panzer Corps from the direction of Zolochiv, and all day the battlegroups of *LSSAH* fought their way into the centre of Kharkov. Manstein's fears about casualties proved to be justified as the retreating Russians used snipers and ambushes to good effect, taking a heavy toll on the attacking German panzergrenadiers. At first, the Russian rearguards contested almost every building, but resistance slackened as the day progressed. To the north of the city, *SS-Totenkopf* moved first east, then southeast, threatening to cut the lines of communication of the Russian forces in and around Kharkov. By the end of the day, Hausser was able to report to Hoth that about a third of Kharkov was in German hands. The troops of *SS-Das Reich* began to move to their new deployment area with many officers complaining bitterly that they had been forced to abandon their thrust into Kharkov just at the point that it was beginning to bear fruit. The battlegroups of *LSSAH* reached and captured Dzerzhinsky Square during the following night after further heavy fighting; at the end of the battle, it was renamed *Platz der Leibstandarte*, a title that it wore for just a few months before the Red Army returned later in 1943. It is now known as Svoboda Square.

With the city being enveloped from the north, Hoth ordered XLVIII Panzer Corps – 6th and 11th Panzer Divisions – to attack to the southeast of Kharkov in order to complete the encirclement. Such a move would put increasing strain upon the rear area units struggling forward with supplies, particularly as both XLVIII Panzer Corps and the SS Panzer Corps would now be dependent upon the same approach roads, and, in an attempt to keep control of matters, a senior staff officer was given the task of coordinating supply movements. Within Kharkov, *LSSAH* continued to drive forward, and by late afternoon on 13 March the western and northern sectors of the city were firmly in German hands and the Russians were clearly abandoning the eastern parts. Fuel shortages and the poor state of the roads prevented *SS-Totenkopf* from completing the envelopment of the eastern outskirts and thus preventing the withdrawal of the city's defenders.

Having taken Graivoron, *Grossdeutschland* drove down the road leading to Belgorod. Moskalenko later wrote that his retreating troops blunted the German advance at Golovchino, but the war diary of *Armee Abteilung Kempf* records that the leading elements of *Grossdeutschland* reached the town in the early afternoon of 13 March and completed its capture before sunset.[24] From there, the division moved on to Borisovka where yet again it was forced to pause while fuel was brought forward to replenish the thirsty armoured vehicles. The Germans had become aware of the arrival of Badanov's II Guards Tank Corps, rushed to the area to try to shore up the Russian defences, and were determined to bring it to battle as quickly as possible; radio intercepts suggested that it was being deployed to secure the road between Belgorod and Kharkov. Shortly before noon on 14 March, *Grossdeutschland* ran into a group of Russian tanks near Borisovka and began a battle that would last for two days.

II Guards Tank Corps had an establishment of three tank brigades and two mechanised infantry brigades, and it started *Gallop* with 175 tanks.[25] By early March, it had already been involved in heavy fighting and had perhaps 90 tanks still operational, but as it moved north its strength was significantly diminished when it was forced to leave much of its mechanised infantry behind. Nevertheless, it still fielded a substantial number of tanks and was a potent force; the tank brigades moved through Kharkov just as the leading SS units began to enter the suburbs, and at first were intended to be used in the city's defence. However, as the threat from *SS-Totenkopf* and *Grossdeutschland* grew to the west and northwest of Kharkov, there was a growing need for an armoured counterattack to try to restore contact with Sixty-Ninth Army, and II Guards Tank Corps was ordered to move into position immediately. Aided by civilians from Kharkov who helped their tanks navigate through the city, the three tank brigades struggled north, then northwest, constantly harassed by Luftwaffe attacks. Just as his corps took up positions in the path of *Grossdeutschland*, Badanov was summoned to the headquarters of Sixty-Ninth Army to discuss how best to use the precious tanks. Throughout its redeployment, the corps had received orders – often contradictory – from a number of different higher commands as it was passed from one formation to another, and Badanov was anxious to sort out the chain of command. Now, the corps chief of staff found himself trying to fight a major battle while his commander was absent.

Throughout 14 March, fighting raged on in Kharkov. *SS-Totenkopf* continued its enveloping movement, reaching Rogan to the southeast of the city in mid-morning and beating off Russian attacks from the east. Fuel shortages proved to be as much an obstacle as Russian resistance for the SS units still engaged within Kharkov, with most Red Army units trying to slip away while they could. Not long after dusk, the SS Panzer Corps declared that it had retaken the entire city; fighting continued against Russian stragglers and partisans for several days, but organised resistance was at an end. There was much rejoicing, and Dietrich – commander of *LSSAH* – was awarded the Knight's Cross with Oak Leaves and Crossed Swords in recognition, and Manstein was awarded the Knight's Cross with Oak Leaves. To the south of the city, XLVIII Panzer Corps began to advance towards the leading elements of the SS Panzer Corps with the intention of encircling the remnants of the Russian units that had pulled out of

Kharkov. Despite the best efforts of Hoth and Manstein, the SS divisions had suffered substantial losses in urban fighting; their collective combat strength had fallen to about 56 per cent of their establishment, though this includes casualties suffered before the battle for the city began.[26]

On 15 March, *Grossdeutschland* advanced to deal with the armoured forces that had been reported by the Luftwaffe to be taking up positions to block the road to Belgorod; these had originally been intended for use by the Russians in a thrust down the Belgorod-Kharkov road in order to help the Russian units falling back from the advance of the SS Panzer Corps, but the advance of *Grossdeutschland* could not be ignored. The reconnaissance battalion, reinforced by the division's assault gun battalion, was the leading German formation, as the assault gun battalion commander, Hauptmann Peter Frantz, later described the action, in an account that shows how the Germans were increasingly emulating the Russian use of 'tank riders':

In the morning the assault gun battalion set out from the east end of Borissowka with elements of the reconnaissance battalion riding on the vehicles. The 1st Battery under Hauptmann Magold ... took over the point position. The battery soon made contact with enemy forces, including tanks. Personal observation and reports radioed by this battery created the impression that the enemy was massing strong forces. While I was still considering how best to carry out an attack against the recognised enemy, one of our reconnaissance aircraft came toward us at low altitude. We immediately broke out the ground identification panels and fired smoke and illumination shells. The aircraft circled twice, in order to determine whether we were really German troops. Then he waggled his wings and dropped a message canister. We quickly emptied the canister and studied the map sketched by the pilot. According to this, 6–8km [3.5 to 5 miles] distant there were about 100 to 120 enemy tanks and wheeled vehicles rolling toward us. This was it! The 1st Battery was pulled back from its present positions to the south somewhat, but not too far. The 2nd Battery was placed in a favourable defensive position ... The 3rd Battery under Oberleutnant Wehmeyer was held back as battalion reserve and security forces were deployed to the southeast. There was a general ban on firing until approved by the battalion. Even while the assault guns were taking on as much anti-tank ammunition as they could hold (the normal quantity carried in an assault gun was 48 rounds, in such cases up to 100 rounds were packed in) the lightly armoured vehicles of the reconnaissance battalion assembled in the direction of Borissowka as ordered ... Then the first T-34s came into view, ten to twelve vehicles. Deployed widely, they came straight toward our hill ... Wave after wave of tanks came toward us. Some veered slightly north into a small valley and disappeared from our view, but part of our panzer regiment was supposed to be in position there or en route. We left the tanks to them. As soon as the specified firing range was reached the battle began. The first T-34s, five or six tanks, blew up. The next wave halted. They too were struck by the frontal fire. The 1st Battery enquired nervously whether it too might be allowed to join in. 'Not yet!' was the answer. Everyone wanted to knock out his share, but it was not yet clear whether all the reported T-34s were in the bag. Only then was the flanking attack supposed to be carried out with 1st Battery. More T-34s continued to move toward us. After it was clear that the enemy had not outflanked us to the south, the 3rd Battery was moved up in the direction of 1st Battery. The two assault gun batteries now began a flanking attack from the south against the enemy armoured forces ... This was one of those rare cases after a successful tank battle when one could accurately count one's own successes. Other weapons had not participated in the engagement at this location and we took possession of the entire field. Forty-three T-34s had been destroyed.[27]

It seems that the true number of tanks destroyed in this ambush was actually 21; the remainder were knocked out when the *Grossdeutschland* panzer regiment dealt with the rest of the Russian armoured force. A junior officer in the panzer regiment described the fighting, which continued through the following night:

Machine-gun bullets whistled through the gardens on the outskirts of Borissowka and shells gurgled eerily overhead, recognisable by their bright red luminous trails ... Radio transmissions by our tanks said that there was feverish activity: enemy infantry was sneaking around our tanks, some were already in their rear; muzzle flashes from every direction, without doubt from enemy tanks.

For three hours there was the sound of heavy fighting; all around the dark night was lit by burning houses. Now and then there was an explosion, hundreds of tracers sprayed into the night sky, the ammunition from a stricken tank. Each man asked himself uneasily: ours or the enemy's? At about 0100 on 15 March three attacks by enemy tanks against Borissowka's northern bridge were repulsed and eight T-34s destroyed. The enemy pulled back for the time being ...

Then came the radioed order: '7th Company reinforce the defences at the north bridge!' ...

We crept across the bridge at safe intervals. Blinded by the glow of the fires, we were still able to see muzzle flashes farther down the street and then the first shells raced past us. We had to get out of there, the enemy had trained all his guns on the bridge. The driver of the first tank quickly realised what was happening: without waiting for orders to do so, he turned the tank off the road and disappeared into the safety of the darkness. The second tank followed closely behind the first; the other two also managed to escape into the dark of night. We stayed close together and formed a circle for protection …

Critical moments now followed. Suddenly the diesel engines of the enemy tanks roared into life scarcely 1,000m away. It wasn't two or even five T-34s, it had to be many more. We had to prepare ourselves for a tough fight!

The morning of 15 March dawned, the roar of engines slowly drew nearer. The tank leader spotted the outline of the first T-34 over on the road. The gunners at their sights were already uneasy, but in the twilight they couldn't yet see their targets clearly. They held their breath and finally released their tension with a happy 'Aah' when the first T-34 finally came into the sight's field of view.

The loader meanwhile waited in feverish tension beside his gun, a shell in his hand and two more clamped between his legs; for every second was vital here … Unsuspecting, the T-34s ground their way through the snow and mud; seven were now in sight and their broadside was too tempting for the gunners.

What if they spotted us too soon? Then it would be better to open fire immediately and without orders. Surely the radio had failed just now! Or had the platoon leader even been put out of action? These and similar thoughts raced through the brain. Nevertheless fire discipline was maintained. Uncertain, the T-34s turned their guns half right and then half left; it was good that we were level with one another. Each gunner had known for some time which enemy tank he had to engage …

Our nerves were stretched to the limit; the tank commanders glanced through their vision slits at the platoon leader's tank. For a moment the calmness they had shown in many battles seemed shaken. Then, finally, the order we were waiting for: attention, safety off, fire! A mighty crash! Four-eight-twelve green, luminous trails of light in a matter of seconds. Between them brief radio transmissions; then only individual shots from our cannon.

Over there, huge jets of flame and smoke. The last T-34 tried to turn around and became stuck. The crew jumped like cats from the turret, but were cut down by our machine-gun fire.[28]

By the end of the fighting, despite its claim that it destroyed over half of the 100 or more German tanks and other vehicles that attacked them, Colonel Vasily Mikhailovich Polyakov's 25th Guards Tank Brigade was reduced to just five serviceable tanks. To make matters worse, communications between the corps headquarters and its various tank brigades broke down during the fighting to the north of Borisovka, making coordination impossible. Unaware of the location of either his headquarters or the other tank brigades, Polyakov ordered the remnants of his brigade to pull back to Belgorod. His chief of staff finally managed to reach safety with the remaining tanks and a large number of wounded men, but Polyakov, one of the heroes of the Tatsinskaya raid, disappeared in the widespread confusion of air attacks and advancing German units, one of tens of thousands of men of all nations who to this day remain listed as 'missing in action'. The other two tank brigades stayed in contact with *Grossdeutschland* over the next two days, but could do little to stop the German advance and lost most of their remaining tanks as a result of combat with German armoured elements and air attacks. Whilst 25th Guards Tank Brigade's claim of German vehicles destroyed does not correlate with the daily totals of available vehicles in the *Grossdeutschland* war diary, it should be noted that the losses claimed by the Germans exceed the entire known strength of II Guards Tank Corps and other Russian armoured formations operating in the area. It is likely that the usual mix of exaggeration, multiple hits on the same vehicle, and the fog of war affected the reports on all sides, as was consistently the case throughout the campaign.[29] Fighting continued in and around Borisovka until the morning of 18 March, with small groups of Russian tanks repeatedly infiltrating closer to the town.

Worse was to come for the Russian tank units. Out of touch with the tank brigades, Burdeyny – the chief of staff of II Guards Tank Corps – suddenly found that his headquarters was under attack:

> At dawn I went into the courtyard from the house where I had spent the night, and I saw movement on the opposite side of a deep valley stretching from behind me to the south of the village of Brodki on some unnamed high ground. At first, I thought that it was 25th Guards Tank Brigade, but, peering through the binoculars, I realised that this was not the case. A motorcyclist rushed to the crest and immediately disappeared behind the reverse slopes of this height, and I realised that before us was either the enemy's reconnaissance unit intelligence or an advanced part of the main body. I couldn't report this to anyone, since the corps commander [was visiting] the headquarters of Sixty-Ninth Army, which was in the vicinity of the Maslova Pristan. A decision had to be made immediately.
>
> Fortunately, it was only possible to break into the village of Brodki from the high ground along a field road, descending from those heights and running along the valley to the eastern outskirts of the village, where as soon as headquarters was established in this village, a security detachment of three T-34s commanded by Lieutenant Petrov

and a platoon of motorised infantry led by Sergeant Levchenko from 4th Guards Tank Brigade had been deployed. We also had protection on the western outskirts of the village – two armoured cars and a platoon of motorised infantry – and we had mined the entry to the village. The direct distance from the highest point of the high ground to the centre of the village was about 1km, or 1,200–1,300m along the road.

Having spotted our staff cars and radio masts, the enemy did not immediately rush into the village. Their reconnaissance had already come under fire from ambush positions and was now cautious, perhaps waiting for the main force to approach. I could see German helmets moving about, the upper parts of half-tracks and the noise of engines. All this happened before my very eyes in a few minutes.

Without wasting time, I sounded the headquarters alarm, and the chief of operations, Lieutenant Colonel Lavrentiev, ordered the officers of the headquarters to assemble on the street and all vehicles and personnel to drive east – to Maslova Pristan, where there was a ferry across the Northern Donets, as we already knew. At the same time, he tasked Captain Oganesyants in the first car to dismount at the eastern outskirts of Brodki and check the readiness of the guard group.

As always in such cases, there was much activity on the streets of the village: people were running and leaping into cars, and then they headed east at speed to Maslova Pristan and the crossing, which was 10–12km [6–7 miles] away from us.

Of course, the enemy immediately noticed the activity in the village, and our intentions were clear to him. He immediately opened fire with anti-aircraft guns and tanks against the village and the vehicles driving east. At the same time, with the support of artillery fire, armoured vehicles, motorcycles, and a few tanks he began to descend from the high ground towards the eastern edge of the village to intercept the vehicles that were leaving to the east.

Our security line was silent, and it seemed to me that a disaster was inevitable. But after letting the enemy advance a short distance, our tank guns suddenly began to fire and heavy machine-guns joined in. My heart eased. Captain Oganesyants had reached the security line in time. The first shots from the guns struck several enemy armoured vehicles and motorcycles, and then one after another two enemy tanks, then another, two began to burn and the other two halted with broken caterpillar tracks. Apparently, the Nazis did not expect such an encounter and spotted our well-camouflaged tanks too late. They were confused, moved around the burned and damaged tanks and then began to withdraw to the high ground from which they had just descended.

On the battlefield were burning and wrecked vehicles and a large number of dead and wounded fascists. However, the enemy continued to fire with anti-aircraft guns and heavy machine guns from the high ground.[30]

Despite driving off the Germans – from the presence of motorcycles, it is probable that this was part of the *Grossdeutschland* reconnaissance battalion – Burdeyny's troubles weren't over. His personal car was hit by gunfire and had to be abandoned, and he finally reached the river crossing on foot. Several of the headquarters staff were left behind, and most – many of them wounded – eventually escaped to the northern Donets in the following days. The last significant armoured formation available to the Red Army to blunt the German counteroffensive was spent, and now the only hope of stopping Manstein's forces was for the weather to turn warm enough to turn the landscape to mud.

On 15 March, while *Grossdeutschland* was dealing with the armour of Badanov's II Guards Tank Corps, *SS-Totenkopf* continued its drive and reached Chuguyev before dawn. Elements of *SS-Das Reich* followed in its wake but turned off the Chuguyev road towards the south, while 6th Panzer Division attacked towards the east just south of Merefa. The following day, the two German spearheads met, encircling the Russian forces to the southeast of Kharkov. Without sufficient infantry to seal off the encirclement, the Germans could do little to prevent many of the Russian troops escaping on foot – some to the southeast, others to the northeast – though as had been repeatedly the case throughout the campaign, they were forced to abandon most of their heavy weapons. Casualties amongst the retreating Russian units were heavy, and seven rifle divisions and two tank corps were effectively rendered incapable of further action in the near future.

Everywhere across the Ukraine, the spring thaw was setting in. Further exploitation of the weakness of the Red Army needed urgency, and the constant fuel shortages continued to hinder Manstein as much as the state of the roads and terrain. The southern sector of the front along the Mius was already settling down for a period of inactivity and the Russians moved several formations north in an attempt to reduce the pressure upon the forces to the east of Kharkov, but despite their commitment *SS-Totenkopf* completed the capture of Chuguyev on 16 March. With the encircled Russian forces to the southeast of Kharkov rapidly dispersing and German infantry beginning to arrive, the German armour turned north to make use of what time remained available to try to gain more ground. The two panzer divisions of XLVIII Panzer Corps were ordered to continue driving back the Russians to the east of the city while the SS Panzer Corps would drive towards Belgorod. While the forces in and around Kharkov laboured to prepare themselves for this next phase, *Grossdeutschland* and the infantry divisions of *Armee Abteilung Kempf* continued their attacks from the west, with *Grossdeutschland* advancing on Tomarovka and beating off repeated Russian armoured counterattacks. Strachwitz might have been unimpressed with the performance of the new Tiger tanks earlier in the campaign, but they were now described as 'outstanding'.[31] Nevertheless, whilst the ground was not as soft as along the Mius, it was clear that the winter campaign season was coming to an end. Manstein contacted Kempf on 16 March to urge greater alacrity on the part of the infantry divisions that were slowly driving back Moskalenko's Fortieth Army:

> 1055: Radio conversation between *OB/Armee-Abt* [*Oberbefehlshaber Armee Abteilung* or 'Commander of army detachment', i.e. Kempf] and *OB/H.Gr* [*Oberbefehlshaber Heeresgruppe* or 'Commander of army group', i.e. Manstein]:
> *OB/H.Gr* states that the infantry divisions are advancing too slowly.
> *OB/Armee-Abt*: The unimaginably bad state of the roads is to blame.
> In response to the comment from *OB/H.Gr* about the *Armee Abteilung* report of yesterday that the road state was good, *OB/Armee-Abt* replied that the roads are only good during the night and early morning when frozen.[32]

Further discussions followed during the day with Busse, Manstein's chief of staff, asking whether the infantry might progress faster if it simply pressed forward along the main supply route used by *Grossdeutschland*; the response was not encouraging. The road was already choked with the supply columns of the armoured formations.

Those armoured formations – primarily the armoured battlegroup of *Grossdeutschland* – continued to clash with Russian tanks. The leading German elements ran into a Russian forming up area north of Tomarovka, rapidly destroying or capturing 22 tanks, but despite their successes much of the road that they had used for their advance remained under Russian tank fire. It took until the evening to secure the road for support units to move up. North of Kharkov the SS began to push towards Belgorod, the next objective for the great counteroffensive, but attempts by *SS-Totenkopf* to move its forces north were hampered by repeated Russian counterattacks around Chuguyev throughout 16 March. As the SS Panzer Corps and *Grossdeutschland* converged on Belgorod, the approach roads became steadily more congested and the *Grossdeutschland* chief of staff suggested that units could be diverted towards the north in order to protect the open northern flank of the division; the suggestion was rejected, as there were no signs of any Russian forces concentrating in that area. Most of the resistance was around Belgorod, but by the afternoon the SS divisions had covered half the distance from Kharkov, with *LSSAH* to the west and *SS-Das Reich* to the east, and *SS-Totenkopf* guarding the eastern flank of the advance; the leading elements of 6th Panzer Division had now reached Chuguyev, releasing the SS division for redeployment to the north. In turn, the German 39th Infantry Division, now operating as part of XLVIII Panzer Corps, was ordered to move to Chuguyev as fast as possible in order to release 6th Panzer Division for mobile operations while the state of the roads still allowed it.

Starting at first light on 18 March, the SS divisions advanced rapidly on Belgorod, crushing all Russian units in their path – the SS Panzer Corps war diary recorded that 'the resistance against the divisions thrusting north was extraordinarily light, allowing the spearheads to reach their first objectives in just a short time'.[33] As the Germans approached Belgorod the level of resistance steadily increased, but by evening the SS divisions had reached and entered the city. Fighting continued in the following days as *SS-Totenkopf* gradually drove back Russian troops that were west of the northern Donets between Belgorod and Chuguyev, while *LSSAH* swung around to face west and thus blocked the retreat of the remnants of the Russian Sixty-Ninth and Fortieth Armies. Some Russian soldiers succeeded in working their way past the SS to reach Russian lines further east, and the largest unit to escape relatively intact – 161st Rifle Division – endured two days of near-constant contact with German troops pressing in from all sides before it managed to escape, moving first north, then northwest. The slowly advancing infantry divisions of Raus' corps finally reached Belgorod on 22 March, just as the spring thaw began in earnest.

As the terrain rapidly turned to mud, both sides took a much-needed opportunity to catch their breath. Russian reinforcements that had been en route for the region finally began to arrive; Twenty-First Army took up positions between Fortieth and Sixty-Ninth Armies, with First Tank Army in reserve to the rear. Whilst reinforcements also arrived for Third Tank Army, it no longer had sufficient armour to justify its title and it was temporarily renamed Fifty-Seventh Army. But whilst the Russians were still able to bring large formations to the front line, the Germans had no such reserves. The best they could do was allow the exhausted divisions of Army Group South some rest, and hope that they could be restored to full strength. Both sides would take advantage of the pause to bring forward replacement drafts and new tanks and guns, and here again, contrast between the resources available to the Germans and Russians was stark. During the whole of 1943, German factories would produce a little over 5,600 new tanks and assault guns; by comparison, the Soviet Union's industrial plants would manufacture nearly 16,000 T-34s alone, and in total some 24,000 tanks and assault guns. Hitler had great hopes and expectations of the newest German tanks – they would need to be exceptionally good if they were to prevail against the Russian forces deployed against them.

CHAPTER 14

PAUSE FOR BREATH

The winter campaign was over. The front line had returned to almost exactly the same positions as the end of the previous winter, with one significant difference: the Russians were left with a large salient around Kursk, projecting to the west. In terms of territory, this was all that they had to show for their dreams of destroying all German forces east of the Dnepr.

Losses on both sides had been severe, and numerically at least – as was almost consistently the case throughout the war – the Russians lost more men and equipment than the Germans in the fighting outside Stalingrad. However, it would be wrong to overstate the importance of this. Firstly, the Soviet Union was in a better position than Germany to sustain such losses. Secondly, the strategic balance had tilted irrevocably. Whilst Manstein's counterstroke recovered the stability of the Eastern Front, the initiative would in future lie with the Red Army. Both sides would rest and re-equip, but with every passing week, the inescapable arithmetic of tank production would work against the Wehrmacht.

Manstein's abiding fear throughout the long campaign had been that a catastrophe far greater than Stalingrad beckoned. If the Russians could reach Rostov and the shores of the Sea of Azov, all of the German forces in the Caucasus would be isolated and destroyed; if the Russian tanks succeeded in seizing the Dnepr crossings, all German units in the Ukraine would be added to the haul. Either outcome would have been terminally disastrous for Germany, and preventing these superseded all other tasks for the commander of Army Group Don. This must include the fate of the encircled Sixth Army, and the question arises: did Manstein believe that it was possible to save Paulus' troops?

It can be argued that, given a freer hand with the resources that were available, Manstein and Hoth could have achieved success with *Winter Storm* – the armoured units stranded in the Caucasus were ultimately released for operations further north, and had they been allowed to join LVII Panzer Corps at an earlier stage it seems probable that the Germans would have been able to reach Sixth Army, even if the latter had persisted in refusing to launch any attacks of its own. But simply breaking through the encirclement would not have been enough. The Russian forces that were gathered to oppose LVII Panzer Corps would have counterattacked with vigour and keeping the corridor open would have taxed the strength of the forces available. It would also have been essential for Sixth Army to withdraw to the west, and this would have required the permission of Hitler – Paulus lacked the self-belief of Hausser and would never have permitted any withdrawal without permission. Even in the unlikely event of Hitler granting such permission, Sixth Army would have had to continue tying down the forces that had surrounded it throughout its retreat – otherwise, they would have been released to attack elsewhere, increasing the likelihood of success of the Russian attempts to reach the Black Sea or the Dnepr crossings.

Manstein was perfectly aware of all of these factors, and wrote about them extensively in his memoirs. He must therefore have been aware that success was very unlikely, perhaps even impossible. Nevertheless, an attempt had to be made – with so many German troops encircled in Stalingrad, it was unthinkable that they should simply be abandoned without any attempt to save them. Once it became clear that a greater catastrophe was imminent and that Hitler – and therefore Paulus – would never change their minds, Manstein showed no hesitation in drawing forces away from LVII Panzer Corps in order to prevent the Russians from achieving a potentially war-winning victory. The decisive manner in which he did so speaks volumes about his personal willingness to write off Sixth Army in order to prevent a far greater defeat.

From the German perspective, the eventual salvation achieved by Manstein was a close-run thing. Any further delays on the part of Hitler could have been fatal – indeed, as has been described, the delays proved to be critical in that they fostered the impression held by the Russians that the Germans were on the run, and resulted in the Red Army moving sufficiently far to the west to be fully exposed to Manstein's counterstroke, but not so far to the west that the German forces were isolated and destroyed. Nor was it sufficient to move several divisions from the west to the Ukraine, and to release the forces that had been tied up in the Caucasus; even once all of the pieces were in place, the counterstroke required the highest level of military skill by the Germans at every level. Despite being worn down by a tough winter and despite the shattering effect that Stalingrad must have had upon German morale, soldiers and junior officers performed admirably. As is consistently the case with the achievements of either side on the Eastern Front, this remarkable martial feat has to be put alongside the pitiless manner in which it was achieved. Most German accounts of these battles concentrate on the military action, with barely a mention of the civilians, and many Germans of all ranks later claimed complete ignorance about the manner in which the local population was treated. But as this narrative has shown, the widespread evidence found by the advancing Red Army of atrocities and forced labour camps makes it almost impossible to believe such protestations; even if many of those who later wrote their memoirs were not personally involved in the mistreatment of civilians, they surely must have been aware of what was happening. By acting in this manner towards the population of the Ukraine, Germany perhaps squandered its best chance of winning the war; the Soviet authorities were not popular with many Ukrainians after the deliberate famines and repeated purges of the 1930s, and many civilians welcomed the Germans in 1941 as liberators. Treating them as potential allies against the Soviet state rather than as little more than slaves would, at the very least, have prevented the rapid growth of the partisan movement, and might have resulted in a very different outcome to the entire war.

The Red Army came close to winning the war in the winter of 1942–43. If Manstein's fears had been realised, it seems inconceivable that Germany could have recovered from such a disastrous setback – at the very least, the wholesale transfer of sufficient divisions to build a new Eastern Front would have reduced considerably the obstacles faced by the Western Allies and might have resulted in an invasion of France at an earlier date, though whether the British and Americans had sufficient amphibious capability in 1943 is open to question. In his memoirs, Manstein suggests that the Russians could have achieved more than they did:

> The first stroke – the encirclement of Sixth Army – was undoubtedly correct. If it succeeded ... the strongest striking force the Germans had would be eliminated.
>
> It would have been better if this first blow had been coordinated with the offensive against the fronts of the Italian and Hungarian armies, in order that every effort should be made from the start to cut off the German forces at Rostov or on the Sea of Azov in one unified and large-scale assault operation. Clearly the available artillery was not equal to the task, and for this reason, presumably, the breakthrough operations had to be staggered. It is also conceivable that the transport situation did not allow the sum total of assault forces to be assembled and supplied simultaneously.[1]

The concluding comment is something of an understatement – it is inconceivable that the Red Army could have concentrated all of the operations of the winter into one grand offensive without stretching its logistic service far beyond breaking point. There is also a degree of hindsight at work in Manstein's assumptions. Before the onset of *Uranus*, there was no guarantee that any of the Russian offensive operations would succeed. In particular, the Russians had to develop confidence in their abilities; nobody, from Stalin down to the junior ranks, would have had sufficient self-belief to propose an operation on the scale that Manstein suggested. Nevertheless, there is some justification in a further comment from Manstein:

> Even after the successful breakthrough against the Hungarian Army, which tore open the German front from the Donets to Voronezh, the Soviet command still failed to press on with sufficient speed and strength in the decisive direction – towards the Dnepr crossings. Instead of putting all its eggs in one basket and simply leaving a strong, concentrated shock group to provide offensive protection to the west, it squandered its forces in a series of far-ranging uncoordinated thrusts at Akhtyrka and Poltava by way of Kursk, against the Dnepr and across the Donets line … In this way it enabled the German command to be stronger at the decisive spots when the time came.[2]

This squandering of resources grew out of the mistaken belief that the Wehrmacht had already suffered irreparable damage, just as Hitler's decision to squander resources the previous summer was based upon an inaccurate assessment of the state of the Red Army. In both cases, realisation of the real situation came too late.

The German strategic objective for 1942 was to secure the Caucasus oilfields and deny their use to the Soviet Union. For much of the year, the oilfields produced little oil for the Russians (and even less for the Germans); whilst the Red Army suffered from fuel shortages at key points of the winter fighting, these were not caused by an overall shortage of fuel, merely the consequence of overstretched supply services that struggled to perform adequately over badly degraded roads. The Germans too were constantly hampered by fuel shortages, but these reflected more than logistic issues; the reality was that, whilst access to the Caucasus oilfields was not critical for the Soviet Union's war effort, Germany was desperately short of oil. The Romanian oilfields had limited capacity and synthetic fuel production was no substitute for access to adequate natural resources. Bearing this in mind, it is easy to criticise Hitler's failure to support

Kleist's army group – just like the Russians during the winter of 1942–43, he believed that the enemy had already been defeated. There was therefore no urgency to complete the campaign.

For the Russians, the chastening setbacks of March were a stark contrast to their euphoric celebrations of December and January. Vasilevsky wrote that Vatutin had urged *Stavka* to permit a rapid advance in depth but Stalin had held back until after the fall of Kharkov – thereafter, he too became infected by the over-optimism that was prevalent in the headquarters of Southwest and Voronezh Fronts. Vasilevsky was dispatched to the latter even as Manstein's counterstroke began, and he later wrote that he realised the gravity of the situation after meeting Rybalko to discuss the state of Third Tank Army. Whilst Vasilevsky claims that the reinforcements that *Stavka* then sent to the sector were instrumental in preventing the Germans from making even greater gains – in particular in the direction of Kursk – he makes no mention of the onset of the spring thaw.

The Russians rapidly started a detailed analysis of the winter's fighting. The organisation of Russian armoured formations was considered once more in order to try to find the optimum mixture of tanks, infantry and artillery. At a higher level, the front line was further reformed, with a new Kursk Front – renamed Orel Front and then Bryansk Front a few days later – created on the northern flank of Voronezh Front. Golikov was criticised for the manner in which his front had ceased to function in a coordinated manner and he was ordered back to Moscow; in 1941, this might have been the prelude to arrest and execution, but Stalin had learned the limitations of such a draconian policy. Instead, the experienced Golikov became deputy defence minister, then head of the army's personnel directorate. The criticism of Golikov seems somewhat unjust – he was ordered to divert his forces south in order to try to help Southwest Front, and once his forces had been spread out in this manner, their defeat in detail was almost inevitable. His replacement as commander of Voronezh Front was Vatutin, who had been widely criticised for his over-confidence. However, his enthusiasm and energy seem to have earned Stalin's approval, and he was promoted to general.

Both sides began to look to the future. Manstein's assessment was that the German position along the Donets remained vulnerable to a powerful Russian attack towards the Dnepr crossings, and he anticipated a drive by the Red Army from the Belgorod-Kursk area towards the southwest. His preference was to allow this advance to commence while concentrating German armoured forces to the north of the Russian assault; when the opportune moment came, he would release these forces in a counterthrust towards the southeast, striking into the flank and rear of the advancing Russians. Whilst this was unlikely to result in the complete defeat of the Soviet Union, Manstein believed that such an outcome was – for the near future at least – beyond the ability of the Wehrmacht. The best that could be achieved was to wear down the Red Army in the hope of then negotiating a separate peace.

The likelihood of Stalin ever accepting such a separate peace was on the face of things most unlikely, but it is worth noting that the Japanese and Swedish governments both offered to act as intermediaries during the temporary cessation of hostilities during the *rasputitsa* season. Whilst the Soviet ambassador in Stockholm, the colourful if elderly Alexandra Mikhailovna Kollontai, was an inveterate Germanophobe, lower ranking diplomats – in particular, Vladimir Semenovich Semyonov and Boris Yartsev – were more inclined to seek a rapprochement with Germany. Stalin was growing increasingly impatient with what he saw as the excuses of the Western Allies with regard to opening a land front in the west, and with his approval, Russian diplomats met German representatives near Stockholm for informal discussions in April 1943. The minimum positions of the two sides left no room for compromise – Stalin wished for a restoration of the 1941 frontier, while Hitler demanded the creation of a satellite state in the Ukraine, together with other economic concessions, and the talks rapidly came to an end.

It is difficult to see how any agreement, on the terms of either dictator, could have resulted in a lasting peace, particularly given the wide awareness in the Soviet Union of German atrocities in the occupied parts of European Russia, the Baltic States and the Ukraine. But Stalin may have been motivated by the failure of the Western Allies to initiate an invasion of the European mainland and their wish to restore Eastern Europe to its pre-war frontiers, by which they meant 1939, not 1941. The talks with the Germans may have been little more than an attempt to exert leverage upon the United States and Britain, but they put into context Manstein's hopes of achieving a military outcome that would make such talks more likely to progress to an agreement.[3]

Manstein's planned counterstroke for the summer of 1943 – the 'backhand blow' as it became known – was not without risk, but played to the strengths of the Wehrmacht, particularly its tactical and operational excellence. However, Hitler was opposed to it on three counts. Firstly, it would once more require the abandonment of Ukrainian territory, albeit temporarily, and he remained adamant that the control of the Ukraine was essential to the war effort of either Germany or the Soviet Union. Secondly, he expressed concern that any such Russian advance, even if only temporary, would result in an adverse political effect on Romania and Turkey. Thirdly, the operation would run the risk that, once the Russians had been allowed to advance, the counterstroke might fail, leaving the Red Army in permanent control of the Ukraine. Manstein was probably not alone in believing that these reasons were little more than rationalisation – the reality was that Hitler remained viscerally opposed to conceding any territory that he had gained, constantly harking back to his order for the Wehrmacht to hold firm before Moscow in December 1941. Consequently, the Führer demanded instead that plans should be drawn up for a 'forehand blow', i.e. one that did not first entail allowing the Russians to advance. The obvious objective for this was the Kursk salient, and there were initial discussions about this during the meeting between Hitler and his generals on 10 March. If this operation was to be adopted, Manstein believed that it would need to be implemented as soon as the ground started to dry out in May – it was vital to attack while the Red Army was still weakened by its setbacks in February and March. Instead, Hitler imposed repeated delays to allow for equipment levels in the panzer divisions to be improved with increasing numbers of the newest tanks, utterly ignoring the fact that Russian tank production exceeded German production by a factor of four and that any delay was of far greater benefit to the Red Army than to the Wehrmacht.

At the top levels of the German regime, the disaster at Stalingrad left its mark. Albert Speer, the Armaments Minister, later recalled a dinner organised by Goebbels in which the latter remarked on the manner in which the British had systematically mobilised their people and industry for war in a manner that Germany had failed to do. According to Goebbels, this was because of Dunkirk – the near-disastrous battle in 1940 spurred the British to make the necessary changes. Stalingrad could serve a similar purpose for Germany, he suggested, concentrating minds on the importance of mobilising for 'total war'. He went on to proclaim this policy in a major speech even before the fighting in the Ukraine had been drawn to a close by the spring thaw, but implementing 'total war' policies proved difficult. The proposed ban on luxuries, freely available to those in the upper echelons of the Nazi Party, was met with protests; Hitler's mistress, Eva Braun, objected to the Führer when she learned that production of cosmetics was to be curtailed. Nevertheless, Speer was able to start implementing changes that would lead to a marked increase in production of armaments.[4]

The Russians, too, looked to the coming summer campaign, as Vasilevsky described:

> The Soviet command got down to drawing up a plan of action and comprehensive
> provision for it immediately after completing the winter campaign – at the end of

March 1943. Already in early April, the general staff was acting on *Stavka*'s instructions in issuing orders for the fronts for them to use the time of the spring thaw for improving defences on all the lines they held, especially their anti-tank defences, and for developing defensive installations and creating reserves on the main fronts, as well as for preparing their troops for action; the latter mainly involved working on offensive fighting and offensive operations. As always, but then especially, the main concern ... was to create strong reserves and assemble enough tanks, aircraft, artillery, ammunition, fuel and other material resources which the troops would need for launching their large-scale offensive operations ...

It seemed that we had done everything possible to organise our offensive. However, soon after we made some essential revisions to the *Stavka* summer plan, envisaging the main attack coming in the southwest direction. Soviet military intelligence managed to discover in time the preparation of Hitler's army for a large-scale offensive on the Kursk bulge and even provide us with the date.[5]

The original intention of the Red Army was therefore precisely what Manstein had anticipated – a further attempt to pin Army Group South to the Black Sea coast. Soviet military intelligence was fortunate to have access to material gathered by the 'Lucy' spy network, based in Switzerland and run by Rudolf Roessler, a Bavarian who had fled Germany when the Nazis came to power. Roessler was contacted by fellow anti-Fascists within the German military, in particular Generalleutnant Fritz Thiele and Oberst Rudolph von Gersdorff, and using their positions in the German Defence Ministry's signals office, they provided Roessler with an Enigma coding machine and a radio, and assigned him an official radio callsign – the signals office was so compartmentalised that those who encoded signals had no idea where they would be sent, and those who transmitted the signals had no idea of their content. Although he was not a communist, Roessler rapidly recognised that the Soviet Union was the strongest enemy of fascist Germany and passed information to Moscow via an intermediary, Alexander Rado, who coined the name 'Lucy' because all he knew about the German network was that Roessler was based in Lucerne. After providing the Soviet Union with information about German plans in both 1941 and 1942, the network furnished lavish details of the forthcoming attack on Kursk; in most cases, the information reached Moscow within ten hours of decisions being made in Berlin.[6]

On 8 April, Zhukov advised Stalin that, in light of this intelligence, it would be better to allow the Germans to attack rather than attempt to forestall them with a Russian attack; once the German armour had been worn down, the

Red Army would still have sufficient time to launch its own offensive. Stalin was concerned that his armies might not be able to withstand a massive German attack, but his senior commanders had few such concerns. This was no longer the army of 1941 or 1942, and with appropriate preparations, the front commanders had no doubt that they could stop the panzer divisions in their tracks. But despite the widespread optimism after the winter fighting, the setbacks of late February and March left no room for complacency and many lessons had clearly been learned, as Shtemenko wrote:

> In planning the 1943 summer campaign we had to look very carefully before we leapt. We could not launch an immediate offensive ourselves. Even to be sure of thwarting an enemy offensive, we had to make careful preparations, reinforcing and concentrating our troops and reserves, bringing up ammunition and building up fuel stocks. It was considered essential, for instance, to have as many as 20 refuellings per aircraft before a large-scale offensive could be launched.[7]

The gloom in German military circles after the Stalingrad encirclement was replaced by cautious optimism when Manstein demonstrated that the Wehrmacht remained a formidable force, but the outcome of the fighting left others in Germany deeply dismayed. The various anti-Nazi resistance groups in both civilian and military life had concluded after Germany's victories early in the war that they would have to wait until there was a major setback before moving against Hitler. There was a general expectation that when such a disaster occurred, Hitler would lose the trust of his generals who would then be prepared to move against him – any attempt to arrest or assassinate the Führer without the support of at least a large part of the army would be doomed to failure and might simply result in the replacement of one disastrous head of state by another from the same political party. The main obstacle was the personal oath of loyalty that every officer had given, but it was hoped that Stalingrad would demonstrate to the generals that they had to act, regardless of their oath. Hans Gisevius, who was intimately involved in several plots against Hitler, described the thinking of the conspirators:

> The moment the Stalingrad disaster was complete, the marshals in the east were to act. They would not renounce their oath to Hitler as head of state or as their supreme commander, but simply refuse to obey him in his capacity of commander-in-chief in the east. This was to serve as a pretext for [Field Marshal Erwin von] Witzleben, as commander-in-chief in the west, to break with Hitler

– still on a purely military basis. In the ensuing confusion [Generaloberst Ludwig] Beck would take over in order to restore a unitary military command. Then, employing [General Friedrich] Olbricht's well-prepared home army, we could carry out a 'legal' *Putsch*.[8]

It is worth noting that at this stage, the intention was to remove Hitler from power, not necessarily to kill him. Gisevius is wrong in that Witzleben had been replaced as commander-in-chief in the west by Field Marshal Gerd von Rundstedt in 1942 after openly criticising the decision to invade the Soviet Union, though he was also unwell at the time and retired from active service in order to seek medical treatment; nevertheless, he had been involved in conspiracies against Hitler since before the war and remained in close contact both with his fellow conspirators and like-minded individuals in the army. Regardless of whether he would have been able to prevail upon Rundstedt to break with Hitler, the conspirators were informed by Kluge, the commander of Army Group Centre in the east, that he would only refuse to obey Hitler if Paulus made a public proclamation to the army and the people of Germany about Hitler's responsibility for the disaster. When Paulus silently surrendered, the plan collapsed and Kluge – who had always been a lukewarm conspirator at best – reportedly told the conspirators that he had reluctantly decided to give Hitler one last chance. Despite this setback, the conspirators still believed that events might turn in their favour:

> We did not abandon hope, in spite of Kluge's defection. Another shock, the mass surrender in Tunis, had been foreshadowed months before. We hoped that we should be able to make use of this opportunity. Unfortunately, we assumed that the Anglo-American forces would take the leap across to Sicily immediately thereafter. At the time virtually no German troops were stationed on that island ...
>
> Beck and [Carl Friedrich] Goerdeler were not swayed from the determination that Hitler must be overthrown. Every day brought new and more terrible casualties. The bombings mounted night after night. Little imagination was required to predict the frightful devastation which we can see today. But could a revolt now be expected of the generals? Scarcely. That much was clear by February 1943. Consequently, at the time Beck gave his consent to assassination, which until then he as well as Goerdeler had rejected for religious and political reasons.[9]

So much was at stake in the critical weeks of the winter of 1942–43. The fate of the entire German position in the Eastern Front was in doubt until Manstein's counteroffensive unfolded successfully, and for a brief time it seemed as if the circumstances upon which the anti-Hitler conspirators depended were about to fall in place. Manstein's extraordinary achievement, built upon the technical expertise of officers and soldiers at every level in the Wehrmacht, settled both questions, but only for the moment. Many of the men of the Red Army had always believed that ultimately, they would win; now they had a better understanding of how they would win. The conspirators who had hoped that a military disaster would create a decisive split between Hitler and his generals now took the decision that the only hope for Germany was for the Führer to be assassinated. Hitler's confidence, badly damaged by the Stalingrad debacle, seemed to recover rapidly in the spring, even though this recovery was entirely due to the efforts of others and not at all due to him. All of them – the men and women of the Red Army, the Wehrmacht, the leadership of both sides, and the disparate resistance groups – looked to see what the summer of 1943 would bring.

NOTES

INTRODUCTION

1   R. Overy, *Goering* (Phoenix, London, 1984), p.176
2   C. Webster and N. Frankland, *The Strategic Air Offensive Against Germany* (HMSO, London, 1961), Vol. IV, pp.501–04
3   R. Wagenführ, *Die Deutsche Industrie im Kriege 1939–1945* (Deutsches Institut für Wirtschaftsforschung, Berlin, 1954), p.29
4   See for example, R. Citino, *The Wehrmacht Retreats: Fighting a Lost War, 1943* (University of Kansas Press, Lawrence, KS, 2012); R. Smelser and E. Davies, *The Myth of the Eastern Front: The Nazi-Soviet War in American Popular Culture* (Cambridge University Press, Cambridge, 2008)

CHAPTER 1

1   M. Cooper, *The German Army 1939–1945* (Scarborough House, Lanham, MD, 1990), p.283
2   See, for example, M. Tukhachevsky, *New Problems in Warfare* (Art of War Symposium, Carlisle, PA, 1983); I. Uborevich, *Operativno-Takticheskaia i Aviatsionnaia Voennye Igry* (Gosudarstvennoe izdatel'stvo, Otdel Voennoi Literatury, Moscow, 1929); G. Isserson and B. Menning (trans.), *The Evolution of Operational Art* (Combat Studies Institution Press, Fort Leavenworth, KA, 2013); S. Krasilnikov, *Organizatsiya Krupnykh Obshchevoyskovykh Soyedineniy. Proshedsheye, Nastoyashcheye i Budushcheye* (Gosudarstvennoe izdatel'stvo, Otdel Voennoi Literatury, Moscow, 1933); V. Melikov, *Problema strategiceskogo razvertyvanija po opytu mirovoj i grazdanskoj vojny* (Naucno-Issledovatelskiye Otdel Voenny Akademie, Moscow, 1935)
3   S. Shtemenko, *The Soviet General Staff at War 1941–1945* (Progress, Moscow, 1970), p.23
4   D. Glantz and J. House, *When Titans Clashed: How the Red Army Stopped Hitler* (University Press of Kansas, Lawrence, KA, 1995), pp.80–82
5   H. Guderian, *Erinnerungen Eines Soldaten* (Vowinckel, Heidelberg, 1951),

pp.353–55

6   A. Vasilevsky, *A Lifelong Cause* (Progress, Moscow, 1973), p.126

7   Vasilevsky, *Lifelong Cause,* p.8

8   Ibid., p.13

9   For an account of the Brusilov Offensive, see P. Buttar, *Russia's Last Gasp: The Eastern Front in World War I 1916–1917* (Osprey, Oxford, 2016), pp.139–293

10   For an account of the Kornilov Affair, see P. Buttar, *The Splintered Empires: The Eastern Front in World War I 1917–1923* (Osprey, Oxford, 2017), pp.209–17

11   Vasilevsky, *Lifelong Cause*, p.21

12   Shtemenko, *Soviet General Staff*, pp.124–26

13   P. Mezhiritsky, 'Reading Marshal Zhukov' in *The Soviet and Post-Soviet Review* (Libas Consulting, Philadelphia, PA, 1995), Vol. XXIII 1, pp.349–50

14   N. Krushchev and S. Krushchev (ed.), *Memoirs of Nikita Krushchev* (Pennsylvania State University Press, University Park, PA, 2004), Vol. I, pp.362–70

15   Vasilevsky, *Lifelong Cause*, p.152

16   G. Zhukov, *The Memoirs of Marshal Zhukov* (Jonathan Cape, London, 1971), Vol. II, pp.43–44

17   D. Glantz, *Kharkhov 1942: Anatomy of a Military Disaster* (Sarpedon, New York, 1998), pp.21–37

18   Shtemenko, *Soviet General Staff*, p.56

19   W. Adam and O. Rühle (trans. T. le Tissier), *With Paulus at Stalingrad* (Pen and Sword, Barnsley, 2015), pp.22–23

20   C. Bellamy, *Absolute War: Soviet Russia in the Second World War* (Pan, London, 2007), p.498

21   E. Ziemke, *Moscow to Stalingrad: Decision in the East* (University of Michigan Press, Ann Arbor, MI, 1987), pp.328–30

22   Quoted in A. Clark, *Barbarossa: The Russian-German Conflict 1941–1945* (Papermac, London, 1985), p.205

23   Quoted in Clark, *Barbarossa*, p.208

24   Ibid., p.209

25   R. Forczyk, *Tank Warfare on the Eastern Front 1941–1942: Schwerpunkt* (Pen and Sword, Barnsley, 2014), p.201

26   Ibid., p.202

27   S. Zaloga and L. Ness, *Red Army Handbook 1939–1945* (Sutton, Stroud, 1998), pp.78–79

28   Adam and Rühle, *Paulus at Stalingrad*, p.29

29   Quoted in F. von Mellenthin, *Panzer Battles* (University of Oklahoma Press, Danvers, MA, 1956), p.153

30   J. Engelmann, *Manstein: Stratege und Truppenführer – ein Lebensbericht in Bildern* (Podzun Pallas, Friedburg, 1981), p.19

31   E. von Manstein, *Soldat im 20. Jahrehundert* (Bernard & Graefer, Munich, 1997), p.177; M. Melvin, *Manstein: Hitler's Greatest General* (Orion, London, 2010), p.65

32   T. Anderson, *Sturmartillerie: Spearhead of the Infantry* (Osprey, Oxford, 2016), p.11

33   B. Lemay (trans. P. Heyward), *Manstein: Hitler's Master Strategist* (Casemate, Newbury, 2010), pp.56–57, 62–63

34   E. von Manstein, *Lost Victories: The War Memoirs of Hitler's Most Brilliant General* (Presidio, Novato, CA, 1994), p.56

35   O. von Wrochem, *Vernichtungskrieg und Erinnerungspolitik: Erich von Manstein, Akteur und Symbol* (Schoeningh Ferdinand, Paderborn, 2006), p.47

36   H. Trevor-Roper, *Hitler's War Directives 1939–1945* (Birlinn, Edinburgh, 2004), p.50

37   E. von Manstein, *Lost Victories*, pp.137–38

38   S. Westphal, *Erinnerungen* (Hase & Koehler, Mainz, 1975), p.55

39   C. Hartmann, *Halder: Generalstabschef Hitlers* (Schöningh, Paerborn, 1991), p.304

40   E. von Manstein, *Lost Victories*, p.268

41   Ibid., pp.268–69

42   P. Schramm (ed.), *Kriegstagebuch des Oberkommandos der Wehrmacht* (Bernard & Graefer, Munich, 1982), Vol. III, p.597

43   For a detailed account of *Mars*, see D. Glantz, *Zhukov's Greatest Defeat: The Red Army's Epic Disaster in Operation Mars 1942* (University Press of Kansas, Lawrence, KA, 1999)

CHAPTER 2

1   Zhukov, *Memoirs of Marshal Zhukov*, p.140; J. Erickson, *The Road to Stalingrad* (Panther, London, 1975), p.389

2   Erickson, *Road to Stalingrad*, pp.167–68

3   Ibid., p.457

4   Vasilevsky, *Lifelong Cause*, p.191

5   P. McTaggart, 'Soviet Circle of Iron' in *WWII History: Russian Front* (Sovereign Media, Herndon, VA, 2006), p.49–50

6   A. Beevor, *Stalingrad* (Penguin, London, 1999), pp.229–30; W. Craig, *Enemy at the Gates – The Battle for Stalingrad* (Penguin, London, 2000), pp.147–48

7   W. von Richthofen, *Kriegstagebuch* (Bundesarchiv-Militärarchiv, Freiburg, N671/9), 12 Nov 42

8   M. Abdullin, *Stranits iz Soldatskogo Dnevnika* (Molodaya Gvardiya, Moscow, 1985), pp.4–5

9   Ibid., pp.12–13

10   Craig, *Enemy at the Gates*, pp.175–76; Beevor, *Stalingrad*, p.239; Bundesarchiv-Militärarchiv Freiburg RH20-6/221

11   M. Axworthy, C. Scafeş and C. Crăciuniou, *Third Axis, Fourth Ally: Romanian Armed Forces in the European War 1941–1945* (Arms and Armour, London, 1995), pp.89–92

12 V. Kharchenko, *Spetsial'nogo Naznacheniya* (Voyenizdat, 1973), pp.67–68

13 Vasilevsky, *Lifelong Cause*, p.195

14 Erickson, *Road to Stalingrad*, pp.465–66

15 H-U. Rudel, *Stuka Pilot* (Black House, London, 2013), p.68

16 Ibid., p.65

17 Richthofen, *Kriegstagebuch*, 19 Nov 42

18 Major Bruno Gebele, quoted in A. Beck (ed.), *Bis Stalingrad* (Helmuth Abt, Ulm, 1983), p.170

19 M. Badigin, *Boy Trebuyet Podviga* (Voenizdat, Moscow, 1980), pp.14–16

20 Tsentralnye Arkhiv Ministrertsva Oborony, Podolsk, 48/486/25, p.287

21 Rossiyski Gosudarstvennyy Arkhiv Literaturi I Iskusstva, Moscow, 618/2/108

22 Manstein, *Lost Victories*, p.271

23 Ibid., p.294

24 Ibid., p.295

25 W. Werthen, *Geschichte der 16. Panzer-Division – Weg und Schicksal* (Podzun, Bad Nauheim, 1958), p.142

26 Badigin, *Boy Trebuyet Podviga*, pp.19–20

27 Tsentralnye Arkhiv Ministrertsva Oborony, Podolsk, 48/486/25, p.290

28 Tsentralnye Arkhiv Ministrertsva Oborony, Podolsk, 48/486/25, p.303

29 O. Selle, K. Marx (trans.), 'The German Debacle at Stalingrad: Hitler Forbids Breakout' in *Military Review* (US Army Command and General Staff College, Fort Leavenworth, KA, 1957), Vol. XXXVII, p.37

30 V. Tarrant, *Stalingrad: Anatomy of an Agony* (Leo Cooper, London, 1992), p.112

31 Craig, *Enemy at the Gates*, p.193

32 Manstein, *Lost Victories*, p.278

33 Abdullin, *Stranits iz Soldatskogo Dnevnika*, p.17

34 Ibid., p.25

35 Ibid., p.31

36 L. Rotundo, *Battle for Stalingrad: The Soviet General Staff Study* (Macmillan, London, 1989), p.188

37 H. Schröter, *Stalingrad: Bis zur Letzten Patrone* (self-published, Osnabrück, 1952), p.108

CHAPTER 3

1 An account of this meeting – albeit not contemporaneous – is available at United States Air Force Historical Research Agency (Montgomery, AL), K113.106-153, *Aussagen zur Problem der Luftversorgung von Stalingrad*

2 F. Morzik, *German Air Force Airlift Operations* (USAF Air University, Montgomery, AL, 1961), pp.145–50

3 United States Air Force Historical Research Agency (Montgomery, AL), 168.7158-335, *Feldgericht des VIII Fliegerkorps 26.1.43*

4   United States Air Force Historical Research Agency (Montgomery, AL), 168.7158-338, W. Pickert, *Aufzeichnungen aus meinem Tagebuch und von Besprechungen über Operative und Taktische Gedanken und Massnahmen der 6. Armee*

5   M. Kehrig, *Stalingrad: Analyse und Dokumentation einer Schlacht* (Deutsche Verlags-Anstalt, Stuttgart, 1974), p.561

6   Ibid., p.562

7   S. Friedin, W. Richardson, and S. Westphal, *The Fatal Decisions: Six Decisive Battles of the Second World War from the Viewpoint of the Vanquished* (Michael Joseph, London, 1956), p.142

8   Irving, *Göring: A Biography* (Macmillan, London, 1989), p.367

9   United States Air Force Historical Research Agency (Montgomery, AL), K113.309-3, *Bericht über eine Auskunft Görings Stalingrader Zusage durch Generaloberst Lörzer*

10 J. Hayward, *Stopped at Stalingrad: The Luftwaffe and Hitler's Defeat in the East 1942–1943* (University Press of Kansas, Lawrence, KA, 1998), pp.240–42

11 O. Selle, p.38

12 Manstein, *Lost Victories*, pp.304–05

13 Ibid., pp.306–07

14 Vasilevsky, *Lifelong Cause*, p.196

15 Ernst von Salomon, quoted in D. Bradley, *Walther Wenck – General der Panzertruppe* (Biblio, Osnabrück, 1981), pp.28–29

16 Quoted in Bradley, *Walther Wenck*, pp.244–45

17 W. Pickert, 'The Stalingrad Airlift: An Eyewitness Commentary', in *Aerospace Historian* (Air Force Historical Foundation, Bolling AFB, DC, 1971), Vol. XVIII, p.184

18 Adam and Rühle, *Paulus at Stalingrad*, p.112

19 Manstein, *Lost Victories*, p.310

20 Vasilevsky, *Lifelong Cause*, p.201–03

21 Manstein, *Lost Victories*, p.314

22 Mellenthin, *Panzer Battles*, p.158

23 Translation of taped interview with General Hermann Balck, 12 January 1979 (Battele Columbus Laboratories, Columbus, OH, 1985), pp.20–21

24 A. Harding Ganz, *Ghost Division: The German 11th Panzer Division and the German Armored Force in World War II* (Stackpole, Mechanicsburg, PA, 2016), p.121

25 H. Balck, *Ordnung im Chaos: Erinnerungen 1893–1948* (Biblio, Osnabrück, 1981), p.361

26 Manstein, *Lost Victories*, p.320

27 H. Scheibert, *...Bis Stalingrad 48km: Der Entsatzversuch 1942* (Pudzun-Pallas, Wölfersheim-Berstadt, 1998), pp.12–13

28 Ibid., p.13

29 E. Raus, *Panzer Operations: The Eastern Front Memoir of General Raus, 1941–1945*

(Da Capo, Cambridge, MA, 2003), p.142

30 W. Paul, *Brennpunkte: Die Geschichte der 6. Panzerdivision* (Biblioverlag, Osnabrück, 1993), pp.233–34

31 Raus, *Panzer Operations*, p.145

32 Scheibert, *Bis Stalingrad*, pp.37–38

33 Raus, *Panzer Operations*, p.151

34 Paul, *Brennpunkte*, pp.237–39

35 Scheibert, *Bis Stalingrad*, p.43

CHAPTER 4

1   D. Glantz, *From the Don to the Dnepr: Soviet Offensive Operations December 1942 – August 1943* (Cass, London, 1991), p.14

2   *Tagebuch Fiebig* 5 December 1942, Bundesarchiv-Militärarchiv Freiburg, ZA-3.947

3   Balck, *Ordnung im Chaos*, pp.364–65

4   The 'Reichenau-Befehl' of October 1941, retrieved from www.ns-archiv.de

5   A. Mayer, *Why Did the Heavens Not Darken?* (Pantheon, New York, 1988), p.250

6   Adam and Rühle, *Paulus at Stalingrad*, p.9

7   Office of the United States Chief of Counsel for Prosecution of Axis Criminality, *Nazi Conspiracy and Aggression* (USGPO, Washington DC, 1946), 'Red Series', Vol. VII, pp.978–95

8   G. Temkin, *My Just War: The Memoir of a Jewish Red Army Soldier in World War II* (Presidio, Novato, CA, 1998), pp.59–60

9   Manstein, *Lost Victories*, p.180

10 Melvin, *Manstein: Hitler's Greatest General*, p.243, 466, 474–75; Bundesarchiv-Militärarchiv Freiburg, RH 21-4/272

11 R. Brett-Smith, *Hitler's Generals* (Presidio, San Rafael, CA, 1976), p.167

12 J. Thorwald, *The Illusion* (Harcourt Brace Jovanovich, New York, 1975), p.65

13 C. Davis, *Von Kleist: From Hussar to Panzer Marshal* (Lancer Militaria, Houston, TX, 1979), p.16

14 Ibid., p.17

15 Temkin, *My Just War*, p.62

16 Balck, *Ordnung im Chaos*, pp.366–67

17 Raus, *Panzer Operations*, pp.154–56; Scheibert, *Bis Stalingrad*, pp.47–48

18 Abdullin, *Stranits iz Soldatskogo Dnevnika*, p.35

19 S. Zaloga, J. Kinnear, A. Aksenov, and A. Koshchavtsev, *Soviet Tanks in Combat 1941–45: The T-28, T-34, T-34/85, and T-44 Medium Tanks* (Concord, Hong Kong, 1997), p.72

20 Kehrig, *Stalingrad*, p.602

21 Raus, *Panzer Operations*, p.158

22 Scheibert, *Bis Stalingrad*, p.58

23 *Kriegstagebuch des Panzerregiments 11* 12 Dec 42, Bundesarchiv-Militärarchiv Freiburg, RH 27-6
24 Raus, *Panzer Operations*, pp.159–61
25 Paul, *Brennpunkte*, p.247
26 Scheibert, *Bis Stalingrad*, p.62, footnote 2
27 Ibid., p.64
28 Rotundo, *Battle for Stalingrad*, p.141
29 Vasilevsky, *Lifelong Cause*, p.213
30 *Kriegstagebuch des Panzerregiments 11* 13 Dec 42, Bundesarchiv-Militärarchiv Freiburg, RH 27-6
31 Scheibert, *Bis Stalingrad*, p.75
32 Quoted in Scheibert, *Bis Stalingrad*, p.80
33 Paul, *Brennpunkte*, pp.250–51; Scheibert, *Bis Stalingrad*, pp.77–78
34 Scheibert, *Bis Stalingrad*, pp.88–89
35 A. Drabkin, *Ya Dralsya s Pantservaffe: Dvoynoy Oklad, Troynaya Smert'!* (Yauza, Moscow, 2007), pp.5–22
36 Scheibert, *Bis Stalingrad*, p.94
37 Drabkin, *Ya Dralsya s Pantservaffe*, pp.32–38
38 Rotundo, *Battle for Stalingrad*, p.121

CHAPTER 5

1 Vasilevsky, *Lifelong Cause*, p.215
2 Raus, *Panzer Operations*, p.173–74
3 Vasilevsky, *Lifelong Cause*, p.216–17
4 Manstein, *Lost Victories*, p.327
5 H. Heiber (ed.), *Lagebesprechungen im Führerhauptquartier: Protokollfragmente aus Hitlers Militärischen Konferenzen 1942–1945* (Deutsche Verlag, Stuttgart, 1962), pp.53–54
6 Glantz, *From the Don to the Dnepr*, pp.21–23
7 G. Rochat, *Le Guerre Italiane 1935–1943: Dall'Impero d'Etiopia alla Disfatta* (Einaudi, Turin, 2009), p.378
8 E. Corti (trans. P. Levy), *Few Returned: Twenty-Eight Days on the Russian Front, Winter 1942–1943* (University of Missouri Press, Columbia, MO, 1997), pp.3–4
9 N. Revelli, *L'ultimo fronte: lettere di soldati caduti o dispersi nella seconda guerra mondiale* (Einaudi, Turin, 2009), p.4, 10
10 Quoted in H. Hamilton, *Sacrifice on the Steppe: The Italian Alpine Corps in the Stalingrad Campaign 1942–1943* (Casemate, Newbury, 2011), pp.14–15
11 Ibid., p.15
12 G. Bedeschi, *Fronte Russo: c'Ero Anch'io* (Mursia, Milan, 2008), pp.144–45
13 C. Gnocchi, *Cristo con gli Alpini* (Mursia, Milan, 2009), p.44
14 For a detailed account of the opening phases of *Little Saturn*, see Glantz, *From the*

Don to the Dnepr, pp.43–49

15 A. Zheltov, *Yugozapadnom Front v Kontranastuplenii pod Stalingradom* in *Voenno-Istoricheskii Zhurnal* (Voennoe izd-vo Ministerstva Oborony Soyuza SSR, Moscow, Nov 1967), p.66

16 Scheibert, *Bis Stalingrad*, p.107

17 Paul, *Brennpunkte*, pp.256–59

18 Scheibert, *Bis Stalingrad*, p.110

19 *Kriegstagebuch des Panzerregiments 11* 17 Dec 42, Bundesarchiv-Militärarchiv Freiburg, RH 27-6

20 Manstein, *Lost Victories*, p.331

21 Paul, *Brennpunkte*, p.260

22 *Kriegstagebuch des Ia 6 Panzer Division* 18 Dec 42, Bundesarchiv-Militärarchiv Freiburg, RH 27-6

23 Paul, *Brennpunkte*, p.261

24 Manstein, *Lost Victories*, p.560

25 Ibid., pp.333–34

26 Harding Ganz, *Ghost Division*, p.127

27 Balck, *Ordnung im Chaos*, pp.367–68

28 Scheibert, *Bis Stalingrad*, pp.120–21

29 Ibid., pp.123–25

30 Quoted in Paul, *Brennpunkte*, p.263

31 Glantz, *From the Don to the Dnepr*, p.56

32 A. Burdeyny, *V Boyakh za Rodinu* (MAK, Moscow, 2016), p.74

33 Ibid., pp.79–80

CHAPTER 6

1 See, for example, Melvin, *Manstein: Hitler's Greatest General*, pp.314–16

2 Manstein, *Lost Victories*, pp.335–42

3 S. Biryusov, *Kogda Gremeli Pushki* (Voenizdat, Moscow, 1961), p.113

4 Paul, *Brennpunkte*, p.265

5 Account by Zollenkopf, in Scheibert, *Bis Stalingrad*, pp.129–30

6 Y. Kravchenko and B. Pribylov, *K Granatomotu Taubina* (Arktika 4D, Moscow, 2011), p.90

7 A. Karpov, *V Nebe Ukrainy* (Politizdat, Kiev, 1980), pp.74–77

8 *Kriegstagebuch Panzer-Regiment 11* 20 Dec 42, Bundesarchiv-Militärarchiv Freiburg, RH 27-6

9 Rotundo, *Battle for Stalingrad*, p.122

10 P. Koshevoi, *V Gody Voyenyye* (Voenizdat, Moscow, 1978), pp.134–37

11 *Kriegstagebuch 17 Panzer Division* 20–21 Dec 42, Bundesarchiv-Militärarchiv Freiburg, RH 27-17

12 V. Krysov, *Batereya, Ogon!* (Yauza, Moscow, 2007), pp.28–30

13 Obergefreiter von Bruch, quoted in Paul, *Brennpunkte*, p.267
14 Scheibert, *Bis Stalingrad*, pp.145–46
15 Adam and Rühle, *Paulus at Stalingrad*, p.95
16 J. Wieder and H. Graf von Einsiedel, *Stalingrad: Memories and Reassessments* (Arms and Armour, London, 1998), p.202
17 Manstein, *Lost Victories*, p.562–63
18 Ibid., pp.336–37
19 Kehrig, *Stalingrad*, pp.633–37
20 Bundesarchiv-Militärarchiv Freiburg, N/547/21 Nachlass Hauck
21 Burdeyny, *V Boyakh za Rodinu*, pp.96–98
22 H. Vasiliev, *Tatsinskii Reid* (Voenizdat, Moscow, 1969), pp.26–62
23 P. Klatt, *Die 3. Gebirgs-Division 1939–1945* (Podzun, Bad Nauheim, 1958), pp.132–34
24 Corti, *Few Returned*, pp.7–8
25 Ibid., p.61
26 2 Lt M Pedroni, 81st Infantry Regiment, quoted in Corti, *Few Returned*, p.244
27 Burdeyny, *V Boyakh za Rodinu*, pp.118–19
28 Vasiliev, *Tatsinskii Reid*, pp.66–77
29 Burdeyny, *V Boyakh za Rodinu*, pp.131–32
30 Vasilevsky, *Lifelong Cause*, pp.219–20
31 *Kriegstagebuch des Ia 6 Panzer Division* 22 Dec 42, Bundesarchiv-Militärarchiv Freiburg, RH 27-6

CHAPTER 7

1 Quoted in Paul, *Brennpunkte*, p.270
2 Ibid., p.272
3 Koshevoi, *V Gody Voyenyye*, p.151
4 C. Vicentini and G. Rochat, *Il Sacrificio della Julia in Russia* (Gaspari, Udine, 2006), pp.44–45
5 Ibid., p.45
6 Ibid., p.45
7 Paul, *Brennpunkte*, p.276
8 G. Zdanovich, *Idem v Nastupleniye* (Voenizdat, Moscow, 1980), pp.47–49
9 Burdeyny, *V Boyakh za Rodinu*, p.141
10 Corti, *Few Returned*, pp.109–10
11 Koshevoi, *V Gody Voyenyye*, p.152
12 P. Rotmistrov, *Stal'naya Gvardiya* (Voenizdat, Moscow, 1984), pp.149–50
13 Rotundo, *Battle for Stalingrad*, pp.127–28; Vasilevsky, *Lifelong Cause*, pp.221–22
14 Manstein, *Lost Victories*, pp.346–47
15 Vasilevsky, *Lifelong Cause*, p.224
16 Quoted in Hayward, *Stopped at Stalingrad*, p.273

17 Manstein, *Lost Victories*, p.348
18 Quoted in Friedin, Richardson, and Westphal, *Fatal Decisions*, p.155
19 Manstein, *Lost Victories*, pp.349–50
20 Unteroffizier Wolfgarten in H. Scheibert, *Panzer Zwischen Don und Donez* (Podzun, Friedberg, 1979), pp.51–52
21 Ibid., pp.52–54
22 Burdeyny, *V Boyakh za Rodinu*, pp.158–61
23 Ibid., p.161
24 Scheibert, H, pp.61–62
25 Scheibert, H, pp.64–65
26 M. Kazakov, *Operatsiya Saturn: Stalingradsleya Epopiya* (Isdatelstvo Nauka, Moscow, 1968), pp.514–15
27 Glantz, *From the Don to the Dnepr*, pp.73–78
28 *Sbornik Materialovpo Izucheniyu Opyta Voyny* (Voenizdat, Moscow, 1943), Vol. VIII, p.63
29 Glantz, *From the Don to the Dnepr*, p.79

CHAPTER 8

1 See for example Melvin, *Manstein: Hitler's Greatest General*, p.321
2 Manstein, *Lost Victories*, p.354
3 Adam and Rühle, *Paulus at Stalingrad*, pp.155–60
4 Vasilevsky, *Lifelong Cause*, pp.224–25
5 Ibid., pp.225–26
6 I. Tiulenev, *Cherez Tri Voyny* (Voyenizdat, Moscow, 1972), p.228
7 A. Mollo, *The Armed Forces of World War II* (Crown, New York, 1981), p.207
8 J. Fest, *Die Unbeantwortbaren Fragen: Notizen über Gespräche mit Albert Speer Zwischen Ende 1966 und 1981* (Rowohlt, Haburg, 2006), p.143
9 M. Miller, *Leaders of the SS and German Police* (Bender, San Jose, CA, 2006), Vol. I, p.308
10 A. Krüger and S. Scharenberg, *Zeiten für Helden – Zeiten für Berühmtheiten im Sport* (LIT, Münster, 2014), p.85
11 H. Peiper, *Fegelein's Horsemen and Genocidal Warfare: The SS Cavalry Brigade in the Soviet Union* (Palgrave Macmillan, Basingstoke, 2015), p.120
12 Vasilevky, *Lifelong Cause*, pp.236–37
13 N. Pustyntsev, *Skvoz' Svintsovoyu V'yugu: Zapiski Razvedchika* (Voenizdat, Moscow, 1966), pp.76–77
14 Ibid., pp.78–79
15 Quoted in L. Veress, *Magyarország Honvédelme a II. Világháború Előtt és Alatt 1920–1945* (Nemzetőr, Munich, 1973), p.369
16 N. Shtykov, *Polk Priminayet Boy* (Voyenizdat, Moscow, 1979), pp.38–39
17 P. Shafarenko, *Na Raznykh Frontakh: Zapiski Komandira Divizii* (Voyenizdat,

Moscow, 1978), pp.140–41

18   F. Adonyi-Naredi, *A Magyar Katona a Második Világháborúban, 1941–1945* (Kleinmayr, Klagenfurt, 1954), pp.98–108

19   Shafarenko, *Na Raznykh Frontakh*, pp.143–45

20   R. Patai, *The Jews of Hungary: History, Culture, Psychology* (Wayne State University Press, Detroit, MI, 1999), p.546

21   Y. Bauer, *Jews for Sale? Nazi-Jewish Negotiations 1933–1945* (Yale University Press, New Haven, CT, 1994), p.148

22   G. Temkin, *My Just War*, pp.79–80

23   Shafarenko, *Na Raznykh Frontakh*, p.147

24   A. Vetrov, *Tak I Bylo* (Voenizdat, Moscow, 1982), p.104

25   Vicentini and Rochat, *Il Sacrificio della Julia*, p.61

26   E. Collotti, *Gli Italiani sul Fronte Russo* (De Donata, Barii, 1982), p.278

27   I. Nosov, *Vysoty Poluchayut Imena* (Voenizdat, Moscow, 1978), pp.12–13

28   Vetrov, *Tak I Bylo*, pp.104–05

29   Ibid., pp.108–09

30   A. Speer, *Inside the Third Reich* (Weidenfeld & Nicholson, London, 2015), p.279

31   V. Shimansky, *Pozyvnyye Nashikh Serdets* (Voyenizdat, Moscow, 1980), pp.47–51

32   Shtykov, *Polk Priminayet Boy*, pp.46–48

33   E. Corradi, *La Ritirata di Russia* (Mursia, Milan, 2009), p.93

34   G. Bedeschi, *Centomila Gavette di Ghiaccio* (Mursia, Milan, 2011), p.313

35   Quoted in Hamilton, *Sacrifice on the Steppe*, p.156

36   Quoted in ibid., p.157

37   Quoted in ibid., p.136

38   For one version of events, see O. Heidkämper, *Witebsk: Kampf und Untergang der 3. Panzer Armee* (Scharnhorst, Heidelberg, 1954), p.22

39   Gnocchi, *Cristo con gli Alpini*, p.21

40   Pustyntsev, *Skvoz' Svintsovoyu V'yugu*, pp.89–90

41   E. Faldella, *Storia Delle Truppe Alpine 1872–1972* (Cavalotti, Milan, 1972), pp.1641–44

42   M. Bellelli, *Luigi Reverberi: un Soldato, un Alpino, un Uomo* (Centro Culturale Comunale, Vavriago, 2009), pp.40–41

43   M. Rigoni Stern, *Il Sergente Nella Neve: Ricordi Della Ritirata di Russia* (Einaudi, Turin, 2014), p.88

44   G. Bedeschi, p.393

45   K. Moskalenko, *Na Yugo-Zapadnom Napravlenii* (Izdatelstvo Nauka, Moscow, 1969), Vol. I, pp.398–99

46   Ibid., p.400

47   I. Nemeskurty, *Requiem egy Hadseregért* (Magvető, Budapest, 1982), pp.198–99

48   C. Vicentini and P. Resta, *Rapporto sui Prigionieri di Guerra Italiani in Russia* (UNIRR, Milan, 2005), p.45

49   Hamilton, *Sacrifice on the Steppe*, p.200

CHAPTER 9

1   Moskalenko, *Na Yugo-Zapadnom Napravlenii*, Vol. I, pp.407–08
2   B. Kleine, *Bevor die Erinnerung Verblasst* (Helios, Aachen, 2004), pp.24–27
3   Ibid., p.33
4   Shafarenko, *Na Raznykh Frontakh*, p.151
5   Shtykov, *Polk Priminayet Boy*, pp.53–55
6   Ibid., p.59
7   Temkin, *My Just War*, p.85
8   Shtemenko, *Soviet General Staff*, p.72
9   Quoted in ibid., p.76
10   Manstein, *Lost Victories*, p.386
11   G. Lübbers, 'Die 6. Armee und die Zivilbevölkerung von Stalingrad' in *Vierteljahrshefte für Zeitgeschichte* (Institut für Zeitgeschichte, Munich, 2006), Vol. 54, pp.87–123
12   H. von Manteuffel, *Die 7. Panzer-Division im Zweiten Weltkrieg* (Traditionsverband Ehemaliger 7. Panzer-Division Kameradenhilfe, Krefeld, 1965), pp.303–05
13   I. Kobylyanskiy, *From Stalingrad to Pillau: A Red Army Artillery Officer Remembers the Great Patriotic War* (University of Kansas Press, Lawrence, KA, 2008), p.75
14   Temkin, *My Just War*, p.90
15   Quoted in Paul, *Brennpunkte*, p.288
16   Manteuffel, *Die 7. Panzer-Division*, pp.307–10
17   Corti, *Few Returned*, p.225
18   E. Klapdor, *Viking Panzers: The German 5th SS Tank Regiment in the East in World War II* (Stackpole, Mechanicsburg, PA, 2011), p.128
19   B. Boll, *Zloczow, Juli 1941: Die Wehrmacht und der Beginn des Holocaust in Galizien* (Zeitschrift für Geschichtswissenschaft, Berlin, 2002), p.898ff; S. Mayer, *Der Untergang fun Zloczów* (Ibergang, Munich, 1947), p.6–10
20   Klapdor, *Viking Panzers*, p.130
21   Ibid., pp.138–39
22   Rotmistrov, *Stal'naya Gvardiya*, pp.158–59
23   Balck, *Ordnung im Chaos*, p.302
24   Ibid., p.308; Mellenthin, *Panzer Battles*, pp.186–87
25   V. Nechayev *Gvardeyskiy Umanskiy: Voyenno-Istoricheskiy Ocherk o Boyevom Puti 9-go Gvardeyskogo Tankovogo Korpusa* (Voyenizdat, Moscow, 1989), p.42
26   Klapdor, *Viking Panzers*, p.144
27   Manstein, *Lost Victories*, p.357
28   Ibid., pp.361–62
29   Quoted in Manstein, *Lost Victories*, p.358
30   Quoted in Adam and Rühle, *Paulus at Stalingrad*, p.206
31   Abdullin, *Stranits iz Soldatskogo Dnevnika*, pp.70–71
32   Balck, *Ordnung im Chaos*, pp.399–401

33   United States Air Force Historical Research Agency K113.309-3, Vol. IX 21/1/43

34   Quoted in Hayward, *Stopped at Stalingrad*, p.304

35   Ibid., pp.320–21

36   Goering's speech of 30 January 1943 in *Bulletin of International News* (Royal Institute of International Affairs, London, 1943), Vol. XX, No. 3, pp.100–04

37   Quoted in Simon Price and Peter Thonemann, *The Birth of Classical Europe: A History from Troy to Augustine* (Allen Lane, London, 2010), p.162

38   *Volks-Zeitung* (Vienna, 4 February 1943), pp.1–2

39   C. Merridale, *Ivan's War: The Red Army 1939–1945* (Faber & Faber, London, 2005), pp.163–66

40   Rotundo, *Battle for Stalingrad*, p.131

CHAPTER 10

1   Moskalenko, *Na Yugo-Zapadnom Napravlenii*, Vol. I, pp.402–03

2   National Archives and Records Administration (NARA) (College Park, MD) Microfilm series T314, roll 509, frames 7–10

3   J. Solarz, *Totenkopf 1939–1943* (Wydawnictwo, Warsaw, 2008), p.18

4   Bundesarchiv-Militärarchiv Freiburg, *Kriegstagebuch 121. Infanterie-Division*, 2–3 July 1941, RH26-23

5   Manstein, *Lost Victories*, p.399

6   H. Boog, W. Rahn, R. Stumpf, and B. Wegner, *Germany and the Second World War* (Oxford University Press, Oxford, 2001), Vol. VI, p.7

7   Manstein, *Lost Victories*, p.400

8   Biryusov, *Kogda Gremeli Pushki*, pp.134–35

9   Paul, *Brennpunkte*, pp.289–90

10   Shtemenko, *Soviet General Staff*, pp.84–85

11   I. Rakobolskaya and N. Kravtsova, *Nas Nazyvali Nochnymi Ved'Mani: Tak Voyeval 46-y Gvardeyskiy Polk Nochnykh Bombaardirovshchikov* (Isd-Vo MGU, Moscow, 2005), pp.204–05

12   Kobylyanskiy, *From Stalingrad to Pillau*, pp.78–79

13   P. Belyakov, *V Pritsele 'Buryy Medved'* (Voenizdat, Moscow, 1977), pp.50–54

14   H. Spaeter, *The History of the Panzerkorps Grossdeutschland* (Fedorowicz, Winnipeg, 1995), Vol. II, pp.5–13

15   Nosov, *Vysoty Poluchayut Imena*, pp.18–19

16   P. Traynin, *Soldatskoye pole* (Voenizdat, Moscow, 1981), p.69

17   Shtemenko, *Soviet General Staff*, pp.97–100

18   Rotmistrov, *Stal'naya Gvardiya*, pp.164–66

19   A. Yershov, *Osvobozhdenie Donbassa* (Voenizdat, Moscow, 1973), p.10

20   I. Krupchenko (ed.), *Sovetskie Tankovje Voiska 1941–1945* (Voenizdat, Moscow, 1973), p.100; Glantz, *From the Don to the Dnepr*, p.87

CHAPTER 11

1   Shtemenko, *Soviet General Staff*, p.106
2   Vasilevsky, *Lifelong Cause*, p.245
3   Glantz, *From the Don to the Dnepr*, pp.151–53
4   A. Zvartsev, *3-ya Gvardeiskaya Tankovaya: Boevoi pit 3- Gvardeiskoi Tankovoi Armii* (Voenizdat, Moscow, 1982), p.44
5   T. Tebart, *298. Infanterie-Division 1940–1943: Ruhm und Untergang* (Kameradschaft der 298.Inf.-Div, 1990), pp.102–08
6   H. Thöle, *Befehl des Gewissens: Charkow Winter 1943* (Munin, Osnabrück, 1976), p.25
7   Vetrov, *Tak I Bylo*, p.115
8   Glantz, *From the Don to the Dnepr*, pp.172–76
9   Bundesarchiv-Militärarchiv Freiburg, *Kriegstagebuch Armeeoberkommando 8*, 5 Feb 1943, T314-54
10 Yershov, *Osvobozhdenie Donbassa*, p.34
11 A. Kuzmin and I. Krasov, *Kantemirovtsy: Boevoi put 4-go Gvardeiskogo Tankovogo Kantemirovskogo Ordena Lenina Krasnoznammennogo Korpusa* (Voenizdat, Moscow, 1971), p.57
12 N. Skripko, *Po Tselyam Blizhnim i Dal'nim* (Voyenizdat, Moscow, 1981), pp.258–59
13 Zdanovich, *Idem v Nastupleniye*, p.66
14 See W. Strik-Strikfeldt, *Against Stalin and Hitler: Memoir of the Russian Liberation Movement 1941–45* (Macmillan, London, 1970) and J. Hoffmann, *Die Tragödie der 'Russischen Befreiungsarmee' 1944–45. Wlassow gegen Stalin* (Herbig, Munich, 2003)
15 Zdanovich, *Idem v Nastupleniye*, pp.66–67
16 C. Wagener, *Der Gegenangriff des XXXX Panzerkorps gegen den Durchbruch der Panzergruppe Popow im Donezbecken Februar 1943* in *Wehrwissenschaftliche Rundschau* (Mittler, Bonn, 1954), Vol. I, p.26
17 Bundesarchiv-Militärarchiv Freiburg, *Kriegstagebuch XXX Panzerkorps*, 12 Feb 1943, RH24-40
18 Quoted in Manteuffel, *Die 7. Panzer-Division*, p.317
19 Quoted in ibid., p.324
20 Yershov, *Osvobozhdenie Donbassa*, pp.39–40
21 Thöle, *Befehl des Gewissens*, pp.51–52
22 Bundesarchiv-Militärarchiv Freiburg, *Kriegstagebuch Armeeoberkommando 8*, 7 Feb 1943, T314-54
23 Spaeter, *History of the Panzerkorps Grossdeutschland*, Vol. II, p.25
24 Moskalenko, *Na Yugo-Zapadnom Napravlenii*, Vol. I, p.429
25 Bundesarchiv-Militärarchiv Freiburg, *Kriegstagebuch Armeeoberkommando 8*, 14 Feb 1943, T314-54
26 Thöle, *Befehl des Gewissens*, p.100

27   Spaeter, *History of the Panzerkorps Grossdeutschland*, Vol. II, pp.39–42

28   S. Mitcham, *SS-Oberst-Gruppenführer und Generaloberst der Waffen-SS Paul Hausser*, in G. Ueberschär (ed.), *Hitlers Militärische Elite* (Primus, Darmstadt, 1998), Vol. I, p.91

29   Moskalenko, *Na Yugo-Zapadnom Napravlenii*, Vol. I, pp.432–33

30   Quoted in Thöle, *Befehl des Gewissens*, p.332

31   Drabkin, *Ya Dralsya s Pantservaffe*, pp.274–75

CHAPTER 12

1   J. Stalin, *O Velikoi Otechestvennoi Voine Sovetskogo Soyuza* (Gosudarstvennoe izdvo Politicheskoi Literaturi, Moscow, 1946), pp.89–91

2   P. Shafarenko, *Na Raznykh Frontakh: Zapiski Komandira Divizii* (Voyenizdat, Moscow, 1978), p.161

3   Shtemenko, *Soviet General Staff*, pp.102–03, 108

4   Vetrov, *Tak I Bylo*, pp.117–18

5   Moskalenko, *Na Yugo-Zapadnom Napravlenii*, Vol. I, p.437; N. Kazakov, *Nad Kartoi Bylykh Srazhenii* (Voenizdat, Moscow, 1971), p.171

6   Kazakov, *Nad Kartoi Bylykh Srazhenii*, p.169

7   Moskalenko, *Na Yugo-Zapadnom Napravlenii*, Vol. I, pp.438–40

8   D. Parker, *Hitler's Warrior: The Life and Wars of SS Colonel Jochen Peiper* (Da Capo, Lebanon, IN, 2014), p.94

9   C. Bishop and M. Williams, *SS: Hell on the Western Front* (MBI, St Paul, MN, 2003), p.170; Parker, *Hitler's Warrior*, pp.356–57

10   Thöle, *Befehl des Gewissens*, pp.123–26

11   Shtemenko, *Soviet General Staff*, p.212

12   Moskalenko, *Na Yugo-Zapadnom Napravlenii*, Vol. I, pp.446–47

13   P. Hoffmann, *The History of the German Resistance 1933–1945* (McGill-Queen's University Press, Montreal, 1996), pp.279–80

14   H. Röll, *Generalleutnant der Reserve Hyacinth Graf Strachwitz von Groß-Zauche und Camminetz: Vom Kavallerieoffizier zum Führer gepanzerter Verbände* (Flechsig, Würzburg, 2011), pp.182–86

15   Hoffmann, *History of the German Resistance*, pp.281–83

16   A. Stahlberg and P. Crampton (trans.), *Beholden Duty: The Memoirs of a German Officer 1932-1945* (Brassey, London, 1990), pp.239–47

17   Quoted in H. Breithaupt, *Zwischen Front und Widerstand: en Beitrag zur Diskussion um den Feldmarschall von Manstein* (Bernard & Grafe, Bonn, 1994), p.64

18   Balck, *Ordnung im Chaos*, pp.465–67

19   Manstein, *Lost Victories*, pp.423–27

20   For a Soviet account, see D. Lelyushenko, *Moskva-Stalingrad-Berlin-Praha* (Nauka, Moscow, 1987), pp.125–28

21   Biryusov, *Kogda Gremeli Pushki*, p.144

22 Kuzmin and Krasov, *Kantemirovtsy*, p.62

23 V. Morozov, 'Pochemu ne Zavershilos Nastuplenie v Donbasse Vesnoi 1943 Goda' in *Voeno-Istoricheskii Zhurnal* (March 1963), p.16

24 For a discussion of this, see Glantz, *From the Don to the Dnepr*, pp.119–20

25 Quoted in R. Neillands, *The Dieppe Raid: The Story of the Disastrous 1942 Expedition* (Indiana University Press, Bloomington, IN, 2005), p.75

26 Ibid., p.1

27 Vasilevsky, *Lifelong Cause*, p.247

28 Zdanovich, *Idem v Nastupleniye*, pp.54–55

29 Bundesarchiv-Militärarchiv Freiburg, *Kriegstagebuch Armeeoberkommando 8*, 19 Feb 1943, T314-54

30 J. Weiss, *The Lemberg Mosaic* (Alderbrook, New York, 2010), p.173

31 *Die Zeit* (Hamburg), 21 June 2001

32 Yershov, *Osvobozhdenie Donbassa*, pp.81–84

33 Bundesarchiv-Militärarchiv Freiburg, *Kriegstagebuch Armeeoberkommando 8*, 23 Feb 1943, T314-54

34 Shtykov, *Polk Priminayet Boy*, pp.71–72

35 A. Yaroshenko, *V Boi Shla 41-ya Gvardeiskaya: Boevoi put' 41-I Gvardeiskoi Strelkovoi Korsunsko-Dunaskoi Ordene Suvorova Divizii* (Voenizdat, Moscow, 1982), pp.65–66

36 Paul, *Brennpunkte*, p.292

37 K. Bailes, *Technology and Legitimacy: Soviet Aviation and Stalinism in the 1930s* in *Technology and Culture* (Johns Hopkins University Press, MD, 1976), Vol. XVII No. 1, pp.63–64

38 L. Ratley, 'A Lesson in History: the Luftwaffe and Barbarossa' in *Air University Review* (Maxwell AFB, March 1983) available online at http://www.airpower.maxwell.af.mil/airchronicles/aureview/1983/mar-apr/ratley.htm

39 V. Morozov, 'Pochemu ne Zavershilos' Nastuplenie v Donbasse Vesnoi 1943 goda' in *Voenno-Istoricheskii Zhurnal* (March 1963), p.26

40 F. von Senger und Ettelin, *Panzer Retreat to Counteroffensive* (US Army Europe Historical Division, Wiesbaden, 1956), p.10

41 Moskalenko, *Na Yugo-Zapadnom Napravlenii*, Vol. I, p.451

42 I. Klochkov, *My Shturmovali Reykhstag* (Lenizdat, Leningrad, 1986), pp.43–44

43 C. Hamilton, *Leaders and Personalities in the Third Reich* (Bender, San Jose, CA, 1984), Vol. I, pp.261–63

44 Bundesarchiv-Militärarchiv Freiburg, *Kriegstagebuch Armeeoberkommando 8*, 27 Feb 1943, T314-54

45 Bundesarchiv-Militärarchiv Freiburg, *Kriegstagebuch Armeeoberkommando 8*, 27 Feb 1943, T314-54

46 Kazakov, *Nad Kartoi Bylykh Srazhenii*, pp.173–74

CHAPTER 13

1 Manstein, *Lost Victories*, p.433
2 Bundesarchiv-Militärarchiv Freiburg, *Kriegstagebuch Armeeoberkommando 8*, 28 Feb 1943, T314-54
3 A. Zvartsev, *3-ya Gvardeiskaya Tankovaya*, p.52
4 Vetrov, *Tak I Bylo*, pp.119–20
5 Ibid., p.121
6 Bundesarchiv-Militärarchiv Freiburg, *Kriegstagebuch II. SS-Panzer Korps*, 3 Mar 1943, RS2-2
7 Vetrov, *Tak I Bylo*, pp.127–29
8 Shafarenko, *Na Raznykh Frontakh*, p.163
9 Thöle, *Befehl des Gewissens*, p.214
10 Shafarenko, *Na Raznykh Frontakh*, p.165
11 Moskalenko, *Na Yugo-Zapadnom Napravlenii*, Vol. I, p.452; Kazakov, *Nad Kartoi Bylykh Srazhenii*, p.177
12 Quoted in Paul, *Brennpunkte*, p.293
13 Bundesarchiv-Militärarchiv Freiburg, *Kriegstagebuch Armeeoberkommando 8*, 8 Mar 1943, T314-54
14 Manteuffel, *Die 7. Panzer-Division*, pp.329–30
15 Moskalenko, *Na Yugo-Zapadnom Napravlenii*, Vol. I, pp.452–53
16 Ibid., Vol. I, p.454
17 J. Restayn, *Tiger I on the Eastern Front* (Histoire & Collections, Paris, 2001), p.96, 104, 116
18 Melvin, *Manstein: Hitler's Greatest General*, pp.423–427
19 Moskalenko, *Na Yugo-Zapadnom Napravlenii*, Vol. I, p.453
20 *Istoriia Vtoroi Mirovoi Voiny, 1939–1945* (Voenizdat, Moscow, 1976), Vol. VI, pp.139–40
21 Quoted in Thöle, *Befehl des Gewissens*, p.270
22 K. Margry, *The Four Battles for Kharkov* (Battle of Britain International, London, 2001), pp.20–22
23 Thöle, *Befehl des Gewissens*, pp.275–76
24 Bundesarchiv-Militärarchiv Freiburg, *Kriegstagebuch Armeeoberkommando 8*, 13 Mar 1943, T314-54
25 Glantz, *From the Don to the Dnepr*, p.383
26 M. Reynolds, *Steel Inferno: I SS Panzer Corps in Normandy* (Sarpedon, New York, 1997), p.10
27 H. Spaeter, *The History of the Panzerkorps Grossdeutschland* (Fedorowicz, Winnipeg, 1995), Vol. II, pp.70–71
28 Ibid., Vol. II, pp.71–73
29 Burdeyny, *V Boyakh za Rodinu*, pp.186–88
30 Ibid., pp.188–91
31 Bundesarchiv-Militärarchiv Freiburg, *Kriegstagebuch Armeeoberkommando 8*, 15

Mar 1943, T314-54

32   Bundesarchiv-Militärarchiv Freiburg, *Kriegstagebuch Armeeoberkommando 8*, 16
      Mar 1943, T314-54

33   Bundesarchiv-Militärarchiv Freiburg, *Kriegstagebuch II SS-Panzer Korps*, 18 Mar
      1943, RS2-2

CHAPTER 14

1   Manstein, *Lost Victories*, p.439

2   Ibid., pp.440–41

3   For a full discussion, see V. Mastny, 'Stalin and the Prospects of a Separate Peace
     in World War 2', in *American Historical Review* (University of Chicago Press,
     1972), Vol. 77, pp.1365–88

4   Speer, *Inside the Third Reich*, pp.350–55

5   Vasilevsky, *Lifelong Cause*, pp.264–65

6   For more information about the Lucy network, see A. Read and D. Fisher,
     Operation Lucy: Most Secret Spy Ring of the Second World War (Coward, McCann
     & Geoghegan, New York, 1981); V. Tarrant, *The Red Orchestra: The Soviet Spy
     Network Inside Nazi Europe* (Cassell, London, 1999)

7   Shtemenko, *Soviet General Staff*, p.155

8   H. Gisevius, *To the Bitter End: An Insider's Account of the Plot to Kill Hitler
     1933–1944* (Da Capo, New York, 1988), p.466

9   Ibid., p.468

BIBLIOGRAPHY

Bundesarchiv-Militärarchiv (Freiburg)
National Archives and Records Administration (NARA) (College Park MD)
Rossiyski Gosudarstvennyy Arkhiv Literaturi I Iskusstva (Moscow)
Tsentralnye Arkhiv Ministrertsva Oborony (Podolsk)
United States Air Force Historical Research Agency (Montgomery AL)

Air University Review (Maxwell AFB)
American Historical Review (University of Chicago Press)
Bulletin of International News (Royal Institute of International Affairs, London)
Die Zeit (Hamburg)
Military Review (US Army Command and General Staff College, Fort Leavenworth KA)
Technology and Culture (Johns Hopkins University Press, MD)
The Soviet and Post-Soviet Review (Libas Consulting, Philadelphia PA)
Voenno-Istoricheskii Zhurnal (Voennoe izd-vo Ministerstva Oborony Soyuza SSR, Moscow)
Volks-Zeitung (Vienna)
Wehrwissenschaftliche Rundschau (Mittler, Bonn)

Abdullin, M., *Stranits iz Soldatskogo Dnevnika* (Molodaya Gvardiya, Moscow, 1985)
Adam, W. and Rühle, O., trans. le Tissier, T., *With Paulus at Stalingrad* (Pen and Sword, Barnsley, 2015)
Adonyi-Naredi, F., *A Magyar Katona a Második Világháborúban, 1941–1945* (Kleinmayr, Klagenfurt, 1954)
Anderson, T., *Sturmartillerie: Spearhead of the Infantry* (Osprey, Oxford, 2016)
Axworthy, M., Scafeş, C., and Crăciuniou, C., *Third Axis, Fourth Ally: Romanian Armed Forces in the European War 1941–1945* (Arms and Armour, London, 1995)
Badigin, M., *Boy Trebuyet Podviga* (Voenizdat, Moscow, 1980)
Bauer, Y., *Jews for Sale? Nazi-Jewish Negotiations 1933* (Yale University Press, New Haven, CT, 1994)
Beck, A. (ed.), *Bis Stalingrad* (Helmuth Abt, Ulm, 1983)

Bedeschi, G., *Centomila Gavette di Ghiaccio* (Mursia, Milan, 2011)

Beevor, A., *Stalingrad* (Penguin, London, 1999)

Bellamy, C., *Absolute War: Soviet Russia in the Second World War* (Pan, London, 2007)

Belyakov, P., *V Pritsele 'Buryy Medved'* (Voenizdat, Moscow, 1977)

Biryusov, S., *Kogda Gremeli Pushki* (Voenizdat, Moscow, 1961)

Bishop, C., and Williams, M., *SS: Hell on the Western Front* (MBI, St Paul, MN, 2003)

Boll, B., *Zloczow, Juli 1941: Die Wehrmacht und der Beginn des Holocaust in Galizien* (Zeitschrift für Geschichtswissenschaft, Berlin, 2002)

Boog, H., Rahn, W., Stumpf, R., and Wegner, B., *Germany and the Second World War* (Oxford University Press, Oxford, 2001)

Bradley, D., *Walther Wenck – General der Panzertruppe* (Biblio, Osnabrück, 1981)

Breithaupt, H., *Zwischen Front und Widerstand: en Beitrag zur Diskussion um den Feldmarschall von Manstein* (Bernard & Grafe, Bonn, 1994)

Brett-Smith, R., *Hitler's Generals* (Presidio, San Rafael, CA, 1976)

Burdeyny, A., *V Boyakh za Rodinu* (MAK, Moscow, 2016)

Buttar, P., *Russia's Last Gasp: The Eastern Front in World War I 1916–1917* (Osprey, Oxford, 2016)

Buttar, P., *The Splintered Empires: The Eastern Front in World War I 1917–1923* (Osprey, Oxford, 2017)

Citino, R., *The Wehrmacht Retreats: Fighting a Lost War, 1943* (University Press of Kansas, Lawrence, KS, 2012)

Clark, A., *Barbarossa: The Russian-German Conflict 1941–1945* (Papermac, London, 1985)

Collotti, E., *Gli Italiani sul Fronte Russo* (De Donata, Barii, 1982)

Cooper, M., *The German Army 1939–1945* (Scarborough House, Lanham, MD, 1990)

Corradi, E., *La Ritirata di Russia* (Mursia, Milan, 2009)

Corti, E., trans. Levy, P., *Few Returned: Twenty-Eight Days on the Russian Front, Winter 1942–1943* (University of Missouri Press, Columbia, MO, 1997)

Craig, W., *Enemy at the Gates – The Battle for Stalingrad* (Penguin, London, 2000)

Davis, C., *Von Kleist: From Hussar to Panzer Marshal* (Lancer Militaria, Houston, TX, 1979)

Drabkin, A., *Ya Dralsya s Pantservaffe: Dvoynoy Oklad, Troynaya Smert'!* (Yauza, Moscow, 2007)

Engelmann, J., *Manstein: Stratege und Truppenführer – ein Lebensbericht in Bildern* (Podzun Pallas, Friedburg, 1981)

Erickson, J., *The Road to Stalingrad* (Panther, London, 1975)

Faldella, E., *Storia Delle Truppe Alpine 1872–1972* (Cavalotti, Milan, 1972)

Fest, J., *Die Unbeantwortbaren Fragen: Notizen über Gespräche mit Albert Speer Zwischen Ende 1966 und 1981* (Rowohlt, Haburg, 2006)

Forczyk, R., *Tank Warfare on the Eastern Front 1941–1942: Schwerpunkt* (Pen and Sword, Barnsley, 2014)

Friedin, S., Richardson, W., and Westphal, S., *The Fatal Decisions: Six Decisive Battles of the Second World War from the Viewpoint of the Vanquished* (Michael Joseph, London, 1956)

Gisevius, H., *To the Bitter End: An Insider's Account of the Plot to Kill Hitler 1933–1944* (Da Capo, New York, 1988)

Glantz, D., *From the Don to the Dnepr: Soviet Offensive Operations December 1942–August 1943* (Cass, London, 1991)

Glantz, D., *Kharkhov 1942: Anatomy of a Military Disaster* (Sarpedon, New York, 1998)

Glantz, D., *Zhukov's Greatest Defeat: The Red Army's Epic Disaster in Operation Mars 1942* (University Press of Kansas, Lawrence, KS, 1999)

Glantz, D., and House, J., *When Titans Clashed: How the Red Army Stopped Hitler* (University Press of Kansas, Lawrence, KS, 1995)

Gnocchi, C., *Cristo con gli Alpini* (Mursia, Milan, 2009)

Guderian, H., *Erinnerungen Eines Soldaten* (Vowinckel, Heidelberg, 1951)

Hamilton, C., *Leaders and Personalities in the Third Reich* (Bender, San Jose, CA, 1984)

Hamilton, H., *Sacrifice on the Steppe: The Italian Alpine Corps in the Stalingrad Campaign 1942–1943* (Casemate, Newbury, 2011)

Harding Ganz, A., *Ghost Division: The German 11th Panzer Division and the German Armored Force in World War II* (Stackpole, Mechanicsburg, PA, 2016)

Hartmann, C., *Halder: Generalstabschef Hitlers* (Schöningh, Paerborn, 1991)

Hayward, J., *Stopped at Stalingrad: The Luftwaffe and Hitler's Defeat in the East 1942–1943* (University Press of Kansas, Lawrence, KS, 1998)

Heiber, H. (ed.), *Lagebesprechungen im Führerhauptquartier: Protokollfragmente aus Hitlers Militärischen Konferenzen 1942–1945* (Deutsche Verlag, Stuttgart, 1962)

Heidkämper, O., *Witebsk: Kampf und Untergang der 3. Panzer Armee* (Scharnhorft, Heidelberg, 1954)

Hoffmann, J., *Die Tragödie der 'Russischen Befreiungsarmee' 1944–45. Wlassow gegen Stalin* (Herbig, Munich, 2003)

Hoffmann, P., *The History of the German Resistance 1933–1945* (McGill-Queen's University Press, Montreal, 1996)

Irving, D., *Göring: A Biography* (Macmillan, London, 1989)

Isserson, G., trans. Menning, B., *The Evolution of Operational Art* (Combat Studies Institution Press, Fort Leavenworth, KS, 2013)

Istoriia Vtoroi Mirovoi Voiny, 1939–1945 (Voenizdat, Moscow, 1976)

Karpov, A., *V Nebe Ukrainy* (Politizdat, Kiev, 1980)

Karsai, E., *Fegyvertelen Álltak az Aknamezőkön: Dokumentumok a Munkaszolgálat Történetéhez Magyarországon, Szerkeztette és a Bevezető Tanulmányt Irta* (A Magyar Izrailiták Országos Kepviselete Kiadása, Budapest, 1962)

Kazakov, M., *Operatsiya Saturn: Stalingradsleya Epopqya* (Isdatelstvo Nauka, Moscow, 1968)

Kazakov, N., *Nad Kartoi Bylykh Srazhenii* (Voenizdat, Moscow, 1971)

Kehrig, M., *Stalingrad: Analyse und Dokumentation einer Schlacht* (Deutsche Verlags-Anstalt, Stuttgart, 1974)

Kharchenko, V., *Spetsial'nogo Naznacheniya* (Voyenizdat, Moscow, 1973)

Klapdor, E., *Viking Panzers: The German 5th SS Tank Regiment in the East in World War II* (Stackpole, Mechanicsburg, PA, 2011)

Klatt, P., *Die 3. Gebirgs-Division 1939–1945* (Podzun, Bad Nauheim, 1958)

Kleine, B., *Bevor die Erinnerung Verblasst* (Helios, Aachen, 2004)

Klochkov, I., *My Shturmovali Reykhstag* (Lenizdat, Leningrad, 1986)

Kobylyanskiy, I., *From Stalingrad to Pillau: A Red Army Artillery Officer Remembers the Great Patriotic War* (University of Kansas Press, Lawrence, KS, 2008)

Koshevoi, P., *V Gody Voyenyye* (Voenizdat, Moscow, 1978)

Krasilnikov, S., *Organizatsiya Krupnykh Obshchevoyskovykh Soyedineniy. Proshedsheye, Nastoyashcheye i Budushcheye* (Gosudarstvennoe izdatel'stvo, Otdel Voennoi Literatury, Moscow, 1933)

Kravchenko, Y., and Pribylov, B., *K Granatomotu Taubina* (Arktika 4D, Moscow, 2011)

Krüger, A., and Scharenberg, S., *Zeiten für Helden – Zeiten für Berühmtheiten im Sport* (LIT, Münster, 2014)

Krupchenko, I. (ed.), *Sovetskie Tankovje Voiska 1941–1945* (Voenizdat, Moscow, 1973)

Krushchev, N., Krushchev, S. (ed.), trans. Shriver, G., *Memoirs of Nikita Krushchev* (Pennsylvania State University Press, University Park, PA, 2004)

Krysov, V., *Batereya, Ogon!* (Yauza, Moscow, 2007)

Kuzmin, A., and Krasov, I., *Kantemirovtsy: Boevoi put 4-go Gvardeiskogo Tankovogo Kantemirovskogo Ordena Lenina Krasnoznammennogo Korpusa* (Voenizdat, Moscow, 1971)

Lelyushenko, D., *Moskva-Stalingrad-Berlin-Praha* (Nauka, Moscow, 1987)

Lemay, B., trans. Heyward, P., *Manstein: Hitler's Master Strategist* (Casemate, Newbury, 2010)

Manstein, E. von, trans. Powell, G., *Lost Victories: The War Memoirs of Hitler's Most Brilliant General* (Presidio, Novato, CA, 1994)

Manstein, E. von, *Soldat im 20. Jahrehundert* (Bernard & Graefer, Munich, 1997)

Manteuffel, H. von, *Die 7. Panzer-Division im Zweiten Weltkrieg* (Traditionsverband Ehemaliger 7. Panzer-Division Kameradenhilfe, Krefeld, 1965)

Margry, K., *The Four Battles for Kharkov* (Battle of Britain International, London, 2001)

Mayer, A., *Why Did the Heavens Not Darken?* (Pantheon, New York, 1988)

Mayer, S., *Der Untergang fun Zloczów* (Ibergang, Munich, 1947)

McTaggart, P. et al., *WWII History: Russian Front* (Sovereign Media, Herndon, VA, 2006)

Melikov, V., *Problema strategiceskogo razvertyvanija po opytu mirovoj i grazdanskoj vojny* (Naucno-Issledovatelskiye Otdel Voenny Akademie, Moscow, 1935)

Mellenthin, F. von, *Panzer Battles* (University of Oklahoma Press, Danvers, MA, 1956)

Melvin, M., *Manstein: Hitler's Greatest General* (Weidenfeld & Nicholson, London, 2010)

Merridale, C., *Ivan's War: The Red Army 1939–1945* (Faber & Faber, London, 2005)

Miller, M., *Leaders of the SS and German Police* (Bender, San Jose, CA, 2006)

Mollo, A., *The Armed Forces of World War II* (Crown, New York, 1981)

Morzik, F., *German Air Force Airlift Operations* (USAF Air University, Montgomery, AL, 1961)

Moskalenko, K., *Na Yugo-Zapadnom Napravlenii* (Izdatelstvo Nauka, Moscow, 1969)

Nechayev, V., *Gvardeyskiy Umanskiy: Voyenno-Istoricheskiy Ocherk o Boyevom Puti 9-go Gvardeyskogo Tankovogo Korpusa* (Voyenizdat, Moscow, 1989)

Neillands, R., *The Dieppe Raid: The Story of the Disastrous 1942 Expedition* (Indiana University Press, Bloomington, IN, 2005)

Nemeskurty, I., *Requiem egy Hadseregért* (Magvető, Budapest, 1982)

Nosov, I., *Vysoty Poluchayut Imena* (Voenizdat, Moscow, 1978)

Overy, R., *Goering* (Phoenix, London, 1984)

Parker, D., *Hitler's Warrior: The Life and Wars of SS Colonel Jochen Peiper* (Da Capo, Lebanon, IN, 2014)

Patai, R., *The Jews of Hungary: History, Culture, Psychology* (Wayne State University Press, Detroit, MI, 1999)

Paul, W., *Brennpunkte: Die Geschichte der 6. Panzerdivision* (Biblioverlag, Osnabrück, 1993)

Peiper, H., *Fegelein's Horsemen and Genocidal Warfare: The SS Cavalry Brigade in the Soviet Union* (Palgrave Macmillan, Basingstoke, 2015)

Price, S., and Thonemann, P., *The Birth of Classical Europe: A History from Troy to Augustine* (Allen Lane, London, 2010)

Pustyntsev, N., *Skvoz' Svintsovoyu V'yugu: Zapiski Razvedchika* (Voenizdat, Moscow, 1966)

Rakobolskaya, I., and Kravtsova, N., *Nas Nazyvali Nochnymi Ved'Mani: Tak Voyeval 46-y Gvardeyskiy Polk Nochnykh Bombaardirovshchikov* (Isd-Vo MGU, Moscow, 2005)

Raus, E., *Panzer Operations: The Eastern Front Memoir of General Raus, 1941–1945* (Da Capo, Cambridge, MA, 2003)

Read, A., and Fisher, D., *Operation Lucy: Most Secret Spy Ring of the Second World War* (Coward, McCann & Geoghegan, New York, 1981)

Restayn, J., *Tiger I on the Eastern Front* (Histoire & Collections, Paris, 2001)

Reynolds, M., *Steel Inferno: I SS Panzer Corps in Normandy* (Sarpedon, New York, 1997)

Rigoni Stern, M., *Il Sergente Nella Neve: Ricordi Della Ritirata di Russia* (Einaudi, Turin, 2014)

Rochat, G., *Le Guerre Italiane 1935–1943: Dall'Impero d'Etiopia alla Disfatta* (Einaudi, Turin, 2009)

Röll, H., *Generalleutnant der Reserve Hyacinth Graf Strachwitz von Groß-Zauche und Camminetz: Vom Kavallerieoffizier zum Führer gepanzerter Verbände* (Flechsig, Würzburg, 2011)

Rotmistrov, P., *Stal'naya Gvardiya* (Voyenizdat, Moscow, 1984)

Rotundo, L., *Battle for Stalingrad: The Soviet General Staff Study* (Macmillan, London, 1989)

Rudel, H-U., *Stuka Pilot* (Black House, London, 2013)

Sadarananda, D., *Beyond Stalingrad: Manstein and the Operations of Army Group Don* (Praeger, Westport, CT, 1990)

Sbornik Materialovpo Izucheniyu Opyta Voyny (Voenizdat, Moscow, 1943)

Scheibert, H., *Panzer Zwischen Don und Donez* (Podzun, Friedberg, 1979)

Scheibert, H., *...Bis Stalingrad 48km: Der Entsatzversuch 1942* (Pudzun-Pallas, Wölfersheim-Berstadt, 1998)

Schramm, P. (ed.), *Kriegstagebuch des Oberkommandos der Wehrmacht* (Bernard & Graefer, Munich, 1982)

Schröter, H., *Stalingrad: Bis zur Letzten Patrone* (self-published, Osnabrück, 1952)

Senger und Ettelin, F. von, *Panzer Retreat to Counteroffensive* (US Army Europe Historical Division, Wiesbaden, 1956)

Shafarenko, P., *Na Raznykh Frontakh: Zapiski Komandira Divizii* (Voyenizdat, Moscow, 1978)

Shimansky, V., *Pozyvnyye Nashikh Serdets* (Voyenizdat, Moscow, 1980)

Shtemenko, S., *The Soviet General Staff at War 1941–1945* (Progress, Moscow, 1970)

Shtykov, N., *Polk Priminayet Boy* (Voyenizdat, Moscow, 1979)

Skripko, N., *Po Tselyam Blizhnim i Dal'nim* (Voyenizdat, Moscow, 1981)

Smelser, R., and Davies, E., *The Myth of the Eastern Front: The Nazi-Soviet War in American Popular Culture* (Cambridge University Press, Cambridge, 2008)

Solarz, J., *Totenkopf 1939–1943* (Wydawnictwo, Warsaw, 2008)

Spaeter, H., *The History of the Panzerkorps Grossdeutschland* (Fedorowicz, Winnipeg, 1995)

Speer, A., *Inside the Third Reich* (Weidenfeld & Nicholson, London, 2015)

Stahlberg, A., trans. Crampton, P., *Beholden Duty: The Memoirs of a German Officer 1932–1945* (Brassey, London, 1990)

Stalin, J., *O Velikoi Otechestvennoi Voine Sovetskogo Soyuza* (Gosudarstvennoe izdvo Politicheskoi Literaturi, Moscow, 1946)

Strik-Strikfeldt, W., *Against Stalin and Hitler: Memoir of the Russian Liberation Movement 1941–45* (Macmillan, London, 1970)

Tarrant, V., *Stalingrad: Anatomy of an Agony* (Leo Cooper, London, 1992)

Tarrant, V., *The Red Orchestra: The Soviet Spy Network Inside Nazi Europe* (Cassell, London, 1999)

Tebart, T., *298. Infanterie-Division 1940–1943: Ruhm und Untergang* (Kameradschaft der 298.Inf.-Div, 1990)

Temkin, G., *My Just War: The Memoirs of a Jewish Red Army Soldier in World War II* (Presidio, Novato, CA, 1998)

Thöle, H., *Befehl des Gewissens: Charkow Winter 1943* (Munin, Osnabrück, 1976)

Thorwald, J., *The Illusion* (Harcourt Brace Jovanovich, New York, 1975)

Tiulenev, I., *Cherez Tri Voyny* (Voyenizdat, Moscow, 1972)

Translation of Taped Interview with General Hermann Balck, 12 January 1979 (Battele Columbus Laboratories, Columbus, OH, 1985)

Trevor-Roper, H., *Hitler's War Directives 1939–1945* (Birlinn, Edinburgh, 2004)

Tukhachevsky, M., *New Problems in Warfare* (Art of War Symposium, Carlisle, PA, 1983)

Uborevich, I., *Operativno-Takticheskaia i Aviatsionnaia Voennye Igry* (Gosudarstvennoe izdatel'stvo, Otdel Voennoi Literatury, Moscow, 1929)

Ueberschär, G. (ed.), *Hitlers Militärische Elite* (Primus, Darmstadt, 1998)

Vasilevsky, A., trans. Riordan, J., *A Lifelong Cause* (Progress, Moscow, 1973)

Vasiliev, H., *Tatsinskii Reid* (Voenizdat, Moscow, 1969)

Veress, L., *Magyarország Honvédelme a II. Világháború Előtt és Alatt 1920–1945* (Nemzetőr, Munich, 1973)

Vetrov, A., *Tak I Bylo* (Voenizdat, Moscow, 1982)

Vicentini, C., and Resta, P., *Rapporto sui Prigionieri di Guerra Italiani in Russia* (UNIRR, Milan, 2005)

Vicentini, C., and Rochat, G., *Il Sacrificio della Julia in Russia* (Gaspari, Udine, 2006)

Wagenführ, R., *Die Deutsche Industrie im Kriege 1939–1945* (Deutsches Institut für Wirtschaftsforschung, Berlin, 1954)

Webster, C., and Frankland, N., *The Strategic Air Offensive Against Germany* (HMSO, London, 1961)

Weiss, J., *The Lemberg Mosaic* (Alderbrook, New York, 2010)

Werthen, W., *Geschichte der 16. Panzer-Division – Weg und Schicksal* (Podzun, Bad Nauheim, 1958)

Westphal, S., *Erinnerungen* (Hase & Koehler, Mainz, 1975)

Wieder, J., and Einsiedel, H. Graf von, trans. Bogler, H., *Stalingrad: Memories and Reassessments* (Arms and Armour, London, 1998)

Wrochem, O. von, *Vernichtungskrieg und Erinnerungspolitik: Erich von Manstein, Akteur und Symbol* (Schoeningh Ferdinand, Paderborn, 2006)

Yaroshenko, A., *V Boi Shla 41-ya Gvardeiskaya: Boevoi put' 41-I Gvardeiskoi Strelkovoi Korsunsko-Dunaskoi Ordene Suvorova Divizii* (Voenizdat, Moscow, 1982)

Yershov, A., *Osvobozhdenie Donbassa* (Voenizdat, Moscow, 1973)

Zaloga, S., Kinnear, J., Aksenov, A., and Koshchavtsev, A., *Soviet Tanks in Combat 1941–45: The T-28, T-34, T-34-85, and T-44 Medium Tanks* (Concord, Hong Kong, 1997)

Zaloga, S., and Ness, L., *Red Army Handbook 1939–1945* (Sutton, Stroud, 1998)

Zdanovich, G., *Idem v Nastupleniye* (Voenizdat, Moscow, 1980)

Zhukov, G., *The Memoirs of Marshal Zhukov* (Jonathan Cape, London, 1971)

Ziemke, E., *Moscow to Stalingrad: Decision in the East* (University of Michigan Press, Ann Arbor, MI, 1987)

Zvartsev, A., *3-ya Gvardeiskaya Tankovaya: Boevoi pit 3- Gvardeiskoi Tankovoi Armii* (Voenizdat, Moscow, 1982)

INDEX